D0296655

BLOODY FOREIGNERS

Also by Robert Winder

NO ADMISSION

THE MARRIAGE OF TIME AND CONVENIENCE

HELL FOR LEATHER: A MODERN CRICKET JOURNEY

BLOODY FOREIGNERS

The Story of Immigration to Britain

ROBERT WINDER

LITTLE, BROWN

A *Little, Brown* Book

First published in Great Britain in 2004 by Little, Brown

Copyright © Robert Winder 2004

The moral right of the author has been asserted.

A CIP catalogue record for this book
is available from the British Library.

ISBN 0 316 86135 9

Typeset in Palatino by M Rules
Printed and bound in Great Britain by Clays Ltd, St Ives plc

Little, Brown
An imprint of
Time Warner Book Group UK
Brettenham House
Lancaster Place
London WC2E 7EN

www.twbg.co.uk

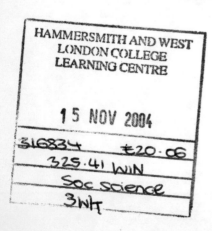

To Hermione, Luke and Kit

Contents

Acknowledgements

P. G. Wodehouse once made fun of a writer by asking why he had given such a lengthy explanation of his book and its purposes, when a simple apology would have sufficed. In this case, however, I can assert without embarrassment that the original idea was a splendid one, since it was not mine. Richard Beswick, of Little, Brown, had for years nursed the impulse to produce a book that would present immigration not as a subject or issue (let alone as a 'problem') but as a narrative, a story, an adventure. So the book fell into my lap more or less fully formed: all I had to do was join the dots of his brainwave.

In the event I was slow on the uptake; I stared warily at the gift horse's mouth, sizing up its considerable teeth. It could hardly be a story of the sort you might find in a novel: there wasn't a cast of characters or an individual consciousness (apart from mine) that could learn something as it went along. It would be false, moreover, to propose individual figures as 'representative' of any one ethnic or national identity, since these are too numerous and tangled already. There is a bias, in most sociology, in favour of big numbers and significant categories. But the differences between people may be more telling than the similarities. Can a rich merchant from Portugal be lumped in with a destitute peasant from Russia, just because they both happen to be Jewish? Can a Hindu represent the Indian diaspora, rather than a Sikh, a Muslim, a Buddhist or a Christian? How many nationalities can be squeezed into a single term such as 'Asian'? Is anyone, in short, 'typical'? A book that straddled so many hundreds of years, and so many millions of people, would have to skate over such distinctions.

I hesitated. But in my hesitation I leafed through histories of Britain, and was struck by the extent to which the topic has been overlooked. Time and again I came across delineations of the national character which failed to view it as the product of a cosmopolitan ancestry. They preferred to see it as something solidly rooted in the soil and climate, as native and natural as an oak or a hawthorn; or else as something geological, a stratum of rock (usually granite) which could be chiselled but not changed. I read accounts of the eighteenth century in which slavery was barely mentioned, and surveys of modern times in which immigration cropped up almost in passing, as an inconvenient side-issue that had little to do with the central thrust of national life. The truth – that Britain has absorbed foreign genes since it was first discovered by continental wanderers – really did seem to have been sidelined. I resolved to take a closer look.

Any anxieties about my own eligibility softened on the grounds that if this wasn't my story to tell, then whose was it? True, I wasn't an immigrant. But I soon saw that we are all immigrants: it simply depends how far back you go. And if personal experience is the criterion, it would not be enough for the author to be an immigrant. He or she would have to be part Roman, part German, part Danish, part French, part Jewish, part Irish, part Caribbean, part African, part Indian, part Chinese, part Greek, and part every other nationality you can think of. No one person could claim to represent the ethnic or religious strands that twist their way through this story. I was, I told myself, at least as unqualified as anyone else. I took heart from a line by Oscar Wilde: 'The one duty we owe to history', he said, 'is to rewrite it.' History is not, as has been said, the past – it is the story we tell ourselves about the past, what we have instead of the past.

Then there was the perplexing question: was this a book about immigration into Britain or England? The United Kingdom is a recent, perhaps temporary federation which has existed only since the Act of Union with Scotland in 1707. If I was narrating immigration to England, then by rights I should include migrants from elsewhere in the British Isles – from Wales until 1535, and from Scotland until 1707. In the end I decided that to regard these as immigrants rendered the usual implications of the term almost meaningless, though I have treated the Irish as international travellers, even in the years when they were fellow nationals. I inclined towards a geographical rather than a political definition, and resolved to narrate the passages into Britain, not simply England.

The story, however, is anglocentric – above all an English story. The great bulk – 98 per cent – of today's foreign-born population (just under four million) lives in England, and nearly half lives in London. Scotland, Wales and Northern Ireland have been only lightly brushed by this tremendous ethnic and cultural alteration; indeed, this might be one reason why they are able to sustain a more coherent (some would say limiting) and folksy form of national pride.

The terms 'Britain' and 'England' are not, of course, interchangeable, and I have tried to avoid using them as synonyms. As a loose geographical description, however, Britain inhabits our history books, dictionaries and everyday speech as the only available term. As a result, I have at times used the term 'Britons' to refer primarily to the English, simply because there is no word for English people – Englons? Englanders? Angles? I am uncomfortably aware, however, that in referring to Britain I am often alluding almost wholly to events in England.

As it happens, Britishness (to turn my cards face-up) seems a likeable and relevant idea in this context: it enlarges the associations of each component nationality, and makes mini-multiculturalists of us all – or polyculturalists, to use the fashionable phrase. Yet the United Kingdom, as has been said, is neither united nor a kingdom any more (indeed, for some odd reason, every time I tapped in the word 'united' – as in 'United Kingdom' – it came out as 'untied').

Suddenly, and inevitably, we are again alert to the pleasures and perils of narrowly defined nationalisms, which seek resonance by being exclusive rather than elastic. In England, the cross of St George (a Turkish knight, by all accounts) has been reinvented as a national flag by greetings card companies and football fans. Britishness, meanwhile, remains a baggy concept with room for a rich assortment of cultural sympathies and identities. A man or woman can cheer for England at the World Cup, Britain at the Olympics, Europe at the Ryder Cup, Scotland against Wales, Sussex in the County Championship, and the West Indies in Test matches. Our loyalties can be fluid and overlapping.

In truth, I was keen not to become enmeshed in such abstractions. The whole idea was to narrate the various passages to Britain as a story, not as an issue. If there was a eureka moment, it came when I saw that an immigrant is only the glum flipside of a much more exciting figure: an emigrant. This sounds (and is) obvious, and if it has any novelty reflects only the fact that the subject occupies us less than it should: the cold shoulder which migrants so often encounter may consist of little more than a massive, frozen incuriosity. There is a built-in tendency to present immigrants as passive or problematic second-tier characters, as guests or mere visitors with certain obligations of deference and gratitude towards their 'host'. Emigrants are much more dashing – adventurous, eager, intrepid, fun. This simple conception drove most of my research. Migrants ceased to be the feeble, dependent figures of so much cartoon mythmaking, and became plucky explorers on the sharp, often painful edge of social progress.

The book appears at a time when immigration is a major national concern. This is not surprising. The world's population is being shaken both by the ease, speed and cost-effectiveness of modern travel, and the seductive imagery – a bragging form of lifestyle one-upmanship – that wealthy nations churn out and broadcast every day. The political heat around the rights and wrongs, pros and cons of migration is buffeted by the simple fact that people are swirling across borders faster than ever. There are colossal economic and demographic forces greasing the wheels. The West has erected an elaborate paper barricade – made up of passports, permits, cards and forms – which aims to prevent the world's have-nots from encroaching too noisily on its haves. But the material rewards of a successful migration from a poor country to a rich one are handsome enough to encourage a spirited defiance of such rules. Indeed, the political and technological pressures usually known as globalisation (though a better term for this might be 'Americanisation') actively promote the modern phenomenon of migration. The liberal insistence on free markets, democratic politics and unregulated corporate power is a potent sponsor of cross-border job seeking. Sometimes, as in the case of the Chinese cockle-harvesters who died on the treacherous sands of Lancashire's Morecambe Bay in February 2004, it has calamitous consequences. But so enviable are the fruits of migration that the amazing thing is not how many attempt it, but how few.

It is strangely easy to forget that immigrants are often, and by definition, entrepreneurial risk-takers and rule-flouters, with a keen sense of individual liberty. The big idea of globalisation, for instance, is that the world should uproot the barriers to the free flow of trade. Yet few of the world's richest countries are happy to extend this freedom to the free flow of labour. Goods, services, capital – these must be allowed to run free. But people must be shackled at all costs. Is this logical? As John Maynard Keynes wrote: 'Migration is the oldest action against poverty. It selects those who most want help. It is good for the country to which they go; it helps break the equilibrium of poverty in the country from which they come. What is the perversity in the human soul that causes people to resist so obvious a good?'

This book is not a polemic. But I did start with the premise that immigration is a form of enrichment and renewal, and have changed my mind only to the extent that I now find it pointless even to brood on whether it can be described as a 'good' or a 'bad' thing. It is like wondering whether it is good or bad to grow old. Nor can immigration be conceived of as a single experience. For the man who meets the woman of his dreams, or makes his fortune, it is a happy process; for the boy knifed at a bus stop by a gang of violent bigots, it is a catastrophe. Most migrations are in-between affairs, involving equal portions of fulfilment and regret. Encounters between strangers, meanwhile, are rarely straightforward; the mingling of peoples has always been accompanied by fear, suspicion and animosity. Migration has never, not for a thousand years, been easy. People have rarely been treated as well as they hoped or deserved, and the roll-call of names who have suffered the worst excess of bigotry is long.

The urge to divide the world into 'us' and 'them' is as strong as ever; recent studies indicate that if children are divided into two logical but random groups – blue eyes and brown eyes, say – it doesn't take long before squabbles break out. Men v. women, Blacks v. Whites, Catholics v. Protestants, Hindu v. Muslim . . . sometimes it appears as if most of the world's energy goes into guarding these corrosive v-signs. Inevitably, as the natural barriers against migration grow porous, some raucous voices are raised in protest. But what if 'we' are 'them', and 'they' are 'us'? The thought raises hackles: so much easier to cling to what divides us than what we share. Perhaps we need a new word: 'thus'?

The title invokes a phrase that has, in contrast, rung down the centuries. In medieval times, Englishmen could speak of 'cursed forrainers'; in Victorian times they talked of 'blasted furriners'. Its an old refrain, a behind-the-hands grumble that has long since been co-opted by immigrants themselves. In 1859 Friedrich Engels poked a man in the eye with an umbrella and soon heard from the man's lawyers. 'Needless to say', he wrote, 'these blasted English don't want to deprive themselves of the pleasure of getting their hands on a *bloody foreigner*.' The book may not have been my idea, but its faults are all my own. Special thanks are due to Toby Eady, Viv Redman and Philip Parr. Above all, thank you to the innumerable scholars whose original work in many specific historical fields I have relied on hugely in the course of assembling what follows.

Introduction

Imagine for a moment that we could watch, from some all-seeing camera high in space, the long history of the British Isles unfolding before our eyes. Among the brief flashes of light and shade (summer and winter), the most striking sight would be the astounding traffic into and out of our ports. Thousands of ships and planes, millions of people, year after year, century after century – our country would seem defined by ceaseless comings and goings. We would not see that some of the arrivals never leave, or that some of the departures never return. We might not detect the endless mixing and stirring of the population. But as the centuries flew past, we would witness the slow advance and steady transformation of a country and a people. It would seem an epic story.

It might also seem surprising. We do not always think of Britain as a country settled at a deep level by immigrants. We prefer to construct mythologies of the national character as something stable, as a still and virtuous point in an often unruly world. Even the most authoritative histories see it as a durable set of genes, ideas and habits, a white page to which, in the last few decades, a few multicoloured flourishes have been added. If they mention immigration at all – as, now, they have to – they usually present it as a self-contained strand oblique to the main thrust of national progress. The arrival of migrants from our former empire is categorised as one of the 'problems' or 'challenges' faced by postwar society. But the long and steady movement of people to these shores before the modern era is forgotten altogether. If anything, we are inclined to think of ourselves as the migrants: as a centuries-old race of inquisitive seekers after fresh and unconquered lands.

It is true that Britons have been relentless travellers ever since the invention of the sail. The heyday of empire saw British ships, laden with British families, criss-crossing the world in search of favourable spots for their farms, chapels, vineyards, plantations, factories, shipping companies, banks or mines. This tradition has not died: indeed, until the apocalyptic-sounding year of 1984, twentieth-century Britain was a net *exporter* of people. Between 1961 and 1981, usually thought of as a time of energetic immigration (according to Enoch Powell and later Mrs Thatcher, who famously pointed out the dangers of being 'swamped'), we ran up a deficit of over a million people. The postwar generations headed for the colonies (or ex-colonies), just as their predecessors had done. This time they went not as missionaries and administrators, but as roving employees or businessmen – economic migrants, to use the fashionable phrase. But just like the earliest settlers, the modern British emigrants sought a better, freer life in sunnier climes, with fresher vegetables, looser morals, fewer nosy neighbours and a pool rather than a pond.

Several million Britons live overseas today, and we rarely dispute their right to do so. Over a hundred thousand reside, to take just one example, on the French Riviera, along the glossy strip of coast between Toulon and Monaco. How we envy them. Emigration is one thing: it strikes us as daring and sprightly. But immigration is something else. It is one of those grim, unsettling words that clangs on our consciences as a duty, an issue – a burden. Of course, it has been and will continue to be all of these things. Britain's surliness towards foreigners is legendary and well documented. Yet immigration – more grandly defined or imagined – is not only one of the biggest stories of British life; it is also one of the most resonant, and one of the oldest. Ever since the first Jute, the first Saxon, the first Roman and the first Dane leaped off their boats and planted their feet on British mud, we have been a mongrel nation. Our roots are neither clean nor straight; they are impossibly tangled.

Why, then, are we so fond of believing that Britishness consisted of some smooth and harmonious racial archetype until the postwar arrival of several million black and brown faces from the Tropics? Overseas settlers have been coming here for centuries. There were French Jews in London, Lincoln, York and Norwich in the twelfth century; the Elizabethan age brought Italian musicians, German businessmen and even Africans, pressed by the first piratical stirrings of the slave trade. Protestants from the Low Countries, seeking religious tolerance, brought new trades and kick-started the Industrial Revolution in the same period. Huguenot refugees arrived from France *en masse* in the seventeenth century, creating a vibrant commercial atmosphere, as did Greek Christians fleeing the Turks (a church was built in Soho for the Archbishop of Samos in 1677). Cromwell readmitted Jews, and the coronation of William III attracted a substantial Dutch population. The heyday of the slave trade brought many black Africans (in 1768 the number of black Londoners was put at 20,000 out of 600,000 – a sizeable proportion, though, like all such statistics, it is probably exaggerated). So the eighteenth century, which seems in our cartoon imaginations a civilised era, all Vanbrugh and Handel (both immigrants), all ballgowns and girls on swings, was busy with black servants running errands or selling pies. They were the lucky ones who had escaped the transports from Liverpool. Some of them married, baptised their children and were buried – all in England.

The Hanoverian monarchs opened fraternal links with Germany, and Victorian Britain hummed with human traffic from all over Europe: scientists, engineers, teachers, labourers, maids, sailors and (following the failed revolutions of 1848) political dissidents and intellectuals. Some 400,000 Irish people – refugees from the potato famine – came to Manchester, Liverpool, London and Glasgow in the 1840s, transforming and reshaping the character of those cities (and while they may, constitutionally, have been British, they were certainly not treated as such). Some 40,000 Italians fled the Mediterranean and, although they were headed for America, settled here; roughly 50,000 Germans were living here by the end of the century. And the Tsarist pogroms in Russia brought perhaps 150,000 Jewish evacuees in the 1890s. Many settled in London's East End; others made their homes in Leeds, Bradford, Manchester, and all stations between Hull and Liverpool – the classic route onwards to America. The imperial fleets were meanwhile sucking Indian (Lascars) and Chinese seamen on to our ships and into our ports (the world's oldest Chinatown is in Liverpool). Migrant workers from all the lands on which the sun never set subtly changed British life – or at least laid the foundations for the not-so-subtle changes that would follow.

Each migration was an adventure: indeed, it is amazing how often an immigrant's journey closely resembles a heroic escape – risky boat rides, midnight treks, cars nosing through dark woods, disguises, the barking of police dogs, hiding-places, secret papers, close shaves, nail-biting escapes and whispers. Yet we habitually see immigrants not as brave voyagers but as needy beggars. Is it asking too much that we look for ways to celebrate the part they have played in our history, instead of clinging to narrower definitions of British or English identity?

The story of immigration has been anything but smooth or uneventful. But then it is doubtful that any nation could have assimilated the arrival of so many people from overseas without stress, and Britain is not unique in falling far short of the ideal. The overseas explorers on these shores have found the natives anything but friendly: our social history includes regular and vindictive race riots. The Huguenots, the Irish, the Jews, the Poles, the Protestant refugees from Germanic Europe, and more recent immigrants from Africa, the Caribbean, India and Asia, have all, in their turn, attracted sometimes furious hatred. They have had to defend themselves, sometimes with their fists (or worse). There is a shamefully long catalogue of violent reprisals against foreigners, and it is added to nearly every day. Blatant racism is deep, ugly, endemic and hard to dislodge. There have been many famous flashpoints just in recent memory. If a monument were to be erected for the victims of racial hatred, it would require space for an awful lot of names.

But it is equally possible to say that in their vexed and stumbling way these islands have been more adaptable than the stereotype of stiff, unyielding John Bull Britishness usually implies. Britain's frequent hostility to immigrants is balanced by many acts of routine kindness between the races. Individual open-mindedness has often defeated our nastier streak, though it is less well recorded, inspiring no court cases, no White Papers, no shocked headlines, no urgent documentaries.

Besides, now that the modern sky is so crowded with planes, all countries are having to grapple with tensions between their historic national self-imagery and the rich plurality of lifestyles they are obliged to accommodate. The agitations of national or ethnic pride stir the politics of country after country, usually in a bloody manner. But Britain, for all its high-profile failings, has not seen 'ethnic cleansing' on the scale of Bosnia, Rwanda, Uganda . . . or Nazi Germany. Enoch Powell famously predicted 'a river foaming with blood', and is often held up as an archetype of British racism – as the mouthpiece for a universal British hatred of the immigrant. But Powell was shouted down and sacked. He has also been proved wrong. His precious river might be shamefully flecked with blood, but it is not foaming, and never has been.

Debates on this subject are invariably fought between optimists and pessimists. The pessimists would say that modern Britain is irretrievably racist. Optimists counter that Britain's record is better than almost anywhere else; that we haven't done too badly, all things considered. Both sides take Britain to be a singular entity, that can be personified and judged – guilty or otherwise. But 'Britain' has always been mixed and mutable. It can harbour good intentions alongside bad ones. So 'we' are at once guilty and not guilty; 'we' profited hugely (and iniquitously) from slavery, but also supported the rebellion against it. Neither cancels out the other. An accurate estimate of the British character must allow room for both strands.

There are other contradictions in the immigration debate. The traditional right-wing–left-wing divide, the contrast between a conservative and a progressive cast of thought, is skewed in this area. Logic suggests that right-wingers should be pro-immigration (on laissez-faire grounds, and because it brings the supply of cheap labour on which free enterprise relies). Left-wingers, meanwhile, with their faith in the idea that personal liberties should be subordinated to the collective interest, might be expected to be suspicious of liberal migration laws, with their individualistic flavour. Yet these positions are usually reversed. Free-marketeers cling to a nationalism which resists any attempt to upset the status quo (not so much laissez-faire as laissez-*nous* faire); while leftists, anxious to harness the springs of wealth-creation to the cogs of social justice, classify immigrants as needy refugees, potential subscribers to an egalitarian world view. This reflex sometimes leads to misunderstandings. I once met an Indian businessman who had sat in on several government meetings about overseas development. 'The funny thing about New Labour', he said, stifling a smile, 'is that they think if you're Indian, then you must be left-wing.'

Champions of a liberal approach to immigration, for their part, often bump into the awkward fact that some immigrants can be far from liberal. What then? Is it a contradiction for a liberal society to insist that it is willing to tolerate everything except intolerance?

In any event such conversations – however worthwhile and necessary – obscure the extent to which immigration is a story. And, like all the best stories, it has happy moments as well as sad ones, comedies as well as tragedies. The list of shameful episodes is long, and growing longer every day. But there are uplifting tales, too – of people remaking their lives. The immigrant experience is not uniform: some people come hurriedly, as refugees; others to seek their fortunes. Many find heartache, but many have prospered. It has been a momentous adventure both for each individual and for the nation they have settled in and reshaped. Gradually, as the generations have passed, the new population has repeatedly managed to slip past the obstacles (even now: Britain has the highest rate of interracial marriage in Europe). The story is not – never can be – complete, but the way Britain has absorbed new people in the last thousand years may be seen as a rough-edged tribute to its sometimes taciturn receptiveness.

Either way, the seeds of a new country have been thoroughly sown. As the story marches on, we can see a constant tussle between kind and cruel impulses, an exhausting two-steps-forward–one-step-back dance towards the Utopian idea of a pluralist, happy, cosmopolitan country.

The metaphors for immigration are usually aquatic: we talk of floods and tides, of being swamped or drowned. We might do better to think of Britain as a lake refreshed by one stream that bubbles in and another that trickles out. The fish might squabble and at times attack one another; conditions sometimes favour the pike, sometimes the minnow. Every so often the incoming stream stirs the still pond, but over time the lake adapts and develops a new, unexpected ecology. Without the oxygen generated by fresh water, it would stagnate.

The modern story of immigration – the explosion encouraged by mass-market air travel – seems a fitting epilogue to the saga of the British Empire, the backwash of our long, volatile relationship with those remote dominions bound by the Union Flag. If this catches us by surprise, then it is a reflection of the incurious attitude we managed to maintain towards our empire for so long. One of the things that immigrants bring with them is a fresh and appraising eye for our own past.

In any case, it is hardly the first time that Britain has been refreshed by foreign blood. And it will not be the last. All over Europe, economists are nervously scanning demographic trends and tripping over one inescapable fact: if national economies are going to grow at a level sufficient to provide pensions for the existing working population, then serious immigration is a necessity, whatever anyone feels about it. Few politicians choose to spell this out as boldly as they should. But immigration, far from being a threat to our way of life, might one day turn out to be quite the opposite: our best hope.

If the story of immigration remains to an odd extent untold, it must partly be because all discussions of the subject swiftly turn into conversations about politics and social justice; into debates about rights, racism, multiculturalism and so on. There is nothing wrong with this: these are important and necessary debates. But somewhere in this process of abstraction the story itself is diminished, becomes the premise of an argument rather than a drama in its own right. It becomes an issue – with pros and cons, and arguments on both sides – encouraging us to be either for or against, according to some crude or subtle measure of socio-political reasoning. It becomes a contest between groups, instead of a tale that resonates on the individual level. Because, above all, immigration is a journey: it involves the packing of cases, tearful goodbyes, a fluttering in the stomach at the crossing of time zones and weather systems, sleepless nights, anxious moments at passport control, exhausting encounters with bureaucracy, an eagerness for new worlds shot through with nostalgia for abandoned ones, a web of kept and broken promises, surprises and disappointments. This tends to be overlooked when debates deal in numbers, and are fuelled by defences of or attacks on our 'record'.

The story of British immigration may also have been neglected because it is so diffuse. We cannot identify a singular migration, like the Great Trek of the Boers, or the massive Irish and Italian evacuations to America: individual events with specific causes, sharp borders and distinctive icons. There is no Ellis Island, no vision of a magnificent, torch-bearing Liberty, in the story of British immigration. Instead, Britain has absorbed migrants at a thousand points and times. Its history is the sum of countless muddled and contradictory experiences. There are happy stories and sad stories, hard-luck stories and success stories, love stories and murder mysteries. It requires a good deal of fabrication and a hearty lack of curiosity to lump the dizzying varieties of immigration – from Huguenot weavers and Indian shopkeepers to South African dentists, from Polish fighter pilots to Jamaican fishermen, from refugee orphans to Russian aristocrats – under a single heading. Some came on steamers from the Caribbean, some trekked overland in the back of lorries, as stowaways or penniless refugees (though a rarely acknowledged fact about refugees is that a high proportion of them are middle class: it takes both means and aspirations to cross half the world, however uncomfortably). Some have come on lilos, in the wheel wells of aircraft, in airless trucks or beneath cross-

Channel trains. Others encountered England at Eton, or Sandhurst, or through investment banks, or in the first-class lounge.

Immigration has given us many institutions that seem built into our heritage: Rothschilds, Warburgs, Barings, Reuters and Cazenove in the City; Marks & Spencer and Dollond & Aitchison in the high street; Trust House Forte and Tesco on our ring roads. Our native architecture has been catalogued by a German, Pevsner. Then there are the literary figures who would not be here if they or their parents had not fixed their sights on Britain – T. S. Eliot, Joseph Conrad, Harold Pinter, Salman Rushdie, V. S. Naipaul, Germaine Greer, Doris Lessing and many others. The most prominent modern historian of these islands, Simon Schama, is himself the son of an immigrant. Immigration has given us shady tycoons (Robert Maxwell), respected generals (Peter de la Billière), noted intellectuals (George Steiner), amazing musicians (Alfred Brendel) and brilliant athletes (Linford Christie). There is much more to this story than the drug-dealing yardies and fiery clerics often deployed as immigrant archetypes. Not everyone knows that nearly a third of Britain's army in the First World War consisted of overseas troops. The Great War remains, to most people, a testament of doomed British youth, the cream of a generation mown down in the poppy fields of Flanders. But a million and a half Indians fought in the war, and regiments from Africa and the Caribbean were quick to join the fray.

Other aspects of British history reveal our multicultural roots to be deeper than we sometimes imagine. The first Indian MP was elected in 1892, and the first black footballer played (for Spurs and Northampton) long before the Great War. Two of the boxing champions of the nineteenth century were immigrants: Thomas Molineaux was a freed slave; Ted Lewis – the showbiz name for Gershon Mendaloff – was the son of immigrant Jews from northern Europe.

Britain has always been invigorated by foreign people and influences, has always been a cross-breed (and it is a characteristic of racial thinking to reckon that only thoroughbreds are worth cultivating). It was formed, in the first place, by a thousand years of invasions, from Rome's to William the Conqueror's. So there may be a few remote Welsh villages that can claim kinship with ancestral Britons, but they certainly form an exclusive club. While the bones of a Stone Age man unearthed recently in the Cheddar Gorge contained DNA that has survived in at least one contemporary Somerset man, that DNA has long since been threaded, plaited, twisted and embroidered with other strands. Most of us, even those who claim direct descent from Cheddar Gorge Man, have immigrant ancestors somewhere in the dense foliage of our family trees, whether we like it or not.

Our national religion is Middle Eastern (via Greece, Rome and Germany), and was brought here by the Western world's first continental drifters, the monks and scholars who roved across Europe. Our language is a fluid compound of German, Roman, Greek and French, and our desert-island books, our national classics, are the offspring of migrants. The Bible is a translation; Sir Lancelot is French; Hamlet is Danish; Shakespeare's blank verse came from Virgil; his sonnets descend from Petrarch. Many of our most popular trees and flowers are immigrants. When the ice retreated the land was impoverished and supported only a tiny number of plant species. The Romans are known to have transplanted the sweet chestnut, the walnut,* the fig and the leek; the Normans carried the seeds of French botany; and the great explorations of empire captured nasturtiums from South America, heather from South Africa, rhododendrons from the Himalayas, hebes from New Zealand, hostas from China and Japan, busy lizzies and begonias from India and gypsophila from Siberia. Lilies, fuchsias, marigolds and magnolia came as strangers and had to adapt to a new climate.

All the rhetoric that seeks to depict modern immigration into Britain as a hazard, putting at risk a thousand-year way of life, plays false with the historical truth: Britain has always accommodated strangers. One of the reasons why it has been able to absorb so many overseas citizens in recent times is that people have been settling here since time began. Immigration is an old, old story, one that defines the texture of British life every bit as significantly as our grand heritage of stately homes – many of which themselves have immigrant foundations.

Of course, over the centuries, there have been shifts in the ideology of national identity. Does it derive from place: the landscape, the soft pastures and hills, the pastoral ideal for which wars have been fought? Is it a set of manners or codes: fair play, thrift and hard work (in the Utopian vision) to which all can aspire? Or is it a question of birth and blood? As Ford Madox Ford pointed out, the first English king, on school rulers, is a foreigner, William the Conqueror, and it is odd how he often seems more 'English' than the crude, hapless Harold, speared – we like to believe – in the eye by an arrow at Hastings.

In the high noon of empire, many true-born Englishmen raised in the Tropics clung fiercely to their customs: teatime, cricket, horseracing, bridge, gin. To the British expat, nationality was and is a quality deriving from a revered set of characteristics, manners and values. But this desire for reminders of home is often interpreted as 'ingratitude' when it is displayed by migrants to these islands. We are shocked if they do not wish to renounce the world they came from. We demand that, when in London, they behave like Londoners.

The pressure of modern migration has led successive politicians to seek narrower definitions of the national character, more dangerously rooted in hotter questions of blood and birth. Today there are competing – or warring – ideas of Englishness and Britishness, and the debate will intensify as 'Britain' loses

*The word 'walnut' comes from the Anglo-Saxon *wealh*, meaning 'far away' or 'foreign'.

credibility as a binding agent. Already, Britishness seems, in the political arguments, an old-fashioned imposition; but unlike many national identities it is by definition inclusive. It might at least be possible for an African or Indian citizen to feel 'Black British', since Britishness is itself a big tent. It may be harder for anyone to feel 'Black English', let alone 'Black Scottish' or 'Black Welsh'.

Daniel Defoe long ago satirised the idea that there was any such thing as an ethnically coherent idea of Englishness. In his famous 1700 poem 'The True-Born Englishman' – written partly to curry favour with England's new Dutch king – he emphasised the stew of foreign influences that bubbled in the English cauldron. It would make a neat contemporary national anthem:

> Thus from a mixture of all kinds began
> That Het'rogenous Thing, an Englishman:
> In eager Rapes, and furious Lust begot,
> Between a painted Briton and a Scot:
> Whose gend'ring offspring quickly learned to bow,
> And yoke their heifers to the Roman plough:
> From whence a mongrel half-bred race there came,
> With neither Name nor Nation, Speech or Fame,
> In whose hot Veins new Mixtures quickly ran,
> Infus'd betwixt a Saxon and a Dane.
> While their rank Daughters, to their Parents just
> Received all nations with Promiscuous Lust.
>
> . . .
>
> For Englishmen to boast of generation
> Cancels their Knowledge and lampoons the Nation.
> A true born Englishman's a Contradiction
> In Speech an Irony, in Fact a Fiction.

This is, if anything, more true today than when he wrote it. Britain has an amnesiac streak, however, when it comes to acknowledging the immigrant blood in her veins.

The transforming movement of recent decades is of a new and spectacular order. The postwar labour shortage created a vacuum which sucked in workers from Europe (345,000 of them), as well as from the collapsing (or liberated) empire. How did they travel? Where did they go (and why)? What did they encounter? What did they abandon? How did they juggle their previous selves with their new situation? How did they cope with the upheaval? How did they reshape both their own lives and the everyday dynamics of life in Britain? We rarely ponder the answer to such questions.

Nor are we always alert or sympathetic to the classic quandary that faces all such migrants: they might come with one eye fixed optimistically on the prospect of a bright future in new surroundings; but the other is always glancing over their shoulder at the home they have left. The process can be chastening. The West Indian playwright and poet E. A. Markham wrote: 'Though there was no particular trauma in leaving home, there was some dismay in England to find the general assumption was that you had left nothing of value behind.'[1] That is a sad comment on the fearful indifference of the country in which he came to live. This may be a reflection of the extent to which racial prejudice is often an abrasive form of incuriosity. Despite several centuries of global adventuring (or perhaps because of them), Britons are characterised by a marked lack of interest in anyone else. This famous insularity may at best lead to a live-and-let-live state of affairs in which, so long as the neighbours are not bothering anyone they can do as they damn well please. But at its worst it can curdle into vicious hostility. The demonisation of asylum seekers as indolent scroungers obscures the fact that immigrants are by definition entrepreneurs. No one more gloriously passes the test proposed by Norman Tebbit's disdainful insistence that people should get on their bikes in search of work than those who have crossed the world in search of a better life. In another, parallel, irony many of those quickest to oppose the persistent desire of migrant workers to come to Britain are also the quickest to exploit the cheap labour they offer. Their houses are cleaned, cars washed, extensions built, coffees mixed, drinks served and children cared for on the cheap, and often in the tax-evading invisible economy, by migrant workers.

Much of what immigration has brought is a matter of texture. Britain's cities embrace an infinite number of flavours or ornaments of immigration – in fashion, music, literature, architecture, retail habits and every sort of food, from curry to cappuccino, from Chinese takeaways and kebabs to pizzas, watermelons and cantaloupes. There are hundreds of different churches, and thousands of cosmopolitan cafés and shops. And as the generations of immigrants advance, British life begins to be more thoroughly (and equitably) porous. Indian newsagents send their children to smart private schools to study medicine, law or economics, so that they will not have to get up at dawn to sort the day's papers. The language of rights assumes a non-racist, egalitarian plateau which is still only barely in view; but though the process of assimilation is a never-ending story of ups and downs, gives and takes, it inches its way onwards through a swirl of triumphs and disasters. And, like a sculpture chiselled by thousands of sometimes clashing hammers, the face of the nation is constantly changing.

In a way it is not a story at all, in the fabular sense of the word; it is a pageant, a picaresque, a jumble of remarkable tales. French Protestants, Jews, Hungarians, Indians, Greeks, Ukrainians, Africans, Cypriots, Chinese, Poles,

Nigerians, Italians, Germans, Swiss, South Americans, Caribbean islanders – some slaves, some millionaires – have been drawn by history or pushed by tragedy. Some have made happy landings; others have found disillusion and misfortune. Many have met bitter racial hostility – though immigration is far from being a black-and-white affair: immigrants have jostled one another every bit as aggressively as they have been jostled by the so-called Anglo-Saxons. This is often ignored by those seeking improved race relations, who fear that if we look too hard at the trees we will fail to notice the size and darkness of the wood. But among the worst enemies of the Russian Jews who arrived as harassed refugees at the end of the nineteenth century were the already assimilated Jews, who saw the newcomers as an embarrassing challenge to their own relatively prosperous social order. The same unhappy paradigms are acted out today in the animosity felt by some West Indians towards Africans, say; or in the local enmities that animate the lives of some Asians in Britain. It often feels safer to cling to generalisations in these delicate fields: almost everyone wishes to avoid seeming racially insensitive. But generalisations that attempt to squeeze a Chinese woman into a category labelled 'Black 'n' Asian', or assumes common ground between Pakistani Muslims and Indian Hindus, to take just two examples, are always going to miss more points than they hit. One of the many ironies in the story of immigration is the speed with which immigrants come to share our national resentment of foreigners.

The pages that follow will seek to catch the drama and the flavours (there is no one prevailing flavour) of this remarkable collective adventure. Britain has been and remains both resistant and accommodating. Every time we sip our ultra-English cups of tea we can, if we wish, savour echoes of the forced labour that cropped the leaves in Asia, or the bent backs of the slaves whose sweaty efforts gave us our sugar lumps. Both on the individual and on the collective level (a national metamorphosis) the story swarms with contrasts, some inspiring, some quite the opposite.

Tolerance and assimilation have moved at a crawl for each successive group of immigrants. The Huguenots of the sixteenth century continued to speak French for a hundred years; the Iberian Jews of the next century hung on to their Portuguese for a similar length of time. It seems that the original immigrants need to die before their descendants can accept themselves – and become accepted – as truly British. But maybe our modern world can move more rapidly. The first stream of postwar immigrants has had a bitter struggle for acceptance, let alone equality, but this has already developed into an intricate politics of identity and citizenship. And the received wisdom (sometimes known as prejudice) can change more swiftly than we tend to think. When Indians and Pakistanis first began to arrive in large numbers, for instance, they were compared unfavourably with the West Indians. A 1958 government working party contrasted 'the skilled character and proven industry of the West Indians with the unskilled and largely lazy Asians . . . feckless individuals who make a beeline for National Assistance'. This stereotype has long been upended – if only to be replaced by others that are equally limiting and unjust.

But while ideological disputes circle, immigrants have their lives to get on with – taking lovers, husbands and wives, being jilted, having children, saving or losing money, drinking with pals, going to church, dancing the night away, scoring centuries, dreaming of better things, nursing grievances or thanking their lucky stars. In so doing, they offer the established residents of these islands something as profound as it is neglected: they hold out the possibility of being British by choice, not by birth. Anglo-Saxon literature dignifies blood above all else; it sanctifies the slaughter of anyone who threatens or challenges the kin or *comitatus*. A cousin is prized more highly than a lover. But Anglo-Saxon literature is uncouth, bloodthirsty and a thousand years old. Surely we can give more recent and civilised ideas a little pirouette in the limelight. The more refined idea of nationhood proposed implicitly by all immigrants, and rejected with vehemence by a few self-styled 'true Brits', coincides usefully with the continuing deregulation of the global market place. In the future, perhaps nations too can best be thought of as competing brands. Perhaps, to borrow the rhetoric of the free market, our future depends on our devising a product attractive enough to compete in the dog-eat-dog atmosphere of the global economy. Far from attempting to deter immigrants, one can even imagine a system of recruitment in which nations compete to attract the brightest and best migrants. Perhaps countries will one day behave like corporations, interviewing and hiring (and firing) applicants according to their own remorseless logic. Of course, there might have to be a relaunch, with bells and whistles, and dancing girls, and a live webcam link-up. The brand might need a new logo (or flag); it might even require a new name: Britland or, if we want to emphasise our buoyant, freewheeling new nature, Swingland. And the ideas for which this new nation stands will almost certainly need to be codified, documented and ritualised into an allegiance not to crown and country, land and blood, but to a set of principles: fair play (if you like), justice, tolerance, dynamism, opportunity, inclusiveness.

There is nothing new in these precepts. It is only a question of giving them a try, on the grounds that immigration is, apart from anything else, the sincerest form of flattery.

CHAPTER 1

The Invaders

The very first immigrant to arrive in the British Isles, some 25,000 years ago, would have been hard put to say exactly where he was, and not only because he could barely speak. He would have been serenely unaware of anything so modern and pointless as his (or anyone else's) nationality. He was simply part of the advance guard of *Homo sapiens*, stepping out on its irrepressible march into all the lands on earth. He would have picked his way, not necessarily in a straight line, through the marshy regions exposed by the thawing of the Arctic snow. With the end of the Ice Age, a habitable land – boggy tundra which slowly bloomed into lush forest – was beginning to emerge above the melting snow. Our man, a hunter-scavenger from the south, needed neither a passport nor even a boat; he could have wandered unchecked through the thick woods that in those interglacial days connected the British peninsula to mainland Europe.

Perhaps he was trailing a mammoth, a bison or a moose; perhaps he was fleeing a rival in love; or took a wrong turn in the Netherlands. Maybe he stopped for a reviving drink at one of the chalky streams in the Kent area, found the water delicious, and decided to stay for a while. It must have seemed a happy place, with woods full of boar and deer, and sweet lakes jumping with fish. Did he realise what he had stumbled on – an entirely new country? Did it occur to him, as he huddled by his fire and listened to the wolves, that he could declare himself king of this damp landscape, and rule in lonely majesty for ever? We'll never know. All we can infer (from the archaeological shards dug up in Berkshire, Devon and Yorkshire) is that the first Britons, whoever they

were and however they came, arrived from elsewhere. The land was once
utterly uninhabited. Then people came.*

Thousands of years later, in 7000 BC or thereabouts, global warming melted
the ice cap and raised the sea level. Water broke through the fragile chalk bridge
that connected the peninsula to the continent and filled the Straits of Dover. But
Homo sapiens had advanced a lot in the intervening years and was able to
overcome this new barrier. Neolithic, Stone Age people came in light skin boats,
cleared land, reared animals and raised crops. The local cavemen could stone
a deer, light a fire and suck the marrow out of bones, but not much else. The
newcomers knew what a spade was. They were small (not much more than five
feet tall) but tough. They took a particular liking to the chalky downland (easy
to till) in Berkshire and Wiltshire, and filled the countryside on either side of the
Ridgeway, and on the fringe of Salisbury Plain, with their villages, mounds,
barrows, earthworks.

A thousand miles to the south and east, great civilisations were beginning to
spring up, in Egypt and Mesopotamia: people were learning advanced new
ways to cultivate and irrigate the land, build towns, monuments and roads,
work together, enslave one another and domesticate animals. Over several
thousand years these new forms of human knowledge drifted towards Britain
in the minds and mouths of migrants.

It would be several more millennia before the next wave of immigration
broke upon our shores. It was an invasion, more or less. The Beaker people
came from the Rhine basin about a thousand years before the Romans. They
were escaping the tribal turmoil of Central Europe and pushing west towards
the known edge of the world. They too came by boat: back then, the Rhine met
the Thames in the swamp that is now the North Sea. Whatever other attractions
Britain held, it was above all the place where the river led, which helps explain
why they set up camps along the Thames valley. They came armed with bronze
swords, and seem, in the dim light of posterity, to have been relatively civilised:
they were clever potters (hence their name) and redoubtable engineers – it was
they (probably) who contrived the remarkable movement of stones from Wales
across the Severn to complete Stonehenge. That grand feat alone suggests that
they brought a new level of social organisation to British life. It is even possible
(given the prominence bestowed on women in their burial mounds) that they
were pioneer feminists.

But we are already committing a historiographical *faux pas*. Prehistory is an
unknown quantity, and it is too easy to infer, from the bones and beads
unearthed by modern archaeologists, that successive waves of migrants

---

*One of the latest theories concerning the lifestyle of the first settlers is that they might
well have been cannibals. Knife-marks on bone fragments found beneath the Eton
boathouse suggest that human flesh was scavenged as eagerly as any other.

'brought' progress, carrying new ideas like so much hand baggage. Historians have a term for such thinking: 'invasion fallacy'. The reality was probably much more subtle. Not everything arrives fully formed; innovations are not smoothly imported. They engage with and are shaped by local conditions. We do not know, for instance, that the Beaker people 'brought' bronze to these islands, thus creating the energetic manufacture and use of weapons that is an enduring hallmark of human life.* Ancient Britain had its own supplies of copper and tin; the Beaker people may have worked with native smelters. Even at this early stage we have to tiptoe between tempting generalisations.

At some point in that long-lost Bronze Age, however, Britain was also populated by southern Europeans pushing north, looking perhaps for somewhere cooler, or for easier hunting. The Latin temperament arrived long before the Romans came, saw and conquered. 'Some Iberian blood', wrote the historian G. M. Trevelyan, 'probably flows in the veins of every modern Englishman; more in the average Scot, most in the Welsh and Irish.'[1] With hindsight, this is a clumsy assertion: it does not seem to have occurred to Trevelyan, even in a chapter titled 'The Mingling of the Races', that Indian or African blood could possibly qualify as 'English'. Nor does he regard 'mingling' as an untidy process: in his hands, it becomes the expert stirring of ingredients by a skilled chef, labouring to perfect that unique and unrepeatable recipe: the Englishman. But Trevelyan is right that the dark, romantic look we often think of as Celtic is more likely to be Mediterranean in origin. The Celts, with their fair skin and red hair, were nowhere near Britain at this time. They were still happily brandishing their swords and howling at one another east of the Alps.

Nevertheless, in most modern accounts, the Celts are presented as indigenous Britishers, victimised aborigines of these islands, oppressed down the centuries by cruel invaders from Italy, Germany, France and (in the new folklores of Scotland, Wales and Ireland) England. In fact, the whole notion of our 'Celtic heritage' is a subject of warm historical dispute. The idea that a single tribe called the Celts overran these islands from Gaul, bringing with them the Gaelic language (from Gaulish), is now sharply contested. Yet we still find it easy to invoke our 'Celtic fringe' as if it were the genuine repository of a rich pagan past. There are indeed many genuine links between ancient Celtic languages and stories but there is also a good deal of political propaganda in the creation of binding national folklores.† This is sharpened by a New Age thirst for cool pagan signs of ancient spirituality. Quite who the Celts were is a

---

*As the novelist John Fowles once wrote: 'If the best stone-age tools are for handling wood and stone, the best bronze-age ones are for killing or subjugating other human beings.'

†'Agreed national histories are inevitably nationalist histories', wrote Simon James in *The Atlantic Celts*, a sharp critique of Celtic mythmaking, 'and are always partisan.'

much more difficult question. The Greeks referred to the barbarians to their north as *keltoi*, but this is skimpy evidence that they were a settled, ethnically coherent Central European tribe. The 'Celts' – the popular name for all the Iron Age peoples who fought their way into France and Britain – were advanced in ironwork and other crafts: they loved elaborate goblets and brooches (and shields). They also loved carousing, making merry and feasting. Traditional history has them coming as invaders, and unusually vicious ones at that: tearing west out of Eastern Europe, they sack Rome like football hooligans at an away match, and don't pause for breath until they hit the ocean. This is now considered unlikely. The brave Gauls with their magic potion who fought off the Romans in the Asterix cartoons were Celts, all right. But the ancient people of the British islands may not have been of the same stock: they might simply have absorbed, to varying degrees, their customs and habits.

Either way, there were no Celts on this side of the Channel until a few hundred years BC. And no one even thought to call them 'Celtic' until the eighteenth century AD, when it became useful to find a term that distinguished the brave, poetic, freedom-loving populations of Wales, Scotland and Ireland from their thin-lipped English oppressors.* The Celts were *arrivistes*. But the Romans didn't know that. So when the legions began to arrive in force a century after Julius Caesar's expeditionary raids in 55 and 54 BC, they assumed that they were dealing with an ancient Celtic province, thus buttressing the legendary status of the Celts. The Druids did indeed hold sway, and there were Celtic names for certain rivers and towns – Avon, Severn, Thames, Leeds – which survive today, but these islands were divided among many warring tribes. The Romans arrived and fought most of them: the Iceni, the Brigantes, the Belgae, the Cantii and the Brythonic. The Romans took the last of those names, gave it a Latin twist, and called us Britons. We should be grateful: we could have gone down in history as Brigands.

Whatever the truth about Celtic society, it does seem undeniable that it was overpowered by the Romans. They brought – and in this case we can use the word without reservation – a quite new concept of social order. They built the famous lattice of roads radiating out from London that is still visible in today's atlases: according to one estimate, three-quarters of the roads in southern England echo the Roman layout. They not only founded towns, but introduced the idea of towns itself. They planted a rough legal framework, the rudiments

---

*Can it be a coincidence that the first appearance of the word 'Celtic' in British political discourse was in 1707, the year of the Act of Union between England and Scotland. Celtic Britain emerged at exactly the same time as Great Britain, in other words; indeed, it can even be seen to have been inspired by the immediate appropriation of 'Britons' – a term which until then referred to the non-English people in these islands – by the new English empire. A new word was required to describe non-Englishness, and 'Celtic' fitted the bill.

of finance, a calendar, the first sprigs of Christianity, the Latin language, an architecture based on stone rather than wood, new culinary habits, superb industrial skills in engineering and glass, novel sports and games, and a distinctive idle lifestyle based on country houses: more than six hundred villas were built during the occupation. They even introduced Britons to the idea of the bedroom – Celtic huts consisted only of a single space for eating and sleeping. Roman merchants and traders followed in the wake of the invasion, married Britannic women, and made lives here. London became a trading post for tin, pearls and slaves (for years, Britain was known as 'the tin islands'). British oysters gathered near Anglesey were shipped off in tanks of sea water and were 'prized' in Rome itself.

The Romans were impressed by more than mere shellfish, though: Caesar himself was notably struck by the Druids. But he probably shared Tacitus' view that 'we are dealing with barbarians'. The Romans may have been happy to plunder the resources of Britain, but they were certainly never going to adopt British customs: they lived exactly as they would have in Rome. They were not farmers, and did not settle the land, as most invaders do: they lived like modern-day expats, in warm, handsome haciendas, surrounded by walls to keep out the plebs.

The Roman occupation lasted for nearly four hundred years. But few of the Roman overseers were Italian, and the army was composed of Gauls, Hungarians, Germans and even North Africans. So, among its other achievements, Rome introduced the first black faces into the British landscape: the skull of an African girl was found in an Anglo-Saxon burial ground in Suffolk, and an inscription in Durham records the life of a Syrian. But, while the occupiers were a multi-ethnic crowd, they were culturally of one mind, and over the centuries the Britons were Romanised too: they wore togas, learned to have baths, shaved, drank wine, sent their sons to school, perhaps even had a stab at rhetoric. The wilder tribes were never truly tamed, so the Romans herded them into the mountains in the north and west (Scotland, Wales and Cornwall) and left them there, behind imposing walls and garrisons. Some of these Britons took to their boats and drifted south across the Channel to the French coast, where they inspected the familiar rocky landscape and nostalgically called it Brittany. Breton and Cornish were closely related and remained mutually comprehensible languages until the eighteenth century; and it was surely a homesick Cornishman who found a new home in the south-west of Brittany, and decided to call it 'Cornouaille'.

The withdrawal of the Roman influence in the fifth century AD ushered in the invasions that established the foundations of modern English – if not British – life. Germanic tribes from Northern Europe swept in and gleefully put out the lights, as they did all over Roman Europe. They were vandals and they delighted in stamping on the refinements of civilised life. If they had intended to settle, they might not have destroyed so many fine stone houses. But they came as raiders, swooping from the sea, snatching what treasure they could find in the monasteries and villas, and leaving as abruptly as they'd arrived. They destroyed almost everything. The English countryside would not have solid roads again until the turnpike programme of the eighteenth century.* Even the language was obliterated: Celtic all but vanished, and Latin itself was shunted aside, except for some solid place names (everything ending in -*chester*) and the odd culinary term: *wine* and *cheese*.

The Dark Ages are so-called mainly because of the figurative sense in which the Roman world, through its literacy, scholarship, urbanity and – eventually – Christianity, was in contrast a lamp of civilisation. But they were also dark in that they passed unrecorded: we know next to nothing about those centuries. The earliest surviving memoir of the times was written by the sixth-century Welsh monk Gildas. He had few happy memories. 'Every colony is levelled to the ground by the stroke of the battering-ram,' he wrote. 'The inhabitants are slaughtered along with the guardians of their churches, priests and people alike, while the sword gleamed on every side, and the flames crackled around.'[2] This is the image that has been given forceful new life by the cinema and popular literature. It is how we see the world inhabited by the archetypal English hero: King Arthur. But there's much askew in the way we imagine Arthur. Should he even be called English? He was, after all, one of those Romanised Ibero-Celts whom the Angles and the Saxons were so anxious to overpower. He was a British rebel (possibly even a Romanophile loyalist) and the Anglo-Saxons drove him and his so-called civilisation into the sea. The Malory-inspired image of him, as an armoured knight on horseback, is five hundred years wide of the mark. He was a Dark-Age brawler, not a flower of medieval chivalry.

Apart from Gildas, what knowledge we have of this period derives mainly from Bede's history of the English Church, written in the seventh century, and he didn't even mention Arthur. But he did largely complete the Anglicisation of Britain. 'This island', he wrote, 'contains five nations, the English, Britons,

---

*Rudyard Kipling summed up the process in a single jaunty verse in 'The River's Tale' (1911).

> But the Romans came with a heavy hand,
> And bridged and roaded and ruled the land,
> And the Romans left and the Danes blew in –
> And that's where your history books begin.

These glib couplets helped create the rum-ti-tum version of English history that presented such an attractive satirical target for Sellar and Yeatman in *1066 and All That*: 'The Norman Conquest was a Good Thing, as from this time onwards England stopped being conquered and thus was able to become top nation.'

Scots [i.e. Irish], Picts [i.e. Scots] and Latins.'[3] He could well have exaggerated
the extent to which these were ethnically defined areas; this might more closely
have resembled a political partition. But since he was himself an Angle, Bede
followed the familiar practice of imposing his own placename: England. Had
he been a Saxon or a Jute we might to this day be living in Saxland or Jutland.*

Which poses the interesting question: who, in this story, are 'we'? The
conquered or the conquerors? In a way it is no surprise that a certain vexation
still clings to the subject of whether we are British or English, because these are
at bottom exclusive entities. At this stage, the English were emphatically not
British. If anything, they were busy appropriating the name of the land they
had invaded. Once again, however, we must resist resting on the assumption
that incomers naturally obliterate all traces of the local lifestyle and replace
them with their own. When the initial rampaging died down, what actually
took place was a merger. The English and the British lived alongside one
another. We know little of the details: they were not busy writers.
Undoubtedly, they often fought like wildcats. But after three or four centuries
they had created a new race and a new language: Anglo-Saxon. The basic
compost of Englishness – we cannot say Britishness yet: the Scots (in Ireland),
the Picts (in Scotland, so-called because of their war paint) and the Welsh Gaels
were all valiantly loyal to their British heritage† – was beginning to ripen and
mature.

Almost everything about the Dark Ages now seems remote and somewhat
comic.‡ There is a cartoon depicting two ancient Britons wagging fingers at
each other as if in civilised argument. The caption says simply: 'Some of my
best friends are Jutes!' Ethnic conflict has been with us for longer than anyone
can remember.

The Jutes were one of three Germanic tribes who invaded and settled the
British Isles as the Romans withdrew. This was an intricate game of musical
chairs, played on a gigantic stage. The Saxons came from northern Germany and
established themselves in the south and west of the island. The Angles came
from what is now central Denmark and made a new home for themselves in the
north and east. The Jutes came from the northern tip of Denmark and took
control of Kent and the Isle of Wight. In one sense they were pushed: everyone

---

*As it happens, England's Anglish origins are more precisely visible in French: *Angleterre*.
They know that deep down we are German, while declining ever to see themselves as
Frank.
†Indeed, it was the Celts who kept the flame of Christianity sputtering through the Dark
Ages. St Patrick took it to Ireland; St Columba carried it back to Scotland by setting up
a monastery on the island of Iona; and Aidan brought it back to England at Lindisfarne.
‡Though some find the era anything but funny. You can almost feel the tears welling up
in G. M. Trevelyan's eyes when he is confronted with the tragic absence of docu-
mentation: 'The most important page in our national annals', he wrote, 'is a blank.'

was anxious to flee the horn-helmeted tribe from across the Baltic – the ferocious Vikings. The Norsemen had good reason to take to their boats. Their own home was a thin, frozen strip of land on the margin of an icy sea. Behind them lay cold and inhospitable mountains. It was often easier to go to the next village by boat than it was to walk, and the sea was the route to both adventure and booty. The flat, defenceless shore of Angle-land and Jutland must have seemed irresistible to these tough warriors and superb sailors. They found they could simply help themselves. So eventually the Jutes, Angles and Saxons upped sticks and moved to Britain (behaving pretty much like Vikings on their way). The Danes moved into the land vacated by the exodus they had caused, so much milder and safer than their own steep fjords. Later they pursued their old victims south and west, invading the new Angle-land, and giving their name to Normandy while they were about it. The Viking raiding parties, like the Anglo-Saxons before them, at first came for boat trips in the summer. But eventually they grew fond of this island and decided to stay. Just like the Romans, they pushed the Britons – the Romanised Ibero-Celts – west and north, into the mountains. Again some fled south to Brittany, where they probably would have been amazed to find the natives speaking a dialect of their own language.

All of this is common – though often neglected – knowledge. Even the truest Brit is a descendant of the invaders who preferred soft valleys and rich monasteries to their own dark woods. Nationalist appeals to ethnic solidarity – in songs such as 'There'll Always Be an England' – suggest that there always was an England. But the first mention of the English in literature – in Bede's description of the Angle boys who inspired Pope Gregory to murmur, '*Non Angli sed Angeli*' – features us as slaves: they were for sale in a Roman market place. And 'we' certainly did not rule the waves: our ancestors were powerless in the face of all those dragon-prowed attacks from the north.

Alfred, the first great English king, was the descendant of Saxon immigrants. But his most immediate and greatest task was to repel those who followed in his ancestors' wake. The Vikings, with their sea power, could strike where they pleased: up and down the coasts and along the rivers. They had fantastic names – Eric Bloodaxe, Harold Wartooth, Wolf the Unwashed, Thorkell the Skull-splitter – and they came with huge spears and axes, smashing and burning, seemingly for fun.* They torched the monasteries at Lindisfarne and Iona, seizing gold and breaking necks. Alfred, assisted by a Channel storm which wrecked a bristling armada off Dorset, resisted them successfully enough to create a partitioned country – Saxon in the south-west, Danish in the north-east.

---

*Though we must always remember that the Vikings may have been dealt a harsh hand by history. We owe our view of their ferocity almost entirely to accounts written by their enemies. Maybe they were not quite so terrible as we think. They did, after all, bring with them the useful word 'law'.

He also came to recognise the importance of sea power – a conviction that spurred Britain to become a nautical people.

Alfred's divided nation lasted for only a century. It took a Danish monarch – King Cnut, in 1016 – to unite the country. Like so many of Britain's conquerors, something in the damp landscape of these islands seduced him into embracing rather than erasing its culture. He became a Christian and built new monasteries, most notably the one at Bury St Edmunds (in commemoration of the East Anglian king slaughtered by Danes). In this period London was a Scandinavian city, with such churches as St Olaf's and St Clement Danes; the leading citizens were Danish merchants. Norse names were scattered across the countryside, too, especially in the north, where any town ending in -by – Derby, Appleby, Rugby, Grimsby – has a Viking signature.

Seen in this light, the Norman Conquest, which often seems to signal the start of the English story, was a civil war between two tribes of Danish expats: the Norsemen of France and the Anglo-Danish heirs of Cnut. It was ignited by the death of Edward the Confessor, who himself had been raised in Normandy and was married to a Norman queen. When the throne passed back to a Saxon, Harold, the Duke of Normandy began to prepare his fleet. William became the Conqueror partly because, as a Norseman, he was invigorated by the prospect of plunder (and England was a ripe prize), but also because he had a decent claim. To some extent, at least, the Norman Conquest was a continuation of the Viking advance.* It added the final ingredient to what, stirred and simmered over the centuries, has come to be seen as the distinctive national stock. What we now think of as the archetypal English character was already, at this early stage, a robust mixture of Mediterranean, Celtic, Saxon, Roman, Jute, Angle, Danish and Norwegian, all moulded and rain-streaked by the British climate and landscape. The Viking burial ship found at Sutton Hoo contained metal bowls from Alexandria, a Swedish helmet, Frankish coins and Celtic ornaments. All that was required was a piquant French sauce: Normandaise. It was very bitter, but the Anglo-Saxon British population had to swallow it for more than two hundred years. Only with the accession of Henry IV, in 1399, did Britain have a king who spoke English as his first language.

---

*This is not what Victorian children learned. Mrs Markham's 1823 *History of England* reminded them that after the Norman Conquest the Saxons outnumbered the Normans, so that 'we are still almost all of us of Saxon descent; and our language and many of our habits and customs sufficiently declare our origin'. This was written only eight years after the Battle of Waterloo, a time when Britain might have been anxious to obscure its links to the continent. In similar vein, popular depictions of the triumphant Duke of Wellington made little of the fact that he had been born and raised in Ireland, and schooled in Paris.

CHAPTER 2

A Norman Province

All around the world, tourist boards advertise trips to Britain with images of the great castles and cathedrals that occupy the commanding heights of our landscape. They seem timeless and typically English. It is rarely mentioned that they are predominantly French – proud monuments to the invasion that signals the end of England's 'dark age'. In the years following his close-run but decisive victory at Hastings, William the Conqueror and his heirs embarked on a construction programme so amazing that within only a few generations the subjugated island north of the Channel was home to many of the architectural wonders of the world. Westminster Abbey was already complete by the time William arrived – it made a handsome venue for his coronation.* But within decades there were other marvels to admire (or fear): the Tower of London was rising grimly beside the Thames; great castles at Chepstow, Colchester, Windsor, Arundel and Ludlow were lording it over the countryside for miles around; and fabulous cathedrals at Winchester, Durham, Canterbury and Norwich were soaring up to the clouds.

The Norman Conquest was swiftly achieved. England fell fast, 'between the third hour and evening', according to the medieval Norman chronicler William of Poitiers. The invader rapidly secured his footing by throwing up forts at Pevensey and Dover, then seizing the land west of London while his troops fanned out through the English countryside. William and his cronies didn't

*Though even this was not an Anglo-Saxon building; it was constructed by Edward the Confessor's Norman Archbishop of Canterbury, Robert of Jumièges.

trouble to win over the population at large: they snatched the levers of power. A whole country was seized from the top down. It was like a corporate takeover.

There was some sharp resistance to be suppressed, however. Harold Godwineson attempted an invasion of his own in the south-west, and the threat of Viking raids along the east coast remained acute. The north simmered for decades. But within a few years an intimidating new feature began to glower over the shires: wooden forts towered above the cowering natives. Then came the creation of larger stone castles, cathedrals and manor houses. The Norman knights drove north into Scotland, pausing on the Tyne to build a stronghold named, truthfully enough, Newcastle. No one could have been in any doubt that there was a fresh power in the land.

The planting of castles was a Norman reflex. The first ramparts were built quickly – more permanent versions in stone came later. By the time of William's death a redoubtable network of more than fifty forts had been raised, both to defend the country against Viking assault and to terrify the locals. Some were weak – the walls or roof would collapse easily or catch fire – but even the rebuilding projects in the succeeding centuries were governed by an aesthetic – Gothic – which had its origins in France. The stone was often French, too, imported from quarries across the Channel.* Canterbury and Winchester were rebuilt by William of Sens and Henry Yevele (who also had a hand in Bodiam Castle). And when Edward I launched the greatest age of English castles in the late thirteenth century – best seen in the Welsh turrets of Flint, Caernarfon and Harlech – their building was supervised by James of St George, from Savoy.

The enthusiastic creation of monasteries and friaries was also encouraged by the new Norman elite. The Benedictine house at Battle (to commemorate the triumph at Hastings) was only the first in what would eventually become a network of twelve hundred religious foundations, some of which, like Tewkesbury, Evesham and Malmesbury, were richly endowed. Then came the Cluniac priories (some thirty-two in all). Even the smaller priories at Northampton and Lancaster were constructed by monks from Normandy. And throughout the twelfth century, monks and friars belonging to the Cistercian, Carthusian, Dominican and Franciscan orders (the first two of which originated in France; the others in Spain and Italy) began to arrive in England. The monasteries were major employers (at Rievaulx in Yorkshire some 500 lay workers were hired as labourers by the 140 monks), and they effected a revolution not just in religious observation but in the financial fabric of everyday life. In developing the practice of sheep farming, for instance, the Cistercians introduced something more than a technical novelty. The

---

*With the masonry came the seeds of a pair of plant varieties – the pink and the wallflower – which would colourfully stud English country gardens for centuries.

replacement of subsistence arable farming with the gathering of wool on roomy estates planted the seeds of an economy built for trade (not to mention one designed to concentrate wealth in the hands of an oligarchy). It might not have been their intention – the whole allure of the Cistercian idea was that it was a retreat from the wicked ways of the world – but it is no accident that the word 'cattle' is related to 'chattel', to the idea of possession. At a stroke, farming became agribusiness and – through the wool trade – a vehicle for international commerce. A pattern of English country life and wealth was laid down which would propel our prosperity for nearly a thousand years.

Few of us remind ourselves of this aesthetic and commercial debt to the Norman conquerors. And, of course, the true picture is murky. Certainly, the first stirrings of the Romanesque style of architecture was visible in tenth-century England; and the realm of Ethelred and Cnut was a growing force in agriculture, commerce and the arts (especially literature) before the Normans arrived. Imperial history, in search of a heroic Anglo-Saxon past for a heroic Anglo-Saxon race, took pains to diminish the impact of the conquest. Edward Augustus Freeman, in his six-volume *The History of the Norman Conquest* (completed in 1877), conceded that it led to 'a most extensive foreign infusion, an infusion which affected our blood, our language, our law, our arts'. But he stressed that it was 'only' an infusion: 'the older and stronger elements still survived, and in the long run they again made good their supremacy'. He felt it was 'a temporary overthrow ... in a few generations we led captive our conquerors; England was England once again'. In this Freeman was loyally upholding a centuries-old trend of regarding Normans as 'them' and Anglo-Saxons as 'us'.* We can hardly miss the urgency of his desire to nourish a continuous national myth that could rally the empire to the banner of Britain's historic resilience.

But what if 'we' are 'them'? Even in recent times (in the war-inspired propaganda of the twentieth century, for instance) we have cultivated a belief in Britain as unconquerable; mighty forces such as the Spanish Armada, Napoleon's war machine and the Luftwaffe, we told ourselves, failed to breach

---

*This was the dominant view, but not the only one. There was a rival tendency to see the Normans as the bringers of civilisation, especially among fans of the Gothic. Thomas Carlyle, in his 1858 life of Frederick the Great, jeered at those who banged the drum for Anglo-Saxon ancestry: 'England itself', he wrote, 'still howls and execrates lamentably over its William Conqueror, and rigorous line of Normans and Plantagenets; but without them, if you will consider well, what had it ever been?' and G. K. Chesterton satirised, in *Orthodoxy* (1909), the urge to sentimentalise Anglo-Saxon roots: 'A man may end by maintaining that the Norman Conquest was the Saxon Conquest.' Freeman's view formed the basis of the history syllabus in schools for years, which helps explain why we still tend to see Harold as a rightful King of England, bravely slain – instead of a malicious usurper or pretender (to the Normans, he was 'the oath-breaker').

our ramshackle but resolute defences. This indoctrination has left a false but distinct impression that we have never been invaded. Indeed, the famous insularity of the British is often attributed to the fact that we do not, unlike our continental friends, have a folk memory of foreign occupation. But this means only that our memories are short and unreliable, because our early history is one of little else.

More fog is spread by the modern tendency to refer to the English as 'Anglo-Saxon'. This misleading categorisation is partly a convenience – a multicultural nation requires a neutral, ethnic-sounding term for the 'host' population; but it owes something also to the nationalist urge to overstate Britain's sturdy connection with those original Alfreds, Egberts and Ethelreds.

Unlike their Angle, Saxon and Viking predecessors, the Normans did not come *en masse* and settle the land. To William and his friends, England was an overseas possession – the jewel in the Norman crown, no less – and it was ruled and exploited like the colony it was: ruthlessly subjugated, then milked for all it was worth.* The occupation was an upper-class affair: only ten thousand or so Frenchmen followed in William's footsteps – less than 1 per cent of the population, and only a quarter of the number that accompanied the Roman Emperor Claudius to Britain in AD 43. But they were the *crème de la crème*: they arrived as, or became, bishops and barons, grandees and magnates. William redistributed the estates of England to his supporters in a land-for-knights deal; lucrative demesnes were awarded in return for the promise to administer local justice and supply troops to the King's reserve army of five thousand well-armed and mobile mounted cavaliers. Thus Odo, Bishop of Bayeux, became Earl of Kent; William Fitz Osbern became Earl of Hereford; Hugh d'Avranches became Earl of Chester; and so on. Other great names abound (they are all listed in the Domesday Book): De Mandeville, Peverel, Lacy, Montfort, Mortimer, Vere, Mowbray. When William died in 1087, one-third of the kingdom was owned by just 180 immigrant lords. And of the sixteen bishoprics in the land, only one was held by a non-Norman.

It amounted to nothing less than the formation of the English aristocracy. Of all the many Norman 'contributions' to British life, this might have been the most far-reaching.† By introducing a feudal system – a land ruled by knights

---

*They were warriors, and organised affairs to be permanently on a garrison footing. The Norman achievement in Britain may be incalculable, but it was secured by methods not much different from the Nazi occupation of France. As William of Malmesbury wrote: 'They are a race inured to war, and can hardly live without it.'

†As R. Allen Brown wrote, in *The Normans and the Norman Conquest* (1969): 'To set down the results of the Norman Conquest is to write the rest of English history to the present day, and to add the histories of all those countries who were to feel the impact or the influence of post-conquest England.' In other words: the sun never set on the Norman Empire.

and barons, each of whom had military and financial obligations to the king – the Norman occupation both laid the foundation stone of the British class system and erected its chief pillar: the primacy of land ownership as the path to power. The first generation of landholders had a plunderer's mentality which did not last. But the structure soon crystallised. A new royal line was established which would endure for two hundred years, or until the present day, depending on your point of view. Indeed, the only ruler since the Norman Conquest who can really claim to be dyed-in-the-wool English is Oliver Cromwell. A social system was born which still occupies the pinnacles of supposedly egalitarian modern Britain. Some of the nation's grandest families can trace the lineage of their property, if not their blood, back to a Norman forebear.* The Normans also gave birth to the longstanding dynastic reflex by which the eldest sons became landowners, the brainy ones went into the Church and the unlucky youngest joined the army.

William's knights were by no means the charming ladies' men of medieval legend. They were advanced horsemen, to be sure, but their armoured cavalry churned through enemies like impregnable tanks rather than fighting for maidens' tokens on jousting fields. They were not averse to splitting a head or slashing off an arm, sometimes on the merest whim. To the population of England they were hired thugs – the word *'cniht'* means a retainer or serving man. And they rode hard (if smooth-shod) over the interests of their new subjects. According to William of Poitiers, the Conqueror was even-handed: 'to no Frenchman was anything given unjustly taken from an Englishman'. But this highly partial view rests heavily on the idea that taking land from the English was entirely just. By the time of William's death, there were only two leading Anglo-Saxon landholders left: Thurkill of Arden and Colswein of Lincoln. The rest of England was in the hands of the new aristocracy.†

The most notable family that could claim a direct line of descent from the battlefield in Sussex was the De Vere clan, which produced twenty consecutive earls of Oxford in a 561-year dynasty that stretched until 1703. Lord Macaulay called them 'the longest and most illustrious line of nobles that England has seen'. The earls distinguished themselves at Hastings, Crécy, Poitiers, Bosworth and in the Elizabethan court. A few corpuscles of their blood, mingled of course with German, English and Scottish, almost certainly flows in the arteries of, for instance, Princes William and Harry.

---

*The editor of *Burke's Peerage*, L. G. Pine, reckons that five out of seventeen English dukes are of Norman descent – a lot, but fewer than the number who claim it.
†The picture painted by William of Poitiers contrasts with the view in the *Ecclesiastical History of Orderic Vitalis*, a twelfth-century Anglo-Norman monk: 'Foreigners grew wealthy with the spoils of England, whilst her own sons were either shamefully slain or driven to wander hopelessly as exiles through foreign kingdoms.'

The feudal society – a hierarchical pyramid by which wealth was sucked upwards (the King taking one-quarter for himself) – gave William the power to maintain a huge and proficient army, which was deployed partly against 'foreign' aggressors (the Vikings, the Scots and the Welsh) and partly as the cutting edge of civil defence. The Saxons were bullied for taxes and brutally punished if they resisted.* The north suffered especially grievously: William's troops laid it waste. It was a brutal episode, though it united a partitioned country by erasing what had long been a national problem, even then: the north–south divide. But what replaced this was an institutionalised racial divide that soon took on the solid outline of a class system. Normans who committed murder were liable for a hefty fine ... unless their victims were English. In the eyes of the overlords, even the free villagers were merely troublesome 'villeins'.

William was, to a large extent, an absentee king. He spent more than half his twenty-one-year reign back in Normandy. So England – and other parts of Britain, too, once the Normans began to plant their castles in Wales, Ireland and Scotland – came for the first time to be ruled by an independent bureaucratic elite. William was canny: the lands he gave his friends and kinsmen were spread far and wide. One noble, Henry de Ferrers (founder of what would later become the Ferrer dynasty, earls of Derby), held land in fourteen different counties. No baron could become an autonomous regional power: each had to work closely with the King and with his exchequer.† The agency through which all this was achieved, of course, was the Domesday Book, a survey of the assets of every town and village in the kingdom, and a vast reckoning-up of exactly what it was the Normans had seized. It's a remarkable document, and we can only imagine the dread that must have accompanied the gathering of information. It wasn't called the Domesday Book for nothing. This amazing tally of the nation's wealth was so-named because, to those who had to endure this intrusive inspection, it resembled Judgement Day.

*The nature and origin of feudalism is a subject that has exercised historians greatly. Some see it as a purely Norman imposition on pre-feudal Britain; others have preferred to view it as the refinement of the Anglo-Saxon system of lordship. It might be that this far-reaching social system derived, in fact, from nothing more than a single brilliant technical advance: the invention of the stirrup. Without stirrups, there could be no cavalry; without cavalry, no knights; and without knights, no Sir Lancelot. Chivalry, after all, is the etiquette of men on horseback. And, like etiquette, it is a French term, firmly rooted in the world of the *cheval*.

†Although the department responsible for taxation wasn't yet called this. The exchequer was named after the large table, covered in a chequered cloth (as in the game of chess: the grid functioned as a medieval spreadsheet for financial calculations), installed by Henry I's new chancellor, Roger of Avranches, early in the twelfth century.

Where previous intruders were initially happy to plunder whatever treasure they could see, and set fire to everything else, the Normans decided from the first to run the country themselves, for their own profit and pleasure. They installed themselves on their new estates and enjoyed the sound of coins clinking into their coffers. One happy by-product of the Domesday survey was that it fixed many of the new nation's place names. Without it, the modern map might read very differently. Some of England's most charming village names reflect their French ancestry: Norton Fitzwarren, Sturminster Marshal, Berry Pomeroy; though for the most part the map remained Anglo-Scandinavian. People's names, on the other hand, adjusted to the new order in ever-increasing numbers. For a few generations there were still children called Alfred, Godwin, Wulfstan and Godric; but soon they became William, Robert, Roger and Geoffrey. The same went for surnames, for those who had them.* Some classic English names – Boswell, Gascoigne, Greville, Neville, Venables and Sinclair – have Norman origins. While Latin remained the official language of law and religious matters, French was the tongue of polite society and of commerce. French terms attached themselves especially to military ranks and official titles – chancellor, lieutenant, sergeant, count, abbot, chaplain and duke – and seeped notably into everyday Anglo-Saxon in the culinary sphere.

There are around ten thousand words of French origin in the English dictionary. The majority of these crept in at a later date, but the Normans certainly implanted a receptiveness to French and thereby helped to create the supple English that was used to such effect by Chaucer and Shakespeare. The English of the pre-Conquest natives was never swamped, but it gained a new dimension of expressiveness. It became rich in synonyms; we frequently have a Latin, a Germanic and a French word for the same thing. We can be skilful (Scandinavian), dextrous (Latin) or adroit (French); on the other hand, we can be sinister (left-handed, in Latin) or gauche (left, in French). But the growth of the language was not only a matter of vocabulary: its conceptual range was broadened, too. If the Angles and Saxons brought a salty lifestyle composed of the *sea, ships, rudders, masts, sails, steering* and *north*, then the Vikings added a sense of *sky, roots, dirt, gasps* and *screams*. It was up to the Normans to add finesse, through *romance, nativity, courtesy, beauty, sacrifice, largesse, feasts, sauces, palaces, ornaments,* and even the Sunday *roast*.

---

*At the base of the social heap, surnames did not become common until the late Middle Ages, when travel began to create confusion between people sharing the same Christian name. In 1465 Edward IV decreed that the Irish be given surnames, much as a modern telephone exchange might order the addition of a new prefix. Surnames described either place or trades: Cork, Weaver, etc. In Norman times surnames were rare, and elongated to ludicrous lengths by hyphens. My favourite is Tollemache-Tollemache-De Orellance-Plantagenet-Tollemache-Tollemache, which suggests an enthusiastic amount of inbreeding.

Intermarriage was encouraged, mainly for political and financial reasons. The Conqueror's niece was married to Earl Waltheof of Northampton; and Henry I, when he became King, set a vivid example to both his barons and his subjects by marrying an Englishwoman, Edith. Local midwives and nannies, meanwhile, were giving the children of these immigrant invaders early lessons in native ways. But outside this upper social stratum it took more than a century for the two populations to merge. Rebellious Britons insisted on wearing beards to cock a snook at the clean-shaven Norman rulers. In 1153, Richard de Lucy could sneer at 'the wiles of the English'; and Richard I's chancellor, over a century after Hastings, was hated partly because he could not speak English. However, at roughly the same time, Richard fitzNigel could say that 'nowadays when Normans and Englishmen live close together and marry each other it can scarcely be determined, that is in the case of free men, who is of English and who of Norman birth'.[1]

So is a conqueror an immigrant? According to the strictest definition, we would have to say that he would at best be an extremely illegal immigrant, a treasure- rather than an asylum-seeker. But at this stage the idea of nationality was at best nascent: there were no customs, only habits. The national gene pool had by now been repeatedly flooded, and the native soil had been double-dug; new and foreign shoots had been grafted on to the grubby rootstock. It doesn't matter which metaphor we choose. The point is that Englishness was not a stable and settled identity: it was always simmering or boiling over, being diluted or reduced. England had foreign rulers, foreign tutors, foreign songs, foreign sports. The Angles, Saxons and Vikings brought people to these shores, brought 'us'; the Normans contributed an upper class. Not all of their leadership was good: some of it was awful; much of it was resented and feared. But within five or six generations – by the end of the reign of Henry II in 1189 – England, if not Britain, had a quite new political, military, commercial and religious establishment.* The institutions created by this establishment are the lasting legacies of Norman influence: the government, the aristocracy, the Church and the army. The Angevin monarchy especially (implanted by the Dukes of Anjou with Henry II) sponsored the development of English common law, an initiative which means that every time we appear in *court* before a *judge* and *jury*, to dispute *debts* and *contracts*, we are resolving our disputes in a celebrated English system that nevertheless has solid French roots.

Royal parks were created for hunting, and the first English handbook on the fine art of the chase was written in French. The Normans also revived the abandoned Roman fondness for gardens, embedding it perhaps for ever in the British psyche. The monasteries led the way, planting vineyards, orchards, vegetables, herbs and flowers. The pattern of village society, meanwhile, was

*As Kipling put it, England was being 'hammered, hammered, hammered into shape'.

laid down in a fashion that would govern country life for centuries: the rich man in his *manoir*; disgruntled tenants in the fields. Our island story, a convulsive saga of class animosity and inequality, would be shaped for ever by the installation of this remote, superior elite. Richard I had the *coeur*, rather than the heart, of a lion, and it lay – despite his heroic role in the Robin Hood legends – in France rather than in England. Even when all Norman influence had been absorbed, and a new line of kings arrived, it came not from England, but from France.

CHAPTER 3

The Expulsion of the Jews

Late in the twelfth century, a man and woman called Arnold and Ode of Cologne trudged from the Rhineland to the Channel coast and embarked at Dieppe for the treacherous sea crossing to Kent. They were pilgrims, heading to Canterbury in search of a miracle; and they were not alone. Since the murder of Thomas à Becket in the cathedral in 1170, the surrounding land had quivered with divine interventions. Mad Henry of Forthwick was led screaming into the tomb, but walked out with his wits restored. A blind woman who touched her eyes with a handkerchief dipped into the martyr's blood regained her sight; the deaf, dumb and lame could all expect miracle cures. In one unnerving drama, a blind man called Robert of Essex was en route to the shrine when he was run over by another blind man on horseback. In desperation he pleaded to the martyr, and at once – a miracle! – he could see! He sprinted the rest of the way to Canterbury.

News of these supernatural wonders spread fast (Thomas was canonised by the Pope only two years after his death); and a prototype tourist industry sprang up in Canterbury, with rascally merchants and cut-throat innkeepers profiting gratefully from the trade in overcrowded lodgings and bogus trinkets. It was not yet the slick package tour described by Chaucer nearly two centuries later, but travellers from all over Europe plodded to the sacred site. They probably passed a few would-be crusaders heading in the opposite direction, east towards Saracen Jerusalem.

Arnold and Ode were praying for a baby. They'd been trying for years, but nothing seemed to work. Canterbury was their last hope. Maybe they bought one of those pewter ampoules of holy water (fresh from the river, but mingled with a drop or two of 'saint's blood'). At any rate, Ode became pregnant. Perhaps out of gratitude, or from fear of the effect the journey home might have on so divine a pregnancy, the couple settled in London. Their son was duly born, and a little later he gained a sister.

Arnold and Ode remained in England, and their daughter eventually married another German, Arnold Thedmar, a noted merchant from Bremen. Their son was also named Arnold Thedmar. He was born in August 1201 and went on to become an alderman of London, as well as a leading player in Anglo-German trade. In 1258 he was convicted of fraud and imprisoned (the charges were trumped up: his real offence was that he opposed Simon de Montfort's baronial attempt to unseat King Henry III), but he was pardoned and restored to eminence only a year later. In his declining years he wrote a book – *De Antiquis Legibus Liber* – a history of the mayors and sheriffs of London.

Arnold and Ode were the kind of migrants we would recognise today: voluntary and unarmed travellers. Many such people came from France, Germany and Flanders to try their luck, beg a favour from a saint, or pursue a trade. There were jobs going in textiles and metalwork, in various crafts and guilds, and given that England was so backward, there were promising business opportunities. The Thedmars found themselves, like many other foreigners, in on the ground floor of a commercial revolution.

In listing the effects of Norman occupation we might have skipped over the most significant: the relative stability it brought to an island that had buzzed with sour warmongering for centuries. The peace was uneasy, to be sure: the enduring popularity of the Robin Hood stories, in which an ousted Saxon patriot fought a nimble guerrilla action against the so-called Norman 'yoke', shows the extent to which a national myth could crystallise around the idea of innate and aggrieved Saxon virtue. The Normans' imposition of a clear national administration and firm defence policy fostered, almost for the first time since the Romans, trade and commerce on an international scale. Hence the Thedmars: people came from foreign parts neither to conquer nor to plunder, but simply to work, live, eat and worship in peace.

Thanks to its holy martyr, Canterbury was cosmopolitan by twelfth-century standards. Arnold and Ode might have raised a few eyebrows, but they would not have faced any official discouragement. The Normans were keen to see England's towns settled by Frenchmen, to prevent the formation of any revolting Saxon strongholds; but immigrants from elsewhere were also encouraged, by the granting of mercantile privileges, to put down roots. Foreigners were preferable to Saxon merchants, as their main interest was clearly commercial rather than political. It was easy for newcomers to obtain royal permits to engage in trade.*

Market day emerged at this time as the focus of urban life, as traders set up stalls in the town centres of Canterbury, London, Bristol, York, Oxford, Lincoln,

---

*Back then, a 'foreigner' could be someone from another county. In Canterbury a Bristol man would have been a foreigner; one from Maidstone merely 'from western parts'.

Norwich and Winchester. Before long, England had become a busy exporter of grain, bacon, sheep, cheese, salmon, lead, tin, coal, honey and leather; meanwhile, boats unloaded wine (partly, but by no means exclusively, for ecclesiastical use), pitch, hemp, iron, timber, cotton, fur, salt, spices, sugar, carpets, oranges, silk and soap. The harbours at London, Bristol, Southampton and the so-called Cinque Ports of Kent and Sussex – and the bigger market towns – Lincoln, Norwich and York – began to hum with foreign accents from France, Flanders, Biscay, Genoa and Venice (the last was, we must remember, around four times bigger than London at this time, and much more civilised). Flemish masons worked on Salisbury Cathedral, and also on the great castles. Foreign cobblers, clockmakers and miners were eagerly sought and handsomely rewarded: in the century after Alderman Arnold, Edward III invited German copper miners over to survey the local landscape and instruct the local people. Perhaps most significantly in terms of British culture, brewers came too. English beer had traditionally been made from malt. It was the Dutch who planted the fruit in Kent that would inspire 'hoppynge beer'. Half of the early English breweries were German or Dutch-owned, and even the English ones relied on expert foreign mixers, stirrers and coopers (we were drinkers first, it seems, and manufacturers only second).

But the biggest business was wool. The Cistercian monasteries had by now become colossal agricultural combines, and the wool trade was the new power in the land. Wool offered exciting arbitrage opportunities to traders from Flanders, probably the most advanced region of Europe, which had a clothmaking industry already up and running. England at this time habitually exported its wool, then imported the woven cloth. The more enterprising traders couldn't help noticing that, while English wool cost up to £15 a sack in Holland, it was only £5 a sack in England. So Flemish and Walloon clothmakers began to cut out the shipping costs and move closer to the source of their raw material. They especially liked the flat countryside of Lincolnshire and Norfolk, which, give or take a windmill or two, was just like home. 'Englishmen', wrote the church historian Fuller, 'knew no more what to do with the wool than the sheep that wear it.'[1] Flemish workers also settled in Cranbrook in Kent, Castle Combe in Wiltshire, and York. One, the judiciously named Thomas Blanket of Bristol, began to produce cloth on a semi-industrial scale. Traders, meanwhile, made royal fortunes, and were royally taxed.*

---

*The prominent place of wool in Britain's agro-industrial past is acknowledged by a smattering of placenames (Ramsgate, Woolwich) and in everyday speech. We can be dyed-in-the-wool, spin a yarn, lose the thread; we can be crooked, fleeced, cloth-eared, sheepish. We can fabricate evidence and unravel a plot. We can be mutton dressed as lamb. Even our broken bones can knit together. Our arguments are often woolly, maybe because we have had the wool pulled over our eyes; but we eat shepherd's pie and retain a taste for homespun wisdom. My own remote ancestors were, more than likely, pretty handy with a bobbin.

Scattered legal records show foreigners engaging in the business world. The court rolls of Grimsby include the bare bones of a protracted squabble between two 'Dutchmen' – Lutkyn Bernston de Hans and Henry Johnson. Bernston sued Johnson twice, in actions involving herrings, eels, crossbows, bars of salt and various hogsheads or pipes of wine (white from Gascony, red from the Rhine). Such traders as these might not have been full-time residents: indeed, their presence was often limited to forty days per annum. But they were granted major privileges – free movement, recourse to the law and so on – to pursue their overseas interests. Their obvious success provoked some stirrings of local resentment which were enough to warrant several royal edicts on 'resident aliens' in 1266.

Throughout this period, the Crown was confronted with a balancing act. It wanted to guarantee the prosperity of the foreign traders, who could be milked for tax; but, though it could afford to ignore public opinion, there were keen baronial interests that needed to be indulged. Officially, however, the foreigners' presence was both appreciated and supported. Edward III would go to great lengths to invite continental weavers to England, even joining a Flemish guild himself. In London there were increasing numbers of Gascon, Flemish, Dutch, Italian and German merchants to handle the trade.

Establishing a pattern that would be repeated many times in the centuries to come, people reacted violently against these showy strangers, who seemed to be doing so well. In 1312 there was what may best be described as a race riot in Norwich, when locals attacked foreign traders, mainly Flemish and Walloon weavers.

The most significant of the new immigrants – the first to form what we would now call a 'community' – were the Jews who ran England's fledgling financial industry. They established families which survived for over two hundred years. To the extent that they thought of themselves as nationals, they probably considered themselves English. They were cultivated, worldly, scholarly and rich.

On Steep Hill in Lincoln stand three ancient stone houses. One is the hall of a local dignitary, Peter of Legbourne; the second seems to have been a synagogue. The third has often been thought to belong to the richest man in Lincoln in the twelfth century, a Jewish moneylender called Aaron. He had business dealings with twenty-five counties. His clients included the King of Scotland, the Archbishop of Canterbury, several other bishops, earls and abbots, and hundreds of ordinary folk. His funds helped build Lincoln Cathedral, the abbeys at Peterborough and St Albans and at least nine Cistercian monasteries. After his death in 1186, his estate was snatched by the Crown, but his cat's cradle of assets was so intricate that a special exchequer (the *Scaccarium Aaronis*) spent years trying to hunt down the debts.

Aaron was merely the most prominent of many. In the centuries of French rule, some three thousand Jews settled in England. They came mainly from Paris and Rouen (at first)* and the Low Countries, having been invited by the Norman and Angevin court. The Church's insistence that usury was a sin was proving to be an inconvenient principle, given its enthusiasm for capital-intensive construction projects (cathedrals), so Jews were invited to perform this important service. Those who came were in any case excluded by the guilds from most other trades and crafts, so in effect they had little choice but to be financiers. They were servants of the King, and required royal permits to set up in business. They were also given special privileges and guarantees: anyone harming a Jew was damaging the King's property (as outrageous an act as poaching a deer). The consequences could be dire.

Thanks in large part to their near-monopoly position (there were some Christian moneylenders, despite the ecclesiastical prohibition), they prospered mightily. They could charge unholy rates of interest, at times as much as 100 per cent per annum. Early in Henry II's reign in the twelfth century, Richard of Anstey (in Hertfordshire) kept a record of his dealings with them. He borrowed forty shillings from Vives, 'the Jew of Cambridge', and paid interest of eight pence a week (nearly 2 per cent – not bad business for the lender) for a year. In a long list of subsequent debts he paid similar rates of interest, between three and four pence in the pound per week. Effectively, whatever amount you borrowed, you had to pay back almost double by the end of the year. But the need for liquid funds was intense, and before long a network of Jewish finance houses stood at the centre of English trade. For a hundred years they flourished. There was a Jewish presence in every major town in the land, as familiar and necessary a sight as a modern cashpoint machine.

Some of the more prominent moneylenders are still radiant names, recalled in the *Dictionary of National Biography*. As well as Aaron of Lincoln, there were Josce of London, Abraham of York, David of Oxford, even Isaac 'the Russian' of Hampshire (almost certainly England's first Russian immigrant). These were powerful men. But this was not a wholly male preserve. Licoricia of Oxford and Belaset of Wallingford were early examples of high-flying women in the financial services sector.†

As the years passed, the Jews branched out a little. Some became doctors,

---

*Leaving Rouen might not have been too much of a wrench: the Jews of that city were twice lynched, in 1010 and 1096 (for resisting baptism). This second eruption of violence almost certainly convinced the survivors that now might be a good time to try their luck with the other French expats across the Channel.

†Licoricia 'donated' £2,500 to support the building of Westminster Abbey – not, one assumes, a cause especially close to her heart. It's likely that such 'donations' were paybacks to the establishment for continued protection. The name Belaset, meanwhile, translates as 'nice assets' – a tribute, no doubt, to her financial muscle.

goldsmiths, pawnbrokers and even laddermakers. There were artists (Marlibrun of Billingsgate), fishmongers (Abraham le Peysoner), crossbowmen (Abraham Balisterius) and cheesemakers (Isaac Furmager). There were rabbis, too, some of them scholars of international repute: Elijah Menahem of London was a leading translator and Judaic theologian, with an impressive library. The most potent community was in London, clustered around a synagogue in what is now Ironmonger Row, near Moorgate. There were other synagogues in Threadneedle Street, Coleman Street, Basinghall Street and Gresham Street. One of the City's cramped alleys still recalls them: Old Jewry.

Initially, they ran a franchise operation: the King charged them fees for commercial privileges while going to them for loans. But after a while it dawned on the monarchy that taxation might be preferable to borrowing, since no repayment was involved. Slowly, and with increasing severity, the Jews' growing wealth was plundered in a series of random and greedy taxes, or 'tallages'. Successive kings viewed them as an almost bottomless war-chest.

Meanwhile, out in the shires, relations began to sour. Naturally, since they prospered, the Jews were hated; though it is important to remember that initially, at least, they were hated no more than any rich French nobleman. But over time their cultural and religious distinctiveness made them the target for obvious prejudice. In 1144 the murder of a small boy, William, in Norwich was hastily attributed to a Jew. The boy became the focal point of a miracle-working sect, and eventually he was even canonised. Other unsolved murders or untimely deaths were readily blamed on the supposedly sinister Jews: if a Jewish doctor failed to save a life, the whole Jewish community might be attacked and fined.

Henry II protected them (they were the goose, after all, that laid several golden eggs in the form of castles and cathedrals), but he also, and with impunity, confiscated a quarter of their wealth in 1187. By this time there was a fresh and sharp new odour in the wind: crusading zeal. The Jews were infidels, and their presence meant some defending of the faith could be done en route to the Holy Land. Nor do the indebted often have generous thoughts about their creditors. When Richard I inherited the throne in 1189, he rode his affluent Jewish financiers hard in order to raise funds for his assault on Jerusalem. At his coronation, London's Jews were attacked, and the following day similar uprisings burst out in Norwich, Lincoln, King's Lynn, Thetford and elsewhere. In York, 150 Jews were herded into the castle and murdered. The twelfth-century mob, it seems, was as easily roused (by thoughtless or malign leaders) as it has been many times since. Many Jews survived only because their contracts stipulated that they had the right to take refuge in royal castles. Winchester's Jews sheltered in that town's castle so often that one of the turrets became known as the Jews' Tower.

When Richard left, his brother John helped himself to huge sums (ostensibly to help ransom brave and good King Richard – hardly a cause close to Jewish hearts). In 1210 John imposed a tax so severe that some Jews decided to leave the country. Those who stayed soon wished they hadn't. It is said that one Bristol Jew was tortured into parting with ten thousand marks by the simple expedient of having a tooth pulled every day until he consented. He was brave: he held out until the seventh tooth.

Resentment of the Jews slowly hardened into official disdain. In the thirteenth century Henry III not only plundered them but began to destroy their legal rights. One by one, they were expelled from town after town, including Leicester, Lincoln, Warwick, Southampton, Nottingham and Newbury. By accepting land in lieu of debts, they had become significant landowners and property agents; but from now on they were banned from owning anything other than the house in which they lived. They were permitted only a single burial ground, the one in London; so the corpses of deceased Jews would be trundled on carts across the shires to their place of rest. Dogs would run after them, barking as the mournful carriages creaked past.

The nobility still needed the Jews to underwrite their more expensive adventures: Richard of Cornwall used Abraham of Lincoln to finance his successful bid for the throne of Germany. But throughout Henry III's reign they were brazenly persecuted. New laws were passed and edicts issued to limit their freedoms: any Jew born, proclaimed the King in his Mandate on the Jews of 1253, 'shall serve us in some manner'. Two years later Henry himself attended the punishment of a Jewish man, Copin of Lincoln, who happened to live near a cesspool where a young boy, Hugh, had been found dead. Copin was tortured until he confessed. The King then ordered that he should be dragged through the town tied to a horse's tail before being hanged. It was a fateful moment: the harrying of Jews had been given the royal seal of approval. A hundred other Jews were subsequently arrested for the murder of the same boy, who later, like little William of Norwich, would inspire patriotic (or anti-Semitic, depending on your point of view) ballads and rhymes. A further eighteen who protested against the injustice were executed.

The mob, unchecked by any official penalties, began to rule. On Palm Sunday in 1263, in London, some four hundred Jews were killed in a festive rampage. The following year saw even more carnage: up to a thousand Jews were surrounded and beaten to death. This, the London Massacre of 1264, immediately entered the pantheon of anti-Jewish atrocities, though in the usual version of England's chequered history it barely rates a mention. A few years later, in 1272, the London synagogue was confiscated and given to some friars. Events were sliding downhill in what now looks like a familiar trajectory. In 1275 the new King, Edward I, issued the *Statutus de Judeismo*, which banned Jews from lending money at interest, thereby ruining the majority at a stroke.

It obliged all Jews over seven years of age to wear a brand – a patch of yellow cloth – for identification.* It was now illegal for Jews to leave the country (for fear they might take precious English money with them), but in 1276 several Jews were deported for tallage avoidance. The expulsion had begun, and it did not end for another decade.

In 1282 Jewish religious observance, even in private homes, was banned. In 1287, in an act of the most blatant extortion, all Jews were arrested, pending the payment of a twenty-thousand-mark tallage.† But the money was no longer there; the cash cow had been milked dry. Two years later, in what looks like a contrived pretext, accusations of coin-clipping – a white-collar crime involving the shaving of silver from the King's currency – were levelled at the Jewish community. There were house-to-house searches, and all suspects (some 680 out of a total Jewish population that some estimates put as high as 10,000) were arrested and sent to London. They were imprisoned in the distinctly uncomfortable Tower; 293 were hanged, and their property was confiscated. Meanwhile, eight Jews were hanged in Bedford, five in Canterbury, four in Norwich. As would so often be the case in the future, the Jews, rather than the mob that was persecuting them, were seen as 'the problem'.

Eventually, in 1290, in an act that would resonate across Europe and be echoed by continental monarchs, the problem was 'solved'. The remaining Jews were formally expelled in a mass deportation. In a hollow spasm of goodwill, the emigrants were treated with conscience-salving grace. Orders were written that no one should 'injure, harm, damage or grieve' them. The exiles were even permitted to take their cash and portable wealth, such as was left; their property and bonds fell to the Crown.

The expulsion of the Jews was both a tragedy and a national disgrace. It has also been allowed to slip the national mind. A. L. Poole in *The Oxford History of England* (no less), fell blithely into the suggestion (or presumption) that the Jews brought the expulsion on themselves: 'The ostentation which possession of great wealth enabled the Jews to display, and their unconcealed contempt for the practices of Christianity, made them an object of universal dislike.'[2] Given that the 'practices of Christianity' included brazen hypocrisy about money, punitive and arbitrary taxes amounting to extortion, the gouging out of eyes and wrenching of teeth, 'unconcealed contempt' would seem a mild and civilised response.‡ One wonders, also, about the strength of Poole's 'universal

---

*The resonance of this is clear enough. But if the medieval Jews were obliged to wear this so-called 'badge of shame', it suggests that they did not stand out physically. The cartoon of the medieval Jew – stooped, hook-nosed, long-bearded – would seem to be a myth. They wore the same hooded cloaks as everyone else, and did not even favour beards.
†Whether such figures are accurate is not clear. H. G. Richardson, for one, believes them to be merely 'picturesque expressions denoting a very large, an incalculable sum'.
‡Though there is no evidence that the Jews displayed even this.

dislike'. There is no denying the existence of lynch-mobs, but these often seem to have been mobilised by desperate debtors. When the Jews of York were massacred in 1190, among the first things to be destroyed was the list of bonds they held. It is possible that the hatred was driven by financial rather than racial panic. There are sufficient instances of peaceful cooperation – joint ventures, even cheerful social encounters – to suggest that, to some extent at least, the Jews were able to live with tolerable ease. Aaron of Lincoln and Gervase of Cornwall set up a joint property company in Mansion House. Jews and Christians are recorded as exchanging jests in the crowd arrested for chasing a deer down Colchester High Street. In polite society there were even good-natured theological debates. Many Jews stashed their valuables with accommodating Christian neighbours when the taxation became punitive. The Jews of Norwich, in 1190, might have been as doomed as their colleagues in York had it not been for the good offices of the local bishop, Hugh, who intervened and saved them. These were pitiless times, and many a Christian lost his life, or at least a limb, thanks to the royal thirst for cash. But even if money was the root of this particular evil, the fact remained that the majority had turned on a single community. England had become a place that could not tolerate foreigners. By the time Edward I expelled the Jews, they had nothing left. They had been reduced, as one chronicler said, to 'prowling about the city like dogs'. Their houses were sold, raising the less than princely sum of just two thousand pounds. Edward spent it on the tomb of his father, and on some new stained-glass windows in Westminster Abbey. The many generations who have no doubt admired them since can rarely have thought of the stricken Jews walking, throughout October 1290, towards the harbours of Kent and London before the 1 November deadline for their departure (All Saints' Day).

One of the boats commissioned to carry them away struck a sandbar in the Thames estuary. The captain invited his passengers to disembark and stretch their legs, then sailed gleefully off the mudflat, shouting to the bereft refugees that they should seek help from Moses. Maybe they tried. But no one came to their aid. The sea did not part. They all drowned.

CHAPTER 4

'Onlie to seeke woorck'

In 1204 the Norman landowners of England lost their possessions in France. Perhaps this stimulated in the aristocracy a sense of England as a home rather than an overseas possession. If it didn't, then the Black Death of 1348 completed the job. Nearly one-third of the population was wiped out by the gruesome disease, which did not discriminate between rank or race as it rippled through the national bloodstream. Disaster, though, can create fellowship; community spirit can thrive beside the wells of loss and bereavement. So the plague – which was merely the worst of several outbreaks in fourteenth-century England – left in its wake a people united by disaster. It also produced a gap in the labour market that immigrants were eager to fill.

The country had by this time been ruled by a cosmopolitan, non-English elite for nearly three centuries, so foreign bosses were nothing new. But shipping was improving, and it was not such a reckless adventure to cross the Channel any more. So, along with the businessmen who sniffed commercial opportunities in the blighted island, ordinary workers began to filter across the grey sea to Kent. News did not travel fast in the Middle Ages: word trudged at walking pace. But by the end of the sixteenth century economic migrants were almost commonplace, if not exactly welcome. Over a third of the 7,143 'strangers' quizzed in 1573 (in one of several nervous surveys of 'aliens' conducted by Elizabethans) said that they had come to these shores 'onlie to seeke woorck for theire livinge'.*

*In a pioneering attempt to distinguish between 'real' and 'bogus' asylum-seekers, the Elizabethan authorities tried to separate those who had come 'for consciens sake' from those who were merely job-hunting. Those who admitted that they had come 'onlie to seeke woorck' were filed under the Elizabethan for 'bogus', and asked, far from politely, to leave at once.

Strangers had been drifting England's way for a long time by then. At the end of the thirteenth century Italian financiers, with royal encouragement, were quick to occupy the position evacuated by the expelled Jewish moneylenders. The Riccardi family of Lucca (in charge of collecting customs payments for the Crown), the Frescobaldi of Florence and the Bardi and Peruzzi families swiftly became opulent virtuosi of the money supply. Successive Masters of the Mint came from Marseille, Asti and Florence. Their influence on England's finance industry is recalled in prominent placenames, such as Lombard Street in the City of London. They even imported the symbols for pounds, shillings and pence, from the medieval Italian *lire*, *soldi* and *denari*.

Under the terms of the *Carta Mercatoria* of 1303, an agreement that granted rights to foreign merchants in return for dues and levies, overseas traders were free to come and go, import and export, enforce contracts and settle disputes. They thrived, though they had to be careful. 'Be obedient to the powerful, keep on good terms with your fellow countrymen,' advised Amerigo dei Frescobaldi, a well-padded banker and Lincolnshire landholder. 'And bolt your door early.' This was sensible advice. But in official circles immigration was encouraged. England was intent on remedying its palpable lack of industrial expertise, and the quickest way to do this was to inspire a brain drain from the continental centres of excellence.

Wool was the central thread of the economy. Not everyone was pleased. Thomas More saw it as tyrannical, an early form of corporatism in the way it cleared the land and challenged the old ploughman's lifestyle. 'Sheep', he observed, 'are eating up men . . . They pluck down towns, and leave nothing standing, but only the church to be made a sheep house.'[1] When the monasteries were dissolved by Henry VIII, many people cheered, since to rustic eyes they were merely grasping wool conglomerates. As an economic initiative, the dissolution of the monasteries was double-edged: England's wool trade was dealt a bad blow. But international trade was expanding in other areas, and England's bureaucrats could see the need to keep pace with continental methods. Henry VIII invited skilled ironworkers from Germany to pound steel in the Royal Armoury in Sussex. Not long afterwards, in 1568, Daniel Hoechsetter, a German smelter from Augsburg, set up one of the first two English joint stock companies when he established a mining firm in the Lake District. He had been authorised to prospect for minerals by Queen Elizabeth, and initially took twelve German workers with him to Keswick to extract copper and silver. At its peak, some years later, his company, the Society of Mines Royal, employed some 150 Austrian and German craftsmen. His descendants were not as astute, though, and the company went bankrupt in 1634.*

*The word 'bankrupt' itself derives from the Italian *'banca rotta'*, a businessman's bench, which was symbolically broken if he failed to meet his obligations.

Daniel Hoechsetter was the beneficiary of some surprisingly enlightened policy-making. When Elizabeth came to the throne in 1557, Lord Burleigh took it upon himself to solve the trade deficit between England and the rest of Europe by importing people. He could have banned foreign luxuries such as hats (£8,000 per annum), satin (£10,000) and pins (£3,000), but he chose instead to boost rival industries here. Italian silk weavers were invited from Geneva with an offer they could hardly refuse: freedom from customs, protection from competition, a house, a church, a school . . . It was a sweet deal, and similar terms were available for foreigners to begin the manufacture of soap, saltpetre (used in gunpowder) and other essentials in England. The energetic acquisition of overseas knowledge was gathering pace, and it had an explicit educational purpose: foreign traders were obliged to hire English apprentices and pass on their skills.

At the other end of the social scale, a few gypsy caravans were popping up in England's muddy fields. Their name – a vague compression of 'Egyptians' – was coined at a time when very few Britons had seen an Egyptian in the flesh. They were first glimpsed – as far as anyone can tell – around 1480. But the earliest written record of their presence dates from 1514, when a witness at an inquest referred to Egyptian women who 'could do marvellous things by looking into one's hand'. Some of the brasher ladies at court were quick to sport vivid versions of flamboyant gypsy costume, but the powers-that-be were not so impressed. Henry VIII passed England's first anti-gypsy law in 1530 after Parliament, fearing that vagrancy might prove disruptive or infectious, was moved to legislate against them. The 'gypsions' were ordered to leave, and banned from re-entering the country. Harsher measures followed. In 1540 a group of gypsies, after a short stay in Marshalsea Prison, was herded on to a ship bound for Norway. In 1554 the death penalty was introduced for anyone caught consorting with them, and it was no idle threat: in Aylesbury, in 1577, six people were hanged under this law. Another five met the same fate in Durham, in 1592, and nine gypsies themselves were executed in York in 1595. The 1598 Act for the Punishment of Rogues, Vagabonds and Sturdy Beggars insisted that they were a rotten and unwelcome menace. But a few long-suffering gypsies continued to slip through the countryside. Perhaps one of them inspired Shakespeare's 'Egyptian mind-reader', who gave Othello's mother the strawberry-flecked handkerchief that caused the tragic hero such heartache.

Unlike the majority of foreigners in Britain, gypsies were of no economic significance and could count on no support from the ruling class. But if the expert immigrants – the weavers, cobblers, glass-blowers and brewers – were sponsored and welcomed by the authorities, they too faced resentment from those less advantageously placed on the social ladder. Increasingly, they were also seen as an unwelcome encroachment. There were quarrels over jobs and rent (migrants down the centuries have tended, with the eager collusion of landlords, to put pressure on housing), and complaints that foreigners worked too hard.* Perhaps no one troubled to publicise the benefits that incoming craftsmen and entrepreneurs might bring. The otherwise righteous Peasants' Revolt of 1381 left foreigners cowering in their churches: some were lynched if they failed a simple test and said '*brod*' instead of 'bread', or '*case*' rather than 'cheese'. In Yarmouth, Wat Tyler's men went on a hunting trip, found three men and killed them. And in London the peasants were in no doubt about who were their most significant enemies: the Flemings. 'There was scarcely a street which was not littered with the dead,' writes one historian.† 'In one place lay a ghastly heap of forty headless corpses.'

As with the Jewish moneylenders of an earlier age, the 'aliens' began to find themselves hedged about by new restrictions and impositions. In 1440 they became liable for a new 'stranger' subsidy of sixteen shillings: some two thousand names appear on the roll of those expected to pay it. In 1453 this became an annual tax of forty shillings. In 1481 the Steelyard, the headquarters of the Germanic merchants who dominated the Hanseatic trade with the Baltic states and the Rhineland, was raided and wrecked. And there were repeated race riots, mainly in London. Two anti-Italian uprisings in 1456 and 1457 caused most of the Venetian, Genoese and Florentine merchants to lose heart and leave. And in 1517 – on what became known as Ill May Day – a London mob embarked on an energetic witch-hunt for aliens, who were seen as rich, sharp-elbowed cuckoos in the otherwise immaculate English nest. Royal troops suppressed the riots, but the Crown then introduced a new set of statutes by

---

*One of the ways in which they pressurised rents was by crowding into small spaces, lowering the price per person at the cost of the price per house. The dramatist Robert Wilson has one of his characters in *The Three Ladies of London* (1590) advising a friend on the management of her properties:

> Madonna me tell ye vat ye shall doe, let them to straunger dat are content
> To dwelle in a little roome, and to pay muche rent.

Wilson clearly felt strongly about this issue. In another play he wrote:

> I would gladly get by living by mine Art
> But Aliants chop up houses so in the Citie
> That we poore crafts men must needs depart.

The same argument could have been heard in London's East End in the late nineteenth century, or in Notting Hill in the 1950s.

†The aptly named J. Arnold Fleming, whose two-volume history, *Flemish Influence in Britain*, was published in 1930. He is usefully alert to the Low Country origins of some standard English fabrics: gingham comes from Guingham in Holland, and the arras through which Polonius was stabbed in *Hamlet* was named after a town famous for its tapestries. Diapers, meanwhile, were originally cloths from Ypres – d'Ypres.

which denizens became liable for a new alien tax – at roughly double the normal rate.*

In Norwich, where refugees had been invited to help restore the city's textile fortunes, the rules were detailed. Foreigners could not sell their products on the retail level, except to fellow aliens. They were not allowed to buy the animal skins they needed to work leather. They were not allowed to operate more than one loom each, or to transport their yarn without special permits from the mayor. And they could not have guests for more than one night. They were accused of pushing up the price of timber and – of course – of spreading plague.

Such anti-foreign backlashes look familiar enough, and offer dismaying evidence that a fiery hostility to strangers has been visible for as many centuries as we have known what to call ourselves. But medieval life was rough, to say the least; and the list of atrocities, while terrible, is relatively brief – the eruptions punctuating long periods when no animosity is recorded. Cardinal Wolsey raided the Steelyard twice in search of pernicious Lutheran tracts. But in 1538, four Dutch Anabaptists were burned at the stake as heretics; and two more followed in 1540. In Amsterdam, more than 150 so-called heretics were killed in similar reprisals, and when the crackdown gathered pace in the Low Countries in 1544, many Protestants fled swiftly to England. It might not have been perfect, but it was the safest haven in Europe. There were tremors, but no pogroms.

So, despite the persistent sense of unease and occasional bouts of violence which surrounded England's immigrants, the trickle slowly became a flood. In 1500 there were three thousand foreigners in London, 6 per cent of the civic population. 'Tottenham', said one alarmed Londoner in Henry VIII's reign, 'has turned French.' When Nicander Nicius visited England in 1545, he wrote: 'Here there dwell men from most of the nations of Europe.'[2] Many refugees were men and women of notable energy and renown. One, a Mrs Dingham van der Plasse, the wife of a Flemish knight, enriched herself by introducing the English upper class to starch, a refreshing new laundering technique which inspired the development of those large frilled ruffs so familiar from Elizabethan portraiture. She was even willing, for the tidy fee of five pounds, to teach English apprentices how to stiffen a collar. Another migrant, Peter Martyr, was an Italian-born Dutch scholar who promptly became Regius Professor at Oxford.

Not all of the Dutch immigrants stayed in the south-east. One, Jan de Groot, set up a ferry service in the far north of Scotland, at a little harbour which would later become legendary as John O'Groats. He was one of three brothers who settled on the harbour's edge in 1496. Soon there were eight De

---

*Denizens were those who had been formally granted – or had bought – the right to live and trade as Englishmen.

Groot families all vying for precedence. Motivated perhaps by the same egalitarian notion that lay behind Arthur's round table, the wily Jan built an octagonal house, with eight entrances and an eight-sided table in the main hall.*

Peter Martyr was well named. He was in the vanguard of a new phenomenon: the Protestant exile. As a new Protestant nation, England obviously attracted persecuted Christians from the other side of the Channel, mainly from the Low Countries. They were by definition self-reliant: much of the doctrinal energy of the Protestant revolution stemmed from ideas of personal responsibility (for interpreting the Bible as well as in moral conduct). They were industrious, thrifty and independent-minded. Protestants rested only on Sundays, while Catholics took a two-day break each week. So Protestants put in more hours; and with their keen sense of self-advancement, this gave them a striking edge in productivity. Later, these qualities would be harnessed into one of the Western world's most powerful commodities: the Protestant work ethic.

In 1548 there were sufficient numbers of 'strangers' in Canterbury to justify the creation of England's first foreign-language church: St Alphege's, a gift to the French from Archbishop Cranmer. Two years later, the growing band of 'strangers' in London won a church of their own: Austin Friars, the roomiest church in the City. The first leader of the London church was a Polish baron, John a Lasco, a former Archdeacon of Warsaw, a Protestant convert and a well-travelled scholar who had visited Erasmus in Basle. He was swiftly accepted as a bona fide VIP: in 1552 he sat on a thirty-two-man commission to revise ecclesiastical law. There were two other ministers, one of whom, Francis Perussel, had been accused of heresy in Paris in 1545. It was he who had founded the French church in Canterbury before moving to London.

Their timing was not good. The church was only three years old when Queen Mary took the throne and attempted to reverse the Protestant cause in these islands. Austin Friars closed its doors and its leaders fled to Germany. But they returned when it was reopened in 1559, and the congregation swelled. A year later, Austin Friars became the Dutch church. The French set up their own in Threadneedle Street, which was then, as its name suggests, a neighbourhood noted more for its looms than its loot. The congregation lived in Southwark, Smithfield, St Katherine's Dock, Whitechapel and Farringdon – all within walking distance of the pews – which regulated its spiritual and secular life.

---

*The greatest Dutch contribution to Scottish life, though, is the game of golf, which began as *Het Kolven*, and involved knocking a ball across ice at a post. In 1457 James II declared that 'golfe be utterly cried down and not to be used', but kings have only so much power. If cricket is a West Indian game invented by Englishmen, golf may well be a Scottish game invented by the Dutch.

They were tailors, weavers, shoemakers, woodworkers, metalworkers, goldsmiths, glassmakers and printers.

It was in this last trade that they made perhaps their most immediate contribution to English publishing. Caxton's press was taken over by the well-named Wynken de Worde, from Alsace, and nearly all of the other leading printers were foreigners. Nicholas van den Berghe, trading under the name Nicholas Hill, published thirty-six books between 1547 and 1553, mostly Protestant tracts. In one of them he wrote a fervent preface thanking King Edward VI for 'the great benefits I have received of this your majesty's realm of England'. Stephen Mierdmann came to Billingsgate from Antwerp, and had three employees to help him turn out fifty editions of various works, including a robust attack on the papacy which he probably wrote himself. Others – William de Machlinia, John Lettou, Reyner Wolf – dominated the new printing medium and gave it a radical, dissident, Protestant flavour. God's word spread, through their hands, throughout England, and helped the Protestant cause, which still had flimsy roots, to prevail.

In 1561 the town of Sandwich on the Kent coast took an enterprising decision. Having identified the need for 'men of knowledge' to boost the flagging local economy, it invited 'five and twentie' migrant householders from London to set up textile workshops by the sea. The settlers – almost all Flemish Protestants – began to arrive in December, and their households turned out to be sizeable. Francis Bolle, for instance, brought his wife Christina and their nine children (four sons and five daughters, ranging from three to eighteen years old). In all, 407 people arrived in the following months. Their workshops prospered, and in 1568 they attracted a fresh batch of immigrants, this time French-speaking Walloons. By now a third of Sandwich was foreign, and since there was insufficient work even on the ever-humming looms, some of them became pirates, preying on Spanish ships in the Channel. The Crown could not afford to turn a blind eye to this, and the French were moved wholesale to Canterbury, which had already felt the brunt of the Sandwich effect and had applied for the same miracle cure.

At this time the cathedral city was a shadow of the place that had once attracted pilgrims from all over Northern Europe. The dissolution of the monasteries had broken the spell cast by Thomas à Becket's shrine, and the vast hostels of Chaucer's day were now almost empty. The city offered a hundred houses to 'strangers', some of whom were already Anglicising their names: Du Bois became Wood; De Bourges became Burgess; Blanc became White. They founded a church and a school, began to turn out bolts of serge and silk, and grew in number. Perhaps 750 people crammed into those first 100 houses, but by 1582 there were over 1,600 in the local congregation; ten years later there were 2,700; and in 1595 the figure had topped 3,000. As in Sandwich, this represented one-third of the city's population, and they were similarly busy: eight hundred looms were soon spinning out fine cloth and silks, and the city achieved fresh fame as a foreign-accented industrial powerhouse.

Once again, Canterbury became an important oasis for new immigrants on the road from the Channel ports to London. Paul Erfo, travelling in a party of fifteen people, paused in Canterbury and was loaned five shillings to help him on his way. A generation or two later, in 1640, a writer called W. Somner, in his already-nostalgic *Antiquities of Canterbury* (one of the first, though by no means the last, laments for the glory of bygone times), complained that the foreign congregation had 'growne so great and yet daily multiplying, that the place in short time is likely to prove a hive too little to contain such a swarme'.

In spite of this 'swarme', the 'stranger' population of Canterbury seems to have lived peacefully enough. In London, foreigners might be called rude names in the street, but in Canterbury the so-called natives were well aware of the prosperity the aliens had helped to foster. They were self-regulating: a committee of church leaders – eventually a formal twelve-man court – ensured that the flock did not stray, and liaised with the mayor on matters of discipline and punishment. They looked after their own but their burgeoning businesses constituted a significant job-creation scheme for the locals. In an annual report to the Crown, the city authorities insisted that the Walloons 'not onely maintaine their owne poore at their owne charge without permitting any of them to beg . . . but also set many hundreds of the English poor on work'.

Envious rivals soon followed the Kentish example. Norwich had already, in 1565, requested 'divers strangers' to help revive the city's flagging cloth works. Maidstone petitioned for sixty families, while twenty were placed in Southampton. England's first mulberry trees were planted in Rye, to sustain a local population of silkworms. Their offspring still cast shadows over the town today.

As always, there were signs of a split in English society. Even as feelings against the recent 'swarme' were growing heated at street level, forcing the authorities to get tough, employers were keen to safeguard their precious craftsmen. Brewing had been a Flemish-monopolised industry for over a century, so in 1554, when a royal proclamation ordered all foreigners who were not denizens (i.e. naturalised) to leave, the brewers, coopers, feltmakers and spinners fought for an exemption and won. The warden of the Dyers Company wrote of two employees threatened with expulsion that they were 'very excellent experts' without whom he could not manage. 'The want of theyme should be a wondrous great loss and hindrance,' he claimed. Who could resist so eloquent an appeal? The commercial argument also won the day in Sussex, where in 1584 the local MP launched a bill to suppress the glasshouses operated by 'divers and sundry Frenchmen and other strangers' in his constituency. He may have been thinking of Jean Carré, who was born in Arras, raised in Antwerp and came to London in 1567. He bought the monopoly to make window glass, set up factories in Rye, Hastings and Knole, and hired foreign Protestants to operate them. Soon they were turning out windows and drinking goblets. It transpired that a great many people liked his glasses, especially parliamentarians, who could afford to fill them with wine: the bill failed.

The moral argument also made its first appearance at this time. 'They are strangers now,' said Sir John Woolley, pleading in a ground-breaking parliamentary debate that people should look on the bright side of immigration. 'We may be strangers hereafter. So let us do as we would be done to.'[3] This simple maxim has not always been closely observed. That it was uttered at all, in the late sixteenth century, would suggest that there were vitriolic anti-foreign sentiments which Woolley felt the need to counter. But it also signals the presence of a tolerant strain in the English temper which has been in perpetual conflict with the intolerant one. A visiting sixteenth-century scholar, Lemnius, found 'incredible courtesy and friendliness' in England. But his contemporary Paulus Giovius found the English to be 'destitute of good breeding and despisers of foreigners'. Although many immigrants, such as those in Canterbury, prospered, others were not so lucky. All would have arrived with hand baggage only, and the first imperative was to scrape by, somehow. Many became beggars, despite the vigilance of their own churches, which recognised the unpleasant side-effects this might have on the immigrant communities' social standing. The luckless foreigners incurred the wrath of the locals in two contrasting ways: they were hated if they became rich, and even more if they remained poor. If wealthy, they were gimlet-eyed exploiters; if starving, they were good-for-nothing trespassers.

This situation was further complicated in Tudor times by political considerations: England did not wish to offend the rulers of the countries from which immigrants came by welcoming the refugees too eagerly.. But the threatened mass expulsion never materialised.* In 1551 a delegation of citizens petitioned the Lord Mayor of London to act against foreigners who threatened, as they thought, their jobs and homes, and there was talk of a cull – a rerun of Ill May Day. Agitators insisted that there were some forty thousand foreigners in London (a figure scoffed at by historians, who suggest a quarter of that

---

*In the summer, two foreign shoemakers were arrested for 'loitering' in London, found not to be denizens, and sent to prison. But after nine days they were released. Even Queen Mary's subsequent anti-Protestant reign made few inroads into the immigrant community. One Flemish merchant, Lyon Cauch, was arrested and executed in 1556, but it is hard to say that he fell victim to purely anti-foreign prejudice, since he was killed alongside thirteen native Protestants.

number at most). But such are the inflationary tendencies of bigotry and mob politics.*

Or maybe the alarmists were simply looking ahead. Not long afterwards, in 1572, France's Protestants, the Huguenots, were victims of an assault so vicious and terrifying that they had little choice but to flee for their lives. On 24 August, St Bartholomew's Day, the open-air wedding of Henri of Navarre and Margaret de Valois sparked an eruption of ill-feeling against the Protestants who had come to Paris for the marriage. Some 2,500 were killed, and news of the blood-letting reached Bordeaux and Lyon, igniting similar riots there. In all, some ten thousand Protestants were butchered. Boatload after boatload of the survivors fled to England and headed towards the centres of 'stranger' strength. Austin Friars, in London, started putting on an extra Sunday service at 7 a.m. to cope with the demand. And the existing community had a lively whip-round to help the newcomers find their feet. In 1565 the church's poor-chest had disbursed some £10 per month; after 1572 it was handing out more than £70. The natives were generous, too: the Bishop of London contributed £320 to the appeal; York gave £70. They might have been motivated partly by a desire to tweak the Pope's nose. The Vatican was quick to disparage England's treacherous and interfering role in assisting the Protestant cause, allowing Bishop Jewel to respond with ostentatious piety: 'Is it so heinous a thing to show mercy?' In the Low Countries England became known as the 'Asylum Christi'.

The trip across the Channel was not for the faint-hearted. The evacuees crossed in tiny rowing-boats, dodging dragoons in the harbour and frigates out at sea. They were reliant on the right weather for success: a sou'westerly might push them all the way to Denmark; a clear, sunny day would make them easy to spot. They carried a Bible, maybe a spare pair of shoes and a few English coins.† It's fair to say that these treacherous journeys were heroic: great escapes. Illegal immigration is a fine-tooth comb. The system catches the clumsy or clueless; only the bravest, the best and the luckiest slip through. It should never surprise us when migrants prosper: nearly all of them has passed an exacting entrance exam.

David Papillon, for instance, had the misfortune to be born on 14 April 1572, a few months before the massacre. It was probably his fault that the family

---

*Not for the last time, immigrants were merely the most obvious, not the most relevant target. The population of London more than doubled in the course of the sixteenth century, from 50,000 in 1500 to over 100,000 in 1600. It was overcrowded all right, but not with immigrants: the real pressure on housing was caused by the 'swarme' of migrants from elsewhere in England.

†The coins were probably forgeries called Lushbournes, minted in Luxembourg. The English authorities hated these threats to the money supply and dealt harshly with anyone caught with a purseful.

stayed in France: his mother would have been in no fit state to attempt a nocturnal Channel-crossing. After many years in their hostile home country, however, the family slipped on to a boat to England in 1588. Alas, the boat foundered and sank off Hythe, wrecked by the very same winds that would soon frustrate the colossal Spanish Armada. David's mother was drowned, but he was saved, and was taken to London to be raised by relatives. Eventually he became an architect and a senior military engineer – in 1646, he successfully fortified Gloucestershire in the Roundhead cause. He was a deacon of the French church, and wealthy enough to build a stately home of his own, Papillon Hall in Leicestershire. One of his sons was Thomas Papillon, who makes a sizeable dent in the *Dictionary of National Biography* as a businessman and politician. He was a director of the East India Company and officer in charge of supplying 'victuals' to the navy.

An even more remarkable success story concerns one of the most prominent of the Italian merchants who settled in Tudor England, a financier named Sir Horatio Palavicino. Born in Genoa, he spent his early life in the Low Countries, and came to England as part of a Catholic revival when Queen Mary appointed him Collector of Papal Taxes. When she died he renounced Catholicism (he was no fool, though: he did not go so far as to renounce the fortune he had won) and became a powerful supplier of capital to Queen Elizabeth and her court. He was officially made a denizen in 1585, and knighted two years later – an honour he repaid by financing and equipping one of the vessels that beat off the Spanish Armada in 1588. He had business dealings across the Channel (Henri of Navarre borrowed a hundred thousand French crowns from him) and acted as a roving foreign affairs attaché, travelling on royal business to France and Germany. He lived in fine style near Cambridge with his Dutch wife, Anne Hoostman of Antwerp, and his two sons, until his death in 1600. Queen Elizabeth might well have shed a few crocodile tears, since his death released her from a debt of nearly thirty thousand pounds, a fortune in Tudor times. As an alien, he could own property but not bequeath it, so his possessions were held in trust until some lucky man could make honest Englishmen of his sons. Up stepped Sir Oliver Cromwell, uncle of the future Lord Protector. He married Sir Horatio's widow, and for good measure betrothed his two daughters to the Palavicino boys.*

We can't afford to generalise from so singular an example. History favours prominent people, the men and women who made an impact and left a clear trail through English life. The majority of the Protestant immigrants in Tudor times did not make headlines. Many were destitute: it was hardship, not gastronomic finesse, that led them to invent one of the classic English dishes –

---

*The Lord Protector himself would eventually marry the child of a French Protestant family: Elizabeth Bouchier, daughter of Sir James Bouchier, a financier.

oxtail soup. English butchers used to leave the tails on the hides; it was early Huguenots who seized on the rejected gristle and turned it into a robust broth. But their names sit on church rolls and in the legal records. And one fact can be readily inferred from a certain pointed silence in the historical record. There are plenty of accounts of trouble caused by angry natives, but not one affray seems to have been started by the immigrants themselves. They were no fools: they had folk memories of persecution; they kept their heads down.

The dramatic effect they had on English trade is not general knowledge. For the last 200 years historians have tended to see us as the fount of industrial innovation, not as the happy recipient of some good fortune. But it is barely overstating the case to assert that England inherited, with this refugee population, the first coiled spring of an industrial revolution that might otherwise have blossomed more richly on the continent. Not every eyewitness saw it that way. Sir Walter Raleigh made a famous objection, arguing, in 1593: 'The nature of the Dutchman is to fly to no man for his profit, and they will obey no man long . . . I see no matter of honour, no matter of charity, no profit in relieving them.'[4] In this, Sir Walter was merely being short-sighted. The French historian Michelet, with the benefit of hindsight, disagreed. 'By endeavouring to separate England and Flanders,' he wrote of the French persecution of Holland in the sixteenth century, 'the French king only stimulated Flemish emigration and laid the foundation of Britain's manufacture.'[5]

The expansion of England under Queen Elizabeth was to a large extent financed by the commercial advances made after 1544, when a ready-made workforce, led by experienced entrepreneurs, arrived on these shores to establish new trades that would drive English prosperity for many generations to come. They helped, perhaps decisively, to consolidate Protestantism in this country, and built an important bridgehead of expertise which amounted, as time passed, to nothing less than a shift in the balance of power between England and France.* And their presence here meant that when an even greater storm blew up in France a century later, throwing before it an even larger wash of religious refugees, there was already a strong community of like-minded souls ready, and sometimes even willing, to welcome them to a new life in a new land.

---

*The French glassmaking industry, for example, melted away altogether in the wake of the Huguenot evacuation. When Voltaire visited London two centuries later, he made admiring remarks about English glass manufacture. The art, he felt, had been brought by refugees and 'was henceforth lost to France'.

CHAPTER 5

Divers Foreign Craftsmen

The Tudor Room at the National Portrait Gallery houses a glittering set of royal and aristocratic images: Henry VII, Henry VIII and his wives, Elizabeth and Mary, along with the earls of Walsingham and Southampton, Essex and Oxford, Sir Walter Raleigh and Sir Francis Drake, Cardinal Wolsey and Thomas Cromwell. They look relaxed, like the cast of a costume drama, and pleased with themselves, as if they knew that they would one day come to represent the first flush of English glamour and authority. This was the period when England became a world power, and began to send navigators out to enlarge and consolidate that power. In one corner stands Sir Francis Drake, fetching in red silk, his hand resting calmly on the globe he circumnavigated, as tranquil and assured as a duke patting the head of a favourite dog.

The subjects might be English. The artists were not. Holbein and Van Dyck, John de Critz the Elder and Marcus Gheeraerts . . . these were the painters deemed up to the task. Even the many works by 'unknown hands' have Low Countries or Rhineland fingerprints. These men were humble labourers who would wander from court to court in search of patrons, and it is not surprising that so many of them congregated in the court of Elizabeth. The growing wealth of the English upper class, and its eagerness to commission bravura images of itself, attracted those who etched in the guiding principles of a native art.

This remained the case into and throughout the Stuart period. Peter Lely was born in Westphalia: his Flemish father was a captain in the Brandenburg army. But he came to England in the 1640s and made his name with a still-famous portrait of Charles I and his family in 1647. He painted Cromwell, and at the Restoration Charles II promoted him as the natural successor to Anthony Van Dyck. He became a denizen in 1662 and was knighted just before his death in 1680. His place at the royal easel was taken by Godfrey Kneller, a Lübeck man, who was appointed court painter by Charles II, James II and then William III. He, too, was naturalised, knighted and made a baronet.

And these are only the most celebrated painters of the time: the list of other overseas-born artists is very long. Antonio Verrio came from Otranto and painted the ceilings of Windsor Castle for Charles I; the engraver Peter Vanderbank, who made portraits of the great and good, and illustrated both *Don Quixote* and the works of Sir Isaac Newton, came from Paris (his son John opened a drawing academy in London); and the Keeper of the Royal Collections for Charles I was Abraham van der Doort, a man who took such pride in his meticulous cataloguing that in 1640, when he failed to locate a miniature requested by the King, he hanged himself (in vain – the work turned up soon afterwards). Willem van der Velde was the century's greatest and most prodigious 'painter of sea-fights' – a dozen of his naval scenes were installed at Hampton Court Palace; fourteen are now in the National Gallery. Simon Verelst and his son Cornelius were noted flower painters.* There were countless others: Adrian van Diest, Balthazar van Lemens, Paul van Somer, Lucas de Heere. A foreign name was virtually a hallmark of quality, so much so that the native-born antiquary Richard Rowlands felt obliged, when he set up a printing business, to locate it in Antwerp and trade under his grandfather's name, Richard Verstegen.

The artists lived alongside scholars and scientists. The historian Polydore Vergil, born in Urbino, was a potent narrator of English history: his chronicles of the Tudors and his edition of the works of the medieval monk Gildas are essential records of a lightly recalled chapter in the national story. The philosopher and engineer Jacobus Acontius came from the Tyrol. Theodore Haak, from Worms, taught philosophy in Oxford and London. Nicholas Kratzer, mathematician, clockmaker and friend of Dürer and Erasmus, became a fellow of Corpus Christi. The Royal College of Physicians had several German fellows. The Italian John Vigani taught chemistry at Cambridge. The Dutch inventor Cornelius Drebbel arrived in 1604 with his compatriot, the astronomer Constantin Huygens. Drebbel built a prototype submarine which sailed down the Thames from Westminster to Greenwich, and also has claims to being the father of the modern fridge: his public demonstration of his cooling device

*Pepys's diary records an encounter with Simon Verelst, a Dutchman 'newly come over'. He was shown a picture of a flowerpot, which he declared to be 'the finest thing that ever, I think, I saw in my life . . . It would be worth going twenty miles to see it.' The Verelsts liked it here. Cornelius's grandson went on to become Governor of Bengal.

drove the eyewitnesses in Westminster Hall out into the street to escape the sudden chill.

Most of the 'foreigners' who came this way were ambitious and knowledgeable. They were innovators, carrier pigeons for the best of continental expertise and craftsmanship. There were perhaps as many as four thousand in London in 1600 (out of a population of some one hundred thousand).* Many of these were transient, of course, not much more than international sales reps. But some were prominent figures in English society: men like George Gisze from Danzig, Dirk Tybis from Duisberg, or the Cologne expatriates Herman Hildebrand, Derich Born and Derich Berk. The commander of Henry VIII's bodyguard had been a German soldier from Nuremberg, and it remained fashionable to put the protection of the royal household in the hands of foreign mercenaries – they were less susceptible to local sedition and plots. By the end of the sixteenth century, however, the Germans in England were starting to feel the resentment of their 'hosts', and Elizabeth went so far as to close the now-ancient Hansa Steelyard. The Hanseatic trade was well established, though, and could not be so easily suppressed. Ipswich, Yarmouth, Newcastle, King's Lynn, Hull and Boston all conducted important business across the North Sea.

These trading links provided a channel of communication along which people could move with surprising freedom. London played host to German cutlers like Johan Kauning, Peter Klein and Gillam Hanwick. Coppersmiths came from Aachen, and one of them, Jacob Buirette, set up shop in Edinburgh, made brass wire, and died a baronet in 1638. The gunmaker Kaspar Kalthoff thrived in London during Cromwell's protectorate, and Cromwell himself encouraged a gifted Dutch clockmaker, Ahasuerus Fromanteel, insisting in 1656 that he be admitted to the Worshipful Company that controlled the trade. Fromanteel had been baptised in the Dutch Reformed Church of Norwich in 1607, and had long been at loggerheads with the Worshipful Company. In 1658 he produced the first pendulum-regulated clock in Britain. He married Maria de Bruijne in Colchester, and they had three sons, all of whom joined the family timekeeping business.

None of this represented the arrival of an immigrant community, in the sense we would understand it now. There were, however, a couple of small immigrant locales. In 1687 twenty craftsmen and their families came from Solingen and set up home in Shotley Bridge, near Durham, to make sword blades. Their company operated until 1832, and many Shotley Bridge swordmakers were in at the beginning of the Sheffield cutlery business.

The most significant engineering project of the seventeenth century involved

---

*It is well-nigh impossible to distinguish the number of 'foreigners' accurately by nationalities. Danish . . . Flemish . . . German . . . to the English they were all 'Dutch'.

Dutch labour (not to mention Dutch capital and management). Cornelius Vermuyden was an embankment engineer who had been born on the sea-threatened island of Tholen, in Zeeland; Holland, it goes without saying, was the unrivalled world leader in the art of keeping the waves at bay (it was not known as the nether land for nothing). James I and Charles I gave him contracts to drain the marshy Thames estuary near Dagenham, and then to do the same to 360,000 acres of waterland in Lincolnshire and Cambridgeshire. The projects were not wholly successful – indeed, his promised fees were initially withheld – but eventually the Crown settled its debt by granting Vermuyden some fifty thousand acres of the reclaimed land as his own property.

The most ambitious of these schemes was the draining of the Fens. In 1630 Vermuyden was invited to dig his channels and raise his dykes to create a vast new acreage of arable farmland. The Earl of Bedford, in partnership with a consortium of Dutch and English investors, backed the project, despite fierce opposition from the local hunters and fishermen, who waged an early form of guerrilla warfare against the mainly Dutch workforce that had been recruited to transform the landscape. These fractious rebels were known as the Fenland Tigers: for generations they had hunted the fish and wild duck that lived in the sedge and reed marshes, and they now busily sabotaged the windmills, chapels, pumps and camps of the intruders. They had supporters in high, godly places who regarded the reclamation project as an offence against the divine order of things.* But the engineers had a more pragmatic argument: reclamation, they said, was progress, and unstoppable. Sheep and oxen were more profitable than eels.

The work took decades. In 1642 the Parliamentary army broke the dykes to impede a Royalist advance. But in 1649 Vermuyden beat off competition from a compatriot (brazenly named Westerdyke) and was commissioned by Cromwell's protectorate to resume (and repair) the work he had begun. By 1652 some forty thousand acres had been drained and turned into agricultural land. It was dry only in summer, and in the course of the drainage the level of the topsoil sank by twenty feet; but a precarious new English landscape had been created. It left in its wake several Dutch-flavoured villages, such as Sandtoft. There's a Vermuyden Gardens in Ely, and a Vermuyden School in Goole.

The man himself went on to drain Sedgemoor, in Somerset, thereby creating a decent surface for the battle that would take place there in thirty years' time. His brother had been a colonel in the Parliamentary army during the Civil War, and he himself went to Holland on a bold and secret escapade as Cromwell's emissary, carrying an amazing proposal for an alliance between the two

---

*'Holland,' wrote Andrew Marvell in a characteristic tease, 'that scarce deserves the name of land / As but the off-scouring of the British sand.'

nations. England and Holland would unite as a joint Protestant power in Europe; Holland could have all of Asia as its empire; England would have the Americas. The plot failed, and so, in later life, did Vermuyden. He married a London woman (one of their children was to enter the Royal College of Physicians), and he was also knighted. But he died in obscurity. In death he was handed, at last, an Anglicised name, entering the record books in 1683, in charming recognition of his labours, as Cornelius Fairmeadow.

The Restoration was a time when science took great leaps forward. The bourgeois energy released by the protectorate, the powerful new sense of self-government and self-reliance, fanned the flames of empirical study. Among the ranks of innovative and pioneering men who formed the inaugural membership of the Royal Society were many foreigners.

Probably the most influential was Prince Rupert (of the Rhine), who, at the tender age of twenty-three, had been a showy cavalry leader for the Royalist cause in the Civil War. He was born in Prague in 1619, and came to England in 1636, where he cut a dashing figure at court. By the end of the war he was commander-in-chief of the King's army that was routed at Naseby. He fled to Germany and Austria, but Charles II invited him back and offered him a seductive pension of six thousand pounds per annum.

Rupert invested energetically in the Hudson Bay Company, of which he was a director, but his military interests now had a scientific flavour: he was a governor of both the Company of Mineral and Battery Works and the Company of Mines Royal. He built a laboratory at Windsor, where he fiddled with new explosive techniques. And he was one of the founders of the Royal Society, along with two other notable Germans, Heinrich Oldenberg and Samuel Hartlib.

Oldenberg was the functionary of the two and became editor of the Society's house journal, *Philosophical Transactions*. Hartlib, meanwhile, was very highly regarded in intellectual circles. A Protestant exile from Polish Prussia, he had come to England in 1628 and opened a school in Chichester. A few years later, in London, his gregariousness and intelligence made him a magnetic promoter on behalf of science and progress. In addition to contributing to the formation of the Society, he set up a charity for refugees. Milton addressed his lecture 'On Education' to Hartlib, praising him as 'a person sent hither by some good providence from a far country to be the occasion and the incitement of great good to this island'.

Other German scholars and thinkers were pioneers in the English enlightenment. Peter Stahl travelled to Oxford in 1659 and gave lectures in chemistry and mineralogy. C. A. Baldwin, a German alchemist, joined the Royal Society in 1676. And one of Robert Boyle's assistants, Gottfried Hanckwitz, hit upon the means to achieve the large-scale manufacture of phosphorus. He changed his name to Godfrey and founded one of Britain's first chemical firms, Godfrey and Cooke.

These men were all Protestants, and religious liberty was the overriding reason why they came, if only because it permitted the exploration of sacrilegious scientific concepts. England had long had French and Dutch churches; now it had German ones, too. The first was created in 1671; it was joined by another, at the Savoy, in 1692. In 1702 Queen Anne's consort, Prince George of Denmark, thoughtfully put a German Lutheran chapel in St James's Palace, thus making it tolerable for the German monarchs who would shortly be taking up residence in London.

This variousness – one would hesitate to call it multiculturalism – paved the way for more radical concessions. For over three centuries the Jews had been banished from these shores; now, at last, the doors began to open for them. A select handful of Sephardic Jews from Spain and Portugal had at various times managed to live here under false identities, posing as Iberian Christians (or Marranos). Sir Edward Brampton, governor-general of Guernsey under Richard III, was actually a Portuguese Jew, born Duarte Brandao. One of Queen Elizabeth's doctors, Roderigo Lopez, was Jewish – a fact which might not have helped when he was charged with treason and executed in 1594.* And Charles I was happy to entrust the corn supply of his army and navy to Antonio Carvajal, who had come to London in the 1630s, masquerading as a Portuguese Catholic. He set up business in Leadenhall Street, and was said to import one hundred thousand pounds' worth of silver each year. He was an active arms trader, too: in 1643 a ship full of his gunpowder was hijacked by the Earl of Warwick and given to Cromwell's Parliamentary army.

These successful men were exceptions, and even they dared not practise their religion openly. But Jewish leaders in Europe were beginning to look to England hopefully as a potential haven. They certainly needed one: in 1648 there were savage pogroms in the Ukraine, where up to a hundred thousand Jews were massacred, the hot flame of anti-Semitism raging out of control. In 1655 Rabbi Menasseh Ben Israel travelled from Amsterdam to London to see if he could persuade Cromwell to recognise and legitimise Jews in England, one of the few countries where the population no longer harboured any lethal resentment of them. It turned out to be a tangled process: typically English, one might have said, in its willingness both to concede the point and avoid anything like a clear statement of the case. Cromwell was well inclined, and passed Menasseh's petition to his council for debate and ratification. The council

---

*Lopez had taken over from an Italian, Giulio Borgarucci, brother of a famous professor of anatomy, who might just have lent his name – Prospero – to one of Shakespeare's most magical characters. There were enough Italians in London to inspire the creation of an Italian section at the Strangers' Church, under the ministry of Girolamo Jerlito.

appointed a committee. The committee discussed it for a while, frowning at the subtle pros and cons while they wondered, as it were, how it would go down in the shires. There was no great enthusiasm for anything like a grand statement of toleration: that would be dangerous. The idea rather seemed to be to contrive matters so that Jews could live and worship in England freely, without broadcasting the fact. In the end, a congress of lawyers came up with a neat solution: since the expulsion order of 1290 had been a royal prerogative, not a parliamentary law, it was no longer binding – it applied only to the Jews who had been resident in England at that time. So there was no need to revoke anything. The Jews were allowed (if not exactly welcome) to come.

Still, the committee carried on wrestling with the details of the case. Menasseh became despondent, and drifted back to Amsterdam. Cromwell, meanwhile, grew impatient, and dissolved the committee altogether. Nothing had been resolved when a group of twenty Jews, led by Antonio Roderigo Robles, arrived in March 1656 and declared themselves Jewish refugees from the Spanish Inquisition. In effect, they were asylum-seekers, and they were shrewd. By identifying themselves as anti-Catholic, they successfully ingratiated themselves with the authorities. They were granted permission to pursue their religion, at first discreetly (they were permitted to 'meet privately in their houses for prayer'), but soon in public. By the end of the same year, Cromwell's council consented to the construction of a synagogue, and a property was leased. The Lord Protector's old enemy Antonio Carvajal was one of the influential figures in this tiny group. He and his sons had been naturalised as English subjects in 1655, which made him the first officially English Jew since the expulsion. On becoming a denizen, he opened a small synagogue in Aldgate and leased a burial ground in Mile End. When he died, he left thirty pounds to 'the poore of my nation'. He did not mean England.

Once again, the eastern fringe of the City grew into something of a Jewish quarter.* But the Jewish presence remained small. By the end of the century there were only a thousand or so Jews in London. Perhaps the folk memory of the expulsion still haunted European Jewry, and made them mistrustful. Certainly, the Restoration of the monarchy under Charles II was a nervous time for these Jews, who had no way of knowing his attitude towards them. But the new King, who had been helped back to the throne by Sir Augustine Coronel (the 'litell Jue' who became the first of his faith to be knighted in Britain), ruled for them, announcing through the Privy Council that Jews could enjoy 'the same favour as previously they have had, so long as they demean themselves

---

*Pepys visited the Aldgate synagogue and was startled by its liveliness and lack of solemnity. 'I never did see much, or could have imagined there could have been any religion in the whole world so absurdly performed,' he wrote in his diary for 14 October 1663.

peaceably and quietly'. When people speak of 'typically English', this, perhaps, is the sort of thing they have in mind: it embraces a mixture of grudging, against-my-better-judgement tolerance with barely disguised distaste. It was not a very stout defence of Jewish rights and interests: they could stay, it was proposed, as long as they didn't make a scene. But this was much better than anything available in continental Europe at that time. The Jews did as they were bid, and kept as low a profile as possible.

In 1663 Samuel Fortrey, grandson of a refugee from Lille, wrote a book called *England's Interest and Improvement*, in which he listed four reasons why migrants were tempted to come. It was, he said, an obliging and temperate land. Second, the English law was relatively solid, not open to capricious distortions, and afforded some protection to the individual. Third, England gave newcomers the chance to make a fortune. And fourth, it offered religious sanctuary. These are not small things. That no one was eager to shout them from the rooftops or pulpits, to proclaim them as honourable national characteristics, is sad, but should hardly surprise us. Patriotic drums prefer to strike more bombastic notes. And this was a time of extreme religious sensitivity, when the smallest (to us) theological alignment could carry a whiff of treason. Catholics and Protestants alike had grown used to keeping one ear cocked for a knock on the door. Discretion, in the seventeenth-century temper, was always the better part of valour.

In its bumbling way, England was providing a precious sanctuary for those persecuted in brasher countries. Soon, however, this newfound tolerance would be tested on a scale never before imagined.

CHAPTER 6

A Refuge for Huguenots

In 1674, when Isaac Minet was fourteen years old, he was sent from Calais to Dover to visit his brother Stephen. The Minets were not rich aristocrats but grocers, so this was not a frivolous excursion. More than likely, Isaac's father sensed that the time was fast approaching when England would have to be their home. The Minets were Huguenots, and all the old tensions were bubbling to the surface again.

For nearly a hundred years, since the Edict of Nantes in 1598, Protestantism had been tolerated in France. In theory. In practice, it was harried without respite. In 1627 Cardinal Richelieu, officially chief minister of Louis XIII but effectively ruler of France for twenty years, resolved to stamp out this heretical stain on the nation's honour. He laid siege to La Rochelle, one of the rebellious strongholds of Calvinism, and starved to death 20,000 of the city's 25,000 inhabitants.* As ever, Richelieu was inspired by more than theological concerns: the Huguenots of La Rochelle were a political force that might, if unchecked, have become part of a confederacy of independent provinces stretching all the way to Lyon. It is a moot point whether the Huguenots were a dynamic mercantile people because they were Protestant, or whether they became Protestant because it matched their independent, driven sensibilities. Either way, they were stamped on.

---

*England tried half-heartedly to relieve the port, sending an army to the Ile de Ré under the Duke of Buckingham. But the invasion failed. One boatload of forty-two refugees made it through the French blockade, however, and landed at Southampton.

When England's Puritans executed Charles I in 1649, some of the worst Gallic fears seemed to have been confirmed: Protestants were regicides. France's Huguenots noisily condemned the removal of a crowned monarch, and emphasised their own royalist sympathies to anyone who would listen, but few did. The net slowly began to close. From 1681 onwards, soldiers were dropping in on Protestant homes, billeting themselves at the owners' expense, and smashing a few windows when they left. These dragoons were deployed as crude papal salesmen, making offers that could scarcely be resisted, let alone refused. Eventually, in 1685, the Edict of Nantes was revoked, and something like civil war was declared on the nation's 'heretics'. Protestant services were banned, the churches themselves were destroyed, trade was restricted and intermarriage outlawed; children were required to be baptised and raised as Catholics, which meant stripping them away from their families to some far from holy convents.

The Minets knew the game was up when the church in Calais was demolished in 1685. Isaac and his mother hid for three days in the house of a friendly (and brave) Dutch shopkeeper, and then tried to sneak down to the harbour. They were recognised, captured and forced under torture to abjure their faith. When they returned home, the dragoons were still camped on their property, bullying, threatening and pocketing everything of value.

The Minets bided their time until, on 31 July the next year, they had another try. They received word from Isaac's brother, who was still in England, that a boat was on its way. In the middle of the night they stole down to the beach a couple of miles east of Calais and waited. There were, they knew, patrols of soldiers and coastguard vessels lying in wait for them and the thousands like them who were fleeing for their faith, and their lives. But they managed to steal aboard and slip quietly across the dark sea to Dover.

Isaac immediately set up shop in Newport Street, London. In 1690 he returned to Dover, where he helped establish the family insurance firm (and a line that led unbroken to John Minet, a leading light at Lloyd's in the twentieth century). He also, in a poignant tribute to the sea-crossing that had saved his life, set up a packet-boat service between Dover and Calais. For the rest of his life, 1 August – the date of his arrival – was a sacred festival in the Minet household, observed with fasts and prayers.

Isaac Minet was one of tens of thousands of French Huguenots who suffered a similar fate, and undertook a similar adventure.* They hid in bales of straw, casks of wine, empty vats or heaps of coal; they were disguised by neighbours or sheltered by friends, and crept across borders or out to sea. Jean Desaguliers

---

*Some historians give the figure as forty thousand. Others suggest that it was twice that number. Even more, some ninety thousand, fled overland to Germany, Holland or Switzerland.

came from La Rochelle to Guernsey and London in a barrel, which might have
been where he conceived the idea for the world's first air-conditioning system –
it was installed in the House of Commons.* A young boy called Henri Portal
hid in a bread oven while the soldiers laid waste to his family's house; then he
travelled from Bordeaux to London in a wine cask.

The journey to England was hazardous, especially for those forced to make
the long detour through Gibraltar. Many were captured and enslaved by
Spanish pirates; others were intercepted by French patrols and sent as slaves to
the galleys of the royal fleet (where they sat six to an oar in hot, cramped, germ-
infested holds). For months they streamed ashore at Plymouth, Bristol and all
the available harbours along the south coast. It was a remarkable refugee
evacuation and England rose to the occasion with some dignity. As early as 1681
Charles II had offered the Huguenots free denizenship, and the churches of
England conducted swift whip-rounds to raise money for the often destitute
newcomers. No doubt the King and his court were motivated partly by political
considerations: France was a hostile power, and our enemy's enemy must, as
the saying goes, be our friend. Then there was the fact that Charles, unlike his
father, knew that he could not alienate the Protestant parliamentarians too
much (although, by this time, he was ruling without a Parliament). And there
was also an economic motive behind the warm welcome. After the Great
Plague of the 1660s, England was short of manpower.†

But aside from these practical considerations, there was also a clear and
frequently expressed sense of religious and sometimes even humanitarian
obligation. England had been primed to sympathise with Huguenots by
numerous Restoration publications about the viciousness of French Catholic
persecution. These had punchy titles like *The Deplorable State and Condition of
the Poor French Protestants Commiserated* or *A True and Perfect Relation of the New
Invented Way of Persecuting the Protestants in France*. One such, written as far
back as 1654 by a minister of the French church, Jean-Baptiste Stouppe,
painted a ghoulish picture: 'My pen falls from my hand in describing these
things; yea, the very thought of them makes my whole body to tremble, my
hair to stand up; a heart of adamant, a hand of steel and a pen of iron could
not express half the horrid prodigies of cruelty and lamentable spectacles
which were seen . . . here the leg of a woman, there the head of a child,

---

*He also established the planetarium, was a fellow of the Royal Society and was one of
many Huguenots whose taste for discreet friendship societies made them energetic
supporters of and apologists for Freemasonry.
†'There is nothing so much wanting in England as people,' wrote Carew Reynell in his
book *The True English Interest* (1674). A decade later, in 1683, an apologia written on behalf
of the Huguenot refugees insisted: 'No country is rich but in proportion to its number.'
Power, in the seventeenth century, was a function of size.

sometimes the privy members of a man, the entrails of another, and sometimes the pieces of another, whom the beasts had not yet made an end of eating.'[1]

When he came to the throne in 1685, the Catholic sympathiser James II tried to calm the situation by censoring or suppressing such publications. But the message had already sunk in, and England was keen to help. House to house collections raised forty thousand pounds, a huge sum for those times. The French churches of London, Canterbury, Southampton and Norwich offered spiritual and financial support, and job opportunities. Soup kitchens were set up in Soho to feed the starving. Even the initial reflex of the people in the street seems to have been hospitable. One new arrival, Jacques Fontaine, wrote a memoir of his first days in Devon, and recorded that the 'good people' of Barnstaple were 'kindness itself' when he and his fellow refugees disembarked. It was a Sunday, and the townsfolk were walking home from church. One man stopped to offer lodgings to the bewildered French families. 'I was as completely domesticated with them as if I had been a brother,'[2] he wrote. The entire shipload found places to stay.*

And what a dynamic injection of fresh blood he and his fellow travellers turned out to represent. Fontaine and his compatriots brought new wool-dyeing techniques which would make Barnstaple famous in the decades to come. One member of his original party, Monsieur Roche, founded the Barnstaple Bank. One went to London, where she met and married Samuel Pepys. Another, Pierre Prelleur, became a flamboyant musician and composer.

Their story was repeated all over southern England. The Huguenots possessed exactly what the country needed: the know-how necessary to transform an agricultural economy into an industrial one. They became spinners in Bideford, tapestry weavers in Exeter and Mortlake, wood carvers in Taunton, and calico workers in Bromley. Featherwork, fans, girdles, needles, soap, vinegar – whole new trades sprang into existence. They revolutionised the silk industry,† and brought new techniques for velvet, taffeta and brocade. Under the patronage of the Earl of Shrewsbury, Huguenots from Liège joined the rudimentary steel industry in Sheffield and at Shotley Bridge. A migrant innovator in thermodynamics (and assistant to Robert Boyle) called Denis

---

*Fontaine worked as a French teacher, a fisherman, a wool manufacturer and a merchant. Eventually he settled in Taunton, where the success of his shop – he sold foreign delicacies such as brandy and hats, mainly to other foreigners – soon attracted the envy of the locals. A case against him was brought before the mayor by a Taunton man who called Fontaine a 'French dog'. The case was dismissed, but Fontaine took the hint, and decided to leave Taunton while he could.

†There was a twentyfold increase in English silk production between 1650 and 1700. By the turn of the century, England was a net exporter of the fabric . . . to France.

Papin cooked a meal for the Royal Society in 1682 using his own invention, a 'digester of bones' – or what we would call a pressure cooker.

It is easy enough to see, in retrospect, that the Huguenots were a vibrant addition to English life. The refugees themselves were often exhausted, scared, bereaved, ruined and broken-hearted. But they made their presence felt with unusual speed. England adopted not just a needy labour force but a group of business leaders who could build on the foundations laid by previous generations of Protestant migrants. By 1640, for instance, textiles were already the major national industry, accounting for 87 per cent of England's exports. So the new refugees came at a useful time, and the refinements and enhancements they brought gave the industry a sharp boost. By the end of the century almost half the freemen of Norwich worked in the manufacture of 'worsted', a cloth that took its name from the village of Worstead just north of the city. The Weavers' Company in London, which in the past had been quick to oppose immigrant firms, was this time quick to applaud new methods. In 1684 two men from Nîmes appeared before the company and demonstrated a new technique for shooting silk. The court judged that 'the like hath never been made in England, and that it will be of great benefit to the nation'. The two men were appointed 'foreign master gratis' and speeded on their way.

The most important Huguenot colonies were in central London, in Spitalfields and Westminster. There were nine French churches in the former;* fourteen in the latter. Various street names in Spitalfields – Princelet Street, Fournier Street – bear witness to the prosperity of the Frenchmen who settled there: the neat roads are lined by large, handsome houses. Some still have the big, glass-ceilinged workshops the Huguenots built at the back for their looms. You can easily imagine the ceaseless clacking of the machines punctuated by sudden chirrups of birdsong – the Huguenots liked birds, and often hung caged canaries in the loft.†

But there wasn't room in these Huguenot strongholds for all those who came. Soon they began to drift into outlying villages such as Putney and Wandsworth. The River Wandle is hardly a landmark these days: it creeps unnoticed into the Thames. But at the end of the seventeenth century it was a vivacious stream which enlivened this small settlement across the Thames from London. Huguenots settled on its banks in numbers: by the early eighteenth century almost a quarter of the population was French. There was a French school and a French cemetery, and several modern roads – Osier Street, Huguenot Place – still recall those francophone days. Wandsworth's clothworkers soon gained fame as experts in coloured fabrics, especially felt

*One of these churches, in Brick Lane, would generations later become a synagogue, and later still a mosque.
†Which gave fuel to the anti-immigrant satirists, one of whom wrote a poem about these 'interloping canary birds'.

(from rabbit fur). The rich scarlet they refined from Brazilian wood was used for the bold uniforms of the East India Company and even, it has been claimed, for the cardinals' hats in Rome. It is delightful to imagine (though difficult to prove) that all of those brilliant red Vatican hats were patiently dyed and stitched for the papists by commercially minded Protestants in south London.

In France, meanwhile, the hatmaking industry that had once thrived at Caudebec in Normandy ground to an abrupt halt. The whole business had, in today's parlance, relocated. Maybe some second thoughts furrowed the brows of the senior executives at the court of Louis XIV. The harrying of the Huguenots had inspired thousands of able and hard-working citizens to pursue their trades in the lands of France's international rivals and enemies. Louis sent his emissary Bonrepaus to London in 1685–6 to evaluate the scale of Huguenot immigration there, and he was dismayed to find the newcomers so busy. 'I am sorely grieved', he wrote, 'to see that our best manufacturers are being established in this kingdom.' When he visited Ipswich, he was so downcast that he offered the Huguenots cash to return to France. Later French economists, with the clarity of hindsight, had an even keener sense of how damaging it had been. 'The epoch of 1685', reported the Lyon Chamber of Commerce in 1753, 'was fatal for our industry, not so much because it deprived us of manpower as because it occasioned new establishments to arise in England and Holland.'

And it wasn't just textiles. French clockmakers had long been expanding the local timekeeping industry. Indeed, the Worshipful Company of Clockmakers had been founded in 1631 partly, if not chiefly, to create an organised English resistance to 'the multiplicity of foreigners', by whom the London-born workers felt 'exceedingly oppressed'. Ninety such watchmakers are listed on the church rolls after 1680. One of these, David Compigné from Caen, made the town clock at Winchester.

The Huguenots also transformed the production of paper. In 1485 England had no paper mills – it relied on France for its supply. But by 1714 there were two hundred factories up and running, enough to meet two-thirds of the accelerating national demand. In 1685 a petition was presented to the Crown requesting permission to produce white paper, which, while not unknown in England, had been of poor quality. The business plan promised 'new invented mills and engines not heretofore used in England', and claimed to have 'brought out of France excellent workmen'. The Crown nodded, and Gerard de Vaux (from Languedoc) set up a paper mill at South Stoneham in Hampshire. One of his workers was the plucky refugee-in-a-barrel Henri Portal. In 1719 he set up his own mill at Laverstoke, where he gave, in gratitude, a job to John Vaux, the son of his one-time sponsor. In 1724 he acquired the monopoly for making paper for the recently founded Bank of England, whose notes were printed on his tough, clean, hard-to-forge Huguenot paper. England's first newspaper press, meanwhile, had been operated by a Huguenot called Jourdain in Plymouth since 1696, and half the booksellers on the Strand, in London, were French.

Clothes, hats, paper, pins, needles, watches, clocks, shoes. At the start of the eighteenth century it was said that 'hardly anything vends without a Gallic name'. Indeed the term for selling – vending – was French. But an even greater contribution to England's life and future came with the Huguenots' financial dealings. Their mercantile experience had taught them both the value and the delicacy of financial instruments: they knew how to handle rents, payrolls and cash flow, but also how to create investments and treat money itself as a commodity. England had until this period been a money-under-the-mattress kind of place. But finance was becoming a major industry, and the Huguenots were happy to take a leading role. It can't quite be true that the French smuggled away 'immense sums, which have drawn dry the fountains of commerce', as a French observer claimed in 1689. But they certainly possessed some liquid assets. Etienne Signoret, a silk merchant of Lombard Street, left a hundred thousand pounds on his death; so too did David Bosanquet. There were at least twenty Huguenots with assets of more than five thousand pounds – the equivalent of modern millionaires.

And they knew how to manage their funds. When the Bank of England was founded in 1694, nearly 10 per cent of its capital – £104,000 out of £1.2 million – was put up by 123 Huguenot merchants. Seven of the twenty-five directors were Huguenots or Walloons; one, Sir James Houblon, became the first governor. Another, John Castaing, founded a stock prices report, *The Course of the Exchange*, which later became the *Stock Exchange Official List*, the third-oldest daily paper in the world. A drop of Huguenot blood in your veins, the saying went, was worth a thousand pounds.

But we have to be careful not to overstate the case. The Huguenot lot was not always a happy one, as the writers and artists of the future were only too willing to describe. The Victorians depicted the Huguenots' arrival with penny-dreadful sentimentality, casting them as stout-souled onward Christian soldiers and surrounding them with 'the aura of martyrdom'. Samuel Smiles's 1868 description – 'The people crowded round the venerable sufferers with indignant and pitying hearts' – set the standard.[3] Meanwhile, John Millais painted a mawkish scene (inspired by Meyerbeer's opera *Les Huguenots*) which showed a white-laced young girl begging her dashing pre-Raphaelite beau to embrace Catholicism and so escape punishment. The girl is feeble, tremulous and uncomprehending; the boy is all manly principle and rectitude. Mrs Gaskell wrote a weepy pamphlet about the Huguenots, inspired by the sad stories told by a neighbour.* The stern Macaulay waxed lyrical on their behalf,

---

*'Cruelties were perpetrated,' wrote Mrs Gaskell, 'which it is as well, for the honour of human nature, should be forgotten.'

insisting that 'even the humblest refugees were intellectually and morally above the average common people of any kingdom in Europe'.[4]

Actually, the Huguenots were by no means 'average common people'. Macaulay was being prompted by the enduring reflex that presumes all refugees to be 'common'. It is a patronising and wrong-headed fallacy, but it has proved of decisive importance in governing how immigrants are viewed and treated. Like all newcomers, they are automatically reserved a place at the bottom of the social pile.

Through the rosy-cheeked Victorian images of brave dignity amid terrible hardship there runs a seam of truth: huge numbers of refugees depended on church handouts after they had fled France with virtually nothing. But the presence of a powerful group of wealthy men among the immigrants was a stimulant and boon. The Huguenots were the opposite of lazy, but they were luckier than many immigrant groups in finding a thriving employment market tilted, if anything, in their favour.

Apart from the impact they had on England's material conditions, they continued to shift the religious constitution of the nation in favour of Protestantism. For the three years after 1685, it was once again in the balance: England had a Catholic King (James II) who was not eager to antagonise France. But the Protestant population was given a boost: suddenly there were as many French Protestants in England as there were Catholics, and they were zealous – they had already suffered mightily for their beliefs. They were activists, printing pamphlets, engaging in theological debates and building churches. The French Church in London was alert to the importance of maintaining a high moral tone, for pragmatic as well as divine reasons. In the 1690s it repeatedly urged its congregation to be disciplined and peaceable, to lay aside its 'proud and haughty airs' and to avoid any suggestion of carousing, revelling or 'lewd conduct', in case these should 'scandalise the English nation which it is so much in our interests not to offend'.

This was good advice in days when multiculturalism was not even a concept. But immigration itself was not really an acknowledged form of behaviour either. Few Huguenots would have called themselves immigrants. The merchants probably thought of themselves as working temporarily from the London office. The rest were waiting for civilisation to return to France so that they could go home and pick up the threads of their former lives. This is true of a great many immigrants, even today. Immigration, indeed, might be a rather grandiose, unequivocal word for what is often a diffident decision, full of hesitations and reluctant compromises. The drip-drip process of acclimatisation becomes immigration only in retrospect.

Having said that, this was a momentous event. In a few short years, the French Huguenots comprised 1 per cent of the population of Britain. When combined with the even larger 'stranger' population that was already here, a significant slice of the national personnel was 'alien'. At first it was concentrated in relatively few areas – London, Canterbury, Norwich and Southampton. In the years that followed, though, the Huguenots filtered into society at large. Genealogists have suggested that Huguenot blood now flows in the veins of three-quarters of English men and women. But their traumatic, dynamic entrance into English life has faded into the background of our national consciousness.*

Not many of the inhabitants of Wandsworth know that the row of dots on the blue and gold quartered shield (representing Surrey) in the borough's crest are teardrops, symbolising the suffering of the Huguenots who settled by the Wandle. Few of the thousands who keep the markets humming in the City are aware that Threadneedle Street owes its name to the weavers who settled in the tenements there.

But what of the thousands who didn't leave their mark? We don't have the testimonies of those who suffered merely private misfortunes, who went mad with grief at the loss of their wives, husbands or children, or died of malnutrition, tuberculosis or a broken heart. We know little of those who came unstuck at the wrong end of an unsolved clubbing down at the docks, their skulls broken when a sudden flash of anti-foreigner fury possessed some drunken English roughs, and their bodies tossed thoughtlessly into the slimy brown river. And we certainly don't have any record of the most common experience of all: the many thousands who lived quietly, bearing up under their own unremarked burdens, perhaps praying daily to be reunited with their

---

*This despite the composition of a hymn written in their honour by Dr Samuel Byles, medical officer of the French Hospital in the nineteenth century. It is a neat summary of the story.

> I tell of the Noble Refugee
> Who strove in a holy faith
> At the altar of his God to bow,
> When the road it was marked with death.
>
> When the despot's sword and the bigot's torch
> Had driven him forth to roam
> From village, and farm, and city and town
> He sought our Island Home.
>
> And store of wealth, and a rich reward,
> He brought in his open hand,
> For many a peaceful art he taught
> Instead of the foeman's brand.
>
> Hey! for our land, the English land.
> The land of the brave and free.
> Who with open arms in the olden time
> Received the Refugee.

nearest and dearest, or stroking their lockets and silver hairbrushes (token heirlooms from their once affluent lives) as they worked all the daylight hours for a pittance, and hated the fact that they couldn't speak English, and who slowly, invisibly, gave up hope of going 'home', and sank from sight.* Or perhaps, as the years went by, they came to feel a fondness for their adopted country, for its rough and sometimes cussed manners, its earthiness, its damp green moods; their hearts might have swelled as they saw their sons successfully taking the reins of the family business, or their daughters successfully married. The Huguenot exodus was torrid, and only with the benefit of several hundred years' distance can it strike us as inspiring. But from that vantage-point we can hardly deny that they came, saw and prospered. Nor that 'we', after a certain amount of bluster and some clenched-fist bitterness, in the end accepted them without much more than a murmur.

*This was the case for at least another century. 'Though far away from France,' wrote Mrs Gaskell, 'though cast off by her a hundred years before, the gentle old ladies who had lived all their lives in London considered France as their country, and England as a strange land.' Victorian Huguenots still spoke French on Sundays.

CHAPTER 7

The Protestant Haven

When William of Orange announced his claim to the English throne in 1688, and then stepped ashore with his troops to pursue it, no one smiled more broadly than the Huguenots. To them, he represented a clarification of the religious uncertainty that had quivered in England under the Catholic James II. But the most immediate effect of William III's coronation in 1689 was to bring a significant new Dutch elite to England. When the time came, the *Dictionary of National Biography*, the A-Z of English life, would be expanded and framed by two immigrants, Jacques Abbadie (a Huguenot) and a Dutch military family, the Zuylensteins. Both crossed the Channel as part of William's train. The King, as kings do, acted quickly to ennoble and reward his friends, who promptly founded English dynasties. Hans Willem Bentinck became the Earl of Portland; Arnold Joost van Keppel became the Earl of Albemarle.

Bentinck's was a remarkable career. As a member of the then Prince William's household it was his busy diplomacy which had secured the nation-building marriage between his own master and James II's elder daughter Princess Mary in 1683. Two years after William's successful invasion against his father-in-law, Bentinck commanded a regiment of horse at the Battle of the Boyne, and subsequently became both the King's most trusted adviser and the most notorious and unpopular schemer in the country. The King had good reason to trust his old friend: Bentinck had persuaded the German princes to look the other way when William resolved to invade England; and had also tended him when he had smallpox, sitting beside William day and night for more than two weeks (and loyally contracting the disease himself). William smothered Bentinck in titles: Baron Cirencester, Viscount Woodstock, Earl of Portland. In the process Bentinck amassed a great fortune and founded a grand family line (one of his descendants would become a noted governor-general of India).* But he, and others like him, perfectly symbolised the King's lack of faith in his new English subjects. There were echoes of what the first William had done half a millennium before.

Not all the new Dutchmen were courtiers. There were engineers, clock-makers, goldsmiths and artists. Louis Crommelin was appointed by the King to oversee the Royal Linen Manufactory in Ireland, and can thus claim to be one of the godfathers of Irish linen. But the most striking and influential import was military. The army that invaded England was full of Dutch and French Huguenot soldiers – nearly ninety of the officers were Huguenots – and William's second-in-command was the German Protestant Duke Friedrich of Schomberg, who went on to command the royal forces in Ireland two years later. Schomberg felt sufficiently proud of his new allegiance to write, in despatches, of 'we English'. And though he died at the Boyne, in reportedly heroic style,† he had already prepared for William an army of great strength and effectiveness. The baton was taken up by such men as Jean-Louis Ligonier, a Huguenot who came to Britain from Switzerland and fought as a cavalry officer in all the major battles of the early eighteenth century, when England's army met the French at Blenheim, Ramillies, Oudenaarde and Malplaquet. He was one of two Huguenot field marshals in the army (the other was Montandre). England had not had a professional army before Cromwell's New Model force, and in the modern science of military tactics and organisation the country lagged alarmingly behind France.‡ Young would-be officers of the Restoration still travelled to Paris for their military schooling and would carry on doing so until Sandhurst was founded – by a Huguenot, General Le Marchand. The combined Dutch–French influence on the High Command after 1688 changed military life, especially in such technically advanced fields as artillery and engineering.

---

*His avarice was chief among the reasons why he was so widely hated. The *Dictionary of National Biography* puts it tactfully, observing merely that 'to legitimate gains he had no aversion'.
†How heroic is open to question. The catalogue to the Museum of London's commemoration of Huguenot life, *The Quiet Conquest* (1985), captioned an engraving of the scene by saying that Schomberg 'dashed into the midst of the fight and turned the fortune of the day'. This might be a fanciful description: the man was eighty-two, and his dashing days were somewhat behind him. The illustration offers a truer picture, perhaps: an overweight and wounded Schomberg is helped from his horse by a Huguenot, Major Henry Joubert, who presumably knew exactly what he was doing, since his father ran a riding academy in Piccadilly.
‡Some of these tactics were sneaky. At the Battle of Oudenaarde, Huguenot drummers confused their former masters, now the enemy, by beating the French retreat.

Other immigrants assisted in military development, too. Albert Bogard, for instance, was born in Denmark in 1659 and began his military career in the Prussian army on the Rhine. The French army offered him a commission, but he was a sturdy Protestant and joined the British army instead, in 1692. He had by that time already fought in eleven battles and twelve sieges, and was probably the most experienced gunnery officer in Europe. As such he commanded a high salary. King William made him a 'firemaster' – an explosives and gunnery expert – and off he went to fight in Flanders. When the army was disbanded in 1697 he was retained, and returned to England as an engineer along with another foreign officer called Schunt. He campaigned in Spain and in 1712 was made Chief Firemaster in charge of the army's cannons. The following year he produced the 'pleasure fireworks' along the Thames that marked the Peace of Utrecht, and in 1722 he became the first colonel of the Royal Artillery, a regiment which he effectively established.

One of his successors was Thomas Desaguliers, son of Jean Desaguliers, the Huguenot inventor of the air-conditioner. Thomas joined the Royal Artillery as a captain in 1745, and became Chief Firemaster three years later. A noted innovator with mortars and rockets in the years he spent at the Woolwich Arsenal, he, like his father, became a fellow of the Royal Society.

By that time the French Huguenots were integral to the fabric of military society. They had helped William to consolidate his grip on England, supported his campaign in Ireland and then fought valiantly in the long sequence of wars (1698–1713, on and off) against their fathers' persecutors, the French, as well as in Flanders, Spain and Austria. Samuel de Péchels, for instance, had seen his mother and sister being dragged off to a convent by the dragoons in 1685; he himself was transported to the Americas. He escaped to Jamaica and found a passage to London, but none of his family were there to meet him. His mother and sister, wife and daughter were all still imprisoned; one of his sons had died; the other was in Geneva. Samuel joined a cavalry regiment and fought under Schomberg in Ireland, founding a military dynasty which would later produce colonels, generals and admirals.

There were five regiments of Huguenot troops in William's army, numbering some 12,000 men; as well as 1,500 French officers. Macaulay wrote that 'among the best troops under his command were the French exiles'. Michelet, in his huge history of France, saw this as faint praise. 'I cannot believe that England,' he wrote, 'with all her glories, her inheritance of liberty, is unwilling nobly to avow the part that our Frenchmen played in her deliverance.'[1] By the time of the English triumph at Blenheim in 1704, twenty thousand Huguenots were fighting against their former countrymen. The navy also found its ranks swelled and its officer class upgraded. The French marshal Vauban estimated, in the early 1690s, that eight thousand or so able seamen had vanished from the French fleet; a good proportion of them wound up below English decks.

In civilian life, meanwhile, the Huguenots were finding their feet on all the influential ledges of society. Louis XIV, perhaps fearing pharmaceutical treachery, had forbidden Protestants to practise medicine; so a number of France's physicians took their skills elsewhere. Gideon De Laune became the William III's doctor, helped found the Society of Apothecaries, and died an extremely wealthy man. Isaac Garnier came to England in 1685 and eventually became Apothecary-General of the Chelsea Hospital (he was succeeded by his son, also called Isaac). In 1716 the French Hospital was established in Bath Street, Clerkenwell. It cared both for the ill and the deranged, such as James Ray, a goldsmith who in 1783 was picked up 'running about the streets like a madman, forsaking his business and crying, "Oranges and Lemons!"'[2] There were Huguenot schools and cemeteries, (such as the one at Mount Nod, in Huguenot Place, Wandsworth) and there was no shortage of refugees to fill them: Protestants continued to be oppressed in France at least until the Revolution.*

The textile industry remained a leading showcase for Huguenot enterprise. As the Huguenots continued to slip across the Channel, the most powerful families began to build large corporations that kept the costume-drama of eighteenth-century high society in silk and taffeta. French fashion was all the rage: Hogarth depicted the congregation leaving the French Church in Soho as daintily dressed, tiptoeing a little sniffily through the ragamuffin English crowd. An anonymous pamphlet in 1735 said of the French immigrants: 'I believe it can be demonstrated that nine parts in ten of that traffic [silk] are in their hands.' The Ogiers operated six firms, and dominated the Weavers' Company. The Bouveries, master silk weavers since the sixteenth century, also went from strength to strength. Edward Bouverie was an eminent merchant, knighted by James II, with an imposing stately home at Cheshunt in Buckinghamshire. His son William would become one of several Huguenot directors of the Bank of England. Another family, the Courtaulds, arrived as refugees from La Rochelle and began as goldsmiths in London until, inspired partly by marriage into the Ogiers, they came to dominate the production of the black crape that became the signature fabric of the Victorian age.

Engineering and technology were given a smart new French polish, too. John Dollond came from Normandy (not, as his name implies, from Holland)

---

*The final flashpoint of anti-Protestant terror was the execution of Jean Calas in 1761. His son, Donat, had committed suicide when he was banned (as a Huguenot) from pursuing his career at the bar. To save his son's soul, Jean Calas rejected the charge of suicide and insisted that his boy had been murdered. Next thing he knew, he himself was accused of the killing and condemned to death on the wheel. The case caused international outrage. Voltaire was moved by it to write his *Treatise on Religious Toleration*.

and studied classics and astronomy while working as a weaver in Spitalfields. Along with his son, Peter, he set up an optics shop in the Strand in 1750 – their speciality was telescopes, which for a hundred years were known in naval slang as *dollonds*. Eventually, after the nineteenth-century merger with Aitchison, they established a firm that would test eyes on almost every high street in the land. Whether it made John Dollond happy or not is another matter: he died, aged fifty-five, of apoplexy. There was also Paul de Lamerie, perhaps the finest worker of gold and silver in English history, who was helping to make London one of the capitals of European jewellery. Daniel Marot, son of a top French architect, brought the regal style to England's palaces: the gilded state coach he made for William III is today the ceremonial carriage of the Speaker of the House of Commons. Pierre Monlong was a gunmaker who came to London in 1684. He became 'Gentleman Armourer' to William III and made two highly wrought flintlock pistols – decorated with allegorical scenes in gold, silver and walnut, they are held by some to be the finest guns ever made in England – which are today in the Tower of London. Hollingworth Magniac, the son of a Huguenot goldsmith, went to China and set up a company – Magniac & Co – that would one day turn into Jardine Matheson.

These and all the other civic advances – in law, science and academia – meant that the Huguenots were in a position to sponsor England's military adventures financially as well as materially. They subscribed heavily to the various royal war-chests, and also played a leading role in the creation of the City's banking and securities industry, which could suck up and disperse a completely new reserve of financial capital for such adventures.* In 1745, when England's companies were invited to sponsor soldiers to resist Bonnie Prince Charlie in Scotland, more than half of the 137 companies which provided men were immigrant-owned, and they pledged twice the manpower of their English colleagues. David Garrick, father of the famous Shakespearian actor, even financed his own naval vessel. It was named *The Protestant Cause*. Huguenots were to make their presence felt in English literature too. The younger Garrick was a driving force in revitalising the reputation of Shakespeare in the eighteenth century. Alexander Pope said of him: 'That young man never had his equal and he never will have a rival.'[3] The writer Harriet Martineau, born in Norwich in 1802, was descended from a refugee surgeon called David Martineau, who ran from the dragoons in 1685. Thomas de Quincey's ancestor fled from Normandy. And Walter de la Mare's great-grandfather was a French refugee called Jean-Baptiste Delamare, who arrived in Britain in 1730. The

---

*In the middle of the eighteenth century, for instance, one-fifth of the gilt-edged securities issued by the English government was held by Huguenots eager to underwrite the national debt.

philologist and doctor Peter Mark Roget, the son of a pastor from Geneva, produced – when he wasn't busy perfecting the slide rule – his thesaurus in 1852. A descendant of the well-heeled Bosanquet family even penetrated into the soul of English cricket by inventing the googly, a remarkable variation even if the first wicket taken with it fell to a ball that bounced four times.

All of this success was especially striking given that, in addition to the corner-of-the-eye hostility they might face in everyday life, aliens were still subject to unusual restrictions and regulations. They paid up to double the going rate in parish dues and national taxes; they were liable for special customs charges on the transportation and sale of their goods; and their employment practices were monitored and hedged with rules. The chattering classes were still well inclined towards them,* but in the 1680s there were formal petitions against the foreign concerns by London's tailors, porters, feltmakers, founders, glaziers, bakers, needlemakers, dyers, shipwrights, barbers, carpenters and joiners. In other words, in daily life they faced almost unanimous opposition.

English people still could not differentiate between the newcomers. They were all bloody foreigners. Again, while it was one thing for the literate middle classes and clergy to feel sympathy for fellow worshippers, or for business leaders to admire entrepreneurs, it wasn't always easy for the man in the street to combine his officially encouraged hatred of France (the national enemy) with a fondness for refugees. He had always been told that the French were frog-eating Papists. And now here they were, grabbing the best jobs and driving up rents. Rumours that the great conflagration of 1666 had been started by the Dutch and French, who supposedly went round 'scattering fireballs', were still circulating twenty years later. As one Dutch report commented: 'It will be a long time before the people of London forget their wild rage against the foreigners.'

Even before the great migration of 1685, when Thomas Papillon and John Dubois became sheriffs of London and Middlesex in 1682, the Lord Mayor of London was urged to intervene on the grounds that the newly elected men harboured plans 'to overthrow the government and cut our throats'. As the numbers of migrants swelled three years later, so too did the volume of the abuse they attracted. By 1709 a travel writer called Sorbière, on arriving in Dover, would complain: 'I was as little regarded as if I had been a bale of goods.'[4] In 1730 the Abbé le Blanc came to England and wrote: 'There are some here who cannot bear the sight of a Frenchman with tranquillity.'[5]

The French were mocked for the easiest reasons: the food they ate and their

---

*The printers and pamphleteers remained busy turning out conscience-pricking reports of the hardships suffered by the Huguenots still trapped in France. One, *Memoirs of a Protestant condemned to the Galleys of France for his religion, written by himself*, by Jean Marteilhe, was translated by Oliver Goldsmith.

wooden shoes; or, alternatively, for their airs and graces. They were regarded as either foppish dandies or leprous scarecrows. The Huguenots colonised the poorer areas of town, and were promptly accused of being the cause of the poverty. There was hot talk about 'the devilish invention' of looms, which were feared by English weavers as threats to their livelihood. And there were sporadic eruptions of violence. 'Yesterday a great company,' said one newsletter, 'fell upon the French weavers, broke all their materials, defaced several of their houses and greatly disturbed the city.'[6] Such protests would continue throughout the eighteenth century. As late as 1769 voices and fists were raised against the master weavers who had been importing new looms from Holland. Louis Chauvet, of Bishopsgate, had seventy-six machines smashed. But two of the agitators were hanged, and in 1773 the weavers obtained special privileges from Parliament (protectionist measures against France) in return for an agreement about employment conditions and rates.

It was a sign of the shift that occurred in the eighteenth century: mob rule no longer called the shots. But this didn't mean that resentment of the newcomers died away. The birth of party politics both permitted and encouraged the taking of sides on the issue of immigration. The Whigs – mercantile, liberal – were in favour of generous immigration strategies, to boost the available manpower: the word 'manufacture', after all, means 'made by hand', and it was axiomatic that more hands meant higher production. 'Labour is the father and active principle of wealth,' wrote William Petty.[7] And in 1752 Josiah Tucker, the Dean of Gloucester, asked: 'Is not that country richest which has the most labour? What is the value of land but in proportion to the numbers of people? Was a country thinly populated ever rich? Was a populous country ever poor?'[8]

One of the keenest defenders of immigrants was the novelist Daniel Defoe, who wrote numerous books and articles in support of the idea that England should eagerly stock itself with foreigners, always based on the assumption that England needed fresh faces and a larger labour force. He repeatedly mocked all those who believed that there was anything sacred about the chemistry of English blood. His most celebrated character, Robinson Crusoe, who often seems the emblematic British emigrant – the emblematic imperialist, indeed, building his gardens in the Tropics – was in fact an alien, the son of a merchant from Bremen who settled in Yorkshire. 'I was called Robinson Kreutznaer,' he says in the first paragraph of Defoe's classic, 'but by the usual corruption of words in England we are now called, nay, we call ourselves and write our name, Crusoe.' The novel has not often been read as a parable of immigration, but we can certainly see Defoe's story of a castaway, labouring mightily and ingeniously to plant his life and leave his mark on a strange and hostile island, as an allegory of refugee life.

The Tory Party and its sympathisers, meanwhile, were nervous about the sanctity of the established Anglican Church, and opposed all attempts to welcome new workers from abroad, however skilled. So here, three hundred years ago, we can see the birth of ideas which still inflame public opinion today: some see immigrants as fresh fuel for the economy and the culture; others view them as leeches. In 1691 a clumsy satire appeared called 'Fire is past but blood is to come'.

> The nation it is allmost quit undone
> by French men that doe it dayly overrune . . .
> They have made our nation grevously to groane
> Under a burthen of great misery.[9]

These sentiments would be echoed many thousands of times in the coming years. In London, Rye and elsewhere Huguenots were beset by angry thugs. One woman was killed when a gang wrecked her house. And when William III floated the idea of free naturalisation for refugees, Sir John Knight, MP for Bristol, declared: 'Let us first kick the bill out of the House, then the foreigners out of the kingdom.'[10] An extract of his speech was printed in a pamphlet: *Consideration upon the Mischiefs that may arise From Granting too much Indulgence to Foreigners*. Not for the last time, a pious-sounding biblical precedent was enlisted in support: 'Thou mayest not set a stranger over thee', he said, quoting Deuteronomy, 'which is not thy brother.'

An anti-foreign mood was already a big part of the national temper. So, however, was its opposite: Knight was condemned for his remarks. The House of Commons ordered that his speech, with its contemptuous references to the 'Froglanders', be burned. This was the era when a John Bull notion of English identity (later caricatured by James Gillray) was being formed, but while some Englishmen could not bear the sight of the French, some welcomed them.

The Huguenots themselves were strong enough to withstand the odd barrage of abuse, and continued to thrive. Their migration remains, even though tainted with the mud of English rudeness, a glittering success story. Of course, many Huguenots lived in penury (as did many native English people). Some were desperate: Judith Leford was hanged in 1734 for killing a newborn child in the workhouse; James Burquois was executed a few years later for stealing ('The weaving business was slack,' he said in his defence). There were Huguenots on the convict hulks that sat in the Thames and the Solent, sometimes for years. Three of them spent seven years on these ships that never sailed; John Dupen, a baker from Shoreditch, suffered this fate for stealing a handkerchief. But on the whole the Huguenots were neither repelled or restrained: between 1734 and 1832 there were sixty-five MPs of Huguenot descent. And their communities were genuine communes in what is now an old-fashioned sense – groups of neighbours who attended the same church, helped one another and clung hard to their French culture. England, it turned out, both tolerated and suited them. Many became proud, almost caricature patriots. The editor of that exquisitely English anthology, Palgrave's *Golden Treasury*, was of Huguenot stock. And the man often acclaimed as the greatest ever Englishman, Winston Churchill, had Huguenot blood in his ancestry. Even the archetypally English dog which adorned record sleeves, listening patiently to His Master's Voice, was Huguenot-trained: Nipper was the pet of the art designer Francis Barraud.

If many of the Huguenots prospered, another group of immigrants caught the full force of the animosity aroused by their success. In the summer of 1709 thousands of Germans from the Rhineland – the 'Poor Palatines', as they became known, partly because they were poverty-stricken, partly because they were luckless – arrived in London. It was one of those mysterious upheavals that no one anticipated, and it was greeted with a marked absence of warmth or hospitality. It might even be (though there is plenty of competition) one of the least edifying episodes in the entire story of migration.

The Palatines came shortly after the birth of party politics, and they soon found themselves the subject of many rancorous Westminster debates. In 1708 the Whigs won the election. Combining humanitarianism and economics in one neat pledge, they moved to clarify and ease the process of immigration. The result was the General Naturalisation Act, which would entitle all foreign Protestants to come to England and, for the price of a shilling, be naturalised. There had been many previous attempts – in 1664, 1667, 1670, 1673, 1689, 1690 and 1693 – to force such a bill through Parliament. On this occasion, as previously, it was opposed by the Tory Party, which argued (this might sound familiar) that such a measure would provoke a 'flood' of unwelcome foreigners. But the Whigs won the day and on 23 March 1709 the Act was signed by Queen Anne. It was the start of a momentous episode in the history of the free movement of people. Alas, it would turn out to be a short and unhappy one.

The farmers who lived along the Rhine were at that time in desperate straits. French armies had repeatedly carved up their land in the wars that ravaged Central Europe, and the new Elector was a determined Catholic, keen to convert his overwhelmingly Protestant peasantry. The winter of 1708/9 had been bitter: the people were cold and ill as well as ruined. They piled into boats and drifted down the river. In spite of the new, welcoming legislation that had been passed in England, many had their sights set on a more distant horizon. The previous winter, forty or so of their countrymen had passed through England en route to New York, where they had found work in the naval stores. The grapevine hummed with suggestions that the colonies out west were the true land of opportunity. The persuasive agents moving through Europe in search of workers for the colonial plantations did not go into too much detail.

But to the Palatines, who wanted nothing more than some fertile land to till and their own Church, they sounded heaven-sent.

Unlike the French and Dutch Protestants, these Germans were ill-equipped for their adventure: they had no money, few friends and little expertise in the urban crafts and trades at which the Huguenots excelled. As a result, they could not inspire the kind of ruling-class support which helped the Huguenots to survive and flourish. But such was the enthusiasm – or need – of the Palatine migrants that the queues at Rotterdam rapidly became mobs. In May, just six weeks after the General Naturalisation Act won royal assent, 852 Germans limped ashore in London. They were starving, diseased and weak. They were met by two Lutheran ministers (one from the High German Church at the Savoy) who came armed with a grant from Queen Anne (sixteen pounds per day) to look after them.

A couple of weeks later, another 1,100 arrived, leaving 600 huddled in Rotterdam waiting for the next ship. On 15 July 2,776 made the trip, and a fortnight after that a further 1,443 disembarked. By the end of the summer, approximately thirteen thousand Germans had been dumped in London's eastern slums. It was an amazingly rapid migration; the Huguenots had arrived, by comparison, in dribs and drabs. The immigrants included many who were unable to provide for themselves: nearly three thousand were children, and many more were old and sick. Only fifteen hundred men were able to state their trade, and most of those (over a thousand) were vineyard workers, not likely to find easy pickings in beer-stained England. They had nothing to do, and nowhere to go. While they dreamed of America, they lacked the means to finance the trip. Most were lodged in the wharves and warehouses at the docks, in Bermondsey and Southwark, but several thousand were sent to what was, in effect, the world's first official refugee camp: a thousand army tents were pitched on Blackheath, and this enormous canvas village soon became something like a fairground attraction. Londoners would wander out to drink beer, lay bets and gawp at the unhappy campers.*

Initially, the local response was at least semi-magnanimous. It was assumed (wrongly, it turned out) that these were religious refugees, like all those before them. One pamphleteer visited the camp and reported that the people seemed 'Innocent, Laborious, Peaceable, Healthy and Ingenious'. Indeed, he added, 'They may rather be reckon'd a Blessing than a Burden.' A good part of England once more rallied round. Each Whig MP donated a hundred pounds to the relief fund the Queen had sponsored; London alone raised twenty thousand pounds. It was an impressive burst of public generosity, and a harbinger of the charitable streak that would become a major fact of life in years to come. Daniel

---

*Someone even produced a little self-help book, *A Short and Easy Way for Palatines to Learn English*. It included such useful phrases as 'Come, let us go to the alehouse'.

Defoe again championed the newcomers. 'Opening the nation's doors to foreigners has been the most direct and immediate reason of our wealth and increase,' he wrote in 1709, 'and has brought us from a nation of slaves and meer soldiers to a rich, opulent, free and a mighty people.'[11] He proposed to settle the Palatines in small colonies by giving them land in deserted areas, such as the New Forest, which they could then render productive. But his plan was rejected. Instead, the government tried to disperse refugees across the country in small groups, and offered five pounds a head to any parish willing to have them.

The mood against the foreigners was starting to harden, though, and there were few takers. The Tories were denouncing the new aliens as a threat (there were rumours that some of them were Catholics, and, indeed, almost a third were), a drain on resources and a menace. One prominent Tory, Sir Thomas Hearne, reported (in a breathless and scandalised manner still familiar today) that some forty of these foreign hooligans had set upon a group of 'honest Englishmen' and been let off with no more than a reprimand. A tiny contingent of two families was housed at Sundridge in Kent, but their house was stoned and surrounded by a twenty-six-man lynch-mob shouting at them to leave or face the consequences. The Palatines left. Queen Anne set a few hundred to work at Windsor, building a canal; a few hundred more were pushed into the army and navy; a hundred or so went to Liverpool to work on the quays. But this barely dented the sluggish mass of the dejected German asylum-seekers in London, and in the end the government came up with a radical solution: deportation.

Ireland was chosen as the promised land. The Battle of the Boyne had only recently been fought, and the British government was anxious to settle this troublesome Catholic territory with loyal Protestants. On the grand level, one of William III's generals, Henri de Massue de Ruvigny, had been made Earl of Galway; why not populate his lands with these anti-Catholic labourers? The refugees left London in August in a huge caravan: 1,300 families, more than 5,000 people, trailed out of the city in 109 wagons. They must have looked like a retreating army as they juddered along the bumpy tracks that led north-west towards Chester, where they were loaded on to boats and transported across the Irish Sea to Dublin. There were attempts to push them out on to lots of vacant or confiscated land, but the Palatines were not impressed: the muddy fields felt awfully like the ones they had fled. As the months went by, most drifted back to Germany. In the end only about a thousand stayed.

The rest of the Palatines were given a whiff of their dream, loaded on to ships and sent across the Atlantic. In April 1710 some three thousand set off for New York on what would prove to be a brutal voyage. Nearly five hundred people died on board. Things hardly improved when they arrived: they were sent to find jobs in the fields and wound up working in gangs under tough supervisors. In Virginia they founded a town, New Bern, but were almost wiped out, first by typhoid and then by a mob, which killed hundreds. No wonder they felt cheated.

By now the atmosphere back in England had changed: the Palatines could no longer count on any political support in London. Jonathan Swift's magazine, *The Examiner*, said that they 'rather chose to beg than to labour', and accused them of breeding disease, 'by which we lost in Natives thrice the Number of what we gained in Foreigners'.[12] A Tory pamphleteer put it more concisely, jeering at the Whigs for having engineered the arrival of this 'scum'. In 1712 the bar came down, and the General Naturalisation Act was repealed. It had been a short-lived experiment, but Tory spokesmen still drew conclusions from it which like-minded politicians would echo for the next three hundred years. In 1714 Bishop Atterbury wrote a tract accusing the Whigs of diluting 'the old honest English stock' with 'different and base species'.[13] 'Naturalisation' had – like 'immigration' today – been successfully muddied. 'This harmless word', said Josiah Tucker, the Dean of Gloucester, 'has by art and industry been made such a bugbear that the very sound of it carries dread and terror.'[14]

All of that ugly talk was utterly of its time. The age-old fear of foreigners was merging with mutterings about racial superiority that would ride in the vanguard of Western thought for the next 250 years. Swift encapsulated it by claiming that the first principle of patriotism was to resent foreigners: he was scornful of 'those who love a Dutchman, a Palatine or a Frenchman better than a Briton'.[15] He spoke, no doubt, for many. But the people of Britain, though, were at this time being asked to welcome at least one foreigner with open arms. 'And, with the Palatines still fresh in the mind, it was fitting that he should be a German.

CHAPTER 8

The Hanoverian Empire

The most important immigrant of the eighteenth century – according to the traditional definition of what counts as important – came on a smart yacht called the *Peregrine*, which sailed from The Hague to Greenwich in September 1712. It was a nasty two-day crossing in horrid weather, and perhaps this contributed to the newcomer's apathy when he finally disembarked. But he was a reluctant traveller anyway. He'd spent six weeks humming and hawing since accepting the formal invitation to take up residence in London, a place he had visited once, in 1683, and hadn't greatly liked. But duty called, so here, eventually, he came. He was fluent in French, but didn't speak English, and though he would live here on and off (mainly off: he was an absentee immigrant) for thirteen years, he never would quite get the hang of it. His name was George Louis, the Elector of Hanover, and he was the new King. Nearly a million people lined the route from Greenwich to Westminster when George I, as he was about to become, climbed into a glass coach drawn by eight horses and, accompanied by two hundred carriages full of dignitaries, made his ceremonial entrance into the city and the national consciousness.

His best feature, as far as England's ruling class was concerned, was that he was a Protestant. The Glorious Revolution of 1688, which ousted James II and welcomed William III, had established the supremacy of Parliament over the Crown: the King could no longer, and never would again, be a divine autocrat. He still had huge formal powers – the appointment of bishops and other notables, for instance – but the Civil List Act of 1698 had guaranteed the Crown funds sufficient only to maintain an opulent court. The monarch now lacked the wherewithal for the whimsical waging of war or – perish the thought – the suspension of Parliament. And the Act of Settlement in 1701 had established that Catholics, for the foreseeable future, need not apply for the top job. There were some Jacobite stirrings in the shires – there would be a couple of boisterous royal 'pretenders' in the years ahead – but the Crown was now a distinctly junior, if pampered, partner in the governance of the nation.

The position remained one of terrific social and symbolic significance, however. So when it became obvious that Queen Anne (James II's younger daughter, who had come to the throne in 1702) would die without producing an heir (though not for want of trying: she had seventeen pregnancies and lost one son at the age of eleven), England's leaders bent their minds to the succession, and the Elector of Hanover was recruited. He would be succeeded by his son and great-grandson, and for most of the century England would be ruled by Germans. George I brought seventy-five servants – gentlemen of the bedchamber, pages, footmen, surgeons, trumpeters, tailors and kitchen staff – including two Turkish grooms, one of whom, Mehemet, was christened and elevated by his grateful master into Ludwig von Köngstreu. England was never more than a home from home, and the English, those regicidal bores, could be kept at a very long arm's length. Far from exploring his new domain, the furthest the King ventured was to Newmarket races. His descendants were no more adventurous: George II spoke German at home to the end of his days in 1760. The Hanoverian Georges, I, II and III, never stopped missing their old homeland, with its grand balls, magical schlosses, fabulous hunting and delicious Westphalian ham for breakfast. 'Oh! My heart will never forget', cried George III, 'that it pulses with German blood.'[1]

The arrival of the Hanoverians meant that the upper layer of eighteenth-century society received a fresh injection of new blood, whether in the form of George I's German inner circle – men like Baron von Bernstorff and Baron Bothmer, who had been George's envoy to London in the years before his coronation – or in the shape of the many German businessmen, bankers, scholars and artists who made the short journey west. In effect, the court of Hanover located its headquarters in London, and the King's trusted advisers were invariably Hanoverian bureaucrats: Bernstorff was often referred to as 'the first and the only minister' to the Crown, which led to some controversy when his opposition to a territorial deal with Prussia turned out to hinge on his ownership of three villages in Mecklenburg. One of the King's apothecaries, too, was from Hanover: August Brande. Some of George's favourite women also came. Melusine von der Schulenberg, naturalised in 1716, was made Baroness of Glastonbury, Countess of Feversham and Duchess of Munster and Kendal; Sophie Charlotte von Kielmansegge (of whom it was said, by the Prince of Wales no less, that she had lain with every man in Hanover) became the Countess of Leinster and Darlington.

By the middle of the century, with George II now on the throne, there were around five thousand Germans in Britain, most of them in positions of some influence. In particular, the officer class of the military acquired a brash, scarlet-coated, heel-clicking glamour.

The artistic world, relying as it did on aristocratic patronage, continued to be good to foreigners. The famous singers at the opera – such as the sopranos Cozzoni and Faustina, and the castrato Senesino – were nearly all continental stars. And many of the most eminent figures in painting were immigrants. Johann Zoffany was German; Henry Fuseli was the Anglicised name of Johann Heinrich Füssli, the Swiss son of a court painter in Zurich; and John Michael Rysbrack was originally Johannes Michael Rysbraeck, from Antwerp. There were many more. Joseph Nollekens, the son of an Antwerp painter, inherited the mantle of the French Huguenot Louis-François Roubiliac. Nollekens was born in London, but grew up in Flanders before returning as an apprentice in the Dutch-run school of Peter Scheemaker. He was the virtuoso of the society bust: his sculptures of the actor David Garrick and the novelist Laurence Sterne won him an entrée into the *beau monde*.

The most prominent artistic figure of the early part of the century, the architect and playwright Sir Thomas Vanbrugh, was the grandson of Gillis van Brugg of Antwerp, who had settled as a confectioner in Manchester in 1667. Sir John himself was raised there, but studied in Paris and served as an officer in the East Somerset Regiment before settling into his role as the builder of massive stately homes – such as Blenheim Palace and Castle Howard – and the Queen's Theatre.

In music, the German genius Georg Friedrich Handel was joined by such compatriots as Johann Christian ('the English') Bach, Karl-Friedrich Abel and Peter Salomon, who was the impresario behind the visits to London of both Haydn and Mozart. Even so quintessentially English a work as John Gay's *Beggar's Opera* owed much of its popularity to the music, which was written by John Christopher Pepusch, the son of a Berlin pastor and musical scholar who, apart from this lively ensemble of folksy tunes, amassed a sizeable archive of ancient music which he eventually left to the British Museum.

All of this Germanic cultural activity was backed by a hearty appetite for trade. Hamburg concerns like Voght and Sieveking set up offices in English coal ports – Leith, Newcastle and Sunderland. And new firms sprang up in London, such as G. W. Soltau & Co. and Spitta, Molling and Co. In 1785 Johan Claiss from Karlsruhe secured an important patent for scales. He was part of an enterprising German community which included Jacob Haas, an instrument-maker and producer of pumps, barometers and thermometers, and Johan Holzapfel, a manufacturer of cutting tools. Rudolf Ackerman, from Schneeberg, set up in London as a coach designer, but also secured a patent for rendering clothes waterproof, and developed lithography. Frederick Koening invented the mechanical printing press on which, a few years later, in 1814, *The*

Times would be printed. Johan Seifert won a Royal Society prize in 1759 (for his crucible); as, two years later, did Jacob Lieberich. Friedrich Accum arrived in 1793 and wrote the first chemistry textbook in English; one of his disciples, Friedrich Albert Winzer, followed, changed his name to Windsor (anticipating the royal choice by over a century) and went on to found the Gas, Light & Coke Company in 1812.

These businessmen didn't even have to deal with English bankers. The City had long been dyed-in-the-wool cosmopolitan, and the most powerful firm of the period, extremely active in the placement of continental capital in expanding British investment funds, was the Dutch merchant house of Gerard & Joshua van Neck. Sir Joshua (he was made a baronet in 1751) was reckoned to be one of the wealthiest men in Europe, having secured the monopoly in tobacco from France. The family entered the blue bloodstream of the elite when one of Sir Joshua's daughters (from his marriage to the French Huguenot Marianne Daubuz) married Thomas Walpole MP. Her sister then cemented the merger by marrying Thomas's brother, Richard.

The other major Dutch-run firm was the partnership of the Goldsmid brothers, Abraham and Benjamin. They were Jewish, and came with their father from Holland to set up as bill brokers in 1763. They soon became bold financiers of government loans and major players on the London Stock Exchange. Benjamin bought sixty acres in Roehampton, south-west of London, and built a grand house on it, with an artificial lake, a ballroom and a library, as well as a synagogue. The party he gave to celebrate Nelson's victory at the Battle of the Nile in 1798 was the major society event of the year, a heady twenty-four-hour gala of masques and fireworks. It was one of many such parties thrown by the Goldsmids, described at the time as 'entertainments to princes and ambassadors reviving the glory of the *Arabian nights*'. Benjamin's business, though, was both precarious and nerve-racking, and he committed suicide in 1808, hanging himself from a silk cord. His brother Abraham followed suit in 1810, in the midst of a resounding collapse which sparked panic in the City. As the *Courier* put it: 'We question whether peace or war suddenly made ever created such a bustle as the death of Mr Goldsmid.'[2]

New German firms sprouted in the shadow cast by these giant concerns. Andreas Grote, whose grandmother had been a Huguenot refugee, came from Bremen and founded a bank in 1776. The family grew fast: he and his wife had nine children; his eldest son produced eleven. Peter Hasenclever set up a firm called Seton & Crofts, and lived (like the van Necks) in Putney with his family. John Baring, the son of a Lutheran pastor, came to England, set up in Exeter as a clothier, and through his son Francis launched one of the most enduring and (until its recent collapse) prestigious houses in the City.

There were only four Georges in this period, and one of them was mad. So the Hanoverian monarchy can hardly be described as a flood of foreigners swamping the good old English way of life. But, as monarchs do, they set the tone. The Hanoverian palette of likes and dislikes would, as the century wore on, inveigle its way into the British mentality, at least in the upper classes. 'Books?' George II is famously reported to have said. 'Prithee don't speak to me of books.' It was a family trait, and the aristocracy came to prefer horse-riding or a game of whist to music, literature, art or science. The arts became little more than status symbols: trips to the opera were primarily social occasions – grand and showy ways to pass the time before (or during) dinner. While the Tudors had been keen on the arts, and the Stuarts had added to this an energetic sponsorship of science, the Hanoverians represented a giant leap backwards. They brought to Britain's fashionable circles an impatience with the subtleties of both arenas, and what seems now a characteristically British disdain for intellectual matters. In the coming centuries British pragmatic genius would often be contrasted with its flimsy sense of aesthetics and style. But this is where we hear it first, in the giddy social whirl of the eighteenth-century court. It might not be a coincidence that the poetic accent of the period – even in the hands of men of genius like Dryden and Pope – is notably mannered and formal. The heroic couplet strikes many modern ears as pedantic, laboured and self-satisfied. The foreignness of the court and its entertainments emphasised the schism between popular taste and so-called high art, a schism that has bedevilled us ever since. To the man in the street, 'art' came to mean something fancy and high-falutin, something foreign. Popular culture chafed against the constraints of fashion, and mocked them. So this period also saw the rise of more earthy forms of culture: the stark cartoons of Hogarth, musical theatre and even the novel, seen as an incorrigibly vulgar form by those on the higher social rungs.

It may be stretching a point to lay the blame (or the credit) for the rise of the English novel at the door of the philistinism of the German royal family. No one can say with any authority that immigration, even royal immigration, has such precise effects. But the main function of royalty, even in the eighteenth century, was to set an example. And the Hanoverian example was bewigged, portly and plump-jowled. It came to form the basis for the classic cartoon caricature of Englishness. But looks can be deceiving. The Duke of Cumberland – nicknamed the 'Butcher' for the ferocity of his reprisals against the Scots after the Battle of Culloden in 1746 – has often been presented as the stereotypically cruel and supercilious English bully, a sadistic public schoolboy with grown-up weapons and a particular hatred of Scots. In fact, he was a young German prince, the son of George II and Caroline of Ansbach.

The licence to be dandyish attracted one of the century's oddest immigrants: Charles Geneviève Louis Auguste André Timothée D'Eon de Beaumont. The unusual mixture of masculine and feminine names was neither an accident nor a sentimental whim: the child, born in Burgundy in

1728, was of uncertain sex. In a bizarre compromise he was baptised as a boy, dressed as a girl and dedicated to the Virgin Mary as both. From the age of seven he/she was educated as a boy, eventually graduating as a doctor of law. A use was then found for the ambiguity of her/his appearance; she was sent to St Petersburg on a secret mission to the Empress Elizabeth disguised as a woman. When he returned to France, it was as a captain of dragoons. He came to London in 1762, where he lived lavishly and in public as a man. Challenged by the Count de Guerchy to prove that he was not a woman in man's clothing, he refused to satisfy the curiosity of the authorities. The public, too, was anxious to know the truth, and there was heavy gambling on the subject. In 1774 the case was resolved against him, and he was ordered to wear women's clothing. A subsequent case was brought by an incensed (and out-of-pocket) gambler. Again the jury decided that Beaumont was a woman. She cut quite a dash, no doubt, in her ringlets and perfume, though she had not forsworn macho adventures: in 1787 she fought a duel, with swords, in her women's costume. This earned her some useful celebrity, and for a while afterwards she gave fencing lessons. In 1796 she was wounded and retired, but she survived until 1810. She had spent the last thirty-six years of her life as a woman, so it was something of a shock when it was discovered, on her death, that she had been a man all along. The examining doctor admitted that her throat was 'by no means masculine' and that her breast was 'remarkably full', but there was no mistaking the more obvious evidence: 'The male organ', he said, was 'in every respect perfectly formed'.[3] He was buried in St Pancras. He had been painted twice: once in a dress, once in military uniform. In 1868 his gravestone was lost during the construction of the railway line out of north London.

It was a freakish time, and Georgian England had a greedy appetite for such mesmerising figures. A captured Aborigine from Australia was paraded before the court in 1789, and a Polish dwarf, Joseph Boruwalski, embarked on a national concert tour with his miniature violin, before settling in Durham to write his memoirs.* For some, the pressures of exile were too great: Franz Kotzwara, a brilliant Polish musician, made a sensational name for himself when he was found to have hanged himself during a daring sexual extravaganza in a Soho brothel.

One who managed to rise above it was Giovanni Belzoni, an actor and engineer born in Padua, who came to Britain when France invaded Italy in 1803. He was oversized – six feet, seven inches – and he made a tawdry living for a while by teaming up with an English giantess (a 'consort of Amazonian proportions') and performing feats of strength at St Bartholomew's and other

---

*His shoes were only six inches long. As if to prove that life isn't fair, his brother was six feet, four inches tall.

travelling fairs. The empire saved and promoted him. In 1815 he was in Egypt, improving the irrigation of the viceroy's gardens by installing pumps, and was then entrusted with the task of ferrying the granite head of Rameses II to the British Museum in London. Inspired by this, he went back as a serious excavator of Egyptian remains, and achieved honour by locating the entrance to one of the great pyramids, part of which – Belzoni's Room – was named after him. He went on to join that long line of illustrious 'British' explorers who were not born in Britain, including John Cabot, Van Diemen (the 'discoverer' of Tasmania) and Sukpiz Kurz, from Munich, curator of the herbarium in Calcutta.

The Jewish community, having gained a foothold under Cromwell, had already begun to expand and move out of the shadows in which it had been forced to hide for so long. The small number of Sephardic Jews from the Mediterranean were joined by Ashkenazi from Northern and Eastern Europe, and the Jewish population swelled from some eight thousand in 1700 to some twenty thousand in 1800. There were still heavy restrictions on Jewish advancement (similar to those inflicted on Quakers and other dissidents) – the military was closed to them, as were the law and the universities – so they retained their traditional and sometimes risky position as expert money brokers and merchants. But here they could prosper. Samuel Dormido, in 1657, had become the first Jew to trade on the Royal Exchange, and such was the rush to follow in his footsteps that a 1697 regulation limited the number of licensed Jewish brokers to twelve.* Several of these men became famous figures as diamond traders and bankers: the Mendes da Costa family lived grandly in Highgate and acquired smart country seats in Surrey and Hertfordshire. Abraham Ricardo was a bigwig from Amsterdam who became an important player in the London Stock Exchange. His son David was educated in Holland but returned to write revolutionary works of economic theory and bought a country house, Gatscombe Park, in Gloucestershire. Other notable families – Ximines, Lopes, del Prados, Salvadors – followed suit. They slid into English high society with speed and care: long family histories in which they had posed as Christians had taught them how to assimilate. Samson Gideon was the son of a merchant in the West Indies who had arrived in London at the end of the seventeenth century. He set up as a money broker and speculator, and soon became the most resourceful financier in the City (his loans helped to suppress the 1745 Jacobite Rebellion). In what would become a significant Jewish trend, he married a Protestant, sent his son to Eton, and drifted away from his own faith, partly in the hope of a peerage, which never arrived.

The Sephardic Jews found homes in the villages just north of London, but

---

*This sounds like discrimination, but in the context of the times it was extremely liberal. Britain was in effect allowing 25 per cent of its new capital market to be run by foreigners.

were not always welcome. As early as 1709 a London pamphleteer complained that his beloved Hampstead was 'overstock'd with Jews'. The first history of Jews in Britain, the *Anglia Judaica*, written by a patriotic Briton called D'Blossiers Tovey in 1738, displayed familiar reflexes: 'unbelievers', it said, were 'like weeds in a cornfield'. But it also opposed the more rabid anti-Jewish sentiments of the day, and rejected the urban myth that Jews stank: 'Both Jews and Christians smell as bad as each other,' it insisted.[4]

The new Jewish community was used to looking after itself, however. The synagogues raised collections for the poor (so successfully that there were reports that other destitute aliens posed as Jews in order to obtain charity), and they could also be ruthless. Jews were ordered to leave the country if they brought dishonour on the whole charitable enterprise, and in 1710 the availability of poor relief was limited to a mere three days.

The eastern quarter of London, meanwhile, was swelling with Ashkenazi migrants from northern Europe. In 1692 a group of German merchants led by Moses Hart built a new 'Great' synagogue in Aldgate. Moses's brother Aaron – author of the first book in Hebrew to be published in London – became, figuratively at least, the Chief Rabbi. Moses Hart was one of the twelve 'Jew brokers' permitted to trade on the Royal Exchange, and he made the most of it. He trimmed his beard, declined to cover his head, and bought a palatial house in Twickenham,* which he decorated with grand Christian art by such painters as Van Dyck, Rubens, Hals and Holbein. He even had a painting of Jesus in the Temple, driving out the money-changers. By marrying his daughter to Aaron Franks, he allied himself to the other pre-eminent Jewish family in Britain at that time: the Frankses were prime movers in diamonds and coral, and supplied the British army overseas. Aaron Franks and Bilhah Hart moved into a riverside mansion right next door to Moses, where they entertained luxuriously, laying on concerts and balls for the people who counted.

Then, suddenly, there was a mini-boom in the number of Ashkenazi Jews. In 1745 Jews were expelled from Prague, and made their way through Holland to Britain. And Germans and Poles began to make the North Sea crossing. These newcomers were by no means struck from the same mould: unlike their worldly co-religionists already established in Britain, they were often landless, unskilled and unprepared. They had never lived outside traditional Jewish ghettos, and their first reflex was to band together. But it gradually dawned on them that there were fewer limits to their ambition in England: to a large extent they could live where they pleased and trade more freely than they had ever thought possible. 'Jews may dwell in any part of the City where they wish,' wrote a surprised Moses Cassuto in 1770. 'They may practise any sort of trade or craft and open a shop in any place outside the City in the suburbs, or even

*Now the West London College, with a wing called Moses Hart House.

in the City if they have practised the craft seven years under a master, in the same way as a Protestant may.'[5] Some exploited these opportunities and found sought-after work in finance or as doctors and surgeons, but most went against what until then was the prevailing stereotype and lived very humbly.

London was fast becoming the busiest trading city in the world, but it needed worker bees as well as queens. England's booming naval power helped create jobs in marine stores and supplies, and some Jews set up as dealers in the seaports. Soon there were congregations in Liverpool, Portsmouth, Falmouth, Hull and Plymouth. Many Jews acted as prize agents, banking the booty lugged home by brash English pirates (or, rather, cataloguing the treasure liberated by our brave seafarers from vile Spanish rogues) and distributing it according to an agreed formula. Naval opportunism was one of the few ways in which a common man could secure himself a nest-egg, and Jewish agents inserted themselves profitably into this aspirational system.

Otherwise, they peddled watches, pencils, ribbons or second-hand rags, and were often seduced into more chancy vocations. In 1795 a magistrate estimated that some two thousand of London's Jews were 'engaged in nefarious practices', and even if this is an exaggeration, it is evident that Jewishness was not synonymous with wealth. Indeed, Jews were stereotyped in popular songs and slurs as scoundrels and beggars. To 'jew' became a verb, meaning to con or swindle. One pamphlet insisted that Jews were 'the subtlest and most artful people in the world'. Some, such as Moses Hart, countered this by leaving their Judaism behind. Others left England behind. In 1733 Britain's Jewish leaders organised the evacuation of two shiploads of their people to Georgia, thus sowing the first seeds of what would become a huge community in the New World.

There was still a powerful lobby which argued that the Jews could – and should – be milked for money: in 1690 the Earl of Shaftesbury had proposed that they be charged with extra taxes and levies. Others clung to this view into the eighteenth century, but money talked. Solomon de Medina had financed the Duke of Marlborough to the tune of some six thousand pounds per annum in the early years of the century, and was rewarded with a knighthood. And William III had his own reasons to be grateful to the Jews: his expedition to England had been funded by a huge loan – two million gulden – from a Jewish financier in Holland, Isaac Pereira, who was rewarded with a plum post in Britain: Commissary-General for Shipping and Supplies.

In the first half of the eighteenth century, naturalisation still needed to be bought. And there remained the religious obstacle: no one could enter the professions or even become a commissioned officer without first taking the Christian oath. In 1753 the Jewish presence was formalised by the Jewish Naturalisation Act – the so-called 'Jew Bill', which removed the obstacles to Jewish participation in British public life. There was plenty of opposition, and though the bill passed easily through Parliament (96 votes to 55), it provoked such a fuss – there were hostile quips about 'the London Synagogue, formerly St Paul's' – that it was repealed after only a year. Still, by the end of the century synagogues were opening in provincial towns.

The largest community remained in London, however, on the fringes of the City. An apprentice shopkeeper in Aldgate called Daniel Mendoza made a name for himself by dealing with rude customers in a most vigorous fashion: he went on to become England's top prizefighter, and wrote the first manual of his sport, *The Art of Boxing*. He was not large (five feet, seven inches) but he was quick and strong: to hold his own against much larger opponents he relied on his speed and what would become classic footwork. After one spectacular success in 1790 he was invited to walk with George III in Windsor Great Park.

Although, to incurious locals, they seemed all the same, England's Jews were a disparate people, hailing as they did from Germany, Poland, Portugal, Holland, Italy, France and Spain. An orphanage was opened in 1703, and a Sephardic school in 1735, to teach English to migrants keen to merge invisibly into British society. And in 1760 the Sephardic and Ashkenazi wings united to form a joint Committee of Deputies, which would lobby for Jewish interests with the government. In an early nod to multiculturalism – the freedom to observe one's own culture and language – their sermons were given in Portuguese rather than English until 1813 (though printed translations were available: Jews were careful to rebut suggestions of exclusivity).

The Duke of Sussex became a keen Hebrew scholar and built a formidable Hebrew library. And, in an odd twist, Lord Gordon, a one-time Protestant fanatic and rabble-rouser of the anti-Catholic (i.e. anti-Irish) mob in 1778, turned to Judaism. He joined the Hambro Synagogue, and when he was sent to Newgate Prison for libelling the Queen of France in 1788, he signed in under the name Israel bar Abraham Gordon, and pinned the Hebrew Ten Commandments to the wall of his cell.

The most notable arrival of this period was Nathan Rothschild, who set up the London branch of his family's business at the end of the century, and presided over the gradual relocation of the firm, which was hard-pressed in its ruggedly anti-Semitic home town. Other migrants included Alexander Schomberg, the son of a German-Jewish doctor, who became a captain in the Royal Navy (and the second British Jew to be knighted). Louis Samuel came from Mecklenburg and became a watchmaker and silversmith in Liverpool; his brother Moses edited an early Jewish literary magazine called *The Cup of Salvation*. Moses' son Montagu turned his name around (to Samuel Montagu) and embarked on a great banking career, initially at the firm of his brother-in-law Adam Spielman in London, and then in partnership with his brother Edwin, a bullion trader in Liverpool. One group came to Britain in a specific commotion. Gibraltar had become British as part of the small print in the

Treaty of Utrecht in 1713 (the climax of the Duke of Marlborough's successful campaigns). By 1776, partly through the influence of the Emperor of Morocco, a Jew called Moses ben Attar, the Rock had a large population of Jewish traders. In 1779, when Gibraltar was besieged by the Spanish, they fled to England.

Meanwhile, out in the English countryside, the rural population was introduced to a new variant on an old form: the wandering Jew. Itinerant pedlars sold the usual range of utensils and fripperies from town to town. They were helped in 1772 by the publication of a Yiddish almanac, which became in effect their timetable, listing the dates of all the significant country fairs and holidays, and charting the movement of coaches and carriages. Some found peaceful places to hang their hats. A jeweller called Samuel Levi tramped with his brother to Wales, where they eventually set up a bank, having taken the precaution of awarding themselves a new name: Phillips. A rag seller called Moss Lyon married and settled in Portsmouth – one of his children joined the navy, the other became a fellow of Wadham College, Oxford. Travellers like these drifted away from Judaism partly to avoid the taunts it inspired, but chiefly because there was no way to observe it: they were usually far from any synagogue, miles from the nearest rabbi.

The Jews were not alone in being deprived of the means to practise their faith. It had been a common problem for all migrants for centuries. But that was gradually starting to change. There had been a Greek church in London since 1674; and Scandinavian churches were springing up, too. But the most significant 'foreign' faith, the one which could still generate hatred and fear, was the Roman Catholic Church. In the eighteenth century, it began to be associated not just with a dwindling band of aristocratic landowners, but with a new immigrant working class: the Irish. They came as labourers, and undercut the locals, especially in the countryside. They were merely drifters, seasonal hands for hire, but it wasn't hard to demonise them and anger the mob. When James McLean, son of a clergyman, was hanged at Tyburn in 1750 for terrorising Hyde Park, a large crowd was there to wave him on his way.

Along with the Irish from the west, the eighteenth century saw the first significant migration from the more distant east. There were already several thousand people of Indian origin in Britain: the gypsies, descendants of the nomadic tribes that spilled out of the Himalayas in the fifteenth century. In spite of their earlier hostile reception, they worked as entertainers, animal dealers, herbalists and astrologers, and were by now an embedded feature of the travelling tinker-and-pedlar circus of rural life. But relations with the Indian subcontinent itself did not begin until 1599, when Queen Elizabeth gave a royal charter to the East India Company. The company had grown fast, and was soon one of the planks on which England's prosperity was built. It inspired the formation of a fleet, which in turn created many new jobs in docks, foundries, warehouses, saw mills and chandleries. Trade accelerated after 1665, when Charles II received an unusual wedding present from Portugal: the city of Bombay. And for nearly a hundred years the trading links deepened. Then, in 1757, Robert Clive's military exploits at Plassey made Britain something more than a trading partner: it became the colonist, the administrative overlord. In a fateful move, London began to collect tax from its vast new colony.

Not many Indians were invited back to their new mother country, but a small number of servants or maids ('ayahs') were brought home as employees. Several are depicted in Johann Zoffany's portrait of Warren Hastings, for instance. Some were engaged for the voyage and then abandoned on arrival. The same thing happened to the Indian crews – the 'Lascars' – hired in increasing numbers by the British merchant fleet. They were popular with shipowners because they worked harder, drank less, and could be hired more cheaply than a Bristol or a Liverpool man.*

Lodging-houses sprang up: the Ayahs' House in London's Old Jewry provided beds for up to a hundred maids at any one time. By the end of the century there were three sailors' refuges in London (in Shoreditch, Hackney and Shadwell) and another in Liverpool. Some were driven to beg. Others had horror stories to tell. One notorious case concerned the Muslim Lascar who, as part of his initiation into the cheeky ways of the British seaman, was flogged, lashed to a mast with pork entrails wrapped round his face, and doused in salt water.

But if the century was characterised above all by its heartlessness and cruelty, there were some pangs of sympathy for these luckless exiles. In 1785, a correspondent to the *Public Advertiser* tried to stir the conscience of the readership by condemning the 'hard-heartedness and insensibility that distinguish the present times', and pleading that some respect be accorded people who, 'though different in colour, religion and country from ourselves, are still our fellow creatures, and who have been dragged from their warmer and more hospitable climates by our avarice and ambition'.[6]

In 1773 curry made its first appearance in a British restaurant, on the menu of a coffee house in the Haymarket. A few years later, S. K. Mahomed arrived in Dartmouth. At the turn of the century he would set up, in Brighton, some sought-after Indian vapour baths, which promised to cure various ailments and restore tired limbs. Today we could call it thalassotherapy. Mahomed brought

---

*There was even a notable South Sea islander, Omai, probably the first man from the Pacific ever to come to Britain. He was brought by Captain Tobias Furneaux in his ship, the *Adventure*, and was felt to be so extraordinary that he was wheeled in to meet King George III. He bowed and said: 'How do, King Tosh.' A heroic-looking portrait of him, painted by Sir Joshua Reynolds, was sold at auction in London in 2001 for £10.5 million.

with him a word – shampoo; from the Hindu *champi*, massage – which would attach itself irrevocably to the British sense of personal hygiene.

The appearance of these Asiatic strangers, coinciding as it did with the first struttings of imperial arrogance and power, generated some glimmer of a serious racial awkwardness. The ease with which the conquest of India had been accomplished, and the avarice of the maharajahs who had smoothed the path for the invaders, perhaps intensified an already sharp British sense of racial superiority. But, of course, the eighteenth century's most significant development in this area was the growing traffic in Africans. The slave trade was churning the world's population in new and alarming ways. Slavery was a thriving business long before most Britons had even heard of Africa, but Britain's impressive sea power was winning it a monopoly of this soul-destroying commerce. And the fledgling, grudgingly uniting kingdom firmly intended to make the most of it.

CHAPTER 9

Servants and Slaves

In 1740 James Thomson wrote the words for 'Rule Britannia'. It was performed as part of a theatrical masque called *Alfred*, which posterity has been happy to lose in its ample folds. But the song has echoed down the centuries, and still swells the larynxes of the promenaders who squeeze into the Albert Hall each summer for the annual singalong. Wagner would later remark that the first eight notes expressed everything you could wish to know about Britishness, and we've been running Thomson's bombastic little lyric up the flagpole ever since, jubilantly or defiantly: Britons, we insist, 'never-never-never shall be slaves'. Thomson knew exactly how to play on the emotions of his audience. In 1740 a man had only to saunter near the docks in Liverpool, Bristol or London, or even scan the classified section of the daily journals, to know that being a slave was absolutely the worst thing that could possibly happen to anyone.

Many blind eyes were turned to the horrors of the Middle Passage, but the slave trade could hardly be ignored. Eighteenth-century England was home to several thousand Africans who carried messages, steered horses through crowds, cooked, swept, busked, scrimped, saved, gambled, drank, slipped into secret doorways, clenched their teeth and cowered in fear, all in plain view of so-called polite society. Most social histories of the period see it as a time of elegant country houses that have now been tenderly restored by the National Trust, a time of girls in lacy gowns on swings, bewigged violinists with florid whiskers and footmen in fancy dress; a neoclassical arcadia, in short, shot through with bolts of sexy exuberance, gluttony and inventive industry. But James Thomson knew more than most what terrors lay behind this civilized facade.* In 'Seasons', a poem enlivened by anti-slavery reflexes, he wrote with disgust of the sharks who would follow the fleets, attracted by the stench of blood and death.

For the most part, though, the slave trade seemed almost natural, part of 'the way things were'. One of Queen Elizabeth's most dashing seamen, Jack Hawkins, had discovered on his 'divers voyages' to the Canary Islands that 'negroes' were 'very good merchandise' in Hispaniola – the Spanish colonies in South America. He fitted out three ships and sailed to Guinea, where, 'partly by the sword and partly by other means', he herded three hundred Africans into his holds. Thousands of miles to the west, he sold them for a treasure trove of ginger, leather, sugar and pearls, and was so proud of himself that he later added the figure of a shackled slave to his coat of arms.

For the next century, slavery remained a small, *ad hoc* business – a form of piracy, a perk for privateers. The Arab-run trade across the Sahara was an enormous business that had been conducted for almost a thousand years: in the course of the eighteenth century, perhaps three-quarters of a million Central African slaves were marched up the Nile to Egypt, and some half a million more were taken on the western routes to Libya. The transatlantic trade was also up and running, operated by Spain and Portugal (not to mention France, Holland and Denmark). But England, with naval supremacy over its Iberian rivals, soon came to dominate it. In 1655 Cromwell grabbed Jamaica from Spain and saw the fantastic wealth-creating potential of slave labour and sugar ('white gold'). After the Restoration Charles II gave it the royal seal of approval by founding a company, the Royal Adventurers into Africa, which was granted a monopoly for a thousand years. Among its members were seven knights, five earls, four barons, two dukes, a marquis and several members of the royal family. In the following twenty years it captured and (under its new name, the Royal African Company) sold ninety thousand slaves across the Atlantic. In 1713 the Treaty of Utrecht deprived Spain of its grip on slavery and handed this trophy to Britain. That one geopolitical transaction would dominate economic life for a century. By the time the trade was abolished in 1807, Britain had snatched and thrashed, bought and sold more than two and a half million men and women (mainly men) into the plantation inferno, in eleven thousand ships.

The profits were enormous.† Britain paid for slaves not with cash but with products, which kept the native population fruitfully employed collecting

---

*He was, after all, given as a gift the governor-generalship of the Leeward Islands, which generated an eye-opening income (for a poet) of £300 per annum.
†One estimate is that the transports accrued to British planters and traders an aggregate profit of a million pounds a year throughout the eighteenth century – many billions in today's terms.

cowrie shells from the Maldives, or in the manufacture of textiles, copper, pewter, cutlery, alcohol and guns at home. The trade had its own coin: the guinea, first struck in 1663 by the Royal Adventurers, and named after the African coast where they 'mined' their raw material. Torrents of bright new guineas splashed into London's mercantile coffers and transformed English life in ways that could hardly have been imagined. The handsome country houses where Jane Austen's heroines could play the piano and discuss such pressing matters as hats and dowries (houses that now seem so essentially and tastefully English), the boom in the arts (sculpture, poetry, music, painting, theatre – all of which required spendthrift patrons) – these and much else besides derived, either directly or indirectly, from the slave trade.

The industrialisation of agriculture encouraged, into the bargain, a wholesale and irrevocable transformation of English (and then British) tastes and manners. As the eighteenth century proceeded, the national diet grew from meagre to gluttonous. Rare tropical delicacies became staples. Potatoes, spices, tea, coffee, tobacco, chocolate and above all sugar entered, filled and sometimes blocked the national bloodstream. All of these were sold initially as medicinal imperatives. The potato was 'a Root of great Vertue' and something of an aphrodisiac;* tea enjoyed 'the repute of prevailing against the headache, Gravel, and griping in the Guts'; coffee was held to 'support the vital flame'; and tobacco, according to its apologists, could 'afford Relief to Arthritic patients'. Sugar could coat almost any pill, and was sold on the grounds that it was delicious. Alongside its excellent by-product – rum – it conquered the national palate with fabulous speed. In 1700, 23,000 tons of sugar were imported. At the end of the century nearly quarter of a million tons came ashore, to be dissolved into sweet confections and beverages across the country. The new hot drinks were perfect for our cold climate: in the 1720s 9 million tons of tea were dumped on to English docks; by the 1750s this had risen to 37 million tons. Coffee percolated with similar speed. The very first coffee house had opened in Cornhill, London, in 1657, and by the time of the Great Fire there were more than eighty in the City. In 1740 there were 550.†️ Not everyone liked it (one customer said it was 'black as soot and tasting not unlike it'), but stirred with sugar it was a popular and enlivening accompaniment to everyday chit-chat, the doing of deals and the reading of the new daily journals that had given such an informative boost to the life of the capital.

---

*It was held to be 'favourable to population' – a slogan not even today's global pushers of fries would dare suggest.
†In inspiring this profusion of cafés, these public forums for conversation, coffee can also be said to have greased the wheels of financial markets, newspapers and intellectual life.

Britain became in one sense the centre of world trade: from the east came tea (China) and coffee (Turkey and Arabia); from the west came sugar and tobacco, harvested by slaves (from Africa). Apart from anything else, this global vacuuming of raw materials gave a powerful boost to an important British industry: pottery. We became a nation of cups and saucers, dainty plates and silver spoons. British ships brought mahogany, cotton, rice, ginger, pimento, tortoiseshell, ivory, gold dust, gum, palm oil, cocoa and coffee. Britain stopped being a land of markets and became a land of shops (and shopkeepers, as Napoleon would soon observe). The consumer society was born. The papers devoted more space to advertising than to news; and by 1759 roughly 140,000 new shops had opened across the kingdom. Much of this dynamic expansion of the retail trade was built on the strained backs of the slaves who laboured, under the lash, in fields far from the snug and increasingly sweet British hearth.*

All this helped the new ideas and theories of capitalism to sprout and blossom. And these theories could be put to the test, because Britain had enough spare capital to experiment. Money markets began to replace land ownership as the elite path to wealth and prestige;† banking and insurance grew into huge international concerns. Without the capital generated by the slave trade, it is doubtful whether Britain could have mustered the resources needed to invade and secure India, or the investments summoned by the first drumbeats of industrialisation. The initial beneficiaries were the cream of society,‡ and many of them recycled their booty by injecting the capital required to build mines and factories at home. The Bristol-based Goldney family pushed the capital they had made from slavery towards Abraham Darby, who in 1709 perfected the art of smelting iron, and can be said to have launched the age of iron, steel and coal. One Member of Parliament, Anthony Bacon, won a contract to supply Negroes to the islands in 1765. The deal netted him £67,000, which went into industrial development around Merthyr Tydfil, at that time a hamlet of shepherds. Bacon bought a lease on four hundred acres and set up a brisk mining operation for iron and coal. Richard Pennant MP inherited the largest estate in Jamaica, funnelled the cash flow into some new slate quarries near Bangor, prospered mightily, and ended up as the first Baron

---

*Between 1700 and 1760, 180,000 slaves were ferried to Barbados to work the sugar cane; 50,000 of them died of disease, malnutrition, overwork, neglect or murder.
†Inspiring Alexander Pope's satirical lines on those who let their land fall into disuse while they themselves 'sit content, On the slow and silent growth of ten per cent'.
‡And the government. Tea was taxed heavily, as a luxury, at 120 per cent – marvellous for the Treasury until it noticed that three-quarters of the tea trade was handled by smugglers eager to evade the steep import duty. That is why Bostonians selected tea as the target for their revolutionary acts. In 1784 the duty was cut to a paltry, but more lucrative, 12.5 per cent.

Penrhyn. The trade also sponsored the nautical advances that would guarantee Britain's empire in the years to come: the first copper-bottomed ship was a 140-ton Liverpool slaver, the *Hawke*, and by 1786 some 124 vessels in the triangular trade were copper-bottomed.

The fortunes founded on slavery, in other words, shaped the structure of British life as decisively and irrevocably as had William the Conqueror's gifts of land to his favoured knights. The Gladstones of Liverpool grew rich and powerful from slave-shipping, so much so that one of their descendants could become Prime Minister. Liverpool Town Hall put elephants and slaves on its crest. Even the Church saw no harm in it. The Society for the Propagation of the Christian Gospel ran plantations in Barbados, and piously branded the word 'Society' on to the skin of each new slave. Some of the more ruthless defenders of slavery found biblical justification for the trade.

Through this period, several thousand black Africans were living and working not in the plantations of the Caribbean but here in Britain, among those who were growing rich on their suffering. Their lives are so ill-documented that it requires an effort of imagination to picture them at all. In the first half of the eighteenth century especially, they left barely a mark. Once the abolitionist movement gathered pace, their story starts to emerge; but we still have only fragments.

In the light of the colossal upheaval caused by the slave trade as a whole – a demographic volcano from which flowed a diaspora which would transform the world – the social ramifications in Britain itself were modest. The *Gentleman's Magazine* of 1764 claimed there were 20,000 'negroe servants' in London alone; and the following year the *Morning Gazette* hazarded the view that there were 30,000 in the country as a whole; in 1788, Gilbert Franklyn suggested that there were 40,000. But these were all alarmist guesses swollen by the desire to have the Africans ferried – out of sight and out of mind, though not, of course, out of pocket – to the fearful labour camps out west.* In 1764, a party for black men and women in a Fleet Street pub (an 'all black hop') was sufficiently unusual to rate a mention in the newspapers. But the African or Caribbean presence was striking enough to ignite heated outbreaks of distaste for 'colonies of Hottentots'. Modern historians have combed parish lists, baptismal and marriage registers, criminal records, sales contracts and property tallies, and have extrapolated these into a more or less plausible

---

*Indeed, the *Gentleman's Magazine*, in citing so high a number, stressed that it spoke of 'a grievance that requires a remedy'. Almost no one has an interest in minimising the number, however. Some modern accounts are correspondingly happy to accept high estimates, to amplify (as if it needed amplifying) the barbarity of the crime. Scobie, in *Black Britannia* (1972), reckoned that there might have been up to 50,000.

estimate of ten thousand.* Many came young; their lives were often brief. Only a brave few were able to puncture the iron ceiling beneath which they were chained.

Initially, they were simply slaves. Some were bought as domestic servants for the better class of home; some were retained by returning plantocrats; others managed to jump ship and slip into the muddy shadows. Their status here was in theory uncertain: technically, no Christian could be a slave, and the Africans who had themselves baptised (or who were sent for baptism by progressive owners) were arguably free. Furthermore, in 1706, Lord Chief Justice Holt declared that 'No man can have property in another . . . there is no such thing as a slave by the laws of England.' A year later he repeated himself: 'As soon as a Negro comes into England, he becomes a free man.'[1] These unequivocal judgments were ignored; sometimes they were evaded by a breathtaking piece of logical sophistry, which insisted (inverting the whole idea of the original assertion) that, since the slaves were the property of other men, they could not be people, and needed to be treated as commodities. Thomas Papillon was one of many who took his black servant 'to be in the nature and quality of my goods and chattels'.[2] The slaves in the colonies were handled in this way, and their existence was tabulated and recorded. The Africans in Britain were deprived of even that dubious right. However, their presence is memorialised in illustrations by Hogarth and other contemporary printmakers,† who present them as vivid satirical eyewitnesses to the greedy antics of their so-called superiors; and in a few passing remarks in newspapers, memoirs and court cases.

Even if they were acknowledged as freemen, though, it did them little good, as they remained barred from paid work. In 1731 the Lord Mayor of London ruled that 'no Negroes shall be bound apprentices to any Tradesman or Artificer of this City'. So inevitably they ended up for the most part in 'service', initially in only the most fashionable households. Black servants soon became an elegant (and cheap) way of complementing and setting off the pale skin of their

---

*One instance of the malleability of such figures is the crime statistic unearthed by Norma Myers: between 1785 and 1789, she found, 0.55 per cent of listed crimes in London were committed by blacks. Assuming an even distribution of crime throughout London's population of 780,000, she estimates that there were 4,290 Africans in the city. It is possible that blacks committed a high proportion of listed crime, if only because they were assumed to be criminal and targeted as such. It is equally possible that they were denied the luxury of legal process, were simply given thrashings by their owners, and therefore did not enter the records. So the true figure could be much higher or rather lower. It could also, of course, be about right.
†Such as William Humphreys, whose *High Life Below Stairs* showed white maids adoring a black butler. When David Garrick staged the play of this title at Drury Lane, the black servants were played by white actors. It might not have been funny otherwise.

owners. A duchess could hardly afford to be seen in public without a dashing black companion, lavishly dressed in brocade and a turban, and given a heroic name like Pompey or Caesar, Scipio or Socrates. They were fashion accessories, more or less: they brought a touch of tamed jungle to the Georgian living room.* As such, they became an everyday feature of life in England, treated by the upper crust in much the same way as they treated their pets.† Adverts would appear in papers like the *Tatler*, the *London Chronicle* and the *Liverpool Gazette*: 'A Black boy, twelve years of age, fit to wait on a gentleman . . . A fine Negroe Boy, can Dress Hair in a tolerable way.'[3]

These were, in comparison with their peers, the lucky ones: silly clothes were better than no clothes at all. But if life in England was marginally less vicious than life in the colonies, it was still slavery, and was administered with historic cruelty. These were forced, involuntary immigrants, pushed against their will into a cold, foreign land. They contradict the stereotype that rabble-rousers have deployed for centuries, because far from wanting to 'come over here' and foul the nest, they never wanted to leave their homes in the first place.

Even so, their presence was bitterly resented. They had to endure calls for their expulsion – which would mean transportation to the chain gangs on the plantations. But there was little comprehension of precisely what that entailed since the Liverpool merchants and investors shielded the public from the ugly truth. The slaves, they said, had been rescued, plucked from certain death in the tribal jungle and liberated into the dignified fresh air of hard spiritual endeavour. Pious tracts were written (the Liverpool merchants commissioned one from a Jesuit) which claimed that the slaves ought to be grateful for having been introduced to civilisation and the radiant light of Christian values. Their lack of gratitude for this munificence began to anger the public. In 1723 the *Daily Journal* wrote: 'A great number of Blacks come daily into this city, so that 'tis thought in a short time, if they be not suppress'd, the city will swarm with them.' And Edward Long, author of a *History of Jamaica* (1774), had as his starting-point the notion that the similarities between Africans and orang-utans far exceeded the differences. They were, he argued in one impressive outburst, 'brutish, ignorant, idle, crafty, treacherous, bloody, thievish, mistrustful and superstitious'.[4]

In this context, it seems meretricious even to ponder, let alone try to assess, what kind of 'contribution' these unfortunate people made to the national life.

---

*And fashion was a fickle mistress. The Duchess of Devonshire wrote once to her mother offering to send her an eleven-year-old boy called Michael, because the Duke had decided he was fed up with black servants. It was 'more original to have a Chinese page than a black one; everybody had a black one'.

†In Maria Edgeworth's 1802 novel *Belinda*, both the pet dog and the black manservant are called Juba.

The doors to advancement were firmly blocked: Africans were forced to contribute their sweat and toil, but weren't allowed to offer anything more. They were unwelcome (except as waiters) at the high tables of industry, the economy, intellectual and political life. Where the Protestant refugees from Europe had been encouraged, and the Jews had been tolerated, the Africans were trapped. Such is the self-fulfilling nature of racial ideas and reflexes. The depiction of their race as inept and unworthy, and the zealous upholding of this image with whips and chains, created people who could all too easily be depicted, on the far side of a vicious circle, as servile, fractious, idle and ill-disciplined. The occasional revolts in the West Indies were publicised to demonstrate the importance of keeping the national foot firmly on the African neck.

In the end, the powers-that-be lost, or retreated, or coolly washed their hands of the whole dirty business. To an often neglected extent, this was because the slaves themselves were able to contrive a shift in the national mentality by inspiring, demanding and sometimes guiding the abolitionist crusade. They fought, and ultimately triumphed, against the injustice that had befallen them. It took a long time. But it was a major achievement, since quite apart from eroding the moral credibility of slavery itself, the abolitionist movement ushered in an appetite for social change and a modus operandi for future protest movements: the establishment of workers' rights, for instance, and the enfranchisement of women.

The Society for the Abolition of the Slave Trade was not formed until 1787, but the pressure for humanitarian advances had been growing for some time before that. John Wesley described the trade as 'execrable' and the Methodist churches preached against it. Individuals such as Thomas Clarkson, Granville Sharp, James Ramsay and eventually William Wilberforce led the public outcry by writing, lecturing and seeking specific legal advances in the courts.* Other clergymen, such as John Newton, echoed their words. Newton was the son of a seaman and had once been captain of a slave ship; but in 1748 he resolved to take seriously the tenets of Christianity, and became a rector. He wrote a hymn ('How Sweet the Name of Jesus Sounds') and produced a string of heated denunciations of slavery.

In liberal society it became as fashionable to declare oneself opposed to slavery as it once had been to have a black boy passing the scones. Dozens of novelists included sentimental black characters battling adversity in the Tropics before finding freedom in England. Women led a boycott of sugar and rum. Josiah Wedgwood, whose pottery business had prospered on the back of tea

---

*Ironically, the prime movers in the abolitionist movement, the Quakers, had at one time been eager slavers. There were eighty-four Quaker members of the original slaving company, and even a slave ship called the *Willing Quaker*.

with two sugars, produced a plaque inscribed with the slogan: 'Am I not a man and a brother?'* The movement became widespread and unstoppable. In 1792, Parliament received five hundred anti-slavery petitions.

The leaders of this movement were heroes, to be sure, and their revolt was inspired by the best of motives. But to present abolition as a merciful blessing bestowed by an enlightened officer class confirms that freedom, for Africans, was automatically in the gift of their British 'superiors' – a patronising suggestion in itself. It denies to the slaves any major role in their own emancipation. Of course, slavery itself limited their influence; they had to engage the sympathies and support of men more powerful than themselves. But African immigrants in Britain agitated hard to persuade others of their right to a better life, sometimes by escaping (often the only form of rebellion available to them), sometimes by behaving in ways that contradicted the stereotypes that maintained the trade in their lives, but also, most stirringly, by rejecting the hand that life had dealt them and rising to positions of prominence in their own right. The Abolition Committee had a black twin, the Sons of Africa, a group of ex-slaves who wrote letters and speeches on their own behalf.

Slavery in Britain had been outlawed, technically, in 1772, when Judge Mansfield, at the Court of the King's Bench, planted a plain legal landmark by finding that the master of a young black man called James Somerset had no right to compel him to board a ship. Somerset had been bought in 1769 by Charles Stewart in Boston. As soon as he landed in England he boldly put himself forward as a test case by declaring himself free, citing a 1771 ruling by Judge Blackstone that 'a slave or negro, the moment he lands in England falls under the protection of the laws . . . and becomes *eo instanti* a free man'.[5] This was simply a restatement of Holt's assertion of 1706, but that earlier ruling had been consistently ignored. Now James Somerset set out to ensure that the same thing would not happen again. He was able to enlist some powerful supporters, such as Granville Sharp, who was a true friend to the slaves. He took on Somerset's case despite having had his fingers burned a few years earlier, when he stumbled across a seventeen-year-old slave, half blind and lame, in the street. The boy, Jonathan Strong, had been pistol-whipped by his owner, David Lisle, a London lawyer and a shareholder in a Barbados plantation. The pistol had been smashed into Strong's head hard enough to fracture his skull. Sharp sent Strong to St Bartholomew's Hospital, and after three months helped him, now partially healed, to get a job as a messenger for an apothecary near Fenchurch Street. Two years later, Strong bumped into his former owner, who seized and prepared to transport him. Strong managed to get an appeal to Sharp, who

---

*These small black-on-white medallions were a bestseller, even in high society; men had them inlaid in gold on their snuff boxes, ladies wore them on bracelets. Thomas Clarkson ordered 500 of them, and handed them out like business cards.

intervened. The case was heard in 1767. The judge was benign: 'The Lad had not stolen anything, and is not guilty of any offence, and is therefore at liberty to go away.' But Sharp then promptly found himself charged by Lisle with robbery, for having commandeered the boy. Advised that he would be found guilty of harbouring a fugitive, and shocked by the extent to which property laws could be stretched to apply to a young man, Sharp was forced to admit defeat.

He devoted the next two years to studying the law. So when James Somerset came to him, he was well prepared, and he needed to be. Somerset was kidnapped by Stewart and spirited on to a Jamaica-bound ship called the *Ann and Mary*, but Sharp secured his release by obtaining a writ of habeas corpus. The case lasted a month. Many black people gathered in the court to hear the verdict, bowing gravely to the officers of the law. The *Morning Chronicle* permitted itself a tender aside: 'No sight could be more pleasingly affecting to the mind than the joy which shone at that instant in these poor men's sable countenances.'[6]

It must indeed have been a moving scene, but again the judgment was largely ignored. Slaves who ran away gleefully from their domestic prisons were denounced by their masters as 'ungrateful villains'. One, who had been baptised and was planning to marry a white woman (a monstrous crime), was seized and dragged on to a westbound ship. He had fewer allies than Somerset; the law was inaccessible to him. So he chose a more drastic form of protest: he shot himself in the head.* In the years that followed, the law that with one hand had guaranteed rights of slaves to be free citizens was quick to protect, with the other, the rights of their owners, many of whom had legally enforceable contracts in their favour.

While the Somerset decision by no means wrought an instant liberation – Mansfield himself emphasised that he had not outlawed slavery, but had merely ruled that slaves could not be forced to leave the country against their will – it did at least change the direction of the prevailing wind. And it helped to bind the growing number of free Africans into something like an immigrant community.† The crowd at the Somerset hearing had proved that there was already such a thing as a slaves' grapevine along which relevant news could

---

*In 1773 Thomas Day wrote a famous, sentimental and popular poem based on the case, called 'The Dying Negro', presented as a monologue by the suicidal man to his fiancée:

> Take these last sighs – to thee my soul I breathe –
> Fond love in dying groans, is all I can bequeathe.

†'Community' is of course modern jargon. It would not have resonated with many Africans in eighteenth-century England, whose most profound sensation was loneliness. They were live-in workers dispersed in smart houses throughout the whole country, far from home and friends, and, as far as they could see, quite beyond help.

travel fast. And after the trial a celebratory black ball was organised in a Westminster pub. People could be mobilised. In 1773, when two blacks were hauled off to Bridewell for begging, they were visited by three hundred of their fellow Africans, who had an impromptu whip-round to raise funds on their behalf. And when the anti-slavery activist Thomas Clarkson went to Manchester in 1787 he was surprised to find a large number – some forty or fifty – African faces pressing round his pulpit.

That even a well-inclined and interested party like Clarkson should have been surprised is an eloquent statement of the extent to which Britain's black community inhabited a twilight zone beneath consideration. Only a few had emerged from the shadows: Job Ben Solomon, a self-taught genius who eventually worked as an Arabic translator for the British Museum; Francis Barber, a poet and protégé of Samuel Johnson; and Francis Williams, used (more or less) as a guinea pig to test the Duke of Montagu's theory that nurture could triumph over nature, who was educated at Cambridge and eventually became a scholar in mathematics and Latin. These men could live something approaching a decent life, even if it depended on and was sometimes hobbled by patronage. Others, through sheer hard graft, were able to purchase their freedom, find work as musicians, shopkeepers or grooms, and live on their own terms – slipping into all-black bars for a drink, chatting with friends, making secret plans. They had to keep their heads down; anyone with 'ideas above their station' was tempting fate. The Duchess of Queensbury had a favourite servant (and maybe more than that) called Julius Soubise. In 1768 Lady Coke reported breathlessly that she had just been to visit the Duchess and found her 'half undressed. She was talking to her Black Boy.'[7] The Duchess encouraged Soubise to become an expert horseman, fencer, sonneteer and fop-about-town. He joined the most fashionable clubs, swaggered at the opera, rode in Hyde Park and pursued women frantically. But upon learning that he had been passing himself off as a prince, the Duchess was heard to rebuke him flirtatiously: 'O! is it so, Master Soubise. I must lower your crest, I perceive.' Eventually, he was packed off to Bengal to establish a riding school. He died when he was thrown from an unbroken stallion. Soubise was pampered and patronised, but this benign oppression was preferable to the callous inhumanity of the plantations.

And there are other glints of light. Quite a few servants were rewarded in the wills of their dying owners, and were able to step into the semi-free world. Lord Mansfield himself had a slave called Elizabeth Dido whom he treated with some kindness: he was once reproached by a visitor for 'showing a fondness' towards her. In his will he formally freed her, with five hundred pounds and an annual legacy of a hundred pounds. Margaret Hamilton gave her servant Joseph Harvey seven hundred pounds on her death bed. 'It is all for you,' she said. 'To make you happy.' Margaret's uncle (who had 'given' her Joseph) was horrified, and made a legal bid to recover the money. He failed on an interesting technicality: he was unable to demonstrate that Joseph Harvey was in any sense still his property.

Cases such as this remained the exception rather than the rule. In general, Africans looked in vain for a helping hand. By the end of the century there were several shabby communities in London (Wapping, Limehouse and St Paul's) and Liverpool – where one road became known as 'Negro Street'. The derelict tenements where they squatted became known as 'rookeries'. One sprang up around the City of London, a good centre of operations for the beggars and buskers, prostitutes and hawkers they were forced to become. One celebrated pair, Billy Waters and African Sal, became a fixed part of the scenery outside the Adelphi Theatre in the Strand. They were immortalised as Staffordshire figurines, and Waters even rated an obituary, which spoke touchingly of the way he had eked out a living for himself, his wife and two children by 'the scraping of cat-gut'. He was not permitted to die with dignity, however: he was forced to pawn his fiddle before breathing his last breath in the St Giles workhouse. Charles M'Gee was another well-known 'chaunter' (he would have been hard to ignore, with his long white hair and one good eye) at Ludgate Hill; and Joseph Johnson, a wounded and discharged seaman, sang sea shanties at Tower Hill.

More celebrated than any of these was Phyllis Wheatley, who came from Boston in 1772, having been taken from Africa as an eight-year-old girl. She was hailed as a poet, a child prodigy, and stayed as the guest of the Countess of Huntingdon. She was examined by 'learned' men, who issued a proclamation of authenticity, declaring that it was indeed the case that 'an uncultivated barbarian' had managed to make some lines rhyme. She was treated in much the same way as Saartje Baartman would be a few years later: as a bizarre circus act. Baartman came to London in 1810 from South Africa, and was given the stage name 'The Hottentot Venus', in honour of her enormous backside.

Most free black women were in an even worse predicament, however. They had only two options: pickpocket or prostitute. In much the same way as black men were feared as sexual predators, black women were vilified as pernicious temptresses, leading astray the otherwise high-minded menfolk of Britain. But they enjoyed brisk trade. Soho was home to a black brothel and one prostitute called Black Harriot is said to have serviced twenty members of the House of Lords. She bought a house on the proceeds and, in a unique social experiment, set up with a Guards officer.*

Harriot was infamous in her time – she merited a mention in an eighteenth-century chronicle called *Nocturnal Revels* – but she could hardly be called a significant historical figure. In fact, only one eighteenth-century African Briton

---

*The experiment failed: the officer ran through Harriot's money, racked up large debts, then abandoned her.

was included in the first *Dictionary of National Biography*: Ignatius Sancho. He was born on a slave ship en route to the Spanish colony of New Granada (now Ecuador) in 1729. His mother died from disease soon after they arrived, and his father committed suicide. The surviving orphan was baptised by a bishop and sent by his owner to London, where he was given to three sisters in Greenwich (who added the name Sancho, a Quixotic tribute to his cheerfulness, to his baptismal name Ignatius). The sisters were not enlightened: they aimed to keep the boy tame by keeping him ignorant. But he had the luck to catch the eye of the Duke of Montagu, one of whose hobbies, as we have seen, was black intellectual development. He gave Ignatius some books. Alas for the orphan, the Duke died in 1749, but Sancho begged the Duchess to take him into her household. She hired him as a butler and it seems he pleased her, because when she died only two years later, she left him a tidy allowance of thirty pounds a year. Sancho, free at last, was reckless with his money, and spent it at the theatre and in gambling dens. In 1766 he spent his last shilling watching David Garrick play Richard III, before swallowing his pride and seeking employment with the new Duke of Montagu. He became the Duke's valet and once again made a highly favourable impression: in 1768 the Duke had Sancho's portrait done in oil – by Gainsborough, no less.

By 1774 Sancho had become too gouty and obese to work as a valet. With the Duke's help, he set up a grocery in Westminster, and this soon became the centre of an informal ex-slave society. It was a salon, more or less: visitors would sip tea and discuss politics, while Ignatius sat at the back writing long letters on current affairs in his thigh-slapping patriotic style. An anthology of these was published posthumously in 1782, and, despite a frosty review by Mary Wollstonecraft, it sold impressively: the ninth edition came out in 1794.

Sancho had voted in the 1774 and 1780 elections. In the latter year he witnessed (and sharply disapproved of) the Gordon Riots, the violent civic unrest inspired by anti-Catholic legislation (there may, at the time, have been fewer Catholics than blacks in London). Sancho condemned the crowd's 'worse than negro barbarity'. When he died, on 14 December 1780, he became the first African to be given an obituary in the British press. He'd been one of London's 'characters' – his popularity was such that he even gave his name to a brand of tobacco – Sancho's Best Trinidado.

He was relatively well loved partly because he was so courteous. His contemporary, Ottobah Cuguano, was more abrasive. In 1787 he published *Thoughts and Sentiments on the Evil and Wicked Traffic of the Slavery and Commerce of the Human Species*. It was a ground-breaking work. The genuine voice, the unnerving outraged howl of the slave, had never been heard before. Not surprisingly, Cuguano seemed dangerous: he preached sedition, and held 'every man in Great Britain responsible in some degree' for the evils of slavery. His language was biblical, and it struck a deep barb into the righteous streak of those who read him. 'Our lives are accounted of no value,' he wrote. 'We are hunted as the prey in the desert, and doomed to destruction as the beasts that perish.'[8]

Other Africans – Robert Mandeville, Jasper Goree, Thomas Cooper – soon echoed him. The loudest and most eloquent, however, was Olaudah Equiano. He was born in 1745 in what is now Nigeria, enslaved as an eleven-year-old boy, and carted off to Barbados and then Virginia. He converted to Christianity, read everything he could lay his hands on, and bought his freedom in Montserrat in 1763. He came to Britain and was baptised at St Margaret's, Westminster. He signed on as a naval employee and in 1772 joined an expedition to the North Pole. His ship, the *Race Horse* (one of his fellow seamen was a fifteen-year-old boy called Horatio Nelson), sailed into the ice and was forced to retreat. In 1776, on another voyage, he ran into trouble off the Mosquito Coast when the captain of a sloop headed for Jamaica attempted to re-enslave him. He was tied up and hung from a mast until the ship's carpenter risked the wrath of the skipper by cutting him down and putting him into a canoe. For several years he worked as a servant, joining that invisible community of half-free Africans in London, but he was always restless and busy. He applied for ordination as an Anglican priest and was interviewed by the Bishop of London, but for some reason his application failed.* In 1792 he married Susanna Cullen, with whom he already had a daughter. The girl died aged four, and Equiano wrote a sad and rebuking lyric on her grave at Chesterton, near Cambridge:

> Should simple village rhymes attract thine eye,
> Stranger, as thoughtfully thou passest by,
> Know that there lies beside this humble stone
> A child of colour haply not thine own.[9]

Equiano wrote his memoirs under the name Gustavas Vassa. They were published in 1788 as *The Interesting Narrative of the Life of Olaudah Equiano, or Gustavas Vassa, the African*. This highly unusual first-hand account of the slave ships found sympathetic ears across the country, swelling the ranks of the abolitionists. The book ran to fourteen editions, and readers were moved and shocked by the scenes Equiano described. 'I had never seen among any people such instances of cruelty,' he wrote of his first encounter with the trade. 'One white man in particular I saw, when we were permitted to be on deck, flogged so unmercifully with a large rope near the foremast, that he died in consequence of it, and they tossed him over the side as they would have done a brute.'[10] This was the kind of thing that Britons had for years tried not to think

---

*He would not have been the first black minister. Philip Quaque had been ordained and sent to the Cape, where he served dutifully for half a century.

about. Now it could no longer be denied. But Equiano was more than a simple eyewitness: he was also an outspoken polemicist. 'To kidnap our fellow creatures, however they may differ in complexion, to degrade them into beasts of burden, to deny them every right but those, and scarcely those we allow to a horse, to keep them in perpetual servitude, is a crime as unjustifiable as it is cruel.' He was an activist, too, lobbying or working with Granville Sharp on several legal cases.

He was briefly involved with the ill-fated scheme to deport American slaves in Britain to Sierra Leone in 1787. Thousands of slaves in Virginia and Carolina had heard about the James Somerset case and joined the British army in the War of Independence in the hope that it would lead to freedom. After the war many of these unfortunate loyalists were betrayed – dumped in Nova Scotia and Jamaica – but a large number returned to Britain as veterans. They were unwelcome and could not find work. London acquired an unsightly new feature: black beggars. The winter of 1786 was bitter, and scores of them died. A new committee for their 'relief' supplied bread, broth and meat, but more was required, and a plan was drafted to ferry them back to Africa. Seven hundred people signed the repatriation agreement, but only four hundred turned up – perhaps the others feared it was a trick, and they would be ferried west, not south. In the end, people were rounded up on the streets and pressed on board two ships in the Thames estuary. Some jumped overboard to escape.* When the ships finally left, they ran straight into a Channel storm which drove them into Plymouth for repairs. Fifty Africans died of fever before the ship left English waters, and thirty more expired on the month-long voyage south. In Sierra Leone, of course, no provision had been made for their arrival, and there was no medicine in their modest supplies. They arrived in the rainy season. Of the 350 black passengers (and 59 white wives†), only 60 lived more than four years.

---

*Their lack of trust was understandable. A few years earlier, in an infamous case in 1781, the captain of a ship called the *Zong* threw 131 slaves overboard, to save water. Slaves who fought for their lives were shackled before being tipped into the sea. When the ship arrived in Jamaica there were 420 gallons of fresh water on board. Far from apologising, or keeping quiet, the shipowners sued the insurance company for declining to compensate their loss. At the hearing, the Solicitor-General, John Lee, affected to find the case open and shut: 'What is all this vast declaration of human beings being thrown overboard? This is a case of chattels or goods.'

† The wives were drunken prostitutes carried on board ship and pushed into 'marriage' by a press gang in London. A visitor to Sierra Leone, Anna Falconbridge, was horrified when she learned from one of the women about this expulsion: 'It is scarcely possible that the British Government, at this advanced and enlightened age, envied and admired as it is by the universe, could be capable of exercising or countenancing such a Gothic infringement on human Liberty.'

While Equiano was lobbying and campaigning in his polemical essays, a gentler voice was influencing public opinion. James Albert Ukawsaw Gronniosaw was a pious young man who narrated his many troubles while thanking God for the countless blessings that had been showered on his unworthy head. He described himself as 'a poor blind heathen' who had been saved by 'the boundless goodness of God'. He was helped in this by a ghostwriter, a mysterious lady from Leominster, and it is likely that the sentimental piety of his prose owes something to her intervention. But his remains a luminous life. He was kidnapped in Africa and sold to a Dutch planter in Barbados. He went to New York as a domestic slave, was given his freedom in a will and arrived in England with high hopes ('I imagined that all the Inhabitants of this Island were Holy') which were soon dashed. In Portsmouth he gave his savings of twenty-four pounds to a landlady, who ran off with them. 'All my promis'd happiness was blasted,' he wrote. He went to Petticoat Lane, where he married a riding mistress, but was driven out during some weavers' riots and headed east, to Colchester. A sympathetic farmer gave him four carrots, which he chewed for a while before giving them to his child. Salvation arrived when a lawyer gave him a job as a builder. He went to Norwich and Kidderminster, while his wife hired a loom and wove cloth. They had three children in total, one of whom died of smallpox. Only when a Baptist minister refused to bury her did dejection finally get the better of Gronniosaw. 'We are travelling through many difficulties,'[11] he wrote, as his story tailed into oblivion.*

Gronniosaw's was a sad life, bravely lived. He was less fortunate than Ignatius Sancho, whose letters indicate that his was a cheerful, well-fed, domestic existence, fully engaged with both the trivial and the pressing issues of the day. But there were similarities in their life stories. Both had friendly relations with whites – Sancho with Laurence Sterne, whom he revered, and Gronniosaw with his wife, whom he loved. Theirs is one of the first instances of a racially mixed marriage that we have, and it seems, in the direst circumstances, to have been a happy one. Both men were able to try their luck in different arenas, and were often dealt with in a kindly manner by those who met or employed them. Both managed to find a kind of social equilibrium, and could not have been unique in achieving that. However, they, like every other black person in Britain, met enmity on a daily basis. In 1786 a man wrote to the *Morning Post* complaining that the country had become 'a refuge for all the blacks who choose to come here'. It seemed not to strike him that they had 'come here', in most cases, anything but voluntarily.

---

*Caryl Phillips used Gronniosaw's memoir as raw material in his novel *Cambridge*. One of the many affecting views expressed by his eponymous slave hero is the contempt he feels for popinjays such as Julius Soubise, fops who forget that they are merely lucky, 'dependent on the bounty of Christian strangers'.

The contrast with previous generations of immigrants could hardly be more obvious. The European Protestants who fled Catholic whips had to suffer resentment, but they prospered mightily, and represent the sunny side of immigration. The Africans represent the opposite, the tragic side. Of course, the greatest legacy of the slave trade was that Britain became infected with a racism which would dominate the twists and turns of migrant life in the future. Whether racism inspired slavery or slavery inspired racism is a historically vexed question. Certainly the whole enterprise was practised with extreme racism – Africans were seen as savages and heathens, and the metaphorical associations of black and white were powerful. But even minor distinctions within Christianity (between Catholics and Protestants, for example) could precipitate fear and hatred. White underclasses (such as the Irish) were routinely characterised as savages, too. So perhaps it's safest to say simply that slavery and racism reinforced each other.

But whatever lay at the root of British hostility to foreigners, through the slave trade it achieved a new, clearer definition. From now on, Britons would think of themselves as 'white', as if this alone was a suggestive and meaningful quality. In the coming centuries, slavery dwindled, but racism did not.* Anyone who did not possess this exclusive pigmentation would face bitter hostility.

The black 'community' of ten thousand or so brought here by the slave trade (even the lucky ones who witnessed its demise) declined with remarkable speed. The sexual imbalance meant that few black men had children (they could not afford them, on the whole). Aside from the handful of exceptions salvaged by history, the immigrants themselves passed away, uncelebrated and unremembered. Across Britain, today, there are people surprised, as a new generation of researchers begins to pass genealogy through more searching racial filters, to learn that they have a black ancestor. They are rare but eloquent reminders of the connection between modern Britain and a time we have since tried hard to forget.

---

*Indeed, slavery is far from dead. It has been estimated that there are 27 million slaves in the world today. Traffickers in people are reckoned to have sneaked 35,000 a year into Western Europe in the last decade of the twentieth century, where they are recruited into the sex industry.

CHAPTER 10

Radical Victorians

If one of the ideas behind the abolition of the slave trade was to boost Britain's image as the moral leader of the civilised (i.e. wealth-creating) world, then it worked like a charm. And it coincided with and was varnished by legislation which confirmed Britain as a land of the free, as well as a home of the brave. In the space of a few decades, Parliament announced the emancipation of both Catholics (in 1829) and Jews (in 1835). Both acts were controversial; both attracted shrill opposition. But both passed safely into law, and Britain found itself in a rather surprising position: suddenly, it was a bright beacon of liberty in a Europe where absolute monarchs stamped on free thinking. Britain, which had the added bonus of its blossoming prosperity, was boasting that it was happy to accept all comers.

There was a contradiction here, of course: the new empire was run in a far from liberal fashion. Nor was the home front all quiet: the Peterloo Massacre in Manchester, in 1819, when troops waded into a crowd of early trade unionists, killing eleven and leaving hundreds wounded, was only the worst of many such disturbances.* But in Europe Britain was known to be a good (if grudging) friend to the displaced, and this became especially useful when the failed continental revolutions of 1848 sent many clever refugees to the only place that would accept them. They were neither indulged nor fêted; they lived quietly

---

*One of those at Peterloo was William Davidson, the illegitimate son of the Jamaican Attorney General and a black slave. In 1817 he'd produced a radical periodical, *The Forlorn Hope*, and been imprisoned for sedition and blasphemy.

and often felt cold-shouldered (they were used to more enthusiastic audiences). But they were more or less left in peace, a priceless commodity. Voltaire had declared as long ago as 1733, in his *Letters Concerning the English Nation*, that this was the land of liberty. 'The Jew, the Mohametan and the Christian transact together as though they all profess'd the same religion,' he wrote, 'and give the name of infidel to none but bankrupts.' In the next century, the wealthy Russian émigré Alexander Herzen, founder of the first Russian newspaper to be published overseas (the *Bell*), echoed Voltaire's words. 'England,' he said, was 'the only country to live in', despite its twin 'follies' of feudalism and Toryism.[1] Freud, after visiting his half-brothers in Manchester in 1875 (they were in textiles), left with an 'ineffaceable impression' of Lancashire, and floated to his fiancée the idea of moving there: 'Let us seek a home where human worth is more respected.'[2] Even Friedrich Engels, no friend of capitalism, said as much in his preface to Marx's *Das Kapital*. 'England', he wrote, 'is the only country where the inevitable social revolution might be effected entirely by peaceful and legal means.' It was, he stated, 'undeniably the freest, or the least unfree, country in the world'.[3]

The uses to which that freedom was put were in one sense logical: England provided the platform for the liberation of Italy, for instance, by tolerating and even protecting one of its leading architects, Giuseppe Mazzini. He came in 1836, having been expelled from Switzerland, and when he sailed up the Thames, staring at the 'indescribably spectacular' rows of wharves and jetties, he could not have suspected that he would remain here, on and off, for the rest of his life. Eventually he would refer to England as 'my real home, if I have any', and in 1871, when he left for what he thought would be the last time (he was wrong), he called it 'the land I have learned to love as my second country'.[4] Not that he had found life easy in Britain. He earned little more than pin money from journalism and lived in monkish austerity, smoking Swiss cigars as his only real indulgence. But his dedication to literature, revolutionary theory and the cause of Italian nationalism never wavered. He was befriended and admired by the cream of Britain's intellectual elite: Mill, Carlyle, Bentham, Meredith (who called him 'one of the chiefs of our age'), George Eliot ('a true hero'), Dickens, Swinburne ('a true king') and Browning. And he created the first institutions devoted to the support of the small but growing Italian community which was beginning to plant its feet in England. In 1840 he started a society for London's Italian artisans, and in 1841 opened a school in Hatton Garden. This was successful enough to embarrass the Catholic Church (which was alarmed by its republican tendencies) into opening its own, more traditional classrooms a few doors down the road. Some forty or so fellow dissidents had followed Mazzini from Rome, and with them he set up a society, the 'Friends of Italy', which both debated and raised funds for their dreamed-of nation state.

Mazzini rose to prominence through a well-orchestrated political scandal in which he proved (by arranging for friends to send letters to him on certain dates) that the Post Office was opening and inspecting his mail. This caused an enormous rumpus. There were long, soul-searching debates in Parliament (*Hansard*'s record of the discussion runs to five hundred pages); Lord Macaulay declared it 'utterly abhorrent'; and Carlyle wrote an emphatic letter to *The Times*: 'It is a question vital to us that sealed letters in an English post office be, as we all fancied they were, respected as things sacred; that opening of men's letters, a practice near of kin to picking men's pockets, and to other still viler and far fataler forms of scoundrelism, be not resorted to except in cases of the very last extremity.'[5] His tone suggests that the invasion of Mazzini's privacy was a tactic rare enough to call for an unusually high horse. The freedom of the individual was a well-polished part of Britain's self-image. Even if it were not a right that could be permitted to trickle down too far, it was certainly owed to a gentleman (of whatever nationality) who numbered among his enthusiasms the poetry of Byron.

Mazzini's rights were upheld, and Britain's reputation as a free-thinking arcadia was buffed to a bright gleam. Many markedly different varieties of desperate people were drawn to it, although some were not what we would normally call dissidents. On the contrary, they were aristocrats or statesmen ejected, often with good reason, by subjects whom they had oppressed. Prince Metternich of Austria and Louis Philippe of France both became part of London's fashionable *beau monde*; later, the French Empress Eugénie made the windy voyage from Deauville to the Isle of Wight to escape the Communards of 1871. She was following a trail blazed by panicky French aristocrats and Royalists after the Revolution and Terror of the 1790s. This was the evacuation made famous by the Scarlet Pimpernel, who spirited a few select members of the upper crust across the Channel to safety.* The frightened French members of the *ancien régime* saw their old enemy Britain in a new light, as rather obliging and benign – as good a place as any to quarrel about rank and generate a lax trail of unpaid debts. 'There must have been many wealthy boat captains plying the Channel ports that summer,' said Gabriel-Denis Deville, one of Louis XVI's Swiss Guards, who managed to bluff his way on to a British vessel at Le Havre.[6]

One refugee was an auditor called Count Deloitte, who escaped to Hull. His grandson set up Deloitte's in 1845, and by the end of the century was the oldest practising accountant in the City. He lived in Southall, where he built the Holy Trinity Church and half a dozen almshouses for the poor. Another refugee, Marie Grosholtz, had learned the art of wax modelling from her uncle. She came alone in 1802, having survived the worst of the Terror, and brought a

---

*The British found an elegant way of easing this particular immigration crisis. In 1795 they repatriated a small army of French expats at Quiberon in a mini-invasion. It was a spectacular failure: 748 émigrés were captured and shot as traitors.

collection of masks with her. She'd taken the masks from the severed heads at the base of the guillotine. This ghoulish exhibition toured the country and formed the basis of the museum that still bears her married name – Madame Tussaud's.

Britain was a nice place to be one of the idle rich, but that didn't stop the French complaining about it: they hated the food, the weather, the clothes – everything. The grumbling marquis or scruffy French priest became a familiar sight in south-eastern haunts. Unlike their Huguenot predecessors, the majority were snobs – too fussy even to dream of taking tradesmen's jobs as weavers or bakers.*

Britain was no stranger to snobs. But it also offered shelter to intellectual outcasts, many of whom were impoverished or in very reduced circumstances. Even before the failed revolutions of 1848 dissidents from Italy (Mazzini), Hungary (led by Kossuth) and Poland were forming small clusters of expatriates – a brand-new chattering class. By far the most significant group was the bickering collection of Germans which gathered in the shade of their great but still little-known leaders Karl Marx and Friedrich Engels. The fledgling Communist League, outlawed in Germany, emerged on this side of the Channel to pursue an energetic debate on the future of the world's political economy. Indeed that Marx and Engels' historic work – from the *Communist Manifesto* to *Das Kapital* – was to a large extent a critique of British capitalism is often forgotten. But both men were keenly aware that the freedom of expression they enjoyed in England was rare, and perversely linked to the commercial liberty which created such polarities of prosperity and grief, and which it became their lives' work to oppose.

Engels was the pioneer, chiefly because he was better connected. He came to Manchester in 1842 to work for his family's cotton-processing firm (Ermen and Engels), and wrote *The Condition of the Working Class in England*, a bitter account of working-class horrors. At that stage he was only a temporary visitor, but in 1849 he settled for good. He married an Irishwoman, Mary Burns, and became a solid member of the Manchester Exchange. When not writing piercing accounts of the brutal English free market in capital and labour, he was a keen member of the Cheshire Hunt ('the greatest physical pleasure I know'[7] he wrote to Marx) and loved fine wine. His daughter's journal records that his idea of heaven was a bottle of 1848 Château Margaux. His manners became so Anglicised that he once wrote to a German club in Manchester to complain that the stiff, pompous letter he had received from the librarian was altogether too

*A handful made more purposeful landings. Marc Isambard Brunel fled Normandy for America before reaching England in 1799, building the Rotherhithe tunnel and leaving as his legacy a talented son, Isambard Kingdom, one of the great architects of Britain's steam age.

'Prussian'. He was the central figure in the German expatriate community, which he generously bailed out of its many financial difficulties. Marx, in particular, was doggedly subsidised (Engels was known as Uncle Angels by Marx's daughters). His genius required patronage: he lived beyond his means, loftily declining a cost-cutting move from Hampstead to Whitechapel on the grounds that the latter 'could hardly be suitable for growing girls'.[8] Engels' money financed convivial outings on Hampstead Heath, where Marx held court over mouthwatering picnics of veal, bread, cheese, fruit and wine. But he was indulged because his work was epic, and his friends knew it.

Around these two swam a small shoal of vociferous fellow exiles. George Weerth pursued a twin-career similar to that of Engels: he was a successful businessman and a radical pamphleteer based in Bradford. The Anglophile poet Ferdinand Freiligrath came and worked unhappily for a German bank in London ('The City lies far from Parnassus,' he moped). He performed sterling service in the export of British culture by translating Burns, Scott, Wordsworth, Coleridge, Keats, Shelley, Byron and Tennyson, and eventually took his courage in his hands and went as far as a German immigrant could go to embrace English ways: he shaved off his beard. Arnold Ruge, meanwhile, a philosopher who had been Marx's editor, had served five years in prison in Heidelberg, and was expelled from Paris in 1849, settled for a quieter life in Brighton, taking in pupils and pursuing gentle hobbies – gardening, billiards, walks on the Downs. At one point he bought a photography business, but it was not a success. He was somewhat rancorous about his failure to lead a more celebrated life in England (Alexander Herzen went to see him, and said that he was 'a grumbling old man, angry and spiteful') and founded the Agitation Club, a forum for political debates about Germany's future, where he could let off steam.*

The Agitation Club had a rival: Gottfried Kinkel's Emigration Club. Kinkel was a philosopher and artist who had arrived in Britain as a celebrity, basking in the glory of his daring escape from Spandau Prison. His arrival was something of an anticlimax, though: there were no cheering crowds of admirers. He travelled in disguise to Leith, and arriving on a Sunday found that it was not easy even to toast his successful escape: he walked for seven hours in search of an inn. His celebrity would prove useful later, however. He gave lectures and was able to live more comfortably than many of his compatriots. He became friends with the banker Grote, and Felix Mendelssohn was a regular visitor. 'England,' he said in 1866, was 'the only country in

---

*In a neat historical echo, Ruge's great-nephew Ludwig fled Germany a century later, having opposed Hitler as a student leader. He came to England, was immediately classed an 'enemy alien', but rose to the rank of major in the British army and ended up staying after the war.

Europe which has never expelled a refugee', and was the least likely to persecute strangers. 'It gives elbow room to every man, a field for his labour and energy, and full liberty to build up his house by his labours, without demanding in return a denial of his principles or the sacrifice of his character.'[9] His wife Johanna was scathing about those of her compatriots who had the nerve to complain of their lot. 'Would you believe it?' she wrote. 'There are still clubs of continental refugees sitting around here, not mixing with the English at all, just carrying on among themselves the squabbles of 1848. Among these people it is the fashion to criticise England.'[10] She wrote a novel about a German émigré, *Hans Ibele in London*, in which she sneered at the lazy braggarts who – when they weren't dropping by to borrow money – were condemning the bourgeois materialist urge to acquire any. 'People say so much about the religious narrowness of the English,' she wrote. 'Yet we had to suffer constant torments in Germany on account of our unbelief, whereas we are left in peace here. The Englishman does not like to quarrel; he is altogether the most peaceful, well-meaning human type you can find, and that is the result of long years of political freedom.'[11] She also appreciated the fact that London was so cosmopolitan: 'At tea parties you meet Persians, Egyptians and so on,' she told a friend back in Germany.

The expats could meet at the German restaurant in the Strand, gulping down Vienna beer while they talked, or they could repair to Schartner's German pub on Long Acre. At the German clubs they could eat creamy meals and gossip about their various factions,* then pop in to the German bookshop run by George Thimm. Like so many before and after them, the German exiles did not see themselves as settlers: they were panting to go home from the moment they stepped ashore. They were displaced refugees, and in the central decades of the century Britain was the only country where they could study and scheme without being harassed by agents of the state. 'The police hinder no one in the development of his talents,' wrote Johanna Kinkel. They had already tried and been expelled from cities such as Zurich, Paris and Brussels, which were closer to home and better stocked with suitable cafés.

In Britain it was a solemn article of faith that the state had no right to meddle or pry into a man's private affairs: that's why there had been such an outcry over the interception of Mazzini's mail. The government, blithe in its sense of superiority, and contemptuous of the power of the written word in any case, had neither the need nor the wish to stoop to such strategies. When Prussia's Prime Minister wrote to the Foreign Office that Marx was plotting an assassination attempt on Queen Victoria, he was loftily ignored. Requests by Austria to clamp down on Mazzini were also dismissed, on the grounds that he

---

*Marx, under no illusion as to his own importance, loftily referred to these rival societies as 'the war between the frogs and the mice'.

had broken no British law. In 1858, when a Frenchman in England, Simon Bernard, was arrested for making the bomb designed to blow up Louis Napoleon in Paris, he was acquitted. One German visitor was impressed by the 'jubilation of English national feeling' that greeted this verdict, which was indeed a stirring rebuttal of French diplomatic pressure. The principles of 'this island of freedom', she declared, had been 'gloriously upheld'.

Herzen saw these shadowy subversives as colourful additions to London life: 'What amazing types of people are cast down by these waves,' he wrote. 'What must be the chaos of ideas and theories in these samples of every moral formation and reformation, of every protest, every Utopia, every disillusionment and every hope, who meet in the alleys, cook-shops and pot-houses of Leicester Square and the adjoining back streets.'[12] And Dickens was quick to satirise anyone who saw them as a threat: 'A complicated web of machination is being spun – we have it on the authority of a noble peer – against the integrity of the Austrian Empire, at a small coffee-shop in Soho. Prussia is being menaced by twenty-four Poles and Honveds in the attic of a cheap restaurateur in the Haymarket. Lots are being cast for the assassination of Louis Napoleon in the inner parlours of various cigar shops.'[13]

The ubiquity of capitalism's fiercest critics seems ironic at a time when Britain was enjoying an explosion of industrial profiteering. But it was not a coincidence. It sprang from the same reverence for individual liberty that allowed capitalism itself to flourish. And it was not tolerance so much as indifference. Just as industrialists were allowed to build companies without having to concern themselves (for now) with restrictive legislation, so the émigrés were not hindered when devising their plans to smash those same industrialists and their rotten system. Britain had an honourable plurality of more or less independent institutions such as the law and the Church, and it had long championed private property above all other considerations, even the national interest. The government was far from all-powerful: society functioned under the twin banners of common law and private contracts. So laissez-faire Britain could be a callous place as well as a benign harbour for those not welcomed elsewhere. The ability to live without interference included the possibility of starving without support. 'The exile is free to land upon our shores,' wrote the alert Chartist editor Joshua Harney in 1848, 'and free to perish of hunger beneath our inclement skies.'[14]

Harney himself, and many like him, perhaps did not fully appreciate how much he owed to the political refugees, for they brought a new radicalism to Britain. The abolitionist movement had already given progressive Britons a notion of the methods required to pursue social justice, and also a taste of success, but now there were other freedoms to be sought – in industrial relations and fair political representation. The ideology of radical protest, given avant-garde glamour by dissident Europeans, dripped through the salons, cafés and (since so many of them earned a living by teaching) classrooms of polite society and into the local intelligentsia. Both the Chartist movement of the 1830s and 1840s and the first stirrings of trade unionism not only had their roots in this intellectual climate, but found several leading figures in what we would now call the immigrant community.

The most astonishing of these was William Cuffey, the son of an ex-slave, who grew up as a tailor in Kent, then came to prominence as a resonant speaker at Chartist rallies. In 1848 he was arrested, charged with planning revolt and, in a ghoulish echo of the fate that had befallen his father, transported to Tasmania. The German involvement was also wide-ranging. Karl Schapper studied theology before being expelled from Germany, and in England he became leader of the Workers' Education Association (with his compatriots Bauer, Lessner and Moll), and fought hard for better schools. Revolution, said Schapper, should be knocked into people's heads through education, not with the butt of a rifle. After 1850 he faded from politics, but his place in the vanguard of egalitarian protest was soon filled by his compatriots. Karl Pfander, a tailor, worked steadily for various working-men's societies until his death in 1876, and was supported by Marx and Engels. Friedrich Lessner, born in Saxony, also became an obdurate political activist through his long involvement with the trade union movement. He lived in England for sixty years, and with Engels and Eleanor Marx he set up the Social Democratic Foundation in 1882, before branching off two years later to form the Socialist League. In 1893 he was a co-founder of the Independent Labour Party. In 1907 he was referred to as 'the oldest living Social Democrat' in the country.

These people contributed greatly to what is often seen as a central tenet of 'Britishness': the dogged pursuit of individual freedom and social justice. Through them and others like them Britain was exposed to a restless, insomniac temper which, certainly at the time, did not seem exactly native. And, if nothing else, the country could pride itself that it had provided a haven for this small but potent army which was regarded elsewhere as rather too hot to handle.

CHAPTER 11

Industrial Revelations

Plenty of patriotic tears were shed, in the late twentieth century, over the demise of Triumph, the classic British car company. Its rugged motorcycles, stately saloons and sporty runarounds – all those nifty Heralds, Stags and Spitfires – had been part of the landscape of British motoring for decades, and a byword for the skills of British engineers. It was not often mentioned that Triumph was the creation of a German immigrant, Siegfried Bettman. Born in Nuremberg in 1863, he came to England as a sewing-machine salesman, but soon saw the potential of British bicycles – the best in the world, at the time – and set up a business to export them to continental Europe. Initially the bikes were built by a Birmingham contractor and sold under the Bettman label, but it soon became clear that a British name was an essential marketing ploy. Bettman, by now in partnership with another Nuremberg engineer, Maurice Schulte, racked his brains for a suitable brand, and came up with a good one. The Triumph Cycle Company added motorcycles to its range in 1902 (during the First World War it sold some thirty thousand to the British army) and cars in 1922. In both fields it produced enduring 'British' models. Bettman himself went on to become founder-president of Coventry's Chamber of Commerce, and mayor of the city in 1913. He was successful, modest, eminent and somewhat unlucky: 1913 was not, as he would soon find out, the best time to be a German businessman in Britain.

It seems to us now that strong elements of anti-German feeling are woven into the fabric of the British character. In fact, they are a distinctly modern contrast to what for centuries had been a long, intimate and fairly happy connection. The Hanoverian monarchy had introduced many German habits into Britain's smart circles, and the marriage of Queen Victoria to Prince Albert of Saxe-Coburg and Gotha cemented the alliance. Victoria was almost 100 per cent German herself (there was a single non-German great-great-great-great-great-grandfather in her family) and she had been raised and chaperoned since infancy by a possessive German governess, Louise Lehzen. So Albert's arrival illuminated a cultural identity that was already firmly embedded. Still, the British Parliament moved swiftly to trim the new consort's powers (or potential powers, in the event of an accident to the Queen): Albert's allowance was reduced from the previous £50,000 per annum to £30,000; and a bill to have him naturalised as British failed. He also had no right to the throne, and the newspapers hooted:

> He comes to take, for better or worse,
> England's fat Queen and England's fatter purse.

When Albert had first travelled to Britain to woo his future bride, he did so in low spirits, despite the company of his favourite greyhound. He knew that he was being looked over as a marriage prospect, and there was every likelihood that the trip would turn out to be humiliating. He and his brother Ernest dawdled before boarding the boat from Rotterdam, then the crossing was slow and rough, and Albert was sick. When he disembarked it was raining. 'They don't exhibit much *empressement* to come here,' wrote the prim and testy Queen, 'which rather shocks me.'[1] The German prince was an immediate hit, however. 'It was with much emotion that I beheld Albert,' wrote Victoria. 'My heart is quite going.'[2] Five days later she proposed.

Albert continued to be lampooned as a mercenary foreign cad, but he performed his public role dutifully. He was President of the Anti-Slavery Society, declaring in his nerve-racking first speech (he was twenty-one) that the trade was 'repugnant . . . the blackest stain on civilised Europe'. And he became Chancellor of Cambridge University in a tightly contested election which the Queen herself found 'unseemly'. The university should have been grateful: German scholarship and educational philosophy were more advanced than their British counterparts, especially in science, linguistics and history, and Albert was able to preside over a steady broadening of the curriculum.* He was

---

*In George Eliot's *Middlemarch*, Will Ladislaw remarks: 'The Germans have taken the lead in historical enquiries, and they laugh at results which are got at by groping about in the woods with a pocket compass while they have made good roads.' The Chancellor of Oxford, the Duke of Wellington, was scathing about such notions: Oxford might not get everything right, he admitted, but at least it would never stoop so low as to embrace German ideas of scholarship.

also a devoted husband to a tetchy queen. His most significant contribution to the national life, however, came with his involvement with the Great Exhibition of 1851. He orchestrated the fundraising for the enterprise, while overseeing and approving both the design of the Crystal Palace itself and the international aspect of the displays inside. Nothing went wrong except for a slight hitch at the opening gala, when a Chinese man in traditional robes, whom everyone took to be a delegate from the imperial court, was placed in the procession between the Duke of Wellington and the Archbishop of Canterbury. It must have been a fine day out for the man, who was actually the owner of a Chinese junk anchored in the Thames. Otherwise the exhibition was both popular and profitable.* Albert public-spiritedly recycled the proceeds into the purchase of much of South Kensington, and authorised the construction of museums dedicated to natural history, science and the arts. The area – and at the time this was green parkland where it was still possible to shoot partridge – became known as Albertopolis, and has (along with the Albert Hall and the Albert Memorial) adorned the capital ever since. His role in the creation of a funeral car for the Duke of Wellington was somewhat less successful. The design he approved was heavy and clumsy, and twice bogged down in the mud in the Mall as the cortège proceeded through London.

Albert's influence in the cultural sphere was direct. He was musical (Mendelssohn was a frequent visitor) and helped introduce British society to Bach, until then a neglected figure. He imported and popularised (through pictures of the royal family at home) the traditional German Christmas, complete with St Nicklaus, decorated fir trees, wrapped gifts, candles and many carols that now seem like ancient national heirlooms – 'Silent Night', 'Oh, Christmas Tree', 'Good King Wenceslas' and many others. German culture was not yet something the British sensibility had learned to fear. It was a *gemütlich* world of quaint woodsmen, charming folk tales, sugar-plum fairies, sausages and chocolates, a sweet, perhaps twee country, religious, musical, Christmassy and in love with children – close, perhaps, to the way we imagine Switzerland today. The Prussian elite had not yet saturated Germany with martial manners, with 'blood and iron'. When Albert tried to rebel against the English insistence that womenfolk should withdraw after dinner, leaving men to smoke their cigars and discuss important matters, such as gambling and horses, in peace, he was warned off by the Prime Minister, no less, who hinted that it might be seen as a bid to 'Germanise' the court. Albert was unapologetic: 'I shall never cease to be a true German,' he wrote, 'a true Coburg and Gotha man.'[3] He and Victoria even spoke German at home. The new science of linguistics indicated that English and German were close cousins in the Indo-European family,

---

*The designer, Joseph Paxton, worked for the Duke of Devonshire, who remarked, on seeing the great glass structure for the first time: 'Fancy one's gardener having done this!'

further consolidating the sense of kinship. High society – despite plenty of 'bloody-foreigner' bashing in popular culture – acquired something of a German accent. A glass of hock before the opera was absolutely the thing.

It would be an exaggeration to say that the presence of a German prince at the centre of the national pageant inspired others to follow in his footsteps, but he exemplified the extent to which Britain offered an atmosphere in which Germans could flourish. As Prussia expanded west and south, Germans left their war-ravaged homeland at a tremendous rate – some two hundred thousand upped sticks and went, mostly to join the mass European settlement of North America. But Britain was close, full of opportunities and well stocked with friends in all the right places. Many young men picked up work as clerks (often in German businesses and banks) in what seems to have been the Victorian equivalent of a gap year – a spell in Britain was an ideal preparation for a business career. German industrialists and engineers, academics, teachers and governesses; German butchers and tailors – they fanned out across the country, rarely forming a sizeable single community. But by 1871 they were the largest foreign-born minority in Britain.

Not many of them were paupers: on the contrary, a remarkable number achieved prominent positions in business, finance and industry. In the process they built several powerful commercial empires, the German roots of which are now rarely visible, having been buried by the next century's Anglo-German animosity. But Britain in the nineteenth century was a magnet for entre-preneurs, who came here for much the same reason as the dissidents and revolutionaries: to escape government interference. As an added bonus Britain was enjoying an amazing industrial boom, driven by the profits that flowed from its imperial possessions and the ingenuity of its inventors. The steam engine, the railway and the mechanical textile mill created unique opportunities for large-scale and often heartless commerce (the freedom to be a pitiless employer was well entrenched). Coal production doubled between 1800 and 1830, and had doubled again by 1845. By the end of the century it would increase twenty times. Iron production quadrupled in only two decades; cotton imports had risen fivefold between 1780 and 1800. The ingredients for enormous change and fabulous wealth were in place. In 1801 there were fifteen towns with more than twenty thousand inhabitants; by 1891 there were sixty-three. Property remained the essential basis of high status (Bagehot observed that the meanest squire earned more respect from the common peasantry than the richest self-made man) but it was no longer the only or even the principal route to wealth and power. And you did not need to be British-born to make the most of the situation.

Ludwig Mond, a research chemist who studied under Professor Bunsen (of burner fame) at Heidelberg, came to England in 1862 to visit the London Exhibition. He was offered a job as a consulting chemist by a firm in Widnes whose general manager, John Brunner, was Swiss. Helped by the financial support of Philip Goldschmidt, a Manchester banker and a relative of Mond, they set up Brunner-Mond in Liverpool. After a rocky start attempting to perfect a new process for manufacturing soda (the boilers kept exploding), the company became the leading alkali manufacturer in the country. 'We are no longer making chemicals,' said Mond in 1882, 'we are making money.'[4] In 1920 the company took over another German concern, the Castner-Keller Alkali Company, and in 1926 swallowed up three more outfits to form ICI, one of Britain's, and the world's, biggest companies. Mond lived quite humbly next to the factory, was no sort of social climber, and spoke German at home with his sons.* John Brunner, meanwhile, became a pillar of the community in the north-west. He was MP for Northwich from 1885 until 1910, built the town's public library, and endowed three chairs at Liverpool University. In 1895 he was made a baronet.

Hugo Hirst, the son of a distiller born near Munich in 1863, was advised early in his life by his uncle that there was no future in a Bavaria that had been annexed by Bismarck's 'arrogant and overbearing' Prussia, which was 'killing all individuality and turning everybody into an invisible part of a gigantic machine of state'.[5] So in 1880 Hirst came to London, first as a clerk in a shipping office and then as secretary to another German, Mr Volckmar, managing director of the Electric Power Storage Company. In 1884 Hirst was dismissed, and opened his own shop in Victoria, selling electric bells, coils and ignition systems. Two years later he went into partnership with another Bavarian, Gustav Byng, and they became successful suppliers of electrical accessories. In 1888 they began to manufacture their own products, bought a large tract of land near Birmingham for their factory, and gave themselves a new name: the General Electric Company. Hirst was one of those immigrants who resolved to be more British, as the saying goes, than the British. He became an Anglican and bought a Berkshire estate, complete with a herd of Jersey cows. He played golf and billiards, and ran a racing stable. He was made a baronet in 1925.

His compatriot Johann Ellermann was the son of a corn merchant from Hamburg who brought his son with him to Hull in 1850, dropping one of their 'n's into the North Sea on his way. Johann trained as an accountant in Birmingham and then, at the age of twenty-four, founded a shipping firm, J. Ellerman & Co., in Moorgate, London. His timing was good: ocean routes were fast filling with British ships, and the business grew at such a pace that he soon bought a more established company, Leyland & Co. When he sold it to J. P. Morgan in 1900 he had made his first fortune, but he did not stop there. He bought a well-known Liverpool line founded years earlier by a Greek

---

*One of whom, Alfred, took over the reins of the company and eventually became an MP, privy counsellor and the first Lord Melchett.

immigrant as well as several other steamship companies. Ships of the Ellerman Line were plying all the major sea lanes, from Liverpool to the Mediterranean, across the Atlantic, to South Africa and Asia. Ellerman became a baronet in 1905 and was reckoned, in 1910, to be the wealthiest man in the kingdom. During the First World War he attracted plenty of enmity, being denounced as a war profiteer, and a German one at that, but he managed to set up a public platform from which to defend himself: he was the largest shareholder in the *Financial Times*, and had major holdings in both *The Times* and the thrusting new *Daily Mail*. He was second only to the Duke of Westminster as a landowner in London, owning 14 acres in Chelsea, 21 in Marylebone, and a handsome 82 in Kensington. When he died he had amassed a record-breaking fortune of £36 million.

Ellerman was not the only German shipping magnate. The founders of Harland and Wolff, in Belfast, were both German. Their company eventually employed eight thousand men and built four hundred ships, among them the *Titanic* and the *Lusitania*.

There were countless others. Jacob Schweppe first fizzed water in Geneva, but came to London in 1792, and built a factory in Drury Lane. Isidore Gerstenburg proposed and funded the first telegraph cable beneath the Channel, and so paved the way for the communications revolution that would lead, eventually, to the telephone. The quickest to take advantage of this amazing new technology was Paul Reuter. The son of a rabbi, he had created the Aachen telegraph and pigeon post before coming to London and setting up his bureau in 1852. It soon became the leading supplier of international news, primarily financial information, to Britain's newspapers, and was one of the driving forces in journalism for the following century.

Joseph Beck, head of the Gas, Light & Coke Company, bought a tract of land in east London, built the largest coal-gas works in the country, and left an echo of himself in the name of the area: Beckton. John Merz, son of a German industrialist and writer (his four-volume *History of European Thought* was a bold bid to unite science and philosophy), was an electrical engineer and the so-called 'British Edison'. His company, Merz & McLellan, developed a network of power stations to deliver electricity to the north-east; later, he was a formative influence on the national grid. Not all of his colleagues admired him, though: an elephant, ran the joke in engineering circles, was a mouse designed by Merz & McLellan. He was killed, along with his two children, when a German bomb flattened his Kensington home in the Second World War.

There were many others in this mould, and they made up a formidable roster of engineering and business leaders. Without them, the British industrial landscape would have looked very different. They were extraordinary individuals and often progressive employers, but, like all entrepreneurs, they needed backers. They found them in the extraordinary network of German or German-descended bankers in the City of London: Barings, Grotes, Samuel Montagu and Rothschilds. Money spoke with a German-Jewish accent. The British government had used Rothschild's international contacts to channel funds during the Napoleonic Wars, and also compensated slave owners with loans from his bank when the pressure to abolish the trade became too great to resist. Later, the Crimean War and the construction of the Suez Canal were funded with Rothschild's cash. Samuel & Montagu, meanwhile, was formed in 1853 and soon established a dominant position in the silver trade. By the time the ampersand disappeared in 1877 (when Samuel's brother Edwin died) it was a top City firm.

The mightiest of all the Germanic money-brokers, though, was Sir Ernest Cassel, who came from a banking family in Cologne and migrated to Liverpool when he was fifteen, carrying a bundle of clothes and his violin. He found employment with a grain merchant, Blessing, Braun & Co., but after a while took up a position at a German bank in London, Bischoffsheim & Goldschmidt, where he shone. By the age of twenty-two he was the manager. In 1875 he was naturalised and married a Darlington woman, but she died three years later. What Cassel did next might be viewed as typically British: he poured himself into his work. He made a fortune in Swedish iron exports and American railways, and recycled it into international banking, raising loans for the governments of Egypt, Argentina, Brazil and Uruguay. In 1895 he underwrote the construction of London Underground's Central Line, and in 1897 bought into Vickers, becoming the manufacturer of a device that would soon be used to furious effect against his former countrymen: the Maxim-gun. He lived in supreme opulence on Park Lane, in a mansion which housed six marble kitchens, a dining room that could seat a hundred, and an entrance hall coated in lapis lazuli. He tried earnestly to broker peace before the First World War, and in 1912 went on a secret (and vain) mission to Berlin to plead for restraint. He was a great friend of King Edward VII – they played cards and talked horse-racing – and became a member of the Jockey Club. In his will he left huge sums to charitable causes: half a million went to the families of servicemen, another half-million to educational institutions. His daughter Edwina became one of the most famous members of the British establishment as the wife of Lord Louis Mountbatten, another German family obliged to modify its name – Battenberg – in the altered atmosphere of the twentieth century.

There were other prominent foreigners in the City. Simon Matthey came from Switzerland in 1790; his son George, after serving an apprenticeship with Percival Johnson, a refiner of gold in Hatton Garden, built a firm that specialised in bullion – Johnson & Matthey – in 1851. The Hambro family emigrated from Denmark in 1839 and created a powerful merchant bank. The Warburgs came from Sweden. And the wonderfully named Julius Caesar

Czarnikow, from Sonderhausen, began in London as a clerk, set up as a commodities trader (sugar from the Philippines and West Indies) and became the first significant importer of sugar beet from continental Europe. In 1875 he was joined by two partners (one German, one Swiss) and together they set up the London Produce Clearing House, a prototype of the modern Commodities Exchange. Julius himself was chairman from 1907 until his death.

Not all of the immigrants were quite so dignified. Abraham Gottheimer was the son of a pedlar from Central Europe who came to London and joined a business that sold 'fancy goods'. In 1859 he set up a discount house in the City, and a few years later established Credit Foncier, a notorious finance company that specialised in new company flotations. On the back of some mysteriously successful dealings in exotic shares – American railways, Portuguese tramways and so on – he became an immensely affluent grandee. He bought what had become a rubbish dump in central London (Leicester Fields), smartened it up, stuck a bust of Shakespeare in the middle, renamed it Leicester Square, and donated it to the city as a grand gesture. He fought hard to become MP for Kidderminster, but was dislodged following allegations of bribery and fraud. He was ultimately brought down by a scandalous court case in which he stood accused of financial fraud and share-rigging on a massive scale. If the story sounds familiar, it is because he is often supposed to have been the model for Melmotte, the corrupt and eventually ruined financier at the heart of Trollope's *The Way We Live Now*.

In the arts, where royal patronage was influential, Germans flourished. The relief of Queen Victoria on the coins of the Royal Mint was designed by Sir Joseph Boehm from Vienna, who also produced the statue of the Duke of Wellington at Hyde Park Corner and the bust of Carlyle on Chelsea Embankment. The royal children were painted by Carl Bauerle, from Baden-Württemberg, while Peter von Cornelius was a particular favourite of Prince Albert. Frederick Lehmann (grandfather of the novelist Rosamond and publisher John) came to London as a portraitist with his brother Rudolf. August Kollman managed to keep the post of organist at the German Chapel in St James's – he had come from Hanover in 1784 – in the family by handing it on to his son George, who in turn was succeeded by his sister Johanna. The sculptor William Behnes and his three sons all thrived. The Duke of Wellington's funeral hearse was designed by Gottfried Semper, a native of Dresden, so, what with Beethoven's funeral march and the presiding spirit of Prince Albert, the occasion was distinctly Teutonic.

In academia, the great Oriental scholar Friedrich Max Müller came in 1846 to study Sanskrit in the library of the East India Company, easily the finest such resource in Europe. In 1849, he visited his fellow Sanskrit scholar Theodor Goldstucker in Berlin, and was arrested. The pair returned to England, Goldstucker to the chair of Sanskrit at University College, London, and Müller as Professor of Modern European Languages. The top Orientalist at the British Museum was another German, Emmanuel Deutsch.

There were German teachers throughout the country, at schools and universities and as private tutors. Professor Hofmann taught chemistry at London University; Dr Leonhard Schmitz was the rector of Edinburgh High School; and Professor Heimann taught German at UCL. The most notable educational theorist was Johannes Ronge, who created the first British children's garden (*Kindergarten*) in his house in Hampstead. It was based on Friedrich Froebel's radical new idea: work through play. Germany had a highly developed reverence for childhood, whereas in England infants (to the horror of the Chartists) were still shoved up chimneys and on to treadmills. But Germany was changing. Froebel's schools were banned by Bismarck as 'dangerous', while in England they were tolerated and then swiftly found a grateful clientele. Ronge trained over fifty teachers, and by 1859 there were fifteen schools following his example. In 1874 he set up the Froebel Society to spread his mentor's gospel.

One particular institution – University College School – was distinguished by its German connections. Two senior teachers were German and many of their students were the children of German emigrés. The dissident German poet-in-exile Ferdinand Freiligrath whose children attended UCS, was eager for them to absorb the merits of Englishness. There might, he admitted, be 'social evils and oppression enough' in this country, but this was balanced and perhaps outweighed by the possibility of 'freedom and national greatness'.[6]

There were German physicians, too. Dr Louis Borchardt, a friend of Engels, had a busy practice in Manchester; and Dr Schaible, in London, estimated that there were forty German doctors in the city.* In 1845 a new German Hospital was founded in Dalston, offering free care for the many tailors, bakers and furriers in the East End. Dr Bronner, a refugee from Baden in 1849, set up an eye hospital in Bedford; Dr Althaus founded a hospital for nervous illness in Maida Vale. The president of the Royal College of Surgeons, Sir William Jenner, was the son of a German. He ministered to Prince Albert during the Consort's final, fatal bout of typhoid. And two Germans – Sir Hermann Weber and Edward Sieveking – served as physicians extraordinary to the Queen. Weber was a keen mountaineer (he shinned up the Matterhorn when he was sixty-seven) and a noted promoter of Alpine cures. He was also a determined Anglophile: in Bonn, he had learned English to read Shakespeare. Apart from his royal duties and his position with the new hospital in Dalston, he treated five prime ministers.

---

*Two of them treated Marx and threatened him with legal action for non-payment of bills.

The employment prospects for women were more restricted. Many worked as governesses in private households; most were wives. One notable exception was a single woman called Malwida von Meysenburg, who left a memoir of her migration titled *Rebel in a Crinoline*. She was aristocratic, but also a free-thinking atheist. A friend of the Althaus family, she followed them to Britain in 1852. Her first impressions were not favourable: 'The dismal, high houses, the grey sky, the noise of the never ceasing stream of carriages, the throngs of pedestrians . . . all this confused and deafened me.' And she was alarmed by the strait-laced attitudes she found. 'I saw that I, who had gone through so many painful struggles to get away from prejudices, would have to face others even more stupid in this country . . . Having to earn my living, I would be dependent on a society so jealous of its savoir faire that it looks upon each deviation from convention as a mortal sin.'[7]

She found a position, however, in Manchester, working for Julia Salis-Schwabe, the wife of one of the little band of shipping magnates that thrived in the north-west. Julia was a liberal activist and a member of the Society of Friends of Foreigners in Distress, which helped raise money for recuperating patients of the German Hospital. So it was a busy domestic scene, full of visits from like-minded Britons such as Richard Cobden and Mrs Gaskell. But von Meysenburg didn't stay, preferring a position in the London house of Alexander Herzen, the Russian émigré. She watched Wellington's funeral procession from the window: 'I was delighted,' she wrote, 'the spiritual and aesthetic element was German.' At Herzen's house she met and grew close to Giuseppe Mazzini, and became busy with relief work in Whitechapel, where there were many poverty-stricken German labourers. An 1854 police report estimated that there were two thousand destitute Germans in what Alexander Herzen called 'the miry bottom' of London. Von Meysenburg wrote, 'Poor German families there are by the hundreds. The work is stamping raw pelts at a German fur factory. Imagine a big barrel in a very warm room, filled to the very top with ermine and sable skins. A man climbs into the barrel stark naked and stamps and works with his hands and feet from morning until night. The perspiration pours from his body in streams. This soaks into the skins and gives them their suppleness and durability, without which they would be useless for more elegant purposes. Thus our rich ladies, with their boas and muffs, though they do not suspect it, are literally clothed in the sweat of the democrats.'[8] She eventually established a club in Whitechapel and campaigned on behalf of women trapped in miserable marriages. She also tried to inspire a women's hospital, an institution that could train women as doctors and nurses, but this was ahead of its time, and she failed to raise sufficient funds.

Amelie Struve, wife of the exiled Gustav (who was struggling to make money out of his vegetarian and phrenological convictions), also tried to raise charitable relief, but was turned down by the Lord Mayor of London, who pointed out that many English workers were in the same plight. She was also opposed by Marx and Engels, who wrote a letter to *The Times* denouncing such charity on the grounds that it would give more useful exiles (such as themselves) a bad name.

The ranks of German unfortunates were swollen after 1871 by the arrival of demobilised soldiers from the Franco-German War: military watches were common in the capital's pawnbrokers'. Some of these expats complained bitterly about their bad luck; others had crackpot schemes to make money. One, Hermann Becker, proposed to import Westphalian foxes to bulk out what he thought, given the English enthusiasm for hunting, must be a dwindling local supply. Most Germans had more conservative notions: many set up as butchers. They gave Britain a new word – delicatessen – and supplied bacon and sausages in almost every sizeable town. The Great British breakfast would have been lost without them.

The German settlement in Victorian Britain was not, numerically at least, a mighty immigration. Fifty thousand in a population of some thirty million is not an eye-catching percentage. But it was unusual in that the Germans entered all tiers of society simultaneously, including the very top, and therefore had a greater effect on British commerce and British sensibilities than their numbers would suggest.

Many of these people may not have defined themselves as German, though. They were, first and foremost, Jewish. The number of Jews in Britain rose from roughly 7,000 in 1760 to 65,000 in 1880, and a good many of these came from Germany. This was true at all social levels: dissidents, businessmen, bankers, clerks, teachers, tailors and labourers: the Jewish drift away from Prussian Germany was substantial. In their eagerness to enter mainstream British life a fair proportion became Christian, but the community as a whole was both willing and able to spearhead (and finance) the cause of Jewish emancipation. In a spirit of liberalism (or indifference) that contrasted sharply with its continental neighbours, the obstacles to assimilation were knocked over one by one. In 1830 Jews were formally allowed to trade in the City; in 1833 the first Jewish juror was permitted to swear an oath on the Pentateuch, rather than the Christian Bible, and the first Jewish lawyers were admitted to the Bar. And, after a typically muddled interlude, Jews were finally allowed to become Members of Parliament. The pathfinder was Baron Lionel de Rothschild, the son of Nathan. He was elected in 1847 after a bruising fight, but was prevented from taking up his seat in the Commons by a law requiring him to acknowledge the Church of England in the oath that accompanied the taking of office. It was not a specifically anti-Jewish tactic – indeed, it was originally an anti-Catholic measure – but it kept Rothschild and Sir David Salomons, elected in 1851, from taking their seats.* The oath law was finally changed in 1858, and both men were able to accept places in the government. Soon afterwards, Britain had a Jewish Prime Minister in Benjamin Disraeli, the son of a poet, critic and stockbroker (Isaac d'Israeli) who had moved to London from Italy.

Disraeli, like many British Jews, was not a zealous upholder of the faith: born here, he was a Christian convert, having been baptised when he was thirteen. He entered smart circles as a dandy, with snappy clothes and cute accessories of gold, velvet and lace. He was petted. When he began fighting elections, though, he didn't command such affection: in Maidstone people shouted, 'Shylock!' He could not have enjoyed so giddy a career had he not renounced his religion. But he was not easily deterred, and anti-Semitism, while an ever-present aspect of his daily life, proved too weak to deny him office.

At this time, anti-Semitism in Britain was infuriating rather than ferocious. One German characterised it as 'exclusion from garden parties, refusal of certain cherished intimacies, and occasional light-hearted sneers'. The poet E. H. W. Meyerstein was dismayed at Harrow when he won the music prize, because the music master refused to announce his victory on the official noticeboard on the grounds that he was Jewish. This was a mean and petty gesture, but, while his Jewishness might have kept him off the noticeboard, it did not stop him winning the prize (or, indeed, being allowed to attend the school). However, Charles de Rothschild recalled his years at Harrow with sardonic horror: 'Jew hunts such as I experienced are a very one-sided entertainment.'

Under English law it was still necessary for anyone wishing to naturalise as British to take a Christian sacrament. For the devout this was intolerable, but for a large number of nineteenth-century immigrants it was no great deterrent. At any rate, the Jewish population in early Victorian England was remarkably quick to integrate itself into the broad mass of public life. At the very least, it was reluctant to draw attention to itself, and conversion was a pragmatic response to the barriers that still obstructed the social acceptability of Jewish men and women.

While those born in Britain did not have to go through the naturalisation process, several scions of the house of Rothschild still married Christians; and all fifteen offspring of the immigrant Barent Gompertz (a prominent figure in the Hambro Synagogue) joined the Church of England and thrived as lawyers, poets, clerics and economists. Hirsch Baer Hurwitz, a Hebrew scholar, became an outspoken critic of Jewish habits, urging that the state ban traditional dress and that the Talmud be destroyed (intellectually, of course). In 1837 he became

*Salomons was fined five hundred pounds for omitting the words 'in the true faith of the Christian'. He was eventually elected several times by his Greenwich constituents before he could take his seat.

a teacher of Hebrew at Cambridge, a job which was not (such were the twists of British etiquette) open to Jews.* But he had by then changed his name to Hermann Hedwig Bernard, and recommended that Jews read the New Testament. He kept his roots well hidden: in his memoirs, Hurwitz declared (falsely) that his father had converted to Christianity before he'd been born. Even his daughter believed this. Many other families obscured their Jewishness so successfully that their children did not speak of it. The financier Ernest Schuster's descendants were anything but keen students of their past. Years later, the poet Stephen Spender grew up accepting a standard cartoon of Jews as big-nosed, avaricious double-dealers, and was surprised to find that he himself was the grandson of a Jewish banker from Frankfurt.

Various Christian missions set out to convert the Jews; some found the task all too easy. 'There is reason to fear that thousands of Jews have scarcely any faith at all,' wrote one dejected vicar in 1814, sensing that he might soon be out of a job. In one sense the Jews' attitude is not surprising: they came to Britain from Central Europe eager for change. And, unlike the Sephardic Jews from the Mediterranean, many of the Ashkenazi had lived in enclosed, besieged communities – they had felt not even the slightest breeze of enlightenment philosophy. Theirs was an ancient church, ripe for reform. Others, of course, were already secular, educated and temperamentally inclined towards progress and breaking with the past; intellectually, they were German liberals.

Many had suffered severe anti-Semitism in Germany and had long since learned to hide their religious habits, if they even had any. Jacob Behrens, for instance, recalling the slights he had suffered in Hamburg, felt that all religion was 'a hollow lie'. When Nathan Adler became Chief Rabbi, he found a sluggish congregation which did not observe the religious calendar, did not circumcise, was happy to conduct burials in Christian cemeteries, and even celebrated Christmas in the German style, if only out of nostalgia for the *Heimat*. One Jewish woman, Julia Davis, renounced her origins and wrote a novel, *Benjamin Phillips*, in which the Jewish protagonist was a greedy murderer. Another Jewish writer, *The Times* journalist Samuel Phillips, peopled his novel *Caleb Stukely* with several Jewish caricatures – dirty scoundrels, the lot of them. In 1851 there were eight thousand seats in Britain's synagogues, but only three thousand of them were regularly occupied on the Sabbath. So less than 10 per cent of Britain's Jewish population was displaying much religious inclination.†

---

*Cambridge allowed Jewish undergraduates for the first time in 1856. Oxford followed suit fifteen years later. The latter's first Jewish undergraduate, Sackville Davis, had entered incognito, and Worcester College proposed to expel him until he threatened legal action.

†'What centuries of persecution had been powerless to do', wrote Lewis Benjamin in 1912, 'has been effected in a score of years by friendly intercourse.'

The next step could not have seemed too big a deal. It was often said that when the Warburg family joined the Church of England, it meant only that rather than skipping synagogue they now skipped church.

As the century wore on, and the number of British-born Jews increased, it became less necessary to convert, and most families sought to uphold their Jewish heritage. Children might be instructed not to marry outside the faith, but this was often ignored.* Henry de Worms was sharply ticked off by the *Jewish Chronicle* for permitting the marriage of his daughter to take place in a Christian church. And many grand Jewish families kept faith with their origins only while the original patriarch remained alive. Lily Montagu, wife of Sir Samuel and an energetic activist for Jewish causes, regretted this as a 'terrible and ominous novelty', but even her own family was not immune.† When her husband died in 1911, he stipulated in his will that his son Edwin would forfeit his ten thousand pounds a year if he married outside the faith. Edwin insisted that he was 'an Englishman, not a Jew' – though as a schoolboy at Westminster he had religiously picked the ham out of the lunchtime rissoles – but he wasn't about to pass up his financial privileges. So, when he sought the hand of a Christian woman, Venetia Stanley, he managed to persuade her to accept Judaism herself, to preserve his legacy. 'As to the religion,' he told her, 'I find it seems always to me the easiest of religions, and makes no demands of me.' Venetia was pragmatic: 'One is happier rich than poor,' she said.

There was also a natural desire to escape or reject the prevailing Jewish stereotype. Fagin, in Dickens' *Oliver Twist*, was depicted as an underworld criminal mastermind, while Trollope's Melmotte was a slippery capitalist monster. These were powerful cartoons; and popular prints vibrated with easy gags based on the same centuries-old folk myths about greedy Jews. These sentiments did not prevent the ennoblement of many prominent Jewish figures – two Rothschilds, Samuel Montagu, David Salomons, Henry de Worms, Sydney Stern, Isaac Goldsmid and several others. By the time of the First World War, Britain had knighted more than twenty Jewish men. In 1869 there were six Jews in the House of Commons; by 1906 there were sixteen. There was a Jewish solicitor-general and a Jewish under-secretary of state for the colonies. The muttering behind their backs continued: many were shocked by Edward VII's friendship with the Rothschilds, for example. But this anti-Semitism, though sad and cruel, was balanced by a principled desire for fair

---

*'Mrs Samuel Sachs', wrote Amy Levy in her novel *Reuben Sachs* (1888), 'had been heard more than once to observe pleasantly that she would sooner see her daughters lying dead than married to Christians.' However, 'Maida Vale was growing used to mixed marriages,' remarks Leonard Merrick in his novel, *Violet Moses*.

†Lily and Samuel were extremely observant. On the Sabbath, when work was not permitted, Christian servants were employed to wind watches and tear lavatory paper.

play. Several public schools – Clifton, Cheltenham and Harrow – opened Jewish houses, with specific dietary and theological schedules. The grandest families in England, meanwhile, were delighted to accept invitations to hunt stags on the Rothschild estate in Buckinghamshire, or swill champagne at one of Clarissa Bischoffsheim's famous parties in Mayfair.

Clearly, these were special cases: an abundance of money has a tendency to dissolve prejudices fast. And this was aided by the wholehearted adoption of a 'British' lifestyle by the immigrants and their offspring. There was, though, a resolute and devout Jewish population of a size sufficient to create its own institutions – synagogues, schools, hospitals, clubs and publications. In 1807 a Jews' Hospital was built in Mile End, near the burial ground reserved in Cromwellian times. It was heftily funded by Abraham Goldsmid, one of the founding fathers of University College, London – a committed anti-sectarian school – in 1837. By this time, the Jews' Free School in Aldgate was packed; by the end of the century, it would be the largest in Europe, with 3,500 pupils.*
Reformed synagogues sprang up in London, Manchester and Bradford. And Isaac Vallentine launched the *Jewish Chronicle* in 1841 under the editorship of Moses Angel (a UCL graduate). London's East End was still the major Jewish township in the country, but affluent families were beginning to beat paths east to Ilford and Redbridge, or along what became known as the 'north-west passage' to Finchley.

There was, in other words a solid foundation on which this new community could build and rely. And it needed to be strong. For even when they married good Anglican girls, even when they converted to Christianity themselves, the families that they joined still often sniffed; not so much at their Jewish origins *per se*, but at what 'people' might think.

The most celebrated figure in this new British-Jewish community was Moses Montefiore. Born in Leghorn, he made a swift fortune on the Royal Exchange trading in groceries and tea. When he retired at the age of forty in 1824, he was wealthy enough to devote the rest of his extremely long life to the cause of international Jewry. He was president of the Jewish Board of Deputies for nearly fifty years, from 1835 onwards, and helped to shape almost every new addition to the growing infrastructure of Jewish life in Britain. His hundredth birthday was a public holiday for Jews all over the world.†

While the ranks of well-off Jewish families grew, another species of far less fortunate migrants continued to make their presence felt both in the streets of the cities and the country lanes of the remote English shires. Many were fleeing conscription in the Russian Tsar's army, a fate well worth avoiding since it

---

*Its colours – blue and gold – echoed the Rothschild crest.
†He was a marvellous advertisement for port. He drank a bottle a day.

meant twelve years in the service, and almost certain death. Now they joined the army of Jewish pedlars who roved the British countryside selling trinkets door to door. They became a familiar sight throughout the kingdom, and to rural people were synonymous with the whole notion of Judaism. It was hard work: 'He is parched in summer and frozen in winter,' wrote Joel Rabbinovitch, describing the pedlar's meagre lot. 'And his eyes wither in their sockets before he gets sight of a coin.'[9] And it was frightening, especially for new arrivals. 'I was a stranger in a strange land,' wrote Samuel Harris, ' and had only sixpence in my pocket.'[10] Harris arrived in Gravesend and availed himself of a scheme run by Jewish relief organisations which gave newcomers a couple of pounds, enough to equip themselves with a pedlar's starter-pack. He set off immediately, walking twenty-odd miles that first day. Three weeks later, he arrived in Birmingham, and then he continued his mazy journey around England, heading south-west to Exeter, north back through Birmingham to Newcastle, and west to Manchester and Liverpool. Roadside inns began to expect him and others like him. 'I lodge twice at Taunton,' wrote one Moroccan traveller, 'at a house where a woman keep a lodging house for de Jewish people wat go about wid de gold tings, de jewellery.'

Many of these pedlars spoke hardly any English. 'Will you buy?' they would ask, holding up fingers to represent pennies. They were easy prey for any local roughs, and several were mugged and killed. Often they would take their wares to Britain's increasingly busy ports, but this was risky, too. A pair of Jewish conjurors boarded a ship in Deal to entertain sailors during the Napoleonic Wars, and were promptly press-ganged into the navy for the entire war. In Falmouth, one of the regular purveyors of rum to thirsty tars on shore leave was a Jewish landlord, Lemon Hart. In Sheerness Henry Russell contributed to the war effort by writing sea shanties such as 'Cheer, Boys, Cheer!' and 'Life on the Ocean Wave', which became the regimental march of the Royal Marines. It's doubtful that many members of that elite service knew that they were swinging their proud arms to a tune penned by a Jewish immigrant.

In London, the Jewish pedlars found a niche which they soon came to monopolise: second-hand clothes. Their cry – 'Old clo! Old clo!' – echoed through the capital's residential streets, as collectors called for wares. These were the Jews who inspired Dickens. At the rag fairs of east London, the piles of raw material these men collected were repaired or converted into second-hand clothes, which were all that most Londoners could afford. The major market was in Petticoat Lane, so called because it had previously been full of Huguenot lacemakers. In 1830 the municipal authorities changed the name, which was deemed too louche for tender Victorian ears, to Middlesex Street.

These Jewish migrants managed to carve out a way of life which was increasingly denied to them elsewhere in Europe, but they were also laying the commercial foundations of a trade that would be of great importance in the years ahead. Just as much as the Rothschilds and Goldsmids, they were pathfinders. And the durability of the changes they wrought in British society, as well as the robustness of the institutions they founded, created a habitable world for the much larger migration which lay just a few years ahead.

CHAPTER 12

Little Italy

A plaque in Covent Garden still marks the spot where, in 1662, an Italian puppeteer called Pietro Gimonde first performed a little play. Samuel Pepys saw the show and described it as 'very pretty, the best that I ever saw'. It narrated the knockabout adventures of a reckless young man called Pulcinella, and it was an immediate hit – literally, since Pulcinella was a fellow who let his fists do most of the talking for him. His feisty misdeeds struck a chord with the brawling British, who renamed him Punch, gave him a long-suffering wife called Judy, and turned him into one of Britain's most enduring comic figures.

If Gimonde entertained the masses, other Italians served the upper echelons of society. Cipriano was a founder member of the Royal Academy; Capezzuolo built the gold state coach used for royal coronations. The Venetian Antonio Canal (better known as Canaletto) spent a decade in Soho between 1746 and 1756, painting the Grand Canal from memory. Giacomo Casanova entertained Londoners in a more direct way. He arrived in 1763 with the vague intention of establishing a lottery. This came to nothing, so he lounged instead at the theatres, in the gambling dens, and at 'all the taverns of good and evil repute'. After an unhappy love affair he filled his clothes with lead and was preparing to leap off Westminster Bridge when he was intercepted by a friend. Shortly afterwards, he had to flee Britain following a gambling scandal.

In the theatres, meanwhile, Italian actors were performing in highly stylised and formulaic stories about the trials and tribulations of two young lovers trying to outwit their grumpy parents. These were 'Italian Mimic Scenes' and they grew into one of Britain's favourite and oddest art forms: the pantomime. In the nineteenth century, they shrugged off their *commedia dell'arte* origins, dropping the original caricatures Pierrot and Harlequin. Instead they became fairy stories stuffed with cross-dressing and crude topical asides.

The Italians didn't always need theatres to stage their entertainment. A pair of tightrope-walkers astounded Edinburgh in 1733, and Italian jesters were regulars at British pageants and fairs. One of them, Joey Grimaldi, is the patron saint of British clowning.* He was born in London in 1779, the fruit of a liaison between an Italian comedian (and dentist) and a chorus girl forty years his junior. The boy was put on the stage early: he appeared at Sadler's Wells Theatre only a few months after his first birthday. 'I'm Grim all day,' he said later, 'but I make you laugh all night.' He became famous as a pantomime clown in *Mother Goose* at Covent Garden, and set the trend for the following century. From Grimaldi's time onwards, when British children laughed, it was likely that they were laughing at an Italian. The pressure began to tell on the home-grown talent, so much so that one British clown, Nelson, felt obliged to do his tumbling and grimacing under the pseudo-Mediterranean sobriquet Signor Nelsonio.

The merrymaking was only the gaudy surface of a far less happy story. Perhaps William Hazlitt sensed this when he remarked, after watching brilliant Italian jugglers at work, that the only response to seeing something done so perfectly was to cry. Many, if not most, of the Italians who moved to Britain led bleak lives. And they had few friends. In 1820 *The Times* published a leading article on the increasing number of barrel organists cranking out their tunes on London's streets. They were, the paper reported, a menace. 'The public have of late been exceedingly annoyed,' it said, 'by the appearance of a number of Italian boys with monkeys and mice wandering about the streets, exciting the compassion of the benevolent.' They 'infested the streets' with their animals, and the racket they made was unendurable. It might well seem to us that 'exciting the compassion of the benevolent' ranks low in the hierarchy of human crimes, but the Italian musicians were certainly regarded as a pest and a nuisance. They were numerous enough (several hundred were plying their noisy trade in the capital) to make a vivid impact: central London vibrated to mechanical polkas and waltzes; hummable snatches of Rossini and Bellini could always be heard above the din of wheels and hoofs. Gustave Doré depicted the organ-grinder as a benign splash of sunshine in an otherwise miserable cage of gloomy tenements, but others viewed them much as modern-day Londoners look upon squeegee merchants.

The organs were often operated by very young boys, at some cost to the

---

*He is commemorated in a stained-glass window in Holy Trinity Church, Dalston, where a service is dedicated to him every year, on the first Sunday in February.

average Victorian hackle. One correspondent wrote in to *The Times* to protest against the roughness with which the police handled them, and scolded those who encouraged 'the hunting down of the poor', but most of the letters took a firmer line, insisting that it was high time something was done. The following year (June 1821), the newspaper suggested that all these entertainers had been brought to England by 'traffickers'. They carried with them, in other words, a whiff of something criminal. The plot thickened, and the number of organ-grinders continued to rise. By the middle of the century there were over eight hundred, and there was a growing sense that they were not quite the hard-up vagabonds they seemed to be, but members of determined and organised gangs.

This was sensationalist, but it turned out to be true. A *'padrone'* – an avuncular-sounding term for an often overbearing boss – would assemble a team of urchins in Italy and arrange for them to travel to London. It wasn't difficult to persuade a hard-pressed mother that her son would be better off, and could contribute handsomely to the family finances, by serving an apprenticeship overseas. The barrel organs were easy to play – all you had to do was crank the handle – so these boys were perfectly competent, and much more likely to 'excite compassion' than the older generation of grinders.* The promise was simple: the boys would sign on with the *padrone* for three years, at the end of which they would return with pockets full of money. Often the *padrone* promised to hand the cash directly to the mother.

It must have sounded plausible to the rural families of Lombardy. They had been ravaged many times by the Napoleonic Wars: conscripted into armies, their livestock lost to invading troops. There had been a typhus epidemic in 1816, and outbreaks of cholera ever since. An economy based on chestnut-picking was wilting under the advance of new agricultural practices, which were clearing nut-rich woodland to create larger fields. A month-long trudge north across the Alps to Germany, France or England had to be worth a try. The mighty Italian exodus, which by the end of the century would swell to some half a million people each year, had begun.

When they reached Britain, reality hit home: the *padroni* stashed the boys in noxious, run-down accommodation in Clerkenwell. The area around Hatton Garden and Little Saffron Hill became known as 'Little Italy':† music was in the air, the men wore yellow neckties and there were babies everywhere, some with earrings (according to one stereotypical report). The *padrone* would sell his boys

---

*Some of these did still exist. In his survey of London's underclass, Henry Mayhew interviewed an old man with 'dancing dogs'; another who was an 'exhibitor of mechanical figures'; and a third, an ex-soldier with a wooden leg, who staged a gun show.
†To those on the outside looking in, at least. The residents called it simply 'the Hill'.

an organ, deducting the cost from their earnings in instalments, and drive them out into the streets. In the summer, they might be sent to seaside resorts, just beginning to become crowded holiday playgrounds; in the winter, they would patrol the roads of central London. Occasionally, they might go to a race-meeting or a fair. The day's takings would be split fifty–fifty with the *padrone*. However, he would often (for their own safety, of course) retain the boys' portion.

The *padroni* did well – one was running a team of fifty 'apprentices'. It was a perfect little rogue-capitalist enterprise, and the favoured apprentices (sons or relatives of the *padroni*) could and did branch out and set up their own troupes. Most of the boy organists, though, did not. They were trapped, beaten, abused and often tricked out of their hard-won earnings. In these early days, there was no one to stand up for them.

This international alms-dealing was a shabby, low-level form of organised crime. It is no coincidence that it resembles the gang structure operated by Fagin in *Oliver Twist*. Dickens himself referred to the public row about the Italian musicians as 'the battle of the barrels'; and his description of Fagin tallies almost exactly with what we know about the *padroni* (though Fagin himself is presented as 'a very old shrivelled Jew').* At any rate, the locations of *Oliver Twist* confirm the Italian roots of his boy villains. When the Artful Dodger takes Oliver to his new home, he leads him through the warren of streets on the southern slope of the Angel, Islington. They drop past Sadler's Wells Theatre and along Exmouth Street into Little Saffron Hill, into the very heart of Little Italy. 'A dirtier or more wretched place he had never seen,' writes Dickens. 'The street was very narrow and muddy, and the air was impregnated with filthy odours. There were a good many small shops; but their stock in trade appeared to be children, who, even at this time of night, were crawling in and out of the doors, or screaming from the inside.'[1]

In 1856 *The Times* resumed its campaign against the street entertainers, this time with more ammunition. 'It is impossible to exaggerate the nuisance,' it claimed. 'We endure them simply as idle people endure dirt and vermin – because we have not the moral energy to get rid of them . . . It is an evil which threatens to make London unendurable.' Once again, the letters poured in. One reckoned that the police were far too soft on these infuriating youths; another suggested that they be packed off to charge Russian guns in the Crimea. One pointed out that the barrel organs were becoming larger and louder (true: hand-held instruments were being superseded by bigger and better carts or barrows) and were literally frightening the horses; another, signed by 'Suffering Woman', complained that the 'rich and influential' people who refused to do anything

---

*The cartoonist George Cruikshank also portrayed Italian street entertainers as Semitic, Fagin-like rogues: stooped, beak-nosed, bearded and with dark, hooded eyes.

about it were insulated from the problem because they lived in grand houses with stout windows, far from the usual routes of the barrel brigade.

A hero of this lobby emerged in the surprising shape of Charles Babbage, mathematics professor and the inventor of a prototype computer – the famous 'Difference Engine'. He pursued musicians through the courts, and even published a pamphlet on the matter, in which he referred to the organs as 'instruments of torture'.[2] Finally, in 1860, he secured a remarkable ruling from a magistrate in Marylebone. Babbage estimated that a quarter of his valuable time was wasted on 'the hindrances occasioned by street bands', and the magistrate was sympathetic. 'No one', he said, 'has a right to play his noisy instruments within the hearing of persons who are pursuing grave occupations.'[3]

In 1863 an MP – Mr Bass, the Brewer – tried to propose a parliamentary bill, but he was talked out of it. In 1864 he tried again, and this time the topic was debated. Gladstone, safe in his smart house, but also motivated by a desire to let people have their fun, thought that to legislate against the musicians would be 'an unwarranted interference with the amusement of the people'. Sir Robert Peel, meanwhile, regarded them as 'an abominable nuisance' and was all for clamping down. To some extent, it was a class issue: the barrel organists tended to cluster outside pubs in working-class districts: people would dance around them as they got drunk. This merely amplified the middle-class distaste. The Act was passed. It fell short of what some agitators had hoped for: for instance, it failed to follow the lead of Paris and introduce a system of licences to regulate and control street music. But from now on, householders were at least in theory entitled to require musicians to move on and leave them in peace.

There were other, more high-minded reasons to object to the trade. The extent to which the boys were abused children was beginning to impress itself on the public. Some cases went to court, and were eagerly reported. Antonio Petinatti accused his *padrone* of failing to honour their agreement. The latter was withholding money he owed, kicking and beating Petinatti, and providing rotten rations: a piece of dry bread in the morning, a 'small quantity of rice boiled up with a little bacon' at night. In another case, in 1858, fifteen-year-old Giuseppe Leonardi died in a workhouse. He was 'one of those unfortunate creatures who are brought over in shoals to this country to perambulate the streets with hand-organs, and to solicit charity,' reported *The Times*. His *padrone*, Luigi Rabbiotti, was charged with responsibility for his death. Rabbiotti had come from Parma in the 1830s and married an Englishwoman. With his brother Antonio he set up as a gang-master, with twenty-five urchins scouring London on his behalf. He operated from a house in Little Saffron Hill. There were non-musical lodgers too – carpenters and asphalt workers – but barrel organs were his main business, and it was a tidy one. He was hauled up several times for mistreating boys and housing them in unhygienic conditions, but had not been deterred. On this occasion, three of his boys came before the court to testify that he was a fair man and a decent employer. And that might have been that, had not an ex-Rabbiotti boy emerged to tell the truth. He testified that his former employer had seized Leonardi by an arm and a leg, and bashed his head against the wall. Alas, the urchin was not believed. The surgeon found that Leonardi had died of natural causes; and Rabbiotti was acquitted.

But the case confirmed the suspicion that these were criminal gangs, exploiting children as pity-provoking props. Social surveys began to reveal the sordid conditions in which the boys lived: fourteen or so to a room in lodgings shared with thieves and prostitutes. These revelations were guaranteed to make Victorian readers shudder. In 1875 a reporter from the *Graphic* visited a den and found crude dormitories, with boys crammed in three or four to a bed – 'huddled together, dreaming of the sunny skies of their native country'. In the same year, a report in the *Lancet* claimed that the Italian quarter was a serious health risk. The *Evening Standard* took one look at the sober medical evidence and leapt to an intemperate conclusion: 'the whole area should be swept away'. The *Telegraph* agreed, raging at the 'horde of unwashed, illiterate, semi-barbarous foreigners, who treat the lives of British children as if they were as valueless as their own'. The business itself continued to thrive. The 1871 census recorded 850 Italian musicians; in 1881, there were 1,240. Some hailed from Paris, fleeing the licensing arrangements (permits were available only to those who already had one year's residence), but most of the new arrivals came directly from Italy. Between 1871 and 1881 some three-quarters of a million people fled the recently unified nation, casualties of the squabbles that accompanied the grand political change. They were assisted by a technical advance – steamships – which would bring even the crossing to America within reach of ordinary migrants. Britain, with its ports of embarkation to the west, became an even more favoured destination. In 1861 there were just under five thousand Italian-born people in England and Wales; by 1901 there were over twenty thousand, and nearly five thousand in Scotland. Half of them lived in London, but there were also sizeable groups in Manchester, Liverpool, Newcastle, Sheffield, Bradford, Leeds and Hull. The figures are imprecise: the Victorian census was not an exact study. One survey by the Italian Ministry of Foreign Affairs in 1872 listed 11,000 Italians in Britain, more than double the British figure. But since many migrants would have ignored both questionnaires, the real number might well have been a good deal higher.

While the British government seemed to think that the feeble Act of 1864 was all it could do to stop the business, the new Italian government started to agitate to halt the exodus of the nation's youth. In 1874 it pressed Britain to impose restrictions on the trade. The Italian ambassador in London spoke of a 'white slave trade' and sought the extradition of the organ masters. The Foreign Office announced that there was nothing it could do: it was up to Italy to withhold passports from such men. While it is easy to see this as a classic dither, it is also a striking example of something more resolute: the British attachment to individual liberty was stronger even than its dislike of shifty foreigners. The Italian ambassador admitted as much by expressing his impatience with British liberalism: 'England is very chary of making restrictions on the freedom of entry of foreigners to these shores. Deposed emperors and kings, princes in trouble, defeated presidents and past presidents, persecuted ecclesiastics, patriots out of work – all find an asylum in little England.'[4]

But there remained a sharp counterpoint to this stout side of liberalism. In Italy, a Child Protection Act was passed in 1889 in a bid to check the flow of juvenile labour abroad. In England, however, it was not so easy to oppose cruelty to foreign children, since we were not notably gentle with our own. Children were still a strong component of the cheap-labour economy. The dangers they faced were well publicised when Charles Fariere, a small boy who begged on the streets with white mice around his neck, was murdered by three morbid villains who then sold his body to King's College Medical School in the Strand (they received nine guineas).

The barrel organists were the advance guard of a process usually termed, rather drably, 'chain migration'. A few hardy pioneers – usually single men – make landfall, drop anchor and send word home. Slowly, their random settlements crystallise into colonies, as women and families swell and stabilise the ranks. Infant service industries spring up to provide familiar food, clothes, books and so on, and gradually the newcomers are able to diversify away from their original speciality and into the mainstream of their new nation's life.

Like all generalisations, this is only broadly true: it has nothing to say about the individual motivations that propelled the travellers. But it is indeed the case that the young, intrepid (or corrupt) entertainers invited friends, relatives or press-ganged children to follow them, until there were whole teams working the streets. Ancillary trades – cafés, delicatessens, barrel-organ makers – began to provide a wider range of job opportunities, and women began to join their menfolk. Firms like Chiappa, Spinelli & Rosi in London and Rubino & Antonelli in Manchester made the instruments that caused such a fuss. Delicatessens such as Gazzano's (Farringdon Road), Terroni's (Clerkenwell Road) and Valvona & Crolla (in Edinburgh) began to serve both their own compatriots and curious Britons. Without knowing it, they were spearheading a revolution in British eating habits.*

But by then the Italian street urchins had exhausted the goodwill of the public, which lazily (if predictably) gave into the prejudice that had existed against all Italians for years. Tobias Smollett ('all the common people are thieves and beggars'), Percy Shelley ('stupid and shrivelled slaves') and Thomas

---

*The first Italian cookbook appeared in 1893 – a collection of recipes by Maria Gironei.

Macaulay ('a race corrupted by bad government and a bad religion') had reflected the general view of the British nation for a hundred years. Now those who hadn't enjoyed the luxury of the Grand Tour had personal experience of Italians themselves, in the form of the *padroni*, and had the worst of these prejudices confirmed. Apart from anything else, these people were Catholics, and while Britain's fear of Popish plots had receded somewhat, there was still a lively hostility to all things Roman. Few seemed to care that a large and varied community was being tarred with the same crude brush. By the end of the century, as we have seen, there were nearly twenty-five thousand Italians in Britain, and the barrel organ was no longer their mainstay. In fact, for the majority, it never had been. Throughout the nineteenth century skilled craftsmen had crossed the Channel alongside the urchins. Some travelled in fully equipped mobile teams (a moulder, a painter, a polisher, a cleaner): they would make statuettes and figurines for sale, or undertake larger tasks – working on a church, a theatre, a museum or a town hall. The organ-grinders came from the hills around Parma, but the plaster modellers were Tuscans. Some of them drifted as far as Glasgow, but most of them stayed in London, sending out street salesmen or producing knick-knacks for the fancy shops in Leather Lane, where Italian picture-framers and looking-glass manufacturers had found an obliging home.

Groups of mosaic workers from Friuli criss-crossed the land, laying down tiles in St Paul's, Brompton Oratory, Westminster Cathedral, the National Gallery, the Tate, the Bank of England and Fife Castle. Some began to accrete into companies. The Art Pavement Company hired 250 Italians to restore Roman mosaics unearthed by new archaeological techniques. Other tiling and ceramic companies sprang up – Grossi in Lewisham, Toffolo in Glasgow, Quiligotti in Manchester and Minoli in Oxford. One of the largest – Diespecker – was the British branch of a German firm, founded by Italians.

Several craftsmen from Como established businesses making barometers, mirrors, pumps and other gadgets. Andreas Molinari set up in Edinburgh as a glass-blower, then moved to London, where he made mirrors in Leather Lane with his English wife and two sons. Giovanni Battista Ronchetti established a similar enterprise for barometers in Manchester and Liverpool, close to the growing fleet of British ships who would be his customers. His shop in Manchester High Street was eventually taken over by a rival Italian firm, Casartelli, which continued to trade until the 1960s. In London, the firm of Negretti & Zambra sold barometers in Cornhill and featured at the Great Exhibition in 1851. It was still trading in Regent Street in the 1970s.

The other trade in which Italians figured prominently was brand new: asphalt. As luck would have it, one of the first roads earmarked for fresh surfacing was High Holborn, and in 1871 the French Asphalt Company was awarded the contract to lay it. Since this street ran right through the Italian neighbourhood in Clerkenwell, the project offered plenty of work for local labourers. The poor men who took the shilling might well have regretted it, though, since it was hideous work. The asphalt was tipped on to the road surface as powder, and then had to be pounded with hot irons until it was molten and could be spread. Workers were not permitted to wear boots – 'in order not to injure the asphalt', as the Holborn and Finsbury *Guardian* delicately put it. Some Londoners moaned that 'foreigners' had been 'brought in' to do jobs sorely needed by British workers, but in truth there were few native takers for this painful and onerous task. When Charles Booth looked into the matter he found that the English labourer 'cannot be induced to undertake this work, alleging, no doubt truthfully, that the heat brings the skin off his feet. We are assured, however, that the feet soon get hardened.'[5] In contrast, the Italians were 'extraordinarily willing and industrious'. One of them, Ghirardani, went on to become an asphalt contractor himself, with offices in the Goswell Road.

For leadership, this community could at first look only to the established Sardinian Church. But the arrival of political dissidents such as Mazzini gave it some much-needed secular leadership (and a supply of Italian teachers for would-be Grand Tourists.) The poet Ugo Foscolo was followed by Antonio Panizzi, who fled a death sentence in Italy and became the first Italian to be knighted in Britain, after a distinguished career at the British Museum. He catalogued the collection and designed the splendid new (now old) reading room. He would have presided over the row of desks at which many other European intellectuals, such as Marx, sat bent over their works-in-progress. Gabriele Rossetti enjoyed some fame as a musician and university lecturer, while his children, Dante Gabriel and Christina, made an even more extravagant cultural splash.*

In 1863 the community gained a spiritual home when St Peter's, Clerkenwell Green, was unveiled. It was the first Catholic church to be built in Britain since the Reformation, and it was an ambitious project. Seating fifteen hundred, it was made from imported Italian marble and looked every inch a Renaissance classic, modelled as it was on the basilica of St Crisogono in Trastevere. The church didn't quite become the vivid focal point for London's Italians, because it was rarely full,† but it was an important cultural symbol. In 1893 it inspired a sight that had not been seen for hundreds of years – a swaying parade of the

---

*Ruskin called Dante Gabriel Rossetti 'a great Italian', though he never set foot in Italy all his life. His sister Christina, meanwhile, wrote what is still one of the central atmospheric elements of the traditional English Christmas, inspired perhaps by thoughts of a Tuscan summer: 'In the bleak mid winter, frosty wind made moan . . .'

†This might have had something to do with the fact that worshippers were charged sixpence for their seat.

Virgin in a public procession through brightly lit streets, and with the smell of Italian food and wine in the air.

Some of the less bashful Italians were happy to pose as artists' models, picking up easy if not lucrative jobs at the Royal Academy, the Slade and the Royal College of Art. One such, Domenico Mancini,* is immortalised in Holman Hunt's *The Light of the World*.

By far the biggest business opportunity for the Italians, though, was in food. As the Clerkenwell community grew, it supported a small service industry in pasta, cheese, ham, bread, olives and oil. And the much-maligned street barrows provided a powerful infrastructure that could support newer and better businesses. The organists from the valleys around Parma had grown up harvesting chestnuts, and now they found that they sold well from the braziers placed beside their musical carts on frosty winter nights. They weren't so popular in the summer months, though, so the Italians turned to another of their own cherished products: ice-cream. Homes in Clerkenwell were soon converted into mini-factories, whipping up confections for their mobile stalls. The ice-cream was manufactured in a swamp of boiling milk and eggs, in dirty garrets (London still had few decent sewers or drains). Often it was mixed and stirred in vats used, in cooler weather, for washing old clothes. Out on the streets it was served in small glasses, which were sloppily rinsed and reused. An 1879 *Lancet* report was quick to blame cholera outbreaks on poisonous Italian ice-cream, and in particular on the filthy glasses from which it was licked. 'For cleaning,' said the report, 'they are dipped into dirty water which contains the mouth secretions of previous buyers, swabbed with a small wet offensive cloth and up-ended on a soiled barrow top.' In time, the ice-cream vendors would come up with an elegant solution: conical wafers. Before then, flat wafers had been used to make ice-cream sandwiches. Salesmen would often tidy them up by licking the edges. The music on the barrows stopped being an end in itself and turned into the tinkling sales pitch that can still be heard today in the gaudy vans that patrol our suburbs and beaches when the sun shines.

The sellers were known as 'Ice Jacks', and they were popular. The most prominent was Carlo Gatti, who began to import ice from Norway in 1857 and eventually set up his own 'ice wharf' at the docks for this crucial raw material. His shop in Villiers Street was also a billiards room and a café; eventually it would become a music hall.

Ice-cream proved especially popular in Scotland. By 1911 there were three hundred parlours in Glasgow alone. The larger producers owned chains of a dozen shops, and there were regular squabbles over pitches and sites. The 'community', if that is the right word for so fractious a rabble, pushed into more upmarket areas, with a better clientele for their wares, but their rivalries became

---

*In the summer he ran an ice-cream stall outside the Lyric Theatre, Hammersmith.

notorious. It was like the *padroni* all over again, a turf war that boiled over into violence. One newcomer, Bruno Serebi, remarked that the first word you needed, as an Italian immigrant in Scotland, was 'fight'. Many were driven out of the ice-cream trade and began to sell that 'British' staple: fish and chips.

The ice-cream clashes didn't help to improve native distrust of the Italians. They had a reputation as crooks and brawlers that was difficult to shake off. Then there was the dismaying fact that in spite of (or because of) this reputation, British women seemed to find them irresistible. Many of the Italian bachelors who landed in London found it all too easy to follow in Casanova's footsteps: British women warmed to their Mediterranean manner. One journalist who tiptoed into an Italian club found it full of drinking and dancing, and noticed with horror that the girls were 'without exception' English. The rate of intermarriage was exceptionally high: of 94 marriages involving Italian men in 1851, 74 were to British women; of the 217 marriages registered in 1881, nearly half were Anglo-Italian.

Although lacking the rich and powerful groups that had proved so helpful to their Jewish and German contemporaries, by the later years of the century there were Italian schools and churches, Italian bakeries and barbers' shops, and an impressive Italian Hospital in Bloomsbury. An Italian Chamber of Commerce opened in 1886, and Italian newspapers such as *Londra-Roma*, *Gazetta Italia di Londra* and *La Scozia* (in Glasgow) found a ready market. Apart from Mazzini's Italian Club, which doubled as a restaurant, and the various political clubs, there was a Mandolin Club, a Cycling Club and even, for a short while, an Italian Cricket Club.

By 1911 Italy was providing Britain with 1,600 waiters, 900 chefs, 1,000 hotel workers, 1,400 bakers and 500 café owners. If the waiters seemed at once charming and aggressive, that's because they had to be. They were not employees. On the contrary, they paid for the privilege of serving at tables, their income coming exclusively from tips (a portion of which went to the proprietor). They would hector diners for loose change even as they poured the wine.

The restaurant boom meant that Italians no longer had to live quite so severe and lawless an existence. A handful began to achieve a more conventional prosperity. Charles Spagnoletti, an able engineer, was hugely successful in the telegraph industry. Anthony Mundella made his fortune in a more traditional British industry while exploiting new technology to the full: his textile firm utilised the latest mechanised looms. Mundella was no satanic mill magnate, though: his four thousand workers were encouraged to join trade unions. In 1862 he won a gold medal at the London Exhibition, and became head of the Nottingham Chamber of Commerce. In 1868 he was the Liberal MP for Sheffield, having campaigned against child labour. Eventually he became President of the Board of Trade – a sign once again that elite figures were often exempt from the racist generalisations (in this case of criminality) with which the mass of their compatriots were so blithely saddled.

Spagnoletti and Mundella were both overshadowed by Guglielmo Marconi. The child of an Irish Protestant mother and an Italian father, he was brought up in Italy, but came to London in February 1896, dismayed by the Italian government's lack of interest in and support for his pioneering work in electronics. That same summer, Marconi demonstrated his new 'radio' on the roof of the post office in St Martin's Lane, which attracted the patronage of two useful customers: the Admiralty and the Post Office itself. In 1901 he sent the first radio message across the Atlantic. Fame and a great electronics company were his, as was the 1909 Nobel Prize for Physics. By now, he was married to an Irishwoman himself, and firmly installed as a leading light of the British engineering establishment.

The German declaration of war in 1914 was received at Marconi headquarters in the Strand, and Marconi returned to Italy as a senator, and argued for Italian involvement in the war (on Britain's side). In 1927 he married for the second time, an Italian this time, and moved back to Italy permanently. He did, however, remain famously fond of the full English breakfast, without which no morning was complete.

By the early years of the twentieth century the fuss over the Italian barrel-organ menace was a remote memory: it had not entirely dissolved, but had been replaced by larger concerns. There were fresh migrations – of Irish, of Jews – to worry about, and besides, London had grown noisier. There were trams, trains, iron wheels on iron tracks, and engines in the streets. Factories clanked with the sound of pumps and turbines. Who cared about the hurdy-gurdy man, with all that going on?

CHAPTER 13

The Labours of Ireland

By far the biggest injection of fresh blood in the nineteenth century came from Ireland, and the fury with which Britain reacted is famous. Few immigrants have been less welcome. These Irish were not the Aran-sweatered fisherfolk of modern advertising.* They were confined in ghettos as ugly as any that have ever disfigured this country. They were penniless, unhealthy, unshod and unclean, lacking even the wherewithal to wash. They were also despised. A people that prided itself on carrying the banner for Christian virtue, that had abolished slavery and emancipated Jews and Catholics (officially), welcomed a new group of extremely hapless immigrants – their own colleagues under the Union Flag, indeed – as if they were rabid and dangerous wild animals.

The Irish had been drifting east for centuries, as beggars, vagrants, tinkers and pedlars. Twice, in 1243 and 1413, they had been expelled by royal statutes – an icy response to people who had been forcibly dispossessed of their livelihood in Ireland as part of the Anglo-Norman estate-building programme. Nevertheless, a steady cargo of seasonal workers and manual labourers buzzed to and fro across the Irish Sea, to do what migrant workers have always done: the dirtiest low-paid jobs. They dug canals, picked fruit, hacked stone out of

---

*As it happens, the traditional Irish Aran jumper is a marketing invention. In the 1930s the German textile entrepreneur Heinz Kiewe was looking for a name for his new line of knitwear. He chose 'Aran' after seeing a documentary about the island. He liked the name, but Irish wool turned out to be unsuitable, so the sweaters were made in the Scottish Hebrides. So are national myths born.

quarries and hauled bales on the docks. These are usually categorised as jobs the fastidious local population is eager to avoid. It has often been said of the Irish, and subsequent immigrant groups, that they came here (or were invited) to do the work no one else would do. But this simple cliché cannot be the whole truth. The 'local population' was not of one mind. The operators of business, fired by the 'invisible hand' of laissez-faire economics, were all for cheap workers. But the labourers themselves were furious, and frequently rioted in defence of the very jobs which, according to the cliché, they were anxious to avoid.* English labourers worked in the same rough trades, lived in equally ugly slums, and resented the Irish labourers who competed with them so successfully. The Irish in London themselves rioted in 1768 in fury over the dreadful conditions in the docks. They received little sympathy: five of the protesters were tried at the Old Bailey and hanged.

If anything, evangelical Britain had reason to be grateful to Ireland, which had tended and kept alight the lamp of Christianity during the Dark Ages. But, of course, it was a Catholic lamp, which after the Reformation barely counted as Christian. So as well as being denounced as lazy spongers ('mumpers'), the Irish were castigated as wage-cutting subversives and Papist spies. These Irish workers were hardly settlers: they were merely camping, hoping to finance their impoverished families back in Ireland. But, as the economic situation at home worsened, so did their hopes of a return.

The potato famine of the 1840s gave the final shove to thousands of starving and unhappy people, who piled into boats bound for Britain's western ports. Since the Act of Union in 1800 the usual immigrant problem of naturalisation had been removed, but these were not optimistic fortune-seekers drawn by the new arrangement. They were driven almost solely by distress and misery. The slightly better-off and more adventurous went to America, where the Irish enjoyed (and continue to enjoy) high repute as tough entrepreneurs. Those who fled east were not only desperate: they were angry and resentful at having to throw themselves on the far-from-tender mercy of the country that was largely responsible for the agricultural and political system that had ruined them in the first place. Even at the height of the famine, they had seen their country's precious textiles, meat and butter heading for the coast under military escort.

There were three main routes to Britain: the short northern passage from Ulster to Scotland; a middle way from Dublin to Liverpool and Manchester; and a southern crossing from Cork to Bristol and London. There were traffic jams on all of these routes, though the busiest was the sea-lane to Liverpool, since that was also the gateway to America. In 1847 some three hundred

---

*There was major unrest in Shoreditch in 1736 when a church builder dismissed his workers in favour of Irish muscle. Irish pubs and slum cottages were attacked by the mob.

thousand Irish people arrived on the Mersey, more than half of whom were in transit before the transatlantic voyage. In all, something approaching one and a half million people fled the Emerald Isle. For Liverpool's marine industry, adjusting to life after slavery, this exodus proved something of a boon.

The 1841 census lists 289,404 Irish-born people in Britain; by 1851 there were nearly twice as many; and by 1861 there were over 600,000. Five per cent of the population of London was Irish, but there were even greater concentrations elsewhere. The Irish made up 13 per cent of the population in Bradford, Manchester and Paisley; 18 per cent in Glasgow; 19 per cent in Dundee; and a full quarter in Liverpool. All of these cities were radically and thoroughly changed in only a few years. The census figures do not include children, and the Irish had large families, even the youngest members of which certainly considered themselves (and were considered by the locals) Irish. So in most estimates the Irish community, by the 1880s, numbered between one and a quarter and one and a half million people – over 3 per cent of the total population.

In the usual sense of the word they were not immigrants, because the Irish were British. Until 1922, when all but the six northern counties achieved independence, the Irish left home as Britons, and were no more foreign than people from Cornwall or Yorkshire.* But immigration is as much a geographical and social uprooting as it is a political transfer. And the Irish who came in the nineteenth century played an emphatic part in the mingling of tribes that created what we now think of as the characteristic British mix.

Besides, Ireland was a strange and unassimilated part of the United Kingdom: its people spoke little English (despite an educational programme in the 1830s to spread the language through the national school system) and they were Catholic, if you wanted to use the polite term – superstitious agents of the devil, if you did not. So they were certainly treated as immigrants – and as the worst and most benighted sort of immigrants into the bargain. Far from being greeted as fellow-nationals, they were seen as barbaric, more or less. They were poor, uneducated, didn't mind a drink and occasionally expressed themselves with their fists. As usual, they were seen as rebellious by nature and simply not to be trusted. They could also (perhaps the gravest sin of all) be surprisingly poetic and merry.

These were sufficient reasons to depict them as members of an alien race. They were lampooned by newspaper cartoonists as grinning apes, and in the

---

*I am reminded of a riposte by a French foreign minister some years ago. He was trying to assure a sceptical audience that the nuclear tests his government was conducting on Pacific islands were perfectly safe, and was asked why, in that case, the bombs were never tested in France itself. The minister sighed. 'But Tahiti', he said magnificently, '*is* France.'

higher journals were labelled 'Celts' – as a people incorrigibly different from (and inferior) to the standard English breed. A Royal Commission in 1836 felt no need to mince words. The Irish were invading our towns with their 'uncleanly and negligent habits'. They brought with them 'filth, neglect, confusion, discomfort and insalubrity'. Like many other groups of social unfortunates, the squalor in which they were trapped was held against them, as if they wore rags and lived in overcrowded slums by choice, as if they ate discarded turnip heads or potato peel because they thought them delicacies. Perhaps it was nothing more than a fearful distaste that led public opinion to shudder at the sight of them. They represented a vivid image of how ghastly life could be – at a time when there were no established social safety-nets – if things went wrong. Britons preferred to see prosperity as a function of thrift and ingenuity, not as a matter of luck, let alone as something that derived from and indeed depended on the exploitation of people like these hopeless vagrants.

A large number of the newcomers, in the absence of any better opportunities, joined the already sizeable Irish contingent in the British armed forces. In 1830 the army was almost 40 per cent Irish; in 1868 there were some 55,000 Irishmen in the ranks (they were not often thought of as officer material, despite the prominence of the Irish-born Duke of Wellington). In civilian life, meanwhile, they were the industrial equivalent of cannon-fodder: factory-fodder. They toiled in construction, gas works, as dockside labour, in coal mines and quarries. Though they were country people, they congregated in cities, the only places they could earn or scrounge a living, and often walked miles to earn a shilling. Awful rat-plagued slums – Liverpool's cellars, Glasgow's tenements, Manchester's 'Little Ireland', the 'rookeries' of east London – mushroomed in what already were the direst quarters of these cities. In one road in York, Britannia's Yard, sixteen two-roomed cottages housed over 170 people. In a telling comment on Britain's housing priorities, the cottages were condemned by a Royal Commission in 1844, but were still being used as cheap housing for the poor (often new generations of immigrants) until shortly before the Second World War. Another York enclave was reported as having just two squalid and overflowing privies for 140 people: the Inspector of Nuisances was moved to describe it as 'the modern Black Hole of Calcutta', a nickname which of course emphasised that this was a primitive and foreign blot on Britain's otherwise splendid urban facilities.

Invariably, the Irish were seen not as the victims of slum conditions, but as their cause. Churchmen and social theorists were convinced that the Irish were reaping what their pernicious Catholicism and innate viciousness had sown. James Froude, the eminent historian, took them to be 'more like tribes of squalid apes than human beings'. Thomas Carlyle, no stranger to racial generalisations, was happy to refer to the Irishman's 'squalor and unreason . . . his fatuity and drunken violence'. The average Irish person, he felt, was 'a ready-made nucleus of degradation and disorder'.

An 1850 report on the sanitary condition of York compared the lovely houses of good Yorkshire folk – 'a cleanly people' – with the miseries of the Irish district around Walmgate. 'The unfortunate sons and daughters of Erin,' it continued, had 'less orderly' habits. Their houses were 'not fit even for pigsties'. This was also the attitude of most newspapers. 'Ireland is pouring into the cities and even into the villages,' cried a *Times* leader in 1847, 'a fetid mass of famine, nakedness, dirt and fever.' Liverpool, said the author, would soon be 'one mass of disease'. Onlookers were quick to attribute these rotten conditions to moral delinquency rather than mere desperation. In 1855 the Liverpool *Herald* said of its Irish slum: 'The lower order of Irish papists are the filthiest beings in the habitable globe. They abound in dirt and vermin and have no care for anything but self-gratification.' Nor were they peaceful. After a summer uprising of Irishmen in Clerkenwell in 1848, *The Times* referred to 'the Irish love of knife, dagger and poison-bowl', and tut-tutted over 'that extravagance of wild sedition which, for want of any other adjective, must be denominated "Irish"'. The papers were quick to report, with horrified glee, the sensational excesses of life in the ghettoes, such as the tendency, when Irish children were given clothes in rare acts of benevolence, for their parents to pawn them and drink the proceeds.*

A few progressive fellow-immigrants such as Engels and Marx saw these morbid settlements as bitter indictments of capitalism, and a handful of Quakers spoke up on behalf of the Irish. 'They laboured', wrote one, Samuel Tuke, 'in the heaviest of employment . . . and were nevertheless thought of as lazy, reckless and violent.'[1] But such men were in a minority. Most people were appalled. The reaction in Scotland was especially severe. 'No Compromise with Popery!' howled the *Scottish Guardian* in 1861. The paper even argued that the famine was a much-deserved divine visitation, a godly punishment for the Irish people's 'barbarous spiritual destitution, its moral and intellectual poverty'. The Scottish Church was rather more militant and Utopian than the Church of England, which had a cannier sense of its secular vested interest. Scotland clung more zealously to the dream of a Protestant Arcadia, and the arrival of so many Catholics was a clear and present threat. 'It must be the time of up and doing,' said one fundamentalist. 'No rest for ourselves and our children until every college, convent, monastery and church of anti-Christ has disappeared from the

---

*The new arrivals were memorialised in sentimental paintings. *The Irish Vagrants* by Walter Howell Deverell (from 1843) features a picturesque pre-Raphaelite group: the man asleep (exhausted, drunk, or both), a woman with a baby, a couple of children begging for a crust. It was easier to shed tears over a painting, of course, than it was to engage with the real thing.

land.' The Glasgow *Herald* observed, in an argument very familiar today, that the Irish had been misled and should be shipped back right away: 'We fear they are induced to leave Ireland under the most disillusive notions of the comfort and abundance that awaits them here.' Bishop Murdoch put it rather more succinctly, proposing in 1848 that the best solution was 'a skinful of bullets'.

It is easy, with hindsight, to see that the chronic urban conditions were caused not by the Irish but by an extraordinary surge in the overall population (from 10.5 million in 1801 to 18.1 million in 1841) with which the social infrastructure could not cope. It was hideously unfair that the Irish, simply by dint of being the most visibly outlandish, should take so much of the blame. But the idea that these poor refugees were a disease-ridden danger wasn't entirely imaginary: the Irish were indeed awash with typhus and dysentery, and the anguish these diseases caused them was matched by the fear they provoked in their neighbours. In 1833 two reporters visited Bristol and found 'hordes' of Irish packed into tiny spaces. One night they came upon thirty people jammed into a single small room. 'At that period cholera was hovering over us, and on the night to which we refer it swooped down on nine out of the thirty, and seven became corpses in the course of a few hours.'[2] Even Engels, who saw the Irish as an exploited proletariat, couldn't help holding his nose when he strayed into the slums of Manchester in the course of preparing *The Condition of the Working Class in England*. He had a principled sympathy for the Irish immigrants, but winced at the sight of the streets where they lived: 'masses of refuse, offal and sickening filth lie among standing pools . . . A horde of ragged women and children swarm about here, as filthy as the swine that thrive upon the garbage heaps and in the puddles.' The people were facile drunks, 'little above the savage'. They had been 'robbed of all humanity, degraded, reduced morally and physically to bestiality'.

Engels insisted that the industrial boom of capitalism could not have happened without 'the numerous and impoverished population of Ireland'. And some members of the British establishment were also quick to see the Irish as a signal economic resource. In 1829 Sir Robert Peel urged his colleagues not to 'condemn too precipitately the incursion of Irish labourers into England. We must . . . consider well the advantages of cheap labour.'[3] Business leaders liked and often employed them, especially as strike-breakers. 'The moment I have a turn-out and am fast for hands,' commented one businessman in a report on the state of the poor in 1836, 'I send to Ireland for ten, fifteen or twenty families.'

It was all right for the factory owners, of course: they didn't have to live next to those stinking slums. For the working classes it was a different matter, and they were resentful. In Scotland, where the Edinburgh–Glasgow and Caledonian canals (projects designed to provide work for unemployed Highlanders) were dug largely by Irish shovels, there was rancour. 'Ireland', wrote the *Trades Free Press* in 1827, 'inundates us with her miserable poor . . .

multitudes are daily poured upon our shores ready to invade the work of every labourer and operative.' This was the voice of the fledgling trade unions, the panicky reaction of a working class that feared the wage-cutting rivalry of a seemingly infinite number of aliens. In the Dumbarton shipyards, in 1855, Protestant dockers threatened to throw their Irish rivals into the furnaces, and there were also bitter riots in Partick and Greenock.*

The Catholic Emancipation Act, which granted full freedom to the pursuit of the Roman religion in Britain, was not passed until 1829. No sooner had it been given royal assent than accusations were made that the country was being swamped. This feeling was given added credence by the way in which a few incautious Catholics greeted the arrival of the 'holy poor' as a divine miracle and a blessing. It gave an ominous boost to Cardinal Newman's idea of Catholic revival, of a 'Second Spring'. But if the Irish fed a Catholic revival in Britain, they also gave a boost to its opposite: nuns and priests were jostled and jeered at in the street, by shop girls as well as by zealots. Others handled the situation in a different way. The Revd Samuel Garratt, who worked with Irish paupers for two years, saw them as lost souls. 'In the very heart of London,' he wrote, 'there exists a race of men with fine natural susceptibilities, more capable than the Saxon neighbours of intellectual development, debased – crushed – dwarfed – unable to stand erect – as men always are when ages of oppression have done their work.'[4] The oppression he was referring to was that of a Catholic priesthood which still urged people to set aside all hope for worldly success. 'It is not the Irish air in infancy,' wrote Garratt, 'or Celtic parentage that has made the Irish in London what they are. It is nothing else but the withering curse of the anti-Christian system which blights where it falls.'

One of the more baleful effects of the Irish migration, then, was that it reintroduced to the British mainland a historic fury that had long been absent: sectarianism. An Armagh-inspired Orange Lodge opened in Manchester as early as 1798, and from then on, all over the country, there were scenes reminiscent of those that still accompany the marching season in Ulster. In 1852 a procession of Stockport's Catholics was banned by a proclamation from Disraeli, no less, who explained that he wished only to 'prevent trouble'. The marchers, as marchers will, ignored him, and insisted on trudging past a gauntlet of banners that read, 'Down with the lousy Irish!' and 'To Hell with the Pope!' The next day, a priest was burned in effigy and the town exploded. Scores of homes were wrecked, a couple of chapels were smashed, one Irishman was killed and another fifty wounded. Furniture was piled up and set

---

*One of many religious rabble-rousers was an unusual immigrant from Italy, the evangelical Protestant Alessandro Gavazzi, who wrote, in one of the anti-Catholic publications that sprang up in mid-century, that the Irish Church was seeking 'to regain her dominion of darkness in this kingdom of Bible light'.

alight. St Peter's Square, in the city centre, was taken and retaken as police advanced and were rebuffed by a furious crowd. In the end, an infantry regiment marched in to restore order and, literally, read the Riot Act. The authorities were in no doubt where the blame lay: of 113 prisoners, 111 were Irish.

The echoes of this revived sectarianism faded but did not die. In 1923 the General Assembly of the Church of Scotland gave tacit backing to a report titled 'The Menace of the Irish Race to Our Scottish Nationality'. It declared: 'the peril is that our Protestant Church will be swamped by an alien population having no sympathy with Scotch history, tradition or custom'. There are still a few God-fearing Scots who refuse to have the colour green in the house. And in Edinburgh and Glasgow sectarian anger continues, sometimes lethally, to disfigure football matches.

The Irish were soon stigmatised as inveterate criminals, and the police, as the representatives of public unease, were quick to harass and arrest them. In York, in 1850, nearly a quarter of the reported crimes were committed by Irish people, a vast disproportion. The most habitual (and necessary) crime was theft, much of it petty. In April 1848 a pair of Irishmen, John McDonald and John Smith, asked for a loaf of bread from a shop. When they were refused (impolitely, no doubt), they grabbed one, an impulsive act of hunger which earned them two months' hard labour. Another couple, Thomas Joyce and John Delaney, were handed three months for 'wandering about the streets with the intention of stealing'. Such imaginative charges were common. There was a seven-day penalty for 'milking cows without leave'. Sometimes the Irish deliberately broke gas lamps in order to be arrested: a roof and a bowl of soup, even in handcuffs, was better than they could often expect outside. The clumsiness of these crimes played some part in the development of the Irish idiot stereotype: too stupid even to nick a loaf and get away with it! The joke-makers don't seem to have realised that the Irish might have wanted to be caught.

There were plenty of Irish or anti-Irish riots – in Cardiff in 1848, in Greenock in 1851,* in Wigan in 1852, in Preston, Blackburn and Oldham. By 1855 Oldham had eleven Orange Lodges, and the English threatened to 'drive the Irish out of town'. The Irish countered that soon they 'would have all Oldham to ourselves'. The outbreaks of violence there and elsewhere followed similar patterns, though they had different causes. In Wolverhampton, trouble was provoked by a battle between rival railway companies, which deployed Irish navvies as rent-a-mobs to disrupt the work of their commercial opponents. So anxious was the London and North Western Railway Company to prevent the

---

*Greenock was the port from which many Scots abandoned their own country and migrated west, landing in a strangely familiar landscape on the other side of the Atlantic Ocean, Nova Scotia.

Shrewsbury and Birmingham Company from completing its link to the Birmingham Canal that it sent three hundred Irish labourers to blockade the route. The police waded in with swords and bayonets, but the local paper, the Wolverhampton *Chronicle*, conceded that the Irish were 'merely the tools of their employers'.

Wolverhampton was typical. In 1851 it had six thousand Irish people in a population of nearly fifty thousand – over 10 per cent. They worked in coalfields, in the ironworks and on the railways, and lived in a slum near Stafford Street (known, in a clear instance of the racial antipathy with which they were treated, as Caribee Island). Once predominantly Methodist, the area now had four Catholic churches (seven by 1866). In May 1848 a clumsy clampdown by the police (they moved in with cutlasses, which some saw as provocative) ran into a two-thousand-strong crowd of stone-throwing Irish residents. The police pushed on regardless and arrested thirteen men. One complained that he had been a victim of what later generations would call 'police brutality'; he showed the court his back, a mass of black and blue bruises. The police claimed that these were self-inflicted injuries, an explanation the court found easy to accept. The man was sentenced to two months in jail.

A couple of weeks later, the air now full of enmity and grievance, a Sunderland constable was attacked. Once again, the police drew their swords: a woman had her arm broken in the mêlée. In July there were further clashes, when the Stour Valley Railway refused to pay wages to its Irish navvies. The navvies ended up fighting the police in a beer hall. So in January 1849, when the police chased a 'suspect' into the heart of Caribee Island, the area erupted again. A modern inquiry would probably conclude that tactless policing was one of the prime causes. A report from that year dismissed the area as an 'open gutter': an overcrowded, cholera-ridden cesspit. Stafford Street was written off as a no-go zone ruled by criminals.

Such clashes were by now commonplace. There were similar riots in almost all of Britain's larger towns. In London, the tension had a political edge, as Irish independence became a prominent topic. In 1867 gunpowder was exploded against the wall of Clerkenwell Prison in an attempt to free some jailed Irish convicts. Six 'civilians' were killed. It was the first Irish terrorist action on the mainland, and (like much subsequent terrorism) its most immediate effect was to slow down the process by which independence might be achieved. Many middle-of-the-road supporters of home rule, outraged by the blast, abandoned the cause of Irish freedom, and its future in Parliament became bleak.

London erupted in something like panic. There were rumours that the Fenians were digging tunnels under the Thames, to blow up St Paul's Cathedral and the Bank of England. A call went out for special volunteer constables to patrol the streets, and no fewer than 166,000 people responded. London had already seen violent Irish crowds a few years earlier, when they had turned out in force to protest against a visit of the Italian nationalist Garibaldi in 1862.* The idea that the Irish were dangerous subversives was becoming hard to dismiss.

It sounds, to modern ears, like a familiar story, and the echoes in the inner-city riots of recent decades are hard to miss (the furore that followed the famine was certainly similar to the storm surrounding the arrival of today's Afro-Caribbean population). Karl Marx was quick to portray the Irish as victims of a purely racial fury. 'The ordinary English worker', he wrote, 'hates the Irish worker as a competitor who lowers his standard of life . . . His attitude is the same as that of the "poor whites" to the "niggers" in the former slave states of the USA. The Irishman pays him back with interest. He sees in the English worker at once the accomplice and the stupid tool of the English domination of Ireland.'⁵ The Oxonian Edward Augustus Freeman, while no 'ordinary English worker', did not contradict Marx. He went to America in 1881 and wrote: 'This would be a grand land if only every Irishman would kill a negro, and be hanged for it.' The parallels are obvious. For Notting Hill, Toxteth, Brixton, and St Paul's read Clerkenwell, Greenock, Cardiff and Stockport. Immigrants clustered in the cheapest, roughest areas, driving the rent up and the tone down. Some of them became wretched, lawless and angry. The police, urged on by a sensationalist or malicious public opinion, moved in to confront the hard core, but ended up having pitched battles with the disaffected residents. Innocent bystanders were harassed and hurt, which inspired a new spiral of fury and injustice. Each time, the caricatures became more boldly drawn, and seemed more true. The Irish were viewed as violent, angry, lazy, noisy, uneducated, scary and drunk (alcohol being the Victorian equivalent of today's drug culture). They were harshly discriminated against in employment, housing and all areas of social welfare; and badgered both by squads of racist citizens and by a police force dedicated to the defence of non-Irish property. Lancashire was for decades a miniature Ulster. For almost the whole century, the Irish migrants were regarded as a palpable and perhaps intractable 'problem'.

It isn't easy to see the misery of the Irish in nineteenth-century Britain as anything other than a tale of brutal prejudice and neglect. But it's not the whole story. Alongside the riots and the slums, the racism and the exploitation, there was a less explosive side to the Irish migration.† Not all the Irish who came to

*Garibaldi was vilified by the Irish because he was strongly anti-Vatican.
†G. K. Chesterton was quick to point out that even the seemingly neutral formulation 'the Irish' was something of a racial slur; as if they existed only in the plural – 'like the measles'. He also refused to accept the prevailing view that they were by definition reckless failures. 'The Irish are not in the least unsuccessful,' he wrote, 'unless it is unsuccessful to wander from their own country over a great part of the earth, in which case the English are unsuccessful too.'

Britain were prompted by straits so dire that they had no other option. It is one of the saddest ironies of migration that people with most reason to leave are often the least able or the last to do so. Some simply had itchy feet, the desire to join relatives or friends across the sea, a yen to explore. Few countries have spawned such energetic travellers as Ireland. Nor was there much logic in the usual caricature of the Irish refugee as a diseased and undernourished alcoholic. The Irish did society's heavy lifting. And they were strong enough to do it, week after week, year after year. Disease and malnutrition cannot have been the norm. They must have eaten more (and drunk less) than the routine myth claimed. There were many reports of the lack of hygiene in the Irish slums. But in 1845 an inquiry by Dr Lyon Playfair found that 'the migratory population of Liverpool is a much more healthy class than the residents of that town'.

The rookeries and slums, meanwhile, even though they were crammed, were simply not large enough to hold the entire émigré population. Manchester's infamous 'Little Ireland' was called that for a reason. It housed only a couple of thousand people. Given that the Irish in Britain numbered well over a million, it was a shameful extreme rather than a typical case. And in 1892, when Engels revisited Manchester, he was obliged to admit that 'Little Ireland had disappeared' (and before the revolution, too). The Irish dispersed more widely across the country than is sometimes thought. They were not simply herded into big-city slums, but lived in smaller towns too, in Colchester and Carlisle, Winchester and Macclesfield, Durham and Derby, Plymouth and Portsmouth – almost everywhere, in fact. Some five hundred lived peacefully in Stafford and were employed as shoemakers; a few hundred worked in the tin mines in Cornwall. Nor were they all labourers: there were doctors, drapers, carpenters, clerks, smiths, cooks, shopkeepers, landlords, domestics and even policemen. In Hull, the chief constable was an Irishman, Andrew McManners, and he was supported in his determination not to make scapegoats of the town's Irish settlers by an Irish surgeon, Edward Daley, and the Irish editor of the Hull *Advertiser*, E. F. Collins.

In Liverpool, unsurprisingly, there was a vigorous Irish middle class (what the historian Roy Foster has called 'Micks on the Make'). The large Irish population supported a significant service industry: the champion boxer Jack Langan ran a thriving pub on the docks (complete with a figurine of St Patrick), while another Irish pub, run by John McCandle, held regular debates on Irish politics. There were Irish butchers and bakers, tailors, grocers and milliners, and of course there were many Irish merchants – export agents for the cattle, butter and oats that criss-crossed the Irish Sea.

The cattle trade was dominated by the Cullen brothers, from Dublin; William Brown from Ballymena traded textiles, expanded into merchant banking, joined the mercantile elite as a baronet, and expressed his gratitude by funding the Liverpool Museum. M. J. Whitty became head constable of Liverpool, founded the *Daily Post* and was proprietor of the Liverpool *Journal*; his brother James was a draper and politician.

One Irish Catholic, Charles Russell, came from Newry to London as a lawyer, and became Lord Chief Justice – proof that the high ground was attainable in practice as well as in theory in the wake of Catholic Emancipation. Russell trimmed his sails shrewdly, and was no sort of Irish nationalist. But Patrick James Foley, whose parents had travelled to Leeds from Sligo in the 1830s, was a distinguished Catholic and supporter of home rule. After school he became a clerk, and worked with various friendly societies, struggling to alleviate poverty and concentrating particularly on burial expenses. He joined a loan club that met in a pub in Whitechapel, seeking to provide some sort of cooperative help to the bereaved, allowing them at least a trace of dignity in their funeral arrangements. This swiftly grew into Pearl Assurance. Foley was one of the four founder members: he became managing director and then president in 1908. He never forgot his roots, though, and it was said of Pearl, which by 1913 was the third-largest life assurance company in Britain, that 'any Irishmen in trouble could get a job' at one of its many offices. Foley also built several Catholic schools in Lewisham.

Nearly half of the Irish in Britain were able to find skilled or professional work, belying the stereotype of the Irish navvy. The influx had a middle-class streak broader than is usually thought. Notable writers crossed the Irish Sea, maintaining a literary tradition in Britain that stretched back to Swift, Sterne and Goldsmith. Wilde and Shaw were formidable London celebrities: the former in the Café Royal, the latter in the Fabian Society. Bram Stoker was another writer who exchanged Dublin for England: his *Dracula* is set largely in Whitby and London.

At the beginning of the nineteenth century, no actor commanded greater public interest than Edmund Kean, who was abandoned as a baby in a Soho doorway and was thought to have been the son of an Irishman. He was small, charismatic, talented and eventually wealthy. One would be tempted to see it as ironic – if it weren't simply an instance of the English sense of class as the decisive measure in human affairs – that Irishness, in the upper reaches of the social scale (the Shaw–Wilde end), could be a glamorous attribute. Matthew Arnold saw it as magical, quick-witted and lyrical, and compared it favourably to stodgy English persistence. Thackeray visited Ireland and said, 'I have met more gentlemen here than in any place I ever saw.' The Irish were 'men shrewd and delicate of perception'.[6] Trollope too swore that the Irish were 'good-humoured, clever, the working classes very much more intelligent than those of England'.[7] Hostile feelings towards the masses ran alongside a sneaking affection for individuals: Paddy might be a rascal, but he had a twinkle in his eye. He might be rash and improvident, as Shaw put it, but he was also brave and good-natured.

Ireland sent forth her radicals too, who entered into and propelled the first stuttering attempts at democratic protest in the Chartist movement. Two of the leading Chartists – Feargus O'Connor and James O'Brien – were Irish. O'Connor was the brawn, O'Brien the brains. The latter came from Dublin to Gray's Inn as a law student, and became, under the pseudonym 'Bronterre', one of the most eloquent revolutionary writers in England, pressing for egalitarian reforms some half a century before they became fashionable. In 1840 he was brought to trial for 'seditious speaking' and spent eighteen months in prison. Afterwards he was the editor of several journals and a popular lecturer on social affairs. O'Connor was the charismatic rabble-rouser of the Chartist rallies and proprietor of the influential *Northern Star*. Some fifty thousand people gathered in Kensal Green to witness his funeral in 1855. Both men had a specific grudge against the British political establishment – they wanted home rule for Ireland – but both gave energy to the grass roots of Britain's protest movement. O'Connor might have given too much: O'Brien and others certainly felt that Chartism was harmed rather than helped by his overblown and noisy approach.

One of the most impressive Irish migrants was a Jewish Dubliner – a Christian-convert evangelist who came to London in 1866 hoping to train as a missionary to China. That didn't work out, so he became a teacher instead, at one of the East End's many 'ragged' – free – schools. In 1867 a cholera epidemic confronted him with the stark details of urban squalor, and he found a new vocation. He set up a school of his own in Hope Street, and a charitable empire was born. The man's name – familiar to many generations of modern children – was Dr Thomas Barnardo. He was rarely candid about his background; indeed, he usually pretended he had grown up as a Quaker. But his name became a byword for charitable philanthropy, and he mobilised public opinion in support of his good causes.

Free state education was not a civic right until 1870; the ragged schools were a loose association of philanthropically financed institutions established mainly for the promulgation of Christian behaviour: they were designed to 'stop crime while it is in seed, and sin before it has broken into flower'. Barnardo engaged the support of Lord Shaftesbury and the banker Robert Barclay. In 1877 he bought two warehouses by the Regent Canal in Mile End and turned them into what would become, in just two years, the biggest such school in London, with over a thousand children. The canal was busy with coal barges ferrying fuel to the gasworks a few hundred yards away. Smoke from the Bryant & May matchworks down the road showered soot on to the children. But in these grimy circumstances the school flourished.* Book-learning was only the half of

---

*Barnardo's original school is now the Ragged School Museum in Mile End, on the literary-sounding junction of Copperfield Road and Ben Jonson Road. It occupies a historic site in one of the few surviving warehouses that used to line the Regent Canal – the waterway that linked the docks at Limehouse to Paddington Station.

it. 'We find in many cases', wrote Barnardo, 'that food is more essential to the boys and girls than education.' They were given breakfast (bread and cocoa), and the kind of cheap dinners for which some modern Londoners pay over the odds: 'lentil or pea soup and bread, varied occasionally by rice and prunes or haricot beans'.

It wasn't all plain sailing. Barnardo's energetic desire to spread the word once took him to a large, fortress-like local pub called the Edinburgh Castle. He strode into the heart of the smoke-filled, gin-soaked room and started offering Bibles for threepence, or New Testaments for a penny. There weren't many takers. In his memoir *Night and Day*, he recalled the pointed lack of enthusiasm: 'I presently found myself on the ground with the flat part of the table pressing on me. Several of the biggest lads leaped inside it, dancing a "devil's tattoo", to my great discomfort.'

Still, he persisted. He avenged himself on the Edinburgh Castle by buying it and turning it into a Christian mission, which became the headquarters of a charitable giant. By the time he died in 1905, Barnardo's schools had educated over fifty thousand children. His orphanages – those famous 'homes' immortalised by the yellow-and-green collection-box houses carried from door to door – had housed twelve thousand more. And in an engaging twist, this resolute immigrant became a keen evangelist for emigration, sponsoring the movement of some eighteen thousand children to new lives in Canada and Australia. He called it 'philanthropic abduction', and it wasn't only the needs of the children he had in mind. He was well aware of the wider social implications of a destitute underclass: 'Every boy rescued from the gutter is one dangerous man the less,' he said. Cartoonists poked fun, as they often will at do-gooders, even when they genuinely are doing good. Cruickshank portrayed a group of men, including a cleric, shovelling tiny children on to a cart outside a gin palace, like so many horse droppings, and called it 'A Sweeping Measure'. Barnardo wasn't deflected. He built a historic archive of before-and-after photographs of the children in his care, designed to demonstrate the excellence of his methods.*

There is one last hint that an Irishman's life in Victorian Britain might not have been quite so dismal as it is sometimes depicted: there were high levels of intermarriage between Irish immigrants and the local population. The surveys are skimpy; the proportion of marriages in which the place of birth is listed as 'not known' is high. But in York and Bristol, for instance, only half the marriages involving Irish people were all-Irish affairs. The Irish, in other words, were not entirely cut off from routine social intercourse; nor can they have been universally detested. E. P. Thompson put it neatly: 'It is not the friction but

---

*Although he was once accused of deception ('artistic fiction') in the 'before' photographs. Maybe the children weren't quite ragged enough for the ragged schools.

the relative ease with which the Irish were absorbed into working-class communities which is remarkable.'[8]

None of this means that the image of the Irish as hard done by is untrue; only that it is not the whole truth. It is interesting, too, to see how rival ideologies can amplify the same myth. English nationalists liked to emphasise the ugliness of the Irish to highlight their own superiority; the defenders of the Irish emphasised exactly the same thing to highlight the wickedness of their English oppressors. Both added crude glitter to the same cartoon. To say, for instance, that the English corralled the Irish into alcoholic penury presents the immigrants as the docile, feckless beasts that their most prejudiced critics would have us believe they were. In fact, the Irish lived and worked in a way not so different from English and Scottish labourers: they scrimped, saved and sent the money home to their suffering dependants. In 1862 the *Irish Times* rejoiced to see news of the monies that had been transferred back to the mother country: 'The remittance sent home by emigrants to their friends in 14 years amounted to upwards of 12 millions sterling. What a tale of industry, thrift and love of kith and kin is here!' Or, as the famous if apocryphal letter from Ireland ran: 'Send more money! You have another brother!'

It has long been all too easy to refer to 'the Irish' when we mean only 'the Irish poor'. It is as if the successful Irish, the witty Irish, the ambitious Irish, the entrepreneurial Irish, the thrifty Irish do not count, truly, as Irish. One of the side-effects of such talk is to decorate the whole idea of immigration with associations of degradation and cruelty. The British poor endured conditions every bit as cramped and poisonous, competing for the same hard and underpaid work, struggling to survive from day to day. The British Empire was a tower of incredible wealth and power, yet its feet were planted in a shoddy stew of neglect and hardship which granted no exemptions for anything so trifling as mere nationality.

The common depiction of the Irish slums as pigsties is so powerful that it is a wonder anyone ever managed to survive or escape them. That they did – that they had more or less passed into the mainstream of British life by the end of the nineteenth century – goes some way towards refuting the generalisation that helped to place them there.

Today, with a hundred years of forgetfulness and the wounds no longer fresh, it is even possible to notice that, awful though the reaction to the Irish was, it fell short of outright tragedy. From unpromising beginnings the Irish developed into a success story: they stepped onwards and upwards into the centre of a country they simultaneously adapted to and altered. Is it superficial to take any pleasure or pride in this outcome? Should 'we' emphasise only the worst aspects of Britain's tolerance? Either way, their story gives hope for any future immigrants to these shores, because the initial discomfort, however extreme, did not last for ever. At the end of the century, as the red-brick turrets of Westminster Cathedral began to rise into the sky above Victoria Station, it was clear that, thanks to the Irish, England (and Scotland and Wales) now embraced a sizeable Catholic population. Inside, there were pillars of Cork and Connemara marble, a bronze statue of St Patrick, and a mother-of-pearl shamrock. Britain was at last a country not merely of religious reform but of religious variety and tolerance, a fact which would be increasingly important as members of other faiths began to congregate in these islands.

CHAPTER 14

Rule Britannia

In 1889 a bizarre (for the Home Counties, anyway) new building appeared in the quiet Surrey woodland on the edge of Woking. It had been commissioned by a German-Hungarian immigrant and scholar, Dr Leitner, and was designed by the Victorian architect W. L. Chambers. Large, square, white, topped with blue and gold cupolas and approached through a huge, elaborate arch at the front, it was an exotic flourish in a rather unexotic corner of England. This echo of Mughal India was England's first Islamic mosque, and it was named after Shah Jehan, the Sultan famous for commissioning the Taj Mahal. Leitner was an Oriental academic – registrar of the University of Punjab in Lahore – and the mosque was conveniently placed for the Oriental Institute in neighbouring Maybury, which was full of Muslim students and teachers. It was soon a busy centre of Muslim scholarship and inspiration. In 1912 a Lahore lawyer, Khwaja Kamal-ud-Din, in partnership with Lord Headley, a civil engineer, took over the run-down building and made it the headquarters of his Muslim Mission.* Kamal-ud-Din was known in English circles as the 'Very Reverend' – a status akin to that of the Chief Rabbi. For years, celebrated Islamic thinkers and activists rubbed shoulders with heavy-suited Surrey stockbrokers waiting at Woking station for the Waterloo train.

The Woking Mosque stands as a reminder that Victorian Britain embraced a wider range of cultural expression than its straitlaced image suggests. In the ports, Britain's energetic merchant fleet continued to attract (or dump) workers

---

*In 1917 it published the first English translation of the Koran.

from the farthest corners of the empire and beyond. The Suez canal was cut in 1869, and the mysterious East began to filter back to England on the homeward leg of imperial voyages. Ships returning from the Orient would tip not just their cargo but their crew on to the docks: they weren't about to pay them for spending time in port. As the imperial administration grew, returning families uprooted Indian maids and servants to look after the children during the voyage, only to abandon them upon arrival. In 1857 the Strangers' Home for Asiatics, Africans and South Sea Islanders was set up on West India Dock Road, and it was soon full of sacked Indian *ayahs*, who could do little but tout despairingly for domestic jobs with families heading east.

The shipping companies were still fond of their Asiatic Lascars and coolies. These men worked harder, for lower pay, and were not nearly so keen on drunken brawls as their local counterparts.* Other nationalities were similarly favoured. The *Baroda*, for instance, left Liverpool in the summer of 1880 with a crew of three Londoners, three West Indians, three Welshmen, two Germans, a Dane, a Norwegian and a Chinese cook. Of course, the industriousness of such interlopers was resented by British members of the labour market: it seemed typical of the sneakiness and treachery of your average bloody foreigner. But the streets around the London docks were soon home to a fluid colony of Indians, Malaysians, Somalis and Chinese. The Chinese contingent, who came mainly from Shanghai, especially after the Blue Funnel Line established a route in 1865, built 'Chinatowns' in both Liverpool and London. In Liverpool, sailors would drop in for a drink at Grossi's Trocadero, a bar beneath the St George's Hotel set up by an Italian Jew; in Limehouse in London, there were over thirty shops and restaurants, and even an impromptu Confucian temple.†

The Lascars were a mixed bunch – the term was applied not just to Indians but to Burmese, Malays, Yemenis, Siamese and anyone else who looked to hail from east of Suez. Most, however, were Bengalis from around Calcutta, and they too established toeholds in the East End, Cardiff, South Shields and Hull.

They had been a constant feature of dockland life throughout the nineteenth century. A parliamentary report on 'Lascars and other Asiatic Seamen' found that there could at any one time be a thousand or so adrift in London alone. On some ships, up to 85 per cent of the crew were Lascars. In the middle of the century, according to one guess, there were around twelve thousand at work on British ships, roughly half of whom spent at least some time ashore in Britain. It wasn't quite slavery, but in many ways it resembled it. British officers and

---

*Lascars cost sixpence per day in food, compared to a shilling for British sailors, and were paid as little as a sixth or a seventh as much. No wonder, despite the common view that 'in a cold climate the Lascar becomes of no value', they were hauled aboard.
†Echoes of the Oriental presence still live on in certain road names: Ming Street, Canton Street, Peking Street, Nanking Street.

bureaucrats would obtain the labour they needed through often corrupt Indian agents (*serangs*). The *serangs* handled the money, much of which disappeared before being passed on to the men they had recruited. It was a system ripe for bribery, and it did nothing to protect the seamen once their ships had cast off. On one voyage early in the century, 28 of the 74 Lascars in the crew of the *Union* died at sea. According to the *serang*, the men had been mercilessly beaten and flogged by the chief mate. Many of those who made it to England floundered. According to some estimates, over a hundred died each year in their winter quarters.

Things were rather different at the top end of the social scale. Rammohan Roy came to London in 1830 as ambassador of the Mughal Emperor, and lived at Bedford Square, where a plaque now commemorates his residence. He campaigned vigorously against the subcontinental practice of suttee – the custom by which widows would be burned on their husbands' funeral pyres – until his death in Bristol in 1833. Duleep Singh was another curious addition to Victorian courtly circles. A Sikh prince, his lands in the Punjab were annexed in 1849 and he surrendered the famous Koh-i-Noor diamond (later to become the jewel in the crown jewels). He was only eleven years old at the time. Singh soon followed the jewel to England, became a Christian and lived extravagantly on the handsome pension he received in return for his domain. He married the daughter of a German banker and an Ethiopian slave; Queen Victoria became godmother of his son, the patriotically named Victor Albert.* His home was the splendid Italianate palace Elveden Hall in Norfolk, which became the headquarters of country-house-living exotic. Singh was by repute the fourth-best shot in the kingdom, and his lavish house parties became famous. In London, he was a member of the fashionable Carlton Club, relaxed enough to complain about the standard of the fish-knives. A spendthrift, he fell somewhat in the royal esteem when he began to voice demands for the return of the diamond, whose symbolic value he had perhaps underestimated as a boy. He became a committed Sikh, and went so far as to ask the Russian Tsar for help in overthrowing the British in Punjab. Surprisingly, he was forgiven by the British, but his party invitations dried up. After his first wife's death, he married an Englishwoman and retired to France. His father's golden chair is still in the Victoria and Albert Museum.

Dadabhai Naoroji was a partner of Cama & Company, the first Indian corporation to be established in Britain. A Parsee from Bombay, he was fortunate in that, as the son of a priest, he was educated on charitable subsidies. He came to London in 1850 as a businessman, leaving Cama to set up his own cotton trading company. When it collapsed in 1881 he turned to politics. He

*'I always feel so sorry for these poor deposed Indian princes,' said the Queen, having her cake and eating it too. Victor Albert, meanwhile, pursued an ineffably British career: Eton, Cambridge, the dragoons, and marriage to the daughter of the Earl of Coventry.

became professor of Gujarati at University College, London, the founder and president of the Zoroastrian Society, and stood unsuccessfully for election as an MP in Holborn in 1890. Two years later he had another try in Central Finsbury. This time it looked like being a close-run thing. The Prime Minister, the Marquess of Salisbury, remarked that he did not believe that 'a British constituency will take a black man', an outspoken comment which was vehemently criticised by many colleagues. Naoroji was an Indian nationalist, a stance guaranteed to unsettle an English nabob. In his writings, he emphasised that India's poverty was to a large extent the result of its having been drained by Britain: up to £40 million was in effect exported to Britain every year.

In running for Parliament, Naoroji knew what he was getting into. Lal Mohan Ghose had campaigned in Deptford in 1885, only to be dismissed as an 'Indian baboo' and 'an advocate of Mahomedanism' (an odd slur, since he was not a Muslim). But Naoroji had his supporters (one of whom was the venerable Florence Nightingale), and Salisbury's tart judgement rallied them. Naoroji, said one, was 'an Englishman as well as an English subject'. The National Liberal Club threw a banquet for him, and he won a famous victory when, after a recount, the seat became his by just five votes. In his maiden speech, he generously praised 'the love of justice and freedom in British instincts which has produced this extraordinary result'. The love of justice was fleeting, however, and Naoroji's admiration for it was bruised at the 1895 election, when he was voted out. It took a hundred years for his achievement to be appropriately recognised: in 1993, a plaque was unveiled on Finsbury Town Hall.

He was not quite a lone figure. Ironically, the anti-Liberal swing that put paid to Naoroji propelled another Indian into Parliament. The lawyer Sir Mancherjee Bhownaggree was elected in that same election as the Conservative Member for Bethnal Green. He too was a Parsee, and the Tories, some of whom had attacked Naoroji as being not only un-English but un-Indian (whatever that meant), announced that Bhownaggree was of the 'numerically small but intellectually great Parsee race'. He won his seat by 160 votes, which was quite a turnaround, since Bethnal Green had long been a radical stronghold. As if to prove that racial slurs were by no means a Tory monopoly, the ejected candidate, the trade union leader Charles Howell, snapped sourly that he had been 'kicked out by a black man, a stranger'. Bhownaggree held the seat in 1900 and became a fixture in government circles connected with the subcontinent.* An imperial loyalist (his Indian opponents referred to him as 'Bow-the-Knee'), opposed to the nationalist rhetoric of India's growing Congress Party, he met Gandhi in 1906 and 1909, long before the latter became the Mahatma.

Bhownaggree played no part in the expatriate revolutionary politics that

---

*A gallery at the Commonwealth Institute in Holland Park is named after him.

would eventually reach a crescendo through the work of Gandhi, Nehru and Jinnah. But just as London had been a home-from-home for Europe's revolutionaries, so Indian nationalists were able to form themselves into something like a movement. Most came as law students, and they would meet at India House, a society founded by a Balliol-educated egg magnate, Shyamajo Krishnavarma, in 1905. Vinayak Savarkar, a Brahmin from Bombay, came on a scholarship and set about translating Mazzini's autobiography, hoping to publicise liberation philosophy. While the wealthy, multilingual Madame Cama spoke out from her base in Paris against the 'tyrannies' imposed on the Indian poor by Britain, the humbler activists at India House campaigned for independence. Some of them practised shooting pistols in the Tottenham Court Road, a training method that did little to endear them to the police.

Far from this intellectual ferment, dark echoes of slavery could still be heard in Britain's ports. In 1861, Dickens found the pubs in the slum area of Liverpool crammed with black faces.* One memoir of the city, Pat O'Mara's *Autobiography of a Liverpool Slummy*, 1834, recalled that these men were rather popular with the ladies. Sailors made attractive husbands: they were away a lot, and couldn't blow all their wages on beer. 'Not only were they accepted by white women as equals,' she said of Liverpool's Africans. 'Many times they were regarded as the white man's superior.'[1] Abolition, and the sentimental affection it had inspired, also helped a select handful of African Britons to achieve some degree of prominence. Ira Aldridge was born in America in 1807 and came to the London stage in 1825, where he 'whitened up' to play a string of Shakespearian leading roles – Lear, Macbeth and Shylock. *The Times* was only half impressed: the 'shape of his lips', felt the theatre critic, had an unfavourable effect on his diction. But audiences loved him, especially as Oroonoko, in Thomas Southerne's stage version of Aphra Behn's famous novel. George Bridgetower was one of Europe's leading violinists. He played first fiddle in the Prince of Wales's band for fourteen years, and one of Beethoven's sonatas was originally dedicated to him (before being renamed the Kreutzer). There was even a black Florence Nightingale. Mary Seacole, a 'nurse and doctress', was born in Jamaica, the daughter of a Scottish soldier. Moved by the sufferings of the empire's troops abroad, she applied to and was rejected by every health agency involved with the war effort in the Crimea. So she went under her own

---

*Herman Melville compared the atmosphere favourably to the seething anger of American ports. In Liverpool, he wrote, 'the negro steps with a prouder pace, and lifts his head like a man . . . Three or four times I encountered our black steward, dressed very handsomely, and walking arm in arm with a good-looking English woman. In New York, such a couple would have been mobbed in three minutes, and the steward would have been lucky to escape with whole limbs.'

steam, and was soon running the British Hotel and presiding over the treatment of the wounded. When she returned, the Guards held a dinner and a benefit concert in her honour, and a bust of her was made by Queen Victoria's nephew. To some, perhaps, Florence Nightingale was really the white Mary Seacole.

All of these people moved through a social landscape poisoned by racial ideology. The leading light of the Scottish Enlightenment, David Hume, had displayed some very unenlightened tendencies in the previous century. 'I am apt to suspect the negroes,' he wrote in 1753, 'to be naturally inferior to whites.' Ideas such as this were something new: while foreigners had often been resented, they had not been thought of as categorically different. In the years after Hume, a racial pecking-order was developed with whites at the top (naturally) and blacks at the bottom, just above the animals. Matthew Arnold, Cobbett, Carlyle and Ruskin, among many others, gave resonant intellectual support to this theory over the next hundred and fifty years.

The roots of racism are labyrinthine and elusive, but by the mid-nineteenth century, such ideas were so firmly entrenched that when the 'lower orders' had the audacity to rebel against their 'superiors', Britain bristled with righteous indignation. The Indian Mutiny of 1857 was seen as the worst form of ingratitude against the civilising empire-builders. And a few years later, in 1865, a similar uprising in Jamaica was put down with unprecedented savagery: Governor Edward Eyre executed over four hundred Jamaican men, women and children, flogged hundreds more, and torched a thousand houses in a bitter reprisal against the rebels. Back in England, Eyre was reproached and applauded in equal measure. Darwin, Huxley and Mill agitated to have him censured, and huge crowds roared out their disapproval of his ruthless act. But some very grand intellectuals leapt to the man's support. Carlyle and Ruskin were chairmen of the Governor Eyre Defence Committee, and were joined by Dickens, Tennyson and Kingsley, not to mention 71 peers, 6 bishops, 20 MPs, 40 generals, 26 admirals and 400 clergymen.*

Partly it was the very ease of the imperial conquest which confirmed in the minds of Britons the concept of inferior peoples. At its largest extent, in 1914, the British Empire covered 12.7 million square miles, of which the United Kingdom itself accounted for less than 1 per cent. It was like an ant carrying a coconut. A vast and dispersed population numbering 430 million people was taxed and governed by a single dank island in the east Atlantic. In a specific miracle of administrative zeal, the Indian subcontinent was ruled by fewer than a thousand British civil servants. Surely this 'proved' that white Europeans were born to rule, dark natives born to serve? Of course, such notions were

---

*A parliamentary inquiry found Governor Eyre innocent of any misconduct, and kindly offered to reimburse him for the legal expenses with which he had so unfairly been saddled.

founded on ignorance; but it was of a specific as well as a general kind. As Salman Rushdie has pointed out, the trouble with so much of British history is that it happened out of sight, overseas. Very few people knew what went on in the colonies. They were happy to go along with the contorted logic of racist thinking, which insisted that the subjugated populations were too dim for cerebral work, yet simultaneously capable of fearsome cunning. The British were the barons: the natives were peasants. One of the by-products of this belief was that racial animosity was often indistinguishable from class distaste: the MCC members who harrumphed about uppity wogs in the Punjab queued in the rain to applaud Prince Ranjitsinhji playing the leg glance at Lord's.

Religion, science and philosophy joined hands to offer a new vocabulary for racial antipathy. Architects built neo-Gothic monsters that celebrated an imaginary medieval Utopia. Even poets did their bit: the sublime or trans-cendent possibilities attributed to the English countryside by Wordsworth and Coleridge gave winsome strength to the idea that ours was a blessed, character-building landscape – our ruined cottages and neglected abbeys glowed with virtue. Christian spokesmen argued that imperial rule had a high, solemn, evangelical purpose, introducing heathens to the light while providing exciting career opportunities for British missionaries. Crank anthropologists and phrenologists (the Anthropological Society was founded in 1863) argued that racial hierarchies could be classified by skull measurements, cranial angles and so on. The French anthropologist Gustave le Bon finally gave a 'scientific' stamp to racialist thinking by constructing an evolutionary pyramid, with white Europeans lording it over less-evolved peoples. Some anthropologists announced (ludicrously, but who knew better?) that blacks were closer to apes than they were to whites.

Le Bon's ideas flowed smoothly from Darwin's recently formulated theory of natural selection: life could be seen not just as a contest between individuals, but as a wrangle between races. Minor distinctions of pigment and physiology came to be seen as species differences, and race became an ambiguous word, referring both to the entire human race and to its constituent parts. Linguists and etymologists lent their weight to the cause by establishing the cultural supremacy of Indo-European languages. Animal metaphors ran amok. In 1865 the *Spectator* insisted: 'The negroes are made on purpose to serve the whites, just as the black ants are made on purpose to serve the red.'

Increasingly, Britain defined itself by its superiority to the dusky multitudes over whom it held sway. This led to a legal difficulty. Was the son of a Viceroy who happened to be born in Calcutta not to be considered British? Could the child of a Chinese sailor born in Cardiff honestly be supposed to be Welsh? Soon the idea that Britishness was a matter of descent, not mere birthplace, began to displace the ancient code, in people's minds if not in solicitors' offices. People started thinking of British identity as the product not of geography, not of culture and politics, but a question of breeding, of blood. Britain was a race, and from here it was only a small step to the idea that we were not just any old race, but a race apart. The British character seemed rooted in green fields and hedgerows, chalk downs with sheep nuzzling the springy turf, and shadows lengthening over a beech wood. Victorian landscape art celebrated the beauties of the countryside as a human achievement, a national characteristic – which in one sense it was. But this was a conception of character from which a Jamaican or a Bengali, a Chinese or a Malay would automatically be barred.

British education acquired a stridently patriotic tinge, and drilled a strong sense of national pride into the students. Sensitive souls shrank from such crude indoctrination. In *Imperialism* (1902), J. A. Hobson tried to denounce the 'false ideals and pseudoheroes' spread by such strategies. 'To fasten this base insularity of mind and morals upon the little children of a nation and to call it patriotism', he wrote, 'is as foul an abuse of education as it was possible to conceive.'[2] But by then several generations of British schoolchildren had already been raised on jingoistic tales of valour against the 'Fuzzy Wuzzies'.

Victorian Britain was not a monolith, however: it was a rollicking, free-trading, libertarian creature. Even its politics were contradictory. On the one hand, there was Disraeli, the Jewish-born imperialist, the self-made man who became a confident elitist and prodded Victoria into becoming Empress of India. On the other, there was Gladstone, the humanitarian inheritor of a slave trader's fortune, the born-to-rule grandee who argued nobly (and in vain) for democracy and self-rule in the imperial possessions – notably Ireland. Not everyone clung to the narrow view of national identity. The Revd W. W. Champneys was one of many eager to emphasise the breadth of the national character, which combined 'the bravery of Celts, the enterprise of Danes, the robustness of Saxons, the chivalry of Normans, the steeliness of Romans'.[3] This broad vision relied on a set of well-polished clichés, so his plea has a comic undertow, but it was echoed by others. In *The Conquest of England* (1883), J. R. Green wrote, 'Celt and Gael, Welshman and Irishman, Friesian and Flamand, French Huguenot and German Palatine, have come successively in with a hundred smaller streams of foreign blood . . . The result is that so far as blood goes, few nations are of an origin more mixed than the present English nation; for there is no living Englishman who can say with certainty that the blood of any of the races we have named does not intermingle in his veins.'[4]

In 1867 *The Times* felt able to report the Fenian bomb in Clerkenwell with remarkable equanimity, urging its readers not to jump to any hasty conclusions about the perpetrators. 'The Irish portion of this mixed community is quite as large as any that could call itself pure Saxon,' it thundered. Anglo-Saxon was in any case a 'very vulgar and inaccurate phrase' for a country that was 'a composite of at least a dozen national titles'. It even found room for a resonant principle: 'All nations, the Irish among them, can settle here, work here, win here, fare with the rest and chance it with the rest.'

These were noble sentiments. It was a shame they were so heavily outgunned by ignoble ones. But they were at least in principle supported by the statute book. The social atmosphere might have been poisoned by racism, but Britain remained theoretically open to all-comers. In 1793 Parliament, alarmed by the French Revolution, had passed a resolution that aliens could be expelled during wartime, but otherwise there were no formal restrictions against them. The 1836 Aliens Registration Act was a move to catalogue immigrants, not a device to evict them.

Nevertheless, nineteenth-century Britain was not a good place to be dark-skinned or foreign. 'Foreigners', declared the *Truth* magazine in 1893, 'are in fact deceitful, effeminate, irreligious, immoral, unclean and unwholesome.'[5] The John Bull image of Britain as a white Anglo-Saxon inheritance by now had deep roots. It was an awkward time for a new generation to arrive. But one was on the way. Far to the east, the pogroms of late-Tsarist Russia were propelling leaking argosies full of Jewish refugees into the Baltic sea lanes. They were heading for Britain, and they could scarcely have imagined, sure as they were of what they needed to escape, quite what lay ahead of them.

CHAPTER 15

The Jewish Evacuees

In 1878, a young man called Michael Marks left Slonim, the small town in Polish Russia where his father was a tailor, and joined the growing exodus of Jews who were evacuating an area rendered increasingly fraught by the Tsar's anti-Semitic spasms. He was nineteen. He landed in Hartlepool with little English, and less money. He signed up for a pedlar's pack and stalked the northern shires, arriving in Leeds, via Stockton, in 1884. There he became a grander sort of pedlar – a sales rep for Isaac Dewhirst, a clothing entrepreneur with a reputation for employing refugees. Dewhirst lent his young visitor five pounds to get him started, and soon Marks had saved enough to pay for his own pitch, a trestle in the open market at Kirkgate, twice a week. In 1886 he married Hannah Cohen, whom he had met in Stockton, and in the same year hired a permanent stall in the new covered market in Leeds. He sold all sorts – nails, screws, pins, needles, buttons, soap, anything handy – and to save time haggling, and to simplify the accounts, he came up with a bold marketing slogan: 'Don't ask the price,' said the hoarding over his stall. 'It's a penny.' It was a brilliant move – goods flew off the trestle as fast as he could pile them up – and it inspired an equally effective business strategy: his role was simply to come up with goods that could be profitably retailed at that price.

He was not slow to see that he was on to a good thing. He opened similar penny bazaars in Warrington, Birkenhead, Wigan, Bolton and Manchester, before realising that he needed help to run such a widespread operation. He tried to engage Dewhirst as a partner, but his old benefactor declined. So he joined forces with Dewhirst's cashier, Thomas Spencer. It was 1894, and a great

British chain – Marks & Spencer – was born. By 1903 there were forty shops across northern England; four years later (by which time Spencer had died) there were sixty. But it was hard work, and the effort caught up with Marks: he died in 1907, at the age of forty-eight. It was left to his son Simon to canonise the founder as St Michael, stitching his name into the labels of the firm's V-necks and the fabric of the nation.

It is a classic immigrant parable, literally a journey from rags to riches. And Marks was not unique. Isaac Moses and his brother, dominant figures in the Houndsditch clothes market (they included among their clients the deposed King of France), were able to turn their rag-and-bone business into an elite formal couturier which later became better known as Moss Bros. Montague Ossinsky, meanwhile, came to England from Lithuania a few years after Michael Marks. He was just fifteen when he left the house of his father, a Jewish bookseller, and made his way to England. He soon found work in a shop in Chesterfield. In 1904 he changed his name to Burton, and five years later moved to Sheffield, where he started to trade in ready-to-wear men's clothing. Traditional tailoring had not moved with the times: it still clung to its old bespoke credo – one man, one suit – and seemed not to have noticed the emergence of a middle class that wanted affordable off-the-peg designs. Within a year Burton had shops in Chesterfield, Manchester, Leeds and Mansfield. In 1913 he was joined by his younger brother, and the firm became Burton & Burton of Leeds. In 1921 it expanded by buying a rival concern, Albrecht and Albrecht, and by 1925 was the biggest retail empire in Europe, with three hundred shops and a workforce of over five thousand. It was an unmissable part of the national decor: there was a Burtons in every high street, all with the same classy bronze lettering engraved on cool marble, surrounded by reliable stonework. Inside, the shops (which by 1939 numbered six hundred) were gentlemanly – Scottish granite and oak. 'Let Burton dress you,' said the slogan – and millions did. The new factories in Lancashire employed twenty thousand on the eve of the Second World War, and the company operated at every level: as manufacturer, distributor and retailer. During the war, it provided 13.5 million items of military uniform for the British army, a quarter of the total demand – indeed it is rumoured that the saying 'Gone for a Burton' was a jocular reference to the sticky end to which many of these clothes were doomed.

Unlike St Michael, Sir Montague (he was knighted in 1939) lived to enjoy the fruits of his success. He endowed chairs at universities in Leeds, Cardiff, Cambridge, London, Edinburgh, Oxford and Jerusalem. A Zionist, he was active at both the League of Nations and the UN.

Marks, Moses and Burton were members of a Jewish flight from the Baltic and Eastern Europe that was transforming the world. America was the destination of their dreams, but not everyone could afford or face so long a journey. Britain was nearer, and it also had an established Jewish population into whose embrace a frightened refugee might fall. It would prove to be more than a transit lounge on the journey to the New World.

Predators had been circling Russia's Jews ever since the partition of Poland in 1772 delivered a large Semitic population into the rough hands of the Tsar. In 1816 Tsar Alexander announced that the 'Yids' were responsible for every iniquity suffered by the noble Russian peasants – they were 'leeches', he said* – and this was only the first in a series of increasingly harsh blows. In 1866 there was a cholera epidemic in Russian Poland, and famine in Lithuania: many fled. In 1869 the emancipated Jews of Habsburg Galicia took advantage of their new freedom by hot-footing it out of there. And as vicious pogroms – side-effects of the Tsarist plan to herd all Russia's Jews into the area called the 'Pale' in western Russia – grew in intensity, there was an even more furious rush to escape. The only Jews permitted to work 'beyond the Pale' were prostitutes: they were issued with a yellow card by way of a pass, which led to baleful instances of young women posing as whores in order to work as secretaries or seamstresses, and then being prosecuted for abandoning their approved profession.

Eastern European governments seemed to be competing with one another over who could most mistreat the Jews. In 1886 Bismarck expelled 'alien Poles' (i.e. Jews) from Prussia. The Russians responded by banishing Jews from Moscow in 1890. In 1900 some three thousand Jews left Romania and walked west, crossing Europe by foot until they arrived on British soil.

The Board of Guardians for the Relief of the Jewish Poor, set up in London in 1859, had little idea that it would soon have its hands so full. Thousands streamed ashore each week and swelled the throng in the rotten no-go areas by the docks. Between 1881 and 1914 some 150,000 Jewish settlers came to Britain for good. This was in spite of the Board of Guardians' attempts to stem the flow. In 1886 the Board issued the following request: 'We beseech every right-thinking person among our brethren in Germany, Russia and Austria to place a barrier to the flow of foreigners.'

This did not stop them from braving the perils of the journey. Documents had to be bought or forged, policemen had to be bribed, borders had to be sneaked across at night. In 1888 Myer Wilchinski told a House of Commons committee that his own evacuation had been relatively easy, since he had sufficient money to buy off the officials who blocked his path. But it was still

---

*In Russia, anti-Semitism might have been to some extent class-hatred in disguise. Certainly, the harsh blow of conscription, with its implication of near-certain death, fell mainly on the poor. Rich Jews were exempted, as the following subversive lyric noted:

> It is right to draft the hardworking masses
> Shoemakers or tailors – they're only asses!
> But the children of the idle rich
> Must carry on without a hitch.

a nerve-tingling nocturnal adventure until he was finally able, with 'a few more bits of silver', to slip across the frontier into Prussia. And then he had to face the predators hovering above the crowd at the docks – ticket swindlers, bogus recruitment officers, luggage thieves and muggers – before boarding a ship at Hamburg. The crossing was overcrowded and filthy. A reporter from the *Evening News and Post* made the trip in 1891 and found himself aboard a floating hovel packed with men and women 'so enfeebled that one might have fixed their age at nearer seventy than thirty'. Below decks, where the Jewish evacuees were jammed together like cattle, the air was dark and poisonous: 'the horrors of the place were increased by the accumulation of filth, which had taken place by the ever-increasing indisposition of the passengers the longer we were at sea'. The Jews were not nautical, and many were heartily seasick. Quite a few changed their minds about undertaking the much longer trip west to America: they didn't want to stay on a boat a minute longer than they had to.

Beatrice Webb, surveying the new ghetto in Charles Booth's *Life and Labour of the People in London* (1889), watched these ship-weary souls arrive, and wept on their behalf. 'For a few moments it is a scene of indescribable confusion,' she wrote. 'Cries and counter-cries; the hoarse laughter of the dock loungers at the strange garb and broken accent of the poverty-stricken foreigners; the rough swearing of the boatmen at passengers unable to pay the fee for landing. In another ten minutes eighty of the hundred newcomers are dispersed in the back slums of Whitechapel; in another few days the majority of these, robbed of the little they possess, are turned out of the free lodgings destitute and friendless.'[1]

The scale and speed of this disembarkation took everyone by surprise: all at once, whole areas of London, Hull and Manchester were distinctly un-British enclaves. Jewish elders overcame their centuries-old reluctance to show their hand in public. Nathan Adler, the Chief Rabbi, called the new arrivals 'unfortunates who have come here to seek rest', and a Jewish bureaucracy was fully mobilised to help. 'There are many', warned Adler, 'who believe that all the cobblestones of London are precious stones, and that it is the place of gold. Woe and alas, it is not so.'[2] Jewish organisations began a major fundraising effort under the slogan 'Giving without a Murmur'. This action was not entirely altruistic: it was motivated also by a fear that the vast unwashed crowd of newcomers could rock what by then had become quite a steady boat.* This was a fear with ample historical precedent. Anti-Semitism had been inscribed in the British character since medieval times, and earlier in the nineteenth century had found plenty of lofty adherents. In *Ivanhoe* (1819) Walter Scott had the grace,

---

*Even Karl Marx did not have much sympathy for these people, or at least their parents. 'The Jews of Poland', he wrote in 1849, 'are the smeariest of all races.'

when describing the 'obstinacy and avarice' of Isaac of York, to point out that such qualities had grown in response to the 'fanaticism and tyranny' under which all Jews had for centuries been obliged to live. But they were, he felt, 'watchful, suspicious and timid – yet obstinate, uncomplying and skilful in evading the dangers to which they were exposed'. This counts as almost charitable in the light of the harsher feelings that would soon displace this caricature. 'The Jews of the lower orders', said Samuel Taylor Coleridge, 'are the very lowest of mankind; they have not a principle of honesty in them; to grasp and be getting money for ever is their single and exclusive occupation.' This is not some tap-room rabble-rouser – it is the author of 'Frost at Midnight', a man who could weep perfect quatrains over the death of a bird.

As the *Jewish Chronicle* nervously put it: 'The letters which spell "exclusion" are not very different from those which spell "expulsion".' Another, more radical Jewish newspaper urged its readers to adopt a low profile: 'Jews, look about while there is yet time!' it cried. 'A pogrom in Brick Lane, at the crossroads of Commercial Road, can be more terrible, bloodier than a pogrom in Balta.'[3] If anything, this made the fearful migrants even more inclined to seek safety in numbers, and they were the opposite of expansive: they huddled together in crowded courts and cottages in central urban areas – behind the docks in London, in the Leylands of Leeds or Strangeways in Manchester.

Some of them took the now-traditional first step and became pedlars. Others became itinerant glaziers, pacing the streets with a box full of glass on their backs, heads craned up in search of broken panes. The rag fair at Petticoat Lane grew into an enormous market, and there was plenty of edgy jostling for pitches. East London's street stalls mushroomed and swelled. At Columbia Road and Sclater Street, the old Huguenot favourites – plants and birds – found an enthusiastic new clientele. Canaries, goldfinches and pigeons were trawled in from Essex and distributed in London, to bring a little touch of country sap and music to the city. Of course, these markets looked, to a passer-by, unruly and squalid, and, since they were happy to trade on Sundays, also heretical.

The Jewish neighbourhoods swiftly evolved a striking new appearance: black hats, long hair, beards, Yiddish signs above the shops, snatches of strange (to the bewildered locals) foreign music from upstairs rooms and kosher butchers. They were, in other words, distinctive and isolated, clustered as they were around the 'hebrot' – small, independent religious societies oblivious to the wider world. To worried Jewish leaders, they seemed to present an easy target for British scorn. In 1880, the *Jewish Chronicle* stated, 'They have no right to isolate themselves from their English co-religionists. They should hasten to assimilate themselves completely.' The following year, the paper repeated itself: 'If they intend to remain in England, if they wish to become members of our community, we have a right to demand that they will show signs of an earnest wish for a complete amalgamation with the aims and feelings of their hosts.' It was a combustible state of affairs and something had to be done. In 1887 Samuel Montagu (by now Lord Swaythling), along with the banker Hermann Landau and the clothing contractor Mark Moses, managed to combine these tiny units into one federation: some 110 synagogues joined, with 16,000 members. But there was a tussle for power over this expatriate congregation: Lord Rothschild and Isaac Goldsmid created their own consortium, the United Synagogue, and the two organisations embarked on a long and sometimes disputatious rivalry.

Jewish bodies strove to persuade Yiddish speakers to learn English. When a baker called Simon Becker set up a shelter in London in 1885, some influential Jewish figures wanted it closed down, since 'such a harbour of refuge must tend to invite helpless foreigners to this country, and therefore was not a desirable institution to exist'. The *Jewish Chronicle* couldn't have agreed more. 'They must either earn their own living without charity,' it said of the helpless evacuees, 'or return to the land whence they came.' Two prominent Anglo-Jews, Frederic Mocatta and Lionel Alexander, visited the shelter and pronounced it unhygienic, and the Board of Guardians forced it to close.

Montagu and Landau financed a refuge in Leman Street. It was called the Poor Jews Temporary Shelter, and it would become a pivotal clearing house for the new arrivals, who could obtain a bed and two meals a day, for a maximum of two weeks: guests who could afford to were expected to pay. No one wanted word to get out that there really was such a thing as a free lunch. The shelter assisted up to four thousand migrants each year.

Still the boatloads came, six ships a week from the Baltic in the 1890s, and not just to London. A huge fire in Lithuanian Kottingen in 1889 provoked the evacuation of an entire community to Sunderland. Commercial competition was enlarging the market by lowering the price: there was a price war on the North Atlantic crossing and fares fell by 70 per cent to just two pounds. There had never been a better time to take the plunge. But what a plunge it was. Boarding houses sent scouts to the pier to escort clueless newcomers to their rotten lodgings, where they could be charged high rent and duped into surrendering what little cash they might have with them. Some were fleeced the moment they stepped off their ships in Hull or London, by thieves posing as porters or guides. Some stepped ashore convinced that they had landed in America – victims of dodgy ticket salesmen. This was a distressing first glimpse of Britain. 'Robbery and chicanery', warned the *Jewish Chronicle*, 'is quite as active in London as on the Russian frontier.'

Women were especially at risk: up to a thousand each year, at the peak of the upheaval, were seduced away from the docks by suave charmers who promised them refuge, before raping them and imprisoning them in a life of prostitution from which escape was almost impossible. The trade was well organised: sex agents in Russia made tidy profits by tricking girls on to boats bound for London, Bombay or Buenos Aires. Sometimes the girls were married to plausible young blades who would sell their 'wives' to a brothel the moment they reached the promised land. The English police were not much interested: the scoundrels were often themselves Jewish, and the authorities did not see it as their business to intervene. The Poor Jews Temporary Shelter sent its own agents to the quayside to undermine the 'sharks and crimps' who hunted there. Another agency – the Jewish Association for the Protection of Girls – was created to see off the pimps and hustlers at Tilbury.

The voyager who made it safely to the East End found much that was familiar: synagogues, cemeteries, Russian vapour baths and Jewish shops. The new arrivals jostled for work, money and advancement, and quickly built a ghetto with its own institutions and commerce, its own cultural and religious life, its own ups and downs. There were Jewish theatres and music halls, Jewish publishers and booksellers, Jewish tobacconists and jewellers – a complete community-in-exile. It was even possible to see signs advertising rooms for rent with the unusual proviso: 'No Christians need apply'. On the corners of Whitechapel, you could lay bets with Jewish bookmakers while chewing on Warsaw sausage, salt beef or *gefilte* fish, with perhaps a bagel or a strudel on the side. The heights achieved by Marks and Burton were a remote fantasy for these people. Most of the new immigrants were mired in a much tougher world. Girls would make matches in winter at the huge Bryant & May works in Wapping, and jam in Millwall in the summer from strawberries carted in from Kent. But by far the most vivid feature of this new commercial landscape was the sweatshop. It was nothing new, but it suited exiled Jews rather well, and they seized on and perfected it. Rather than seeking employment on the General Labour Exchange (difficult for people who spoke little English), new arrivals could join tiny clothing contractors in basements or lofts. It wasn't much – it might even be ghastly, if you ended up mashing rabbit pelts into imitation-mink coats – but it was better than nothing. Jewish entrepreneurs had it made: they could take advantage of the lavish supply of cheap and desperate labour which staggered off the ships every day. The earlier generation of Jewish pedlars had established a foothold in the second-hand clothes business, and built large markets in Houndsditch and Petticoat Lane. Now they stepped up a rung, and created a network of tiny, cut-throat tailoring concerns which could turn out clothes more cheaply than had ever been thought possible.

These Jewish enterprises could keep the Sabbath sacrosanct, which solved the difficulty many Jews faced in jobs that required them to work on Saturdays. The sweatshops ran on Sundays instead, arousing the annoyance of British rivals, who lobbied for strict Sunday-trading laws largely to prevent the Jews from snaffling up business when everyone else was closed. An impromptu Jewish Labour Exchange sprang up on the Whitechapel Road: men and women would huddle there while employers picked out who they needed. It was, said one scornful Home Office report, a 'pig market . . . You will see masters (you will recognise dealers at once by their gross bellies) scurrying about like poisoned mice among the dishevelled men.' One Jewish tailor recalled the crowd of blighted faces with bitterness: 'Many of them like myself, "greeners" willing to work at anything that would bring them the scantiest means of existence; some married and with families, and all with that enquiring, beseeching look that half-starved, helpless hopeless beings must of necessity possess . . . The majority looked like so many unwashed corpses.'[4]

The world of sweated labour was hideous. The little textile shops lay outside the scope of factory regulations, and they were rough places. Nor were they charities: hands were hired, exploited and fired purely according to demand. Masters would pay newcomers an insignificant apprentice wage, but when the apprenticeship was completed they often found it cheaper to cut loose the qualified man and take on another desperate trainee. They were free-wheeling and aggressive business units which relied on a strict and highly competitive division of labour: one house would prepare leather for shoes, another would cut out the uppers and soles, another would stitch them together, another would close and finish them. It was called 'outwork', and it was a production line without a factory floor, turning out low-cost clothes at ultra-high speed. The work was so sporadic that most trained workers were lucky if they worked two or three days a week, which put them on or below the breadline.

A labour-saving Jewish invention helped the entrepreneurs if not the workers: Isaac Singer's sewing-machine (he was part of the same exodus, but developed his revolutionary device in America, before retiring to Dorset) was purpose-built for such a market. There was a booming retail trade in 'cheap elegancies' – the working man now aspired to something smarter than rags – and if the hard work could be done by packs of foreigners no one cared about, well, so much the better. Beatrice Webb's investigation found over a thousand such workshops in east London, most of which made coats, and nearly all of which had fewer than a dozen labourers. There were another thousand in Manchester, where looms shuttled to and fro in bigger, smarter houses than could be found in Whitechapel. Smaller industries clacked away in Liverpool, Glasgow, Birmingham, Hull and Newcastle.

They were textile dynamos, flexible and responsive to the smallest whim of fashion. They created a ready-to-wear industry in a Britain that till then had relied on German imports. They were also filthy and unstable. In London they had colonised the once-grand multi-storey houses built by successful Huguenot families, and had divided them into tiny hutches which hummed with activity round the clock. 'At all hours of the day and night', reported the *Lancet* in 1884, 'the street resounds with the rattle and whir of the innumerable sewing machines, the windows shine with the flare of gas.' Individual firms might rise or fall – workers tried their luck as masters by setting up their own rooms, only to sink back into the queue of labourers again – but the system as a whole thrived, at least for a time. Men and women toiled ceaselessly in hot, steam-filled rooms, their heads surrounded by dust, threads of cotton and wool, and fumes from dyes, glues, and the gas used to light the dim cellars.

Some were blatantly enslaved: Lewis Lyons, an early Jewish trade unionist, wrote articles deploring the captive conditions in which nine-year-old Jewish girls were shackled to the machines, turning out neat new tennis aprons for the ladies of Surrey and Sussex. But this was a desperate last gasp of semi-slavery: newer, larger factories with the most modern steam-powered machines were ushering in the age of mass production. The sweatshops' days were numbered. (Although the practice would be energetically revived by a later generation of Bangladeshi settlers in the area.)

The new Chief Rabbi, Hermann Adler, refused to denounce the trade, claiming that, while ugly, it was not as bad as the alternative: starving. But among the thirty thousand Jews in London in 1890 was a new, radicalised generation. These recent settlers refused to take so timid a view, and a few of them formed an energetic circle of political agitation. To them, sweating was a blatant expression of capitalism at its most pitiless, and they worked hard to provoke sentiment against it.

Aaron Liebermann had come to London as a student in 1875, after dropping out of his studies at the St Petersburg Institute of Technology. As with many of the restricted number of Jews permitted to pursue further education, he had learned enough to become a revolutionary. He was as alienated from his own Jewish culture as he was from the capitalist plutocracy. The Jews, he ventured, were 'a parasite class'; Yiddish was nothing more than a badge of slavery. He himself spoke several languages and was able to earn a living in London writing articles on behalf of 'the oppressed masses'. Within a year he had organised the Hebrew Socialist Society, which urged workers to organise and resist.* Unsurprisingly, the Jewish authorities flinched: noisy protests were the last thing they wanted, and they quietly persuaded Liebermann to take his ideas off to New York (where he committed suicide in 1880).

His place was taken by his friend Morris Winchevsky, a literary figure who had trained as a priest in Lithuania before converting to radical atheism, and now worked at the Seligman Bank in the City. He started a Yiddish newspaper,

---

*Five of the founders were tailors; they were joined by a milliner and a cabinetmaker. They pledged in their manifesto to besiege 'the system . . . As long as there is private ownership, economic misery will not cease.' In the event, they spent perhaps more time than Liebermann intended discussing the thorny issue of the trouser-pedlars who might technically be thought of as mini-capitalists on the make, and who therefore could not be admitted to the society.

the *Polish Yidel*, which later became *Die Tsukunft*. In 1885 he launched a monthly magazine, the *Arbeiter Freind* (Worker's Friend), which pledged to 'change entirely the present order of tyranny and injustice . . . the workers must unite and organise themselves'. From his office in Commercial Street, he churned out articles on the poor conditions that were ensnaring Jewish workers. Many of these pieces dramatised the struggle of the 'greener', the newcomer struggling to find his feet in the cut-throat labour market of east London. Sometimes the magazine scolded Jews for refusing to stand up to the tyranny of overwork and poor pay: 'What good is talk when Jewish workers are complaisant and smug and nothing perturbs them?' At other times it collected evidence of English anti-Semitism and warned readers to be on their guard. Always, it repeated the mantras of early communism. This was bold talk, an early vibration of the raw ideal ('Workers of the world, unite!') that would soon burst upon Europe. It brought a characteristic Jewish dimension to Britain's often somnolent political discourse, being more Utopian and ideological than native protests, which sought not to change the world but merely to secure better pay and conditions.

Winchevsky's group of thinkers and schemers met at 40 Berner Street in the East End, and soon became known as the 'Berner Streeters'. William Morris was a frequent visitor. They were ambitious not just to improve the lot of London's Jews but to alter the social injustice that plagued all working-class Londoners. 'Jewish happiness', insisted the *Arbeiter Freind* in 1888, 'will come only with the happiness of all unhappy workers . . . Jewish emancipation must come with the general emancipation of humanity.' This was heady stuff, and when, in 1889, a march led by a German band waving banners on behalf of 'Jewish Unemployed and Sweaters' Victims' was confronted by fifty policemen at the Great Synagogue, the *Jewish Chronicle* felt bound to disown them. 'It becomes our duty to declare that they are not Jews,' it railed. That night, the Berner Street club was destroyed in a brawl between the police and rival revolutionary groups.

A good part of this radical Jewish energy addressed itself to specifically Judaic concerns: those who wished to change the world had to start somewhere. One favourite target was the wealthy MP Samuel Montagu, who himself, while backing almost every philanthropic Jewish agency in town, hated the young ideologues: 'the influence of a few Atheists over Jewish working men can no longer be ignored,' he said in 1889. Three years later, a group of political agitators sat on the steps of a synagogue on Yom Kippur, provocatively eating ham sandwiches and sparking a riot which became known as the Battle of the Ghetto. Montagu was right: many Jewish workers were inspired by such calls to arms. They saw men like him not as helpful paternalists but as gloating exploiters, and Jewish London had fast become one of the boiler-rooms of international socialism. The first thing Lewis Smith did, when he came to London in 1872 after spells in Poland and France, was to found a Lithuanian tailors' union in Whitechapel.

His was the first of many. In 1896 there were a dozen small Jewish trade unions; in 1902 there were thirty-two. Individually they had little power. One, the Jewish Boot Finishers' Society, tried to strike in support of its claim for an extra penny per pair of boots, but the wholesaler simply found another supplier willing to fulfil orders at the existing rate. Solidarity was not a potent Jewish force. Indeed, when in 1889 some ten thousand so-called tailors (i.e. sweated labourers) went on strike and demanded a twelve-hour day (with one and a half hours for meals), the community was divided. Lofty figures such as Montagu and the Rothschilds donated funds to support the strikers, and thousands turned out on the rallies that marched through Hackney. But others thought it bad form. Just as Jewish socialists blamed Jewish capitalists for the low esteem in which the whole community was held, so bourgeois Jews dissociated themselves from such radical criticisms of mainstream society. The *Jewish Chronicle* was firm. 'It is questionable policy on the part of poor foreigners', it said, 'to give an exaggerated idea of their numbers by parading through London, and thus excite further prejudice against their entire body.' The strike didn't end until Montagu brokered a deal: hours would be reduced in return for a no-strike pledge. Montagu, still being satirised as a capitalist tyrant in the *Arbeiter Freind*, called it 'the happiest day of my life'.[5]

Between 1870 and 1901 there were various Factory Acts, which eventually set a limit of twelve hours (including meal breaks) on the working day (half a century after the Chartists had begged for such a rule). But the inspections were not very stringent. One official toured a sweatshop, found a maze of burst pipes, blocked toilets and filthy rags and reported that conditions were 'very good'. The regulations also had unforeseen drawbacks: many women still worked twelve-hour days, but were paid for only ten and a half, the legal maximum.

The Utopian, rebellious streak in Jewish London found an unusual leader in Rudolf Rocker, a Catholic German activist who learned Yiddish out of sympathy for a people he saw as typifying the victimised masses. Rocker was born in the Rhineland in 1873 and felt the full force of Prussian authority when, at the age of ten, he became an orphan – a child of the state. His father had been a typographer, and Rocker too had a literary sensibility, which expressed itself in a romantic love of underground philosophy. In 1893, banished from the Rhine valley, he attended a Jewish anarchist club in Paris, and was smitten: men and women freely mingling, engaged in exciting discussions about modern life and its injustices – this was his ideal milieu. Once in London, he became librarian at the Communist Workers' Educational Union and began to explore the strange Jewish world to the east. 'Could anything spiritual grow on these dung-heaps?'[6] he wondered, after a tour of Tower Hamlets. He moved to Shoreditch in search of the answer. There he met a slim young woman called

Millie Witkop, who was selling copies of the *Arbeiter Freind*. She was only eighteen, but had already earned enough money in appalling sweatshops to pay for her parents and sisters to follow her to England. When she subsequently accompanied Rocker on a trip to America, they made headlines by travelling as a pair of free lovers who had declined to marry. 'When love ceases to be free', said Witkop, 'it is prostitution', a statement guaranteed, if not calculated, to put the couple on the front pages. New York reacted with surprising prudishness: it put them straight back on the boat to England.

Rocker became editor of a Yiddish weekly in Liverpool until, in 1898, he returned to London as editor of the *Arbeiter Freind*, for which he wrote twenty-five articles on historical materialism – among the first Yiddish critiques of Marx's ideas ever published. Once again Britain, still a triumphant capitalist–imperialist force in the world, was able to give an admittedly shaky platform to Europe's most radical political impulse.* If you peeked over the top of your Yiddish magazine in one of the anarchist clubs or pubs, you might even have seen a small man sitting in the corner taking notes: his name was Vladimir Ilyich Ulyanov. Soon he would change it to Lenin.

In 1903 Rocker led demonstrations against the latest pogroms in Russia. Some 25,000 people shuffled into Hyde Park to hear speeches deploring the massacres. Rocker toured Leeds, Glasgow and Edinburgh, appealing for a united Jewish revolt against iniquities closer to home. He was tall, blond, handsome, energetic and a bold speaker on everything from class war and theology to Shakespeare and Beethoven. 'He united us,' said one disciple. 'Rocker was our rabbi!' The leaders of traditional Judaism in Britain were less impressed.

In October 1904, the *Evening Standard* – a sparky new paper with a mission to sensationalise – offered its readers an alarming picture of where these people lived. It was all gloomy alleys and stealthy footsteps running through patches of shadow, with fleeting echoes of strange passwords and shards of foreign vocabulary. Here you might find the 'thin' Galician, the 'foxy-looking' Lithuanian, the 'restless' Pole and the 'muddled-headed' German. In their boozy clubs designed to 'tempt poor flies into the trap' the architects of future unrest sat drinking and gambling – 'too lazy to work, they find in the mischievous propaganda they spread a capital means of bringing grist to their own particular mills'. The article ended with a dig at the supposed hypocrisy of these malign beasts. 'They spend night after night in the haunts mentioned and the card rooms that abound in the neighbourhood, gambling away the last coin that should have gone to their underfed wives and children, and returning home to rave afresh against society and the iniquities of those who do not go and do likewise.'

---

*'London, or England', Aaron Liebermann declared, 'is the only place where we Socialists can operate openly.'

This was a fanciful and loaded picture, a good example of the common tendency to build prejudices against an entire community by emphasising its most vivid strand. But it chimed with the first impressions of many outsiders, who looked on London's new ghetto with anguish. Whitechapel, it was said, had become a 'new Jerusalem', teeming with vicious and angry rejects from the rest of Europe. When Jack the Ripper embarked on his grisly series of slaughters, public opinion was quick to assume that he must be one of those pitiless ruffian Jews.*

Those who examined the ghetto more closely, however, found a somewhat different story, a tale of thriftiness, good sense and stoic resolve. In 1896 Henry Walker visited Whitechapel with the intention of writing a religious tract about the squalor of heathen life, but found to his surprise that 'this great and squalid colony is a peaceful and law-abiding population ... the Jew is never intoxicated'. And the Booth Report of 1889 stated that 'the children of Israel are the most law-abiding inhabitants of East London. They keep the peace, they pay their debts, and they abide by their contracts; practices in which they are undoubtedly superior to the English and Irish labourers among whom they dwell.'[7] Booth's writer Beatrice Webb was amazed by the furious ambition of the people she saw: 'The Jew is unique in possessing neither a minimum nor a maximum; he will accept the lowest terms rather than remain out of employment; as he rises in the world new wants stimulate him to increase intensity of effort.' Another pair of social investigators, Russell and Lewis, reported in *The Jew in London* (1900) that immigrants set a far higher store by education than the natives. 'They sometimes lament', they wrote, 'that *englische kinder* – i.e. children brought up in England – are inferior to those educated abroad. The zeal of Jewish parents for their children's advancement is very noticeable. For this end they will make every sacrifice.'

This was not the English way, and the Trades Union Congress of 1894 had listed as one of its grudges against cut-price Jewish workers the fact that they were willing to work for fifteen hours a day on nothing more than 'cold coffee and bread and cheese'. The sweatshops were easy to dislike. Displaced workers, resentful of the sharp competition in the labour market, found common cause with idealistic liberals, who saw the sweatshops as ugly expressions of unrefined capitalism. But the alternative view was put by the Aliens Commission Report of 1903: 'The development of the three main industries – tailoring, cabinet-making and shoemaking – in which the aliens engage has undoubtedly been beneficial in various ways; it has increased the demand for and the manufacture of not only goods made in this country (which were formerly imported from abroad) but of the materials used in them, this

*Although no anti-Semitic mob went hunting for the culprit, as might well have been the case if the murders had occurred in Berlin or Vienna.

indirectly giving employment to native workers.' The myth that Jews were stealing British jobs was undermined by the boom in many ancillary trades – textiles, tools, dyes, buttons, needles. The expansion of the garment business was also a job-creation scheme for non-Jews.

Like many immigrants, the Jews initially occupied a lower rung of the social ladder than the one they had occupied in Eastern Europe. But this meant they were better equipped to scramble upwards than the long-suffering Anglo-Irish proletariat, who anyway had minimal expectations of life. This was the sunless, joyless world explored by Jack London in his brief and pungent masterpiece, *The People of the Abyss*. Disguising himself as a tramp and taking to the streets, London shared his bread (and the occasional coin secreted in his shoe) with the rough, dispirited men he ran into at hostels and shelters. At one point he eavesdropped on a conversation about these bleeding foreigners.

> 'But 'ow about this 'ere cheap immigration?' one man demands. 'The Jews of Whitechapel, say, a-cutting our throats right along?'
> 'You can't blame them,' was the answer. 'They're just like us, and they've got to live. Don't blame the man who offers to work cheaper than you and gets your job. He can't help it. Wages always come down when two men are after the same job. That's the fault of competition, not of the man who cuts the price.'[8]

To Jack London, the condition of the poor, stuck in 'the abyss', was a crime against humanity. The contrast between the unprecedented wealth of west London and the unprecedented squalor of its eastern quarter was savage. He was strident in his desire to enlighten anyone who thought that the capital's beggars were somehow taking the easy option. 'It is softer to work for twenty shillings a week, and have regular food, and a bed at night, than it is to walk the streets,' he wrote. 'The man who walks the streets suffers more, and works harder, for far less return.'

All of this was many miles away from the stereotype of the Jew as an international money-man. But the stereotype stuck. The same Jews who were hated as misers could also be castigated as inveterate, feckless gamblers who hung around pubs betting on horses and cards with their last penny. Morris Winchevsky captured this latter tendency in a plaintive lyric, narrating the plight of a sickly child waiting for her father to come home. But he is:

> In another room,
> Dirty and small,
> In a fine house,
> Full of Jews.

Wages and silver watch gone,
Whilst sitting by a table
Both lost in cards.[9]

This Jewish commune found its most eloquent spokesman in Israel Zangwill. Born in east London in 1864 – a 'Jewish cockney' – to immigrants from Latvia and Poland, he went to the Jews' Free School in Spitalfields, did well there and stayed on as a teacher. He was thus well placed to describe the members of the mass migration ('humble products of a great and terrible past') from Eastern Europe to the new docklands ghetto. In a series of successful novels and plays he opened people's eyes to an entirely new world. His work triumphed on both sides of the Atlantic. One of his plays, a parable of assimilation set in New York called *The Melting Pot*, contributed a resilient phrase to the English lexicon. A noted humorist (he collaborated with Jerome K. Jerome), he wrote stern philosophical dramas – *The War God* was a tense dispute between Bismarck and Tolstoy – alongside drawing-room comedies. His intention, he once said, was to subvert 'the conception of a Jew as a mixture of Fagin, Shylock and Rothschild', but he did more than that. In his most celebrated novel, *Children of the Ghetto*, he captured the garrulous tumult of immigrant life. Early on, the heroine, Esther, walks through Whitechapel to the soup kitchen: 'A female street-singer, with a trail of infants of dubious maternity, troubled the air with a piercing melody; a pair of slatterns with arms akimbo reviled each other's relatives; a drunkard lurched along, babbling amiably; an organ-grinder, blue-nosed as his monkey, set some ragged children jigging under the watery rays of a streetlamp.'[10]

Late in life, Zangwill lived in Sussex (walks on the Downs, with ponies for the children) and pursued liberal causes: he was vice-president of the Men's League for Women's Suffrage and an active Zionist – H. G. Wells called him 'the champion of the Jewish race'. But his plays began to fail, and his books fell out of print fast as the society he described faded from view. Those still-crowded streets have become home to new populations of immigrants from even further afield, who have plied the same trades – textiles, leather, food – suffered the same insults, and experienced many of the same clashes between material ambition and spiritual pride. Perhaps things don't change quite as much as we think.

Somehow, the community described in Zangwill's novels sweated its way towards commercial salvation. It elbowed its way out of the East End of London towards Ilford and Redbridge, or north to Stamford Hill and Golder's Green. In Manchester, it clambered up Cheetham Hill, planting synagogues to mark its ascent. A few Jewish words – such as 'nosh', from the Yiddish word for a snack – wormed their way into the cockney idiom. And Jewish businessmen began to tread confidently in English boardrooms. If Jewish peddling gave us

Marks & Spencer, and the Jewish rag trade gave us Burton's and Moss Bros, then Jewish street trading in east London threw up Jack Cohen.

He was born in the East End in 1898 and worked as a child in a sweatshop. In 1915 he escaped by joining the Royal Flying Corps, and after the war was a notoriously noisy trader – 'I'm not asking for five! I'm not asking for four! Three shillings the lot!' – in a street market. Eventually his stall, like that of Michael Marks, turned into a shop. It was called the Tea and Soap Company. 'Pile 'em high,' urged Cohen, 'and sell 'em cheap.' Perhaps the piles were so high that they obscured some of the letters on the sign – before long, Cohen's company became Tesco. The truth was more prosaic. Cohen went into partnership with T. E. Stockwell, and it was the initial letters of their names that inspired the famous logo. Still, he stuck cheerfully to the stereotype of Jewish shopkeeping – 'Always keep your hand on the money and be ready to run!' – and opened Britain's first supermarket in 1956. He was knighted in 1969. His daughter, Shirley Porter, became a controversial mayor of Westminster.

Other Jewish immigrants who hauled themselves out of the ghetto included Jacob Kramrisch, a leading light of the tobacco industry; Montague Gluckstein and Nathaniel Lyons, who founded the quintessentially English Lyons tea shops; and Reuben Gliksten, who supplied the walnut dashboards for some of Britain's swishest cars (and celebrated by buying Charlton Athletic Football Club).

While first-generation migrants struggled with all the unfamiliar aspects of life in a new land – new laws, new habits, new resentments, new food, new working practices, new everything – their children were energetically groomed to become purposeful members of what for their parents was merely a refuge. A Jewish Lads' Brigade was formed to promote Anglophilia: far from seeking to connect Jewish children with their own cultural origins, its aim was to speed the process of assimilation by ironing out what its commander, Colonel Goldsmid, called 'the ghetto bend'.

This is a now-familiar immigrant paradigm which popular opinion often prefers to ignore: the children of migrants, lacking financial capital of their own, devote themselves to the acquisition of knowledge, which converts into affluence when they become the bankers, lawyers and doctors of migrant folklore. And in Britain there were such routes from penury to wealth. Olympic champions (such as Harold Abrahams), parliamentary giants (such as Manny Shinwell* and Lord Hore-Belisha, who gave his name to the amber globes beside the country's zebra crossings), industrial magnates (Simon Weinstock), even a viceroy of India (Rufus Isaacs) were all born in Britain to immigrant parents. Marcus Samuel immortalised his father's business – trading in shells –

*In 1938, when an opposition MP in the House of Commons told Shinwell to 'go back to Poland', Shinwell crossed the floor and slapped him in the face.

by building a transport and oil company called . . . Shell. He was hailed as 'the godfather of oil' by Admiral Fisher.

Others literally fought their way out of the ghetto. Boxing became a Jewish passion, and in Ted Lewis and Jack Berg it produced a pair of energetic world champions. Those not so good with their fists became entertainers. Chaim Reeven Weintrop was born in 1896, the youngest of ten children. At the age of twelve he appeared in a talent show as 'Fargo, the Boy Wizard', and a few years later, still a teenager, he walked to Southampton and bluffed his way on to a ship. He jumped off in New York and melted into the city as an illegal immigrant. After sharpening his showmanship in vaudeville, he returned to Britain, was wounded in France in the war, and emerged as Bud Flanagan, the comedian and singer who captured the essence of cockney music-hall wit with Chesney Allen in 'Underneath the Arches'.

Dozens of artistic luminaries sprang from similar backgrounds: Harold Pinter, Arnold Wesker, Steven Berkoff, Carol Reed, Muriel Spark, David Bomberg, Anita Brookner, Victor Gollancz, Isaac Rosenberg, Siegfried Sassoon, Peter Sellers, Jonathan Miller, Bernice Rubens, Peter Schaffer. The British stage and screen, the British page and canvas are all unimaginable without such figures. Many were provided with their platform by the Winogradsky brothers (from Odessa), better known as Lew Grade and Bernard Delfont. Isidore Ostrer built the 300-screen chain of Gaumont cinemas, while Sidney Bernstein built up a leisure chain he called Granada, in memory of some fine walking holidays in southern Spain. Lilian Baylis was born in London in 1874, and after accompanying her parents to South Africa returned to England where she reopened the Sadler's Wells Theatre in Islington. Michael Balcon grew up in Birmingham and went on to become the creative force behind the Ealing Studios (as well as the grandfather of a leading modern actor, Daniel Day-Lewis).

Musicians, businessmen, surgeons, cab drivers, dustmen, comedians, designers, journalists, judges, teachers, nurses, cooks, shopkeepers, electricians, soldiers, publishers, actors, firemen, boxers, philosophers: there have been geniuses and blackguards, and everything in between. Almost every field has been touched and changed by this Jewish odyssey. There was even a remarkable imperial adventurer called Morris Cohen. Born in 1887, he was expelled from the Jew's Free School for theft at the age of ten, and sent to Borstal. He wriggled his way to Canada, where he worked on ranches, and after he shot a pair of cowboys who called him a filthy Jew he always wore a revolver. In Canada he befriended many migrants from China, declared that they were the only people who had never persecuted Jews, and learnt Chinese, which allowed him to act on their behalf in property deals. This made him rich. In 1914 he enlisted in the Irish Guards and was put in charge of the Chinese labour force, which was deployed to dig trenches and lug supplies to the front. After the war he went back with them to China, where he became known, from his habit of packing a pair of pistols, as 'two-gun Cohen'. In 1925 Chiang Kai Chek made him a general, and he led troops against the Japanese until he was captured in Hong Kong in 1941. He managed to survive, however, and eventually returned to Britain, and settled in Manchester, telling stories about his remarkable life to anyone who would listen.

At the beginning of the First World War there were three hundred thousand Jews in Britain. Often, they had to run an unpleasant gauntlet of Jew-baiting disdain. But they were spared the obliterating agonies that would soon crush whole populations on the continent.* Indeed, one migrant to Manchester, Chaim Weizmann, was able to influence the future course of international Jewry decisively. He came to Britain in 1904 from Russia, and became a professor of chemistry at Manchester University. In 1915 he helped the then Minister of Munitions, David Lloyd George, to develop bomb-making chemicals for the front; the episode gave him access to the ear of a future Prime Minister. He took full advantage of it. In 1917 Arthur Balfour, the Foreign Secretary, issued his famous 'declaration' in support of 'a national home for the Jewish people . . . it being clearly understood that nothing shall be done which may prejudice the civil and religious rights of existing non-Jewish communities in Palestine'. Weizmann later played a leading role in the negotiations that led to the creation of Israel in 1948, and became the first president. Britain truly had proved to be something of a new Jerusalem.

It is easy in retrospect to regard this remarkable migration – the arrival of over a hundred thousand very foreign foreigners – as a lively parable of assimilation and success. They engaged with and enriched the country in which they made so gloomy a landing. But of course it was anything but smooth at the time. Jewish landlords and sweatshop bosses were by no means models of courtesy or patience: they could be as ruthless as anyone. But there was not much time for social niceties: the migrants were climbing without ropes, clinging on by their fingertips. While patriotic cartoons celebrated the courage of level-headed soldiers proudly sporting pith helmets in a jungle or hill station far away, a bitter battle for survival was being fought and won only a mile or so from the grandees in Westminster. Somehow, it didn't thrill the nation in quite the same way.

---

*'The Englishman', wrote I. Kaplan in the *Arbeiter Freind*, describing the striking but moderate local dread of the immigrant, 'will bar him from his own factory or workshop, but he has never yet organised a mass attack on the foreigner.'

CHAPTER 16

The Anti-Alien Backlash

In the summer of 1903, the farmers and miners at Great Wyrley, a small village half a dozen miles north of Walsall, were listening out for noises in the night. In the space of seven months, five horses, three cows and some sheep had been slashed in the belly with a sharp knife. One pit pony had died. The attacks seemed random, almost recreational, and the police were baffled. Then they arrested the twenty-seven-year-old son of the local vicar. His name was George and he was a solicitor. He'd won the Bronze Medal from the Birmingham Law Society, and established his own practice in that city. He'd also written a learned book on railway law. He was, it would seem, quite an odd person for the police to suspect of horse maiming. The only evidence they had was a series of anonymous letters that named George as the guilty party. A more telling mark against him, perhaps, was that his surname was Edalji. His father, the vicar, was a Parsee who had married an English girl. When the case came to court, George was found guilty of both animal mutilation *and* fraudulent letter-writing, and sentenced to seven years' penal servitude.

Inconveniently for the police, the horse maiming did not stop, and the 'Great Wyrley Mystery' began to attract press comment. People asked why Edalji might have written anonymous letters incriminating himself, as the police insisted. It looked like a clear miscarriage of justice. The former Chief Justice of the Bahamas took up the cause, and three petitions from ten thousand people arrived at the Home Office. In 1906 Edalji was released, grudgingly and with no compensation, after serving three years. Liberal opinion was shocked. Justice might have been done, but injustice had not been undone. He remained struck from the legal register.

Among those intrigued by the case was Arthur Conan Doyle, who rose to the occasion with vigour, defending Edalji at length in the *Daily Telegraph* in January 1907. He went on to write a book about the case in which he was able, at last, to play the part of his hero Sherlock Holmes, observing and deducing for all he was worth. He knew Edalji was innocent, he wrote, the first time he met him. The accused was reading a newspaper in a hotel. 'I recognised my man by his dark face, so I stood and observed him,' wrote Doyle. 'He held the paper close to his eyes and rather sideways, proving not only a high degree of myopia, but marked astigmatism. The idea of such a man scouring fields at night and assaulting cattle while avoiding the watching police was ludicrous.'[1] Elementary! Doyle's intervention was persuasive. The Law Society readmitted Edalji, and he was a solicitor in London until his death in 1953.

That Edalji was suspected and arrested in the first place exposes the racist reflex at what is usually called 'the heart' of British society. That he was subsequently released and then championed by so prominent an author shows also that redress was possible, that harsh prejudices could be both opposed and overturned. Migrants were beginning to make their presence felt in some unlikely fields. At the turn of the century Britain had sullen manners and crude racial instincts; yet it was still an incomparably open country. There were Jews in Parliament, Germans and Italians in boardrooms, Indian civil servants and doctors, lawyers and even African missionaries.* A runaway American slave called William Wells Brown was amazed, in 1852, by the ease with which a man of his colour could move through London: 'In an hour's walk through the Strand, Regent Street or Piccadilly', he wrote, 'one may meet half a dozen coloured men, who are inmates of the various colleges in the metropolis.' Joseph Renner Maxwell graduated from Oxford in 1879 and boasted: 'I was not subjected to the slightest ridicule or insult, on account of my colour or race, from any one of my fellow students.' A black doctor, George Rice, ran several hospitals in south London and lived with his family in Woolwich; his daughter, Lucinda, presided over a prep school. Formal institutions began to spread their wings, or at least their feathers: the African Association was founded in 1897 by a Trinidadian student, Sylvester Williams; similar societies were launched in Edinburgh and Liverpool in 1904. The first Sikh society was founded in 1908, the first Sikh *gurdwara* in 1911 in Shepherd's Bush. The composer Samuel Coleridge-Taylor became Professor of Composition at the Guildhall School of Music in 1903, and went on to become one of Britain's

---

*Aziz Ahmad travelled to Glasgow from Lucknow as a Christian missionary and worked on behalf of the Lascar underclass, lecturing, setting up a refuge and raising funds, behaviour so original that the police investigated him before concluding that he was 'not worth shooting'.

leading young composers until he toppled over at West Croydon railway station, at the age of only thirty-seven, and died of pneumonia. He had suffered many racist slurs, but had also been helped to rise above them. When a student at the Royal College of Music called him 'Coaley', a fellow teacher intervened to insist that Coleridge-Taylor had 'more music in his little finger' than the rude youth had in his entire body. The route of his funeral procession in Croydon was lined, for more than three miles, by hat-doffing admirers paying their respects.

An African actor called Peter Lobengula trod stages in 1899. Joe Clough from Jamaica became England's first West Indian bus driver, on the number eleven route from Wormwood Scrubs to Liverpool Street. And a young Sri Lankan chancer called Isaac Uriah 'Khaki' Brown made a name for himself when he checked into the Royal Hotel in Grimsby as Prince Makaroo of Zululand, met the Mayor, and tried to exchange fake vouchers for money. He turned out to be an engineer on steam trawlers. The papers referred to him as a 'well-dressed dusky personage', and in court he stuck (almost) to his story, swearing that he was the heir to Abyssinia. The court was gullible, but not that gullible. He was sentenced to three months' hard labour.

There were even a couple of black professional footballers. Arthur Walton stood in the goalmouth at Preston North End, while Walter Tull drove forward from midfield at Spurs and Northampton before being transferred to Glasgow Rangers in 1914.

Tull was remarkable. At a time when startled English children would tentatively rub the skin of a black man to see if the colour came off, he might have become a major sporting star had the First World War not intervened and obliterated all such hopes. He joined the army, fought at the Somme, and in Italy in 1917 became, as a second lieutenant, the first black officer in British military history. He managed to survive until the final months of the conflict, when he led an assault on a German trench in France and took a bullet in no man's land. His commanding officer wrote to Tull's brother that he had 'lost a friend'.

The steep gradient of Tull's upward mobility hinted at the birth of a radiant new era in the British attitude to foreigners. Tull's grandfather had been a slave in Barbados. His father had come to Kent and worked as a joiner in Folkestone. Following the death of his mother in 1895, Walter was raised in a Methodist orphanage in Bethnal Green and encountered fewer obstacles than his father. There were some racist hoots from opposition football crowds, but he must have thought the world was changing for the better. Egalitarian ideas do not advance steadily, however: they sneak forward, then shy back. And Britain's liberalism was about to lurch backwards.

The Jewish migration from the East was starting to inspire a crescendo of anti-alien feeling, the logical conclusion of the fearful patriotism roused by a series of imperial struggles: the Indian Mutiny, the Boer War and, especially, the long siege of Mafeking. It would have abrasive political consequences, not least for the small number of Armenians who managed to limp their way to Britain after the Ottoman Empire, in its death throes, attempted to crush this scholarly, Christian colony on its eastern border. The population had been attacked several times between 1895 and 1909, but at the beginning of the First World War the ethnic cleansing reached new heights (or depths) when half a million Armenians, one-third of the population, were slaughtered. A couple of hundred thousand survived a forced march to Syria and Palestine to become refugees; a fortunate handful made it on to Britain and America. The episode raised the temperature in Whitehall – as a vexed dimension of the Eastern Question, it led to high-level resignations – but it was a bad time to be seeking pastures new.

In Britain, the newly arrived Jews were the chief victims of the anti-immigration lobby. And there was an added dimension to the British sense of racial superiority: a fastidious distaste for the masses, for crowds. Industrialisation, and the new transport systems, were creating larger, ever more visible and frightening armies of civilians – at the docks, at railway stations, at factory gates, in urban slums. People were no longer seen as individuals, families or villages. They suddenly crystallised behind a definite article and became 'the people'. Seen *en masse*, they looked barbaric. Intellectuals winced. 'Many, too many, are born,' wrote Nietzsche. He proposed 'a declaration of war by higher men on the masses . . . The great majority of men have no right to existence.'[3] It was easy, it turned out, for ideologues, philosophers and journalists to harbour or broadcast ill-feelings against crowds, which seemed the enemies of romantic individuality. A few voices tried to resist this impulse to dehumanise men and women into mere groups, and argued against the tendency to speak of them as if they were moved by a single will or lacked individual sensibilities,* but few could resist the temptation to deal disdainfully with 'the masses'.

Popular novelists leapt into the fray, inspired by silly predictions that over seven million immigrants would soon swamp these shores. The visionary socialist H. G. Wells captured this aspect of the Zeitgeist in 1898 with his fantasy *The War of the Worlds*, which described an apocalyptic battle between civilisation and alien invaders. A few years later, in 1902, he spoke with enthusiasm about eugenics, controlling human breeding in order to eliminate 'inferior races' for ever. 'If I had my way,' wrote D. H. Lawrence, 'I would build a lethal chamber as big as the Crystal Palace . . . I'd go out in the back streets and main streets and bring them all in, the sick, the halt, the maimed; I would lead them gently, and they would smile a weary thanks.'[2] In the decades to come, such vivid

*'Fifty men are not a centipede,' wrote G. K. Chesterton.

fantasies would find the most squalid expression. At this stage, they merely made it easy to consider whole groups of people as worthless or superfluous – as a burden or a problem. There was little factual logic in the idea that Britain was being swamped. As it happens between 1871 and 1910, nearly two million Britons emigrated, far more than the number who arrived. So the 'influx', dramatic as it sometimes seemed, did not warrant anything like the uproar it provoked. If anything, the new arrivals were only replacing those who had left.

But in 1886 the *Pall Mall Magazine,* reaching for the tired vocabulary it had deployed against the Irish and Italians, described England's new Jews as a 'pest and a menace', and warned of 'a *Judenhetz* brewing in East London'. In 1887 the Conservative MP for Tower Hamlets, Captain Colomb, wondered 'what great states of the world other than Great Britain permit the immigration of destitute aliens without restriction; and whether Her Majesty's Government is prevented by any Treaty obligations from making such regulations as shall put a stop to the free importation of destitute aliens into the United Kingdom'.[3]

Soon there was a virulent chorus of voices raised in protest at the process (1887 was a year of heavy unemployment). Arnold White wrote to *The Times* condemning the foreigners who were 'replacing English workers and driving to despair men, women and children of our blood'. He had already chaired a debate on the subject in Mile End, where anti-alien Conservative MPs were opposed by Jewish leaders such as Sir Samuel Montagu. Something of a political alliance developed: there were private members' bills and government inquiries on the topic. In 1891 White founded a society 'For Preventing the Immigration of Destitute Aliens'. The society's secretary, William Wilkins, wrote one of several tracts called *The Alien Invasion,* which blamed Jews for stealing jobs and forcing up rents by living in tight spaces.* The *Evening News* began a campaign against the 'foreign flood', and the Conservative MPs for Bow and Stepney campaigned fiercely against their new constituents, whom they called 'Yids', and managed to create a noisy faction in their party that demanded action. 'East of Aldgate one walks into a foreign town,' said Major Evans Gordon, the vociferous MP for Stepney. The modern Englishman lived, he felt, 'under the constant danger of being driven from his home, pushed out into the streets, not by the natural increase of our own population but by the off-scum of Europe'.[4] The parliamentary hopeful David Hope Kyd wailed that intermarriage was leading to 'the extermination of the British working man in the East End of London' – a sentiment which might have had more force had he shown any sympathy for the working man before.

---

*One reason the East End was so crowded was that the railway programme was smashing through neighbourhoods with brutal energy. Between 1891 and 1901, some 1,500 homes in Whitechapel were demolished; thousands of people were 'dishoused'.

It is easy enough to depict such agitators as block-headed bigots. But many –
White, for one – were also noted philanthropists and social theorists struggling
to alleviate poverty in London's slums.* The Earl of Dunraven, chairman of a
House of Lords Select Committee, was motivated at least partly by perplexed
feelings of sympathy when he asked: 'Are there no poor of our own among
us? . . . Have we so light a burden to bear that we can conscientiously hamper
ourselves with an additional load?' Churchmen dressed their anti-immigration
feelings in humanitarian cladding, claiming that the ghetto was overcrowded,
which was true. Sometimes the disguise wore thin, though. The Revd G. S.
Reaney wrote of east London's Jews that 'their very virtues seem prolific of evil,
when like some seed blown by the wind they fall and fructify on English soil'.

The campaign chimed with public opinion and drew supporters from
all sectors of society: nationalist Tories and Anglicans, resentful trade
unionists, nervous Jewish grandees† and socialist ideologues all found a
home in the anti-alien movement. The pugnacious editor of the *National
Review*, Leo Maxse, wailed about 'odious Hebrew domination' and warned
of German-Jewish conspiracies. In 1901 Arnold White wrote in *Efficiency and
Empire*, 'The island of aliens in the sea of English life is small today. It is
growing. Rule by foreign Jews is being set up. The best forms of our national
life are already in jeopardy.'[5] The Trades Union Congress passed several
resolutions calling for strict legislation against the immigrants who were
stealing their members' jobs. William Wilkins claimed that forty-three trade
unions supported some form of anti-alien legislation, the most powerful being
the Dockers' Union.

Against this united front of left and right, the Liberal Party, whose faith in free
trade extended to people as well as corn, was weakening. But a few prominent
figures fought to prevent popular sentiment gelling into policy. Beatrice Webb,
one of the few to penetrate the world of the sweatshop when compiling her
report for Charles Booth, was adamant that its squalor was not the fault of any
foreign hand, but the product of native economics. 'If every Jew resident in
England had been sent back to his birthplace,' she wrote, 'the bulk of the
sweated workers would not have been affected, whether for better or worse.'[6]
In an argument somewhat ahead of its time, she blamed the consumer society
for the hardships suffered in the textile industry – the grasping and unregulated
landlords, the ruthless factory bosses, the margin-squeezing wholesalers and the

---

*East London's biggest problem was sanitation: it did not have clean water until 1903.
As Winston Churchill once said, the Empire might rule the waves, but it could not flush
its own sewers. The fishheads rotting in the street were ugly, and the words 'dirty' and
'foreigner' began to be coupled with an invisible hyphen.
†Benjamin Cohen was a Tory and voted for the Aliens Act in 1905. So too, naturally, did
Evans Gordon, who was sponsored by Lord Rothschild.

complacent public, whose desire for cheap clothes was fed by the sweat and sometimes the blood of others. In praising London's Jewish workers as intellectually superior to and emotionally richer than the average Briton, Webb perhaps fell prey to a common temptation. Eager to exaggerate the merits of her subjects, she played into the hands of those keen to see them as cunning subversives. Polemicists on both sides of such arguments were reluctant to admit that the Jews might be ordinary – people like anyone else.

On London's streets, Olive Christian Malvery, an Indian woman of mixed ancestry from the Punjab, became an activist on behalf of poverty-trapped immigrants. She wrote a sharp series of articles in *Pearson's Magazine* (1904) describing their plight. To research her story she had dressed as a down-and-out Italian flower seller and moved through the hostels of London's fetid underbelly as a tramp. But she took care to wear fetching hats and ribbons. 'I realised very speedily', she wrote, 'that a little ingenuity and originality would be worth a fortune to those who wring out a mean living by appealing to the passers by.'

The young Winston Churchill lent his weight to the immigrant cause. In 1904 he wrote a letter to *The Times* arguing that there was no good reason to abandon 'the old tolerant and generous practice of free entry and asylum to which this country has so long adhered and from which it has so greatly gained'. Elsewhere he sneered at that 'loathsome system of police interference', by which 'the simple immigrant, the political refugee, the helpless and the poor may be harassed and hustled at the pleasure of petty officials'.*

The Tories, with their solid majority, could easily have introduced a bill limiting entry into Britain – which was what many of their MPs and supporters, the so-called 'restrictionists', had been demanding for years. But they did not. Perhaps they were given pause by the obvious injustice of the Dreyfus case in France; maybe they were too preoccupied by the war in South Africa, not to mention the remorseless Irish question. In the streets, the pressure to take action was mounting, however. In 1900 the British Brothers' League was founded. It was dedicated to the anti-immigrant cause; its meetings were patrolled by muscular bouncers who would swiftly eject anyone who looked as though they might not 'fit in'; and it grew fast. In 1902 it collected 45,000 signatures on a petition against aliens. As a pressure group it lost its potency after 1903, when the Immigrant Reform Association took up the baton, and robbed the Brothers' League of its respectable (parliamentarian) face. A Royal Commission on Alien Immigration in the

---

*Fine sentiments, and no doubt sincere. But 1904 was the year Churchill left the Conservatives and joined the Liberals. The constituency he found to fight for his new party – North-west Manchester – had a sizeable population of Jewish settlers.

same year proposed that applicants should be filtered, in order to keep out the 'undesirable' element.

Finally, in 1904, after over a decade of lobbying and election promises by the Tories, a bill was proposed. It failed – there was much high-minded dispute over how to define 'persons of notoriously bad character' – but the political momentum was irresistible. On 10 August 1905 the Conservative government ironed out the flaws, appeased the restrictionists and passed the Aliens Act.

It was a fateful day: for the first time, Britain was a club with sharp restrictions on membership. Of course, there had never been a shortage of animosity against foreigners, but here it was translated into, and dignified by, official policy. The legislation might more aptly have been termed the Anti-Aliens Act. Immigrant ships – those with more than twenty foreign passengers – could be refused entry. Customs officers were invited to turn back those unable to support themselves. While aimed above all at Jewish migrants from the Baltic, the Act could be invoked against any would-be immigrants. For the century that followed, immigration would cease to be a right and would be buffeted by the shifting whims of party politics. Parliament would redefine and qualify both the idea and the practice of immigration and citizenship. Each time, these unruly concepts would be hedged with fresh restrictions.

Herbert Samuel MP, scion of the banking family and later Home Secretary and High Commissioner of Palestine, was mortified. In Parliament, he wondered what the Conservative Prime Minister Disraeli (the centenary of whose birth had just been celebrated) would have thought. 'On 19 April you covered his statue with flowers,' he told the jubilant Tories. 'But the day before that you introduced a bill which might exclude from this country such families as his.'[7] A culture of official harassment and suspicion, exactly what Winston Churchill had warned against, was installed on the frontiers. It would prove a good deal harder to dismantle than it had been to erect.* Voices were raised most eloquently against the Aliens Act only after it had been passed. 'I have never been so ashamed of this House of Commons', said a sober Josiah Wedgwood MP as the applause died down, 'as I have been today. I have some regard for the traditions of my country. We have never seen such a unanimous spirit of persecution in this House since the time of the Popish Plot in 1678.'†[8] Ford Madox Ford, meanwhile, set to work on a book called *The Spirit of the*

---

*The first victims of the hostile new mentality were gypsies, several hundred of whom had been squeezed out by French and German authorities and deported from Holland. Britain deported them straight back.

†Wedgwood had a clear sense of the way hostility to aliens could acquire political backing. 'You always have a mob of entirely uneducated people who will hunt down foreigners,' he said. 'And you always have people who will make use of the passions of the mob in order to get their own end politically.'

People: An Analysis of the English Mind, which shook its head over the government's new, narrow definition of nationality. 'In the case of a people descended from Romans, from Britons, from Anglo-Saxons, from Danes, from Normans, from Poitevins, from Scotch, from Huguenots, from Irish, from Gaels, from modern Germans and from Jews, a people so mixed that there is in it hardly a man who can point to seven generations of purely English blood, it is almost absurd to use the almost obsolescent word "race". These fellows are ourselves.'[9]

This was salutary. But Ford's book was published too late to influence either legislators or electors. And though it is debatable whether politicians lead or simply reflect public opinion, there seems little doubt that the Aliens Act gave official sanction to xenophobic reflexes which might, with the proper discouragement, have remained dormant. One particular target was the Chinese community of seamen. They had never shown much inclination to assimilate, since they weren't planning to stay. To the average, ill-travelled Englishman they seemed very strange indeed. In 1875 Thomas Wright had written in *The Journeyman Engineer* that 'the wholesale importation of coolie and Chinese labour going on in some ports abroad is a thing to give pause to the thoughtful'. That was a polite way of putting it: the thoughtless saw no need for any such pause. When a Commission of Inquiry into Liverpool's Chinese in 1906 noted that 'a number' had married local women, the rumour mill began to broadcast the view that the Chinese were seducing the nation's sixteen-year-olds and luring them into opium dens. The *Sunday Chronicle* published an article on 'Chinese Vice', and the Tory MP J. Havelock Wilson stated with a shudder that blushing 'slips of white womanhood' were being seized as the 'body slaves of laundry lords'. This was the sheerest prejudice, fuelled by a general fear of 'yellow peril', of a numberless Asiatic horde that would spill across every obstacle. Perhaps it was inflated too by a guilty conscience: British companies were making fat profits by controlling the Chinese market in opium. Long before poppies became a symbol of British wartime sacrifice, they were the badge of imperial drug barons in Singapore and Shanghai.

In response to the public outcry, the chief constable in Birkenhead confirmed that there were indeed three shops which sold opium, but added that it 'amounts to no offence against the law and no crimes due to it have come to the knowledge of the police'.[10] The Chinese were, he declared, 'very peaceable, law-abiding men'. In 1907 Liverpool City Council called the Chinese 'the embodiment of public order' and felt that they 'maintained cordial relations with English neighbours' (some of whom were delighted to drop their clothes off at the marvellously efficient laundries which the Chinese were opening).

None of this changed the mood in the docks. 'You know, we know and they know', said the Cardiff *Maritime Herald*, 'that a Chinaman isn't worth a toss as a seaman; that his only claim to indulgence is that he is cheap.' In 1908 there were riots in the London docks when British seamen lashed out at Chinese competitors: angry navvies blockaded Chinese crews signing on at the Board of Trade offices in the East India Dock Road. The employers, until then willing to argue that their hard-working Chinese coolies were vital to their enterprises and must be protected, could no longer rely on political backing for their stance. They gave in. In 1911, during a strike of seamen in Cardiff, the Chinese broke ranks, offered to work and suffered harsh reprisals.

Popular literature was quick to use the Chinese as comic-strip villains. Arthur Conan Doyle's 'The Tale of the Twisted Lip', set in the wharves near London Bridge, is a story of shady Malays and fierce Lascars, although the 'dusky personage' assumed by everyone to be a low-life turns out to be loyal and resolute. The journalist Arthur Ward explored the same area and, as Sax Rohmer, created the mysterious figure of Dr Fu Manchu in 1913. Rohmer said that his character – a svelte arch-criminal – was inspired by a chance glimpse of a tall, elaborately dressed Chinese man slipping through Limehouse Causeway one foggy night. Later, this strange subculture was also dramatised in *Broken Blossoms* (1919), a Hollywood film about the love affair between an English girl and a Chinese poet who came to war-torn Britain to bring 'the peace of Buddha to the warring West'. The girl's father could not countenance so unconventional a match, and murdered his own daughter, before being murdered in turn by the poet, maddened by lost love into abandoning his pacifist principles. It is a rather moving Romeo and Juliet story, but it failed to make an impression on the easy Fu Manchu stereotype of stealthy monsters. In *London Saunterings* (1928), L. Wagner said that, owing to our 'insular prejudices, John Chinaman has been very much maligned. In novels and plays he is set forth as a trickster and villain of the deepest dye.'[11]

Just before Christmas, in 1910, the popular fear of dangerous immigrants seemed to gain substance when three policemen were shot in Houndsditch. The men were investigating a noise complaint when they were gunned down. The police were soon able to confirm that the gang behind the shootings was an anarchist cell. The *Daily Mail* told its readers that 'even the most sentimental will feel that the time has come to stop the abuse of this country's hospitality by the foreign malefactors'. The chief suspect was the mysterious Peter Piatkov, or 'Peter the Painter'.* The atmosphere of mistrust was still electric when, two weeks later, there was another incident. A tip-off alerted the police to the presence at 100 Sidney Street of two Latvians who resembled the faces on the 'wanted' posters pinned up after the Houndsditch murders. The police went to investigate and were met by a burst of gunfire; this time one was killed. For the

---

*Some years later, it became a common myth (probably because he had a moustache) that Piatkov was Stalin.

next two hours, shots were exchanged between the police and the trapped renegades. The army arrived, with the Home Secretary, Winston Churchill, acting like a colonel in the vanguard. Eventually the house was set ablaze. Two bodies were recovered, but the man they wanted, Peter the Painter, had vanished.

There were other terrorist outrages. The House of Commons, the Tower of London, Nelson's Column, London Bridge and three railway stations were attacked. An Indian nationalist, Madan Lal Dhingra, assassinated the diplomat Sir William Curzon Wyllie in 1909.* London developed the siege mentality described by Joseph Conrad in *The Secret Agent*, a novel inspired by the detonation of a bomb at the Greenwich Observatory in 1894. Conrad (himself a celebrated immigrant) was able to describe the blast with cool sarcasm, as an act of 'peculiar stupidity and feebleness' carried out by dolts or slobs. But most Britons reacted in less subtle ways.

This general anti-foreign shiver soon found a new and specific target. As Britain lurched towards war in Europe, the position of Britain's German immigrants became first fragile, and then fraught. The Germans successfully supplanted the Jews as public enemy number one. The country was gripped by spy fever, by tales of the hidden hand, of the enemy in our midst. Britons cast nervous glances at Germany's growing military and industrial might. As early as 1871, in *The Battle of Dorking*, George Chesney had imagined a German invasion of Surrey. In 1900 *How the Germans Took London* by T. W. Offin foresaw landings in Essex backed by a stealthy fifth column of German clerks in Britain. In 1903 Erskine Childers' *The Riddle of the Sands* raised fears of sinister forces poised to spring from behind every sandbank or patch of fog off the east coast. The hero of *The Enemy in Our Midst* by Walter Wood (1906) exclaimed: 'We've given a welcome to every bit of foreign scum that's too filthy to be kept in its own country!' Authors of migrant descent joined the patriotic chorus. William Le Queux, born in Chateauroux in 1864, estimated in *Spies of the Kaiser*, that there were five thousand traitors at large, while E. Phillips Oppenheim, in *The Secret*, went somewhat further, and imagined 290,000 such men, 'who have served their time, and know how to shoot'. Arthur Conan Doyle, the 'hero' of the Great Wyrley Mystery, gave ten shillings and sixpence to the Brothers' League and wrote a Sherlock Holmes story that hinged on the minting of fake coins by a sinister German doctor in Berkshire. And just before the outbreak of war, one MP, Sir John Barlow, asked for an official comment on the rumour that there were fifty thousand Mauser

---

*Dhingra insisted that the shooting was premeditated and political – an act of 'patriotism and justice'. He was hanged. Gandhi, in London at the time, wrote that Dhingra was 'egged on to do this act by the undigested reading of worthless writings'. India House was closed down.

rifles and a pile of ammunition hidden in a cellar near Charing Cross, just waiting for the call to arms.*

In spite of all this, the Aliens Act was weakly enforced. It became law in January 1906, and inspectors were installed at fourteen ports, but it was soon obvious that it was clumsy and unworkable. As customs officers were only allowed to vet ships with more than twenty passengers, migrants took care to travel in smaller groups; some 40 per cent escaped inspection at a stroke. And the appeals system worked in the favour of those immigrants who were detained. In 1906, 935 migrants were denied entry; but of the nearly 800 appeals, more than half were upheld. A good deal of trouble and expense had prevented just five hundred people from trying their luck in Britain. The Liberal government, now back in power, urged the new Immigration Boards to give the 'benefit of the doubt to any immigrants who allege that they are flying from religious or political persecution'.

If Europe had remained at peace, then the Aliens Act might have simply fallen into disuse, at least for a while. But armies were on the move, and as Britain tottered towards trench warfare, the opposite happened. The First World War tightened and sealed the Aliens Act for good.

The day after the declaration of war in 1914, the Aliens Restriction Act was rushed through Parliament, along with a Trading with the Enemy Act, which obliged all German-owned businesses to be confiscated. The presses of London's three German newspapers ground to a halt. Twenty-one suspected German spies were arrested. The next day, a crowd gathered in Old Ford Road and bashed in the windows of the bakers and butchers they could identify as German, and boxed the ears of anyone who looked like 'Max von Sauerkraut'. A similar mob went looking for trouble in Keighley after wild and highly improbable rumours that a German woman had been seen dancing in the streets. On 7 August the General Staff resolved that all Germans should be interned, but the following day the government insisted that only non-naturalised Germans of military age need be detained. By the end of the month, 4,300 of these had been rounded up.

That was not nearly enough for some people's liking. Keighley erupted again when an Irishman accused a German butcher of serving poisoned pies. The butcher responded by punching his customer in the face. The Irishman returned with a gang and set fire to the shop. Three other German butchers'

---

*An enquiry that allowed Lord Haldane to reply, with haughty sarcasm, that he was grateful to the Honourable Member for 'bringing before the House this illustration of a class of alarmist statements to which credence is too often given by thoughtless persons'. Haldane himself, the Lord Chancellor, was a conspicuous admirer of German culture. 'I was threatened with assault on the street,' he wrote in his autobiography, 'and I was on occasion in some danger of being shot.'

shops were wrecked and looted (clearly the pies were not considered too toxic to steal). It took over a hundred police to quell the uprising. The mayor said the trouble was caused by Germany's actions on the continent, which was true. But he declined to curry favour with popular indignation. There was, he declared, 'no excuse why people should attack in a cowardly and un-English fashion the homes of unfortunate Germans who found themselves in England.'[12]

Trouble was stacked like tinder throughout the country, ready to be ignited by anything from a perceived failure to show enough respect to the Union Flag to an impatience with the speed of service in the bread queue. At Deptford, in October, a German shop in the High Street had bricks hurled through the window. Soon there was a crowd of five thousand or so throwing stones and setting fires. One frightened butcher fled over the rooftops with his family. Furniture was tossed out of the upper windows of a confectioner's to the cheering crowd below. The riverside streets echoed to the sound of breaking glass. The police surrounded the German shops, but could not hold back the hooligans. In the end, a 350-man troop of soldiers arrived with rifles to clear the area. A few days later, a pub owned by Mr Ingledew, presumed to be Austrian, was pelted by another huge crowd. Along the Old Kent Road, in Greenwich and Brixton, German butchers were obliged to cower or make a run for it. One put up a notice saying that he had been naturalised as British in 1909, but the crowd was too enraged to read it, believe it, or care either way. His shop was ruined. In Catford, the police managed to interrupt an attack on a German-owned pub called the Old Tiger's Head, but a shop owned by a German who had lived here for over thirty years was destroyed. In Crewe, the pubs closed and spat out a crowd of drunken patriots eager for some fun. They attacked two shops owned by a naturalised butcher. Less boisterous sectors of society also did their patriotic bit. Fifty golf clubs passed motions forbidding Germans and Austrians from teeing off on their loyal, uncorrupted stretches of green and pleasant land.

It wasn't immediately clear where all these quarantined Germans could be put. Alexandra Palace was full of refugees from Belgium; our brave and hapless ally had been crushed in the first days of the war, and it would take months to create space for thousands of German prisoners as well. Indeed, over the winter, some three thousand German detainees were released.

The newspapers adopted the 'stir-it-up and slam-it-down' technique that would become familiar over the next century. Northcliffe's new scandal sheet, the *Daily Mail*, called for the sacking of poisonous German waiters,* and then

---

*'British Waiters Only', ran a headline in August 1914. 'Too Many Germans'. In October it urged its readers: 'Refuse to be served by a German or Austrian Waiter.' In response, many hotels did sack their German staff.

indignantly blamed the apathy of officials when the men they had fingered were assaulted. Indeed, if the birth of a new party politics – more populist, less elitist, quicker to pander to the instincts of the man in the pub – was partly responsible for the chilling of the British attitude to foreigners, then the rise of the popular press was an equally strong force. This was especially true when, the following spring, the *Lusitania* sailed out of Liverpool and was sunk by a German submarine. A week earlier, eight trawlers had been sunk by these fiendish new vessels, but the *Lusitania* was something else: a thousand passengers were killed, most of them civilians fleeing to America. The news broke on a Friday (7 May), and the reaction was immediate. Lord Derby called the Germans 'a race of cold-blooded murderers', and a priest wrote in the Liverpool *Courier* that if 'popular fury' could engineer the expulsion of all Germans from the city and the country, it would be 'a blessing in disguise'. Many leader-writers and letter-writers expressed the same view. The *Manchester Guardian* objected to those who, 'without the mob's excuse of ignorance', wrote 'thinly-veiled incitements to violence', but the *Daily Mail* ran articles pointing out that German prisoners were 'coddled ... to the disgust of all right-thinking women and men'. The Manchester *Evening Chronicle* didn't mince a single word in a headline that exclaimed: 'Germans Gloat Over the Murder of Women and Children!' The *Weekly Dispatch* asked: 'How many Germans are living in this country, and not in gaol? What are they doing here? Why do we allow them to mix with decent people?' And *John Bull*, the famously jingoistic mouthpiece of British nationalism (and the biggest-selling weekly journal in the country, as it never tired of boasting), went one step further. 'I call for a vendetta,' wrote the editor, Horatio Bottomley. 'A vendetta against every German in Britain, whether "naturalised" or not ... You cannot naturalise an unnatural beast – a human abortion – a hellish freak. But you *can* exterminate it. And now the time has come ... No German must be allowed to live in our land. No shop, no factory, no office, no trade, no profession must be open to him ... the moral leprosy of the tribe to which he belongs must be emphasised by a boycott in every station of life.'[13]

This was chilling, even in such dire circumstances. The *New Statesman* called it 'a gospel of murder and atrocity ... the most disgraceful passage we have ever read in an English paper'. But it had the desired effect: riots against German enterprises broke out the day the magazine appeared. In Liverpool dozens of shops were attacked, and the police made sixty-seven arrests as they tried in vain to head off the assault. Bootle, Salford, Birkenhead and Manchester all echoed to the sound of angry yells and thrown stones. A fountain-pen factory owned by a 'supposed German' was smashed. German butchers', fruiterers' and jewellers' were besieged by a crowd of some ten thousand furious locals. A clothes shop run by an Englishwoman unwise enough to be married to a German was stoned. *The Times* estimated that the spree caused forty thousand pounds' worth of damage: two hundred establishments were 'gutted'. Liverpool City Council received over five hundred claims for compensation; Manchester received over a hundred.

In the end, weather came to the Germans' aid: rain put an end to the episode. But in London there was no such divine reprieve. War was declared in nineteen out of twenty-one police districts. Smithfields, the meat market that supplied the German butchers, was surrounded. A meeting was called to 'deal with alien shopkeepers', and out marched the vengeful mob, shouting, 'You drown the women and children, and now we'll drown you!' One German was chased down Holborn until he hopped on to a bus; another hid in a horse trough. A party at a barber's shop in Kentish Town was interpreted by roving thugs as a celebration of the 'hideous tragedy', and the premises were attacked. The East End came to a standstill. Looters pushed carts through the streets piled high with stolen furniture and food. In Bermondsey, the crowd attacked a baker's shop, despite the presence of a picture in the window showing the owner's two sons, both of whom were in the British army. In Derbyshire, the London Tea Stores was attacked on the grounds that its owner, Mr Bakewell, was rumoured to be German. In fact, he was from Derby, and he defended himself stoutly against the furious mob. He and his sons fired shots at the crowd and killed a man. Bakewell himself was charged for it.

That wasn't the only case of mistaken identity. Mahomed Palowkar, the son of an Indian and an Irishwoman, had left his wife Elizabeth and their children when he went to seek his fortune in Australia. For once, Mahomed's dark skin would have been a social salvation, but in his absence angry neighbours thought Elizabeth's surname sounded German and showered her with abuse. Her sons could not help: all four were serving in France. She hastily changed her name to Wilson.

An even worse fate befell the Smith family, who lived on the Suffolk coast. Their son, a scholar and linguist who had studied in France and Germany before the war, was widely rumoured to be a German agent. The villagers managed to persuade themselves that he was in the German navy, and that his parents were flashing signals to enemy ships in the night (Scarborough had been shelled in December 1914). The Smiths were ostracised and the chief constable expelled them from the county. Mrs Smith was so hurt and fearful that she hanged herself. Her entirely untreacherous son, it turned out, was a language teacher in South America, on his way home to join the army.

The riots grew ever more calculated and dangerous. Mr Hilbrond had lived in Walton-on-Thames for twenty-eight years; he owned a jewellery shop. On 15 May he was alarmed to find the word 'German' scrawled on his window. He closed the shutters, but in the evening a crowd gathered outside and threw stones. The police called the fire brigade, but someone cut their hoses. It was a long night. Hilbrond's was one of two thousand properties attacked in London that weekend.

For day after day, and night after night, England's streets rattled to the sound of breaking glass, yells and the pounding of angry feet. It was a bleak episode, and it hastened the processing and internment of the Germans. Not long before, at Queen Victoria's golden jubilee in 1887, London had been full of affable royals from Hohenzollern, Hesse and Prussia.* German London, German Liverpool, German Bradford . . . a historic and mostly amicable association came to an unruly end. The fact that many had come here because they were disgusted by the Prussian militarism of Bismarck and later the Kaiser was dismissed. There was a war on, after all. Britons were losing children, fathers, lovers and friends in the trenches every day.

It is easy, a hundred years later, to be appalled by the loutish instincts of the mob. But it could have been worse. Just over a hundred Germans died in the internment camps – by no means a large number in an age when typhus, flu and tuberculosis could carry people off at will. And amid all the smashed property and drunken rampaging, all the calls from *John Bull* for 'extermination', not one German civilian in Britain lost his life at the hands of the mob. Many were roughed up, many more were shamefully forced out of business, but lynch-mob law did not prevail. The legal authorities diligently (although perhaps with heavy hearts) stepped to the defence of Britain's Germans. Across the country, regiments of confused soldiers were hustled out with fixed bayonets to defend people they'd been indoctrinated to think of as 'the enemy' and to grapple with their own countrymen. It can't have been easy. A Manchester magistrate admitted that he could comprehend riotous feelings,† but insisted that 'this sort of conduct does no good, and must not be continued'. The police interned aliens often for their own protection, and courts began to hand out stiff sentences for affray: one woman was given fifty-two days for breaking windows. A week after the sinking of the *Lusitania*, Parliament received a petition with a quarter of a million signatures, requesting the removal of all Germans. The government swept them up at the rate of a thousand a month. They were packed into temporary camps at Frimley, Newbury (in horse-boxes at the racecourse), Stratford (a former jute factory), Hawick, Lancaster (a disused wagon works) and Olympia. Some were herded into prison ships moored off towns like Ryde or Gosport (the socialist Rudolf Rocker was sent to one off Southend).‡

*Prince William, the future Kaiser, went home with an intriguing military novelty – a machine-gun – whose potential he would recognise all too quickly.
†So could D. H. Lawrence. After the loss of the *Lusitania* he wrote, 'I am mad with rage . . . I would like to kill a million Germans – two million.' He might have made an exception for one or two. His wife Frieda, after all, was German.
‡In all, 30,000 military-age Germans went to the camps. Among their number were 9,000 who had appealed unsuccessfully against their internment. But 7,150 appealed and won their freedom.

For some, this wasn't enough. The *Daily Mail*, in particular, kept up its campaign, going so far as to name and shame six men it believed to be 'Huns at large'. A huge camp was built on the Isle of Man: its rows of huts would eventually hold 23,000 prisoners, half the population of the island itself.

It might have been true that an internment camp was the safest place for a German immigrant to be, cooking up his seagull pie or listening (as inmates could at Alexandra Palace) to the camp orchestra. There were serious riots against Germans in Britain every summer during the war years. In 1916 Lord Kitchener was killed when his ship hit a mine near Scapa Flow, and the public response was swift. 'Intern them all!' cried the front page of the *Evening News*, as if the mine had been planted there by a teacher from Bradford or a clerk from Camberwell. The following July, after an air raid killed fifty-seven people, rioters set out across north London, vandalising shops in Islington, Tottenham and Highgate. The suffragette Sylvia Pankhurst tried to argue that the riots were not specifically anti-German – that they had more to do with the prevailing poverty in the local population. And it is true that there were some opportunist hooligans: a heady adventure could be celebrated with some nocturnal booty, a nice roast or a wedge of black pudding. Certainly, too, a few Russian and English shops were looted in the general mayhem. But Pankhurst's critique in seeking sociological motives for the unrest (she had her own axe to grind, after all) was guilty of overlooking the obvious. Every one of the fourteen shops attacked in St Pancras during one riot was German-owned. If mere hunger was the motive, it was strange that it had to be sated with German sausage. And the violence which ruined 150 bakers across London, nearly all run by Germans, actually led to a bread shortage.

Some of the more notable German businessmen, with contacts in the right places, were able to avoid internment. Chemical and engineering businesses were vital for the war effort, and their German bosses were indulged, as were the bankers. But other companies, such as the Osram Lamp Works, were commandeered, and the Anglo-Persian Oil Company was handed to British Petroleum, which had itself begun life as the British subsidiary of the Europische Petroleum Union of Bremen. Thirty-two German piano manufacturers were snatched, and well-brought-up young ladies across the country wondered whether it was treasonous to carry on playing the Steinway or Bechstein in the drawing room.* In all, property worth £58 million was transferred to British owners, and investments worth £27 million were frozen. A sizeable series of debts to German creditors (£18 million) was cancelled.

---

*There was a particular crisis over the manufacture of mouth-organs, which were essential accoutrements of war (light, portable music for the troops), but were, almost exclusively, German-made. British toy-makers were pressed to begin production immediately.

Following moves in 1915 to have Sir Ernest Cassel and Sir Edgar Speyer removed from the Privy Council, a court ruled that they need not relinquish their positions. John Brunner received letters calling him a 'German swine'; his colleague Alfred Mond, another privy counsellor, went so far as to take two men to court for slander when they accused him of giving shares to enemy aliens. But conspiracy theorists were given their most powerful ammunition when one of Mond's munitions factories in Silvertown, east London, caught fire in 1917. Fifty tons of TNT exploded and destroyed a square mile of the City. Sixty-nine women workers died in the blast, the worst home-front explosion of the war.

Prominent figures wrote 'loyalty letters' to *The Times*. But the witch-hunters were in full cry. The *Evening News* suggested that the house of Sir Felix Semon, who had been Edward VII's doctor, was a secret gun emplacement. Sir Edgar Speyer's wife was asked to remove her daughters from a London school, and Speyer himself was asked to resign as chairman of a hospital. Eyre Crow, an assistant under-secretary at the Foreign Office, was vilified for having married a German woman.

The banker Baron Schroder was still a German citizen when war was declared, and his bank might easily have been confiscated as being the property of an enemy alien. But pragmatism prevailed: the banks closed for three days to avoid financial panic, and by the time they reopened Schroder had become a British citizen. His fast-track naturalisation was supported by the Governor of the Bank of England and the Home Secretary, both of whom pointed out that his fundraising power would be vital to the war effort. His change of nationality was buttressed by a royal licence to live and trade in London, but it was a tense time for the Baron. Like all Germans, he was the butt of countless slights and suspicions. He might well have had divided loyalties: his eldest son was in the German army, and would soon be killed on the Russian front. 'I feel', he said, 'as if my father and my mother have had a quarrel.'[14]

Many Germans took the decision to Anglicise their names. In addition to the famous royal conversions – Saxe-Coburg-Gotha to Windsor and Battenberg to Mountbatten* – the writer Ford Hermann Hueffer became Ford Madox Ford†; Loewe became Low; Ansbacher, Ansley; Schloss, Castle; and Waldstein, Walton. The composer Gustavus von Holst was born in Cheltenham of Swedish ancestry, but dropped the Germanic 'von' from his name just in case. 'A

---

*Prince Louis of Battenberg had been First Sea Lord at the outbreak of war but was forced out of office largely because of prejudice against his 'German' (actually Austrian) roots. For once, the suspicions had some substance: Battenberg held on to his name until 1917, and changed it only after the King commanded him to give up his German titles.
†That Hueffer felt obliged to change his name tells us much about the temper of the time. His father was from Munster, but Ford was born here, had fought on the Western Front and been gassed for his trouble. His loyalty to the Crown was beyond doubt.

German name will be an inconvenience and a hindrance so long as we live,' wrote Albert Rotherston to his brother William Rotherstein (later Sir William, a successful painter), explaining the vowel shift. 'It is not giving the children a fair chance, because the bitterness will never go.'

In truth the bitterness had only just begun. Two hundred years of mainly amicable Anglo-German links were brutally ruptured in the mind and smoke of trench war.

CHAPTER 17

Brothers in Arms

On 26 September 1914 a group of soldiers filed ashore in the sunshine at Marseille, in the south of France. A band played the 'Marseillaise'; the French crowd cheered and waved flags. The troops belonged to the Indian Expeditionary Force, and looked like a mini-Raj: white officers, brown troops. It had been dispatched the moment war broke out, and was racing to the aid of the British Expeditionary Force heading for the front in Belgium. The so-called Old Contemptibles were marching towards a patch of land already sanctified by much gloriously shed British blood. Malplaquet – where the Duke of Marlborough had seen off the French in 1709 – was just a few miles to the south; Waterloo was a day's march north. But if the historical echoes were inspiring, the situation looked bad. There were only five divisions in place, and the German advance through Belgium was astonishing: the British would not be able to hold out for long, especially since all they had for artillery was a few puny cannons, and all they had for barbed wire was what they could rip from fields. The Indians – the Lahore and Meerut divisions – were riding to the rescue.

No one knew how these reinforcements would perform. They were paid only fifteen rupees (about a pound) a month, and had never been deployed in so strange and cold a landscape; not many of them had even heard of Germany – let alone Belgium – and they could not easily think of a reason why they should be taking up arms against the Kaiser (whoever he was). Moreover, there were many Muslims in these Indian regiments, and the fact that Turkey was aligning itself with Berlin meant that these soldiers were being asked to fight perhaps the world's most powerful Islamic leader, the Khalif. Could they be trusted?

After a day learning how to handle the Lee Enfield rifle, the Indians were squeezed into khaki uniforms and bussed to the front at Ypres, in the hope that they could at least delay the German push for Calais. They arrived on 21 October and were hurled into action immediately, first at Ypres and then at Neuve-Chapelle. They fought – and died – gallantly and in great numbers. On 22 October 119 Bengal sappers and miners were tossed in as line-plugging infantry and killed in the sort of manoeuvre that would characterise the coming years. At Neuve-Chapelle 500 were killed, and nearly 1,500 wounded, in horrible fighting. Those who survived into the winter improvised a weapon – a long, thin tube packed with explosive which could be poked into enemy barbed wire. It was called the Bangalore Torpedo.

These men were merely the advance guard of what would become a colossal army: ultimately, the subcontinent would supply 1.4 million men to the Allied war effort: more than Scotland, Wales and Ireland combined. They were lured by deceptive posters in Hindi and Urdu – 'Easy life! Lots of respect! Very little danger! Good pay!' Only 10 per cent of these men served in France and Belgium. The rest were sent to warmer battlefields in Gallipoli, Salonika, East Africa, and the Middle East (where they successfully and at huge cost protected the Persian and Iraqi oil fields, without which British forces would have ground to a halt). Fifty-three thousand Indians died; sixty-four thousand were wounded; nearly four thousand were taken prisoner. Twelve were awarded the Victoria Cross for exceptional valour.*

What passing bells for *these* who die as cattle? The conventional iconography finds space for the dashing Australians and New Zealanders in Gallipoli, but otherwise it is a tragic collage of Flanders mud, trenches, barbed wire, big pushes, anthems for doomed youth, horrendous slaughter, the flower of a generation mown down and brilliant red poppies. We have embalmed the war as an undying emblem of obedient British sacrifice. The figures are bald, however: Britain contributed 5.7 out of 8.5 million men. The missing three million? Nearly a third of the armed forces? These are not much mentioned.

The British Empire responded eagerly to a call which promised for the first time to treat all of its members as equals. The men of the Caribbean (such as C. L. R. James, for one) were at first rebuffed by a War Office which assumed

---

*Victoria Crosses were not easily won. One of the dozen was Gobind Singh. At Cambrai, in 1917, Singh was ordered to ferry a message through two miles of machine-gun fire. His horse was shot, but he crawled to his destination. He returned with a reply, and the same thing happened. When a fresh message was prepared, he volunteered again, claiming that he alone knew the way. For the third time, his horse was shot from underneath him. Somehow he still got through.

Sir Peter Lely (1618–80). Lady Charlotte Fitzroy, later Countess of Lichfield. 'Slaves were fashion accessories; they brought a touch of tamed jungle into the living room.' *(York Museums Trust/York Art Gallery, UK/Bridgeman Art Library)*

William Hogarth (1697–1764). *Noon, 1736.* Affluent Huguenot churchgoers tiptoe past the ill-kempt natives. *(Grimsthorpe Castle, Lincolnshire, UK/Bridgeman Art Library)*

French Huguenots Land. (Engraving by C. Durand.) The Huguenots were the first refugees Protestants seeking a refuge from the storm. *(Mary Evans Picture Library)*

Gustave Doré (1832–83). *Dance to Organs* (1870). The Italian hurdy-gurdy men were fun for some, a pest to others. *(Mary Evans Picture Library)*

Gustave Doré (1832–83). The Irish in Whitechapel. 'Send more money,' ran the apocryphal letter to an Irish émigré worker. 'You have another brother.' *(Mary Evans Picture Library)*

Russian Jews in the Poor Jews Temporary Centre, Leman Street, east London, 1890. The local MP referred to them as the 'off-scum of Europe'. *(Mary Evans Picture Library)*

'Don't ask the price – it's a penny.' The market stall opened by Michael Marks in Leeds grew into a colossal retail empire. *(Marks & Spencer Archive)*

Bombay infantry, *c.*1915, Nearly one-third of the Allied troops in the First World War were not British: one and a half million troops came from India alone. *(Getty Images)*

Lascars at the Royal Docks in London, 1930. Indians and South Asians were eagerly recruited on to Britain's ships. They were paid only a fraction of a British seaman's wage. *(Corbis)*

Italian immigrants in London, 1935. Four years later, the cry went up to 'collar the lot!' *(Mary Evans Picture Library)*

They came as if on their way to a dance. 22 June 1948, the *Empire Windrush* arrives at Tilbury Docks. 'Three cheers for the Ministry of Labour'. *(Getty Images)*

West Indian girls in the British army. Military life was a revelation – like peeking through the curtain of an exclusive club. *(Getty Images)*

Handsworth, Birmingham, 1964. The new Labour government declared that 'the number of immigrants entering the United Kingdom must be limited'. *(Mary Evans Picture Library)*

The Italian procession in Clerkenwell, 1989, a ceremony that dates back to 1893, when the Virgin was first carried swaying through London's streets. *(Andes Press Agency)*

The Jamme Masjid Mosque in Brick Lane, once a Huguenot church and then a synagogue. Hundreds of years of migrant prayers have resonated in these bricks. *(Andes Press Agency)*

Gerrard Street, Soho. In 1957 there were fifty Chinese restaurants in Britain. Six years later there were 1500. *(Corbis)*

Banglatown. Migrants from Sylhet settled in streets once colonised by Irish and Jewish families. *(Andes Press Agency)*

The Regent's Park Mosque, London. By the end of the twentieth century there were over 900 mosques in Britain. *(The Travelsite)*

Join the queue. Asylum-seekers outside Lunar House in Croydon. *(Rex Features)*

that black soldiers would be unreliable and 'too conspicuous on the battlefield'. But steamers began to leave Jamaica for Europe, ferrying over ten thousand Caribbean troops to the theatres of war. In one way, the War Office's lack of faith worked in these men's favour. They were not trusted as front-line troops, and were rarely deployed as mere cannon fodder; like the army of coolies recruited in China for menial work,* they were used as labourers, hauling supplies and stores.† For the most part they were ill-equipped, poorly housed and badly fed; some mutinied. After the war, they were sent packing, four thousand of them to Cuba to cut sugar.

The West Indian contribution, however significant, was dwarfed by India's. They were front-line soldiers, as well as medics, lumberjacks, miners, sappers, cooks, railwaymen, drivers, builders and engineers. Several thousand Indians (the figures are vague) drowned at sea in a navy still heavily crewed by Lascars. And there was a handful of Indian fighter pilots, one of whom, Second-Lieutenant Indra Lal Roy, was a bona-fide ace. He had come to Britain at the age of ten to go to school (Colet Court, the smart feeder school for St Paul's in London), and applied to the Royal Flying Corps in 1917. He was told that the best option for a man of his 'background' was to be a mechanic. But he had come on the recommendation of a General, so was admitted. He completed his training shortly before the end of the war, in June 1918. Just a few weeks later he had shot down ten enemy aircraft, a dazzling hit rate. In July, he took one risk too many and was shot down. He was awarded a posthumous medal. He was nineteen.

The Indians were as eager to 'kill more bastered Germans' as anyone. And if the officer class dealt with them patronisingly, seeing them (in many contemporary accounts) as chaps who could put up quite a good show under fire, but not for long, the army itself went to elaborate lengths to observe India's various dietary or sartorial strictures – Sikhs were even permitted to wear turbans rather than helmets. The British public greeted them with undisguised affection. Troop trains were met by animated crowds; people 'salaamed' new arrivals with good-humoured glee. The Royal Pavilion in Brighton, a stately pile of Mughal pinnacles and minarets, was converted into a military hospital, and Indians studying medicine in British universities were drafted in. Such grand hospitals were models of their kind. There were even complaints that India's wounded were better treated than English victims, which was probably

---

*It is possible to glean the esteem in which these Chinese labour platoons were held by glancing at the military-issue phrasebooks provided for the officers in charge. They were full of peremptory commands such as 'The inside of this tent is not very clean' and 'If you are not careful, I will be compelled to punish you'.
†At Taranto, in Italy, they showed signs of what was to come by forming a cricket team which won twenty-seven of its thirty matches.

true. But, as the Viceroy of India insisted, it was justified on the twin grounds of 'gratitude and justice'.

The injured Indians were impressed by their new surroundings. 'If there be paradise on earth,' one Sikh wrote home, 'it is this, it is this.'[1] The food, the religious facilities, even the burial ceremonies, were spot on. They could play hockey, read books, listen to music and watch films. Recuperating soldiers were taken on tours of England's sights: the Tower of London, St Paul's Cathedral, Buckingham Palace and London Zoo. They were even permitted a frivolous hour or two in Selfridge's, the amazing store recently opened by an American immigrant. All of this was refreshing; it was also good propaganda. India was full of praise for the mother country.

As time wore on, however, less dignified tendencies began to rise to the fore. British society remained terrified by the idea of improper sexual liaisons. Walls began to rise around the hospitals. Barbed wire started to climb up the walls. Apart from the occasional day trip, the men were becoming prisoners. 'I have never experienced such hardship in all my life,' wrote one inmate. 'True, we are well fed and are given plenty of clothing; but the essential thing – freedom – is denied . . . we have found our convict station here in England.'[2] Compounding this was the fact that Indian soldiers were underpaid, sometimes receiving only a quarter of the wage given to a British Tommy.

The war experience was an eye-opening education in the ways of the imperial world for many young Indian men. Some felt that the gain in military self-esteem advanced the movement for national independence by fifty years. But even in the short term it was a potent episode. The troops were amazed by the grandeur and power of British life, but also by its miseries and inequalities. They felt both the absolutism of the officer class and the curmudgeonly decency of its masses. They were serving, fighting, suffering and dying as equals under the flag. Surely the old myth of the ignorant, fire-eating 'Bombay baboo' was gone for good. Who could seriously imagine a return to the old master–slave relationship between men who had fought shoulder to shoulder?

But after the war, that is exactly what Britain tried to enforce. The empire troops were shooed off home with undisguised alacrity, and the 1905 and 1914 Aliens Acts were bolstered by a new law which would carry their restrictive rules into peacetime. In July 1919 the grand Peace March in London, a parade to celebrate victory, was purged – by official decree – of any representation by the empire troops that had helped to make it possible. It was a crushing insult, and it set a tone which has only recently wavered.* Perched on a Sussex hill, half-strangled by brambles, stands a white marble memorial to the Indian dead of the First World War. In 2001 a commemorative gate appeared on London's

---

*Empire veterans were invited to parade for the first time in 2000, eighty-two years after the end of the war.

Hyde Park Corner in honour of the overseas soldiers who fought for Britain in both wars. But apart from these and a few other modest memorials,* the role of the empire soldiers is largely forgotten.

Things turned sour almost as soon as victory was declared and the troops took off their uniforms. The official national mood of rejoicing and relief was itchy with indignation and grief. The economy was punch-drunk, and the seamen were on strike, causing chaos at docks already overcrowded with demobbed troops looking for a job or a ship home. It would have been amazing if there hadn't been the odd hand raised in anger. In the event, there were plenty, and most were raised against the Indian, African and Chinese seamen who had been hauled aboard in numbers to fill the gaps left by the recruitment drive. The recruitment of Chinese coolies to the steam rooms of the British fleet had been hamstrung in 1916, when a French ship, the *Athos*, was sunk in the Mediterranean, drowning 543 Chinese labourers who were being ferried to the war zone. But by the end of the war, nearly a quarter of the crew of Britain's merchant fleet was Lascar, and not everyone was happy about that.

The First World War was the first time that Britain's working class had travelled overseas in numbers, and when it returned home, it brought with it a sharpened hatred of all things foreign. Ironically, a slight exception was made for the Germans, who were grudgingly admired for their courage. But years of longing for home aroused in the average British breast a sense that foreign manners, foreign food, foreign weather, foreign insects and foreign people were altogether a cut below. In an ideal world, the troops would have returned with a vow that they had thrown their last punch; in our less than ideal one, they came with fists already clenched against anyone who could plausibly be depicted as 'not one of us'. The large pool of Lascar seamen, several thousand of whom had set up as residents of the major ports, were the nearest and easiest target. Many were dismissed by 'patriotic' shipowners anxious to make room for brave veterans from the trenches. 'There are 11,000 demobilised soldiers to be reinstated,' said one official as he sacked an Indian employee. 'And they must have first chance.'[3]

In one sense it was undeniable that the surviving troops, who had endured the mud, the blood, the shrapnel, the gas, the lice, the oversized rats and all the other horrors of life in Flanders and France, deserved everything that could be given them. But the discrimination was sharp and tactless. There were bitter protests when four Indians were hired by a colliery in Lanarkshire, even though these men had served in the army, and had the medals to prove it. And things took a brutal turn in Glasgow in January 1919. The city was in uproar: a huge seamen's rally was policed by ten thousand troops and four tanks. The

---

*There is a monument to the Indian war dead at Neuve-Chapelle, and a plaque in Westminster Abbey.

authorities were fearful that it might turn into a Russian-style Bolshevik uprising. Then a mob of white sailors chased their Sierra Leonese rivals from the docks with sticks and knives, and surrounded the hostel where they cowered. Fifty policemen eventually escorted the besieged black sailors into custody. In February nine Adenese (British subjects, of course) were hired in South Shields as stokers on a vessel, but the union stepped in and refused to let them sail. In April there was a four-day brawl in London's docklands, fuelled by sermons in the newspapers about the impropriety of 'liaisons' between black men and white women. In Liverpool, where the Elder Dempster Line to West Africa had long relied on crews recruited in the Tropics, a seaman called Charles Wootton was hounded into the Queen's Dock and stoned to death by a mob.* There was more trouble in Salford, Hull, Newport and Barry. In the Cardiff witch-hunt three black coalers were killed. 'I did it', said one of the ringleaders, Gordon Maskell, 'for the benefit of the seamen of whom I am one, and cannot get a job because of those niggers being here.'† Like Liverpool and Salford, Cardiff had its own black 'colony'. In 1919, it was forced to shelter behind a police cordon.

In each case, the police tended to arrest the black seamen, even though they were clearly the victims of the violence, rather than its architects. The papers egged them on. The Glasgow *Herald* suggested that the riots were caused by black sailors angered by the 'alleged preference' of the shipping agents for British seamen. The Liverpool *Echo* reported that 'in every case the coloured men were the aggressors', an observation undermined by revelations that some of the men had been attacked in their beds.‡ The courts, as they had before, tried to redress the balance. In Liverpool, only seventeen of the twenty-nine black seamen brought to trial were found guilty, whereas all thirty-six of the white men were convicted. In Cardiff, all eighteen white defendants were found guilty, whereas the twelve 'coloureds' were all released. But sometimes the magistrates succumbed to primal promptings. John Marden, who kicked and waved a knife at a policeman, was given a one-month sentence (the court reacted to news that he had sixty-one previous convictions by conceding that he was 'no saint'). But Mohamed Abouki, arrested on the same day for hitting a policeman with a stick, was handed six months.

Politicians were swayed by popular anger. Questions were asked in the House about the possibility of 'interning these people' – there was, after all, space in the camps now that the Germans had been sent 'home'. But it was

---

*A community centre for black children in Liverpool is named after him.

†He was given a mere three months' hard labour. 'Now for the Chinese!' he was heard to roar, as his mob elbowed its way through Cardiff.

‡The *Echo* also felt that this was a good time to publish the opinion of its editor that 'the average negro is nearer the animal than is the average white man'.

decided instead to attempt a programme of voluntary repatriation. Committees were set up, ships were booked. Repatriates were offered a free ticket, a five-pound golden handshake and a couple of pounds' travel expenses. To general bemusement, most of the migrant seamen refused. Some were married; some liked it here, despite everything; some had little to return to; some were simply bloody-minded and disinclined to be cowed. A few perhaps had the temerity to believe that this was their home, and that 'repatriation' was a meaningless term. The SS *Kurmansk*, which had room for eight hundred passengers, left Cardiff with just sixty-three Indians and fifty Adenese.

The refuseniks were tough and brave. They'd spent their lives in and around docks, and docks were riotous places. They were used to brawls; they might even have seen worse. It is impossible to know what they felt about such things, but perhaps they reckoned that they could weather this storm, that it would all blow over.

There was plenty of public horror over these uprisings. *John Bull*, which reserved its harshest language for Germans and Jews, actually leapt to the defence of the migrant seamen and criticised the National Sailors and Firemen's Union for its 'disgraceful' refusal to permit them on British ships. 'One black has died,' it wrote, 'yet he was a Briton who had defied the Hun and his devilries for the sake of Britain.' Meanwhile, at least one official urged restraint, if only for tactical reasons. Viscount Milner, the Colonial Secretary, was worried that anti-black fury in Britain would inspire an equal and opposite reaction overseas. On 23 June he wrote a 'Memorandum on the Repatriation of Coloured Men'. 'I have every reason to fear', he explained, 'that when we get these men back to their own colonies they might be tempted to revenge themselves on the white minorities there. We need to make it clear that His Majesty's Government is not insensible to their complaints . . . If we wish to get rid of the coloured population whose presence here is causing so much trouble we must pay the expense of doing so ourselves.'[5]

His fears were confirmed a week later when the SS *Santille* left Cardiff for Jamaica carrying 147 repatriates, who smashed the fixtures and fittings of the ship. Soon afterwards, the SS *Ocra* dropped more repatriated Jamaicans on to the wharves of Kingston. The first thing the new arrivals did was go out looking for white sailors to beat up, and they ransacked a few white-owned shops while they were about it. These outbursts gave ammunition to the hard-liners who insisted that these men had been trouble all along, and thank God we were rid of them.

It required a bold leap of imagination to see the few thousand empire labourers in the ports as serious threats to employment. But the labour market, though notionally undersupplied, was an arena of lively dispute. The women who had filled the factories to supply the war effort were now encouraged to vacate their workbenches and return to so-called domestic bliss. But the suffragette movement, having squeezed a foot in the door of the male domains of work and politics, was not about to return to a world of mops, buckets, ovens and sinks. The handful of migrant workers represented, apart from any specific rivalry over jobs, a further challenge to the old assumptions. The once unshakeable faith in British supremacy was endangered by these itinerant colonials; and they aroused a combustible emotion – fear. There was a vague, but monstrous, dread of the lawless horde, the savage multitude, and even civilised voices fell under its spell. 'The quiet, inoffensive nigger becomes a demon when armed with a revolver or razor,' suggested the *Guardian*. Britain was possessed of an urge to nip this horror in the bud.

A little reflection would have been enough to persuade the demobbed troops that none of this was the fault of the black sailors themselves: shipowners still liked the fact that they were cheaply hired and easily fired,* and bosses were motivated too by a racist sense that an African was 'better suited' to the heat and grime of a ship's furnace than a Lancastrian or even an Irishman. But reflection was a lot to ask of the dazed veterans, who had so recently winced under artillery bombardments. They returned home to find their places in the civilian workforce filled by deckhands from overseas. Some Indians had left their ships and found work in factories: Lever Brothers in Port Sunlight and Tate & Lyle in east London were notable employers of imperial labour. These men were thought of as cowardly profiteers: not only had they avoided the terrors of war, went the myth factory, they had even sneaked into the beds of the true patriots. While good men died, these layabouts were swanking about on Easy Street with the wives of wounded heroes. It was intolerable.

In the spring and summer of 1919 five men were killed and two hundred arrested. When set against the ocean of blood that had been spilled in the preceding four years, not to mention the murderous influenza epidemic that was still rampaging around the world, this was a minuscule tragedy. But it wasn't a question of numbers. The postwar riots put the seal on the mean-minded attitude to foreigners that had elbowed its way to the top of the political agenda at the turn of the century. The trenches of the First World War should, perhaps, have provided an eloquent argument against nationalism, should have inspired a burgeoning desire for a more tolerant, less pugnacious approach to international affairs. As Winston Churchill, the Minister of War, remarked: 'What would happen, I wonder, if the armies of both sides decided, suddenly and simultaneously, to lay down their weapons and insist that the dispute be resolved by some other means?' But this, alas, was a charming whimsy. The bristling desire to repel boarders that had become official policy before the war now had few

---

*On the ships, this was partly the union's own fault. In 1911 it had successfully doubled the wages of white firemen on British ships, while leaving the pay of black seamen where it was.

opponents. Vengefulness (as officially expressed by the Versailles Treaty) outranked conciliation, and the huge contribution that the empire's dark-skinned subjects had made on the battlefield was allowed to slide from memory. In an act of supreme ingratitude, or perhaps merely one of war-weary exhaustion and rancour, a rude new sign was mounted on the door: 'Keep Out'. There were more than enough patriots willing to keep the letters bold and freshly painted.

CHAPTER 18

Casualties of War

Victorious Britain continued to see itself as a muscular peopler of other lands, not a refuge for foreigners. But people from Europe and further afield – Africa, the Caribbean and India – began to be enticed by the increasing ease of steam-age travel as well as by their own curiosity or need, towards the imperial capital.

National independence movements, meanwhile, were gaining strength and credibility in the distant dominions, and students came from afar to see what made the empire tick. The grandiose principles of the nineteenth century – which loftily conferred citizenship and free entry to its colonial subjects – were starting to strike opinion-formers as luxurious anachronisms. The promises had been made at a time when Britons could not imagine that they would ever have to be honoured. Colonial traffic had always been a mainly one-way affair: a matter of good, white Christian folk striding on to their verandas overseas. In the broken-spirited atmosphere of the peace, it began to look as though migration might become a two-way street.

In 1915 the country's bureaucrats equipped themselves with a powerful new weapon: the passport. Various species of royal or official papers – harbour permits, letters of safe conduct – had been in use for centuries, and state-backed passports had been available since 1858 as optional guarantors of national identity. But now, with the smoke of guns and gas across the Channel providing cover for tougher rules, passports became compulsory. For those obliged to carry and present them, they were no more than a nuisance. But for governments, they were a redoubtable new weapon in the attempt to control the national population.

After the war, Britain at last resolved to ration citizenship. A series of parliamentary acts, most of which emerged as ad hoc responses to specific 'problems', examined prevailing notions of national identity and hedged them with fresh restrictions. Inch by inch, prejudices gelled into policy. Entry to the UK became a privilege, one that from now on would be protected by booklets, photos, distinguishing marks, lists, stamps and politics. In 1925, for example, the government reacted to the ongoing trouble in the ports by tightening the laws governing the employment of migrant crew. The Special Restriction (Coloured Alien Seamen) Order required all non-Britons to register with the police. Though aimed at 'non-domiciled' aliens, the police and customs officers in the ports were not fussy. In Glasgow sixty-three Indians resident in Britain were forced to register as aliens; and in Cardiff, Fazel Mohamed, a thirty-nine-year-old seaman born in Peshawar, but married to a British woman and the father of three children, was categorised as 'alien' the moment he stepped off his ship. In Liverpool, the Indian population was subjected to an early form of stop and search. In 1927 they mustered into a rally to protest against police harassment. One surprising ally was the India Office, which feared the destabilising effect the police's behaviour might have on the increasingly volatile subcontinent itself. It was becoming awkward enough to insist that India was British without having to explain that Indians were also 'aliens'. The persecution of coloured seamen, the India Office wrote in a memo to the Home Office, was being taken to 'indefensible limits'. In 1931 the government retreated half a pace by creating the Certificate of Identity and Nation, a sort of second-class passport. But this only confirmed to the Lascars that they themselves were seen as marginal.

In 1931 further steps were taken to restrict passports. They could now be granted only to people with 'a definite offer of employment'. As everyone knew, this was not the way shipping worked – the most definite offer that could be expected was a whistle on the docks at dawn on the day men were needed. The only Indians who were exempt, in a lordly flourish, were people 'of good character and established position'. Not for the first time (or the last) the cut of a man's jib was more telling than the colour of his skin.

In 1935 the authorities changed tack and tried bribery: shipping companies were offered a subsidy to employ 'British' – that is, white – seamen. This backfired immediately. Shippers found it profitable to employ cut-price colonials out of sight in their boiler rooms and galleys, while claiming the subsidy as if the workers were British (which many of them were, of course – whatever the colour of their skin). As a result, the sustained effort to cut the number of African, Chinese and Indian men in the fleet was a dramatic failure. In 1919 some 20 per cent of the seamen were Indian; in 1929 it was 23 per cent; and by 1938 it had risen to 26 per cent (over fifty thousand men). All the campaign achieved was to jolt into life a movement for Indian rights in Britain, echoing the louder, Gandhi-inspired clamour for independence which was disrupting the subcontinent itself.

Several energetic Indian activists began to surface in public life. Uphadhaya (better known as 'Paddy') was a teacher and writer from Bombay who came to Britain in 1922, spoke at Communist Party meetings in Scotland and London, and tried to organise his compatriots into a union. He also distributed pamphlets, which were translated into English by the imam of a mosque in Wimbledon. In 1923 he founded the Indian Seamen's Association, which held rallies and debates on the inequalities to which Indian crews were subject. In 1925 he spoke harshly against discrimination and called for a strike. He had a good case: white seamen were paid over nine pounds a week at the time, Indians under two pounds, and shipping lines often 'forgot' to pay even the tiny compensation – a hundred rupees – owing to families whose menfolk had died at sea. But Paddy was still seen as a troublemaker: he was accused of 'fomenting revolutionary plots' by an MP, interrogated by the police and banned from public speaking. At its height, in 1931, his association had six thousand members, and Paddy proudly designed a flag to wave on their behalf.

Indian sailors were not easily unionised, though: they were too disparate and individualistic, not to mention poor and vulnerable, for that. Uphadhaya's career was cut short when the India Office, citing him as 'distinctly dangerous', requested that his passport be cancelled. Moves to have him classified as an alien and deported, however, foundered on the delicate issue of Indian sovereignty: if he was an alien, how could Britain continue to insist that Bombay was British?

More prominent even than Paddy was the man once described as 'India's finest orator': Shapurji Saklatava. He came to England in 1905, aged thirty-one, as a manager for Tata, the iron and steel company, and quickly became involved in the politics of protest. Initially a Liberal, he married an Englishwoman and for a time confined himself to arguments about Indian home rule. But after the Russian Revolution in 1917, his politics turned to the left, and he became one of the first members of the British Communist Party. In 1921 he became the Labour Party's candidate in Battersea, and won the seat. The Mother of Parliaments suddenly found herself having to accommodate something quite unprecedented: an Indian communist on her green benches. Saklatava was especially popular, it was rumoured, with (newly enfranchised) women, but one taxi-driver was quoted insisting that he had fought with Indian regiments in the war, and could vouch for the fact that they were made of damned good stuff. When an opposition aide ventured the view that the good people of Battersea would surely prefer 'an Englishman' as their candidate, he was shouted down with cries of 'Shame!' Saklatava was attacked much more bitterly for being a 'Red' than for being an Indian. Race was the lesser slur.

In his anti-imperial speeches, Saklatava spoke of imperialists as sharp-fanged capitalist predators. In 1923 he told his fellow MPs that the seventy-four mainly Scottish-owned jute mills in Bengal were able to report profits of £23 million between 1918 and 1921 through the simple expedient of exploiting penniless Bengali labourers. But these low-cost operations in India had shattered Scotland's own jute mills around Dundee, forcing many closures and steep unemployment. Two populations, one at home and one overseas, were starving in order to enrich a handful of Scottish capitalists. Was this sensible economics, let alone enlightened politics? Saklatava didn't think so.

In 1926, he gave a rousing speech at the start of the General Strike, and was arrested and thrown into Wormwood Scrubs. Three years later he lost his seat in Battersea, but he carried on waving his unfashionable banners until his death in 1936, at which point – in the traditional British way – everyone agreed that he had been a fine fellow whom it had been a privilege to know. Some British volunteers in the Spanish Civil War in 1937 even found themselves serving in the Saklatava Battalion, hastily named in his honour.

The other leading Indian activist in Britain was Krishna Menon, a barrister who came to England for a conference in 1924, stuck around for a few months to pick up a teaching qualification, and stayed for twenty-five years. He swiftly became the secretary of the India League, the major pressure group for national independence, and by 1930 was in touch, from his office in the Strand, with twenty-six branches around the country: Bournemouth and Birmingham, Bradford and Bristol, Leeds, Liverpool and many other towns. Along with a small gallery of other Indian intellectuals – barristers, booksellers, shipping clerks, prison officers – he took full advantage of one of London's lovable oddities: the weekly pulpit near Marble Arch known as Speaker's Corner. There he would waylay passers-by with sensational facts: Britain had ten times as many doctors per thousand members of the population as India, and God knows how many more nurses; average life expectancy on the subcontinent was a shocking twenty-three years, and falling. It was hard to sustain much confidence in the idea of the Raj as a bright beacon of civilisation in the face of this sort of information, and Menon was a charismatic presenter of the sorry truth. He wrote for the *New Statesman* and the *Guardian*, and as a publisher was the editor of a ground-breaking series of educational books: the Pelican series of paperbacks. He engaged Bertrand Russell as chairman of the India League and established connections with some forty MPs.

Inevitably, he was drawn into narrow factional disputes with rival Indian organisations, such as Saklatava's association and Swaraj House, an Indians-only club opposed to Menon's more inclusive society. But the various groups were able to unite in their opposition to the crackdown on civil disobedience in India in 1931, when eighty thousand Indians were jailed in a four-month show of force. The publicity they were able to give to certain notorious cases – the man who was locked in a tiny cage for five months for refusing to salute the government at the appointed hour; the group beaten mercilessly by the police for daring to show respect to the Congress Party's flag – made him a forceful player in negotiations about British withdrawal. 'So long as the British insist upon governing India,' wrote Bertrand Russell, 'they have no right to ignore what is done in their name.'[1] Menon helped to ensure that the public could not plead total ignorance.

In 1934 he became a Labour councillor in St Pancras and discovered a new career as an impresario for public education. He dreamed of having as many libraries in the borough as there were pubs, and inaugurated an annual arts festival. He tried and failed to become an MP. The Labour Party ruled him out by saying that he was close to too many communists, neatly sidestepping what was probably the real reason: his views on Indian independence were at odds with those of the leadership. So he stayed in St Pancras, supervising air-raid shelters and public works while pressing for independence in India throughout the war years. In 1955 he became only the second man to be given the Freedom of the Borough.* By then, though, Menon was no longer a local government official: he had until recently been India's first High Commissioner to Britain, and was soon to return to the land of his birth as Minister of Defence.

Menon always viewed the British as his target audience – he enjoyed preaching to the unconverted – but he was buoyed by a small audience of Indian exiles who were putting down roots in England. There were Lascars, of course, and Punjabi pedlars, who had taken over where the nineteenth-century Irishmen and Jews had left off by selling handy items out in the streets. Neither of these groups were too keen on speeches and pamphlets, or indeed educational paperbacks: they had more urgent needs. But there was also a sprinkling of Indian businessmen, doctors, lawyers, and writers, scholars, teachers and shopkeepers. An Indian Chamber of Commerce was founded in 1927, and a few years later nearly fifty companies classed as 'Indian' were trading in Britain. There was an Indian bookshop near the British Museum; the poet Tambimuttu was the editor of *Poetry Today*; Mulk Raj Anand was a fringe guest of Bloomsbury; and Rabindranath Tagore, whenever he visited London, would create a majestic Orientalist stir.† There were Indian guest-houses, even Indian estate agents. In 1931 the Bombay Emporium opened near the

---

*His one and only predecessor was George Bernard Shaw. The freedom of St Pancras was not handed out lightly.
†Tagore was knighted in 1915, two years after receiving the Nobel Prize for Literature. He kept the Swedish honour but handed back the British one in 1919, in protest against British policy in the Punjab.

Tottenham Court Road, providing the first glimmer of what would later become an indispensable part of British life: the Asian shop. In Portobello, you could buy curry powder, poppadoms and mango chutney; and in Glasgow, in 1935, there were three Indian grocers'. Veeraswami's restaurant, in Regent Street, was essentially a Raj creation: a little slice of the Gymkhana Club in London run by an Englishman, William Palmer, for the delectation of spice-loving royalty. But other Indian restaurants and cafés sprang up in its shade: a pair of students from northern India founded Shafi's, in Soho, and homesick Indians, or nostalgic British colonials, could feast on curry at the Taj Mahal on Cambridge Circus, the Koh-i-Noor in Rupert Street, the Rajah on Irving Street, Singh's in Aldgate, the Anglo-Asia on the Brompton Road or the Café Indien on Leicester Square. There were restaurants in Glasgow and Cambridge. A few offered 'outside catering' – ancestor of the takeaway. Something big was simmering in these small ventures, along with the coriander, turmeric and ginger: a wholehearted culinary revolution was afoot which would alter not just the British high street but the British palate.

Out of the limelight, away from the gaze of both the contemporary and the historical news archive, Indians were pursuing dignified private careers. Dr Harbans Gulati left Lahore University in 1916, worked his passage to England on a ship and signed up at the Charing Cross Hospital Medical School. He was a GP in cosmopolitan Battersea for forty years, a magistrate, a Conservative London county councillor and the driving force behind a new concept in healthcare: meals on wheels. The Punjabi-born Dr Dharm Sheel Chowdhary worked as a doctor in Essex and was, in the Second World War, a captain in the Home Guard – a rather atypical member of Dad's Army. He was famous (these were pre-NHS days) for tearing up the bills of impoverished patients, and a local primary school was named after him. Dr Chuni Lal Katial, meanwhile, became Britain's first Indian mayor at a time when the role required more commitment than usual. His borough of Finsbury was blitzed during his term of office.

In all, there were up to a thousand Indian doctors working in Britain in the inter-war period, heartily refuting the supposition that endemic end-of-empire racism would have made such appointments impossible. They didn't make waves: they were too busy concentrating on their patients' health. Dharm Sheel Chowdhary's wife, Savitri, noted, 'It is best not to make oneself conspicuous.'[2] She and her husband were the only Indian people in the village, and she gave up vegetarianism partly to conform, in much the same way as many Indian men shaved off their beards. No doubt there were many who flinched when dark hands examined their white skins; no doubt many malicious jeers and taunts were thrown behind the new GP's back. But Savitri Chowdhary wrote that she could not remember 'a single incident' of racist abuse arising from 'the darkness of my skin', and her husband was 'idolised'.

The Indian 'community' in Britain during the inter-war years was never large, rarely numbering more than seven or eight thousand. Size isn't everything, though, and this modest settlement was historic, since it was the first hint of a much greater migration that would soon gather in the decolonised world. They moved cautiously, like sappers exploring unknown terrain. They were visibly foreign, but also extremely 'British'. They spoke a classical form of English, and could quote Macaulay, Dickens and Shakespeare; they were polite, patient, and wore suits and ties. They even loved cricket. Far from being the incoherent, wild-eyed savages of imperial propaganda, they were articulate, well-informed and persuasive. The British Empire had been buttressed by the stereotype of 'dusky' native helplessness. These industrious settlers did much to undermine the plausibility of this world view.

The beginnings of a substantial Indian* presence coincided with a similar drift of people – mostly students – from Africa and the Caribbean. A select group of affluent young West Africans were sent to university in Edinburgh, Oxford, Durham and London, with a view to instilling in them the proper Christian qualities needed to hold any position of influence back in their home countries. As with the continental dissidents of the Victorian age, they quickly formed political clubs and societies, most of which were dedicated to national independence.

They were a tiny (in 1925 the Colonial Office estimated that there were only 125 African university students in Britain) but vociferous group. There was the African Students' Union, the West African Christian Society, the African Progress Union, the Society of Peoples of African Origin, the African Society and the Anti-Slavery and Aborigines' Rights Protection Society (which merged to become ASAPS – the As Soon As Possible Society), and the Union of Students of African Descent. There was even a short-lived African newspaper, the *African Times and Orient Review*, founded and edited by an Egyptian, Dusé Mohammed Ali.

All these organisations were enraged by the race riots in the ports. They campaigned (sometimes with one voice) for better pay at sea and better hostels on land. They also began to express larger concerns about the nature and conduct of imperial rule. The Nigerian Ladipe Solanke wrote to the British journal *West Africa* to refute an article in the *Evening News* which depicted his country as a godless jungle of cannibalism and black magic, with human meat on sale in the markets. His letter sparked a protest which succeeded in eliciting, from the organisers of the 1924 Empire Exhibition at Wembley, a promise to monitor and control press coverage of Africa.

*At this stage, 'India' still refers to India, Pakistan and Bangladesh. It would not fragment into separate – warring – parts until 1947.

Inspired by this minor but pleasing success, Solanke became an ardent rebutter of newspaper reports and was a driving force behind the creation of a new body, the West African Students' Union. He had, he explained, a dream: that Africans must unite in common cause and lay aside their minor differences and refuse to be 'hewers of wood and drawers of water for the other races of mankind'. He was secretary-general of the union for twenty-five years, emphasising always the fact that Africa had a vivid past, if not a preserved history of its own, long before Europe, and specifically Britain, had arrived. While his comrades-in-arms concentrated on the case for national liberation from colonial rule, he pressed for fair trade in cocoa, and opposed the formation of a price-lowering cartel of British buyers. He also kept one eye firmly on the colour bar, which was being raised with increasing determination by many British hotels and supposedly public spaces.

It wasn't easy for an African to find a bed for the night, either in a hotel or a rented flat. Glaswegian dance halls bounced Africans away from their doors with nonchalant and practised ease. The Residential Hotels and Caterers' Association insisted, when challenged, that the bar was solid and would be maintained. There was no question, this time, of racial prejudice being linked to class antipathy, because the African students were neither poor nor ill-educated. Oluwole Ayodele was a law graduate of Jesus College, Oxford, and a student at the Middle Temple, when a hotel in Lancaster Gate refused to give him a room. He sued, successfully, for fifty-five pounds, a triumph that probably owed something to the fact that he was unmistakeably a gentleman: his father was chairman of the Nigerian Printing and Publishing Company, and his uncle was a tribal grandee. The Colonial Office was embarrassed, and realised that future leaders of its dominions were being given a sharp and dismaying lesson in British bad manners. The fact that the pan-African* movements of the inter-war years acquired a distinctly Marxist flavour did not win them many friends in influential circles. C. L. R. James might well have been frozen out for this reason after he arrived in Britain from Trinidad to further his ambitions as a writer. But he had a significant ally in the great West Indian cricketer Learie Constantine, who had settled in Lancashire in 1929 and needed help with his autobiography. James arrived in Plymouth in 1931 and spent a few months in London, acquiring a ticket for the British Museum Library and firing off his first impressions in half a dozen newspaper columns for the Port of Spain *Gazette*, which described his arrival as the 'homecoming' of a Thackeray-loving Anglophile. Eventually, he journeyed north to join Constantine in Nelson and was granted an unusually privileged view of British society.

*The other term for pan-Africanism was 'Ethiopianism' – Ethiopia being taken as the symbolic catch-all for African interests.

Constantine, though a black immigrant, was a cricketing celebrity (the first West Indian to score a century in England) whose social life was a round of lunches, dinners, speeches and talks with the cricket-loving Lancastrians. Neville Cardus, meanwhile, offered James cricket-writing work on the *Manchester Guardian*, which was ideal, allowing him to pore over his Marx and Trotsky, and develop a refined radical philosophy.* Excited by Constantine's resolute cricketing maxim ('They are no better than we'), he helped write the first notes in the programme of Caribbean liberation and self-government, and spoke at Labour Party and workers' meetings in the north-west. Many of his concerns turned out to be of little interest to his new audience, which wanted a few extra pence in wage packets (or any sort of wage packet) at home, and couldn't muster much enthusiasm for revolutionary movements in remote colonies. Constantine might have made the Caribbean famous, wrote James, but people were still 'hazy' as to its exact whereabouts: 'The majority thought the West Indies had something to do with India,' he remarked. Preparing a speech on a park bench, James was once approached by a boy who asked him, in a guileless way, where his spear was.

The leading figure of the small West Indian circle was the Jamaican émigré Dr Harold Moody, who had arrived at Paddington Station in 1904 as a medical student, before becoming a doctor in Peckham. He had married a (white) nurse and had four children, and was increasingly devoted to the cause of racial equality. In 1931 he was the first president of the League of Coloured Peoples, a coalition of often argumentative factions dedicated to the removal of the colour bar and the promotion of racial pride. 'How can the Englishmen respect us', he said, urging the more radical extremes to unite on the simple central issue, 'if we do not respect ourselves?' He wrote letters to *The Times* and published pamphlets which patiently argued for black rights. His words didn't always fall on receptive ears in black audiences, and were sometimes drowned out by bolder rhetoric, such as that favoured by the more radical George Padmore.

In 1936, C. L. R. James went along to listen to the glamorous Padmore. He had been a Communist Party activist in Moscow, had been jailed by German Nazis, and was now stirring things up in the United States. These were radiant battle honours, so it came as a surprise to James to discover that George Padmore was the pseudonym of a man he already knew, a childhood friend and fellow-Trinidadian called Malcolm Nurse: the pair had once swum together in the river in Port of Spain. Inspired, James himself went to America in 1938 to help ignite the sentiments that would later inspire the civil rights movement.

---

*He remained loyal to the idea that class, not racial, conflict was the essence of progress. He later described Marcus Garvey's drive for Afrocentric black power as 'pitiable rubbish'.

After fifteen years of patient agitation he was interned as a Communist and expelled. He made his way back to London somewhat dispirited, feeling that he had wasted his time and energy. His later life was spent writing the elegant, plaintive works of criticism and argument that made him the undisputed *éminence grise* of the Caribbean diaspora.

In the 1930s, as employment began to pick up after the crashes and crises of the previous years, men and women from the Irish Free State began to pour across the sea once again.* This time they were genuine foreigners (though Eire remained a member of the Commonwealth until 1948), but they slipped into Britain's factories, building sites and offices with barely a voice raised against them. Their predecessors had been hated as viciously as any minority in history, even though they had come as fellow countrymen. Now, hardly anyone seemed to object. In 1934, 11,000 came; in 1935 it was 14,000; and in 1936, 24,000. Ramsay MacDonald, called upon to explain his government's policy with respect to this sudden surge, said there was 'no evidence that they came here with the specific purpose of obtaining, when unemployed, assistance from public funds'.

If things were getting easier for the Irish, they were getting harder for Britain's Jews. Though only a weak flaring of the venomous feelings in continental Europe, anti-Semitism was a growing force in British life. There were marches and rallies, and one notable running fight along Cable Street in east London, where, in what was by now a well-established British sport, stone-throwing civilians 'clashed' with the police. Oswald Mosley's marches were unequivocally designed to taunt London's Jewish inhabitants, and in the years to come many of them would recall with bitterness the anti-Semitic jibes and jeers (and blows) which fell upon them. But however odious, persecution on this scale was no deterrent to those fleeing – or being expelled from – the far more menacing oppressions of Nazi Germany. By 1939 some 226,000 had left the Reich for America, Palestine, Britain, France and anywhere else they could get to. Almost every country in Europe tried to close its doors, so many made their way to Shanghai, one of the few genuinely open ports in the world.

The British government fidgeted nervously. No one wanted another surge of refugees. Anglo-Jewish organisations, even as they pleaded for a relaxation in the rules, vowed that 'all expense will be borne by the Jewish community, without ultimate charge to the state'. In the event, they were biting off more than they could chew, because between 1933 and 1939 some sixty thousand Jews arrived in Britain – far too many for voluntary bodies to support on their own.

---

*Indeed, the pattern of their arrival exposes the extent to which the ebb and flow of economic migrants is largely self-regulating: people do not lightly gamble their savings and hopes on labour markets that are already tense and overflowing.

In all, one-third of Germany's Jewish population managed to escape before the borders were closed, and inevitably this was the third most able to leave: the third that had connections, could afford bribes, had contacts abroad, spoke a foreign language or two, knew how to shuffle bank accounts and could read the warning signs most clearly.

The Kitchener Camp in Kent was hastily turned into a holding pen for evacuees in transit to America. It could hold up to three thousand, and was soon full. Many private citizens stepped forward. Harold Macmillan sheltered forty Czechoslovakian exiles in his country house in Sussex, and the families of two more future prime ministers – Jim Callaghan and Margaret Thatcher – put up refugees in their homes. The *Daily Mail*, true to type, ventured the opinion that all of this proceeded from a 'misguided sentimentalism' which would end in tears. 'Once it was known that Britain offered sanctuary to all who cared to come', it declared, repeating one of its pet prejudices, 'the floodgates would be opened, and we should be inundated by thousands seeking a home.'

Parliament wobbled. When a motion calling for the accelerated entry and naturalisation of Austrian refugees was proposed, it was defeated. And the Prime Minister, Neville Chamberlain, while yielding to no man in his contempt for events in Germany, was obliged to point out that 'outlets for settlement' in the empire were 'limited' (Australia, Canada, Rhodesia and so on were deemed overcrowded). There was an international conference on the subject at Evian in Switzerland, which generated more fine words than firm pledges. On Britain's behalf, the government of Tanganyika offered to make fifty thousand acres available, and there was the possibility of a modest tract of land (a hundred thousand square miles) in British Guiana. But otherwise there was nothing to be done. Lord Winterton, meanwhile, attacked people-trafficking. There was 'big money' being made, he told the House of Commons, 'in this most cruel traffic of illegal immigration'.

But Sir Samuel Hoare, the Home Secretary, promised 'sympathetic consideration' to refugees from the Austrian Anschluss, and the former Prime Minister Lord Baldwin launched a fund to raise money for these people who had been 'despoiled of their goods' and 'driven from their homes', and who sought only 'a hiding place from the wind, a covert from the tempest'. It was, he declared, a matter of national pride: 'The honour of our country is challenged,' he said.[3]

The government gave the nod to a scheme to accept five thousand Jewish refugees for training in agriculture, with a view to their subsequent deployment in the colonies, but this was only scratching the surface. The preferred destination for these Jews was Palestine, which was still mandated British territory, but events in the Middle East were already developing into a lethal stand-off. In 1938 Jewish terrorists blew up an Arab fruit market in Haifa, killing seventy-four and wounding 129. The Mufti of Jerusalem responded by calling for a ban on the sale of land to Jews. In 1939 there was an Arab revolt, a general strike and open fighting between Zionist Jews, Arabs and the British military almost every day. From July 1938 to July 1939, 670 Arabs and Jews were killed.

There was a major British military presence in Palestine, which was unable to keep a lid on the peace, and anyway would soon be needed elsewhere. So the government acceded to Arab demands that Jewish immigration be halted, and even patrolled the eastern Mediterranean with gunboats in an attempt to deter refugee ships, and turn them back to wherever they had come from. British vessels actually fired on one vessel attempting to drop 1,400 Jews on to the beach at Tel Aviv, and killed two unlucky émigrés.*

Britain's final gesture towards Germany's Jews before the outbreak of war was to hammer shut the exit routes by which they might have escaped. And in December 1940, a year into the war, the government turned down a request from Luxembourg that it admit two thousand Jews on the grounds that these people were not in any immediate danger. By then, of course, England had been blitzed and food was scarce. It was not an easy time to be magnanimous. But the official Foreign Office line was to treat Germany's Jews simply as German nationals.

None of this prevented the migration of Jews; it simply raised the price. The last few years of the peace were a good time to be a shady shipping agent or harbour official on the Black Sea, the Aegean or the eastern Mediterranean. Even British consular officials could be tempted. One, a Major Dalton, passport controller at The Hague, was found to have plundered three thousand pounds from desperate Jews in return for the relevant papers. When he was exposed, he shot himself.

However, if there was no energetic programme to save Germany's Jews by offering them sanctuary in Britain then nor was there much resolution in the attempt to stop them from coming. William Beveridge, later famous for the report that launched the Welfare State, went to Vienna in 1933 to form the Academic Assistance Council – which in effect sponsored something of a brain drain out of Central Europe. The British Medical Association opposed such moves, fearful that these foreign cuckoos might elbow aside their British colleagues. Perhaps they were simply fearful of being outshone: in 1992 the Royal Society would boast seventy-four immigrant scholars or their children among its members – sixteen of them Nobel Prize winners.

Among the sixty thousand men and women who managed to join the Jewish

---

*When Chaim Weizmann discussed this episode with the Colonial Secretary, Malcolm Macdonald, he accused him of being worse than Hitler. Macdonald muttered something about 'strategic necessities', which Weizmann described as 'bunk'. The meeting was not a success.

community in Britain was a dazzling array of cultural and scientific talent. If Britain (however half-heartedly) proved to be their lifeline, then they more than repaid their benefactor with their contribution to its future vitality. The Siberian-born neurosurgeon Ludwig Guttman, for instance, struggled to Britain in 1939 and received a warm welcome. 'Thank you, Hitler,' said the Minister of Pensions in 1945, 'for sending us men like these.' A specialist in spinal injuries and paraplegia, he was able to set up, when the bloody dust of war had settled, a unique institution, Stoke Mandeville Hospital, which he presided over under the affectionate sobriquet 'Poppa' Guttman.

Any consideration of this galaxy of exiled Jews leaves one a little winded. If Hitler hadn't prevailed then there would be a sizeable hole in Britain's *Who's Who* (not to mention America's). Sigmund Freud came to London in 1938, died a year later, but made a deep impact on British life through the work of his daughter Anna, who established a child therapy clinic in north London, and his grandson, the painter Lucian. Max Born, meanwhile, was one of the leading lights of what Hitler called 'Jewish physics'. He came to England in 1933 and stayed for two decades, returning to Germany a year before receiving his Nobel Prize.*

The effect on British life of tangled, fateful careers such as these can hardly be overstated. The evacuation included musicians such as Otto Klemperer, Georg Solti, Alfred Brendel, three-quarters of what would later become the Amadeus String Quartet and a trio who founded between them both Glyndebourne and the Edinburgh Festival†; it brought scientists such as Hermann Bondi and Max Perutz; philosophers such as Isaiah Berlin and Karl Popper; economists such as Friedrich von Hayek; publishers such as André Deutsch, George Weidenfeld, Walter Neurath and Bela Horovitz; and numberless authors. Arthur Koestler, who concluded his odyssey through occupied France and Portugal by arriving in Britain in 1940, was locked up, for want of a better idea, in Pentonville Prison. Somewhere in this commotion was a future editor of the *Financial Times*, a controller of Radio Three and a head of the British Council. In the 1930s the upper echelons of British life were given a tremendous infusion of new energy. That such characters were able not only to survive but to thrive in Britain is a tribute chiefly to their remarkable gifts and will power, but it suggests also that the image of Britain's established elite as a sniffy and impregnable clique is sometimes too sharply etched. The anti-alien movements that sprang up after the First World War had badly dented Britain's reputation an as open-door nation, but it remained, especially when compared with the terrifying alternatives, an authentic haven.

---

*Among his many bequests to the country that gave him sanctuary was a grand-daughter, born in Australia, called Olivia Newton John.
†Carl Ebert, Rudolf Bing and Fritz Busch launched Glyndebourne as a classic piece of English pastoral, and Bing later went to Scotland to create the Salzburg of the north.

Jan Ludwick Koch was able to escape Czechoslovakia through Budapest and make it to Britain in time to join the army. By D-Day, as a British officer called Robert Maxwell, he was a young man with a big future.The Hungarian Alexander Korda had left Berlin some years earlier, in 1926, and was already building a powerful production unit – the Korda studios in Denham – which turned out a series of upbeat propaganda films when war finally came and ran up three Union Jacks outside; wags said there was one for each British employee. In 1933 he was followed by Imre Pressburger, who changed his name to 'Emeric' in the hope that it sounded more English before teaming up with a scriptwriter, Michael Powell, to form one of most dynamic partnerships British film has ever known. Aby Warburg, scion of the banking family, moved his famous library from Hamburg to London in the same year, and hired Ernst Gombrich to preside over it. Gombrich himself then spent the war monitoring German broadcasts, before settling down to write his *Story of Art*.

Some of east London's Jewish proletariat winced to see these people arriving in England in such superb style, and garnering sympathy for their plight into the bargain. The residents of the East End had suffered harsh treatment in their own faltering and equally desperate bid for freedom. The new arrivals weren't stepping off the docks into foul-smelling sweatshops and being hooted at by yobs on the street; this was the *haute-bourgeoisie*, and it was moving elegantly, if nervously (complacency was no longer possible), into nice houses in Hampstead or along the Finchley Road, a thoroughfare which London's black cab-drivers (many of them Jewish) were quick to dub Finchleystrasse.

One of the more remarkable migrations of this or any other time was driven by the zeal of a single man, a British Stock Exchange clerk named Nicholas Winton. His own Jewish parents had left Germany at the end of the nineteenth century, but he had been baptised as a Christian, and said later that he was motivated by humanitarian rather than religious feelings. In 1938 he went on a fact-finding mission to Prague and was horrified by the plight of its Jews. He lobbied the Home Office and charitable agencies (both Jewish and Christian) and secured approval for a scheme to evacuate as many endangered children as possible to England.* As long as he could obtain the pledge of a new home (and a financial guarantee) for each child, he could go ahead with the plan. Not all, or even many, of the homes that volunteered to take part in his scheme were Jewish, and Winton had to endure some criticism from Orthodox Jewry which objected to placing Jews with Gentile families. But trains were hired, lists drawn up. The transports began.

Winton's first carriages left Prague on 1 December 1938. The children, whose

---

*An attempt to create a similar scheme in America failed when Congress insisted that separating children from their parents was 'contrary to the laws of God'.

parents had successfully inveigled them on to the relevant lists of evacuees, were taken to the burned-out synagogue or the station by their tense, uncertain families. Bewildered boys and girls hung numbers round their necks, and took as much luggage as they could carry. Some had been prevented from packing precious toys, stamps or coins on the grounds that these were of value and could not be exported. Officials wrapped wire round the luggage to ensure that nothing could be slipped in at the last minute. There were hugs and tears, sobs and cries. And then the train hissed and clanked forward, rolling west towards Belgium, the Channel and safety.

At the Belgian border, Nazi guards climbed aboard, stormed along the train looking for stowaways, ordered the children on to a siding and ripped through their bags in search of jewels, cash or anything else worth stealing. However, when they finally arrived in Harwich the children received chocolate – a special gift from Cadbury's, one of the scheme's sponsors. They were put up in a holding camp just outside the town, or transferred on to the Liverpool Street train to meet their new guardians. Some wolfed down the chocolate immediately, before anyone could take it back; others thought it too precious to eat, and let it moulder in their suitcases as the world tumbled into war.

The trains, eight of them in total, rolled on throughout the following year. They chugged towards the Channel ports from Czechoslovakia while the BBC and the newspapers appealed for more volunteers to take in the children. In all, some 669 children were unloaded from boats in Harwich. One boy endeared himself to onlookers by fishing out his violin and playing 'God Save the King'. Some of the others were tiny – just six or seven; some were teenagers. Some of the hosts were saints, others cynics. Some took refugees in the hope that they might make good wives or husbands for their own children; others saw a chance to secure cheap servants. Winton himself admitted that not all the families that signed up were gentle; some were insensitive, others abusive. Some children were given toast while the rest of the family ate roast beef; some found themselves being hauled off to Christian churches and prayer meetings with a view to completing their salvation by driving Jewish doctrines out of them. Others got lucky and found themselves in country houses. Lord James de Rothschild housed twenty-four in the family seat in Buckinghamshire, of whom one, Jack Helman, came upon some local boys when he was out playing football. When they told him, to his great astonishment, that maybe they'd see him for another kickabout the next day, he hurried back inside to confide the incredible news that 'someone who's not Jewish wants to see me tomorrow'.[4]

It was of necessity a hastily improvised scheme, not fussy about details, and by no means a guarantee of happiness. Many of the children who arrived spoke little or no English; most of them ended up bereft. Only a handful saw their parents again, though it was not until after the war that they learned the precise and awful nature of the events that had claimed their lives, and which they

themselves had so narrowly evaded. But, while far from ideal, and shot through with broken hearts, it was still a luminous deliverance. 'I wouldn't claim that it was a hundred per cent successful,' Nicholas Winton said years afterwards. 'But I would claim that everyone who came was alive at the end of the war.'[5]*
At the beginning of September 1939, the last *Kindertransport* was stopped in its tracks by the declaration of war.

There can be few more vivid demonstrations of the sense in which migration is not always, or even, merely a career move. Nor is it ever an exercise to be undertaken lightly. Magnified by the extraordinary circumstances that propelled these children away from the hot flames at their heels, this episode gave us images of migration powerful enough to shape or fix the way we think about the subject today. All immigrants – all those who come as refugees, at least – seem in this light like pale, frightened children: lonely, needy and grief-torn.

It's no great leap from this to the contemporary depictions of immigrants as plaintive and dependent, as hungry mouths to feed, as takers rather than givers, as a burden rather than a source of energy. As a nation, Britain had sought primarily, and until the eleventh hour, to keep these children away from its shores. That its resolve slackened, that the window was permitted to open wide enough to let this stirring evacuation proceed, was in one sense nothing more than a typically British accident: muddled, unplanned, improvised, and conducted with contradictory dashes of personal warmth and official frostiness. For the rest of the century, Britain would continue to pursue this between-two-schools policy, gritting its teeth against immigrants but then admitting them; growling at newcomers while declining to take fierce steps against them; posing as an enemy while acting as a friend. Beneath the official superciliousness and alarm lay a stout refusal to kow-tow to baser instincts. Winton's scheme was a rescue mission, but also a personal whim. That it was not organised on a larger scale is tragic. It may have been a shining instance of low-key British altruism, but it could not quite obscure the abrasive sharpness of the national feeling about foreigners at this benighted time.

---

*Winton was belatedly recognised for his achievement in 1983, with an MBE. Twenty years later, he was knighted. Aged ninety-three, he confessed to being 'somewhat embarrassed by the fuss'.

CHAPTER 19

Imperial Friends and Foes

In the late summer of 1939 a pretty young Dutch-Irish girl called Eda van Heemstra was hastily evacuated from a boarding school in Kent by her mother, who feared that south-east England would soon be struck by a thunderous aerial bombardment. She was by no means the only child to be steered away from the flightpath of the anticipated German bombing campaign. Indeed, she was one of the few able to take refuge by the simple expedient of going home. Home, however, was Holland – Arnhem, of all places – and it would prove to be even more pregnant with peril than the place she had fled. A few years later, in one of the final paroxysms of the war, Arnhem would be pounded into rubble. The girl survived, and in 1948 she was able to return to England to pursue her theatrical career. Like many gorgeous young actresses, she gave herself a marketable stage name: Audrey Hepburn. She would soon become the radiant epitome of English beauty.

In many ways the Second World War was a reprise or continuation of the First, but this time it was a war of rapid movements, sudden retreats, vast distances and pulverising power. It was also the first clash in which civilian populations were as vulnerable as armies. The conflict rolled across Europe and the world like a hurricane, juddering borders, engulfing and dispersing entire peoples as it went.

Once again Britain summoned its colonial subjects to arms, and once again they came. Political protest had done little to dislodge the famous colour bar but the exigencies of war toppled it in a flash. In October 1939, the Colonial Office announced in both Houses of Parliament that all British subjects from the colonies, of whatever race or colour, were 'on the same footing as British subjects of pure European descent'. In practice, only the RAF took this ruling to heart: ten thousand West Indians entered its hangars and cockpits. The army and the navy both continued to rule out coloured officers.* The Indian army, meanwhile, tossed an unprecedented three million men into battle. Lascars, Africans and Orientals sweated below decks on the great Imperial Fleet, or were sucked into gaps in the mines, munitions factories and forests of Britain itself. Round and round the world they went, from Orkney to Trincomalee, in a demographic upheaval which would have resonant consequences. When the guns fell silent, it was at first hoped that life could return to normal, that things could once more be as they had been before 1939. But the technology that had made the conflict so far-flung and destructive – air power – had altered the world's horizons for good. The propaganda deployed to bolster and refuel Britain's fighting spirit, meanwhile, emphasised our insular bloody-mindedness – we were an unassailable fortress; we would fight on the seas and oceans – at precisely the time when it was no longer even close to the truth. The battleship was obsolete; the sea was no longer a moat.

The insular reflex won through, however.† The authorities knew that the internment of Germans in the First World War had been bungled, and were anxious not to make the same mistake again. But such were the animosities aroused by war that the pressure to round up so-called 'enemy aliens' became irresistible. That many were Jewish refugees was a complication no one quite had the energy to unravel: they continued to be treated as German nationals. The machinery of internment cranked into action all over again.

At the outbreak of the war there were about eighty thousand potential 'enemy aliens' in Britain. Many – the recently arrived refugees – were already semi-prisoners in twenty-seven far-flung centres – hotels, racecourses, castles and country houses. They were awaiting dispersal as civilians, and it was a simple enough matter for the government to take over these camps (like the Kitchener Camp in Kent with its three thousand inmates, at least eighty of whom were doctors) and convert them overnight into internment blocks.

Tribunals were set up across the country to process all alien suspects. There were three categories into which people might be placed. They could be refugees who had been 'subject to oppression'; those who had 'definitely thrown in their lot with this country'; or potential hostiles. Filtering

---

*Only one black Briton, Arundel Moody (the son of Dr Harold Moody), received a military commission during the war.
†Once again, the overseas dimension of the war effort was energetically overlooked. The dreadful saga of the Burma/Thailand railway, for example, became an emblem of Oriental brutality visited on British prisoners of war. In fact, of the 100,000 who died in that infamous project, 90 per cent were indentured Asian slaves. They do not feature greatly in David Lean's film *Bridge on the River Kwai*.

foreigners into these classifications was a cumbersome bureaucratic procedure, and in the early days few fell foul of it. In October and November 1939 some 35,000 cases were processed and only 348 men were interned, just 1 per cent of the total. By the following March, some 72,000 cases had been investigated, and only 600 had been interned. No doubt some of the interned men did not deserve to be locked up, but the very low conviction rate reveals that this was far from a knee-jerk reaction. It was cautious, painstaking and restrained.

But the situation began to change in the spring of 1940. Britain suffered a string of humiliating reverses. In April, the attempted invasion of Norway was repelled by a small German garrison. The government, in the name of morale, was happy to let it be thought that Norway had fallen only through the deceitful efforts of cunningly placed Nazi spies. No one wanted to ascribe the failed invasion to our own military or diplomatic incompetence, least of all Churchill (one of its architects). There was an anxious outbreak of spy fever, and all foreigners were suspects. The *Daily Mail* shouted about the 'enemy alien menace', and called for 'doubtful aliens' to be interned immediately. The *Telegraph* spoke of 'a gigantic conspiracy'. *The Times* urged 'ceaseless vigilance' on its sleepy readership. The previous month, the Home Secretary, John Anderson, had noted the way in which the newspapers were 'working up' feelings about 'aliens'. In a letter to his father, he wrote, 'I shall have to do something about it, or we may be stampeded into an unnecessarily oppressive policy. It is very easy in wartime to start a scare.'

Indeed it was. Britain was not yet at war with Italy, but the papers included Italians in their angry commentaries. The *Daily Mirror* went on the offensive with the claim that gullible Britain was home to 'all kinds of brown-eyed Francescas and Marias, beetle-browed Ginos, Titos and Marios'. They were 'indigestible', the paper thought, and were creating a 'seething cauldron' of 'potential betrayal'.*

On 10 May Winston Churchill was promoted (partly on the back of the failure of his own Norwegian invasion plan) to leadership of the cabinet and the nation. On the very same day, German armies burst across the Rhine and charged towards Paris. Luxembourg fell in a day; Holland collapsed soon afterwards; Belgium had surrendered by the end of the month. Churchill had to fight to prevent his colleagues from capitulating there and then: many senior politicians felt that a rapprochement with Hitler was the only hope. Within days, the little boats of southern England were criss-crossing the Channel to rescue the trapped British Expeditionary Force at Dunkirk. The evacuation was skilfully transformed from an abject military reverse into a national triumph,

---

*A slur that even the *Daily Express* found hard to stomach; it described the anti-Italian fury as a 'medieval witch-hunt'.

but the outlook was still worse than grim. The next assault would fall on our own airfields and cities.

The nation was on full alert. Sir Neville Bland, Britain's Minister to Holland, wrote a panicky tract, based on what he had seen in the Netherlands, about the 'Fifth column menace'. 'Every German or Austrian servant', he wrote, 'however superficially charming or devoted, is a real and grave menace.' All across Britain, he warned, lay 'satellites of the monster' waiting to be roused into action.[1] His story gained credibility when, at the end of May, a British woman of Russian ancestry was arrested (along with an officer at the American Embassy) for feeding military secrets to Germany. The government was on record as believing that 90 per cent of the aliens in Britain were 'well disposed', but it had neither the time nor the resolve to weed out the treacherous minority. If the innocent had to suffer, then so be it. There was a war on.

On 10 June Mussolini threw in his lot with Germany and declared war on Britain. There were at least nineteen thousand Italians in Britain, and with the nation in such peril on so many fronts sympathetic treatment was a luxury that could not be afforded. That very day an irritated Churchill issued his celebrated order to 'collar the lot', and the internment programme roared back to life.

That night, mobs gathered in Italian districts in Soho, Liverpool, Glasgow and Edinburgh, armed with stones. All of the seventeen Italian shops in Greenock were ruined. The next day, the Italians were led away; in Edinburgh, two hundred officers set out to arrest all that they could find. In the 1930s there had been many American-inspired depictions of Italians as gangsters and hoodlums, so it was easy to ignite popular sentiment against them: Italian cafés and shops were ripped to pieces. The authorities had previously compiled a list of 'desperate' characters who would be picked up when the time came, and the time had come. They swooped on 'known Fascist clubs' and bars. In two weeks, over four thousand Italians were arrested.*

Shops and cafés put up signs proclaiming their loyalty: 'This firm is entirely British,' said the Spaghetti House in Old Compton Street; Bianchi's in Frith Street tried another tack, declaring that it was Swiss. Bertorelli's sign said: 'The proprietors of this restaurant are British subjects and have sons serving in the British army'. In Leeds, an organ grinder (there were still a few remnants from the old days) wrote a placard which said: 'I'm British and the monkey is from India'.

The authorities were resolute. London's hotel trade suffered the loss of chefs and managers from the Savoy, the Ritz and the Café Royal. The Sardinian owner of a small milk bar on the Strand – Charles Forte – was also hauled off.

An early convert to total war, Churchill pushed for both mass deportation and an acceleration of the internment programme. In the following three

---

*A number were interned for their own safety, and for some arrest came as a relief.

months, more than 27,000 people were rounded up. Once again, the Isle of Man was usually the end of the line, but people were funnelled through transit camps in converted schools – such as the Oratory in London – hospitals, stables, derelict wharves, mills and anywhere else where a straw bed and a padlock could be found. In time, over seven thousand were pushed on to ships and deported. Britain surrendered utterly to the simplest national distinctions. Foreigners were guilty until proven innocent. No one even bothered to pretend it was fair, though locking up German Jews alongside Nazi prisoners of war was pushing unfairness to new levels.

For once, it wasn't enough to have influential friends. Peter Jacobsohn was living in Hampstead with his mother, an Anglophile who had translated *Doctor Dolittle* and *Winnie the Pooh* into German. They had fled Germany when the liberal magazine they owned fell under Nazi supervision. In 1935 Jacobsohn had written a pamphlet urging that the magazine's editor, Carl von Ossietzky, be awarded the Nobel Peace Prize (he had been imprisoned by the Nazis for preaching pacifism). His petition was backed by luminaries such as Bertrand Russell, H. G. Wells, Virginia Woolf and Aldous Huxley, and Ossietzky was awarded the prize.* Nevertheless, in Britain five years later, Jacobsohn was interned, in spite of a no doubt eloquent plea from John Betjeman.

The arbitrariness of the process was often absurd. Aliens in Cambridge were arrested, on the grounds that the city was a 'restricted area' – not too far from Sandringham, perhaps? – while foreign students in Oxford were not. The Austrian historian Dr Franz Borkenau was the author of *The Totalitarian Enemy*, but this cut little ice with the police. They raided Hampstead Library, a noted alien haunt, and captured the Hungarian editor of the *Picture Post*, along with some twenty BBC announcers or translators. Max Braun was the deposed leader of the Social Democratic Party in the Saar; he had fled in 1935 to avoid certain execution. Even he was interned. In one of the Isle of Man camps, over 80 per cent of the internees were Jewish refugees, and there were 332 British-born children. They were part of a talented and privileged diaspora blessed with the wit, the resources and the good fortune to escape Nazi Germany: artists, journalists and photographers, lawyers and novelists, actors and musicians. Of the 1,500 men in the camp, 121 were artists or writers; there were also 113 scientists, 89 engineers, 68 lawyers and 50 doctors or dentists.

The idea that they might be significant and valuable allies was drowned by the fear that they might also be the core of a fifth column. There were a few plaintive objections. The young Michael Foot wrote a famous article in the *Evening Standard* titled 'Why not lock up General de Gaulle?' And even

---

*This prompted Hitler to declare that in future no German would be eligible for such decadent and laughable foreign baubles.

Churchill conceded that the internees included men 'whose sympathies were wholly with this country'. He continued, 'I am very sorry for them. We cannot . . . draw all the distinctions which we would like to do.'*

Some of the prisoners had been this way before, and knew exactly what to expect. Karl Wehner had come to England as a language student just before the First World War, and had passed through the entire apparatus of internment: a police cell, a temporary billet at Olympia, a converted cruise liner off Southend (where he feasted on great food – steak! roast pork! – along with the German tennis team), and the formal hut camp at Knockaloe on the Isle of Man. After the war he returned to Frankfurt and became a journalist, but following the Berlin Olympics in 1936 he joined the huddle of expatriate German journalists in London. When war broke out, he was in Holland, trying to get money out of Germany. He managed to charm his way across the Channel, but was arrested when he landed and hauled off to Brixton Prison, where he ran into the one-time correspondent of a Hamburg newspaper with whom he was, as it happened, supposed to be having lunch that day. Along with many German Jews (half the inmates at Olympia were Jewish) and various other anti-Nazi dissidents and dignitaries, he was transferred to a Butlin's pleasurama in Clacton. The inmates were not happy campers, despite the presence of a pool, a football pitch, shops and a smashing Pirates' Grotto. It had, said one grumpy resident, 'everything the exuberant imagination of a bank-clerk could dream of'. One day, Wehner found a rough letter 'D' chalked on his door. He had no idea what it meant. Detain? Deport? Destroy? Wehner braced himself for another stint on the Isle of Man. In all, he would spend over seven years of his life in internment camps, the final months of which, as the camp began to empty of refugees and bulge with Nazi prisoners-of-war, were by far the most unsettling.

By June 1940, the camps were overflowing, and hasty preparations were made to ship the internees as far from Britain as possible. The *Duchess of York* took 1,700 German merchant seamen, 500 military prisoners and 400 others to Canada.† The next transport was an elegant Blue Star liner, the *Arandora Star*. It seemed a bit luxurious for the short crossing to the Isle of Man, where most of the passengers presumed they were heading. But it was stuffed with 374 British officers and crew, 712 Italians and 478 Germans, and set sail for Canada on 1 July. The following morning, it was torpedoed and sunk. The U-boat

*One of his favourite scientific advisers, Frederick Lindemann, was born in Baden Baden, and schooled in Darmstadt and Berlin. Lindemann was the son of an Alsatian scientist who had married an American and lived in Devon. Despite being the son of a naturalised Briton, he was refused a commission in the First World War because of his birthplace. But as a professor of philosophy at Oxford he was a concise communicator, an early prophet of radar and an eager advocate of aerial bombing as an instrument of war.
†The military prisoners had the best cabins, as part of a reciprocal deal to ensure good treatment for British PoWs.

captain who torpedoed it (Günther Prien, the fearless 'Bull of Scapa Flow') ignored the swastika fluttering above the deck – the sign that it was carrying German prisoners. Either that or he thought it was a ruse. Most of the Germans on board the *Arandora Star* were seamen, and knew what to do: they stripped off their clothes and jumped into the water. The Italians, however, were landlubbers: some clung to the sinking ship's rope ladders; others were trapped below decks. A few survivors recalled the ship's death rattle: a fatal groan which sounded, to those who heard it, like the high keening scream of distant geese. The sea was awash with bodies bobbing between boats and rafts.

Some elements of the press, not discouraged by politicians, tried to blame the passengers for the loss of life. 'Aliens Fight Each Other in Wild Panic,' said the *Daily Herald*. The sinking was shrouded in official secrecy: no one knew exactly how many people had been lost, nor (since there had been no detailed embarkation lists) could anyone be sure who they were. For Britain's Italian community it was a staggering blow. The authorities were happy to let it be believed that all the drowned men were prisoners-of-war, knowing that few British tears would be shed on their behalf.

By the middle of July, nearly seven thousand internees had arrived in Canada, dodging the U-boats on every voyage. The *Dunera* left Liverpool, sailed north and was hit by a torpedo off Scotland. It proceeded to limp, short of supplies and in terrible shape, all the way to Australia. The voyage took almost two months, and grim stories began to surface about the appalling conditions on board. The passengers had been prodded on to the ship at the tips of bayonets; many had been relieved of their valuables. They had been locked in airless holds with closed hatches; shaving and washing were almost forbidden – lice were rife; the lavatories were overflowing. There were rifle-butt assaults and muggings by the crew. In Melbourne and Sydney, piles of unlabelled luggage were picked over by men who were visibly emaciated and ill. There were British troops on board, under the command of Lieutenant-Colonel Scott, who, while convinced that the Jewish passengers were subversive liars, 'not to be trusted in word or deed', felt that the captured Nazis on board were 'fine, honest and straightforward'.[*2]

One of the guards detailed to oversee the initial boarding of the *Dunera* was so shocked by what he saw that he wrote a letter to his father, describing the whole procedure as 'a thoroughly bad show'. This mild reproof would not usually have been enough to send shock waves through the system, but his father happened to be a senior official at the Foreign Office. Eyebrows were raised, and they were accompanied by some very red faces when it became evident that some of the abused passengers on the *Dunera* were survivors from the *Arandora Star*. They had been plucked from the sea, returned to Greenock,

---

*Scott and two of his NCOs were court-martialled for their behaviour on the *Dunera*.

then shuttled down to Liverpool to rejoin the queue at the docks. This inhumane excess was neither planned nor officially approved, but it was a sign that the machinery for deporting aliens was haphazard and out of control. Not before time, questions started to be asked in Whitehall.

The selection process for internees on the *Arandora Star* had, it transpired, been almost random. And the average age of the Italian dead, it turned out – to the consternation of the few who knew – was nearly fifty; 10 per cent were over sixty. Elderly men had been sent to their deaths. Rab Butler's inquiry criticised both the Home Office and MI5, for pursuing a strategy which allowed Germany to accuse Britain of putting Jews into camps. It was bad propaganda, as well as bad behaviour.

News of conditions in the camps themselves started to come fully to light. It emerged that the list of banned publications included, ludicrously, *The Times* and the *Oxford Book of English Verse*. A commander in Bromley was found to have stolen money and jewellery from his charges. The whole process, as one memo put it, was 'dunderheaded'. Somehow, at a time when London was being blitzed and the nation's Spitfires were cartwheeling and somersaulting in the skies over Biggin Hill, the whole policy was reversed. The government ordered the release of all internees, and by the end of 1940 some ten thousand had been discharged. By the following summer, only 1,300 were still being held.

The internment of aliens is a sad and sorry story – no one's finest hour. But it was a brief episode in a ghastly war. The internees themselves bore their misfortunes with resigned good grace; on the whole, they accepted what was happening as inevitable, possibly even understandable. When Max-Otto Ludwig Loewenstein (later Mark Lynton) was in Manchester, he was visited by a plump, bespectacled, cartoon-like 'Man from Intelligence', who explained to the assembled company, in impeccable German, that the entire policy of internment was 'cretinous', but that they had to be patient. 'Most of us did not bear the slightest grudge then,' wrote Lynton in his memoir of the episode.* 'Nor, oddly enough, ever afterwards.' Another internee, Teddy Schwartz, asked 'What can you expect from the English? You make allowances.'

Some of the camps were purpose-built barracks, but at Douglas, a row of boarding-houses on the edge of town was fenced in; at Huyton, the internees

---

Accidental Journey (1995) describes how he was escorted on 12 May to a camp in a field outside Bury St Edmunds, bussed to Liverpool and held in the camp at Huyton (where some elite prisoners received regular hampers from Fortnum & Mason, much to the bewilderment of the guards). He then travelled to Canada on the *Ettrick*, half of whose passengers were battle-hardened Nazi prisoners; spent the Atlantic crossing unblocking the horrendous latrines; worked a passage back to England on his release in January 1941 to join the Pioneer Corps along with six future Nobel Prize winners; joined the Royal Armoured Corps; and eventually (while still officially an 'enemy alien') became a major in intelligence. He attended at both the fall of Berlin and the Nuremberg Trials.

lived in *Coronation Street*-style terraces ringed by barbed wire. They were still prisons, though, and some inmates suffered claustrophic breakdowns – camp fever. But for most they were tolerable, or better. Some of the Italians, whose ranks were soon swollen by prisoners-of-war, had a memorable time. In the Isle of Man, they ate well and worked in the fields, far from the din of a fight in which they had little interest. Ennio Camisa was plucked from the family delicatessen in Soho where he had worked since 1920, but found that he loved island life: three square meals a day and a healthy outdoor routine. 'We weren't like prisoners,' he recalled. 'It was like a family.'[3] In the Orkneys, Italian prisoners built the Churchill Barrier, an artificial breakwater to protect the British fleet at Scapa Flow. They also built a lovely Italian chapel beside the sea near Kirkwall, and were pleased to find that many of the freckle-faced local girls thought they were simply marvellous – handsome, dashing and sad. In the German-Jewish camps, meanwhile, there were easily enough professors to hold classes on art history or classical mythology, just as there were enough chefs to ensure that the food was edible. Hermann Bondi came from Vienna with his parents in 1938 and studied mathematics at Cambridge until he was led into captivity. He was transported to Canada, but returned to become an influential member of the team that devised Britain's radar defence; later, he won a Nobel Prize for Physics. In Quebec he gave what Max Perutz, a fellow internee and later a famous scientist and author in his own right, remembered as a brilliant course in vector analysis. As an incarcerated alien, Claus Moser took up number-crunching as an assistant to a statistician who was recording camp flows, a useful first step in a career that would eventually lead to his becoming head of the Central Office of Statistics. For him internment was 'a bit of an adventure', though he added that for the older generation of internees, such as his own father, it was 'almost beyond understanding'.

The camps were alive with the sound of music, too. The Amadeus string players, who soon became known as the 'Wolf Gang', were by no means alone. MittelEuropa had landed: it was high-minded and exacting, and it was falling on a population of hymn-singers and music-hall balladeers. The musical world, once again, took on a distinct Germanic tinge; its velvet-plush walls reverberated with Beethoven and Mozart, Schubert and Brahms. Ralph Vaughan Williams, though he had agitated for the release of interned musicians during the war, was troubled. 'They have great musical traditions behind them,' he wrote. 'In some ways they are more musically developed than we are, and therein lies the danger.' The very prowess of Austrian music-making, he felt, might 'entirely devour the tender little flower of our English culture. The Austrians have a great musical tradition, and they are apt to think that it is the only musical tradition.'[4] This is not the voice of some anti-foreign little Englander. On the contrary, it is a clear confession of cultural inferiority.

Despite his reservations, though, Vaughan Williams became one of the Anglo-Austrian Music Society's patrons, and urged it to embrace, rather than shoulder aside, British music-making.

In a way, he was echoing the fears of those doctors who had resented the arrival of medically trained German refugees before the war, or the irritation of trade unionists who feared that foreign workers would embarrass their British colleagues. Much has been made of the sense of superiority which Britons have often brought to their dealings with foreigners, but such condescension often masked something more like nervousness. Britain's cultural insularity, a famous if contradictory reflex in a nation whose interests spanned the earth, had contrived to resist some of the grander European artistic movements: modernism and the avant-garde in art, music and literature. Now, through this infusion of maestros and impresarios, Britain began to realise that there might be something to it, after all.

The war years were a period of tightly policed borders. It wasn't easy for anyone to pass through. But one group of people arrived *en masse*, if not all at once. The Poles, squeezed between Hitler to the west and Stalin to the east, embarked on journeys in which the best and sometimes the only road led to Britain.

There had been a small community of Catholic Poles in England since the late nineteenth century. Joseph Conrad was its most notable member, but perhaps 1,500 of his compatriots came with him as evacuees from unsuccessful uprisings against the assorted rulers of Prussia, Austria and Russia. In 1894 a Polish church, St Casimir, was consecrated in Shadwell. The declaration of the Polish Republic in 1919 led to the establishment of an embassy and various other forums for cooperation, such as the Anglo-Polish Club, which was founded in 1932. By then, there were about five thousand Poles in Britain. They made clothes in London, dug coal in Lanarkshire and worked in the (still foul) salt works in Cheshire. They built a new Polish Roman Catholic church in Devonia Road, Islington. These were neither strong nor ancient ties, however, and there was little infrastructure to support what was about to arrive. When Poland fell to the twin invasions of Hitler and Stalin, its army scattered: there was a stampede north to the Baltic and south to Romania. A new government-in-exile landed in London, bringing some three thousand officials and loyalists with it, and settling in South Kensington and Earl's Court, an area which soon became known as Little Poland.

Some of the newcomers had relatively easy passages. General Sikorski took refuge in Romania, and travelled from Bucharest to Paris in the company of the French ambassador – he arrived in London with his dignity and his epaulettes intact. A miniature navy – three destroyers and a pair of submarines – steamed resolutely into Rossyth, and the rump of a merchant fleet (thirty-eight ships –

three of them troop carriers) also slipped across the North Sea to swell Allied tonnage. Many of the Poles who had made it to France and joined up with the army there managed to leap into the little boats that chugged away from Dunkirk. By the summer of 1940, some twenty thousand had made it safely to Britain.

A much larger number – some eighty thousand – followed a more arduous path. The mythology of the Second World War does not always remind us that Stalin invaded Poland only days after Hitler did, in accordance with the agreed carve-up of territory. In the process, he forced the potentially troublesome middle class of eastern Poland into camps in Siberia and Kazakhstan. It is possible that more than one and a half million Poles were transported to the east at this time; nearly a million of them died, mostly from starvation, over the next two years. Somewhere in this population was a doomed army. Four thousand Polish officers had been executed in March 1940 in Katyn Forest near Smolensk and dumped in a mass grave. More than twenty thousand others had suffered the same fate at various sites. Only under glasnost in the Soviet Union were these details confirmed, and the extermination of these Poles remains one of the most neglected atrocities of an atrocious century.

No one was coming to the rescue of those who were experiencing a slower death in the camps. In June 1941, however, when the Nazi–Soviet Pact was destroyed by the German invasion, they were rapidly identified as useful members of the Allied war machine, and liberated. Stalin initially wanted them in the Red Army, a proposal which was successfully resisted. Instead, they were delivered through the Caspian Sea into Persia and Palestine, where they were rehabilitated as an active fighting force. This was General Anders' army, and it was a precious if dishevelled gift to Churchill's war planners. It was deployed in the Middle East, North Africa and Italy, where the Carpathian Cavalry and the Podolski Rifles fought their way north. Some of it swelled the Polish forces back in Britain, training for and dreaming of the day when they would launch a vengeful assault on Germany itself. General Anders petitioned Britain to help evacuate the civilians as well, but his pleas fell on unreceptive ears. 'In Anders' protests,' wrote Churchill in an official minute, 'we see all those elements of instability which have led to the ruin of Poland through so many centuries, in spite of the individual qualities and virtues of the Poles.'

Ultimately, a large Polish military presence was stationed in Britain during the war, with an even larger number falling under its dominion overseas. The Royal Air Force accepted fourteen thousand Polish airmen from October 1939. From bases at Eastchurch in Kent and Northholt in Middlesex (where a war memorial commemorates their sacrifice), they were nimble aces in the Battle of Britain,* and tireless bomber crews. Many were stationed in the east of Scotland and deployed in coastal defence, but Polish units fought everywhere, and

---

*Polish pilots shot down one in seven of all German planes destroyed in the Battle of Britain.

formed part of the force which was thrown on to the Normandy beaches in 1944. Polish intelligence units, meanwhile, played a decisive part in the cracking of the German Enigma code, having long before appreciated that modern code-breaking required mathematicians, not rugby blues.

The Poles were heroes, and were much mythologised as such – eager, brave, talented, incomprehensible and palpably our friends. Despite the entrenched belief that one Englishman 'was worth ten bloody foreigners', the public cheered them on, as they did the Czech pilots whose homeland had been overrun in a similar fashion, and who served on similar terms. But in government circles the Poles were thought to be a slightly awkward case: an expatriate chattering class of defeated cavaliers. Nor was it always clear under whose flag they were fighting: the Polish government-in-exile, based in the Rubens Hotel near Victoria Station, was keen to regard them as its own, while London's war planners insisted that they answer to British orders. Churchill, for one, was greatly irritated by what he saw as footling and ill-timed Polish demands – for their own uniforms, say, or their determined rudeness to our dear ally in Moscow. The Poles could also be noticeably and embarrassingly hostile to Jews, a tendency which became clear when some Anglo-Polish Jews were sent to Polish units on the assumption that their shared nationality would foster a tight-knit camaraderie. When they arrived, they were warned that they would be first up against the wall when the war ended. In early 1944 two hundred Polish Jews deserted and demanded, despite being informed that they would be shot, transfers to British regiments. The War Office preferred to think of them merely as shirkers, a stance which became hard to maintain when the Polish Foreign Minister-in-exile said he'd 'gladly be rid of them', and when the *Jewish Chronicle* began to publish reports of the anti-Semitic abuse being doled out in some Polish circles.

The Poles, in other words, often seemed infuriating. But from the Polish point of view, the British – especially those in power – seemed oblivious to the scale of the many tragedies and horrors that had befallen them.* Perhaps, too, Churchill, his colleagues and the public at large had a guilty conscience. It was obvious, long before the war moved towards its final negotiations at the Yalta Conference, that there was going to be no restoration of a free and independent government in Warsaw. In his previous discussions with Stalin, Churchill

---

*The émigré magazine *Truth* ran a poetic critique of Britain's impatience with so-called Polish pride:

> A little 'sensitive'? Are we surprised?
> Four times partitioned, murdered, robbed, despised . . .
> No man has taken Oxford from us, yet:
> No man says 'Give us Scotland, and forget.'
> But if he did, I fancy we should strike
> The same proud poses that you so dislike.

(knowing that he was playing a weak hand) had pointedly failed even to mention Poland. So the issue of what to do with the Polish army loomed large in government circles as the war entered its endgame. And it intensified when assorted civilians and dependants began to join the throng. The Poles had been flung so far and so fast that many new attachments had formed: some of the soldiers had Romanian, Italian or Egyptian wives – and surely they didn't expect our hospitality. Polish civilians who had been deported to Stalin's camps, meanwhile, continued to drift in the footsteps of the troops. In 1943 two thousand Polish women trekked south from Russia to India, and worked their way across the Pacific to Australia, South America and Mexico. They did not have a clue what might have happened to their relatives or friends, but their eyes were fixed on Britain as the only place where they could be reunited with their families.

There were soldiers, civilians, government officials, men, women, children, orphans and exotic wives – 160,000 in all. Churchill, swallowing his personal reservations, rose to the occasion, as he so often did, in the House of Commons: 'His Majesty's Government', he promised, 'will never forget the debt they owe to the Polish troops . . . I earnestly hope that it may be possible to offer the citizenship and freedom of the British Empire, if they so desire . . . We should think it an honour to have such faithful and valiant warriors dwelling among us as if they were of our own blood.'[5] This was a resonant but misleading pledge. Privately, senior figures were praying that they could push the Poles home, however gravely their country had been damaged or changed. 'It is much to be hoped', said Herbert Morrison, the always pessimistic Home Secretary, 'that a situation in which we are obliged to offer British nationality to large numbers of Poles will not arise.'[6] He was worried that other foreigners who had helped the war effort would claim equal consideration, and he was joined by Ernest Bevin, the Foreign Secretary, who also pushed for repatriation. Churchill, though, in one of his final acts as Prime Minister before his election defeat in 1945, succeeded in cowing his cabinet into an acceptance that the Poles were 'a special case'. He even wanted the Polish army (which was costing some £2.5 million per month) to be stationed in Germany as part of the postwar military system. A deal was struck, although not with the Poles themselves – they took no part in these discussions, and probably would have walked out in disgust if they had. A new unit would be established: the Polish Resettlement Corps. It would be a foreign legion, not itself military, but under military control. It would perform civilian tasks in industrial and agricultural reconstruction, and would also function as a labour exchange, assigning Poles to jobs in sectors of the stricken economy. For the first time ever, a major group of immigrants would be formally welcomed, embraced and given assistance.

The first step was to disband the Polish army. In March 1946 General Anders was summoned to Downing Street and told, by Clement Attlee and Ernest

Bevin, that the decision had been taken. He was then informed that his men would be urged – but not forced – to return to Poland. They could, if they so desired, sign on with the Polish Resettlement Corps and take their chances here. Enrolment in the Corps would be for two years; members would be deployed in bomb disposal, farming and rebuilding alongside demobilised British troops. It wasn't the most attractive offer that has ever been made to a bereft people, but it was all there was. Of the 160,000 eligible for the scheme, some managed to secure tickets to America and elsewhere, and nine thousand decided to return to Soviet-ruled Poland. But 120,000 accepted their lot and resolved to stay.

Those traditional opponents of migrant workers – the unions – were among the first to make their voices heard over all this. The government was hoping to send two thousand Poles into the coal mines each week. In response, the National Union of Mineworkers banned all Poles from its pits, even though there was an estimated labour shortage of a hundred thousand men in the industry. The National Union of Agricultural Workers and the Amalgamated Union of Engineering Workers also vetoed jobs for Poles on the grounds that there had not been 'full consultation'. Other unions agreed to Polish workers only through gritted teeth, and after insisting on clauses which allowed them to boot out the Poles if there were any British lads who needed work. There was a suspicion that the trade unions were toeing the Soviet line by denouncing the Poles as capitalist troublemakers. 'I ask you,' said the leader of the Communist Party of Great Britain in 1947, 'does it make sense that we allow 500,000 of our best young people to put down their names for emigration abroad, when at the same time we employ Poles who ought to be back in their own country?'[7]

Maybe these attitudes were a surly response to the fact that the Poles were (and still are) legendarily hard workers. Perhaps the unions were afraid that their members would be shown up. Two Polish ex-soldiers joined a factory where workers were expected to produce five hundred pins a day. They felt that no one would mind if they produced twelve hundred, but they were sacked. 'Heaven forbid that you should work with excessive speed or enthusiasm,' wrote Karol Zbyszewski in one of the many new Polish newspapers.* 'For you would be well on the way to creating enemies for yourself.'[8]

Slowly, as the months passed, the unions came round to the scheme. The National Union of Mineworkers achieved a significant victory for its members by agreeing to accept Poles only in return for a five-day week. In January 1947 there were 2,764 Poles working in British industry; by October there were 43,000. By the end of 1948, 65,000 of the members of the Polish Resettlement

---

*The *Dziennik Polski* was the biggest, achieving sales of 31,000 in 1951. It printed news about Poles in Britain as well as reports from home: it even printed the names of Polish pools winners. There were many others – the intellectual journal *Kultura*, for instance. As Brendan Bracken remarked, if you put two Poles in the Sahara Desert, they would certainly start a newspaper.

Scheme had been placed in full employment. And by 1949, with fewer than five thousand people unplaced, the Polish Resettlement Corps was wound up, ahead of schedule and at a cost to the nation of £122 million, far less than it would have cost to maintain them as an unemployed burden on our resources, and far less than the tax revenues that would soon be skimmed from their pay packets. Winding up the Corps, Brigadier Carden Wroe said: 'Thanks to their determination and industry, many Poles are earning good wages and are altogether content with their lot.' That might have been going a bit far – many Poles were disillusioned and miserable. But no one could deny that the scheme had been a success.

The Poles were offered naturalisation, and while they didn't rush to fill out the papers – they were not giving up on their dream of a return to a free Poland that easily – the Home Office was soon processing 1,600 applications a month.* They were also offered language training and vocational courses: fishing in Aberdeen, forestry in Leith, tailoring in Hereford. A few, the lucky ones who had managed to get some of their money out of Poland, set up small businesses on their own. In the spring of 1950, there were 177 Polish farms, 128 Polish watch-repair shops, 78 Polish furniture dealers, 70 Polish photographers and 50 Polish boarding-houses. These businesses were keen to employ other Poles, so jobs could be found, so long as you weren't too fussy. Lawyers worked as nightwatchmen; teachers washed dishes.

At first, the Poles continued to live in camps, the upgrading of which rarely involved more than the removal of the barbed wire that had hemmed in prisoners of war. They were noted scrimpers and savers; expert scavengers for firewood. Some hoarded their meagre gains and sent off parcels of food, clothes and medicine to Poland, where conditions defied belief. But they rapidly drifted into hostels before disappearing off the official register and into civilian life. As with previous migrations, a service industry mushroomed to employ and support them. There were Polish delicatessens, selling rye bread, sausages and pickled herring. There were cafés, clubs and bars all over the country. There were twenty-one Polish schools, and a Polish university was set up in Earl's Court to satisfy the aspirations of the demobbed troops. Students could sit exams and obtain external degrees from the University of London. There was a Polish library, and Polish books were published and circulated. The Polish Army Choir had been a great hit in the war and remained hugely popular. There were a couple of hundred mostly Polish pubs, and even Polish comedians. One astonished radio listeners by announcing, on April Fool's Day, in a perfect impersonation of Hitler, that he was thinking of invading North America in order to protect the rights and

*Jewish Poles tended to be at the front of the queue for naturalisation. They had absolutely no intention of going back to Poland, 'free' or not.

interests of the many German people there. Marian Hemar, meanwhile, raised laughs in his revue at the White Eagle Club in London by joking, à la Henry Ford, that Poland could choose any future it liked, so long as it was black.

There were still occasional episodes of bad-feeling. Ill-wishers accused the Poles of racketeering, prospering while the heroes of El-Alamein were shunned. When a Polish thief went on the run with a revolver, the papers warned of lawless aliens on the loose in our peaceful little Eden. One opinion poll reported that 56 per cent of Britons thought the Poles should 'go home'. But these were isolated incidents. There were no race riots, no attacks on Polish businesses. For the most part, the Poles continued to be thought of as valiant Churchillian warriors. Certainly, no group of foreigners had ever melted into British society with such speed and so little clamour. An influx the size of the Jewish disembarkation at the end of the nineteenth century provoked no major backlash, no new Aliens Act, and very little racist mythmaking. Ealing, in west London, became something of a Polish enclave, with churches, schools, cafés and plenty of heavily accented chatter in the streets.

The Poles had many advantages over most immigrants, though. They were white, often middle class, Christian, industrious, free-thinking, free drinking (always popular with the locals) and – most important of all – devoutly anti-German. They were victims of terrible events, and arrived at a time of chronic labour shortage: after their initial trepidation British workers realised they had no reason to feel hard done by. It probably helped, too, once the Iron Curtain had descended, that there was no possibility that they would be joined by hordes of their countrymen. Indeed, contact between the Polish immigrants and their homeland was soon severed altogether.

If their immigration was smooth, though, it was also because the authorities were for once moved to provide both practical and rhetorical support. It might have made a good model for future migrations. In the event, it proved a one-off. In the years to come, those who came would be greeted with bristling antipathy at all levels of society. Britain became famous not for its liberality, for the breadth of its international connections or for its respect for foreign peoples, but for a notorious xenophobia.

The word is mostly defined as a nationalistic hatred of anything foreign, but at its root is the Greek word *xenos*, meaning 'guest'. So xenophobia is, literally, a fear of guests. This does indeed seem a distinctive national terror. Guests might eat all the food! They might outstay their welcome! For a people whose bungalows were their castles, the thought of unexpected visitors, the inconvenience of having to lay an extra place at supper, was enough to make anyone turn pale.

CHAPTER 20

The Empire Comes Home

On the home front, the war years had their festive side. Socially – even sexually – some traditional shackles were loosened. Women strode off to work in what had previously been a man's world, and still had the energy to go dancing in the evening. Racketeers had a field day; crime soared. Anything went. And a million and a half American troops came as temporary immigrants to whoop it up in the shires before climbing into their bombers, or heading for the beaches of Normandy. They splashed their money around in the pubs and dance halls, tempted eager girls with generous supplies of stockings, chocolate and cigarettes, and handed out sweets to the children. The invigorating effect of their presence is well known: aside from anything else they sired some 22,000 Anglo-American children.

Among their number was a sizeable force of 130,000 black troops. The American army was strictly segregated, and in Britain continued to impose strictures on black soldiers which were shocking even to the littlest Englander. The government did its best to accommodate the American insistence on a form of apartheid, but many Britons leapt to the defence of these victimised allies. Ostensibly, the war was being fought on behalf of underdogs, and the callous manners of white American troops (especially their Military Police) rankled. In Belfast, a bus conductor confronted white soldiers who were busily hurling black troops off the crowded vehicle and told them, 'No colour bar here, mate.' And there were many appreciative testimonials on behalf of the abused men. 'We find the coloured troops much nicer to deal with,' said a canteen worker in Hull; 'I love the Americans,' said a West Country farmer quoted in the *New*

Statesman, 'but I don't like those white ones they've brought with them.' These were common views. 'The Negroes could teach our boys some manners,' said a publican quoted in *Stars and Stripes*. Yankee soldiers were infamous for sneering at the British way of life as dim, small, backward and cheap. The black infantrymen were much more courteous. 'Everyone here adores the Negro troops,' said one Wiltshire woman.[1]

Not everybody was so enthusiastic. One over-eager Conservative MP, Maurice Petherick, wrote himself into the footnotes of racial shame by crudely urging the Foreign Secretary to send the black troops to North Africa, perhaps, or 'to go and fertilise the Italians, who are used to it anyway'. The *New Statesman* cheerfully recounted the story of a society lady who decided, in the spirit of doing her bit, to invite some American GIs for lunch. She wrote to the commanding officer, suggesting that he send six men, adding 'No Jews Please'. On the appointed day she opened her door to find six large black soldiers on her doorstep. There must, she stammered, have been some mistake. 'Oh no, ma'am,' said one of the soldiers. 'Colonel Cohen no make any mistake.'

The extent to which the black soldiers inspired both sympathy and applause brought wrinkles to the foreheads of senior American officers. 'The small-town British girl', wrote a baffled General Eisenhower, 'would go to a movie with a Negro soldier quite as readily as she would go with anyone else, a practice that some of our white troops could not understand. Brawls often resulted, and our white soldiers were further bewildered when they found that the British press took a firm stand on the side of the Negro.'[2] Some of this friendliness can be attributed to the genuine camaraderie and laying down of grievances inspired by the war; some flowed from nothing more substantial than the British weakness for lads in uniform. Much the same hospitality was extended to the West Indian men who joined the services. Those working on RAF bases were embraced as friends by their neighbours; some even resolved to come back once the fighting was over.

But after the war the situation changed rapidly, and not for the better.

Naturally, Britain celebrated victory with a stream of patriotic films, books, combat magazines and triumphalist histories and memoirs, all of which clung to the old idea of Britain as a sorely pressed but invincible island race. The war, according to such retrospective propoganda, had been a matter of wit and courage under fire, daring raids, never-say-die tight corners, stoic endurance during the air-raids – a masterpiece of spirited improvisation and derring-do. It was all thoroughly heroic. But such mythmaking obscured the extent to which Britain, victory or no victory, had been ruined by the war. The nation was exhausted, bankrupt and broken. There was rubble in the streets; the shops were empty. No one could say when rationing would end: austerity – make do and mend – would remain the watchword well into the 1950s.

The world outside showed no disposition to stand still. Europe was awash with displaced persons, evacuees, released prisoners of war, orphans and widows. In the postwar months, millions of people were 'on the move', looking for new homes or old. Britain, despite the fact that it was facing an acute labour shortage, hoped at first that it could avoid giving a home to any of these problematic wanderers. We had, it was felt, enough on our plate with the Poles. But a committee of the great and the good – the Foreign Labour Committee – was charged with the task of plugging the labour gap. It had a million jobs to offer, it estimated, in agriculture, hospitals, mining and other essential industries, and it was eager to scoop up the most useful elements of the shifting continental population. In April 1947 the Ministry of Labour employed thirty-three people as recruitment officers in Germany and Austria, and announced that four thousand foreigners a week were on their way. As a hasty first step, 118,000 prisoners of war sailed from America and were set to work in agriculture. They were, in effect, chain gangs. Many of the other newcomers were temporary or transient, but when the dust settled 180,000 foreigners had made their home in Britain, truffling for jobs in its war-shattered towns.

Among the most welcome were the Italians. In 1947 just 350 Italians risked a landing in Britain. By 1949 some 6,500 had arrived to work in factories, foundries and brickworks. And in the decade that followed, roughly 8,000 Italians came every year. Many travelled from the blighted southern region of the war-torn peninsula, and some came on specific assignments. Seven hundred Italian bricklayers were invited, along with four chefs to make them feel at home, to the clay fields around Bedford, where they formed the nucleus of a community that would soon number 8,000. A similar settlement of leather-workers and cobblers landed in Peterborough, to make shoes. The Coal Board produced leaflets in Italian, emblazoned with photographs of grimy-but-happy miners, requesting sixty workers per week. In an echo of their attitude towards the Poles, the miners' union rebelled and the policy was abandoned.

As before, the Italians brought with them a busy culinary supply train. In 1946 the Gaggia company of Milan devised a new machine for making coffee, and Britain embarked on a frothy love affair with steamed milk. Restaurants with romantic names like Otello or Sorrento began to create the decor – red tablecloths, candles in Chianti bottles, amaretti biscuits – which for a while became synonymous with glamorous continental gastronomy.

Within a few years, some 345,000 European nationals had been recruited for work in Britain. The biggest intake came from the new United Nations camps. One scheme called Balt Cygnet funnelled 2,500 Baltic workers. A more ambitious venture, Westward Ho!, brought 78,500 refugee workers and dependants from Eastern Europe: Ukraine, Romania, Bulgaria and Yugoslavia, as well as the Baltic and Poland. They worked on the land or in heavy industries such as coal and steel. Almost three-quarters of the recruits were men. The economy needed workers, not communities; producers, not dependants. But there were jobs for women too, and the male character of the initial recruitment drive was balanced with plans – Blue Danube, North Sea and the Official Italian Scheme – that looked for 'a field of single women . . . to tap'.

Very few of these migrants were Jewish: hardly any Holocaust survivors were permitted to settle in Britain. Indeed, in November 1945 the Jewish Brigade of the Army of the Rhine went on strike in protest against British inaction. The Foreign Office line was that it favoured the Zionist dream of a homeland in Palestine, and in 1945 one hundred thousand Jews travelled there on steamers. As the horrifying extent of the death camps began to emerge, the government agreed to take a thousand young survivors. Only 732 could be found. They became known as 'the boys', though eighty of them were girls.

The airlift was organised by the Central British Fund and by Jewish refugee organisations, and it followed hard on the heels of Victory in Europe. On 14 August 1945 a dozen Lancaster bombers carried three hundred children, who had been incarcerated at the Theresienstadt camp, out of Prague. They were given chocolate, oranges and wedges of white bread – so delicious that it was widely assumed to be cake – and flown to Carlisle, where they were met by Leonard Montefiore and a small team of helpers. Forty of them had tuberculosis, and the dentist who examined them in their Lake District hostel found that many had not cleaned their teeth for five years, but this was the least of their problems. They were bereaved, bitter and broken-spirited: there were tears, rages and fights over food. Further transports arrived in the following twelve months: the boys were housed in hostels or on farms, and slowly their rehabilitation began. They ended up as leatherworkers, watchmakers, doctors, architects, businessmen and management consultants. One, Hugo Grynn, survived Auschwitz and arrived in Midlothian in February 1946. He became a noted rabbi and broadcaster, and recalled football matches against a team of local Scots. The Scots would lose, then start a punch-up. Welcome to Britain.

In a fervent attempt to demonstrate that the British Empire was still a vibrant concern, the 1948 Nationality Act expansively gave all imperial subjects the right of free entry into postwar Britain. A few voices were raised against this immodest proposal. Lord Altrincham warned his fellow peers that a 'Borneo head hunter' might one day take his seat on the plush red benches. But in the House of Commons, David Maxwell Fyfe (for the Conservative opposition) spelled out the historic principle in blunt terms: 'We are proud', he said, 'that we impose no colour bar restrictions . . . We must maintain our great metropolitan tradition of hospitality to everyone from every part of our empire.' The passage of the bill was a grand gesture, and its implications were going to be explored sooner than anyone imagined. The world, it turned out, was not going to obey this attempt to rewind its clock. The era when a small country like Britain could blithely give citizenship to a billion people all around the world was already over. The further reaches of the British Empire, meanwhile, had already resolved that with the war over they would remain passive possessions of the Crown no longer. The sun was beginning to set all over the map.

The ten thousand West Indian troops who returned – or were sent back – to the Caribbean after the war soon found that they had little to celebrate. Military life had been a revelation – like peeking through the curtains of an exclusive club. They had seen with their own eyes the possibilities in the so-called mother country, whereas the Jamaica they returned to was still devastated after the tremendous hurricane of August 1944 – the worst for forty years. Ancient trees had been toppled, fruit groves trampled; roofs had been whipped off like napkins. Even before the storm, the economy was in tatters. The price of sugar – by far the dominant export – had sunk to the point where the crop was hardly worth harvesting. Fields of cane ran wild and died, and there was no work for the men who once hacked sweetness from the hills. The Caribbean tourist boom was a long way off. The Western bourgeoisie couldn't yet run to swanky winter breaks on these palm-fringed beaches. Aside from a tiny trade in coffee and rum, there was little to do but subsist on fish from the ocean, and whatever yams, mangoes, bananas, maize or breadfruit poked through the rubble.

The only valuable export was labour. Caribbean workers knew all about this: they had known little else. Even within their own islands they often had to trudge for miles in search of piecework on the plantations, and for years they had been hopping over to Florida to pick fruit. In the first half of the century, up to 150,000 Jamaicans (a tenth of the population) went job-seeking in North and Central America. Many had been ferried to Panama to dig the canal.

America may have been the nearest major employer, but Britain, though far off, was now an attainable destination for more than just the odd writer or cricketer. It was also, thanks to the empire, much more familiar. The colonial administration had given West Indians a grounding in Queen and Country, in Shakespeare and Tennyson, in W. G. Grace, *Kennedy's Latin Primer* and the Lord's Prayer. They had grown up singing 'There'll Always Be an England' and 'Land of Hope and Glory' at assembly. Many of their Christian names – Nelson, Milton, Winston – derived from British heroes. A reverence for Britain had been carefully planted. Now, modern steamships brought the land itself within reach.

The returning servicemen broadcast their war-tinted views on the mother country. In addition to the RAF – Trinidad Squadron and Jamaica Squadron – recruits had joined the army – the British West Indian Regiment – or worked as navvies, radar and searchlight operators, cooks and foresters. Over a thousand men from British Honduras had been ferried to Scotland to chop timber, leading the Duke of Buccleuch to express some traditional anxieties about the safety of the virginal local lasses on his estate. This was an uncommon reaction, though. Britain at war had treated the West Indians with a soldierly respect. Many of them left with a bolstered self-confidence and a sense of equality. In Britain, they had seen some shocking sights: apart from the clamorous intensity of the war itself (after which a Caribbean island must have seemed a quiet backwater), they had witnessed white men and women labouring in the fields; white men and women cursing and swearing; white children begging in the streets. They had also seen opportunity. Britain was a worker's paradise – six jobs for every man, or so they said. For people with birthrights so gnarled by slavery that they felt rootless and exiled even at home, for whom even their own sun-kissed islands smacked of imprisonment, the prospect of crossing the ocean to make their own way in the world was hard to resist.

And then, in the last week of May 1948, a ship sailed into Kingston harbour. She was a captured Nazi troop ship that had been refitted and renamed: *Empire Windrush*. She had sailed from Palestine to Mexico looking for an unusual cargo – people. Sixty Polish women who had staggered from Siberia through India, Australia and New Zealand to Mexico were already on board. They were heading for England. And they were soon to have company.

The *Empire Windrush* was high, white and handsome. She could be seen from all over town: the two funnels jutted over the rooftops. She looked roomy and opulent, and seemed to represent all the wealth and dazzle of the wider world. Some of her cabins had already been booked. A few West Indians from the RAF were in the Caribbean on temporary leave; the *Windrush* had come to fetch them. But there was space for a few hundred more. Word spread that tickets were cheap: the Jamaican newspaper the *Gleaner* advertised them for £28 10s (half the usual fare).* In the shops, cafés and fields men counted their pennies. 'During its three days in port,' wrote the *Gleaner*, 'the *Windrush* became easily the most popular ship that has docked in Kingston harbour.'†

Hindsight encourages us to see the *Windrush* as predestined, part of the tidal drift of colonisation and decolonisation – indeed, as the inevitable first step in what would later become known as 'colonisation in reverse'. But at the time she was a one-off, a once-in-a-lifetime, never-to-be-repeated lifeline. Many accounts of the migration from the Caribbean to British shores emphasise that the men were imported labour, invited to do the menial jobs that the cosseted or war-weary locals did not fancy, but this was not the case in 1948. Later, companies such as London Transport and the new National Health Service would indeed canvass in the West Indies to fill the gaps in their labour supply, but this first voyage was not planned. An enterprising skipper simply took the intitiative

---

*It might have been a bargain, but it was six months' wages for most Jamaicans.
†'If there was a ship big enough,' said the poet James Berry, who travelled to Britain on the *Orbita* in the following year, 'everyone would get away.'

and advertised for trade to fill his half-empty ship. The rest was history. The
British authorities did not even know that a shipload of migrants was on its
way until the *Windrush* had left Jamaica far behind.

Nor were the passengers united in their motives. One of them, Vince Reid,
was only thirteen, and had little choice in the matter. In England he would join
the RAF before training as a teacher and becoming, eventually, a college
lecturer. Another, Cy Grant, had found the return to colonial ways
insupportable. 'Jamaica was a colony,' he said later, as an actor in Britain. 'And
having been to the library and read a few books, I didn't want to live in a
colony. When I went back to Jamaica it was shocking. I would say thirty
thousand men were thrown back without any planning. It was bad.'[3] Others
had more private concerns. Edwin Ho, from Guiana (the passengers were not
all Jamaican), was fleeing a gambling debt: he had come a cropper in
Georgetown to the tune of $35,000, and had to make himself scarce. He wanted,
as he said, to escape his parents footsteps . . . 'to make my own way in life'. He
joined the ship in Trinidad. A good boxer, he triumphed in an onboard bout
against a Jamaican champion. His picture even appeared in the London *Daily
Express*, and a pair of promoters offered to find him fights when he arrived. Ho
declined, a decision he would later regret when he wound up in a foundry at
Telford.

Not all of the passengers had been able to afford the fare. Some secured their
passage in lotteries – the so-called 'pardner' schemes by which all the members
of a small community would chip in sufficient to buy one ticket, which would
go to the lucky winner as a loan. But otherwise the trip required a certain level
of financial and family backing. So the majority of the people who boarded the
ship were adventurous and optimistic, young men looking for wider horizons.

It was frequently said of them that they believed the streets of London to be
paved with gold. But as Trevor and Mike Phillips pointed out in their anthology
of *Windrush* memoirs, this was often a patronising attempt to characterise them
as naïve and passive. In truth, they would have settled for streets paved with
pennies. Altogether, 492 passengers (nearly all of them men) made the trip.
They had thin wallets; their only assets were their wits and the sweat of their
labour. But they were skilled workers – sign painters, builders and mechanics.
Nearly half of them already had jobs (in the armed forces) or contacts in Britain.
They were travelling hopefully, ignorant of the fact that they would soon be met
by small but noisy crowds with placards saying 'GO HOME'. Several later said
that if they had known what lay in store for them in dank, sour Britain, they
would have jumped over the rails and swum home.

The voyage was long and slow. Much to the delight of the crew, many
passengers were seasick. The men nipped at their rum and risked their cash
on cards and dominoes, a pastime which led to such anguish for the losers
that the captain banned it. Aldwyn ('Lord Kitchener') Roberts, one of the top

calypsonians in the Caribbean, set up his band and threw impromptu parties.*
Other men took their chances against Edwin Ho in the boxing ring. That was
about it as far as onboard entertainment went. Between bland meals – meat
and boiled potatoes: a dour foretaste of things to come – the men strolled on
the decks and compared notes. Some hoped for a nice little office job and a
house; others planned to save all they earned and wire it home as soon as
possible. The returning servicemen, who had tasted life in Britain, were
nudged in the ribs and asked what English women were like.†

There were no great dramas. Half a dozen stowaways flitted between
hiding-places, cadging food. The Polish women, nearing the end of their
incredible trek, kept themselves to themselves.‡ The ship paused briefly in
Cuba and Bermuda, where the passengers went ashore to stretch their legs.
They were dumbfounded to be herded, at a cinema, into a 'blacks only'
enclosure. It was their first brush with segregation, and it shocked them, not
least because they thought themselves – knew themselves – to be British
citizens. A minor scuffle broke out, but no one wanted to endanger his
precious berth by getting involved in a brawl. Still, it gave the men something
to think about as they marched back up the gangway. Out at sea a couple of
Jamaican wireless operators set up their game of dominoes right outside the
radio shack, so they could monitor the news. They heard that the *Windrush*
was being shadowed by a warship, HMS *Sheffield*, which was under
instructions to turn them back if they made any trouble. It was as if they were
being treated like an enemy, like invaders. And then a blunt memo went up
on the ship's noticeboard. 'I could not honestly paint you a very rosy picture
of your future,' it said. 'Conditions in England are not as favourable as you
may think . . . Hard work is the order of the day. If you think you cannot pull
your weight, you might as well decide to return to Jamaica, even if you have
to swim the Atlantic. No slackers will be tolerated.'⁴ There was no mistaking
the meaning of this: they were not wanted. Most of the West Indians scoffed,
but one or two were chilled. They hadn't even arrived, and already they were
being shown a cold shoulder. *Even if you have to swim the Atlantic?* God: what

---

*One of his songs, written on the voyage, went:

> London is the place for me,
> London that lovely city.
> You can go to France or America, India, Asia or Africa.
> But you must come back to London city.

†One, Alford Garner, recalled that during his war years in the RAF the women had 'just
loved us'.
‡Though they did express sharp displeasure with their travelling companions. The wife
of one returning Jamaican serviceman was distressed to see her husband being 'openly
insulted' because of his colour.

if they had made a fearful mistake? Life in Britain was not, by the look of it, going to be easy.

In Whitehall, the authorities, caught off balance, responded with what now seems typically British equivocation. A blizzard of official memos blew from ministry to ministry. On 7 June, in Parliament, with the *Windrush* still at sea, the Minister of Labour, George Isaacs, said: 'The arrival of these substantial numbers of men under no organised arrangements is bound to result in difficulty and disappointment. I hope no encouragement will be given to others to follow them.' And a Privy Council memo of 15 June, to the Colonial Office, emphasised the need to prevent the *Windrush* from sparking a trend. We should not make any special efforts to help these people, it said: 'Otherwise there might be a real danger that successful efforts to secure adequate conditions for these men on arrival might actually encourage a further influx.' The Ministry of Labour responded on 19 June by expressing its hope that the immigrants could be 'dispersed' in small parties, so they would 'cease to be recognisable as a problem'. The ship hadn't even arrived, yet already the 'influx' had become a 'problem'. The Colonial Secretary, Creech Jones, declared: 'These people have British passports and they must be allowed to land.' But he could not resist adding a contemptuous coda: 'They won't last one winter in England.'

Such were the agitations of racial unease that a country which had recently seen off thousands of German bombers, and was absorbing 120,000 Poles with negligible fuss, was quaking at the prospect of a few hundred migrant workers from the Tropics. But in 1948 the euphoria of victory had faded. Bread, petrol, tea, sugar and bacon were still rationed, and so was jam, oatmeal, semolina and macaroni. Debris lay in heaps. A paper shortage was cramping newspapers and school books alike. There was a dockers' strike over pay. The Church warned that gambling was a 'national epidemic'. Demob happiness was giving way to demob fury. Below the surface the economy was stirring (industrial production rose by 12 per cent in 1948), but it was not yet possible to taste the fruit. Dentists and doctors were refusing to cooperate with the new National Health Service, on the grounds that it would lower standards (not to mention salaries). In 1947 there had been awful floods and a national fuel crisis. People had little to spare, emotionally or financially. Many threw in the towel and left – the working population shrank by a hundred thousand in 1948 – and the government was powerless to prevent it. Britain was far from feeling great.

By now the *Windrush* was nearing British waters. The passengers began to talk more urgently about what lay ahead. The servicemen who knew the po-faced ways of British bureaucracy cautioned their shipmates to be ready with their papers. As the ship nosed its way upriver, some of the stowaways jumped into the drab khaki waters of the Thames estuary, to the amusement of their fellow passengers. Lord Kitchener watched them go and thought them brave: 'I was wondering if these fellas are not afraid of alligators,' he said. 'Because that water seemed to me it must have some kind of reptile in it.'

The *Windrush* slowed to a halt on 22 June, and was surrounded by a flotilla of boats packed with sightseers, eager to see this weird and now-famous ship. They waved and shouted greetings, and the men on the high decks shouted back. When the ship docked, one of the passengers, Oswald Denniston – never slow to see or seize a chance – lifted his hat, gave a brief speech of thanks and proposed three cheers for the Ministry of Labour.* A grateful nation rewarded him with the first job gained by a *Windrush* migrant: he became the nightwatchman (four pounds per night) in the underground shelter at Clapham Common where half of the travellers – the ones with nowhere to go – were sent to bunk down.†

The official sent to greet the ship had made an honest attempt to set an amiable tone. His name was Ivor Cummings, and he had an African father, which perhaps allowed him to sympathise with the new arrivals more than most – he had been refused a military commission thanks to the King's Regulations, which insisted that officers be of European descent. 'I now want to address my friends who have nowhere to go and no plans whatsoever,' he said. 'I am afraid you will have many difficulties, but feel sure that with the right spirit and by cooperating as I have suggested, you will overcome them.' One of the passengers, Sam King, recalled that 'Everything humanly possible was done to help us.'‡

The selection of Clapham as the location for the emergency hostel was one of those random acts which turn out to have decisive consequences. The shelter had been used as a camp for German and Italian prisoners during the war; now it lay empty. Had the *Windrush* jobseekers been housed in Hampstead or Wimbledon, then the history of those areas might have been very different. As it was, the newcomers headed for the nearest labour exchange, a mile or so down the road in Brixton. Within weeks, most had found jobs in foundries, as electricians, on farms, on the railways or in hospitals. The roots of a new population, and a new cultural atmosphere in Brixton, were planted within a few days of their arrival.

The West Indians had been housed and had found jobs that needed doing. But concern remained. The Prime Minister, Clement Attlee, was prodded by a

---

*Denniston would head straight to Brixton market with trays of melons brought from Bermuda. He was still selling fruit there fifty years later.

†The *Daily Express* celebrated his good fortune with a headline: 'Jamaica's Oswald Given Job'. He was handed two blankets to huddle into, and there he lay, brooding perhaps on the price of fruit for his market stall.

‡King eventually became mayor of Southwark. 'If I hadn't left,' he said much later, 'I'd be a peasant farmer.'

group of worried backbench MPs into making a statement. His letter – dated
5 July, just two weeks after the *Windrush* docked – attempted to soothe their
anxieties, but even he could not help flinching at the prospect of more ships
from the west. 'It is traditional that British subjects, whether of Dominion or
Colonial origin (and of whatever race or colour) should be freely admissible to
the United Kingdom,' he wrote. 'That tradition is not, in my view, to be lightly
discarded . . . If our policy were to result in a great influx of undesirables, we
might, however unwillingly, have to consider modifying it.' It is something, at
least, that his first reflex was to cling to rather than forsake the honourable
tradition of free entry. But the mere fact that the *Windrush* should have so
rapidly engaged the attention of the Prime Minister says plenty about the
panicky reaction of the politicians.

The *Windrush* did not trigger an immediate surge of similar voyages. In the
following year, 180 West Indians came to Liverpool on the *Orbita*; the year after
that, a mere 39 Jamaicans sailed on a Spanish ship, the *Reina del Pacifico* (the fare
by this time was seventy-five pounds, an obvious disincentive); in the whole of
1950, only a few hundred took the leap. They weren't universally vilified: bus
conductors sometimes waived the fare for West Indian nurses out of gratitude
or respect, and some boarding-houses defied the stereotype and opened their
doors to weary Jamaicans with bulging suitcases in tow. But as their numbers
grew, so the response grew more frosty. People began to shift seats on buses;
patients in hospitals screamed at nurses to keep their filthy black paws to
themselves; so-called Christians moved uneasily to new pews so they could
pray for tolerance in comfort.

The photographs that recorded their arrival in Britain's ports are expressive.
Walled in by suitcases, the men sport suits and hats, sometimes rakishly tilted
back on their foreheads; the women are in sensible skirts and dapper coats.
They came as if for a dance, putting their best feet forward. And they were
jilted.

Nor can anything disguise the extent to which this was simple racism. Irish
workers were pouring into Britain in the decade after the war at the rate of sixty
thousand per annum, a migration that dwarfed the trickle of hopeful jobseekers
from the West Indies. They laid tarmac for the new motorways and toiled
away on construction and reconstruction sites across the country. But they no
longer attracted the derision endured by their fathers and grandfathers. In
1955, a government working party insisted that 'it cannot be held that the same
difficulties arise in the case of the Irish as in the case of coloured people . . . The
outstanding difference is that the Irish are not – whether they like it or not –
a different race from the ordinary inhabitants of Great Britain.' It was official:
the British and the Irish were of the same 'race'. Those of a different race, it
went without saying, presented difficulties.

The migrants themselves put a brave face on it in letters home, and often enclosed money, a sign of how well they were doing.* But the social facts were grim. England – they had not yet explored Britain – seemed ghastly: inhospitable, cold, and sour. They could hardly help noticing how deeply they were resented: they only had to keep their ears open on a bus. Dispiriting signs that greeted their often vain search for lodgings: 'No Blacks. No Dogs.' The breezy wartime invitations to tea were no longer forthcoming. The Guyana-born poet E. R. Braithwaite served as a fighter pilot in the RAF during the war and assumed, when it was over, that he would be a welcome addition to postwar life. He went to Cambridge University and left with a degree in Physics, only to find all the doors wedged shut. 'Great was my amazement and chagrin,' he wrote, 'when, time after time, I was denied employment, with elaborate casualness and courtesy . . . In due course I was forced to confront the fact that, relieved of the threat of German invasion, the British had abandoned all pretence of hand-in-hand brotherliness and had reverted to type, demonstrating the same racism they had so roundly condemned in the Germans.'[5]

It was true. The striking suspension of racism during the war years – the famous spirit of 'hand-in-hand brotherliness' – was swiftly revoked. Perhaps it was only ever a temporary recruit. Now officers attached to the British West Indian Regiment as part of their National Service were offered a bonus (known casually as 'wog money') to compensate them for the fact that they would be working alongside blacks. As with so many previous migrations, the heart of the animosity was pumped by something very like fear. British newspaper readers looked at the pictures of the newcomers stepping off ships and trains, and blushed. The national guilty conscience was pricked into tetchy life. Anyone with the smallest sense of history knew in their bones that Britain's fortunes had been founded on the massive dislocations of colonial rule. A century of imperial reflexes had inspired a truly British terror of 'the native': ever since the Indian Mutiny, all those dark-skinned hordes had been depicted as barbarous fiends, always on the lookout for innocent British maidens to despoil (no one looked too closely at the extreme ruthlessness with which the mutiny was stubbed out – the rebels had asked for it, hadn't they?). So as fresh crowds of eager West Indians landed in Britain, anxiety swelled into rage. In an all too typical irony, those lured by the employment problem were quickly held to be the problem. 'Thirty thousand colour problems,' wailed the cover of the *Picture Post*. We were, so the argument ran, being deluged. Something had to be done.

---

*Remittances to Jamaica would soon become the country's second-largest source of foreign currency.

CHAPTER 21

Welcome to Britain

Sybil Phoenix was a nursing secretary in post-war British Guiana when she went along to listen to an up-and-coming British politician address a West Indian audience on the merits of seeking employment in British hospitals. 'He made it sound attractive,' she said later. Her mother had died when she was ten, and she had been raised by unkind relatives, so she was more than willing to be seduced by such exciting blandishments. The politician's name was Enoch Powell, at that time a willing collaborator in the postwar recruitment drive. He would shortly change his tune in dramatic ways, but Sybil Phoenix was one of those captivated by his early promises. She sailed to England in 1956.

She arrived at Paddington station and was astonished to see a white woman sweeping up dust and rubbish on the concourse. 'I'm only accustomed to seeing white women who's painted devils but do nothing,' she said. 'They don't even sweep their own homes. They have six of us to do it for them.' Then she embarked on an even tougher journey through London's derelict housing stock in search of a bed. The best she could find was an overpriced basement in Paddington. It was a converted – or semi-converted – coal cellar. 'Every time you light the gas, after about fifteen minutes the water starts running down the wall. I cooked my first Christmas dinner in the country under an umbrella.'

She didn't think that she would be able to bear it, but honoured her childhood pledge to give orphans a better break than she had enjoyed herself and became a foster mother in Lewisham. She gave a home to over a hundred children, eleven of whom went on to university. Having trained as a milliner, she opened a youth group (the Moonshot Club in Deptford), organised choirs, helped to motivate the early race relations groups, and became a Methodist lay preacher. In 1971 she was awarded an MBE, and was briefly the mayoress of Lewisham.

Hers was a brave career, often punctuated by disaster. She lost her own daughter Marsha in a car crash, and in 1981 the Moonshot Club was burnt to the ground in an unsolved blaze, perhaps started deliberately by racist fire-raisers. Thirteen young black people were killed, and Phoenix had to organise a memorial service for them. 'I couldn't eat – the smell of burned people – for a long time. I couldn't keep anything down. Within three months I'd lost nearly two stone.' But she remained resolutely committed to her life's work. 'I was born a member of the British Empire . . .' she said. 'I'm nothing but British.'[1]

In the decade that followed the voyage of the *Windrush*, nearly a quarter of a million migrants, first from the Caribbean, then from partitioned India, Africa and Hong Kong, made their way to the country whose authority they were at last shrugging off. To white Britain, it was a disconcerting shock, but no one should have been surprised. The shuffle of foreign feet on British soil was the natural consequence of a centuries-old interference in world affairs. The long saga of European expansion, which had installed a quarter of a billion white people in far-off lands, was drawing to a close. There would, as a reaction to the hangdog austerity of the postwar years, be an equally forceful wave of emigration as disillusioned Brits headed for roomier, sunnier and less wounded landscapes. But this process was not as noticeable, to most people, as its mirror-image: the immigration of once-colonised people to the homes of their former rulers.

Ever since the abolition of slavery, Britain, as represented by its commercial grandees, had blanched at the prospect of having to pay anything more than the most brazen minimum for its employees. And at first it seemed as if colonial workers could continue to be exploited in this way. To fuel the continuation of plantation economics and the pleasant profits that flowed from them, enormous numbers of men were spread across strange lands by officials who spared few thoughts for the demographic impact of their actions. It was called indentured labour, and it swept Africans, Chinese and Indians across the Seven Seas to work in conditions that did not differ greatly in practice from those that had prevailed under the out-and-out slavers. In the years when the world was its playground, Britain – like other European empires – tossed its toys around with an immense, careless lack of consideration for the consequences. The indentured workers, on five-year contracts, were deployed and displaced by the erratic whims of the imperial business cycle. This often involved a disdainful attitude towards cultural taboos. Hindu strictures against sea-voyages, for instance – travellers would effectively be excommunicated from their caste, making a return home difficult if not impossible – were outweighed by commercial logic, or by the spirit of adventure. Gandhi himself was expelled from his caste when he went to Britain in 1881, despite many solemn pledges that he would fulfil his religious commitments (abstinence from wine, women and meat) wherever he was. He was one of a number of upper-class professionals or merchants to push off from the Indian coast. Half a million Indian workers were lured to Kenya, Uganda, Sri Lanka, Zanzibar, Fiji, Mauritius, Trinidad, Guiana and South Africa.

Now, as the political agent of this extreme disruption grew weak, many of these people were left stranded in emerging nations where they had only loose and temporary moorings. The partition of India in 1947 cut the Punjab in two and inspired the displacement of some two million people, a commotion that was punctuated by hideous massacres as Hindus, Sikhs and Muslims tried to make their way to their particular safe side of the new national boundaries. The emergence of Chairman Mao in China sent a million non-Communists into Hong Kong and beyond, while the growing strength of African independence movements left the imported communities from India exposed and vulnerable to nationalist furies that saw them as an imperial hangover and imposition. In colony after colony, across Africa and the West Indies, the lowering of the Union Jack left people stranded, with little but the theoretical promise of British citizenship to keep them warm. The great age of empires – it stretched from 1500 to 1900 – had sent almost fifteen million Africans and Asians spinning outwards in a colossal, continent-spanning diaspora. Now, as Europe picked through the ruin it had visited upon itself during the Second World War, and the curtain came down on the entire colonial circus, a small number – a fraction of those entitled to do so – plotted a path to the mother country. They had no way of knowing that mother would be anything but pleased to see them.

If the migrants had any illusions, they were swiftly relieved of them, sometimes at painful personal cost. The empire had been widely resented, but also – despite everything – admired. Britain had managed to portray itself in a misleadingly good light. Colonial subjects were not told about the poverty of Britain's cities, or the coldness of their civic norms. Years of missionary and educational propaganda, stunning feats of engineering, impressive admini-strative efficiency, buckets of pageantry, and conspicuous displays of wealth and power had all left their mark. Britain seemed high and mighty, in every sense: in Gandhi's words, it was 'the land of philosophers and poets, the very centre of civilisation.'[2] In contrast, the economic forecast in the countries agitating for independence was gloomy. The colonies were not mixed economies possessing the ability to weather storms: they were passive producers of commodities and raw materials. Indeed, one reason why Britain was abandoning them was that the dominions had been milked so thoroughly that the inevitable fight to keep them was not economically prudent. Financial hardship – perhaps the biggest 'push factor' in any migration story – prodded the newly liberated peoples to pack their bags.

The *Windrush* was not actually the first ship in this story.* But it became the symbol of Caribbean migration because it was the first to be met by newsreel cameras, and the first to raise scarlet flushes of alarm in British newspapers and the House of Commons. This jittery first response set in motion a new generation of anti-alien feelings that would drive policy for decades.

The new arrivals continued to find jobs with relative ease. Some, no doubt, exaggerated their qualifications (it wasn't rare for people who had once painted a door to style themselves 'decorators'). A few were able to pursue more individualistic careers as traders or musical performers. For most, Britain by and large lived up to their expectations of a jobseekers' paradise – certainly relative to Jamaica, where unemployment was running at 40 per cent, and where 90 per cent of those lucky enough to be in work earned less than two pounds a week. If some of the jobs were not those that had featured in the migrants' fantasies, at least they were a start.

But Britain's children (and, more relevantly, their parents) saw black people as the caricatures dreamed up by Enid Blyton. They were 'golliwogs', dubbed by Blyton Golly, Waggle and Niggar – and 'you can't tell one from another'. No one frowned when a character in Blyton's *The Mystery of the Vanished Prince* (1951) remarked of the dark strangers: 'We've got two at our school. One never cleans his teeth and the other howls if he gets a kick at football.'[3]

Such patronising attitudes soon coalesced into resentment. In an echo of the unrest that followed demobilisation after the First World War, there were race-riots in Liverpool in 1948 and Deptford in 1949. These were only minor precursors of the much worse troubles that lay ahead, but they were enough in themselves to sour the social atmosphere. In the summer of 1948 Britain's Caribbeans could cheer when Arthur Wint of Jamaica sprinted away with the Olympic gold medal in the 400 metres at Wembley (the RAF band struck up 'God Save the Queen' to celebrate his victory), but on the way home it was quite possible that someone might make monkey noises at them, or beg them to turn around and wave their tails.† Life in England was clearly going to be an uphill, into-the-wind slog.

However, even unhappy migrants soon drop anchor. The government was anxious to disperse the newcomers across the country, but this proved impractical, partly because the refusal to accept them was so widespread, and partly because of the powerful reflex, shared by all migrants, to stick together, to create oases of familiarity. The trade unions continued to grimace at official pleas to offer jobs to West Indians; some, such as the Transport and General

---

*In late 1947 a ship called the *Ormonde* brought 108 migrant workers on the same route without generating a comparable bow-wave of concern.
†Years later, another gold medallist, the sprinter Linford Christie, would observe that when he won he won for Britain, but when he lost he became the 'Jamaican-born athlete'.

Workers' Union, threatened to strike if forced to take on the men of Jamaica and
Barbados (on behalf of their existing members' jobs, naturally). 'We cannot
afford,' said the General Secretary of the TUC, Frank Cousins, 'that these people
should be allowed unrestricted entry into this country.' It was the same story
in Britain's thousands of unploughed fields. 'We appreciate of course that these
people are human beings', said the General Secretary of the National Union of
Agricultural Workers in 1947, as if this were a rare concession, 'but it would
seem evident that to bring coloured labour into the British countryside would
be a most unwise and unfortunate act.'[4] This may have been a plausible
reflection of the national mood, but such statements also shaped the national
mood. As before, the debate became a row between white-collar pragmatists
who appreciated the need for cheap, pliable labour and were pleased to see the
immigrants, and a group of resentful plain dealers. Between these two extremes
lay the huge, largely placid majority of the British population.

Who knows what might have happened had the government provided
anything resembling political leadership, as was forthcoming for the Poles,
Czechs, European volunteers and even prisoners-of-war? No such assistance
schemes were available to the West Indians. On the contrary, official pamphlets
and posters tried to dissuade them from making the trip. One Home Office
booklet said that British people were not talkative, warned that the food might
seem drab, and recommended, after much thought, that hot water bottles might
be 'a source of great comfort'. That was as far as the hand of friendship
extended. New arrivals were thrown into an unfriendly labour market and a
tougher housing market, and abandoned to their fate. As E. R. Braithwaite put
it: 'There seemed to be no clear positive policy relating to their entry, no
planned dispersal to anticipate and avoid local saturation, and no orientation
scheme to ease the confrontation between the host community and the
newcomers.'[5]

Inevitably, in such circumstances, they clustered in select locales. South
London, thanks to the *Windrush* voyagers, was the first port of call for
subsequent migrants from Jamaica. The *South London Daily Press* was on sale in
Kingston: would-be expats could scan the classifieds, marvelling at the wages
on offer in this scintillating wonderland called Lambeth. Trinidadians and
Barbadians drifted to Notting Hill and Paddington; Guyanese congregated in
Tottenham and Wood Green; Montserratians plumped for Stoke Newington
and Finsbury Park. The markets in these neighbourhoods acquired new accents
and flavours: pineapples, bananas, yams, sweet potatoes, mangoes and chillies
sat alongside apples and pears from the English countryside.

That these tended to be grimy parts of town was not a coincidence: migrants
were unwelcome in all but the poorest neighbourhoods. They were at the back
of the queue when it came to council housing (and quickly understood that
they would be resented if such housing were allocated to them), and it was

almost impossible for them to buy their own properties: even if they had the capital, mortgage lenders automatically saw them as bad risks. Landlords and landladies turned them away the moment they saw the colour of their skin or heard their accents on the phone, usually adding apologetically that it wasn't them, you understand, who had the problem with blacks, but the other residents. Lugging their suitcases vainly from street to street, they had little option but to occupy the cheapest urban areas – Moss Side in Manchester, Handsworth in Birmingham – where industry was dying and the housing had often been blasted by German bombs. In these places they fell prey to mean and unregulated landlordism, which was sometimes the work of other, rival immigrants. The infamous Peter Rachman, for instance, who owned a hundred properties in west London and terrorised his Caribbean clientele with bouncers, dogs and draconian rent demands, was himself a refugee. In recognising that desperate men with little alternative could be pressured into paying over the odds for squalid rooms, he epitomised the miserable downside of a liberalism that turned a blind eye to exploitation. As he swanned around Notting Hill in his Rolls-Royce, he would 'persuade' white tenants to leave his target areas by surrounding them with black neighbours. Then he would cram their former properties with recent immigrants, who of course had little choice, as most other landlords refused to rent them a room. The immigrants needed people like Rachman, even though dealing with him inevitably led to connections with his shady underworld, which proved difficult to shed later. And it would be wrong to say that the immigrants were paragons of virtue: they were nearly all young men, and like most young men they liked a bet and a drink. It was also true that they didn't do a lot of entertaining at home (that would have been difficult, as most lived three to a room), so they took to the streets for their social life. To prim, stay-at-home Britons, this seemed brazen and debauched.

While white Britain's attitudes hardened, the immigrants' opinions of their new home continued to decline. Most may have secured jobs, and were earning much more than they could have in the Caribbean, but Bermondsey was no Barbados, Tottenham no Tobago. When Daniel Lawrence polled the West Indians of Nottingham in the 1960s, he found unanimous disappointment. 'We never realised that it would be so different . . . It was a big shock . . . We was told all lies back home . . . I was not expecting it . . . We adored the royalty you see so much . . . We thought we'd be treated nice here . . . I never knew there was so much colour bar . . . I thought the people of Britain would be good and affectionate – now most of them are against us . . . I did not know I was coloured until the English told me so . . . I expected people to be nice – it's like a slap in the face . . . The money's quite good but nothing else.'[6]

A few years later, the hero of V. S. Naipaul's *The Mimic Men*, Rahul Singh, gave voice to this disenchantment when he arrived in London, looked at the monuments he had so long elevated in his imagination, and felt nothing. There was nothing sacred about stones that had seemed in books so noble, so magnificent. So while the South African playwright Ronald Harwood could disembark at Southampton in 1951 and kiss the quay ('This is the greatest day of my life'), Caribbean travellers of the 1950s generally felt no such euphoria.[7] The landscape was so dull compared to what they'd left behind – all those squashed houses, all those terraced miles and gloomy alleys. 'Like brick cliffs,' said the writer and television producer Mike Phillips. 'Grey, gloomy, lowering, threatening.'[8] And then there was the weather. 'Everything you touched was cold,' said Bernie Grant, later Labour MP for Tottenham. 'The food was cold, the furniture was cold, the table was cold.'[9] Mike Phillips arrived in January. 'You breathed and smoke came out of your mouth.'[10]

Nevertheless, the attraction of the jobs on offer outweighed the miserable weather and hostile neighbours. The cost of the steamer ticket was still out of reach for most West Indians, and for half a dozen years after the *Windrush* the exodus remained a mere trickle. Then, suddenly, it gathered pace. In 1954, 24,000 West Indians arrived; in 1955, there were 26,000. Similar numbers came in the next two years, as British firms began actively touting for workers. In 1956 London Transport resolved to recruit nearly four thousand new employees, mostly from Barbados, making full use of an immigrant poster girl: a lovely young bus conductress standing on the rear deck of a Routemaster, looking composed and perfectly at home. Applicants were loaned the transatlantic fare – it would be deducted from their pay packets on arrival in a sweet, no-lose deal for the company. Those who saw a longer-term future in England, meanwhile, began to send for wives and children (many of whom had been left with their grandparents while their mums and dads scouted out a new future for the family). By 1958 some 115,000 people, mostly single men, had sailed east from Kingston and Port of Spain, and juddered their way to Southampton and London. The *Daily Gleaner* called it 'Westward Ho! in reverse'. This was an expression of glee, but in 1955 the Chief Minister of Jamaica, Norman Manley, concerned by the brain- and muscle-drain from his country, visited Britain to see for himself what was happening. He appointed his son Douglas to write a formal study of the subject, which found that, though there was 'a good deal of colour prejudice', there was also 'a large reservoir of goodwill from Brits'. His main concern was the loss to the Caribbean of such a large slice of its productive workforce. And the migrants were not, Manley insisted, dregs from 'the bottom of the barrel', but, 'the more skilled elements'. The following year, the British Governor-General of Jamaica confirmed that migrants came from the 'better-off' classes.

Jamaica was by no means the only island dented by emigration. In 1953 an Italian shipping line stopped at Montserrat and unearthed an eager seam of workers looking for a passage to Britain. There was no mystery to it. The local wage for cotton-pickers (the island's chief employment) was not quite a pound per day for men, and even less for women. In this context, expensive transatlantic tickets were still a good investment. When an airstrip was built on the island in 1956 (supposedly to support Montserrat's trade in cotton, sugar and limes), it quickly attracted long queues to its departures hall. The effect was both swift and far-reaching. In the decade to come, over four thousand Montserratians – a quarter of the island's total, and an even larger chunk of its working-age population – would travel to Britain. In 1951 Montserrat had earned nearly ten times as much from cotton as from remittances sent home by overseas workers: by the end of the decade, cotton generated only a quarter of the sum remitted home from abroad.

This was a typical tale. Remittances home were so much more lucrative and reliable than local wages, and emigrants became prestigious. There were leave-taking parties for those about to embark, and homecoming feasts for those returning from their glamorous tour overseas. A man who could jingle the coins in his pocket while telling London stories over a bottle of rum could become a local celebrity. His relatives enjoyed status symbols that marked them out as having an absentee worker in the family: a fridge, a flushable loo, a radio, or a motorbike. By now it was clear that Britain didn't want them. But count the pound notes: how bad could it be? In a painful irony, at a time when the emigrants themselves were beginning to strike rancorous Britons as parasites, those who stayed in the Caribbean could also be dismissed, by their own friends and relatives, as idle scroungers.

The government kept looking at the subject, and looking away again. In 1955 it noted the marked increase in immigration, but concluded that there was plenty of work available, and no serious race problem. Lord Salisbury, the Lord Chancellor, was sufficiently concerned to call for controls, but the old liberal, laissez-faire orthodoxy prevailed. The government did nothing. In one way, it was merely stepping on to the path of least resistance. It declined to take any overzealous measures to prevent immigration, while refusing also to stand up for the migrants themselves. This was something of a ministerial compromise: the Home Office was keen to limit the numbers of Commonwealth migrants on law-and-order grounds, while the Colonial Office believed that any restriction would 'send the wrong message' to the colonies. The Home Office was reminded of the damage done to Caribbean goodwill when the great cricketer Learie Constantine had been turned away from the Russell Hotel by a colour-conscious receptionist. For now, such arguments were persuasive enough to win the day.

The pressure of events in the Indian subcontinent, meanwhile, obliged the government to go along with the policy that later became known as 'divide and quit'. The results of partition were, as Gandhi had feared, explosive. After years of colonial severity, historic religious antagonisms spilled into violent unrest. Impoverished, war-weary and homeless, thousands of Indians responded eagerly to the prospect of a new life in Britain. It was a country they understood well, and, within limits, liked.

Despite the long tradition of Indian academics and politicians coming to these shores, and the enormous number of Indian soldiers who had travelled and fought with the British in two world wars, the community of Indians in Britain was small: in 1949 there were only a hundred in Birmingham. Now, Sikhs from the partition line, Hindus from Gujarat, Muslims from East and West Pakistan, from Bombay and the divided Punjab, from Mirpur and Sylhet, came through Suez in search of a more prosperous future. In many cases they found it, and the villages of India and Pakistan, like the islands of the Caribbean, came to be studded with 'England houses' – dwellings funded by remittances from expatriate workers.

In 1955 just over 5,000 Indians came; in 1956, 5,600; and in 1957, 6,600. Nehru confessed to some annoyance, not because his country was losing so many productive workers (India could afford to spare them, to be honest), but because the arrival of so many uneducated Indians in the mother country might embarrass him. His years at Harrow had left him with a keen regard for English manners. 'In my likes and dislikes I was perhaps more an Englishman than an Indian,' he wrote. 'I returned to India as prejudiced in favour of England and the English as it is possible to be.'[11] One of the things he acquired was a touching faith in self-government, which earned him nine years in a British jail.

Among the first Indians to embark were the Eurasians or Anglo-Indians, the products of mixed marriages during Britain's two-century affair with the subcontinent. Around thirty thousand such people landed in the years following the war. They were both British and Indian (though such was the temper of the time that they more often felt like neither); they were neither nationalists nor activists; and were markedly committed to integration and a quiet life. They were often Christian, and spoke good English; yet they still missed home. In a way they were lucky: they were able to sink beneath the surface of waters that had not yet grown choppy.

The same could not be said for the Sikhs. Ever since the Indian Mutiny in 1857, when the Sikhs remained loyal to the Crown, they had been favoured and admired as soldiers. Sikh regiments served in all the theatres of the two world wars, and were installed as garrisons in Hong Kong and Singapore. Not suffering the Hindus' constraints against sea travel, they had also gone in large numbers to East Africa to build the railway. Having a migrant worker in the family was akin to having a son in the army, so Sikh villagers were relatively at ease with the idea of themselves as itinerant employees, especially since their status at home in the Punjab was tenuous: as adherents to a fusion of Hindu and Muslim doctrines, they were open to abuse from both, and though they came to be the largest component of the Indian population in Britain, they were a small minority in India itself (less numerous even than the Christians). They were quick to see Britain as a promising option.

Where in Britain, though? One early Sikh migrant, Darshan Singh, had arrived in 1938 and, like so many, tramped the northern roads as a pedlar. He began by working out of Bradford, but then set up a shop in Leeds. Others followed. He was soon functioning as an informal labour and property exchange. Leeds, and the other textile towns of Yorkshire, began to sprout communities of Sikhs.

Like their migrant ancestors, the Sikhs preferred to work for themselves, if they could. Many, like Singh, sold door-to-door goods both to fellow Sikhs and to a wider public. It was exhausting, after-hours work – evenings and weekends – but the light at the end of the tunnel was the idea of a shop: self-employment, no overtime bans and a licence to work as hard as one wished. In the workplace, the Sikhs kept themselves to themselves in ways that often struck their white colleagues as aloof. They neither drank nor gambled – characteristics usually mocked as 'not joining in' – and they often brought in their own lunchboxes rather than risking canteen food (the cultural suspicion and unease was mutual). There were rows about hours and hygiene: one Midlands factory fielded so many complaints about the habits of Sikh workers that it built them a special lavatory. It soon transpired that the Sikh facilities were much better looked after than the native ones. Some companies – the Post Office and the Transport Authority – tried to impose dress regulations, but these soon came unstuck. Perhaps surprisingly, the Sikh obligation to wear long hair under turbans found much public support. The army had set an important trend by permitting Sikh troops to wear the turban, and the country seemed happy to follow the regimental example. Small victories such as this did not mean that Britain was rallying to the migrant cause. The anti-migrant bullies tended to drown out the milder voices in their favour, and discrimination certainly prevented migrants from getting the jobs, the salaries, the housing and often the neighbourly respect they wanted and deserved.

The Sikhs lived as cheaply as possible, in an atmosphere of some suspicion (they had landed in a part of Britain not known for cosmopolitan curiosity). The locals saw them as filthy, long-haired brutes (the feeling was often mutual: the Sikhs, like many migrants from supposedly primitive lands, saw the British as degenerate and culture-free). Nearly all of them were men, and in Britain all-male gatherings spelled trouble, stirring rough associations with football crowds, urban riots and closing time at the pub. They moved into big, often dilapidated period houses, clubbing together, sharing rooms, all – to

English eyes – higgledy-piggledy. It was a precarious beginning, but it had tangible benefits: the links and friendships forged in the crowded Sikh households fostered a vibrant exchange of contacts and ideas.

There were jobs for them, at least. In Southall, the Woolf Rubber Factory became noted for its willingness to hire immigrant workers. It was conveniently near Heathrow Airport, and swiftly became a home from home, an offshore Punjab for Hindus, Sikhs and Muslims alike. Urban mythology had it that hapless Indians who asked to be taken to Piccadilly or Oxford Street were dumped in Southall and told that Buckingham Palace was just up the road. The area became the capital of Asia-in-Britain: the Methodist church became a Sikh *gurdwara* in 1958; a social club was transformed into a Hindu temple.

In the later years of the decade the Sikhs were joined by the first wave of migrants from further north: people displaced by the construction of the Mangla Dam in Mirpur, Pakistan. This was a five-year project: it would eventually drown 250 villages by sluicing water into the valley. For once, those who liked to speak of 'floods' of refugees were close to telling the literal truth. Mirpuris joined the queue at Heathrow and looked for a way to support themselves. Like the Huguenots and Jews before them, they went to work in clothes, food and metalwork (which in the twentieth century meant not gold and silver but steel and aluminium). Some joined the Poles and West Indians in factories. Others, discouraged by the odium in which they seemed to be held, started their own businesses. Inch by inch, they began to write the classic immigrant parable all over again, starting work as hired hands or door-to-door salesmen before setting up small businesses of their own.

The banking system was wary, so Asian entrepreneurs went their own way, planting the seeds of a self-sufficient economy of their own. Apart from providing fellow migrants with jobs (in restaurants, shops and ancillary trades), they provided a market for migrant moneylenders, brokers, agents, distributors, consultants and go-betweens. This in turn allowed the community as a whole to subsidise the creation of places of worship, schools and clubs. By happenstance more than design, the migrants from India and Pakistan established a stronghold within, but separate from, the rest of British society. They were a self-catering minority, with their own bankers, lawyers and doctors, and their own service and support industries. These were growth areas, and they flourished. If some fell into the economy often known as 'black', who could be surprised? People raised under imperial administration had an acute and well-founded sense of tax as a form of theft.

Britain responded to this largely invisible development with dumb clichés: recent events had made anti-Semitism untenable, but it was still possible, in jokes, to depict the Irish as imbeciles, black chaps as good-for-nothings, Indians as simpletons, and the Chinese as wily and inscrutable. And prejudices do not go down without a fight. In the 1950s it was felt that the West Indians –

Christian, English-speaking, strict and hard-working – were a far more promising addition to the social fabric than these idle Eastern ne'er do wells, who would undoubtedly head straight for the nearest welfare handout.

Contrary to the usual insistence on assimilation as the recipe for successful immigration, a high degree of cultural independence seemed to be more useful. An investigation conducted by Robert Davison in Nottingham in the 1960s uncovered a remarkable contrast between two pioneering groups of immigrants. Eighty-seven per cent of Jamaicans said that they felt British before they came; while 86 per cent said it was fine by them if their children 'felt' English.* In stark contrast, only 2 per cent of Indians and Pakistanis claimed to feel British before their arrival; and only 6 per cent were willing to accept the idea that their children might feel English. So much for the insistence that immigrants should 'fit in' – the common cry of those outraged by foreigners in their midst. In practice, those who tried the hardest to fit in were those most actively discouraged from doing so. Those who were able to form their own communities, develop their own economy and conduct their own affairs – such as Jews, Indians, Pakistanis and Cypriots – found themselves better equipped to advance towards the mainstream.

Contrasts such as these are vexatious, defying any neat summaries of cause and effect. It has been argued that the racism directed towards black Caribbean islanders was more vicious than that which laid siege to Indian communities. It has been argued that Indian culture had not been so assaulted and weakened by imperial considerations, whereas centuries of slavery had uprooted almost every tradition around which Afro-Caribbeans might rally. The one thing they did have was British background and identity; but on arrival this was snatched from their grasp. Jamaican migrants to America were noted as entrepreneurs. Not so in Britain, where they had no access to the credit on which such ventures relied.

How many times, throughout history, have immigrants had to contend with the accusation that they are lazy, grasping, on the take? How many times will they have to deliver luminous counter-examples before we cease to believe it? There aren't many universal truths, but people do not lightly burn their small hoard of money or burden themselves with loans merely to put their feet up at someone else's expense. They do not leave their homes and families because they are risk-averse. They travel, like medieval labourers, 'onlie to seeke woorck'; or, like the pious pastors harried out of the Continent by Catholic armies, for religious and personal liberty. The European and Irish migrations were, in the decade after the war, more substantial, but, without the stain of

---

*Exactly the same number – 86 per cent – however, confessed to disillusionment with Britain.

racial suspicion, attracted no vitriol. There were few complaints, for example, about Hungarians. When the Soviet tanks rolled into Budapest in 1956, over ten thousand of them became Hungarians-in-exile. Most were anti-Soviet dissidents and, therefore, our friends. As George Mikes remarked: 'Everybody is Hungarian.' He went on to explain what would happen if you asked a fellow émigré in London for advice:

> They happen to know a Hungarian cobbler round the corner who is a genius of his craft and a Hungarian tailor who puts Savile Row to shame. We all know where to buy Hungarian salami, sausages and apricot brandy. We all go to various Hungarian restaurants where they cook exactly as our mothers did. We go to see Hungarian dancers in Shaftesbury Avenue, to listen to Hungarian violinists at the Wigmore Hall, to applaud Hungarian runners at the White City, to watch Hungarian football players at Wembley . . . I do not know quite how it is with others; but I personally have not seen an Englishman in London for over two years.[12]

Perhaps it was just that migration, quite simply, had gone 'mass market'. Like so many other aspects of modern life, it was operating on a new and larger scale than people could easily grasp. The numbers were such that it was becoming more and more tempting to speak of immigrants as groups rather than individuals – and then tar them all with the same broad brush. No one noticed, for instance, when a four-year-old boy called Charles Saatchi came with his Jewish family from Baghdad and embarked on a career that would straddle the summits of British marketing and art. Distinct from the fuss over the drift from the Caribbean, India and Pakistan, some migrants were able to slip into Britain without attracting any attention at all.

Cyprus, for example, struck incurious Britons as more a military base than a colonial possession. So when, in 1955, war broke out on the island and many Cypriots began to appear in London, there was no clear sense of what to make of them. Were they Greek? Turkish? Armenian? British? The census of 1931 had noticed over a thousand 'Cypriot-born' people in Britain, but many of these were born to British military families serving time in the Med. The war itself was a confusing three-way conflict. Greek nationalists were rising against British authority with a view to liberating the island. But since they also pledged to tie the future of Cyprus to Greece, the Turkish population were opposing them. The untidy struggle ended temporarily on 19 February 1959, when Cyprus became an independent republic.

Throughout the four years of war, Cypriots left at the rate of around four thousand per annum. But when the British finally withdrew, many of the best jobs on the island – on military bases or in the bars and restaurants patronised by the forces – melted away. In the following year or so, around 25,000 Cypriots came to Britain.

Unlike the West Indian and Indian migrations, which sent single men abroad in search of sustenance through remittance, the Cypriots came in husband-and-wife teams, with well-formed ambitions and expectations: they wanted their own houses and their own businesses. Husbands took jobs in catering, hotels, grocery or hairdressing; wives found piecework in the immigrant mainstay, textiles. They became seamstresses producing or finishing garments at home – a cottage industry and a hangover from the outwork system employed by London's sweatshops. It wasn't well paid, but it was flexible: they could work late at night when the children were asleep, and it didn't require very good English. There was an almost festive, try-anything spirit in these people: coffee shops, butchers', bakers', haulage firms . . . it didn't really matter, so long as it was possible to envisage running the books one day. Cyprus itself was resembling a mini-India – there was talk of partition. And like the Indians, the Cypriots aspired to self-employment. In London, too, the Turkish and Greek communities nudged away from each other. Duplicating the topography of the landscape they had left behind, the Greeks (in the majority by four to one) favoured Camden, while the Turks set up on their eastern flank in Stoke Newington. Haringey became the second biggest Cypriot town in the world.

More by luck than judgement, perhaps, they had come at a good time. The internment of so many Italians in the war had left vacancies in catering. The Cypriots established snack bars and takeaways both in the areas where they lived and in the West End. London society acquired a taste for moussaka and kebabs, pitta bread, hummus and taramasalata. Dancing on tables became a Soho craze. Like curry, this was perfect student nosh: inexpensive, filling and with exciting ethnic overtones. College kids who would one day go on to become barristers could drip honey, nuts and oil on to their essays.

One Cypriot immigrant, Reo Stakis, was doing the same thing for Scotland. He came to Britain before the war as a lace salesman, and in 1945 bought a café in Glasgow. There he followed the example of the Berni brothers and served up cheap steaks and Black Forest gâteaux, offering affordable gastronomy to the mass market. 'He taught them', someone once said, 'to use a knife and fork.' In the end he built a chain of forty-six hotels in Scotland, which he sold to Hilton Hotels for over a billion pounds in 1991. He went shooting three times a week and was knighted for his services to the British palate and pillow.

At any other time, the Cypriots might have attracted angrier social scrutiny. As it was, they didn't find it hard to uphold the traditions and moral standards they too saw as endangered in corrupt Britain. They formed voluntary associations and built a new Greek Orthodox church in Camden; they established Saturday schools where their children could learn Greek; they produced newspapers and held flamboyant weddings.* Like many immigrants, they looked around their new home and noted with horror the disdain in which the local old people were held: neither revered nor indulged, neither pampered nor humoured, but packed out of sight into what were, in effect, orphanages.

In all, there were, according to Home Office estimates, 210,000 people from the Commonwealth living and working in Britain by 1958. Three-quarters of them were male. By all historic measures, this was an extraordinary and rapid migration. Over half of the newcomers – 115,000 – were West Indian; 55,000 were Indian or Pakistani; 25,000 were West African; and 10,000 were Cypriot. Nearly half lived in London – as always, by far the most eclectic and absorbent city in the land. Elsewhere, the largest settlements were in Birmingham (25,000), Manchester (8,000), Liverpool and Leeds (6,000 each).

White Britain grumbled. The migrants themselves had every right to be disappointed by and fearful of the social atmosphere through which they moved, but there were no major confrontations. Then the mood curdled. The postwar reconstruction boom was running out of steam; unemployment jumped to half a million. As far as the West Indians were concerned, most welfare costs they incurred were met by their own Caribbean governments, but details such as this were not going to get in the way of arguments that grew more hysterical by the day. In Kenya, the occasional savagery of Mau Mau rebels was breathing fresh life into the demonic popular stereotype of black men as machete-wielding savages (evidence that the esteemed British officers and administrators who supervised the incarceration of Mau Mau suspects could also be barbaric torturers was not widely broadcast). The national mood hardened. In 1957 the press reported that sixty-six immigrants were being prosecuted for living off immoral earnings in London – and was happy to imply that most were West Indians (and 15 were, but, given that 64 salt-of-the-earth Brits had been arrested for identical crimes, less than one-tenth of such felons were Caribbean migrants).

While resentment rose, the migrants themselves started to see a new chill in the air. In the summer of 1958, Britain's Teddy boys – named for their cod-Edwardian costumes and quiffs – grew ever more boisterous. With National Service ending, they were free to act out their own urban version of working-class gang culture. They aspired to be bad and feared. They would fight whoever was up for it – even one another, if necessary; they ripped up clubs and cinemas on their Saturday-night sprees. Given half a chance, they would

*In Cyprus, marriages were arranged almost as energetically as they were in India. And emigration was good for your image. A mediocre-looking Cypriot émigré might well seem more attractive, or at any rate more eligible, than his rivals back in Nicosia.

harangue anyone with black skin, and even had a rustic-sounding phrase, for their rumbles: they would say they were going out 'black-burying'. In Nottingham, in the summer of 1958, West Indians stopped going out at night – it was too dangerous. The question arose: when would the angry and beleaguered West Indians reckon that enough was enough, and start to fight back? Even more important: what would happen when they did?

The unrepentant Oswald Mosley saw another angry rabble on which he could pin his hopes. He set himself up in an office in Notting Hill and produced inflammatory leaflets – 'Take Action Now ... Protect Your Jobs ... Stop Coloured Immigration ... Houses for White People ... People of Kensington, Act Now'. Pamphlets issued on behalf of his 'Union Movement' featured pictures of blacks with spears entering Britain. Parliament tried to resist: 'We have no intention', said Rab Butler, 'of allowing extremist elements to take advantage of the situation.'[13] There were reports that black cafés and houses were being terrorised; Butler 'universally condemned' such actions. George Rogers, the Labour MP for North Kensington, urged the government to limit the entry of coloured 'undesirables' into 'overcrowded' constituencies such as his own. He did, with some prescience, argue the case for the recruitment of black policemen, but he couldn't resist speaking in shocked terms of the 'tremendous influx' and referring to its inbuilt taste for 'vice, drugs, prostitutes and the use of knives'.

In August 1958 there was, in effect, a two-week fight. Urban riots had erupted in many a previous British summer, and this one had familiar battle-lines. On the 23rd, a pub brawl in Nottingham was apparently sparked by an angry confrontation after a black man was seen talking to a white woman. It soon turned into a serious affray: a thousand whites took to the streets to 'express their anger'. The mob was quelled by police with Alsatians and fire-hoses in an action that left eight people hospitalised. In London, MPs were quick to call again for immigration control, especially after the following evening, when a pack of youths went 'nigger-hunting' in Shepherd's Bush and Notting Hill. They attacked five black men with bars, leaving three dreadfully injured. The nine boys in the gang were all under twenty. At their trial they pleaded guilty and were given four-year sentences. But the damage had been done. Extremists, not for the first or the last time, were setting the agenda.

A week later, Britain's nastiest Teds, and anyone else who thought they were cool and tough, headed for Notting Hill. Some four hundred white men launched two all-night attacks on black people and shops. A petrol bomb was thrown into a black home. Where were the police? They didn't seem anxious to intervene. On the third night, blacks prepared to fight back. They knew what was coming, so they made petrol bombs of their own and hunkered down on rooftops. This time the police moved. There was a street fight involving hundreds of young whites shouting, 'Down with niggers!' ... 'Keep Britain white!' and waving banners – 'Deport all niggers!' In truth, they seemed just as happy to fight the police, but their intention was unmistakeable. Mosley's Union Movement held a rally in a nearby road. 'Get rid of them,' a speaker urged the crowd. 'Go on boys,' women called down from windows. 'Go and get yourself some blacks.'

Two weeks later, sentencing four of the arrested youths to imprisonment, Mr Justice Salmon delivered a famous judgment. 'You are a minute and insignificant section of the population,' he said, 'who have filled the whole nation with horror, indignation and disgust. Everyone, irrespective of the colour of their skin, is entitled to walk through our streets in peace, with their heads erect, and free from fear.'[14] These were fine words. But having the right to walk free from fear was not quite the same as being able to enjoy or luxuriate in that right. And if it was true that the bully boys represented only a 'minute' section of the population, they were certainly not 'insignificant'. There were six thousand West Indians in Notting Hill; and half that number in Nottingham. For them, these racist vigilantes were very significant indeed: petrol-soaked rags were coming through their letter boxes at night.

Once again the law found itself standing against political leaders and media magnificos too easily seduced by the electoral advantage attached to mollifying the noisiest sectors of public opinion. But while Salmon's was a classic judgment, and true in the technical sense that the number of riotous racists was indeed small, its noble sentiments did not really penetrate the fog of prejudice. If it had, it would have generated an earnest and lordly anti-racist campaign among the nation's politicians and opinion-formers. This was not forthcoming. Of course, there was a stream of categorical denunciations. The Prime Minister, Harold Macmillan, condemned the riots and insisted that all British subjects, whatever the colour of their skin, shared the right to walk the streets without fear. But he also nodded at the idea that he would look at the 'problem' caused by immigration. Most newspapers agreed. To restrict immigration would be 'shameful' and 'the easy way out', said the *Observer*. The riots were a 'blot on our national good name for tolerance', said the *Daily Sketch*. But even to call what had happened a 'riot' was to go along with the idea that there were two sides to it. The nights of violence in Notting Hill were no riot, but an aggressive rampage against people who only as a last resort fought back. Sadly, the 'solutions' all seemed to target the victims rather than the aggressors.

There were suggestions that a 'moratorium' be imposed on passports until things cooled down. Questions in Parliament challenged ministers to say what they would do about immigrant 'problems': illiteracy, unemployment, drugs, crime, prostitution and benefits fraud. Martin Lindsay, Conservative MP for Solihull, insisted that a multiracial society was endangering the 'national character'. There were cries of horror when the Home Office announced that 'coloured unemployment' had doubled in recent months (no one seemed to realise that the immigrants were simply the first casualties of the economic slowdown). A Gallup poll showed that over 25 per cent of people felt that the blacks were to blame for whatever trouble befell them. Other polls revealed that 80 per cent of the population favoured controls, and the Conservative party conference that autumn promised to impose them, given a chance. At other times, such knee-jerk reactions would have been called 'giving in to terrorism', but it was evident that the challenge for politicians was purely tactical: how could they impose such widely desired restrictions without seeming merely racist?

Alarmed by such a prospect (remittances home had grown into a serious economic asset), Jamaica's Prime Minister, Norman Manley, returned to London, where he was rudely jostled in the street by uncivil Britons. Again he stressed that his compatriots were by no means 'the deadbeats of the West Indies' but its skilled scrimpers and savers; and he went on to remind his hosts that the driving force behind this migration was the acute rate of unemployment (25 per cent, out of season) back in the Caribbean. The Nigerian Minister of Health also visited London in September to discuss Notting Hill, though his concern was a little different. He wanted assurances that the several thousand Nigerian students in Britain would not be confused with the 'influx of West Indians' who seemed to be causing so much trouble.

Such pleas for consideration fell on confused ears. British politicians found it hard to see beyond the idea that the immigrants were the problem. And they were slaves to the time-honoured administrative presumption that where there were 'problems' there must also be 'solutions'. Working party after working party was invited to assess 'the social and economic problems arising from the growing influx into the United Kingdom of coloured workers', and you needed only a sketchy sense of linguistic priorities to see where this was leading. The rubric assumed that the problems 'arose from' the 'influx'; it did not address itself to the bullying behaviour of the natives. In retrospect, the term 'coloured workers' looks chosen with care, given that a more accurate description of these people at that time was British citizens.

In the end, the government did not act on these acrid impulses. There was no sign that immigration was rising and there were hopes that the problem would solve itself in time. But in the spring of 1959 more bad news burst out of Notting Hill. Kelso Cochrane, a thirty-two-year-old Antiguan carpenter, went to hospital in Paddington on a Saturday night to attend to his broken thumb. He was getting married a few weeks later. On his way home he was ambushed by a gang of six youths. When they had finished with him he was dead from stab wounds.

Everyone expected another 'riot', but the police moved in firmly to patrol the streets, and the Duke of Edinburgh dropped in on some local youth clubs as an expression of royal goodwill. The killers were never found, however, and the impression stamped on public opinion was that the district was a lawless no-go area. It was true that the events of the previous summer had hardened the West Indians into a defiant and angry community. What was crystallising – in the bitter shouts of 'Who killed Kelso Cochrane?' at public meetings – was a polarising world of 'us' and 'them'. Cochrane's funeral saw over a thousand West Indians line the route to Kensal Green Cemetery; hardly any of them knew the victim, but they recognised him as one of their own and gathered round his memory. They wore formal dress and laid flamboyant wreaths; some wept and wailed. In a way, it was the original Notting Hill Carnival: the first formal parade of Britain's new, unified West Indian population.

The nation as a whole, shocked both by the murder and by the sight of this West Indian community on the march, allowed itself to assume that immigration itself was the root cause of all this bloodshed. The Home Secretary, Rab Butler, agreed that the situation was 'disquieting' and that anti-immigration legislation could not be ruled out. The fact that migration from the West Indies seemed once more to be increasing meant that ministers could no longer see any end to it. Though many fancied themselves free-marketeers, they did not trust the market (in particular the employment market) to effect its own cure, did not believe that migration would dip as soon as jobs became scarce. Would-be emigrants in Jamaica and St Lucia, Trinidad and St Kitts kept hearing from friends or relatives who had found work, so they kept coming to join them.

A ministerial committee in 1961 looked at the figures, and the projections, with foreboding. It riffled through evidence that the 'coloured immigrants' tended to live in unhygienic 'colonies' – a rather breathtaking criticism, given Britain's long experience of such things. In passing, it noted with pride the tolerance of the British people as a whole. But all the talk revolved around race. The cabinet did not convene committees to discuss the insatiable love of violence among Britain's young working-class white males, the riotous tough-guy pride that would later rip through the nation's football grounds. On the rare occasions when immigrants fought back, people were quick to see it as an expression of their latent aggression. No one observed that they were, if anything, taking their cue from the Britons who swarmed around them. The publisher Naim Atallah, one of many Palestinians displaced by the founding of Israel in 1948, certainly found that pugnacity was the only language these British understood. For three years he was jeered at by workmates at British Electric. 'One day I rebelled. I think I hit someone with a spanner. After that we became friends. I was one of the boys after that.'[15]. Courtney Griffiths, who came from Jamaica in 1959 and became a barrister, made a similar discovery when he secured the help of his brothers to sort out racist school bullies. 'We waylaid them. We waited outside school and gave them the most serious kicking. Thereafter I never had a problem in school at all. I became a firm favourite with teachers and other pupils.'[16]

There were further cabinet discussions in the spring and summer of 1961, but while the politicians debated immigration statistics, and wondered how they could sweeten the pill of outright exclusion, daily life grew rougher. The police, in particular, seemed convinced that the best way to stop the violence was to send these people back home. Of all the failures of policy and will at this time, this might have been the most grievous. The police were invited to patrol immigration not by protecting people but by harassing them.

In October 1961 the government declared, with an air of reluctant acquiescence, that legislation was forthcoming. Nearly 300,000 immigrants had arrived in little more than a decade. It couldn't go on. The new arrangement would take the form of a work permit scheme, which had been carefully devised to exclude coloured workers without discriminating against them too explicitly. Migrants would be divided into three camps: those with job offers, those with credible skills or qualifications, and those without either of these desirable commodities. Quotas were set for this last category, which, as everyone knew, was the one to which the immigrants they had in mind were most likely to belong.

The proposal did not have unanimous backing in government: the Treasury took up where the now fading Colonial Office had left off and protested that such controls would harm the flexibility and dynamism of the economy. But Home Office concerns about social harmony trumped such arguments.* Rab Butler described the proposed Commonwealth Immigrants Act as a 'sad necessity' but suggested that popular pressure made it inevitable. In a memorandum he admitted that the beauty of the plan was that it could be portrayed as colour-blind, though it 'was intended to, and would in fact, operate on coloured people almost exclusively'.[17] The Labour opposition spoke out: Hugh Gaitskell called it 'a miserable, shameful, shabby bill'; fine words, though not sufficient to stop it becoming law.

It has often been said that such a strategy should have been pursued much earlier, so that immigrants could have been given a softer, better-managed landing. But migration from the Commonwealth was remarkable, and only in fantasy could it have passed off without at least some friction. We might even wonder that there was not more. And neither the ghastliness of Nottingham and Notting Hill nor the rottenness of everyday injustice was enough to shrink

---

*The Treasury's fondness for cheap imported labour might have been myopic. Britain was committing itself to a future of tense industrial relations, overmanning and weak investment at a time when robot-built cars, ships, planes, motorbikes, televisions and radios were starting to pour off hi-tech foreign production lines. Many of our own labour-intensive products would soon be overpriced and out of date.

the queues at Britain's ports. And the migrants came with open eyes – by the early 1960s, no one could pretend that they were heading off to bask in goodwill or live in pampered ease on this happy-go-lucky island in the North Sea. Some historians have been shocked to hear – to take one example – that nearly half of the respondents to one survey vowed to go home if they won the pools. But this only confirmed what was obvious: many were only here for the wages; they felt everything else about Britain stank. If anything, the surprise was that so many – over half – said that they would stay. Despite its acidic manners, Britain was not the worst, not even close to the worst, place to live.

Still, the famous open door was about to close. Less than fourteen years after the *Windrush*, so-called Conservatives were wrecking a historic national principle. Indeed, the story of a decade is framed and explained by this heartfelt political U-turn. In 1948 Britain had promised free entry to all of its imperial subjects. There was an element of bluster about this, but it was nevertheless a high and hopeful pledge. Now it was in tatters. Fateful distinctions were being drawn between 'authentic' Britons and a second-tier level of subjects who could no longer count on Britain as their home, and who could be deported. And no one had any doubts about who would inhabit the second tier. What seemed subtle to mandarins struck almost everyone else as clumsy. It was obvious that this was an attempt not to stop immigration *per se*, but to halt black immigration. The small print exempted the Irish – an independent nation – from the restrictions that were imposed on West Indians, many of whom were still British subjects. It was not quite what people had a right to expect from those who would shortly be told that they had never had it so good.

CHAPTER 22

The Door Closes

The Commonwealth Immigrants Act was passed on 1 July 1962. Soon afterwards, an embarrassing question began to hover in the corridors of the Home Office. In 1961, 130,000 migrants had entered Britain, a colossal increase – roughly equivalent to the previous five years put together. In the six months leading up to the act, another eighty thousand had arrived.

It began to look as if the attempt to raise the bar only urged greater numbers to flock beneath it. Britain's subjects in the Commonwealth, alert to the narrowing of their options, took the now-or-never decision to head for Britain before the door slammed altogether. At the end of the year, a sobering fact emerged: in the three-year period from 1960 to 1962, a period of intense political hostility to immigration and one which culminated in the passing of a historic Act of Parliament designed to contain it, more migrants arrived in Britain than had disembarked in the whole of the twentieth century up to that point. The country would never be the same again.

In the twelve months following the Act, only 34,500 people came to Britain, many of them in the six months before it became law. Migration from the West Indies, in particular, dipped sharply, to around fourteen thousand per year between 1963 and 1966. But a new passage to Britain was opening in the East: Indians and Pakistanis, some displaced or unsettled by partition, were continuing to arrive in large numbers.

This migration was different in character from the one Parliament had hurried to forestall. Most of the pre-1962 migrants were single men, who usually came with only a short stay in mind: a working trip to Britain was becoming an established rite of passage for young men in the Commonwealth, a duty they owed to their families and villages. After the Act, however, these itinerant labourers had to think twice before leaving Britain, since they might not be able to return. The migrants' mantra – one more year, one more year – froze into an open-ended and unpredictable commitment to the country they were stuck in. And while the government was able to argue (and indeed believe) that it had acted decisively to control a situation that was threatening to become chaotic, in imposing a limit on the number of overseas workers it was willing to welcome, it succeeded only in fireproofing the front door. The back door remained ajar. For humane reasons, the Act allowed family reunification, and the result was the very form of migration that many Britons feared most: permanent settlement. Single men sent for their wives and children, just as their predecessors had done. In 1961 only one-sixth of the immigrants were women, and few children came: life in Britain was precarious. But in 1968 there were fifty thousand 'dependants', and by 1971 women and children made up three-quarters of the total. In a decade, Britain was home not only to migrant workers but to migrant families and communities.

People from Africa, China, India, Pakistan and the West Indies were creating a home from home in whichever British locale would have them. The original point of the migration – to support the family at home – dissolved. Now that the families were here too, they saved less and spent more. They built churches and clubs, spread new languages, customs and tastes across the cities in which they lived. Unlike Britain's own imperial evangelists, they were not missionaries, and did not seek converts. Instead they promoted, by example, new appetites, colours, sounds, fashions, prejudices and sensitivities.

While Germany created a low-level social category – the guest worker – with limited civil rights, Britain extended a broader range of freedoms. And as foreign communities began to settle, so they became more assertive. Sikhs, who at first took pains to blend in, demanded and won the right to put their turbans back on and let their hair grow. Caribbean migrants from different islands were pressed into a racial solidarity that began to express itself at the annual Notting Hill carnival which, while it looked like an authentic Caribbean party, was a distinctly British event: nowhere else would Jamaicans and Trinidadians, St Lucians and Guyanese have linked arms in quite this way.

Gestures such as these – akin to an Englishman wearing a tie on his way to the club in Mysore – were interpreted by some Britons as acts of gross cultural ingratitude. The mood in the areas where migrants settled remained malign and fraught. Britain's working-class culture emphasised the manly, the loyal, the muscular. Fortified by drink, it could be aggressive and uncouth. Caribbean islanders in London or Birmingham moved through a daily barrage of four-letter words and physical intimidation. These were the people dramatised as the 'Lonely Londoners' by the novelist Samuel Selvon: crafty dreamers and schemers slipping through and sometimes slipping up in a dangerous and alienating wasteland.

Far from establishing a strict quota, the Act initially set no limit on the number of immigrants. It was hoped that the process of issuing the vouchers – the wait involved – would be deterrent enough. But many were convinced that the Act was too mild, so the government (through a new unit set up by Prime Minister Macmillan, the Commonwealth Immigration Committee*) decided to ration vouchers to nine hundred per week. This was hardly draconian: it allowed for an annual migration of more than 45,000 people. But nor did it contain much slack. The queue swelled, and soon the backlog was embarrassing and controversial. By 1963 there were delays of up to fifteen months, and the pressure mounted: another bolt was needed on the door. The Home Secretary, Henry Brooke, called the 1962 Act 'inadequate'; sterner measures were explored and then imposed. No country was allowed to take more than 25 per cent of the available vouchers – a move specifically intended to trim the number of applicants from India and Pakistan. Britain's bureaucrats blanched when they learned that there was already a waiting list in the subcontinent of some 270,000 people. The government decided to stop chipping at the margins and announced a wholehearted rethink. In the name of efficiency, it resolved that no more applications for C-vouchers – the third-tier level: unskilled labour – would be considered until further notice.

This was the firmest move yet, but it made little difference. In the following twelve months, the number of immigrants rose sharply – up to 68,000 – and Britain's sullen attitude to foreigners of colour, never far from the surface, came barging to the forefront of the public agenda. The 1964 general election was characterised by an outspoken expression of racist dread. In the Midlands constituency of Smethwick, the Conservative candidate, Peter Griffiths, bucked the national swing against his party and took the seat by brazenly playing what would soon become known as the 'race card'. His supporters told voters: 'If you want a nigger neighbour, vote Labour.' Political analysts noted that such tactics, while disgraceful, were clear vote-winners. By now the term 'immigrants' was fast becoming a polite euphemism for 'coloured people', and a significant proportion of the electorate wanted fewer of them. The fact that in 1964 Britain suffered a net loss of seventeen thousand people – emigration was outstripping immigration for the first time since 1957 – was not much emphasised. Immigration was presented and discussed as if it were a brand-new factor in world affairs. There was wide agreement, even among those who pleaded for tolerance, that the 'problem' could be solved only by having fewer 'coloured people'. It was taken as read that the modern migrants were not properly (i.e.

*Among its members were Reginald Maudling and Enoch Powell.

racially) equipped to be British. That the 'problem' had anything to do with the powerful racial prejudices of the British people themselves was rarely allowed to influence either conversation or action.

In one sense the clumsiness of the 1962 Act was consistent with characteristic British traits: a distaste for absolutist solutions, a preference for muddle over clarity, a refusal to be entirely guided by the promptings of either conscience or prejudice. Torn between respect for the idea of equality, and nervousness at the implications of such concepts, Britain pursued a policy which reflected both its generous and its mean streak, often simultaneously. We shall never know what would have happened had the Act not been pushed through. Migration might have surged; it would hardly have petered out. But migration might well have been to a large extent self-regulating; there is a clear correlation, in recent British history, between migration figures and the supply of jobs: when unemployment rises, immigration falls.*

The Labour government that took office in 1964 swiftly declared itself happy to go along with the Tory strategy it had so heartily denounced in opposition. It not only declined to repeal the 1962 Act – it set about strengthening it. Influenced by an angry pulse of public pressure, the party's manifesto admitted that 'the number of immigrants entering the United Kingdom must be limited'. By now there was a queue of some 330,000 voucher applications pending, and in theory there were half a million dependants of recent immigrants entitled to come to Britain. Steps had to be taken. In 1965 a White Paper emphasised the 'very valuable contribution' of immigrants to the economy, while outlining a clear willingness to manage without them. The quota of vouchers was cut from 20,000 to 8,500 per year (a thousand of which were earmarked for tiny Malta) and – again as a specific deterrent to migrants from India and Pakistan – now, no more than 15 per cent would be available to any one country. The majority – five thousand – were expected to go to qualified professionals, as and where there were shortages. Doctors, teachers or engineers had a chance, and fee-paying students were welcome; others would be wasting their time. Further qualifying rules were toughened: children over sixteen could not be admitted as family members and children under sixteen could not join relatives other than their own parents. Immigration officers were given the right to deport migrants convicted of crimes.

The message was unequivocal: migrants were not welcome. Not even the passing of a contrasting piece of legislation in the same year – the Race Relations Act, which made outright discrimination illegal – could disguise this,

---

*Ceri Peach showed that the giddy rise of immigration in 1961–2, the beat-the-bill rush, was the only exception to the rule that migration fluctuates in line with employment possibilities.

and it was a view echoed by numerous politicians, of whom Enoch Powell was only the most prominent. A new institution – the Race Relations Board – was created, too, but it was a weak agency obliged to handle day-to-day complaints rather than root causes.* In the following year, 1966, England won the World Cup, and spawned, as one of the symptoms of a boastful national pride, a new political party, the National Front. For Britain's newcomers, these were lonely years. 'I used to cry in my little room at night,' recalled Balraj Khanna, an Indian painter, who arrived in 1960. 'I used to say to myself, why the hell did I come here? Why don't I go back?' Pride kept him where he was. 'It would have been a moral defeat,' he said.[1]

Decolonisation continued to present Britain's government with a throbbing headache. In 1967 there were clear signs of a looming crisis in Kenya. The new nation, under Jomo Kenyatta, had committed itself to 'Africanisation' since independence in 1963 and there were specific fears in London that a horde of Kenyan Asians – up to eighty thousand of them – might try to leave and head for Britain. In 1963 the Conservative Home Secretary, Henry Brooke, had declared that it would be 'out of the question' to deny the Kenyan Asians entry. 'It would be tantamount to a denial', he said, 'of one of the basic rights of a citizen, namely to enter the country of which he was a citizen.'[2] But that is precisely what happened. Kenya's relatively prosperous Asian population was vulnerable and exposed, and by 1967 Kenyatta was inviting them to leave in no uncertain terms. The more far-sighted, or perhaps the more nervous, began to land in England in the autumn. Around a thousand a month filed into Heathrow; newspapers pictured them jostling for documents in Nairobi. In London, there was more talk of a ban, and the Labour Home Secretary, James Callaghan, duly introduced a bill to exclude them. The Kenyans, fearing the worst, jumped. In the first two months of 1968, thirteen thousand came in another helter-skelter, beat-the-ban rush. The government reacted hastily, and on 22 February the cabinet suggested a quota on the number of Asians it was willing to accept. Only 1,500 non-patrial (i.e. non-white) Kenyans would be admitted each year. Given that there would soon be a waiting-list for papers numbering over seven thousand, this was strict. It was also blatant racial discrimination; Kenya's British-descended settlers, deprived of the imperial protection that had buttressed their profitable and expansive lives in the Happy Valley, were welcomed 'home', but the so-called 'Asians' – some of whom had been living in Africa for generations – were warned that they could not expect the same treatment. They were British subjects, with British passports, but they were not going to be allowed into Britain. Another member of the Labour

---

*In its first year, the Race Relations Board handled 982 complaints, of which 734 were dismissed as unproven or unprovable. Over half (143) of those upheld were criticisms of racial stereotypes in advertisements.

government, Richard Crossman, referred to them as 'Kenya Asians with British passports', as if they had come by these precious documents by some form of subterfuge. A fair amount of diplomatic tap-dancing was required to fudge the fact that, as part of the small print of Indian independence, Britain had agreed that expatriate or diaspora Indians would look to Britain for protection, not to Delhi. The Kenyan Asians were not slaves; they were volunteers. Some 32,000 of them had been indentured to the East African Railway in the early years of the twentieth century, but most had returned to India at the end of their three-year contracts. The majority of Indians in Kenya had travelled, just like British imperialists, in search of commercial opportunities created by the British Empire. And in British Kenya they formed a merchant class that greased the wheels of the colonial economy. The descendants of these pioneers were now being refused entry to the nation they and their ancestors had served.

Arguments such as these did nothing to block or even slow the bill, which was introduced on 27 February 1968. It immediately ran into a storm of criticism. *The Times* declared: 'The Labour Party has a new ideology. It does not any longer profess to believe in the equality of man. It does not even believe in the equality of British citizens.' Others were even more vehement. In the *Spectator*, Auberon Waugh, rarely noted in later life as a friend of the underdog, called it 'one of the most immoral pieces of legislation to have emerged from any British Parliament'. The Archbishop of Canterbury condemned it; barristers and law professors pointed out that it was a violation of almost every international law you cared to name.

On 1 March 1968, however, nearly four hundred Members of Parliament voted in favour of the bill. While they were about it, they plugged some of the cracks in the 1962 legislation. Full citizenship was available only to those with a parent or grandparent born, adopted or naturalised in the UK. The nation, in a frantic hurry, was a taking a profound step. Ninety-nine times out of a hundred this legislation would favour whites. The scion of a colonial administrator who'd gone to the Caribbean, India or East Africa fifty years ago could saunter back to England, point to his grandfather's birthplace and claim full citizenship. The Caribbean, Indian or African civil servant who'd worked alongside him could not. In theory, if his black grandfather had been born in Bedford before relocating to Barbados, he had just as much right to full British citizenship as the Governor-General. But how often had that happened?*

In the end, the government made an exception for the Kenyan Asians. The quota was raised first to 3,000, then to 3,500, then to 5,000. In doing this, a sorrowful pattern was set. Britain had protested furiously against the arrival of

---

*A few months later, in October, a new Race Relations Act was passed. Britain found itself able to promote discrimination with one hand, while outlawing it with the other.

the Kenyans, and then admitted them anyway. It was a circuitous route to the worst of both worlds. Sikhs who had been expelled from their homes settled in Ealing and Leicester feeling alienated, unpopular and nervous. This seemed a peculiarly British way of doing things. Other nations might have spoken high-mindedly and morally on behalf of the Kenyans, and then excluded them anyway. Britain did the opposite: having tried and failed to keep them out, it lost all claims to the moral high ground. Plenty of Britons rose to the occasion: charities helped the Kenyan Asians to settle and apologised for the wilder statements of their leaders and fellow countrymen. But public opinion was gripped by the idea that Britain was under siege.

The Kenyan Asians were placed in an impossible situation. Thrown out of Africa for being too pale, they landed in a place where they were too dark. Enoch Powell was saying that Britain must be 'mad, literally mad' to permit such an unhealthy influx, and warning of the carnage that would inevitably accompany such folly. 'Like the Roman,' he said, in a speech that has entered the folklore of modern British politics, 'I see the Tiber flowing with much blood.'[3] Powell is often taken to personify Britain's racist instincts. And it is true that in some polls three-quarters of the respondents agreed with him. More than 300 of the 412 Conservative constituency associations saw him as a brave prophet. Dockers went on strike in his support, and the National Front daubed 'Powell for PM' on inner-city walls.

But liberal Britain retained the upper hand. The elite squirmed. By firmly equating cultural purity with racial integrity, Powell was throwing his weight behind a national assumption which years of diplomacy had sought to conceal: the last thing the mandarins wanted was to be embarrassed by this sort of talk at dinner with a Commonwealth head of state. And moralists were out-raged. Tony Benn accused Powell of raising 'the flag of racialism over Wolverhampton, a flag which is beginning to look suspiciously like the one that fluttered over Dachau and Belsen'. A more exacting rebuttal was delivered by Edward Heath, who ignored his own members, sacked Powell from the shadow cabinet for his intemperate words, and exiled him to the political fringe.

It wasn't long, however, before Heath, as Prime Minister, found himself presiding over an almost identical debacle. There were still pools of potential British citizens all over the former empire, and in 1971 Heath's government passed its own Immigration Act to make sure that they would not have automatic access to the mother country. It reaffirmed the importance of patriality and introduced specific new tiers of membership: essentially, the white Commonwealth – Australia, Canada and New Zealand – retained the right to come to Britain; the remainder did not. The United Kingdom was now officially a family, a tribe. The politics of immigration – or the fear of immigrants, which amounted to the same thing – had become the motor of the national identity.

Powell, ironically, was having the last laugh: just as he had argued, to be British you now had to be able to show descent from an ancient rustic land of oaks and meadows.

No one really knew how many people had come to Britain recently. Home Office figures suggest that roughly 70,000 people had arrived in each year of the decade, but the 1971 census found that the foreign-born population had grown by only 125,000. The statistics were semi-fabricated, extrapolated from data produced in the sending countries and passenger surveys. The more notable trend in the 1960s was the soaring rate of emigration. Britons unhappy with life at home voted with their feet and headed for Australia, Canada, New Zealand and southern Africa. The exodus rose from 72,000 in 1962 to 112,000 in 1964 and 161,000 in 1966. The Conservation Society saw this as 'a substantial loss' and, by implication, a substantial gain for the destination countries. Hardly anyone made the point that the same might well be true of those people who came to Britain.

It wasn't long before British resolve was once more tested by the stamp of faraway feet. Uganda, with its 74,000 Indians (two-thirds of whom had sensibly retained their British citizenship), was looking like another Kenya, only worse. In May 1970 President Milton Obote proposed a similar campaign of Africanisation, and matters took a brutal turn in January 1971 when Idi Amin deposed him, took power and wasted no time in declaring that the days of the Ugandan Asians were numbered. The following summer, he announced that he had been advised by a dream to give them three months to leave – a form of politics with which it was difficult to negotiate. The clock was ticking.

At first, the Ugandan Asians did not believe it: Amin was bluffing and, in any case, Britain would surely not stand for it. But as the weeks turned into months it was clear that there was no opposing this implacable decree. There were letters in the newspapers, one in the *Uganda Argus*, for example, which said, 'Never in history an African has ever had an Asian friend. To Asians I say bye-bye.'[4] A prosperous class of small businessmen – grocers, doctors, dentists, tailors, barbers, mechanics and teachers – began to pack their belongings.

Harold Wilson's Labour government in the sixties had set a limit of three thousand on the number of Ugandans who would be allowed to enter Britain in any one year. At that rate, it would take over twenty years for all the Ugandan Asians to be admitted. And there were signs that Britain was not willing to budge on this point, no matter how bad the situation became. A thousand signatures were collected and handed to Bolton Council in a petition objecting to the Ugandans' arrival. Leicester Council, having housed a number of Kenyans, went so far as to take out an advertisement in the *Uganda Argus* to warn people away: 'In the interests of yourself and your family, you should accept the advice of the Uganda Resettlement Board and not come to Leicester,' it pleaded. There were the usual rabble-rousing politicians on hand, too, to declare that further migration was intolerable.

Amin's statements were so rash, however, that public sympathy in Britain swung behind the Ugandans' cause. When he declared his approval of Hitler – on the grounds that he had faced up squarely to the Jews – Amin became easy to depict as a monster whose victims required Britain's help. The Attorney-General, Peter Rawlinson, put the moral-historical case firmly enough: 'A state is under a duty to accept on its territory', he said, 'those of its nationals who have nowhere else to go.' Alec Douglas Home, the Foreign and Commonwealth Secretary, remarked on television: 'If homes elsewhere in the world cannot be found for them, we must take these unlucky people in.' For the opposition, Shirley Williams agreed that Britain had a 'clear obligation' to Uganda's expelled Asians, though she recommended also that they be dispersed around the country as widely as possible.

The Uganda Resettlement Board was formed to supervise the migration. Five thousand Britons, some of them recent arrivals themselves, offered lodgings to the refugees, and there was a national fundraising campaign for clothes, blankets and other supplies. The Ugandan Asians were sent to temporary reception camps on sixteen military bases in West Malling, Greenham Common, Newmarket and elsewhere. They carried a maximum of fifty pounds, and such baggage as they could bring in by hand: they were virtually destitute. A Department of Employment study of the first 1,500 arrivals found, however, that only 12 per cent of them were unskilled: the rest were professional, commercial or skilled workers. Perhaps that is why the ever-pragmatic *Economist* was moved to dedicate its cover on 19 August to an encouraging message: 'We know many of you didn't really want to leave your homes and jobs in Uganda. You know we didn't really want you to come before, because we have problems with homes and jobs here. But most of us believe that this is a country that can use your skills and energies . . . You will find that we, like other countries, have our bullies and misfits. We are particularly sorry about those of our politicians who are trying to use your troubles for their own ends. And we're glad your British passport means something again.'[5]

Flights out of Entebbe airport that autumn took the form of an airlift. Canada had offered 5,000 entry documents; Britain made room for 28,000. The dispersal policy backfired, however: the Uganda Resettlement Board produced maps with 'red spots' where migrants should not live, which simply pointed the Ugandans to the most attractive locales – those with established communities of African Asians, that is – while convincing the public in those areas that they were already overloaded. But more than 21,000 Ugandans passed through the resettlement camps and into British life. They settled in now-familiar sites: west London, Leicester, Birmingham and the textile towns of Yorkshire. By the following July, only two thousand of them remained homeless, and many of the camps had already been wound up. The Ugandans, alongside the Kenyans, soon made their mark, showing commercial zeal and an entrepreneurial streak that Britain was slow to admire or celebrate.

Vijay Patel arrived in Britain from Kenya as a bright sixteen-year-old with a tiny handful of petty cash: his father, a timber merchant north of Nairobi, had died when Vijay was six; his mother, a schoolteacher, set up a nursery and raised her children alone, in a single room. Vijay came to London in 1968 and signed up for A-levels in north London, washing dishes at night to keep himself going. He went on to study pharmacy at Leicester University and in 1975, at the age of twenty-five, armed with a loan from a benevolent (or far-sighted) uncle, he opened a chemist's at Leigh-on-Sea in Essex. That first outlet grew into a chain of twenty-one pharmacies, which in turn sponsored the formation of a medical wholesaler – Waymade Healthcare. In 1982 he was joined by his elder brother Bhikhu, and the business continued to grow. In 2001 the brothers were named joint Entrepreneur of the Year, having assembled a fortune estimated at over £250 million.

Manish Chande followed a similar path. He fled Uganda before the expulsion, trained as an accountant in Britain and went into the property business, eventually setting up Trillium, a management company which, when it won the contract to administer the real-estate assets of the Department of Social Security, became the biggest commercial landlord in the country.

In 1975 Naresh and Mahesh Patel, two brothers who had come to Britain from Kenya, took over a declining food company, gave it a new name – Europa Foods – and began to invade British high streets. And in 1983 Moni Varni, raised in Malawi, came to Britain and set up a rice mill in west London. The explosion of Indian and Chinese restaurants was creating a demand for rice on an entirely new scale, and Varni went on to build a purpose-built factory in Rochester, with direct access to the water. He was one of several East African rice barons in the country, and indeed was following in the mighty footprints of Rashmi Thakrar, who had been expelled from Uganda in 1972 before building the Tilda rice plant in Essex.

It wasn't only in commerce that East Africa made its mark. John Sentamu grew up in Uganda, walking twelve miles to school each day until a missionary gave him a bicycle. He went on to train as a lawyer, but left the country when Idi Amin came to power. He was fortunate: he went to Cambridge to study theology, and became a prison chaplain at a remand centre, and then a vicar in Tulse Hill. Eventually he would become Bishop of Stepney and the first black member of the General Synod of the Church of England. This was not enough to make him immune from the prevailing racial suspicion of his adopted country: he was once pulled over in his ecclesiastical car and interrogated by the police.

While the Ugandan Asians might have dominated the headlines, they were not alone in stepping ashore in Britain at this time. In 1972, as Britain negotiated its entry into the European Economic Community, some two hundred thousand people arrived from overseas. The majority were Commonwealth citizens, and the manner in which the white Rhodesians fleeing the civil war in their country were greeted with comradely fellow feeling must have rankled with the Africans who had battled in before them. When refugees fled Hungary in 1956, or Czechoslovakia in 1968, there were waves of public sympathy in their favour. Radio broadcasts pleaded for lodgings and clothes. 'Give a room to a Czech refugee,' they begged. The Lord Mayor raised £2.5 million for the relief of the Hungarians, and parliament approved asylum for 15,000 without igniting protest marches. The east Europeans were recognisable to Britain as freedom-lovers seeking shelter from state tyranny, and their willingness to uproot themselves and build a life elsewhere was no less momentous. But the same was true of the Kenyan and Ugandan Asians. Those who fled communism were independent-minded members of the middle class – musicians and readers – but so were the African Asians. The Hungarians and Czechs did not necessarily speak English, but so long as the migrants were white, it seemed, as Ralf Dahrendorf wrote, that Britain remained 'like Ancient Rome: whoever wanted to come was made welcome, and soon taken into the fold'. The London School of Economics, of which Dahrendorf became director in 1974, had long been an eager forum for overseas students and teachers.

Britons, meanwhile, were beginning to discover holidays in the sun. Lawrence Durrell was writing rapturous tributes to the crystal water and sunlight of the South, and Elizabeth David's cookbooks were gracing kitchen shelves with sumptuous lists of ingredients barely available in British shops. It didn't seem likely that there would be much migration from such sublime climates to muddy old Britain, but the Italians were coming again, and this time they had grander plans than organ-grinding. Britain was awash with trattorias and pizzerias; pasta became as popular a British staple as shepherd's pie, and a lot easier to find. Migrants came in large numbers to staff hotels, restaurants, bars and cafés. By 1971 there were over a hundred thousand Italian-born people in Britain.

The island neighbours of Italy were also willing to leave the sunshine of the Mediterranean. Between 1959 and 1974 nearly 70,000 Maltese left their island; many went to Australia, but 41,000 came to Britain. Theirs was primarily an economic migration; Cypriots were fleeing their island for a much more pressing political reason. In 1974 a Greek plot to assassinate the president, Archbishop Makarios, led to a Turkish invasion – a move to protect the Turkish minority on the island. A line of partition cut Cyprus in two: 65,000 Turks moved north of the boundary; 20,000 Greeks were pushed south. It was a wrench for all of them. Many displaced Turks did not settle in their designated area, despite the incentives dangled before them, and left. About eleven thousand came to Britain, where they swelled the existing community in north-east London. Turkey found itself controlling nearly half of Cyprus, but only a quarter of its people. There were energetic attempts to lure the migrants back, and some responded: the *Daily Telegraph* reported that 5,000 Turks had left Britain, and that 6,000 were about to. But these were no more than guesses: these people might just as well have been nipping home for a visit, a wedding, a christening or a swim.

These crisis-driven evacuations from Africa and the Mediterranean were dwarfed by the much larger and steadier stream of migrants from India and Pakistan.* They were arriving in a country with few gaps in the workforce and a shaky economy which was humming with industrial unrest. The once sought-after Commonwealth workers were now 'surplus colonial labour'.

The Sikhs, who had settled in London, Birmingham and Leicester, were joined by Parsees from Bombay, Gujarat and East Africa, Hindus from Bombay and Delhi, and Muslims from the Punjab and Bengal. To the average Briton, all of these Indians and Africans looked the same: they were all 'Pakis'. But they spoke many major languages – among them Hindi, Urdu, Punjabi, Gujarati and Bengali – which were about as mutually intelligible as English and Italian. As a result, their common language was often English. The Parsees, in particular, were historic migrants who had transplanted themselves from Iran to India in the past: they had already, as a people, successfully formed a home away from home. In India, they were simultaneously assimilated and distinct: different but equal, as the new jargon of multiculturalism would have it.

In Britain, sharp as the differences between them were, the 'Asians' found common cause in their mutual identity as 'bloody foreigners'. They moved, following the Sikh example, into large and crowded houses. They'd rent rooms to friends, friends-of-friends or workmates: there might also be a West Indian couple, an Irish couple, a child or two, a grandmother and a couple of students. An eight-roomed house might well, at busy times, hold more than a dozen adults and half a dozen children. It was a squash for all of them, and there would be plenty of shouting matches about hot water, electricity, the leak in the roof and so on, but the owner would collect his weekly rent, and soon amass enough to pay off some of the mortgage and put a deposit down on a shop. The property business opened up career opportunities for agents and brokers

---

*This was in contrast to the situation in the West Indies. Between 1971 and 1975, there were only seven thousand more departures than arrivals in the Caribbean Community.

willing to target the Indian clientele. But there was a strong culture of interdependency, and powerful social pressure against profiteering. It wouldn't do to get bad-mouthed back home, let alone here in England – aside from anything else, it was bad for business.

While the Hindus and Sikhs from India tended to hail from towns and cities, the Muslims from Pakistan were different: rural recruits lined up by declining British industries as factory-fodder, sometimes by local agents. Initially they came from a specific area – Mirpur, the dam-torn countryside close to the disputed border with Kashmir. It was agricultural hill country, a landscape of tiny farms and smallholdings. There were neither railways nor roads, and there was very little wealth; instead there were potent family ties and an imposing calendar of religious obligations. All three generations lived under one modest roof; marriages resembled mergers and acquisitions. Brides were legal tender, both as portable family assets and as one of the few available means of social advancement.

In other words, it was not at all like Britain. But there was, among the Mirpuris as with the Sikhs, a strong tradition of military service. The region had a surplus of men, and many had fought for the British army. And unlike India's Hindus, the Muslims of the northern Punjab had no religious or caste injunctions against overseas travel. There was a surge of migration from the area after 1960, when those displaced by the continuing construction of the Mangla Dam spent their compensation money on a ticket to Britain. They were relatively unskilled, and settled in the textile belts of Yorkshire, Lancashire and the Midlands, where they found work in an industry that retained some connection with their own background. By 1971 Bradford had a population of thirty thousand Pakistanis, around 10 per cent of its total.

Employers in Huddersfield, Dewsbury, Burnley and Blackburn could hardly believe their luck, as hordes of cheap labour arrived to work hard in their increasingly cash-strapped businesses (exposed, as they now were for the first time, to genuine competition from the former empire). Local populations, however, often took a dimmer view, as the migrants brought strange accents to familiar streets. It might not have helped that many of them chose to settle in places still capable of classing someone from a few miles south as foreign. Ironically, too, the very cheapness of this new supply of labour, and its casual nature, papered over the under-investment that was dooming the textile industry to a rocky future.

It wasn't only the Britons who put up walls. The Muslims themselves were reluctant to sever any ties with their homeland. Few previous immigrant communities had been quite so determined to cling to the culture they brought with them. Unlike many West Indians, who idealised Britain and had to swallow much humiliation when they arrived, the Pakistanis had no false hopes: they arrived with the warnings of their elders ringing in their ears.

Britain held out the promise of good wages, but in most other respects was a wicked place, with a pinched approach to family responsibility, and a chronic fondness for drink. It was materially privileged and spiritually null. Domestic life for Muslims was a dominant, often a domineering force, and it contrasted fiercely with the norms of British mainstream society. They faced social and economic problems that simply never arose for others. It was not easy for them, for instance, to climb on to the property ladder, since it required them to disobey the stern Islamic injunction against borrowing or lending money at interest.

They were not slow, however, to effect sharp changes in the urban landscape and the national lifestyle. Asian-owned corner shops sprang up everywhere – there was even one on the Hebridean island of Lewis. Open all hours, these handy family-run affairs became, collectively, a potent business. A substantial industry developed to fuel and support them – producers, processors, traders, wholesalers, distributors, retailers, cooks and waiters. Families could survive and in some cases prosper; employees could become employers. As a result, the Indians and Pakistanis in Britain were able to develop a powerful and self-sufficient economy. At one point, in the Dewsbury area, there were 37 off-licences, all of them owned by a handful of teetotal Pakistani families. Before long, Asian names were beginning to appear on the lists of Britain's richest men. Some of them were emphatic rags-to-riches stories comparable to the early careers of Michael Marks or Montague Burton. Anwar Pervez came from a farming family in Pakistan in 1956 and drove buses in Bradford before opening a convenience store in Earl's Court in 1962. It turned into the Bestway chain and busily acquired grocery shops across the country. In 1999 his wealth was estimated at £130 million. His Bestway Foundation, which funnels money to schools in needy areas, earned him a knighthood. Others – such as Lord Bagri and Lord Paul – took their seats in Parliament.

In 1970 there were two thousand Indian restaurants in Britain. Most of them were operated by Bengalis from Sylhet, who had a long tradition as ships' cooks in the British merchant fleet. They served Anglo-Asian food designed to appeal to (or fool) the ignorant British palate, and went along with the determination to call them all 'Indian' as a marketing convenience. The curry houses were decorated in red and gold, neo-Raj style; they were cheap and open till late, partly because their original clientele consisted of fellow settlers who lived in houses with few cooking facilities. But it wasn't long before the late-night curry became an irreplaceable part of the British evening out. Immigrant waiters could look on with bemusement as groups of loud-mouthed Brits ordered vindaloo extra hot, washed it down with brimming trays of lager, made rude remarks about the drinks-wallah, and sometimes sprinted out without paying, just for a laugh. Within a few decades, chicken tikka masala (created to satisfy the British fondness for gravy) had become the biggest-selling ready-made dish in the country.*

Karamjit Khera came from the Punjab in 1958, and began work as a bus driver in Glasgow. He moved south, opened a grocer's shop in Nottingham, and in 1976 started a food trading business which became, as Hyperama, the biggest importer of Chinese food in the country. Shahad Hussein, meanwhile, was a cookery teacher until, dismayed by her experiments with Marks & Spencer's Indian dishes, she boasted that she could do better and became their food consultant. Perween Warsi went further, making samosas in Derby so successfully that her company, S & A foods, thrived. In 1995 she was named Woman Entrepreneur of the Year.

The most successful of all the food suppliers was Gulam Kaderbhoy Noon, the inventor of Bombay Mix and the founder, in 1990, of Noon Products, the biggest producer of ready-made Indian meals in Europe. He was born in Rajasthan and took over the family sweet business at the age of seventeen. In 1969 he moved to Britain and opened up as a supplier of sweets to Indian restaurants, but in 1988 he risked everything on a £650,000 loan to build a food-processing factory in Southall. His timing was spot on: he strode unaccompanied into the accelerating demand for 'convenience' food – a marketing euphemism for filling meals that could be simply warmed up and munched in front of the television. In the process, he cracked open an entirely new sales outlet: within a decade, some 75 per cent of 'ethnic' food sales – a market estimated by Charterhouse Securities to be worth £650 million per year – would be sold as own-brand products through the giant supermarket chains. Noon's factory in Southall sucked in 150 tonnes of ingredients each week, and churned them out again as Chicken Jalfrezi and Thai Red curry.

Many Indian and Pakistani émigrés became prosperous and prominent figures, but the most common migrant experience was social exclusion. Every survey confirmed that settlers from Africa, the Caribbean and the subcontinent were over-represented in the categories of low pay, bad housing and unemployment. Nissim Elijah came from the Bombay civil service in 1962, only to find himself taking a giant career step backwards. 'In India I had five hundred people under me. I had a chauffeur-driven car. Here I was just a messenger.'[6] Within a few short years, however, similar polls began to reveal that the Asians were also over-represented in white-collar work and educational qualifications. In 1976 nearly a quarter of Asian and West Indian graduates were employed in manual trades, compared with only a tiny

*A fact nicely celebrated when Damien Hirst produced a song, *Vindaloo*, as a football chorus during the Euro 96 tournament in England. Thousands of pot-bellied English fans united around an Indian word for Indian food, and turned it into an impromptu national anthem.

percentage of white graduates. But by 1981, according to the Labour Force Survey, a full third of Indian males in Britain were classed as 'professionals'. That was a higher percentage than white Britain could boast.

And there were enough success stories to show that Britain – if you were lucky, energetic, or both – offered migrants the chance to blossom in commerce, the professions, the arts, academia, sport and even politics. The clothing line Ciro Citterio was founded by Rasiklal Thakrar in Birmingham. And one unusual entrepreneur, Shami Ahmed, came to Britain when he was two, grew up in Burnley, started producing trendy baggy jeans and gave his company the most demotic name he could imagine: Joe Bloggs. Having made a fortune from that venture, he is now a major shareholder in an earlier immigrant business, Moss Bros.

While all of this was new and transforming, the East End of London was the scene of a historic reprise. The Huguenots had built a cottage textile industry in these tight streets, and it had been taken over first by Jewish migrants from the Baltic, and then by Irish labour. Now a new population was operating the looms and the shops (though not the pubs). It was squeezed out of Bengal by the wars between India and Pakistan that preceded the birth of Bangladesh, and it was swollen by a series of ruinous floods. It was the last of Britain's great seaborne migrations. The Bengalis came on ships from Chittagong and Chalna, and disembarked at the same docks, lodged in the same streets and worked in the same steam-filled rooms as had the Jews a century before. In 1963, the centre of this area, the seamen's district near Cable Street, began to be demolished, and the Bengalis were pushed north to the eastern flank of Shoreditch. It was poor – only 20 per cent of the houses in Bethnal Green had their own bathrooms – and it had not yet recovered from the wartime bombing raids. It was also the heartland of the National Front. By 1970 the party was fielding ten candidates in the general election; in 1974 it fielded fifty-four. In a by-election at Newham South, the National Front candidate out-polled the Conservative and attracted more than 11 per cent of the vote. In a protest outside one of its meetings a month later, a protester was killed.

The unhappy story of the nineteenth-century Jewish aliens was played out once again. In the alleys around Brick Lane, where Jack the Ripper had butchered women, an area described by one local rector in 1880 as 'a land of beer and blood', there was a new blood sport: 'Paki-bashing'. It was the age of the skinhead: in April 1970 a pair of Asian hospital workers were attacked in an incident that sparked a nasty bout of brutal harassment. A few days later, a young man was murdered, and at the end of the month a gang of British bruisers stormed down Brick Lane, injuring five Pakistanis as they went. Daily life for the Bengali and Pakistani families in the area became torrid: the streets were no-go areas, especially at night, when the 'patriots' did their drinking. In 1976 John Kingsley Read of the National Front greeted news of a fresh racist murder in Southall with the infamous words: 'One down, a million to go.' Girls were kicked on their way to school, stones were flung at windows, eggs and tomatoes were hurled at families who risked setting foot outdoors. It wasn't safe to wait at bus stops or to go shopping. *The Times*, reporting this 'wave of racial violence', noted with alarm that some Asians were taking self-defence classes. The migrants were charged with failing to report crimes promptly to the police, though the law seemed a remote ally in such cases. When Shakur Miah was stabbed in the shoulder, in the rush hour on a crowded street, not a single witness came forward to corroborate his story.

There was worse to come. In May 1978 a Bengali clothing worker called Altab Ali was murdered just off the Whitechapel Road. Some seven thousand people walked alongside his coffin on a protest march from Brick Lane to Downing Street. The stage was set for a race war. The following month, an aggressive army of 150 youths battered their way down Brick Lane, smashing windows, uprooting flagstones and damaging cars. In the following weeks, there were marches and counter-marches, nearly all of them involving bloodshed. The police strategy was familiar and simple: arrest the anti-racist protesters. When they tried to set up pamphleteering pitches near the National Front salesmen, they were moved along on the grounds that their presence was likely to cause a breach of the peace. When the Bengali community began to formulate strategies of their own to defend Brick Lane and its residents, the police disparaged such efforts as vigilante law.

It was a period of steady, awful persecution. The victims fell in a bitter and one-sided social war fought on the streets of the nation's poorest neighbourhoods: Ishaque Ali was beaten up in Hackney; Kayimarz Anblesaria was kicked to death at Bromley-by-Bow underground station; Akhtar Ali Baig was stabbed in East Ham. And it wasn't confined to London: Satnam Singh Gill was knifed in Coventry; Samira Kassam, who had three small sons and was pregnant with another, was killed when raiders set fire to her house in Ilford; Ahmed Iqbal, a thirteen-year-old Bangladeshi boy, was stabbed on his way to school. The previous day, Ahmed had bravely gone to help another Bangladeshi boy who was being beaten up, only to be told: 'We'll get you tomorrow.'[7] His assailants were as good as their word.

The authorities seemed to have no idea what to do. A combination of deliberate agitation, police indifference and political neglect was allowing a bonfire of anger and injustice to burn on the streets. Time and again, politicians and the police seemed to imply that it was all the immigrants' own fault: if they hadn't been there, they wouldn't have been attacked.

In 1978 the National Front, wedded to vandalism as a form of political protest, moved its headquarters from leafy Twickenham to Great Eastern Street, the epicentre of this trouble. The police did not see this as likely to cause any breaches of the peace, or at any rate were helpless to prevent it. Instead, they arrested fifty anti-racism protesters who demonstrated against the move. The Greater London Council proposed — in theory, to defend suffering Bengalis — the creation of council blocks exclusively for their use. Liberals accused the GLC of building a ghetto; bigots labelled the plan favouritism. The residents themselves rebelled against the proposal, knowing that it would place them in an even more exposed and besieged position. They clung to the idea that people should and could live in a mixed society.

Not everyone was fighting. In 1976 a remarkable new twist was given to an already remarkable building on the corner of Fournier Street and Brick Lane. The Huguenots had opened a chapel on this site in 1743. It then became a Wesleyan chapel before, in 1898, it was transformed into the Spitalfields Great Synagogue. Now it was the Jamme Jamshid Mosque. Over two hundred years of migrant prayer resonated in its stones.*

The streets around Brick Lane were fast becoming 'Banglatown', a self-contained and private community of some 50,000 Bangladeshis. Like their migrant predecessors in the same terraces and blocks of flats, they were creating a new home in their own image. Sweets, cassettes, videos, clothes, magazines and food from the sub-continent jostled brightly in the cramped shop windows. More than forty curry houses sprang up in Brick Lane alone. Young men sized up the beginnings of life on the Internet, while their ageing fathers still dreamed of finding 'unspoiled' village girls to be their brides. To the outside world, however, crime remained the key 'angle' in the story of immigration.

The fallout from Brick Lane soon drifted west to Southall. But there was no sanctuary here, either. As in Brick Lane, there had been innumerable acts of violence against the migrants, and they climaxed in the election campaign of 1979. The National Front organised a meeting in Southall Town Hall, and though it was evident by now that these 'meetings' were nothing more than provocations, the council refused to ban it. Protesters gathered. Police moved in to 'keep the area clear' – but clear of whom? As the day faded, the crowd grew. Eventually, the authorities tried to shove people along the Broadway and the High Street. Scuffles broke out at once. There were charges and counter-charges. A veritable army of four thousand policemen fought three thousand mostly Asian demonstrators (there were some white allies). Then the National Front members arrived for their meeting. Under heavy police protection, some turned and gave Nazi salutes on the steps. In the ensuing crush, a teacher from New Zealand, Blair Peach, was killed. Witnesses said that he was whacked on

---

*Just around the corner, in Princelet Street, is one of London's newest and most necessary museums: a gallery dedicated to the celebration of immigration.

the head by a policeman, but the truth never fully emerged. There was an all-night vigil over Peach's body at the Dominion Theatre, just across the road from the Victory pub, where Gurdup Singh Chaggar had been stabbed to death by a gang of white youths some months earlier.* The British public was left with another abiding image: of a bloody pitched battle between angry migrants and the police.

And it wasn't as if this was the only story. Britain was changing more rapidly than could be easily explained by breaking news. Leicester, in particular, was fast becoming not only the largest Asian immigrant community in Europe, but the first city in England with a majority of what sociologists still called 'black' inhabitants. In 1972 the town council warned that 'the entire fabric of our city is at risk'; a generation later, it could cheerfully celebrate its diverse and varied temperament. Leicester was no beauty spot: it was a steady and anonymous town with a quaint past and modest habits. Its motto – *semper eadem*: always the same – was proving to be misleading in one way, but at a deeper level was beyond dispute.

There had been mini-Chinatowns in London, Cardiff and Liverpool for almost a hundred years, small communities famous above all for their laundries, which kept Britain's seagoing folk in clean clothes. But the decline in oceangoing shipping was threatening to make these businesses obsolete, as was the birth of a new gadget: the domestic washing-machine. So when Chinese people began to travel in greater numbers on direct flights from Hong Kong they turned to catering as their prime source of employment.

As with the Bengalis, their timing was good: there was a sharp public appetite for inexpensive and filling food. In particular, there was a large new student population hungry for cheap, ready-made nosh. But the Chinese migrants were at a linguistic disadvantage: many spoke poor English, and restaurants were awkward operations for them to run. Necessity, not for the first time, proved inventive, and came up with the takeaway. Takeaways had low overheads and were cheap to establish. They coincided with the expansion of self-service shopping and self-service refuelling, and thrived on the mushrooming market in meals that could be eaten in front of the television by men and women returning home from work too tired to mess around with pots and pans. In 1951, there were perhaps five thousand Chinese in British ports; twenty years later there were ten times that number. Nearly all of them, 90 per cent, worked in catering.

The majority came from Hong Kong. After the Communists took power in China in 1949, many Chinese spilled over the border into the six hundred

---

*The case came to trial and the judge, while finding the defendants guilty, declared that he discerned no racial motive in the attack.

villages that made up the New Territories. Some of these were soon hugely reliant on remittances from Chinese workers in Britain. Both village life and the local economy were dominated by emigration. Migrant workers earning sixty pounds a month in London would remit perhaps twenty-five pounds straight back. Most of the money would repay the loan that had got the worker abroad in the first place, and what was left would swell the family fund for future travellers. Successful families built 'sterling houses'. In some cases, half of a village's income might come from these private subsidies, an important act of conservation which some saw as a form of conservatism, since it insulated villages from the need to modernise and permitted antique social orders to survive unchanged.

The Chinese were unique among those who have made landfall in Britain by spreading themselves across the kingdom. In some towns and villages, they were not just the only Chinese family in the area, but the only foreigners of any stripe. They were discreet, unassertive to the point of being uncommunicative, and never expressed anything like racial or cultural solidarity: there were no Chinese marches through London, no running battles between English and Chinese youths outside the school gates. Their working hours were so antisocial that it would not have been easy for them to join British daily life even if they had wanted to, and they did not want to.

The Chinese swallowed the nightly racial slurs that came their way with barely a murmur.* They had a self-sufficient economy and social life, though neither of these was well upholstered: they kept their heads down and neither sought nor attracted political attention. One of their most striking qualities was their willingness to entertain a most unBritish idea: the fourteen-hour day. The local fish and chip shop had traditionally been open only for brief periods at lunch and teatime. The most common experience for urban holidaymakers at the British seaside was arriving at the fish bar just as it was closing. Chinese fryers and basters changed all that. They took over the majority of the nation's fish and chip shops, and rescued for posterity a supposedly great British institution. In the north of England, particularly, it was a wholesale takeover.

Soon Britain began to acquire the taste for Chinese cuisine. In 1972 a cookery book, *Chinese Food*, edited by Jill Norman, publicised the beguiling nature of Oriental flavours: the fusion of garlic, ginger, spring onions, sugar and chillies that was Anglicised as 'sweet and sour'. In 1975 the first Michelin star was awarded to a Cantonese restaurant; and in 1983 a Manchester restaurant, Yang

---

*As ever, there were exceptions. In St Helen's, Lancashire, in 1963, a gang of English customers at a Chinese restaurant loosed off volleys of abuse and tried to leave without paying. There was a fight and one of the customers was killed. Six of the restaurant's staff were arrested and charged with manslaughter: five were from the same village, and had the same surname. All five were shareholders in the restaurant.

Sing, was named Restaurant of the Year by the *Good Food Guide*. White Britons began to know their Szechuan from their Cantonese, and a wok was as essential as a frying pan. At first the Chinese restaurants in Soho were designed for Chinese customers – Gerrard Street was the nearest thing to a community centre they had, a meeting-place for social and business conversations. But it soon enticed adventurous British regulars who deemed it a mark of taste to go to places where the Chinese themselves ate, a badge of authenticity worth more than any rosette.

In 1957 there were 50 Chinese restaurants; six years later there were 1,400; by 1970 there were 4,000.* As with the Indian restaurant business, this was merely the retail tip of a sizeable commercial iceberg: there were food importers and processors, barbers' shops, travel agencies and gambling rooms, newspapers and bookshops in the economic hinterland behind it.

But the sixty thousand or so Chinese in Britain in the early 1970s had little sense of cultural solidarity. In 1970 two Chinese associations were set up, but neither lasted more than a year. The would-be members were too dispersed and too busy. Chinese life was in any case more than anything a family business. The lineage culture in Hong Kong was all-powerful. In some villages, marriage outside the family-name group would have led to abuse or ostracism. The entry into Britain was a classic chain migration: young men were sent to establish a toehold, and then sponsored the later arrival of relatives and co-workers. The result was a pyramid structure which resembled that of the Italian *padroni* in the nineteenth century. The restaurants might form into chains of ten or more, owned by brothers, cousins and nephews (and run by sisters, daughters and nieces).

The unobtrusiveness of this community was often pilloried as sinister. There was talk of 'secret Triad gangs', and, as the restaurateurs worked chiefly in cash, they were not averse to understating the size of the flow through the till, or the number of employees, to the taxman. Nor were they above withholding that information from the employees themselves; ownership was a time-honoured path to wealth. But as time passed, and the children of the first generation began to enter British schools and streets, the initial severity of this awkward social profile softened. As the novelist Timothy Mo (Cantonese father, English mother) put it in *Sour Sweet*: 'The Chens had been living in the UK for four years, which was long enough to have lost their place in the society from which they had emigrated but not long enough to feel comfortable in the new.'[8] For many British readers, this opening line was an astonishing revelation. In the furore over immigration, no one tended even to mention the Chinese. Their extreme quietness made them invisible. There was an irony here. One of the

---

*For the sake of comparison, there were at this time around five hundred French restaurants in the country.

most common accusations made against immigrants was that they refused to 'fit in'. And the group of immigrants who made the least effort of all to fit in were the Chinese, who kept themselves to themselves and socialised almost entirely with their own families. Yet they were the least disliked. They kept their distance, and Britain seemed to like it just fine that way.

By now the 'immigration issue' was firmly associated with the Commonwealth. So it was easy to forget that these migrations were dwarfed by more traditional groups. In 1951 there were 716,000 Irish in Britain; twenty years later, there were a million – nearly 2 per cent of the population as a whole. They no longer faced the abuse and discrimination that had greeted their forebears; they were able to drift easily into British life. They were no longer a discernible type, except in the media, where a jaunty Irish brogue was a positive advantage – it was voted 'most friendly accent' in a survey of viewer preferences. The world was shrinking, and the Irish, with their shared cultural heritage and identical colouring, became first friendly neighbours, and then simply 'us'. Simultaneously, those from further afield crystallised into 'them'.

The mass media did little to erode this distinction, and Britain's politicians, and many of its people, made neurotic attempts to keep 'them' away. But it was an unequal battle: quick-witted individuals have a clear edge over clumsy bureaucracies. The opponents of migration are always up against powerful human forces – love, lust, curiosity, hunger, fear and hope – and they are usually outmatched. And a nation historically wedded to freedom would always have a hard time striving to curtail it.

CHAPTER 23

Little England

When Margaret Thatcher became Prime Minister in 1979, her supporters hoped for a revival of the values that had made Britain 'Great': industry, thrift, bravery and resolve. This vision did not encourage the recent migrants from the Commonwealth, for whom this description of the British character shivered with unpleasant historical associations. But Thatcher went further. On *World in Action* she insisted that enough was enough, and that she, for one, was here to put things right. 'Some people have felt swamped by immigrants,' she said. 'They've seen the whole character of their neighbourhoods change.'[1] On one level this was an observable truth. But for a British prime minister to use a word favoured by those *The Economist* had once labelled 'bullies and misfits' was no small matter.

Before her remarks, only 9 per cent of British citizens felt that there were too many immigrants; afterwards, 21 per cent admitted they were worried. Mrs Thatcher's supporters argued that it was a politician's job to draw the public's attention to uncomfortable truths. Opponents suggested that such rhetoric was self-fulfilling. It was easy to forget that at this time immigrants amounted to 4 per cent of the population. Was it possible for so small a minority to 'swamp' a mighty imperial nation?

Within a year, however, Thatcher showed that bloody-mindedness could work both ways. In 1975 the *Daily Mail* had drawn attention to the refugee crisis in South-east Asia by flying ninety-nine orphans out of Vietnam to safety. But the Labour government had turned a short-sighted eye to the increasingly dire sufferings of the Boat People, who were spilling out into the South China Sea in vast, forlorn flotillas. It pledged to take only 1,500 out of nearly a quarter of a million such drifters. There were some historical arguments for this neglect. For once, Britain was not one of the key colonial powers: the Vietnamese were being squeezed by China, America and the Soviet Union, and France had withdrawn only twenty years before. But theirs was a tale of woe to surpass almost any that had been heard. After three decades of war and ruin, through alternating famines and floods, the Chinese population of Vietnam was effectively walking the plank. China itself had shut its borders, so there was only one way out: by sea. Vietnamese officials 'helped' the Chinese by selling them boats, or passages on boats. They bobbed out into the ocean, using atlases to navigate, looking for ships with foreign flags. They were attacked, robbed and sunk by Thai and Indonesian pirates. Thousands drowned. Refugee camps in Hong Kong, Malaysia and Thailand overflowed; new boatloads were towed out to sea again and dumped. It was a calamity.

Britain remained wedded to a policy of deterrence: if word got out that you were kind to strangers, more would come. In this they took their lead from the President of Singapore, Lee Kuan Yew, who in 1978 refused to accept the Boat People and declared: 'We would be encouraging those responsible to force even more refugees to flee.'[2] Vietnam, meanwhile, was ostentatiously threatening to honour the UN Declaration of Human Rights by permitting all the Chinese who wished to leave to go – at once.

When Thatcher came to power she sent Lord Carrington to Hong Kong. The government agreed to accept 10,000 Boat People in Britain, along with another thousand or so who had been picked up by British ships. If this was partly motivated by a desire to take the pressure off what was still a British colony, it was also a positive, humanitarian gesture. Three charities came together to resettle the refugees, who were housed in reception centres, given language lessons and helped to contemplate a new life. In all, some fifteen thousand Vietnamese came to Britain at the end of the 1970s, and, unusually in modern times, no one was encouraged to ignore the extent to which they were truly desperate. Senior politicians gave a clear signal that we were rescuing them from the twin evils of communism and drowning, and invited the public to rise to the occasion. Not everyone was listening. When Peter Vo arrived in Bermondsey, his wife was stoned by the locals. And Van Duy Tu was far from welcome in Sydenham. The day after he arrived, National Front stickers were posted on his door. Someone shot an air rifle through the letterbox. But these were ghastly excesses, not the norm. Perhaps the British people reserved a soft spot for those in peril on the sea, but for whatever reason the plight of the Vietnamese struck a chord. Britain stood by.

In case anyone got the wrong idea, the government acted fast to make it clear that this was a one-off. The 1981 Immigration Act imposed new, elaborate restrictions on entry to Britain. The Home Secretary, William Whitelaw, said that it was high time we ditched 'the lingering notion that Britain is somehow a haven for all those whose countries we used to rule'. This idea had actually been officially laid to rest in 1962 and 1971; this was just rubbing it in. There were now three levels of nationality: full British citizenship, dependent territories citizenship and British overseas citizenship. Only the first had full rights. This completed the process begun twenty years earlier: only overseas people of demonstrably 'British descent' could be automatically considered for membership of the club. Everyone else had to apply through the increasingly tight procedures of formal immigration, which were shaped by what the government decreed the country needed: nurses, teachers, scientists, engineers and, to a lesser extent, cheap labour. About 50,000 arrived each year.

As before, the legislation was put to the test almost before the ink was dry. The Falkland Islanders had been classed by the Act only as 'dependent' citizens with no automatic right of abode in Britain. This might have played some part in convincing those in power in Buenos Aires to chance their luck. When the Argentine invasion came, however, Thatcher emphasised that the islanders were 'British in stock and tradition'. Michael Foot, the leader of the opposition, called them 'fellow citizens'. And Enoch Powell popped up to observe that the islanders were 'British people in . . . British territory.'

This imposition of further controls came in the year following another long and fractious summer. In 1980 there were street fights in Bristol, Deptford and Southall. Triggered by fury over the police's stop-and-search campaign, these were also protests against the conditions of everyday life. 'We are living', said one Liverpudlian, 'in a concentration camp with fringe benefits.' The riots in Brixton exploded any dreams of racial harmony in Britain. And Liverpool's Toxteth, home to Britain's oldest black community, was in torrid shape: 52 per cent of young black men were out of work and angry. The police cracked down: Toxteth residents were stopped, searched and detained. When Lester Cooper complained about the harassment of his son, he was stopped and searched himself . . . sixteen times in the following two years.

The area erupted after a particularly provocative arrest. Streets were barricaded against charging riot police. The rioters were organised, throwing bricks on command like Wellingtonian volleys. The fight went on for three days: 150 buildings were destroyed; 800 people were injured; and there were 500 arrests. The police were mildly reprimanded for their heavy-handed tactics and instructed to lay off the borough. As a result, it soon became what it had not been until then – a safe haven for criminals and a busy hive of law-breaking.

Southall, now radicalised, continued to be a flashpoint. On 3 July 1981 a skinhead band played at the Hambrough tavern in the Broadway. A fight broke out between Asians and skinheads, and, when the police intervened, between Asians and the police. The infamous Victory pub was burned out. The next year, a forty-strong gang attacked houses in the East End, threw stones, flashed Nazi salutes and shouted: 'Fucking Pakis Out!' One resident rang the police; six hours later, they still hadn't come. When he complained, adding that a campaign of intimidation had been going on for three years, he was told that the best thing for him and his family was that they leave.

In the decade that followed, very little changed. By 1993, according to Home Office figures, there were 32,500 racially motivated assaults per year. The majority had a common theme: the victims could not count on the police for protection or on the courts for justice. In 1986, seventeen-year-old Naeem Lone went with his father to visit his uncle's shop in Newham. When they left, at about 10.30 p.m., they ran into a post-pub crowd of bullies armed with sticks and poles. Lone later recalled lying in the road, watching as a white girl sat on his father, whacking his head with a shoe. The police suggested they close the shop. Incidents such as this were so common that they ceased to be news, until the determination of Stephen Lawrence's parents provoked a front-page search for the murderers of their son (led by the *Daily Mail*, unusually), and pricked Britain's conscience.

There was a major bureaucratic effort to oppose racist violence in theory. But it wasn't always effective. 'Those opposed to racism,' wrote Keith Thompson in his angry book *Under Siege* (1988), were 'trapped in a strategy that only adds to the problem'. The anti-racism campaigns of local councils – and in particular the priority given to consciousness-raising – sometimes aggravated the problem. Instead of providing any physical protection for those in danger, the councils sent their employees on anti-racism courses.

Nor was the violence all white against black. The animosities that divided the subcontinent found fresh expression in British streets. On 16 January 1984 a Punjabi newspaper, defiantly anti-Khalistan (the state demanded by the Sikhs), was bombed by militant Sikh nationalists; an assistant editor was killed. On 10 June, 25,000 Sikhs marched in London from Hyde Park to the Aldwych to protest before the Indian High Commission against the Indian army's assault on the Golden Temple in Amritsar a week earlier, when the sacred Sikh Library had been burned and the temple ruined. Nationalists chanted, 'Khalistan zindabad!' A newspaper – the *Khalistan News* – was launched shortly afterwards, along with a radio station, the Voice of Sikhs.

British onlookers were bemused. Anyone could see that the desecration of sacred sites was an outrage, but a rally on this scale, addressing issues in a distant land here on British soil, was something new. It was a sign both that the planet was contracting, and that Britain was in some ways a microcosm of the wider world. In 1986 a Sikh politician was shot in an off-licence in the Broadway, Southall, but most Britons still couldn't tell a Sikh from a Hindu or a Muslim, so they were at a loss to know what they were fighting about.

Conversations about immigrants had by now become as good as

meaningless. Immigration itself was steady, so when people expressed a view about 'migrant culture' or 'migrant behaviour', they were really only seeking euphemisms for coloured people. But since a growing number of Britain's non-whites were actually British-born and -raised,* a new term was needed. They began to be known as 'ethnic minorities'. Partly this was promoted by egalitarian activists seeking recognition for the idea of a multicultural rather than a mixed society. By pressing people back into the groups to which they belonged, however, it suggested that racial destiny was both limiting and inescapable. To people who had undertaken grave risks to plant themselves in a new country, this was not always easy to bear. And it sustained some old and easy prejudices, the most enduring and wrong-headed of which was the idea that immigrants were endemically violent and required firm treatment from the law. In a great many cases, migrants had fled violence, not sought it out. In Britain, violence was thrust upon them. Yet the cliché of the aggressive migrant would not die.

Perhaps it was that no one liked admitting, despite weekly evidence from the nation's football stadiums and casualty wards at closing time, that Britain's urban culture was itself incorrigibly tough and brawling. Riot and affray had been popular national sports for centuries. The rioters of Toxteth, Bristol and Brixton were behaving not like immigrants, who had historically kept their heads down, but like the British working class in Bank Holiday mood. While some British nationalists insisted that the country was importing nothing but trouble, many immigrants themselves felt that their children were being corrupted by coarse British manners. Alienated at school and at the job centre, some had caught the British disease. A handful mimicked one of the most obvious yet unsayable aspects of British working-class life: this was a great place to be lazy, rude, hostile to education, angry, impatient and rough. The legal system locked them up with a knowing sigh. Their (often devout) parents despaired. To the extent that we could still talk in terms of 'us' and 'them', we could only conclude that 'we' dragged 'them' down to our own level.

By 1985 Bradford's Asian population numbered some fifty thousand. In the same year the city's Drummond Middle School became the centre of a nationwide controversy over education. The school had five hundred pupils, and 85 per cent of them were Asian. The headmaster, Ray Honeyford, wrote a waspish article about the way his pupils were educated: his argument was primarily with the politicians who set the agenda. The council had abandoned the policy of assimilation – teaching immigrant children in the standard British manner – in favour of multiculturalism, which encouraged them to work within their own cultures and languages. So children pursued different curricula, in different tongues, and in Honeyford's eyes this was cumbersome,

---

*In 1985, it was estimated that there were one million children of immigrants in Britain.

inefficient and divisive. The newspapers enjoyed discussing whether girls
should be allowed to skip swimming for modesty's sake, but Honeyford had
raised a serious point. However, he had done so intemperately. Bradford had
an Asian mayor, and over two hundred Asian community organisations, most
of which were persuaded that the headmaster was 'against' them. He was
sacked.

The episode both symbolised and launched a debate about cultural rights.
At best, there had been inspiring efforts to realign Britain's racial priorities
through education. A 1963 report on schools made no mention of the challenge
posed by immigrant children; a 1966 report included only a paragraph or two.
But a 1975 report, *A Language for Life*, addressed the issue squarely, emphasising
that schools should embrace multiracial subjects and expand the number of
languages they could offer. There was pressure also in favour of ethnic or
religion based, rather than mixed, schools, which cut sharply across the
comprehensive ideal of British education. The Jews' Free School, once the
biggest in Europe, had proved the first of many, and now Islamic schools were
starting to open. Each time this happened there was a spat about the relative
merits of assimilation and separatism. There were moves, meanwhile – by
Jamaicans, for example – to send their children to Caribbean schools rather than
abandoning them to the British educational system.

Things had changed. The quality of British schooling was one of the reasons
for the reverence in which the mother country was held by the first generation
of postwar immigrants. The schools of modern Britain were serving them less
well. In Birmingham, it was revealed that over half of the city's black teenage
boys were leaving school without a single GCSE. The novelist Mike Phillips
was shocked to find that even reading was scoffed at. 'There was one teacher
who would always come up to me with a grin and ask, "What are you reading
now, Phillips?" One day I told him, *The Meditation of Marcus Aurelius*, which is
what I had been reading. And he pissed himself laughing.[3] It was not only the
teachers who were intimidating: classmates could be raucous too. Simi Bedford
came to boarding school from Nigeria in 1948, and took refuge in sheer
excellence. 'I was top of the class in all the teams. I could do anything. I had to.
Otherwise I would have been pulverised.'[4]

But academic achievement was only part of the story. What place should
religious instruction have in a cosmopolitan country, and how should it be
taught? Should there still be a Nativity play in schools like the Drummond?
Come to think of it, what about Christmas trees and Easter eggs? The idea of
replacing Christmas with a multicultural substitute, 'Winterval', was much
derided, but it was a sign, as clear as the empty churches that littered the British
countryside, of a momentous cultural change.

Did we aspire to be a nation full of sharply defined groups? Or did we want
to be blended? A melting pot? Or a salad? Naturally, some blending was

inevitable, and in Britain's case it really could be called desirable: the rate of intermarriage was the highest in Europe, and the 2001 census recorded 238,000 children in the cumbersome bracket 'mixed race'. The question remained: should this process be applauded, resisted or (on the grounds that it was none of our business) ignored? There were increasing efforts, as the century drew to a close, to raise public consciousness of the racial undertones in the media, in children's books, in everyday phrases and all other aspects of our cultural life. This was often rebutted as hollow and self-serving 'political correctness', but it did alert people to the casual offence that lay embedded in everyday transactions. And on the whole, it worked: people did stop saying 'Nigger'. Anyone who thought this kind of stricture oversensitive and beside the point had perhaps not paused to wonder what it was like to be on the receiving end of such slurs. When Michael La Rose came from Venezuela to Hornsey in 1960, as a six-year-old boy, one of the first remarks addressed to him, when he handed over his money in a sweetshop, was: 'Thank you, you little wog.'[5] Welcome to London.

No one could deny by now that Britain's railways, hospitals, shops, cafés and restaurants would have ceased to function without migrant workers. As early as 1971, half of the hotel staff in London were born abroad. And survey after survey was suggesting that Britain was attracting high-calibre people. A third of the Filipina women who came to work in healthcare or childcare (often as private nannies) had been through tertiary education. And the fortunes made by Asian entrepreneurs in the 1970s and 1980s indicated that it was possible to prosper in Britain. The net worth of the top 100 Asians in the year 2000, published in *Eastern Eye*, amounted to £10.6 billion. This was concrete evidence of the energy and drive that migrants had brought with them.

Public life was full of migrants or their offspring, too. The cultural landscape of Britain would have been empty without migrant writers, musicians and sports stars. English sports fans were learning to soften their much-publicised xenophobia when it came to their own team. Even so, racism was never far away, especially in football, where a whole generation of players, from Clyde Best and Laurie Cunningham to Sol Campbell and Emile Heskey had to contend with seething abuse from the terraces. Some of this was pantomime hooting – fans would cheer the black players on their own team while howling at those on the other side. But it was still ugly.

And professional footballers, no matter how abused, were the privileged few. For many more, life was very rough indeed. Britain was still a country in which boys such as Stephen Lawrence and Damilola Taylor could be murdered for no reason other than their colour. But it was also a country in which immigrants were becoming confident enough to turn the tables by poking fun at their 'hosts'. Indian music and comedy was growing more fashionable by the day, and immigrant life was giving a vivacious twang to every city in the land. There was something else unusual in the air. In a nation famous for the crude yobbery of its football culture, international stars and the replica shirts of many nations adorned Britain's pitches. Youngsters sported the colours of a wide range of different nationalities. There were few countries in the world where this was true. Britain was changing faster than many people thought.

CHAPTER 24

Asylum Madness

Just as the nineteen eighties had begun a year early, with the election of Margaret Thatcher, so too the nineties jumped the gun. The pressure on the Berlin Wall built up fast, and broke through even faster. The idea that the disappearance of this geopolitical fault line might promote or permit a surge of immigration from east to west seemed beside the point. And immigration as such was no longer an overriding preoccupation in Britain; most of it had been choked off. There were endless cultural, political (and physical) battles going on, and some diehards continued to insist that they were all caused by over-immigration. But the major portion of Britain's ethnic minorities was already British. Immigration itself was not the hot topic: we were no longer being 'flooded'. The settling-in process – a painful one, to be sure, still scarred by widespread unpleasantness – was already well advanced. No one could seriously propose to turn the clock back. Even the National Front could not scare up much support. In 1974 it had taken 3 per cent of the electoral vote; in 1979 it managed just 1.4 per cent; in 1983 it sank to 1 per cent, and in 1992 it dropped even further, to 0.9 per cent.* It was dying.

The 1991 census, meanwhile, revealed that 3 million (5.5 per cent) of Britain's 55 million people belonged to ethnic minorities. Nearly half lived in London, a sign that this was to a great extent a metropolitan issue: cottage and church-hall Britain remained barely touched. But it also emerged that immigrants were

---

*Even the adoption of a new, more respectable name – the British National Party – could not arrest this slide into the margins of public life.

having more children: Bengali families had, on average, 5.3; Pakistani families had 4.8; and Indians 3.8. White Britain remained wedded to a stolidly nuclear 2.4 per family, and was growing at a much slower rate. Moreover, some immigrants were doing their best to shore up Britain's faith in family values. Ninety per cent of Indians married, against only 79 per cent of whites. Nearly half of Caribbean families were single-parent units, a dazzling figure. But 21 per cent of white families were too, against only 8 per cent of Asian.

While the census confirmed the stereotype that Asian family ties were strong, other surveys revealed the truth behind another cliché. The much-touted Indian faith in education was borne out by the fact that nearly 10 per cent of Indian-born people were in the professional sector, against only 5 per cent of whites. And one 1990 study discovered that 24 per cent of Asian students retook their exams in search of better results, compared to a meagre 10 per cent of white students who thought such diligence worthwhile. It even emerged that you were seven times more likely to be millionaire if your name was Patel than if your name was Smith – even though Smiths outnumber Patels by ten to one.

For three decades, the pressure of migration had swept aside the obstacles placed in its path. Time after time Britain had been obliged to admit displaced people, much to the fury of those who wanted a tougher, even an implacable line. And now there were crises almost everywhere you looked: wars or uprisings in the Balkans, the Gulf, Colombia, Somalia, Rwanda, Sierra Leone, Sri Lanka, Afghanistan and Iraq. Often, Britain was involved militarily. The sturdiest efforts of politicians to put a lid on migration foundered on the endless unruliness and ferocity of life in the outside world. When it came to migration, tough talk rang as hollow as the belief that a state could control its own currency. Immigration was about to take on an entirely new form. And the government would not be able to control it.

In 1986 a Sri Lankan, Viraj Mendis, lost the last of his legal challenges to the Home Office's request (really an order) that he leave the United Kingdom. On the surface, he had a plausible case: he had lived in Manchester for thirteen years – longer than the usual residential qualification period – and he certainly had what most people would call a 'well-founded fear' of persecution in the country of his birth. Though Sinhalese, he had campaigned on behalf of the island's Tamil minority – not a position likely to win many friends in Colombo. When he arrived in Manchester in 1973, he was an engineering student; since then he had been a fervent activist for humanitarian causes and groups. But he had run out of legal options: he had overstayed his visa by more than a decade, and his application for asylum had been turned down flat. In the eyes of the British authorities, he was suspect for another reason: he had objected to the presence of British troops in Northern Ireland.

Mendis declined to go quietly. He had lived with the threat of deportation for years, and by now was an experienced protester. Two years earlier, when he received the Home Office letter informing him that he had no right to remain in Britain, he had contracted a short-lived marriage. This time, he decided on a publicity stunt. With the support and blessing of Father John Methuen, a fellow peace campaigner, he took refuge in the (Catholic) Church of the Ascension in Hulme. He was not exactly in hiding – friends and supporters knew where he was – but the newspapers that sent reporters to the church to interview him liked to present him as a renegade or desperado whom they had somehow managed to track down to his secret hideout.

As such, Mendis became, as the months rolled on, the focal point of a new national conversation about human rights. Eventually he became an icon. For some, he was merely one of too many immigrant troublemakers with whom we had no choice but to get tough. For others, he was an authentic symbol of injustice and a proper challenge to our national conscience. For the Home Office, he was above all an affront. He could not be allowed to get away with it.

The police came in the early hours of 18 January 1989. There were over fifty of them, including immigration officials. They smashed their way in before dawn, with drills and rams, and surrounded their prey. Some were embarrassed to find that the monster they had been assembled to seek out was a single, unarmed man in a pair of cheap pyjamas. Mendis had handcuffed himself to the radiator in a forlorn and final act of defiance. He was led out into the frosty Lancastrian morning, still in his pyjamas, and hustled down to London in a police car. There he spent an unpleasant day at Pentonville Prison (one cheerful prison officer welcomed him in as a 'commie shithead') before being pushed, back in handcuffs, on to a plane bound for Colombo.

Mendis came to no harm. He was closely monitored by the British government, which knew that its own reputation was at stake. After a while, he was offered asylum in Germany, where his new wife was a refugee worker. He joined the International Human Rights Association, which he continued to represent for some years.

The violence surrounding his deportation made the front pages tremble. There was a natural British respect for the tough line, for the iron fist in a velvet glove – but this looked like an iron fist in an iron glove. And it smacked of desecration. Dawn raids on churches . . . had it really come to this? It seemed extreme, to say the least. There were angry exchanges in the House of Commons. Opposition MPs shouted '*Sieg heil!*' and 'Jackboots' as the Home Secretary, Douglas Hurd, tried to deny that the police action had been disproportionate. Several bishops expressed shock at the violation of holy soil, not to mention the damage to holy property. Hurd responded like a headmaster ticking off youngsters in a playground, warning them not to make a 'habit' of giving shelter to such law-breakers.

The Mendis raid coincided with another migrant 'story'. Salman Rushdie's *The Satanic Verses* had been making headlines since its launch the previous autumn. Most reviewers of the novel saw little to alarm them, but many Muslim readers (and non readers) saw plenty. Within weeks the book had been banned in India, South Africa, Bangladesh, Sudan, Sri Lanka and Pakistan. The situation was rich with cultural ironies. Rushdie, who had become a leading light in Britain's liberal culture, was himself an immigrant, born in Bombay (as the Raj bureaucrats insisted on calling Mumbai) and raised in Karachi. His book, an exploration of fanaticism, was falling foul of fanatics. On 14 January, while the police finalised their plans to prise Viraj Mendis from his radiator, copies of the book were burned in Bradford, evoking images of medieval (not to mention Nazi) intolerance. Books hadn't been burned in Britain in recent times. Even *Lady Chatterley's Lover* was only given a laborious court case.

The following month, six people were killed when police tried to suppress an anti-literature riot in Islamabad, Pakistan's capital. And on 14 February, the Iranian Ayatollah Khomeini issued the now famous *fatwa*, offering everlasting glory and a tidy sum of money to anyone who would kill the blasphemous author. It was now a major international issue: in Belgium, two Muslims who defended Rushdie's iconoclasm were shot; so was the novel's Norwegian translator. The Italian and Japanese translators were both stabbed. The author himself would require police protection for a decade, and was the target of much opprobrium. But the more significant aspect, for white Britain, was the way in which the affair dramatised the presence of so many Islamic fundamentalists settled here among us, who had as much right as anyone to call themselves British.

This was precisely the kind of situation that those who had warned about the perils of multiculturalism had feared might come to pass. Which was the higher priority – freedom of speech or the right to religious conviction? There were more than enough niceties here to keep everyone confused. Defenders of free speech found themselves sucked into an alliance with the enemies of multiculturalism, who gleefully included Rushdie himself in their anti-immigrant polemics. It was a genuine conundrum. Senior statesmen retreated behind the sovereignty defence, insisting that it was intolerable that any foreign government should threaten a British citizen on British soil, while occasionally letting slip a 'private' view that Rushdie was a pest.

A quirk of the publishing industry – the long wait for publication of the novel in paperback – created the perfect forum for an extended row. The newly formed Action Committee on Muslim Affairs tried to block the paperback, while the Committee for the Defence of Salman Rushdie attracted the left-leaning intelligentsia to the author's case. Muslim Britain found itself harangued not by its familiar antagonist – conservative Middle England – but by a liberal elite that it could usually rely on for support.

Over and above the sorry details of the case, the episode gave Britain a sharp reminder that there was a new element in the social landscape, one which had no desire to 'blend in' or adapt to British ways. Fundamentalist Islam had been furrowing Western brows ever since the fall of the Shah of Iran in 1978, but despite minor skirmishes, it had not seemed a truly brazen force until now. However keenly Muslim scholars tried to insist that book-burners and *fatwa*-launchers were not at all representative of the mainstream, the images of religious rage were hard to budge. The letters pages of the national press gave a platform to anyone wishing to declare that the law on blasphemy was racist because it applied only to Christianity. Religious 'leaders' appeared on television programmes to argue that their voices were suppressed. All of which did little to erase the impression, to some, that an uncompromising force was on the warpath. When spokesmen for radical Islam started declaring that what they really dreamed of was a day when the black flag of Islam would fly over Downing Street, even the keenest liberals flinched at the prospect that their own principled support for tolerance could turn out, in extreme cases, to be a shield for its opposite: intransigent intolerance. Even the word 'tolerance' became a subject for debate, implying as it did a hierarchy of rights in which a benign elite graciously 'tolerated' the outlandish habits of its inferiors. Public servants were sounding oddly old-fashioned, speaking warmly about ethnic minorities in tones reminiscent of a memsahib praising those absolutely *marvellous* native wallahs who served such wonderful cocktails on the veranda.

In an age when the politics of self-esteem demanded that people honour or indulge their own desires, the Rushdie affair invited people to brood on a more literal definition of 'tolerance': the willingness to put up with things you did not necessarily like.

At a time when Britain was full of a sense of closed worlds opening – perhaps the countries of Eastern Europe would flower like long-dormant bulbs* – the Mendis and Rushdie sagas produced an introverted contrast. Immigration, after a brief hiatus, was once again a major national concern, and again it was synonymous with trouble. Anti-racist politics had made deep inroads into public life. It was no longer easy to cast aspersions on 'bloody foreigners' with a clear conscience: there were laws against that kind of talk. But in late 1989 Britain marched towards the new decade with slumped shoulders and narrowed eyes.

There was a fresh burst of migration on the way, and it was diffuse and

---

*Britain, to a large extent, was able to applaud unreservedly, insulated as it was from the consequences. Fifteen thousand asylum applications had been made to Britain in 1989, a good proportion of them from Eastern Europe. Germany received 200,000 asylum applications, France 54,000 and even Switzerland 36,000.

impossible to pin down. It had no geographical centre; it involved almost the whole world. According to UN figures, there were 75 million people living outside the country of their birth in 1965; ten years later there were 84 million; and ten years after that 105 million. By 1990 the figure had risen to 120 million, and by 2000 some 150 million people would be classified as migrants. In a single generation, the number had doubled – a demographic phenomenon that had no precedent.

In theory, globalisation – a liberalising philosophy that promised to promote economic convergence between nations on a so-called 'level playing field' – should have suppressed the appetite for migration, rendering it easier and cheaper for expanding corporations to invest in developing countries. Capital could move more easily than people, and by smoothing its passage, so the theory went, there would be a diminishing need to travel in search of work.

It wasn't turning out like that. Globalisation, far from levelling the playing field, was introducing steep new slopes. This was merely the continuation of a long-established trend. In 1870 the per capita income in the United States was nine times that in the world's most needy countries; a hundred years later it was fifty times greater, and growing. A 1996 UN report suggested that the wealthiest people in the world (the top 20 per cent) pocketed 70 per cent of the world's income in 1960, but 85 per cent in 1993. Free-traders from the affluent world focused their efforts on stripping away obstacles to their own large and multinational concerns. But as they opened up new markets, the weaker industries in the countries they 'liberated' were badly exposed. When Mexico was obliged to dismantle its trade defences, five hundred engineering companies went out of business.

The pressure to migrate intensified. Customs officials, police, local councils, immigration authorities and Home Office analysts surveyed Britain's borders with alarm. In 1972 there were thirteen thousand asylum claims in Western Europe; twenty years later there were half a million. And the figure was still rising. By the end of the century, the UN would estimate that there were some nineteen million refugees in the world, a small proportion of whom (just 2 per cent) had the resources, luck or nerve to make it to Europe. But if the percentage was small, the number – 380,000 – was big enough to make most governments cower. While Europe celebrated half a century without a major war on its soil, there was violence and tyranny elsewhere. And this coincided with falling air fares and quickening communications. Nowhere in the world, the sign at Heathrow boasted, was more than a day away. Which was great for the British in one respect – it brought exotic holidays within reach – but the reverse was also true. The developing world, which for centuries had been depicted in British iconography as the home of teeming, boisterous and thankfully remote peoples, could now view Britain as nothing more than a short, cheap journey away.

All European countries mulled over the implications of this: Germany fretted about its long and porous border to the east (a subject that had preoccupied previous generations with dismal consequences) and had age-old nightmares about the Asiatic horde; Italy looked across the Adriatic at the ruptured Balkans, and wished the water was wider. Britain's anxiety was more generalised and more specific. It was a rich, already cosmopolitan country. There were established networks of almost every nationality and religion, with clubs, churches and shops well embedded in the landscape, and with their rights protected by law. There was a welfare state which in a crisis would guarantee health, education, housing and money to live on. It might not have been as lavish as the Swedish equivalent, but it was certainly better than what was on offer in the Sudan or Somalia. Britain also had a large, deregulated economy and a fluid service sector, perfect for casual jobseekers. For the most part, it was – even allowing for the long litany of racist maulings and aggressive bullying – a relatively honourable, tolerant and law-abiding place, one of the few countries in the world where the police would not bully you for papers. There were no identity cards: centuries of rugged individualism had produced a country that relied on trust rather than proof, one that still lionised and defended private liberty. It would take more than a few lorryloads of stowaways to overturn such a doughty tradition.*

As an added attraction, there was the English language: Britain was still close to the heart of the world's greatest linguistic empire, and was also the embarkation point for the remainder of the English-speaking world. From here, the argument went, a man or woman might strike out for Canada or Australia, or even take aim at the real prize, America – still the world's most alluring destination, even for those who claimed to hate everything it stood for.

British officials pondering these strong forces had an additional and precise worry. Nearly two centuries after Napoleon had sketched out the idea, the Channel Tunnel was open. It had run wildly over budget and its unveiling was greeted with the usual British chortles of derision. But Britain was no longer an island: people could tunnel in. Alongside this physical opening there was also a gaping loophole in the bureaucracy of migration to Britain. The world was about to walk through it.

There was, at this time, a clear difference between refugees and asylum-seekers. Refugees, or their champions, would cite the United Nations Declaration on Human Rights of 1950 which entitled them to flee persecution and oppression at home. They needed to be able to demonstrate that they had a 'well-founded fear', and they would be looked after, temporarily at least. Political asylum was a different matter. Technically, it was supposed to apply

---

*Throughout the 1980s, the asylum-seekers in Britain came to no more than four thousand each year, a number that made few headlines.

only to those evading arrest in another country – where, by implication, they could not expect a fair trial. It was designed for such people as Alexander Solzhenitsyn, or a Romanian gymnast making a break for it at the Olympics. The wall between the two categories was melting, though, and it was increasingly hard to see the difference. The newspapers drew a rough line between asylum-seekers (genuine) and economic migrants (bogus). But this distinction, too, soon collapsed – rightly, since this was primarily a bureaucratic convenience of our own. Were we saying that we were happy (or at least willing) to accept people running from a secret police force, but not those fleeing from starvation? It didn't matter much, either way. Growing numbers of people in search of a better life gatecrashed the hitherto modest system of asylum, and very soon overwhelmed it.

The response was characteristic: the British authorities sought to make the life of asylum-seekers as uncomfortable as possible, partly to discourage others and partly to pacify those who accused the government of being a 'soft touch'. It didn't work. In 1990 a hundred passengers without documents arrived at Heathrow in the average month; a year later there were 650 each month. In 1989 and 1990 combined there were 45,000 applications for sanctuary; in 1992 alone there were 57,000. This was only a fifth of those who applied to Germany, but Britain wasn't too interested in Germany. There were beggars on the pavements and the trains. London in particular seemed to be awash with them. If anyone paused to think, it was obvious that these people had troubles of their own: some had walked all the way from Romania for the privilege of sitting on a damp concrete step on London's South Bank with a hand held out. But much as Victorian Britain sought to stamp out those blasted Italian barrel organs, public opinion regarded the migrants as a mere pest. The new term 'asylum-seeker' rapidly acquired a sarcastic prefix: 'bogus'. The British public came to believe that all migrants were false: none had a right to be here; all were helping themselves at our expense. There was sharp political pressure on the government to get tough.

Far from Westminster, the engines driving international migration were being strenuously stoked. In 1993 the civil war in Somalia took a critical turn, and the capital city, Mogadishu, was bombarded. Thousands fled, and some had the luck, courage or means to make it as far as London. Britain's imperial presence still resonated for Somalis, many of whom were the descendants of men who had worked on British ships in the distant past. Somalis soon leapt to the top of the national asylum rankings, which automatically put them close to the top of the British unpopularity stakes. No one cared that a good number were university-educated government officials, engineers, doctors and teachers; in exile, such qualifications would prove to be all but worthless. In the razor-edged atmosphere of anti-migrant Britain they had to watch their windows and their backs. They were alive, which was something to be grateful for, but there were few other bright lights on their horizon. They were housed in rotting rooms, often with rough and antagonistic neighbours. They clustered in cafés in Kentish Town and advice centres in Newcastle and elsewhere, where they queued for the phone to see if they could find out what had become of the relatives and friends they had left behind.

The British National Party was beginning to agitate against migrants again. These foreign spongers were given favourable treatment and precedence over honest Brits, they declared. They were stealing our houses, our birthright and our jobs.* In a predictable echo of the internment crises that stirred the home front in both world wars, the official response was to tighten the laws and incarcerate people. Special holding centres were prepared. A brick prison at Campsfield in Oxfordshire opened at Christmas 1993, and at once became the scene of an extended uprising: there were hunger strikes, protests on the roof and a mass breakout over the twenty-foot fence. Liberal observers remarked that something had changed in Britain: it was now possible to imprison people who had not committed any crime. But the majority of the public, inspired by its favourite papers, sighed with disgust: you try to help people, and look how they thank you. As it happened, Britain suffered a net loss of people in 1993, but you wouldn't have known it at the time. We were being flooded, deluged, swamped all over again.

In 1996 the government passed the first of several Asylum and Immigration Acts. The idea was to deter asylum-seekers partly by making their lives even more miserable, and partly by punishing anyone who helped them, even if they did so unwittingly. Travellers who failed to claim asylum immediately – 'on entry' – were no longer eligible for housing, and were not permitted to work for six months. Rejected claimants were not entitled to any benefits, even if they were appealing against the decision. Fines were imposed on the transport companies that – usually inadvertently – brought them in. Lorry drivers and rail operators already faced a £2,000 fine for each person found on their vehicles. Employers too could be fined up to £5,000 for hiring an illegal worker. And airlines were penalised for carrying passengers without papers.

When Peter Lilley, Secretary of State for Social Security, tried to remove benefits from asylum-seekers altogether, a law lord ruled it illegal – another case in which important freedoms were being upheld by the vigilance of an independent judiciary in defiance of the vote-currying whims of elected politicians. It was hard to spot, amid all the fuss, that those claiming asylum

---

*The 1995 Labour Force Survey put unemployment among white Britons at 8 per cent. Among Afro-Caribbeans it was 24 per cent, and among Pakistani and Bangladeshi immigrants 34 per cent. If a Bosnian was depriving anyone of a job, it was most likely to be a Bengali.

amounted to only a small percentage of the people coming to Britain each year. Legal immigration was still running at 50,000 per annum – a manageable and necessary figure which was more than matched by emigration. But the Immigration Service was hinting that unofficial or illegal migration might amount to at least twice that. In 1995 and 1996, some twenty thousand illegal immigrants were arrested, and the assumption was that the authorities were catching only a fraction of the people they were after. Thousands more travelled perfectly legally, on tourist, student or business visas, and then simply stayed, drifting out of reach of law-enforcement agencies. Only the most desperate stowed away in the backs of lorries.

The existing system for processing asylum-seekers was neither large nor quick enough to keep up. Claimants were waiting a year or more to have their cases heard, and when, as usually happened, they were finally given the thumbs-down, they had the right of appeal, which took another year. It was fast becoming an embarrassing bureaucratic quagmire, and the government decided to revamp the entire department by moving it to new offices in Croydon which would be equipped with the latest state-of-the-art computer system for logging and monitoring applications. Work began on the installation of the £77 million network. But it kept crashing, and the move was postponed.

And then, just when the system couldn't take any more, there was another crisis. In the summer of 1995, smoke started belching out of the Soufrière Hills, volcanic heights in the southern part of the Caribbean island of Montserrat. For the next two years, ash and mud spewed on to the land below. Montserrat, an island only a quarter the size of the Isle of Wight, was in grave danger. The capital, Plymouth, was evacuated in 1996; the island's airport lay in the likely path of any major volcanic flow.

The volcano finally blew its top in June 1997, in a series of eruptions that continued into August. There were only nineteen casualties – the area had been abandoned – but the land and the homes on it were utterly ruined, buried under volcanic rubble. For weeks, it was snowing sulphur in Montserrat.

The island was a British overseas territory, a palm-fringed Anglophone oasis with red telephone boxes, Anglican churches and a plume-topped governor from the Foreign Office. It enjoyed exactly the same status as the Falkland Islands, so Montserratians looked forward to the kind of British assistance that had been showered on the South Atlantic a decade earlier.

It was not exactly forthcoming. The government muttered something about budgets, crossed its fingers and hoped that the volcano would cool down. The island's governor wrote to the Foreign Office asking for the construction of a thousand homes in the safe northern part of the island; the request was turned down. But many Montserratians couldn't stay where they were, and they started leaving in July, paying their own way or relying on donations from charities or relatives already overseas. In August the British government relented, and announced an assisted passage scheme to provide the remaining evacuees with the means to leave. Within a year, roughly 3,000 people had done so, and by the spring of 1998 some 7,500 islanders, two-thirds of the population, had abandoned Montserrat. Almost half came to Britain.

There was no official reception scheme. The Montserratians were tossed into the British social system with hardly any guidance or resources. In an act of seeming political generosity, it was confirmed that they would be treated as British citizens; but this turned out to mean that they were treated like homeless British citizens, and ignored the sense in which what had happened to them was exceptional. For the most part, they had to rely on sometimes tenuous contacts and a couple of fledgling charities. It was not one of Britain's most splendid initiatives, even after 1997, when the new Secretary of State for Overseas Aid and Development, Clare Short, came to power pledging to agitate on behalf of the underdog and fight world poverty. The occasion was tailor-made for humanitarian grandstanding, so there were frowns when Short remarked, in August 1997, just two months after the island had been half-buried, that the Montserratians needed to shut up and stop begging for aid. It would, she said, be 'weak politics' if she simply threw money at these constant pleas for help. 'It will be golden elephants next.'[1]

Britain had spent over £45 million on the crisis so far, on housing, transport, food and other aid. But the scale of the disaster was enormous: the island had been smashed; sewerage and plumbing were blocked and broken; power lines were down; factories and fields were buried. Government departments were skilled buck-passers, and urgent requests for help drifted between the UK and the Caribbean, sometimes running out of energy before they found anyone who would act. Clare Short's remark confirmed that Montserrat was being viewed above all as a damned nuisance. Her words echoed around the Caribbean.

It was the phrasing as much as the message: those 'golden elephants' suggested that Montserrat was demanding luxuries. Short apologised, but the damage was done. The Foreign Secretary, Robin Cook, launched a steering group to coordinate government action, and the Montserrat Project was set up to take over from the Red Cross and other agencies providing relief work. The Montserratians, however, arrived in Britain, like so many migrants before and since, with a dazed sense that they were not wanted. They had done nothing wrong; they did not even want to be here. Britain, alas, did not seem to want them here either.

At any other time, the arrival of the Montserrat volcano victims might have roused or ruffled British public life. But in the mid-1990s they were a footnote in the story of asylum-seekers. Increasingly desperate men and women were crossing the Channel in rowing boats, or hanging on to the undercarriage of Eurostar trains. Some were risking (and losing) their lives: one stowaway jumped from a passenger ferry into the sea when he was apprehended,

thinking that he could swim for it. He drowned. An Iraqi refugee was killed
when he jumped on to the roof of a passing train from a bridge in Normandy.
Others were crushed by wheels or electrocuted by high-voltage cables. One
large group attempted to walk through the tunnel to England: they cut through
a fence near the entrance, but were spotted by a security guard as they set off,
and intercepted by police a few miles later. Some were lucky: one group of
sixteen Romanians (five women, two men and nine children) squeezed into the
electrical compartments beneath a Eurostar train, and attracted the attention of
staff at Waterloo Station by knocking for all they were worth when they arrived.
One of the children was just three years old. A cross-Channel ferry picked up
two Lithuanian men who were trying to float across one of the world's most
crowded sea lanes on a pair of inflatable lilos. The men had been paddling for
ten hours, but were only seven miles from the French coast.

Dover had long since abandoned any attempt to provide a kindly British
welcome to these determined infiltrators. The local newspaper called them 'the
scum of the earth'. Grumpy officials in the freight yards of Kent ran thermal
sensors along the lorries. And if they weren't trying that hard – only checking
one lorry in ten – who could blame them? What was the point of being
thorough? If they found anyone, they called the police. And the police just sent
the immigrants off to Croydon.

By 2001, the freight company English, Welsh and Scottish Railways owed
nearly half a million pounds in fines for allowing illegal immigrants to enter
Britain on its trains. They challenged this on the grounds that there was nothing
they could do to prevent it, as they were not allowed to search trains at the
French end. But since the British government had no power to fine French
companies which should have checked their wagons, it fined the British ones
to the hilt. Sometimes the carriages had intact French seals on them, declaring
that they had been checked and vouched for – but there were still people inside.
There was something like rage, in Dover and Folkestone, that their colleagues
across the Channel weren't exactly straining to prevent people making the trip.
As it happened, in Zeebrugge and Calais, security staff were pounding on lorry
doors in random checks, and catching a dozen migrants a week. But this too felt
like a hopeless task. The fugitives would be escorted to the outskirts of Calais,
only to wander back the next day for another try.

Britain had had a long time – a hundred years – to prepare for the 1997
handover of Hong Kong to China. So this was one crisis that the government
could at least see coming. And one of its top priorities was to avoid a mass
migration of Hong Kong citizens to Britain. In 1981 Mrs Thatcher's cabinet
acted with unusual foresight to nip that possibility in the bud. There were over
three million potentially British people in Hong Kong, and negotiations with
China were about to open. Before the subject (let alone the subjects) became

heated, Britain calmly passed an Act that stripped them of the right to settle in
the United Kingdom. Instead, they were awarded a junior form of nationality,
which gave them diplomatic protection and access to Britain, but no rights of
residence. The only people who would be able to avoid living under Chinese
rule after 1997 were those who could claim patriality – an ancestral tie to
Britain. Some twenty thousand people of British descent qualified for this A-
list. The rest would not be considered. The thousands of South Asians (mainly
Indians) who had been attracted to the island were left entirely in the lurch.
China expressed a willingness that they be treated as UK nationals. Britain
declined.

To the British public, this sort of thing seemed abstract, a technicality, and far
in the future. We had grown blithe about such matters, and were to a large
degree unaware of the extent to which nationality, even on paper, was a
concrete thing with immediate benefits.* Opposition was muted. But it was a
stinging slap in the face to the millions of Hong Kong Chinese. Unsurprisingly,
there was much talk of betrayal. No one knew what was going to happen when
the lease reverted to China, but the fact that Britain was going to cut loose the
people who had turned the island into such a commercial powerhouse seemed
both mean-spirited and timid. In 1989 the clampdown on the protest in Beijing's
Tiananmen Square jolted Britain into a few hasty concessions. To forestall what
it feared, once again, might be a sudden exodus from the colony, Britain granted
residential rights, provisionally, to fifty thousand selected citizens – mainly civil
servants and other essential personnel. But it was too late: the more prominent
businesspeople in the colony had already resolved to dismiss Britain from their
sights, which were now fixed elsewhere: on America, Australia, Canada and the
Pacific Rim. All of these places were eyeing up Hong Kong's people with some
enthusiasm, creating points schemes for would-be migrants and actively
seeking to headhunt those that they knew would import trading acumen and
contacts across Asia. If Britain imagined itself to be the promised land, it was
deluding itself. When the time came, those fifty thousand passports would turn
out to be more than enough: Britain was so successful in getting across its
unwelcoming message that even this small quota was not filled.

It made for a tangled retreat from the region. There was much diplomatic
embarrassment when Portugal announced much more generous terms for the
people of Macao, which was being handed over in a similar fashion in 1999. It
promised full Portuguese nationality to 450,000 residents, fewer than 10,000 of

---

*The exiled writer Kenan Makiya, in contrast, was in no doubt that his Iraqi nationality
was a 'ball-and-chain'. In *Cruelty and Silence* he wrote: 'The day I received the letter
granting me British nationality in 1982 was one of the happiest days of my life. Now I
could travel without restrictions . . . Never again would I have to go to an Iraqi embassy,
posting friends at the corner of the street to check up on whether I came out again.'

whom had any ancestral links with the mother country. The people of Hong Kong read the news and shook their heads. Britain had lost all confidence when it came to its ability to embrace foreigners, so one of the most vibrant migrations of the late twentieth century passed it by. While Vancouver boomed, the Hong Kong Chinese did not come to Britain in any numbers. Several columnists, mainly in the *Financial Times*, pointed out that their arrival would have done the British economy nothing but good – these people were a rich commercial asset. But it was too late.

The Treaty of Maastricht, meanwhile, was granting precisely the rights Britain was denying the Hong Kong Chinese to over 250 million Europeans – a hundred times the number of people Britain had gone to such lengths to exclude. By the time the Union Jack came down, and the royal yacht slipped out beyond Kowloon for the last time, Britain had a new Labour government, and the episode was decorated with a telling coda. As soon as power was transferred, Britain granted full passports to all its remaining colonies. Perhaps this was meant to look like a criticism of the shabby policies that had been constructed with respect to Hong Kong; perhaps it was intended as a grand and honourable gesture. But in practice it involved little more than opening up Britain to the threat of migration from such formidable outposts as Gibraltar and St Helena.*

Like a leaking oil tanker lumbering in a vast turning circle, Britain was wheeling away from its past – its historic empire – and committing itself to collaboration with countries it had, for several hundred years, regarded as bitter enemies. It was inevitable that such a major reorientation should be accompanied by the gnashing of many teeth, and there were some vociferous opponents of the sea-change. Euroscepticism flourished among those who regretted the passing of the old order. They might not have been allowed to go on about Fuzzy Wuzzies any more, but they could say what they damn well pleased about the French. And they were a force strong enough in 1997 to help topple a prime minister (John Major) and condemn the party that had governed Britain for nearly two decades to a crushing electoral defeat.

There was still a tremendous din at the Channel ports, and in the newspapers. But the real drama was to be found behind closed doors. Croydon, the Surrey headquarters of the immigration service, was turning into a morass of queues, lost files, hesitant decisions and unenforceable rulings. Before leaving office in 1997, the Conservative Home Secretary, Michael Howard, announced new plans: more detention centres, a smarter computer network and a programme of nationwide dispersal (to ease the pressure on local councils in the south-east, which inevitably were feeling the pinch). But many asylum-seekers who'd had

---

*An unlikely eventuality in St Helena's case – the island didn't even have an airport.

their applications rejected were disappearing, and more were arriving every day. The system, if that is the right word for something so disorderly, was failing.

Would a change of government make a difference? The new Labour administration, represented by the new Home Secretary, Jack Straw, ostentatiously tore up a heartless deportation order that had been served on a young Nepalese who had been adopted by a British citizen. Then the vast waiting-list for asylum was slashed by granting an amnesty to thirty thousand people who had been kept hanging on, in most cases, for over five years. These measures were greeted by Tory jeers, as if Straw were undoing much of their fine work.*

Straw also decided to accelerate the modernisation of the bureaucracy, and pushed the Immigration and Nationality Directorate into its new premises, shedding over a thousand staff on the way, in the optimistic belief that the new technology could take the strain. But the computer system was still crashing on a regular basis, and so, at the worst possible moment, the entire British machinery of asylum and immigration thudded to a virtual halt. In December 1998 the backlog for processing applications was 64,000. A couple of years later, it had almost doubled: 114,600 people were waiting to hear what their fate would be. Laws and principles needed to be upheld, of course, but questions started to be asked about whether it was worth the effort and the money. Britain was spending hundreds of millions of pounds a year on a weeding-out process which simply didn't work. There were almost fifteen miles of shelved paperwork waiting to be investigated; letters went astray; phones went unanswered. When new regional offices opened in Liverpool and Leeds, asylum-seekers who had been housed in the north were summoned to Croydon, while their opposite numbers in the south were ordered to attend hearings on Merseyside. It began to sound like a Kafka short story: The Appointment (or, more accurately, The Disappointment). Croydon became a byword for British clumsiness. The government retained the detention-camp idea: soon there were almost two thousand inmates at some forty centres. But most were held for only a week or so and then packed off to the local councils, to make room for new arrivals. Newspapers reported that a room in one of the centres cost as much as one at the Ritz Hotel.

It was easy enough to scoff. Looked at from another angle, however, Britain was doing its clumsy best to be fair. When a group of Bosnian refugees claimed asylum in Italy, they were herded into a football stadium before being sent back to where they'd come from. High-speed police launches raced across the

*The jeers were rendered hollow by the fact that the previous Conservative administration had granted a similar amnesty, for exactly the same reasons, a few years earlier.

Adriatic trying to intercept migrant speedboats (there was an organised fleet of illicit-trafficking vessels in Albania) and prevent them from approaching the Italian coast. In contrast, by remaining doggedly wedded to the idea that it should accept anyone with a genuine claim, and the illusion that it was possible to investigate individuals from faraway war zones and come to any sort of an informed decision about their situation, Britain was at least trying to behave with some sort of propriety, and with diligence. The bombing of Serbia and the war in Kosovo in 1999 created a million displaced people, and since Britain was implicated in their displacement, it could hardly abandon them altogether.

In 1999 the government tabled and debated another bill, which it touted as giving muscle to a system that would be 'firmer, fairer, faster'. It pushed ahead with the programme of dispersal, and ran into a prickly outbreak of not-in-my-backyard protest groups. There was clear logic to the proposal – Kent County Council had 1,200 teenage boys under its jurisdiction – and several thousand asylum-seekers were sent off to Liverpool, Leeds, Manchester and Glasgow. But the refugees were nervous and unhappy, and regional Britain soon made its feelings clear.* In Hull, two Afghans were attacked and stabbed in the city centre, and a Kurdish teenager opened his door the day after he arrived, was whacked by a stone and blinded in one eye. This was not a great advertisement for the birthplace of William Wilberforce, and those asylum-seekers fled back south again. Sixteen rebounded from Glasgow for similar reasons.

In Dover, Oldham, Sunderland and elsewhere, a relaunched, better-dressed British National Party went on the offensive – in every sense of the word. 'Vote Labour if you want asylum-seeker neighbours,' said a pamphlet distributed in Sunderland, in a clumsy echo of the racist slur that had scandalised (or thrilled) the electors of Smethwick in 1964. Nor was the Conservative Party above this sort of inflammatory talk. Its manifesto for a forthcoming local government election was unequivocal, deploying the full arsenal of migration clichés: 'Labour has made this country a soft touch for the organised asylum-racketeers who are flooding this country with bogus asylum-seekers.' Its authors would insist that there was 'nothing racist' about this – indeed, it stressed that one of its major concerns was to dampen support for the BNP. It was simply that we couldn't, with the best will in the world, admit so many people, they explained, because this only encouraged racial antagonism. Even if this were true, it bore an unnerving resemblance to what people were saying before the Second World War, when it was argued that we couldn't accept Jews because to do so might provoke anti-Semitism. In Sunderland, meanwhile, careless talk such as this contributed to tragedy: an Iranian was stabbed and killed and the authorities,

---

*At Wath, near Rotherham, Throckmorton in Worcestershire, Sittingbourne in Kent, in Gloucestershire and Sunderland . . . the story was always the same. The asylum-seekers would encourage crime, they said, spread drugs and knock property prices.

as so often in the past, acted against the victims, rather than the perpetrators, and closed the town to asylum-seekers in order to cool the hot social atmosphere. The BNP celebrated a victory with martial rhetoric: 'All it needs', it crowed, 'is one more push'. There were, at this time, just over a thousand hapless foreigners – a disparate bunch, from sixty-three different countries – housed in a city of nearly three hundred thousand people.

The government continued to tighten the restrictions and toughen the penalties. Asylum-seekers were required to complete a twenty-page form (in a language they might not know) and deliver it to Croydon within two weeks. Failure to do so would be deemed non-compliance, and was a path to certain rejection. This led critics to insist that it was merely a dodge, an easy way of increasing the number of exclusions. In 1999 a voucher scheme was introduced to replace the small cash payments granted to asylum-seekers – a humiliating procedure which more or less branded the recipients as imposters: the scheme lasted for a year. Some 48,000 asylum-seekers received vouchers worth £26 million through a system that itself cost £15 million to run.

Almost everything else backfired, too, partly because so many steps were being taken on the odd supposition that migrants were willing to give ten thousand pounds to racketeers to sneak them into Britain so that they might be parked in a detention centre in Durham drawing thirty-five pounds a week in vouchers. But the idea that these people were spongers was tenacious. Candidates rejected for non-compliance usually appealed, incurring a further round of weighty legal costs to the public purse. And the continuing inefficiency of Croydon meant that many forms vanished without trace, even when they had been sent by recorded delivery. The official policy in such cases was to reject the lost application out of hand. If it could be demonstrated that the form had been filled in and delivered, the rejection still stood, which meant more work for the appeals court. Sometimes young, unaccompanied children were rejected for non-compliance. Campaigners argued that this too was deliberate, part of a strategy to make asylum-seekers' lives so intolerable that they would go somewhere else.

Church groups, charities, refugee-support agencies and a few newspaper columnists attempted to counter the prevailing public opinion of asylum-seekers by treating them as individuals and broadcasting their stories to anyone who would listen. One pseudonymous Kurdish refugee from Iraq interviewed in the *Guardian*, claimed that he had been shot by the police, and had paid $7,000 to a trafficker to get him to Britain, only to be hoodwinked and dumped in Turkey. He was able to raise another $3,500 from relatives, and a fortnight later he was sealed into a lorry with a dozen others. He made it to Britain, but his troubles had only just begun. Along with a fellow Kurd he was sent to Croydon. He endured a ten-hour wait to pick up his form, and, not trusting the post, returned on the appointed day having completed it. He spent nine hours waiting in what turned out to be the wrong queue, then learned that the correct queue was now 'closed'. He left his form at the building, but was refused a receipt. A month later he received a letter saying his application had been rejected due to his failure to return his form. A solicitor working on his behalf extracted a confession from the Home Office that his form had been lost. He even secured an apology. But the rejection stood. He appealed, was given 'leave to remain' pending a decision, and embarked on another lap of the system. After a year, no one had yet asked him who he was, where he was from or what had happened to him.

No one could pretend that stories like this were exceptional. If anything, they were the norm. Out in the shadier sectors of the British economy, corner-cutting landlords were doing very well out of asylum-seekers. There was no shortage of bogus asylum-support agencies in housing and legal advice. The supermarkets enjoyed the voucher system while it lasted, too, since they were not permitted to hand back change, so could pocket the difference – a carrot to tempt them into supporting the scheme. On the ground, this had some poignant side-effects: asylum-seekers would fret at the till, trying to obtain the maximum amount of goods for their vouchers, juggling a strange currency and making last-minute exchanges to extract every last penny from their allowance. As the queues lengthened behind them, the public reputation of the asylum-seekers dipped a little lower.

The new millennium offered an opportunity to take stock. The figures showed the life of Britain's migrants to be anything but uniform. A Cabinet Office Report, published at the beginning of 2002, showed that one in 20 Indian men was a doctor, compared to one in 200 white men; while 45 per cent of Chinese men were in professional or managerial jobs, compared to 25 per cent of white and Indian men. Black Caribbean women (the success story of the survey) earned a tidy £30 more per week than white women, but Pakistani and Bangladeshi women earned £34 less; only 20 per cent of Bangladeshi women wanted paid employment compared to 80 per cent of Caribbean women. In all, ethnic minorities accounted for 6.7 per cent of the working population of Britain – 2.4 million out of 33 million. Some – many – were thriving; but there was no disguising the extent to which Britain's Muslims were lagging on nearly every material indicator. One-third of Bangladeshi men worked as cooks or waiters. Along with Pakistanis, they were more than twice as likely to be unemployed as the white population; three-quarters of their children lived in households that earned less than half the average national wage.

There were signs that this bleak situation was not set in stone. Twice as many Pakistani and Bangladeshi girls took A-levels in 1998 as white boys. But is was not yet possible to feel the ramifications of such cold data. On the contrary, most of the figures conformed to the time-honoured recipe for heated social unrest, and in 2001 the streets of Oldham and Bradford echoed to the sound of youthful Muslim anger. In both cases, the immediate spark was a march by British Nationalists, but the bonfire had been well-prepared. Years of multiculturalism and political nervousness had created sad, neglected ghettos. Indeed, Sir Herman Ouseley's report into the disturbances sounded oddly reminiscent of Ray Honeyford's bleak prophecy: he charged the local authorities with having permitted segregation to embed itself too deeply; there were schools in Oldham that were 98 per cent Bangladeshi; and Bradford's 54 mosques had done little to promote the integration of its large (17 per cent) Muslim minority.

Britain responded to this disquiet by focusing with fresh intent and fury on the new arrivals. Every year, the number of asylum-seekers was hitting record highs: in 1999 there were 71,000; in 2000 there were 97,000. The backlog for processing applications was still awesome – the waiting-list was 103,000 people long, and the average response time was well over a year. By now, the old distinctions had all but disappeared: newspaper references to asylum-seekers doubled; allusions to refugees halved. Over a billion pounds was being spent on handling this population, much of it on job-creation schemes for British workers hired to monitor and operate the asylum-rejection machine. It was costing an awful lot of money to keep these people in poverty.

And there was never any time to draw breath. In February 2000 an internal flight in Afghanistan was hijacked and steered to Stansted Airport. The plane was surrounded by police marksmen, and for four days there was a familiar stand-off, a classic airport drama rendered singular by the fact that the hijackers didn't seem to be demanding anything. When eighty-five passengers were released unharmed, the truth began to seep out. The hijackers were asylum-seekers. Sixty-six men were later escorted from the plane: they wanted confirmation of their status as refugees and sanctuary in Britain. Naturally, the newspapers spat bile when it was reported that the first port of call for some of the passengers was a night in the Stansted Hilton. More ominously, the incident forged a link between asylum-seekers and terrorism that would only add to the vitriol they already attracted.

A few weeks later, the *Sun* declared 'Victory' in its 'Britain Has Had Enough' campaign to do something about London's beggars. It called them 'the grasping nomads of Eastern Europe', which was also reminiscent of the language used against Jews in the 1930s. It was true – they were annoying. But the lack of sympathy for their many misadventures was remarkable. These travellers had walked thousands of miles to escape persecution in Romania and Hungary, wading across rivers and begging for food as they went. The leader of the opposition, William Hague, reacted by proposing to keep them, and all such migrants, 'under lock and key'.

Migration, it was becoming clear, was dangerous. People were being killed all the time. On land they ran the risk of being broiled, refrigerated or suffocated in a container truck. At sea, it was even more perilous. When Spanish authorities clamped down on the short crossing from North Africa across the Strait of Gibraltar, migrants aimed instead for the Canary Islands, a much longer and more hazardous journey, in open boats. Many drowned. Albanian smugglers often tipped people into the Adriatic once they had safely pocketed their money. They were especially keen on Chinese passengers, it seemed, because they were small, so you could squeeze more of them on to a boat. In 1999 one of these boats capsized, killing 59 people, 39 of them Chinese. In China itself, the vanished were becoming commonplace. Young men would undertake the voyage to London, carrying with them the hopes and savings of their families, and would never be heard of again.

Britain woke up to the full horror of this seedy business in the summer of 2000. A customs officer in Dover opened the back of a lorry and recoiled from an infernal scene: a pile of dead bodies. Fifty-eight Chinese asylum-seekers had been asphyxiated in a lorry partly packed with tomatoes. The air vent that would have allowed them to breathe had been closed. The Dutch lorry driver was charged with manslaughter, but no one could pretend that he alone was culpable. The collapse of communism had opened up land routes from Asia. Smuggling gangs operated an organised black economy: ten thousand pounds or so would buy flights from China to Moscow, Prague or Bucharest, and a few inches of space in a truck across Europe. The journey would often end up in Rotterdam, the ancient stepping-off point where the Rhine meets the North Sea. The city had its own Chinatown, where the so-called Snakehead gangs handled the details. At any one time there would be several hundred Chinese hopefuls waiting to be sent across the Channel; they would be herded into one of the two thousand lorries bound for Britain each day. If by chance they were detected and turned back* they would be found a berth on another vehicle.

The Dover tragedy injected a new word into the vocabulary of migration: Sangatte. The French authorities in Calais had converted a disused factory – once used to house tunnelling equipment – into a holding centre for the vagrants who were clogging up the streets and parks of their Channel ports. They provided food and shelter, but no cash. Sangatte was a vast row of metallic hangars from which, on fine days, people could see the white cliffs of Dover to the north-west. Some had travelled halfway across the world; they weren't about to let a small strip of water stand between them and their goal. Sangatte became the departure lounge for the final leg of the trek. It could be rough: there were fights between Kurds and Afghans, who formed rival gangs to control and profit from the lucrative trade in fake papers and routes into Britain; agents would charge five hundred dollars for a berth on a lorry. But in many respects Sangatte resembled the internment camps in the war. 'Engineers,

---

*The police could inspect only a fraction of the lorries. For a while, they were helped by a team of eight sniffer dogs, who had good noses and were productive. But the team was soon cut back to five dogs.

doctors, professors, jurists,' said one of its directors. 'The amount of grey matter coming through here is impressive.'

Across the Channel, much of Britain's own migration policy increasingly resembled the siege mentality of wartime. Once again there was pressure to 'collar the lot'. In April 2001, P & O announced that they had found 1,600 asylum-seekers in the previous three months. There were new detention centres in Dover and at Oakington near Cambridge. The smartest, Yarl's Wood in Bedfordshire, opened in November 2001. It was designed to hold a thousand people, which meant that the notorious Campsfield prison could be closed. But Yarl's Wood turned out to be Campsfield all over again. The following February, inmates set fire to the building, which blazed out of control; twenty-seven detainees escaped in the confusion. In Glasgow, there were fights between asylum-seekers and the other residents of the rotting estate blocks in which they were housed. A Kurdish man was murdered.

No one could see an end to it. And the specific hostility towards asylum-seekers filtered into a general impatience with immigrants of all sorts. The BNP continued to attract violent support for its repeated claims that foreigners were cornering the market in housing, jobs and grants. How this squared with the news that 30 per cent of children born to Muslim families were living in poverty was hard to explain, but vexed Britons did not want explanations: they wanted action.

The obliteration of the World Trade Center on 11 September 2001 was the final straw. It provoked widespread feeling that asylum-seekers were all potential terrorists. And that opinion was reinforced when some determined fundamentalists were indeed found hiding in the fold of Britain's asylum system in Manchester.

When the figures for 2002 were published, there was an uproar: 110,700 people had sought asylum in Britain. This was bad enough in itself, for most. But even more venom was generated when the imbalance with the rest of Europe was revealed: Italy, larger and less densely populated than Britain, received only 7,300; Spain, twice the size and with an even smaller population, took only 6,179.

Once again, attention focused on the hopelessness of the processing system. In 2002 nearly 55,000 applications were turned down (two-thirds of the total number of decisions made); but only 13,000 people were deported, a long way short of the government's target of 30,000. Deportation was difficult, expensive, often unjust, and always embarrassing. It involved rousing families at dawn and escorting them, sometimes with crying children in tow, to an airport. Any sample of the asylum-seeking population revealed it to be a cross-section of the world's trouble spots: Afghanistan, Iraq, Somalia and Zimbabwe were all well represented. No one could pretend that sending people back to these places looked good, and it was evident that many (if not all) such deportees were being returned to cruel fates that they had risked everything to escape.

Life was hard for those processing the claims, too. Migrants routinely arrived without any documentation, having been instructed by their agents to destroy it, in order to slow down the checking process. The procedures for seeking asylum had become well grooved, and many migrants had been coached. If they came by air, for instance, they learned to loiter as long as possible before presenting themselves to customs and passport control, making it harder to identify their flight. They knew that Britain occasionally favoured certain nationalities – so sometimes it was smart to claim to be Iraqi, while a month later it might be better to be an Afghan. Customs officers grew bored with hearing the same stories. Many people claimed, for instance, that they had fled after being spotted at an 'opposition rally' at home. They weren't attending the meeting, they insisted (attendance was something that could be checked), they were just arranging the furniture. When this chair-arranging defence became overused, new stories were contrived. Meanwhile, there were 'Ghanaian' women who couldn't speak a known Ghanaian language, and Kosovans who looked like Serbs. Language students were rustled up as interpreters, a job which many asylum-seekers themselves could have done, if they had been permitted to work.

The paperwork was morale-sapping, but slowly the tide began to turn. The government hired 1,200 new asylum and immigration officials (almost exactly the number that had been sacked a few years earlier when the system was 'streamlined'). And the mountainous backlog finally started to shrink: from 114,000 at the beginning of 2000 to 35,000 at the beginning of 2002.[2] The number of new arrivals began to decline too: from 23,000 in the first quarter of 2002 to 16,000 in the same three months of 2003. Naturally, the government was encouraged to claim that its firmer, faster and fairer tactics were working. In truth, the fall merely reflected the fact that fewer people were entering Europe as a whole. Perhaps, like all the previous surges of migration, this one was beginning to play itself out?

No one can be sure. It is clear, however, that Britain responded to this most recent crisis like a grumpy old man trying to repair his fence, cursing and throwing up his arms at the number of people burrowing through. The idea that Britain might be the beneficiary in this process – that it was acquiring much needed energy and brainpower – was the furthest thing from most people's minds.

CHAPTER 25

Fortress Britain

The debate roared on. A few plaintive voices spoke up on behalf of battered people. Medical bodies suggested that Britain was treating asylum-seekers in an 'inhumane' way; lawyers implied that locking them up might even be illegal. Others argued that asylum-seekers were being stripped of all dignity – dealt with on the assumption that they were guilty until proved innocent. It could not be right, these voices said, that people in such trouble should be handled so harshly.

The propaganda flowing the other way was more systematic, however. Politicians and tabloid newspapers colluded in what amounted to a sustained, below-the-belt advertising campaign designed to promote feelings of fear and fury. There were exceptions, but the shriller voices raised against asylum-seekers revealed an alarming truth about the mass media. They have always thrived on bad news, of course, but on the hot topic of Britain's new foreigners, they seemed eager not just to report discord but to sow it. The headlines tumbled out, day after day: 'Immigration madness . . . 1 in 4 Asylum Seekers Ends Up in Britain . . . Asylum Cheats "Playing the System" . . . You Pay for Taliban Thug to Live Here . . . Asylum-Seekers Set for £1 Million Leisure Bonanza . . . Asylum: the Joke's on Us . . . Buying a Stamp? Sorry, We Only Serve Asylum-Seekers . . . Judge Lifts Lid on Immigrant Marriage Scam . . . Asylum Blamed for Aids Crisis in Britain . . . Luxury Life of Asylum-Seekers . . . Asylum: What a Shambles'. It was a torrent of abuse, often based on absurd figures. There was even one wild and entirely fictitious report that asylum-seekers were spit-roasting the royal swans.

The result of this wholehearted opinion-mongering was predictable. The British public was badly misled. There cannot, indeed, have been many matters of national importance on which it was more deluded. One *Reader's Digest* survey in 2001 found that two-thirds of Britons thought there were too many immigrants. Most (four-fifths) felt that Britain was a 'soft touch' and should tighten the policing of its borders. These large majorities were instantly convertible into heavy political pressure and clamorous headlines. Politicians on all sides felt duty-bound to talk tough on the subject, to gratify this clear majority. Newspapers boosted ill-feeling, and then reported it as news. But the small print revealed the depth of public ignorance on the topic. When respondents to one poll were asked how much money they thought asylum-seekers were given each week, the average guess was £113. The true figure was £36.54. The sample also believed that Britain's immigrants made up 20 per cent of the population. The true figure was 4 per cent. Another poll found that the average Briton believed that we were taking in 25 per cent of the world's refugees. In fact, Britain was taking just 2 per cent.* There was a nearly unanimous sense that Britain was by far the most attractive destination for the world's migrants, and that the rest of Europe, especially France, was happy to wave them towards us rather than honouring its own obligations. In fact, Britain stood twelfth in the table of European nations in terms of the number of asylum-seekers it accepted relative to the size of its population.†

All of this misinformation meant that the debate was unusually rancid and polarised. Both sides wrote and spoke as if they were in the minority. Little English columnists poured scorn on the lily-livered pinkos who wanted to turn the whole country into a refugee camp, while the lily-livered pinkos themselves posed as brave moralists surrounded by a nation of thugs and morons. Anti-immigration spokesmen posed as truth-tellers willing to say the unsayable, and complained bitterly if they were ever smeared as 'racist'; their opponents insisted that there were indeed racist undertones, if not overtones, in such arguments. The airwaves hummed with what sarcastic observers called bogus attention-seekers. In all of this heckling of opponents, it was almost impossible to find a calm reckoning of what was happening and where it was leading.

This was partly because there were no authoritative statistics. The

---

*In most polls since 1982 more than half of the respondents felt that immigration should decrease. However, a majority was also willing to grant that immigration in the past was a good thing.

†In one respect, Britain did operate a more benign strategy than some of its European neighbours. France, Germany and Italy accepted only persecution by the state as a justification for granting asylum. Britain took a broader view, recognising that non-governmental militias or gangs were just as capable of brutality as state-employed ones. Inevitably, this wider definition was rounded on as yet more evidence that we were a 'soft touch'.

government published numbers on asylum-seeking, and they always made headlines. The peak of 110,000 in 2001 allowed alarmist migration hawks to assert that a crowd the size of the population of Cambridge was pouring in every year. They did not add that a similar-sized crowd was leaving each year.* Gross figures were batted to and fro with little attention given to their significance.

There was one crucial figure that remained unknown: the number of undocumented migrants who had not claimed asylum but were living and working in the increasingly large black economy. One estimate put the size of this hidden workforce at four hundred thousand, a terrific number. Even if such guesses were accurate, there was no suggestion that this influx was here to stay. Given that these illegal jobseekers had no access to either social services or healthcare, no employment rights and no leverage in the housing market, this was highly unlikely: they were simply a mobile force of cheap labour, flowing in to pick crops, pack food and clean cars. There were occasional reports of chronic employment abuses in the little-regulated areas of casual work.

The best word for what happened at the end of the twentieth century might be prohibition. The long sequence of political reforms from 1962 added up to a wholehearted attempt to restrict immigration – especially coloured immigration. The legal routes to Britain were blocked: the fence was now so high that the state was willing to issue work permits and residential rights only to such professionals as it needed or wanted. In 2003, 42,000 foreign nurses were working for the National Health Service – a single London trust noted that it had nurses from sixty-eight different countries on its books. Doctors, too, were actively recruited: in 2001 more than five thousand were licensed to practise in Britain, a full third of the listed medical practitioners in the kingdom. Ironically, at a time when the National Health Service was announcing that it needed 20,000 new doctors, some 3,000 were in limbo in the refugee system, waiting for their claims to be dealt with and not allowed to work. There were major financial implications here: it costs approximately £250,000 to train a doctor. Why bother, when they could be picked up on the world market, ready-trained?† In 2002 the government gave itself a target: 15,000 consultants and GPs and 35,000 nurses, midwives and health visitors to be hired by 2008. If all of these were poached from abroad, Britain would save itself more than four billion pounds in training costs.

If you were not qualified for one of the understaffed professions, though,

---

*It can only be an assumption that this was the case, because the government stopped logging emigrants in 1999. It certainly had been the case up to then.
†Some sending countries – Jamaica, the Philippines, South Africa – began to complain at official levels about the brain drain they were suffering in order to plug this gap in Britain's healthcare system.

Britain had become a hard country to enter legally. But this did not stop people migrating any more than the banning of alcohol in America made people stop drinking. It simply criminalised them, or at least demanded of them increasing inventiveness to slip through the loopholes.* In the longer term, it promoted outlaws: people-trafficking became an industry. It would be wrong to argue that attempts to limit immigration actually caused the number of would-be migrants to soar, but it certainly diverted the flow into a shadowy area of racketeering, and gave powerful succour to the development in Britain of a large lawless economy. Food processing, cigarettes, building work, domestic workers, hotels, childcare, agricultural work ... all aspects of casual labour were influenced. Ersatz job centres and short-cut recruitment agents sprang up on street corners or in lay-bys. Contractors could pull up a truck in the early hours and fill it with people – Afghans, Bosnians, Somalians, Iranians – willing to pick up some cash for a day's work in a service station or a restaurant. According to some guesses, the illegal economy was soon worth some eighty billion pounds per year – four times the size of the black market in France or Germany. The imposition of the minimum wage, meanwhile, had a similar effect. For the Indian stonemasons imported to work on the construction of a lavish new Hindu temple in Wembley, it was great news: their wages rose from 30p per hour to £3.70. But elsewhere the regulation did not guarantee that all Britons would receive such a boost. It simply meant that those who earned less disappeared from the tax returns. Employers didn't stop hiring; they just stopped declaring. Britain became a no-questions-asked, cash-or-nothing economy which, in many ways, and despite the constant prospect of ever-closer union with Europe, was increasingly American in its social reflexes. It was a vibrant, laissez-faire, sink-or-swim, energetic, risky and potentially lawless place, with growing areas of the inner-cities falling outside political control or official influence, patrolled by gangs armed, increasingly, with guns.

It was occasionally possible, through the swirl of bad blood, to detect tangible grounds for optimism. To counter the popular idea that it was a burden, the Treasury released figures suggesting that the immigrant population was contributing more in tax (£31.2 billion) than it received in benefits (£28.8 billion). It also performed a valuable international aid service, transferring up to two billion pounds back home each year, and in some cases financing the maintenance of villages with few other means of support.† In Britain, migrant workers did indeed 'take our jobs', but most of these were in

---

*When the government imposed restrictions on children, for instance, declaring that anyone over the age of sixteen could no longer be termed a dependant, customs officers noticed a sharp rise in the number of 'fifteen-year-olds' coming to join their parents in Britain.
†This was a hundred times the amount that Britain gave to the UNHCR to help support displaced people.

the so-called 3-D category: dirty, dangerous and difficult. If they didn't do them, it was hard to see who would. Migrants allowed the local population to trade up, through tertiary education, to more desirable jobs, and provided the cheap labour that kept business humming. Their willingness to tolerate low wages (high by their own standards) provided a safety valve that allowed billions of pounds' worth of inflationary pressure to hiss out of the economy.*

Some argued that immigration was not just desirable, but essential, if the consumer boom was to be sustained. The birth rate required to maintain an even keel is 2.2 children per woman. In the European Union as a whole, the rate is running at only 1.4; in the UK, it is a slightly more fertile 1.7. But even so, the population will shrink without immigration. Those who fretted about long queues in the supermarket or congestion on the roads saw that as a blessing, but people remain an indispensable asset to any economy, especially in a medically advanced world of increasing age spans. In 1950, according to United Nations figures, there were six workers per pensioner in Britain, enough to underwrite a solid pension system. As the century ended there were only four. If Britain's labour force was not replenished by young newcomers, it would be too small to support the swelling group of over-sixties. Migrants tend to be young, but, even more usefully, not too young. They arrive ready to work, so the state does not have to bear the costs of their childhoods. It could be said that far from putting up a keep out sign, we should have been laying down the welcome mat.

The other enduring idea about migrants – that they are lazy – was also much to the fore in the millennial fury about scroungers and 'health tourists'. If anything exile promotes hard work, and legions of overseas builders, shopkeepers, cleaners, hotel and restaurant workers, nannies, agricultural labourers and drivers work superhuman hours. Such observations found it hard to compete with the shriller insistence that modern migrants were inveterate criminals. Undeniably, there were foreigners involved in serious crime. Balkan, Chinese, Arab and Latin American gangs had all entered the British underworld in recent years. But they did not invent the market they were supplying. Britain could hardly pose as an innocent victim of their corrupt ways.

Hostility to these modern migrants was as powerful as the ancient fears that have disfigured these islands many times in the past before fading, almost invariably, into indifference. The debate has followed the same lines as previous uproars, and there is little to suggest it will not subside along the same lines,

---

*In 1991 there were 227 social workers from overseas working in Britain; ten years later there were 1,175. This was hardly surprising: a social worker from southern Africa could earn ten times more in Britain (£24,000) than at home. As a result, more than half of the 3,000 trained social workers in Zimbabwe have moved to Britain.

too. One can fly in the face of the facts only for so long. It is childlike economics, for instance, to argue that migrants are stealing 'our' jobs, 'our' houses and, in the most frenetic arguments, 'our' women. Economies are neither static nor fixed: they thrive on movement and change. The arrival of more mouths does not mean less for everyone if the new mouths produce more than they consume. Today's migrants come, like the Flemish weavers in the Middle Ages, in search of jobs, but they create as many jobs as they fill – not least, of course, in the bulging bureaucracies created to monitor them and assess their right to be here.

If it were true that migration is economically harmful, then America would be a minnow, not a superpower. A hundred years ago, Francis Walker, superintendent of the US census in 1880 and 1890, wrote that it was time to call a halt to the exodus from Europe. These people, he said, were 'beaten men from beaten races, representing the worst failures in the struggle for existence'. This spectacular misjudgement is echoed in Britain today. Thirty per cent of Britain's foreign-born population have professional jobs, against 25 per cent of the native population. And a third of refugees have professional qualifications. Yet it is still routine to depict all migrants as beggars or pickpockets.

It isn't easy, in the torrential generalisations that dominate the subject, to imagine individual plights. But picture yourself as a migrant from the Commonwealth who, after some natural disaster, has been granted residency. You're on a plane to Britain. All your troubles should be over. You speak English, though not quite well enough to waltz into a conversational job. On the flight to Gatwick you are handed a sheet of paper with a résumé of information about life in Britain, from which you learn only that the weather is colder than might have been expected, that jobs are hard to come by, and that the plugs are different. Never mind. On the whole, you feel grateful and well intentioned. This historic and powerful nation has promised you board and lodging until you can stand on your own feet again. You know that, compared to home, this is a wealthy nation, a land of opportunity. You have two young children with you who were doing quite well at school, and though you know it's not going to be easy, you are optimistic that they will at least be able to continue their studies in this affluent and civilised place.

At Gatwick, you are escorted on to a bus, which inches through the traffic towards central London. You are dropped off into a slightly run-down terraced house on a featureless road clogged with traffic, none of which seems to be moving. It's some sort of hostel, and a few of the other passengers on the bus disembark at the same time. Two of them will be sharing a room with you. Your children will be in another room with other children. There's a dark shower and a lavatory down the corridor. Breakfast, you are told, is at eight o'clock.

The first couple of days are confusing. You are sent on a series of errands to various offices to sign on for entitlements. You do not want to spend your small supply of cash, but the trains and buses are expensive. Each time, you wait for hours before being handed lengthy forms. You know that you cannot afford to make any mistakes when filling them out, but they're in a strange language, so you keep trekking back to the advice centre to ask for help. On your fourth visit the people there are starting to show their impatience.

After a few weeks in the hostel someone arrives in a taxi and takes you to a flat near Paddington Station. It's only temporary, they say, but it'll be better than the hotel. Hotel, you think – was that place really a hotel? We have hotels back home – the ones the English people come and stay in – with swimming pools and air-conditioned rooms and conference facilities. You're beginning to think that Britain isn't quite what it was cracked up to be. On your long walks between appointments (you can no longer afford public transport), you notice lots of people like yourself: dazed, somewhat lost, and more than a little afraid. Several times you ask for people's help and there is no mistaking the annoyance in their replies. Still, the flat is a big improvement. It has three rooms and a bathroom. There's only one mattress, though, and little other furniture. At the advice centre they scribble down the address of a place that specialises in cheap household goods and allows you to buy on credit. But the goods aren't that cheap, and the interest rate seems astronomical. Still, you have no option: you buy some furniture, sign the papers, and pray that the money you've been promised starts coming through soon. It's been years since you have been in debt, and the idea makes you queasy.

There are other problems: there's no electricity and the phone doesn't work. It's winter, and the nights are freezing. You and the children sleep in one bed to keep warm. Outside, late at night, people shout as they walk by, and you can hear glass breaking. You have to venture out to make a call to the electricity company from the phone box, but your English isn't good enough and the person on the other end of the line eventually hangs up. You decide to go in person (more bus fares) and manage to make yourself understood. They promise to hook you up a week tommorow; it will cost forty pounds, which you don't have. You still have no electricity, but you are starting to get post. The housing people say they need your National Insurance number. You don't have one. The Town Hall demands it too, explaining that you can't receive any of the small weekly payments you have been promised without it. Back at the advice centre you are told that the local authority is wary of handing out the precious numbers because they are cracking down on benefit fraud. At home, you were a teacher. You were thinking that you would start making an effort to find work soon, but it is a full-time job just trying to get the lights switched on. A nice-sounding woman calling herself a housing assessor rings to say she needs your income support record. You have not the faintest idea what she is talking about.

You have at least found a place where other people from your country congregate. It's in Finsbury Park in north London, quite a long way from your flat, but you go there every day now to see people and discuss what is happening. You are down to your last few pounds, and the people here have a collection on your behalf. You don't like taking it, but the children have to eat. You go to the housing people and mention that, if at all possible, you'd like to live near Finsbury Park, where you know people. The man tells you that most of the people you came over with are still in hostels – that you are ahead of the game because of the children. He makes you feel selfish and ungrateful.

You need to improve your English and wonder whether it is possible to sign up for a course. There seem to be colleges on every corner, but the fees are huge if you want to start immediately and the waiting-lists are long. You hope it's not going to be like this for the children. You still haven't heard any more from the education authority since they said their hands were tied until you had a permanent address. The children themselves are quiet and fearful. They avoid going out. They really would love a television, but you can't afford one.

You pick newspapers out of bins to practise your English and are shocked by the headlines that you can understand. 'Scroungers!' they shout. 'End This Asylum Madness! . . . And Still They Come!' There are photographs of people who look like you. In one you see someone you know – a doctor from back home whose children were at your school. He's sleeping on a deckchair in the park with his mouth open, like a drunk.

One day you are walking back from the shops when you feel faint: hunger probably, you haven't eaten all day. So you and the children sit on some steps. You've only been there for a moment, catching your breath, when a few small coins are dropped into your lap. The shame of being seen as a beggar brings tears to your eyes. You try to tell yourself that you are lucky, that things will improve, but some of the stories your compatriots tell are soul-destroying.

One has been here for a year now. His fourteen-year-old son was walking home from school when he was set upon by a gang of English boys. They whacked him with a plank and stole his bus money. Your own children will, you hope, be starting school at some point. But they have no friends and hardly anyone has even talked to them. And the schools around here sound frightening: no respect for teachers, high truancy and a lot of bullying. You begin to think you'd be better off teaching them yourself.

You apply for teaching jobs but quickly realise you are going to have to lower your sights. None of your qualifications seem to count for anything here. People look at your CV as if it's a pack of lies.

Finally, after much pleading, you get to see the only mixed-sex school in your area, but the news isn't good. They can take your boy, but not your girl. But the coursework looks very basic anyway – subjects your son learned two years ago. You decide to wait until you can find a school which both your children can attend, even if this means moving flats or travelling. It crosses your mind that you could start your own school for refugee children, but where on earth would you begin?

Increasingly you find yourself wondering: What kind of a country is this? Plenty of times now you've heard people muttering that you should bloody well be packed off back to wherever you came from. A few weeks ago you felt as if you were being rescued by this great country, by these kind strangers. You wonder if you'll ever feel that way again.

Such a picture may or may not be typical, but it is certainly common. However, how many countries in the world could and would provide a flat, a school, a hospital and some petty cash for someone down on their luck? Until the last half-century or so, it was not on offer even here. Systematic help for refugees is still one of the world's newer and braver ideas. It is odd that so many Britons – some because it offers too little, others because it offers too much – find it a source not of pride but of shame. Immigration is, after all, a compliment, a tribute to our opportunity-rich economy, our humane (if overstretched) social services, our already polyglot culture, our historic civil liberties, and our rickety but ancient reputation for fairness and justice.

It isn't hard to feel that the protagonist of this migrant parable deserves a better break. But such sentiments inevitably clash with the bigger picture. How many immigrants should we take? On what basis should we select and reject them? These are quandaries that cannot be addressed without bitter argument and a high degree of injustice. We have grown accustomed to believing that where there are problems there must be solutions, and that the failure to find them can signal only incompetence or ill-will. In this case, the closest thing to a simple answer is that immigration will remain a powerful (even irresistible) force in world affairs while wealth remains so unevenly distributed. Only when it is no longer so urgent or desirable to migrate in search of a better life in Europe or America will the pressure ease.

Friction, meanwhile, is inevitable. And on this point there are, again, two opposing views. Leaving aside the barmier claims that migrants are all disease-ridden, criminally inclined scoundrels who have no place in our well-mannered, sceptred land, there is a sensible argument that they have been arriving on a scale that stretches our strained welfare resources, provokes social unease (true, though holding the migrants alone responsible is mischievous) and provides, in some cases, cover and opportunity for criminals. The opposing argument states that the demonisation of asylum-seekers is both vindictive and misjudged. It looks at a system that imprisons young children for months, and concludes that we are neglecting our moral duty. It suggests that asylum-seekers bring cultural enrichment as well as entrepreneurial drive: above all, they are individuals striving to live by our own ideals for self-improvement and betterment.

The awkward thing about these two extreme views is that they are both true, or at least contain truth. Immigrants are not all the same. They represent the full spectrum of human types: dreamers and schemers, rascals and rogues, saints and villains. Looked at *en masse*, it is possible to say that the numbers represent a social challenge to which our country may not be equal. But the individual predicaments that comprise this mass can produce a lump in even the toughest throat: parents whose children have been hacked at with machetes in front of their disbelieving eyes; families whose homes have disappeared in mudslides or earthquakes; professors running for their lives because of an abstract political doctrine that brands them parasites; peasants whose crops have failed; devout people whose rulers have a different religion; romantics who have fallen in love with someone of the wrong sort, or the wrong class, or the wrong sex. There is no easy way to impose quotas on predicaments such as these.

In early 2004 London's newspapers once again transmitted sour warnings about the avalanche of migrants poised to land on Britain. The European Union was due to be enlarged in May, and itchy-fingered editors were happy to imagine entire populations heading straight for benefit-rich Britain. 'Asylum UK' sang the *Daily Mail*; the *Daily Express* warned of a 'huge gipsy invasion'. Many alarming figures were bandied about, but the most reliable guide remained the 2001 Census – a survey of some 20 million homes. It showed that Britain's population had risen by two million in the previous decade, and now stood at 58,789,194 (a full million lower than the prevailing estimates). Migration, netted out, had swelled the figure by approximately 50,000 per year in the previous decade: three and a half million people had come to live in Britain; three million had left. It meant that 7.9 per cent of the total population belonged to a so-called ethnic minority, and fewer than half of these were immigrants: the majority had been born here. Britain was eagerly accepting up to 150,000 new residents (in line with government targets), and reluctantly processing a further 103,000 (or 110,000 according to the OECD) asylum-seekers each year. If the south-east felt 'swamped', it was partly because of the steady drift within the British Isles: the Census noted that the population of Scotland had sunk by 2 per cent in a decade, depressed by the number of evacuees heading for London.

In the context of a world where such comings and goings had become a fact of life, in a world that contained an estimated 175 million such migrants, Britain was being only lightly brushed. But by most historic measures it was still a sharp demographic explosion. And to the average Briton it remained a confusing modern phenomenon, one whose consequences could not easily be glimpsed.

Scholars began to construct 'theories' of migration – explanations that put political and cultural considerations alongside the usual economic logic of push-pull, and which sought to rethink the relationships between migration, welfare, sovereignty and 'globalisation'. They tended to celebrate migration in principle, and even wondered whether the low rates of immigration in nations such as Japan were contributing to economic stagnation; and tickled away at the so-called 'liberal paradox' – the philosophical difficulty Western democracies face when they seek to deny the very freedoms on which they themselves were founded. In the gaps between these yawning abstractions, newcomers continued to set foot on British soil, much as they always had. Senior economists emphasised that they were likely to enhance prosperity, since the majority were in the energetic 16–24 age group. Social studies emphasised that whereas in the last two decades of the twentieth century six women arrived for every five men, migration had once again become the province of single men. It remained to a huge extent a story for south-east England. Only 2.5 per cent of migrants made their way to multi-cultural Wales; just 2.2 per cent settled in the cosmopolitan north-east; a skinny 0.7 per cent crossed the water to Northern Ireland. In England, Chinese and Indian children were the top performers at school. New ceremonies were introduced to ritualise the award of citizenship; new schemes were proposed to store asylum-seekers overseas (in someone else's backyard). The system continued to groan. But the ancient pulse of national life – the rhythmic flow of people coming and going – continued to thud away like a heartbeat.

At some point we may arrive at a public consensus over how many migrants we, as a society, can admit; what we can offer and withhold; how we can deter those we reject; and how we can police them. In the meantime, we can only note that the contrasts evident in the mass of migrants are also true of British people: we too can be either flamboyant or stolid, honest or treacherous, selfless or sleazy. In the end, we may have to admit that immigrants are just like us. The Labour MP Oona King (a black Jewish Briton) put it as well as anyone when she said that she knew Jews who hated blacks, and blacks who hated whites. 'You see,' she joked, 'we're all the same underneath.' It is hard to imagine a time when Britons might be obliged or eager to pay £5,000 to an obvious criminal for some false papers and a place in the back of a container lorry bound for Baghdad. But if life really is a lottery, as the old proverb has it, then take a long look at that person in the queue in Croydon, or cleaning offices in Manchester, or delivering pizzas in Leicester, or mowing grass in Canterbury. It is an uncomfortable thought, but it really could be you.

The Identity Parade

One of the most suggestive tableaux in English historical folklore concerns the celebrated moment when Henry Stanley tracked down David Livingstone in his missionary camp near Lake Victoria. Livingstone was already a radiant figure, haloed by mystique, and the search for him in the unmapped headwaters of the Nile had the kind of fabled overtones of the lunar landing a century later. Stanley's famous greeting expressed the drama of the moment more precisely than any photograph. 'Dr Livingstone, I presume.' It seemed so frightfully English, so patently tailored to the occasion. After a long, momentous and death-defying journey of exploration, aching with sweat, thirst and fatigue, Stanley still had the wit to obey the understated niceties of clubland etiquette; he addressed Livingstone as if hailing a colleague through a mist of after-dinner pipe smoke. The ostentatious courtesy of his remark, with its pointed insistence on the need for sober decorum at such a time, was wonderfully aligned with the classic imperatives of English composure and reserve. God was in his heaven; all was well with the world; we could still count on the English to keep up appearances. That the encounter was in fact between an ambitious Welsh-born American and a pious Scot was insufficient to prevent it from becoming an enduring English myth.

The English are famously – sometimes proudly – xenophobic. Foreign languages are 'mumbo-jumbo', 'double Dutch' or 'all Greek to me'; sports commentators find it hilarious when their colleagues stumble over a foreign name, whereas a cultivated immigrant who slightly mispronounces an English word is thought an utter dunce. Tributes to this tendency are so common, and chime so neatly with our good-natured talent for self-deprecation, that the contrary view is less often heard. Yet there is a national knack almost amounting to genius for appropriating foreign influences and co-opting them as our own. This might be an extension of the way Englishness imposed itself on the Scottish, Welsh and Irish members of the British union: they were free to provide folksy decor – kilts, bagpipes, male-voice choirs, jigs – but the serious issues were dominated by English manners and beliefs. This grew into a reflex condescension, which expanded into a feverish colonial itch. Centuries of hoisting our flag over other people's possessions ingrained in us a magpie instinct. The Victorian mania for museums, the urge to trawl exotic artefacts into orderly British collections, fostered a suave willingness to think of foreign bodies not merely as British-owned, but as British. The long controversy over the Elgin Marbles – the sculptures retrieved from the Parthenon in the nineteenth century – still founders on an obstinate sense that they really are British, on the grounds that they were just lying there unwanted and that 'we' picked them up.

On the face of it, such a presumptuous cast of thought is at one with Britain's stolid reputation as an introverted fortress. It can, however, express itself in surprising ways, as an easygoing ability to embrace any foreign prowess we might admire. Perhaps the boldest example of this is the ascent of Everest. It was wholeheartedly celebrated as a major British triumph, proof that we were still paramount explorers, could still attain summits. The plain facts of the matter – that a New Zealander and a Nepalese had reached the top – were swept into oblivion by a wave of national pride.*

Perhaps it was easy for a colonial nation to imagine that Tenzing and Hillary were British underneath. But there are many instances of national highlights turning out to be expressions (sometimes fervent, sometimes opportunistic) not of patriotism but of Anglophilia. Hardly anything seems more British than the music of Handel, an immigrant composer who became little less than the orchestral spin doctor to the new British monarchy – indeed, to the Empire. When George I inherited the British Crown, he requested, as part of a public-relations campaign to impress his new subjects, a riverside concert. His chosen composer contrived the perfect soundtrack. Handel had already spent three years in London as the guest of Lord Burlington in Piccadilly, so he knew

---

*Britain was not alone in indulging such sentiments. Tenzing Norgay wrote about the pain he suffered when India and Nepal, hoping to anoint him a hero of their own, sought to detach him from Sir Edmund Hillary and the team of which they were both a part. It remains common today for Sherpas employed by foreign expeditions to be prevented from setting foot on top. This is partly to ensure they do not qualify for a 'summit bonus', but also to maintain the subtle imperial pecking order in which climbing with heavy equipment is less celebrated than ascending with a lighter load. 'We' were mountaineers; 'they' only porters.

enough of English musicology, such as it was, to strike the right note. Indeed, his *Water Music* so impressed the King that it was replayed three times that very night. And this was only the beginning. Shortly before his death, George I signed Handel's naturalisation papers, so the composer was on hand to produce a coronation march for the new King, George II. The resulting music gave the Hanoverian dynasty, and the Crown, an evocative new theme: 'Zadok the Priest' has been played at every British coronation since. Like 'Rule Britannia', Handel's music evokes images of plumed Horseguards parading down the Mall, solemn celebrations in the Abbey, fleets pushing out to sea, and the Union Flag fluttering from a brilliant white flagpole. But it was the work of a migrant crowd-pleaser with perfect pitch.

Along with the *Messiah* (1742) and the *Music for the Royal Fireworks* (1749), these resonant compositions have been integral to defining and broadcasting the grandeur of British royalty for over 250 years. Even the *Messiah*, Britain's favourite oratorio, acquired a profound patriotic tinge. When Wagner visited London in 1855, he saw an audience rise to its feet during the 'Hallelujah Chorus', for all the world as if it were the national anthem. 'True, Handel was not an Englishman by birth,' wrote Samuel Butler, 'but no one was ever more thoroughly English.'[1] Handel, in this view, was simply a passive medium for the expression or transmission of a force larger than himself: Englishness. Had Butler been privy to Handel's saltier asides on British musical appreciation he might have been more willing to consider the notion that the composer did not merely 'capture' the peculiar character of the British soul, but helped to invent it.* And by presenting it as a bold, resolute chorus, he was flattering it outrageously. The Britain championed in his music is heroic, united and devout. It seems apt that the first classical music ever recorded (on an imported Edison phonograph) was a chorus from his *Israel in Egypt*, performed at the Crystal Palace Handel Festival in 1888. By then, Handel lay in Westminster Abbey, sanctified as a British legend.

There are other such instances. In his book on Anglophilia, *Voltaire's Coconuts*, Ian Buruma recalled the sentimental crescendo at the end of the 1935 film *The Scarlet Pimpernel*, when Leslie Howard, playing the dashing hero who has been flitting across the Channel to liberate the harassed friends of the British aristocracy, returns with his beloved and sees ahead of him the white cliffs of Dover. The music swells beneath his keel. 'Look,' he murmurs, only a little tired after his brave exertions in France. 'England!' It's a scene of blunt patriotism, charged with love for the familiar landscape and all it seems to represent: freedom, ease, dependability. Yet this image was contrived by three Hungarians. The producer, Alexander Korda, was busy putting this and other great moments

---

*Handel once said that to impress London concertgoers, the composer had to hit them smack between the ears – nothing less would do.

of British history on to the British silver screen; the writer was his fellow émigré Lajos Biro; and the actor, hired specifically because he epitomised the English gentleman, was Leslie Howard – whose real surname was Stainer, and whose parents were immigrants.

Korda and his cohorts were part of a sizeable overseas contribution to British cinema which has produced more than its fair share of such native-seeming archetypes. The bumbling army officer Colonel Blimp – an affectionate tribute to the jolly good chap – was the creation of another Hungarian, the screenwriter Emeric Pressburger. Other film-makers such as Joseph Losey (*The Servant*) and Karel Reisz brought foreign perspectives to their visions of Britain's emotional landscape and fortified a cherished upstairs–downstairs mythology. Was the portrayal of the butler in *The Remains of the Day* based on an inherited sense of the hidden traps of a class-conscious society? Or was it moulded by a Japanese sense of ceremony and restraint, of a sort we might expect from an author (Kazuo Ishiguro) who was born in Nagasaki? Of course, we can concede that a foreign sensibility might easily see us more vividly and in bolder outline than we see ourselves. It was not a coincidence that the presiding inspiration for the film came from Ismail Merchant, whose loving visions of Edwardian manners won him six Oscars. But we must also recognise that, like Handel, these artists were not merely absorbing the local character: they were dramatising a notion of Britishness that was already a lucid, well-formed part of the imaginative baggage they brought with them. If we so desire, we could even see such works as sycophantic or heartfelt thank-yous, repeating the easiest caricature of Britishness. Artists carry their own aesthetic idioms with them. While Japanese painters in London could make Hyde Park look like Kyoto in the cherry-blossom season; an English artist travelling the other way could hardly avoid representing Japan as the spitting image of Buckinghamshire.

It is enough to remind us of something now very unfashionable: a Jewish joke. In England in the 1950s there were two Jews, refugees from the war, whose paths would cross from time to time. Their conversations always followed the same pattern.

'How's your health?'

'Wonderful. Couldn't be better.'

'Family all well?'

'Thriving.'

'Business?'

'Booming.'

'So what's the matter? Why so glum?'

'Oh, it's these damned British. You know ... it's subtle, insidious, ever-present. You can feel it in a handshake, see it in a glance. I just feel I'll never truly fit in, never be fully accepted.'

'Oh, that,' said his friend. 'Listen, all you need to do is get yourself some proper English clothes. Go to Savile Row. Wrap yourself in tweed. It makes all the difference, I tell you.'

Several months later, they met again. This time, the man was dressed like a duke, but he still looked depressed.

'My God,' said his friend. 'You look just the ticket. But why the long face? Health all right?'

'Fit as a fiddle.'

'Family?'

'No, everyone's fine.'

'Business?'

'Couldn't be better.'

'So what is it? Don't tell me you still feel excluded.'

His friend lowered his eyes gloomily. 'It's worse than that,' he said, in a voice more mournful than ever. 'We lost the Empire.'

There were several versions of this gag in circulation in the 1950s. One featured a German immigrant who was offered naturalisation. 'What?' he exclaimed. 'Without India?' Such jokes bought laughs by depicting immigrants as pretentious, as having ideas above their station – they were put-downs. These days, they're more likely to make us blush than smile. But we can still enjoy the acute sense of immigrant disappointment: the revelation that the country they have joined was falling short of their high expectations.

When people say that migrants are 'more English than the English', it often means only that migrants are aping the more pronounced characteristics of Englishness. The Hungarian writer George Mikes, who came to London in 1938 and never left (and found an obliging publisher in a fellow Hungarian, André Deutsch), poked fun at this habit in *How to Be a Brit*. 'I have spent the best years of my life becoming a true Englishman,' he wrote, 'and now the whole country is turning alien.' This was a joshing reference to decimalisation. 'When the furlong, the chain, the rod, pole and perch, the peck, the bushel and the gill are gone,' he sighed, borrowing the why-oh-why intonation of the golf-club bore, 'Britain as an island will have disappeared.'[2]

A recent reincarnation of the same joke – the what-ho Indian couple in the television show *Goodness Gracious Me*, with their love of a pint down the local before the Sunday roast – tickled funny bones because the characters forlornly mimicked a form of Englishness that scarcely exists any more. Today, when some boroughs and towns (Brent, Newham, Leicester) have populations in which white people are in the minority, such presentations of 'Englishness' – it is hard to see anything as characteristic of 'Britishness' these days – are even more blatant caricatures. Indeed, it is barely a surprise when an Ascot-and-Henley *Spectator* columnist who cheers Enoch Powell's speeches and describes Africa as 'bongo-bongo land' turns out to be no scion of the ancient shires but a Greek millionaire, Taki Theodoracopoulos. Immigrants often align themselves with national stereotypes with special zeal. Three of the greatest tyrants in history – Napoleon, Hitler and Stalin – were all born outside the nations they inspired, misled, brutalised and came to represent.

One could even say that 'Englishness' is by definition a foreign idea – a silhouette visible only from afar. Only those equipped with the means of comparison can discern the outline of our national character. If societies reveal themselves most transparently in the assumptions they do not question, then it is inevitable that these remain unquestioned by natives, and hence hidden.* Of course, the national character as seen from afar can often be comically dated. A British Council Survey in 2001 discovered that Britain is still thought of – in Japan, Nigeria, Greece and China – as a land of top hats and afternoon tea, kings and queens and arrogant racists. Nearly everyone believed contemporary British achievements such as the Internet (the brainchild of Tim Berners-Lee) and Viagra (perfected in a Kent laboratory) to be American inventions. In Britain itself, meanwhile, men and women continue to define themselves more boldly by what they are not than by what they are. Englishness, tiptoeing between rival nationalisms, sometimes feels like nothing so much as an absence, meaning little more to most people than 'not foreign'. National identity is often a statement of opposition to outside forces; a form, more or less, of protest.

Englishness, then (which ought to be less nebulous than its ageing relative Britishness), is Janus-faced. To a foreigner, it appears as a caricature; to a native, it is a defence mechanism; to both, it suggests some indefinable yet vital essence of this soil, this history, this climate, this topography. There are anthologies of poetical tributes to its pastoral charm, its bewitching sense of proportion, its greenery, its soft, refreshing rain. John Betjeman (descended from a Dutch furniture-maker who came to London in the 1820s) was writing from the heart when he described the sadness he felt watching Kent recede behind him as he stood on the lurching deck of a ship. 'Those lucky people waving from the shore,' he wrote. 'They can go back to change their books at the library, read the evening paper, fix the black-out curtain, put the kettle on, let the dog out, or go to a lecture on the Home Guard.' This homesickness was sharpened by wartime anxieties, but he later gave a fuller summary of what his England was all about:

---

*For example: the chief characteristic of an Englishman, to an Australian, is that we whinge. And who, reading the endless jeremiads in our newspapers about the railways, the schools, the neighbours, the government, the price of houses, the average wage, our national football team, the plight of women who work, the plight of women who don't work, the violence and ignorance of our teenagers, the weather and a hundred other things that are 'collapsing', can deny it?

> For me, at any rate, England stands for the Church of England,
> eccentric incumbents, oil-lit churches, Women's Institutes, modest
> village inns, arguments about cow parsley on the altar, the noise of
> mowing machines on Saturday afternoons, local newspapers, local
> auctions, the poetry of Tennyson, Crabbe, Hardy and Matthew Arnold,
> local talent, local concerts, a visit to the cinema, branch-line trains, light
> railways, leaning on gates and looking across fields . . . heavily ticking
> church clocks, modest post offices, creeper-clad warden's cottages,
> rusty croquet hoops on rectory lawns, swinging inn signs and well-
> stocked gardens where brick paths lead through thyme and
> vegetables.[3]

The two most important words in this passage are 'For me'. Betjeman did not
hide the extent to which he was writing about himself, his own inclinations
and fancies; but some of his admirers have taken this whimsical self-portrait
as if it were a sharp-eyed summary of English life. Much the same has
happened with George Orwell's delineation of England as a stoic land of 'solid
breakfasts and gloomy Sundays, smoking towns and winding roads, green
fields and red pillar-boxes'.[4] This is more recognisable than Betjeman's
Sunday-afternoon Utopia, but only slightly: indeed, in adding industrial
grime to the picture, Orwell ups the pathos without greatly enlarging the
angle of vision. Neither is inclusive; both invite not a nod of recognition but
a pang, a sob over the dissolution of a homely, unpretentious ideal. John
Major's famous vision of Britain as a place where old maids cycle home after
evensong owes more to Betjeman's ecclesiastical reverie than to any
recollection of his own – it can hardly have been characteristic of his childhood
in Brixton. And Bill Bryson relied on similar atmospherics in his lavishly
popular paeans to British life. Again, he was loved not for delivering a good-
natured outline of his own sensibility and preferences – for Ordnance Survey
maps, musty bookshops, footpaths through bracken, smoky railway stations
and Marmite on toast by a cheap gas fire – but for nailing the national
character on the head.

Orwell himself once pointed out that those who describe books as
fashionable usually mean only that such books are popular with people under
thirty. By the same token, people who contrive thumbnail sketches of national
identity are usually lamenting the passing of their own youth, the fraying of
the iconography with which they grew up. A cross-section of Britain today
would include the ticking of church clocks and the stack of shoes at the door
of a mosque; the scarlet blaze of a letter box and the smell of corn grilling at
the Notting Hill Carnival; the bleat of new-born lambs and the rasp of Muzak
in shopping malls; sponge cakes in village halls and the flash of gold and
turquoise in a passing sari; the fine mist of water sprinklers on suburban

lawns and the blare of police sirens at night; the lilt of choirs heard across fields and the roar from the nearby dual carriageway. There is no coherent picture in such disparate glimpses, nor should we try to construct one. If anything defines modern Britain, it is variety, the sense of often clashing flavours.

By the same token, our national identity is no longer easy to summarise. When people speak of the 'typical' English character, they are usually picturing a figure who might be played by Edward Fox or Hugh Grant (or, in its more abrasive incarnations, Bob Hoskins or Michael Caine). And this is only partly because of Hollywood's insistence on the deployment of English actors in roles that call for a supercilious, foppish, shifty or sadistic disposition. In seeing our national characteristics manifested in Nelson or Churchill or Florence Nightingale, we are only choosing which aspect of the national character we wish to emphasise. We rarely propose Ronnie Biggs as 'typical', for this would define us as a nation of roguish crooks and chancers. We rarely cite Harold Shipman, Hindley and the Wests as emblematic, for who wants to be a nation of perverts and murderers? We choose our stereotypes, and then permit them to govern us – as slogans or advertisements of our identity.

One of the reasons why traditional definitions of national identity carry a weaker charge than before is that they are class-specific, and thus not universal, at a time when Britain itself is in any case losing coherence as a binding agent in our affairs. In popular culture, 'Britain' grows ever more remote, a historical, public-school notion cherishable only by retired colonels and mandarins. Devolution, meanwhile, is both responding to and sponsoring a disintegration of the British idea into more compact units of pride which emphasise identities that can plausibly be projected as non-English. Scottish, Welsh and Irish folklores are paraded as bright tokens of subjugated national identity, thriving on a delight in not being English, and leaving Englishness as a bewildered grey area stranded between vivid banners: Burns Night, St Patrick's Day and the Eisteddfod are celebrated with more vibrancy and brio than St George's Day, even in Guildford. The limitations of such narrow identities are clear enough: the kilts-and-thistles iconography of Scottish nationalism sprang a leak when Scotland announced, in 2003, an 'aggressive drive' to encourage immigrants, an acknowledgement that poor economic growth and weak business dynamism were linked to the absence of such migrants. But even within England itself the regional gulfs are deep: Truro and Teesside are divided by more than miles; Tower Hamlets rarely compares notes with Tunbridge Wells. The fact that the most obvious symbol of national pride – the flag of St George – has been co-opted by such uninspiring loyalists as the British National Party and football hooligans only adds to the sense in which patriotism, for many English people, had become troublesome and embarrassing until it was given a brilliant new gloss by the rugby team that won the 2003 World Cup in Australia.

But it is immigration, above all, which exposes the traditional sense of national identity as a mirage. It leaves us with so few credible national archetypes, no single banner beneath which all the varieties of modern Briton can rally. In its place, in the absence of a common flagpole on which we can hoist our colours, we have an identity parade. Recent culture has supported a crescendo of identity politics along sexual, religious and many other lines. What we are – what we feel – often seems more significant than what we do or think. And no social signifier is as powerful as ethnic identity.

One of the most obvious effects of modern migration is the way in which settlers from the Commonwealth, having built a permanent presence in the national life in the face of much hostility and nervousness, have initiated discussions on what it means to be British today. What is it, though, this thing called 'ethnic identity'? Like all such abstractions, it is a problematic amalgam of separate and sometimes contestable inferences, in common parlance little more than a euphemism for unmentionable racial facts: above all, a matter of blood and descent. Modern genetic research is often hijacked by this impulse to pin people to their roots like butterflies to a frame. The not-so-tacit and frankly reactionary assumption is that, wriggle as we might, there is no escaping our biological destiny. But ethnic identity must be more than merely a biological or genetic property: it is overlaid with religious and linguistic overtones, with historical, sexual and culinary traditions and taboos. And it is usually held to be supranational: Chinese migrants and their children seem irreducibly Chinese, just as a Geordie in Japan remains incorrigibly English.

'Ethnic identity' is an especially slippery concept because it has been tugged in so many different directions. On the one hand, the world is cross-pollinating: migration and intermarriage are stirring once-distinct racial characteristics into a stew. On the other, ethnic allegiances flow into the vacuums left by pinched national mythologies, offering the satisfactions of belonging to peoples who feel fragmented and atomised. On the one hand, the world grows homogeneous and at the mercy of mass-processed global norms, especially in the field of what is amusingly known as 'popular' culture: the most centrally planned, conventional and inescapable culture of them all. On the other, marketing and fashion pursue an energetic policy (divide and sell) to herd people into easily defined consumer niches. So even as 'ethnicity' becomes more questionable as a way of categorising people, it grows ever more tenacious. The children of migrants are often more outgoing than their parents, keener to explore and absorb the culture of the country they were born in rather than the one their parents left behind; but their children occasionally revive rather than abandon the convictions of their grandparents. In the process, subtle new 'ethnic identities' are born every day.

Terms stretched this far eventually wilt. And 'ethnic identity' is one that becomes less meaningful the more widely it is used. Initially, it had a religious implication: it meant non-Christian. Today it is more commonly a political construct, a label applied either by the dominant ethnic group (implicitly defined as having no ethnic identity to speak of) to describe people with different beliefs, different habits or a different skin colour; or by minorities insisting on their own cultural and political rights. Either way, it is schismatic, promoting the idea of differences too extreme to be bridged. It harbours a sense of superiority: it carries the word 'minority' as a shadow, and can be used as an adjective, as if ethnicity were a mere accessory – as in 'ethnic' food, furniture or clothes. It becomes a mere style. The sari can be flaunted by anyone as a badge of adventurous and cosmopolitan tastes.

There are similar contradictions in what at first sight appear to be sternly opposed points of view: the hard-line, immigrants-are-ruining-our-country argument, and the more liberal impulse to defend, help, support and encourage migrants. They disagree, but are united by an assumption that 'ethnic' denotes a junior role in our affairs, a dependent status that requires 'our' intervention. Hawks reckon that someone who hasn't been reared on the Book of Common Prayer, who hasn't sung 'Jerusalem' a thousand times or laughed at Morecambe and Wise, can possibly be British. They go on to insist that migrants should abandon whatever nasty habits and beliefs they have brought from overseas, defer enthusiastically to local prejudices and do their best to 'fit in'. Doves argue, on the contrary, that settlers here need the support of their own, not British, culture – that they are entitled to import their own ways of life and that Britain's uglier impulses of racism and discrimination must not be allowed to restrict this process. Hawks reckon that immigrants should be taught English and must learn to love *Coronation Street*. Doves think that they must not lose the connection with their own 'cultural heritage'. Broadly speaking, these are the gulfs between nationalists and pluralists; between those who wish to raise a telescope to their eyepatch and pretend that Britain has not changed and those for whom it has not changed enough. At times, the gap between these two positions seems irreconcilable. But both share a reflexive, belittling superiority to the 'ethnic identities' they denounce or defend. Both presume seniority, feel that a certain level of deference or gratitude is appropriate. Neither argues that what the migrants feel or believe is none of our business.

There are signs that the sometimes inflexible ideologies that have dominated the politics of identity are breaking down and dispersing. There is already a narrative behind the seemingly uneven flow of intellectual developments in this area. Broadly speaking, the first generations of Commonwealth migrants were expected to assimilate, to 'fit in', to adapt to their new home and discard the cultural inheritance they brought with them. This was the view expressed with reckless eloquence by Enoch Powell and his more rabid supporters. When combined with an unimaginative refusal to believe that Caribbean or Indian people were capable of such a feat, it took childish forms: 'Get out of our country . . . Britain for the British'. Far from prevailing, this attitude created a backlash, and a contrary idea that in a free country migrants were at liberty to observe whatever cultural customs they liked gained ascendancy. This was multiculturalism, and it too created as many enemies as it did friends. What seemed considerate to some seemed divisive and patronising to others: the idea that people should not adapt was just as simplistic as the demand that they should. Moreover, in seeming so rooted in gestures of protest, in a rejection of the prevailing 'British' value system, it set different cultures on conflicting paths. Most crucially, it failed to imagine a common ground between or above cultural difference, a civic platform where all people could meet on equal terms as fellow citizens. In the political arena, multiculturalism (by now an ungainly substitute for 'racially mixed') began to seem a logical impossibility: a nation had to reconcile entitlements and rights, policing areas where they infringed on each other; it could not gratify all urges to power. So the search party moved on again. These days, the buzzword is 'polycultural', which suggests a richer and less hermetic relationship between different peoples.*

In all of this theoretical bantering on identities and rights between ethnic categories, however, it is unsettling that these groups are discussed as if they are things rather than people. This serves no one but the enemies of migrants: those whom you wish to keep out or deport you must first dehumanise. There is nothing so likely to make a British audience melt as an individual plight, and nothing so likely to harden its heart as the translation of individual pleas into collective demands. People who would wince at the prospect of separating a pregnant mother from her children and pushing her on to a plane can easily be persuaded to 'repel boarders'. People who would not dream of refusing help to a child fleeing torture can applaud the removal of 'bogus claimants'. But it takes an effort of imagination to see these amorphous and unwelcome groups as individuals, with ideas and projects, sorrows, talents, fears and hopes of their own. And this extends to all generalised projections of racial or ethnic identity. They trample over and bury the much more resonant, and much less threatening, traces of individual lives.

Migrants have written often and heatedly about the claustrophobic side-

---

*Strictly speaking, 'multi-' and 'poly-' mean the same thing – 'many'; the first is Latin, the second Greek. But there is now a distinction: multicultural suggests an array of discrete cultures; polycultural suggests a mixture of ingredients too closely entwined to be distinct, a whole greater than the sum of the parts. In emphasising the connections rather than the barriers between cultures, it is plainly the more cohesive and optimistic, though equally unlovely, term.

effects of such thinking, whether in its most brazen form (racism) or in one of its better-intentioned guises. The cultural priority given to 'roots' – a stab at profundity based on a loose sense that 'root' causes are the ones that matter – is so strong that it can lead us to neglect what is happening to the branches and leaves. Thus 'black' artists are often assumed to be addressing 'black' audiences or 'black' issues – which they sometimes are and sometimes are not. Thus Afro-Caribbean boys in British schools are crushed between high expectations at home (the severity of West Indian parenting is famous) and rock-bottom expectations at school, where one slip of the pen in English lit. and it's off to woodwork for the lot of them.

The identities created in opposition to such prejudices can be equally limiting. 'Somehow', wrote the Montserrat-born writer Ferdinand Dennis, who sailed to Southampton when he was eight, 'I had journeyed from being a Jamaican child immigrant in Britain to becoming Black, a Black Briton . . . Being Black meant being radical, dreadlocked, anti-establishment, belonging to the "other" Britain united by a common experience of racism.'[5] Men such as Dennis felt 'imprisoned' in such a narrow identity, trapped by this strange collusion between enemies and friends. They declined to settle for so narrow and limited a role.

Many such categorisations, be they racist or anti-racist, have collapsed under the weight of their own clumsiness. To speak these days of both Sinhalese and Bengalis – let alone Chinese and East Africans – as 'Asian' is as sloppy and indiscriminate as it would be to twin Swedes and Portuguese. To think of Nigerians, Jamaicans and Guyanese as essentially, primarily 'black' is to overlook cultural distinctions as marked as those that distinguish Wales from Italy. Just as a retired English teacher in Spain might not feel the least twinge of kinship with the lager louts who maraud along his beaches in the summer, waving their Union Flags and backsides in the faces of perplexed local citizens, so many Jamaicans were quick to notice and dismiss the so-called 'smallies' among their fellow travellers – people from the more diminutive Caribbean islands. Don't try to tell a Trinidadian of Indian descent (such as V. S. Naipaul) that he seems no different from his Afro-Caribbean compatriots. And what does a Sri Lankan in Britain 'feel'? Asian? Buddhist? Tamil? Sinhalese? British? English? None of these? All of them? There is no answer to such questions, just as there is none available to the Britons whose parents were part of the Indian exodus from East Africa when they are confronted with the unthinking enquiry: 'Where are you from?'

Nothing is dissolving stiff conceptions of 'ethnic identity' faster than the steady rise of a new category: mixed race. Understandably, there were some murmurs of discontent when the category was included in the 2001 census, inviting respondents to pinpoint their 'ethnic and cultural background'. 'Mixed' might mean something biologically, but it makes little sense as an ethnic identity. It was only a census form – a necessarily blunt attempt to get a handle on the changing nature of Britain's population – so some of the public complaints about its insensitivity may have been overcooked. But it did indicate again the priority still attached to racial background as a categorical imperative.

Ethnic identities are the leopard's spots of modern sociology: they are usually thought to be indelible. If that is true, however, why then do migrant families, and the social agencies agitating on their behalf, so often worry that children, when exposed to new influences, might 'lose' their ethnic identity altogether? If it is immutable, how can it be so easily imperilled, so lightly mislaid? In this context, ethnic identity is not even skin-deep, but a cultural construct requiring constant nurture and maintenance.

In pondering whether ethnic identities can be lost or supplanted, people usually limit themselves to judgements about what people other than themselves should do with theirs. So I often wonder what I would lose if I lost mine. How does Britishness express itself in me? In a fondness for Chinese duck, Indian chicken, Jamaican coffee and French bread? In a reverence for Mozart, or a devotion to writers from Buenos Aires, Prague, Chicago and St Lucia? In a liking for mountainous scenery, or a dislike of crowds? In a preference for sunshine over rain, wine over beer? In a secular fondness for cathedrals, or a weakness for cricket? In an automatic attachment to liberty, privacy, justice, order, freedom of speech, fresh water, limitless electricity, sexual freedom, a plentiful supply of food, hot baths in winter, easy access to doctors and lawyers, all-night shops, helpful neighbours, milk deliveries, more-or-less reliable postmen, telephones, holidays in the sun, libraries, televised football, old people's homes, sewage works, rubbish collection, zebra crossings, National Trust scenery, garden centres, cinemas and the hundreds of other fine things people take for granted as natural rights rather than social achievements?

Is this a typically British list? Yes.

Is it exclusively British? Absolutely not.

This is where the proposition that ethnic or national identities are decisive and inviolable really founders, because if I have anything to declare in my cultural luggage it is primarily to do with class. The set of tastes and attitudes listed above might be shared by anyone of similar background and education from Argentina to Zimbabwe, from Denmark to Palestine, from India to Venezuela. An Egyptian lawyer has more in common – in terms of what he or she expects out of life – with a Canadian lawyer than with the beggar who lives at the bottom of the street. The coolness so often interpreted by migrants as ethnic hostility is sometimes class sensitivity in disguise. Indeed, given that ethnic minorities are often thought of as junior members of society, it is all too easy for ethnicity to be sublimated into the already firm hierarchies of class consciousness. 'Ethnic' can even be a slur, meaning little more than 'peasant' or 'uncivilised'. Britain's immigrants have often found themselves in such a cruel double bind. Relegated by racism to the bottom rung of the social ladder and the lower tier of the labour market, they are then resented by workmates and neighbours for having ideas above their station, for making so insultingly evident their distaste for their surroundings, their desire to haul themselves and their children up to better things. In groping for a better deal, they often find themselves with the worst of both worlds.

There will not soon be an end to such discussions of identity and belonging; indeed it is important that these subjects are debated. But it is now a fact that Britain, and especially England, is a nation of knotted ethnic roots. We only have to tune in to the range of languages accessible on our radios, or glance at our skyline, to be reminded of it. There are 900 mosques and 150 Hindu temples in Britain; along with 365 synagogues, 250 Sikh *gurdwaras*, 160 Christian churches with Caribbean origins and 20 Buddhist houses. There are dozens of parishes for the Greek, Russian and Serbian Orthodox churches, while London's own Catholic churches are full of the Spanish, Portuguese, Polish, Italian and Filipino faithful. There are Armenian, Eritrean, Coptic, Ethiopian and Syrian Orthodox churches, too. In the history of these churches – legible from the names in their archives of births, marriages and deaths – is written a dazzling array of human life. We can see almost the same jostling of different flavours in any restaurant listing.

The attempt to pretend that all of this is merely a marginal aspect of British life has long since worn thin, yet it is still resilient. We continue to see 'white' as a non-colour – an absence of ethnicity – when a few primary-school experiments with prisms are enough to tell us that it is a joint venture between blue, red and green. This is in part because the political response to the 'threat' of migration has produced an ever-narrowing definition of national identity, one that relies ever more stringently on traditional blood ties. Whether politicians were bowing to public pressure or creating it is debatable. There are polemicists for both sides: some argue that successive governments led an otherwise placid populace into racism; others say that politicians were just giving voice to prejudices that afflicted the nation as a whole. Whatever the cause, the effect was both plain and unfortunate. At precisely the time when the national character was being diluted, attempts were made to distil it into its 'pure' form. The legal constraints imposed on immigration legitimised the feeling that modern migrants were invaders who needed to be fended off, and breathed life into the old idea that these newcomers did not belong here. Men or women who in 1948 were unquestionably British found themselves recategorised, first as 'coloured immigrants' and eventually, at the sad end of a sorry story, as 'asylum cheats'.

One of the other ways we trick ourselves into seeing Britain as ethnically stable is by habitually comparing ourselves with America. We – so this cosy myth runs – are the original, the work of art; America is the processed, mass-market reproduction. Americans collaborate with this myth by portraying us, in their popular culture, as quaint, dated, eccentric and listless versions of themselves. But the contrast is loaded. America is almost entirely composed of relatively recent migrants. Perhaps, if instead we compare ourselves to Japan, a nation with which we have much in common – both being small, crowded, rainy, industrious groups of islands with faded imperial airs and exorbitant house prices – then a different picture emerges. It is we who look like the melting pot, we who represent a vibrant image of plurality and variety.

To summarise: 'ethnic identity' is a catch-all intended to make rough-and-ready distinctions, for political and cultural reasons, without giving offence. Such catch-alls are inevitably loose; ultimately, they risk becoming drop-alls. But one cannot dismiss as trivial or insignificant something that means so much to so many, which implants and controls such fervent allegiances. It may be portable, a magic lamp dazzling enough to generate contrary ideas about identity. But it does mean something, and people mean something by it. However carefully we may think we have picked it to bits, it will always reform itself into something gritty and obdurate. Ethnic pride is intensified by opposition or hostility; it feeds on humiliation, and is made strident by it. This, if anything, makes pressing the need for a national identity spacious enough to encompass rather than resist the glittering ethnic blur of which Britain is now composed. This is a historic quest, one of the key political adventures on which Britain is now embarked: the search for a national identity in which ethnic conformity does not play a dominant part.

Such a nationality is not quite unprecedented. Germany and Italy are both federations of once-competing sovereignties. American patriotism manages to include a boisterous mixture of ethnic populations in its emphatic anthems. The architects of modern Europe seek to promote pride not in a nation but in a federation. But multicultural experiments often fail. India's Muslims insisted on their own territory, created Pakistan, and have ever since regarded their closest neighbours as their direst foes; Israelis and Palestinians, Greek and Turkish Cypriots – all resist co-habitation; Yugoslavia made a Mephistophelian pact with ethnic pride and fell into self-lacerating slaughter. The hot conflicts between Tamils and Sinhalese in Sri Lanka, or the Hutu and Tutsi in Rwanda stand as frightening reminders of the flammable nature of ethnicity: ethnic pride leads to ethnic rivalry leads to ethnic violence – it has a will not just to power but to autonomy. If the search for a British identity attractive enough to tranquillise the furies of the constituent parts is to prevail, then England, Scotland, Wales and Ireland can hardly afford to remain attached to the idea of themselves as convincing ethnic categories in their own rights.

The quandary remains: national identities need to be malleable and supple, but have to cohere around something. In the past, racial purity sufficed, and despite having been given a bad name so often, the concept still has teeth. But now in Britain the national identity needs to rely on something more interesting than racial typology. In a denationalising world, it needs to be nimble enough to embrace or ignore ethnic qualities rather than insulting them and elevating them into rivalries. It will need to articulate principles and values, rather than clinging exclusively to a selective mythology of past victories. It will need to occupy a civic terrain where private interests overlap to form the public sphere. And it will need to retreat from the private and spiritual arenas, freeing people to be as different-but-equal as they please. It needs to be symphonic, something more than a mere brassy fanfare. It probably needs to cohere around a lucid set of individual rights, so that the group to which any man, woman or child belongs is incidental rather than decisive. One thing is certain: the evolving national identity will be the product of long and angry disputes, and cannot be set in stone – it will always be a work-in-progress. But one day, perhaps, it will be natural for people to claim, as the Polish-born Jacob Bronowski once did, that they are British by choice . . . and proud of it.

Of what might such an identity consist? Why might anyone feel proud to be British? The sources of pride in our history are well established, though less well publicised than the sources of shame that inspire regretful mutterings in every pub and café in Britain: the laughable railways and pallid schools, the rotting hospitals, the cash-starved universities, the puerile politics, the frequent sporting disappointments, the managerial blight behind the Millennium Dome and the new Wembley Stadium, the greed and corruption in boardrooms, the police excesses, the trashiness of tabloid Britain and its infatuation with celebrity, the spectres of paedophilia, gang crime and murder, and lots more besides. It ought to be easy to be proud of a nation that gave birth to such resilient ideas of private liberty and public probity, a nation that threw off the twin yokes of an authoritarian religious supremacy and absolute monarchy long ago, in favour of a sturdy form of self-reliance and popular cooperation; a nation which believes in law rather than force as a solution to arguments a nation with a well-tempered mistrust of extremism; and a nation in which a well-ordered philosophy of public service still finds effective expression in the restrained and civil way in which most people behave. We can add that Britain has, in spite of everything that can be said about racism and injustice, an exceptionally long tradition of tolerance towards foreigners. For a thousand years, when the countries of their birth could not endure them, people have been able to thrive – or at least survive – here. The hope of this book is not that we can console ourselves with this outstanding fact while declining to lift any further fingers in that cause. It is simply that in narrating and celebrating it – admitting it, in some cases – our own national pride can feel less clenched, less besieged.

Some of the recent incarnations of our most cherished national traits stand in need of such revision. When we congratulate ourselves for the way we stood alone against Hitler, we have to remember that we didn't do any such thing. We stood together, supported by troops and workers from the British Empire. When we salute the postwar egalitarian ideal that produced the Welfare State, or the Reithian ethic that aimed to elevate public culture, we need to recognise the contribution of immigrants to this heady atmosphere, and to applaud the way the humanitarian goal has been widened by migrants to include a hitherto neglected insistence on racial equality as well. When we dwell on the diligent and unpretentious good manners that once typified England – the much-satirised diffidence in the face of queues, courtesy in the face of mishaps, patience in the face of adversity – we need to realise that such traits may be more common now in migrant Britain, with its strong family loyalties and principles of obligation, than in the brash, every-man-for-himself mainstream.*

The national sensibility is under pressure and changing at a time when national sovereignty itself is under pressure as a concept: sometimes it even takes on the appearance of an anachronistic hangover from the age of empires. So it is clear that a new identity will not arise smoothly and without provoking cries of anguish from the wounded. It may well be a painful process: identities have often seemed worth dying, and killing, for. At the very least they inspire wrath. So when David Blunkett, for instance, suggested it would be wise for immigrants to learn English, a modest enough practical proposal, he was howled at by some as urging 'linguistic colonialism'.† When Robin Cook waved a flag for foreign dynamism, suggesting that chicken tikka masala was now the national dish, he was rounded on by others as a traitor. The fact that opposition came from different quarters was barely noticed: opposition always claims to be on behalf of 'the people'.

There was a similarly blank reaction to the Parekh Report, a state-of-the-nation summary of life in 'multi-ethnic' Britain published, with new-millennium resolve, in 2000. Nearly all of its recommendations were uncontroversial and just. It argued for a national consensus built on the idea of inclusiveness. It

---

*Is it a coincidence that Leicester, the city with the highest proportion of ethnic minorities in Britain, has emerged as the city with the best health (measured by the low incidence of heart disease) and the lowest murder rate in the country?
† Blunkett caused offence not so much because of what he said, but because of when he said it. Hardly anyone disagreed with the idea that learning English was prudent; but his decision to propose it as part of a response to the riots in Oldham and elsewhere seemed to suggest that poor language skills were a major cause of urban violence. A common language probably is a prerequisite for an open and equal society, happy to converse with itself. But at such a time, this sounded like blaming the victims, not the thugs.

urged us to celebrate, not merely tolerate, minorities, to think of Britain place, not a race. 'While cherishing cultural diversity,' wrote the chairman, Bhikhu Parekh (who came from Gujarat in 1959), 'Britain must remain a cohesive society with a shared national culture.' It should stand for 'fairness, equality and common belonging'.[6] So far, so good. But the report committed a tactical faux pas in raising a few more radical banners. In arguing for a 'community of communities', and clinging to the idea of 'multiculturalism' as an essential right, it failed to allay the worries of those who fear a loss of national integrity and coherence. These are reasonable and non-racist concerns. Where, after all, does the balance of rights lie between the 'community' and the 'communities'? By arguing that 'Britain' had racist connotations strong enough to require a new national name, the report assured itself of a stormy passage in the media, which sank enthusiastically to the occasion and denounced it as an ungracious slur by the enemy within.

In most respects, this angry response was – as kneejerk reactions often are – as illogical as it was intemperate. People who had the week before screamed that Britain was 'flooded' or 'swamped' by migrants now swore that they were such a tiny minority (a paltry four million out of sixty million) that they had no right to address themselves to the major institutions of nationhood. But beneath the hysteria there were some cogent criticisms. It was noted that, in mocking both the flag and the very idea of 'Britain', Parekh and his colleagues were happy to consign a proud history to oblivion. And the report seemed coy about the fact that many of its authors were themselves immigrants, prospering in a Britain which, contrary to their thesis, was both receptive to their talents and happy to reward them with a key role in its future. In casting aspersions at the racist connotations of Britishness, it disparaged the equally notable anti-racist, progressive streak in Britain's past. The racism in old Britannia is unmissable; but the report did not emphasise that it has almost always been opposed by a larger and more liberal tendency. Today, as in the past, racist spokesmen speak for many, but not for enough. When Enoch Powell declared in 1968 that Britain was 'mad, literally mad' to be permitting such high levels of immigration, he was sacked. And when Robert Henderson wondered, in *Wisden* magazine in 1995, whether England's foreign-born players could really be counted on to burst a lung for their country, the press pounced on him.

This cuts both ways: too brazen a rebuttal of traditional symbolism will only inflame defenders of the faith. Racism, like terrorism, cannot easily be 'fought': opposition only gives it fuel. It needs, if anything, to be tamed, defused, exposed. Similarly, if progressive ideologues reject national emblems, then these can too easily be monopolised by rougher-tongued nationalists. In all of these ways, a report which deserved better risked dismissal as a fashionable pose, a wearisome piece of gesture politics, a publicity stunt. Orwell sounded a warning bell over half a century ago: 'In left-wing circles it is always felt that there is something slightly disgraceful in being an Englishman, and that it is a duty to snigger at every English institution.' In pleading for togetherness, the Parekh Report seemed to conform too breezily with this stereotype, and generated the opposite of what it had desired: a heated and polarised spat between antique reflexes.

So the search is still on for a middle way, a way to loosen and expand the notion of Britishness without disposing of it altogether, a way to include a range of impulses and characters it has not been asked to accommodate before. One of the things it does not need to include, of course, is a narrow-minded obligation to jeer at foreign sports teams – the behaviour semi-encouraged by Norman Tebbit's famous cricket 'test'. If we entertain the idea of a man like Tebbit as a migrant himself – to South Africa, say – it is easy to see how woolly such a notion was. He might never have intended to stay. He might, as his business thrived, have permitted himself a small prayer: Next year in Colchester. But what if the years turned into decades, if his children started leaving university and marrying locals, and showed no wish to return to dingy old England? And what if a slide in the currency eventually made it no longer feasible to sell off his business and retire to soothing English lawns? What if, in order to participate in the politics of his new state, he felt it necessary to acquire a fresh passport? Should he cheer on the Springboks at Twickenham and the Proteas at Lord's? No one should expect him to. He might support South Africa when they played New Zealand, if only because his daughter was dating a prop forward from Bloemfontein. But in any contest between his old country and his new one, the pantomime ties of childhood would win out every time. Expats often become more rather than less loyal to their birthplace. It helps them stand out; it is their unique selling point.

It used to be assumed that geography was not only a handy marker of national identity – especially in an island nation like Britain – but the essential driver of ethnic differences. It is true that nationalism, in its folkloric manifestations, has often sought to locate the unique recipe behind sovereign characteristics in the contours of the land itself: thus Scottishness is a heather-clad highland, Englishness a grassy meadow. And geography clearly influences culture to the extent that landscape and climate are major factors in the creation of religious, gastronomic, social and sexual manners and dogmas. The siesta did not catch on in cold, dark England; nor was it luck that Protestantism and its work ethic thrived in the chilly north of Europe (hard work keeps you warm).

Aviation technology has set us free from such emphatic considerations, though if we are honest, we have to concede that humans have always been nomadic. In early times, people would move in search of food or water, to escape famine or flood. The convulsive drifting of the world's population has eroded geography as surely as the sea nibbles at the shore. The ethnic diversity of Britain is a fact, not a matter of opinion, and the past is less than ever a reliable guide to the future. These days, geographical boundaries look more like lines – endlessly fought over and pushed this way and that – between merely political (not even linguistic) cultural entities. It is ideological pressure that has led to their being seen as ethnic frontiers. Modern scientists insist that the genetic variance between nationalities is far and away to small to account for the cultural and behavioural differences between nations. Humans, they say, differ from each other by only one genetic dot in a thousand. In the light of discoveries such as these, humankind really does share a genetic ancestry, really might be that hippy ideal: one very big if not always happy family.

History is not photography: it does not 'capture' the past. If anything, it is closer to an expressionist painting, thickly crusted with gaudy slabs of oil. The story we have so often been told, and have repeated, about Britain's past has been subject to many makeovers and revamps. This applies especially to celebrations of our own ethnic identity – the attempt to suggest that our strange and remarkable history has or had a racial logic to it. But the confident clarity of the received wisdom – the 'traditions' that we invent and sustain – is partisan. There is a much more errant and haphazard story surrounding the sharp-edged tale usually offered as the national narrative. A consideration of the way Britain has welcomed, denounced, thought of and forgotten about immigrants leaves us with a hazy, blurred and ill-defined picture. What we cheer as sea-changes or turning-points – Agincourt, Blenheim, Plassey, Trafalgar, Waterloo, the Somme, Dunkirk, the Blitz, the Battle of Britain – often turn out to be merely the favoured emphases of the opinion-forming class, highlighting just one path through the endless, untidy flow of our affairs. All that Whig history which insisted that the story of Britain was the tale of an advance, an ascent to prosperity and enlightenment, has an unavoidable postscript: how else can it end but with an exhausting climb-down? That is where we are now: the story we tell ourselves, doggedly and with an angry lump in our throat, is that we are a giant in decline. Naturally, we are eager to find someone to blame for this state of affairs.

Kings and tyrants have known for centuries that the best way to fuel a clannish surge of national pride is to wage war on a foreigner. At the time of writing, the fight is with the foreignness in our midst, the very people who hold out the promise of the rapprochement that could be wrought by the mingling of different people within a single nation. If it is impossible to predict what shape the national identity will take in the future, it is at least clear that the campaign to broaden it has been inspired and led by immigrants themselves, uncomfortable with a definition that does not include them. Whatever form it takes, historians of the future will be forced to conclude that it was imported, stretched and updated by migrants as a distinct contribution to the ongoing story of Britain. Who knows, perhaps they will look back in wonder that we, in the dim and distant twenty-first century, could have expended so much spirit arguing over the importance of a few variations in skin pigmentation and physiognomy, of a few minor differences in the way people celebrate or dispute the existence of God. Perhaps they will say a little prayer of thanks that they don't think like that any more.

Notes

Just as we all come from somewhere else, if you look back far enough, this book is directly descended from a family of scholarly forebears. It could not have been begun, let alone finished, without the distinguished work of historians in each of its many fields. Grateful thanks, and sincere apologies for the oversimplifications that have almost certainly crept in, are due in particular to the following historians: Cecil Roth and H. G. Richardson, for their detailed investigations of Jewish life in medieval England; Andrew Pettegree, Daniel Statt, H. T. Dickinson and Laura Hunt Yungblut for their exhaustive work on Continental Protestants in England; Robin Gwynn and Tessa Murdoch for their redoubtable accounts of Huguenot life; Peter Fryer, Kenneth Little, Folarin Shyllon and James Walvin for their inspiring studies of black Britons since the days of the slave trade; and L. P. Curtis, Sheridan Gilley, Roger Swift, J. A. Jackson and Lynn Hollen Lees for their resolute recreations of Irish migration in Victorian Britain. Rosemary Ashton has drawn our attention, after long years of neglect, to the significance of German refugees in Britain in the nineteenth century; Lucio Sponza and Terri Colpi have done the same for the Italians; as have Keith Sword and Norman Davies for the Poles. Lloyd Gartner, V. D. Lipman, Harold Pollins, Bernard Gainer, David Fishman, Bernard Wasserstein and others have rescued the story of the Jewish migrants in recent times. Colin Holmes has set imposing standards in his authoritative summaries of modern immigration; Rozina Visram has written the standard histories on Asians in Britain; and Mike and Trevor Phillips, among others, have heroically preserved the stories of the *Windrush* generation. Jonathon Green's anthologies of interviews with recent migrants are indispensable.

In 1904 Ford Madox Ford (then Ford Madox Hueffer) began his assessment of the national mood in *The Spirit of the English People* with the following pointed remark: 'England, almost more than any other, is the land that has been ruled by foreigners, yet the Englishman, almost more than any other man, will resent or will ignore the fact.' If this remains to a surprising extent true, it is certainly not the fault of those mentioned above and below.

Introduction

1 E. A. Markham, 'Taking the Drawing Room through Customs', in Ferdinand Dennis and Naseem Khan (eds), *Voices of the Crossing*, Serpent's Tail, 2000, p.5.

1 The Invaders

1 G. M. Trevelyan, *History of England*, Longman's, 1926, p.6.
2 Gildas, *The Ruin of Britain and Other Works*, trans. M. Winterbottom, Phillimore, 1978, p.27.
3 Bede, *A History of the English Church and People*, ed. Leo Sherley-Price, Penguin, 1968, p.38.

2 A Norman Province

1 Quoted in A. L. Poole, *The Oxford History of England*, vol. 3: *From Domesday Book to Magna Carta 1087–1216*, 1954, p.191.

3 The Expulsion of the Jews

1 Thomas Fuller, *Church History of Britain*, 1655, quoted in J. Arnold Fleming, *Flemish Influence in Britain*, Jackson, Wylie, 1930, p.124.
2 A. L. Poole, *The Oxford History of England*, Vol. 3, p.353.

4 'Onlie to seeke woorck'

1 Thomas More, *Utopia*, quoted in J. Arnold Fleming, *Flemish Influence in Britain*, p.93.
2 Quoted in Andrew Pettegree, *Foreign Protestant Communities in Sixteenth Century London*, Clarendon, 1986, p.13.
3 Sir John Woolley, in Simon D'Ewes, *Journals of all the Parliaments during the Reign of Queen Elizabeth*, 1682, p.509, quoted in Andrew Pettegree, *Foreign Protestant Communities*, p.291; Lemnius, quoted in Edward Smith, *Foreign Visitors in England*, London, 1889, p.40; Paulus Giovius, quoted in *ibid.*, p.40.
4 Sir Simon D'Ewes, *Journals*, p.509, quoted in Robin Gwynn, *Huguenot Heritage*, Sussex, 2001, p.151.
5 Quoted in J. Arnold Fleming, *Flemish Influence in Britain*, p.127.

6 A Refuge for Huguenots

1 'A Collection or Narrative Sent to the Lord Protector', 1655, quoted in Robin Gwynn, *Huguenot Heritage*, p.162.
2 Jacques Fontaine, *Mémoires d'une Famille*, Huguenot Proceedings, Vol. I, No. 2.
3 Quoted in R. A. Shaw, R. D. Gwynn, and P. T. Shaw, *Huguenots in Wandsworth*, Wandsworth Borough, 1985, p.8.
4 Huguenot Library, reproduced in Tessa Murdoch (ed.), *The Quiet Conquest*, Museum of London, 1985, p.318.

7 The Protestant Haven

1 J. Michelet, *Histoire de France*, Vol. XIII, Paris, 1860.
2 Indemnity bond for a lunatic, issued by French Hospital, 1734, included in Tessa Murdoch (ed.), *The Quiet Conquest*, p.84.
3 *Ibid.*, p.141.

4 Quoted in Edward Smith, *Foreign Visitors in England*, p.30.

5 Quoted in *ibid.*, p.39.

6 Quoted in Robin Gwynn, *Huguenot Heritage*, p.149.

7 William Petty, *Treatise of Taxes and Contributions*, 1662, quoted in Daniel Statt, *Foreigners and Englishmen*, University of Delaware Press, 1995, p.45.

8 Josiah Tucker, *Reflections on the Expediency of a Law for the Naturalisation of Foreign Protestants*, 1752, p.19, quoted in *ibid.*, p.45.

9 In 'Fire is Past but Blood is to Come', quoted in Robin Gwynn, *Huguenot Heritage*, p.147.

10 Quoted in Daniel Statt, *Foreigners and Englishmen*, p.116 and Robin Gwynn, *Huguenot Heritage*, p.152.

11 'Brief History of the Poor Palatines', *The Review*, 1709, quoted in H. T. Dickinson, 'The Poor Palatines and the Parties', *English Historical Review*, 1967.

12 *The Examiner*, 7 June 1711.

13 Francis Atterbury, *English Advice to the Freeholders of England*, 1714, quoted in Daniel Statt, *Foreigners and Englishmen*, p.195.

14 Josiah Tucker, *The Elements of Commerce and the Theory of Taxes*, 1755, quoted in *ibid.* p.213.

15 *The Examiner*, No. 2, 28 December 1710, included in *Prose Works of Swift*, ed. H. Davis, Vol 6, p.95.

8 The Hanoverian Empire

1 Quoted in Christopher Hibbert, *George III: A Personal History*, Viking, 1998, p.373.

2 Quoted in *Dictionary of National Biography*, Vol. 8, Oxford, 1890, p.81.

3 Quoted in *ibid.*, Vol. 5, p.834.

4 D'Blossiers Tovey, *Anglia Judaica*, 1738, ed. Elizabeth Pearl, Weidenfeld & Nicolson, 1991, p.38.

5 Quoted in Harold Pollins, *Economic History of Jews in England*, Associated University Press, 1982, p.59.

6 Quoted in Gretchen Gerzina, *Black England*, John Murray, 1995, p.145.

9 Servants and Slaves

1 Lord Chief Justice Holt, 'No Man can have property in another', *Salkeld's Reports*, Vol. 11, p.666, quoted in James Walvin, *Black Personalities in the Era of the Slave Trade*, Allen Lane, 1973, p.15 and Gretchen Gerzina, *Black England*, p.96.

2 'The Will of Thomas Papillon', 1700–1, quoted in James Walvin, *Black Personalities*, p.15.

3 *Liverpool Chronicle*, 1768, quoted in James Walvin, *The Black Presence*, Orbach & Chambers, 1971, pp.79–80 and Folarin Shyllon, *Black People in Britain 1555–1883*, Oxford, 1977, p.13.

4 Not to mention their predisposition to 'artifice, duplicity, haughtiness, violence, rapine, avarice, meanness, rancour and dishonesty' (Edward Long, *History of Jamaica*, Vol. 1, 1774, p.4, quoted in Peter Fryer, *Staying Power*, Pluto, 1984, p.158).

5 William Blackstone, *Commentaries on the Laws of England*, Oxford, Vol. 1, 1773, p.127, quoted in James Walvin, *The Black Presence*, p.24.

6 *Morning Chronicle and London Advertiser*, 24 June 1772, quoted in Gretchen Gerzina, *Black England*, p.130.

7 Quoted in James Walvin, *Black Personalities*, p.21.

8 Ottobah Cuguano, *Thoughts and Sentiments on the Evil of Slavery*, London, 1787, p.112, quoted in James Walvin, *Black Ivory*, HarperCollins, 1992.

9 Plaque on wall of St Andrew's Church, Chesterton, Cambridge, quoted in James Walvin, *An African's Life: The Life and Times of Olaudah Equiano 1745–1797*, Cassell, 1998, p.188.

10 Review in *Public Advertiser*, No. 16761, 5 February 1788, quoted in Peter Fryer, *Staying Power*, p.109.

11 *A Narrative of the Most Remarkable Particulars in the Life of James Albert Ukasaw Gronniosaw, an African Prince, as Related by Himself*, Leeds, 1814, p.23, quoted in Gretchen Gerzina, *Black England*, p.21.

10 Radical Victorians

1 Quoted in E. H. Carr, *The Romantic Exiles*, London, 1933, p.5.

2 Quoted in Ernest Jones, *Sigmund Freud: Life and Work*, Vol. 1, London, 1953, p.195.

3 Friedrich Engels, Preface, *Das Kapital* [1886], Allen & Unwin, 1938, p.xiv.

4 *Fortnightly Review*, 1 March 1871, quoted in Dennis Mack Smith, *Mazzini*, Yale, 1994, p.214.

5 *The Times*, 15 June 1844, quoted in *Life of Thomas Carlyle*, Vol. 3, London, 1923, p.264.

6 Quoted in R. R. Palmer, *The Year of the Terror*, Blackwell, 1989, p.338.

7 On 3 May 1861, quoted in Rosemary Ashton, *Little Germany: Exile and Asylum in Victorian England*, Oxford, 1986, p.62.

8 Marx to Engels, 15 July 1858, quoted in *ibid.*, p.110.

9 Quoted in *ibid.*, p.166.

10 Letter to Kathinka Zitz, 31 May 1854, quoted in *ibid.*, p.188.

11 *Ibid.*, p.194.

12 Alexander Herzen, *My Past and Thoughts*, Vol. 3, p.1180.

13 'Household Words', 26 April 1851, Charles Dickens, *Uncollected Writings*, ed. H. Stone, 1969, p.255.

14 *The Star of Freedom*, September 1852, quoted in Bernard Porter, *The Refugee Question in Mid-Victorian Politics*, Cambridge, 1979.

11 Industrial Revelations

1 Letter to King Leopold, 1 October 1839, included in *Queen Victoria in her Letters and Journals: A Selection*, ed. Christopher Hibbert, John Murray, 1984, p.55.

2 *Queen Victoria in her Letters and Journals*, p.56.

3 Quoted in Richard Hough, *Victoria and Albert*, Richard Cohen Books, 1996, p.71.

4 Quoted in Peter Morris, *Dictionary of Business Biography*, Butterworth, 1981, p.291.

5 Letter from Hugo Hirst to Edward Hirst, 23 October 1915, quoted in R. T. Davenport, *Dictionary of Business Biography*, p.275.

6 Freiligrath to Bulwer Lytton, 7 February 1947, quoted in Rosemary Ashton, *Little Germany*, p.81.

7 Malwida von Meysenburg, *Rebel in a Crinoline*, London, 1937, p.129.

8 *Ibid.*, p.209.

9 Quoted in Betty Nagar, *Jewish Pedlars and Hawkers*, Porphyrogenitus, 1992, p.62.

10 Quoted in *ibid.*, p.62.

12 Little Italy

1 Charles Dickens, *Oliver Twist*, Oxford, 1949, p.55.
2 Charles Babbage, *A Chapter on Street Nuisances*, 1864, p.3. quoted in Lucio Sponza, *Italian Immigrants in London*, Leicester University Press, 1978, p.176.
3 Quoted in *ibid.*, p.176.
4 *Chambers' Journal*, 29 September 1877, quoted in *ibid.*, p.153.
5 Charles Booth, 'Industry', in *Life and Labour of the People in London*, Vol. 4, 1902, p.35.

13 The Labours of Ireland

1 Samuel Tuke to Jonathan Pim, 26 August 1847, quoted in Sheridan Gilley and Roger Swift, *The Irish in the Victorian City*, Croom Helm, 1985, p.79.
2 A. Carrick and J. A. Symons, *Medical Topography of Bristol, Transactions of the Provincial Medical and Surgical Association*, quoted in *ibid.*, p.79
3 E. Strauss, *Irish Nationalism and British Democracy*, quoted in *ibid.*, p.109.
4 Samuel Garratt, *Motives for Missions*, London, 1853, p.214.
5 Karl Marx to S. Meyer and A. Vogt, 9 April 1870.
6 Quoted by Sheridan Gilley in Colin Holmes (ed.), *Immigrants and Minorities in British Society*, Allen & Unwin, 1978, p.89.
7 Quoted in *ibid.*, p.89
8 E. P. Thompson, *The Making of the English Working Class*, Victor Gollancz, 1980, p.480.

14 Rule Britannia

1 Pat O'Mara, *Autobiography of a Liverpool Slummy*, 1834.
2 J. A. Hobson, *Imperialism*, 1902, quoted in Ron Ramdin, *Reimaging Britain*, Pluto, 1999, p.114.
3 *The Record*, 15 May 1851, quoted in Sheridan Gilley in Colin Holmes (ed.), *Immigrants and Minorities*, p.86.
4 J. R. Green, *The Conquest of England*, 1883, quoted in *ibid.*, p.87.
5 *Truth* magazine, Vol. 34, No. 879, 2 November 1893, quoted in Lucio Sponza, *Italian Immigrants*, p.120.

15 The Jewish Evacuees

1 Beatrice Webb in Charles Booth, *Life and Labour of the People in London*, Vol. 1, 1889, p.583.
2 Circular address in *HaMeliz*, Vol. 28, p.287, quoted in Lloyd P. Gartner, *The Jewish Immigrant in England*, London, 1960, p.24.
3 *Die Tsukunft*, 12 November 1879, quoted in *ibid.*, p.107.
4 Myer Wilchinski, 'History of a Sweater', *Commonweal*, 26 May 1888, quoted in David Fishman, *East End Jewish Radicals*, Duckworth, 1975, p.45.
5 Quoted in Lloyd P. Gartner, *The Jewish Immigrant in England*, p.126.
6 Rudolf Rocker, *The London Years*, London, 1956, p.80.
7 Quoted in Harold Pollins, *Hopeful Travellers: Jewish Migrants and Settlers in Nineteenth Century Britain*, London Museum of Jewish Life, 1986.
8 Jack London, *The People of the Abyss* [1903], Journeyman Press, 1977, p.80.
9 'A Character Sketch of Jewish Life in London', *Polish Yidel*, No. 1, 25 July 1884, quoted in David Fishman, *East End Jewish Radicals*, p.141.
10 Israel Zangwill, *Children of the Ghetto*, Heinemann, 1892, Meri-Jane Rochelson (ed.), Wayne State University Press, 1998, p.73.

16 The Anti-Alien Backlash

1 Arthur Conan Doyle, *The Story of Mr George Edalji*, Egan, 1985, p.35.
2 D. H. Lawrence to Ottoline Morrell, in *Selected Letters*, 1978.
3 *Hansard*, Vol. 311, 1887, quoted in Bernard Gainer, *The Alien Invasion*, Heinemann, 1972, p.166.
4 W. Evans Gordon, *The Alien Invasion*, quoted in V. D. Lipman (ed.), *Three Centuries of Anglo-Jewish History*, London, 1961, p.113.
5 Arnold White, *Efficiency and Empire*, G. R. Searle (ed.), Harvester, 1973, p.80
6 Beatrice Webb, *My Apprenticeship*, quoted in Bernard Gainer, *The Alien Invasion*, p.98.
7 *Parliamentary Debates*, Vol. 145, 1905, quoted in *ibid.*, p.198.
8 *Parliamentary Debates*, Vol. 114, 1919, quoted in *ibid.*, p.208.
9 Ford Madox Ford, *The Spirit of the People: An Analysis of the English Mind*, London, 1904, p.44.
10 Letter to the Home Secretary, 7 December 1906, quoted by J. P. May in Colin Holmes (ed.), *Immigrants and Minorities*, p.117.
11 L. Wagner, *London Saunterings*, Allen & Unwin, 1928.
12 Manchester *Guardian*, 31 August 1914, quoted in Panikos Panayi (ed.), *Racial Violence in Britain in the Nineteenth Century*, Leicester University Press, 1996, p.67.
13 *John Bull*, 15 May 1915, quoted in *ibid.*, p.73
14 Interview with Henry Tiarks, quoted in Richard Robert, *Dictionary of Business Biography*, Vol. 4, p.123.

17 Brothers in Arms

1 16 January 1915. Quoted in Rozina Visram, *Asians in Britain*, Pluto, 2002, p.183.
2 2 December 1915. Quoted in *ibid.*, p191.
3 Quoted in *ibid.*, p.199.
4 *Cardiff Mail*, 3 July 1919. In Panitis Panayi (ed.), 'Riots', p.100.
5 'Memorandum of the Repatriation of Coloured Men', 23 June 1919, quoted in Panitos Paranyi (ed.) pp.104–5.

18 Casualties of War

1 Bertrand Russell, *Condition of India*, London, 1933, p.xiii.
2 Savitri Chowdhary, *I Made my Home in England*, quoted in Rozina Visram, *Asians in Britain*, p.295.
3 Lord Baldwin, radio broadcast, 8 December 1938, in *Keesings Contemporary Archives*, 1937–40, p.3361.
4 Quoted in *Into the Arms of Strangers*, director Mark Harris, 2000.
5 Quoted in *ibid.*

19 Imperial Friends and Foes

1 Quoted in Peter and Leni Gillman, *Collar the Lot*, Quartet, 1980, p.102.
2 Quoted in *ibid.*, p.254.
3 Quoted in Jonathon Green, *Them*, Secker & Warburg, 1990, p.96.
4 Letter to Ferdinand Rauter, quoted in Daniel Snowman, *The Hitler Emigrés*, Chatto & Windus, 2001, p.180.
5 Winston Churchill, *History of the Second World War*, Vol. 5, Cassell, 1950.

6 Quoted in Keith Sword, Jan Ciechanowski and Norman Davies, *The Formation of the Polish Community in Great Britain*, London, 1958, p.233.
7 Quoted in Paul Foot, *Immigration and Race in British Politics*, Penguin, 1965, p.118.
8 Quoted in Keith Sword, Jan Ciechanowski and Norman Davies, *The Formation of the Polish Community*, p.382.

20 The Empire Comes Home

1 Quoted in Juliet Gardner, *Over Here*, Collins & Brown, 1992, p.152.
2 Quoted in *ibid.*
3 Quoted in Mike Phillips and Trevor Phillips, *Windrush: The Irresistible Rise of Multi-Racial Britain*, HarperCollins, 1999, p.47.
4 Quoted in Vivienne Francis, *With Hope in Their Eyes*, Nia, 1998, p.31.
5 E. R. Braithwaite, Preface, in Onyekachi Wambu (ed.), *Empire Windrush: Fifty Years of Writing about Black Britain*, Victor Gollanez, 1998, p.15.

21 Welcome to Britain

1 Interviewed in *Windrush*, pp.127, 129 and 329.
2 M. K. Gandhi, quoted in Shompa Lahiri, *Indians in Britain*, Frank Cass, 2000, p.42.
3 Enid Blyton, *The Mystery of the Vanished Prince*, London, 1951, p.72.
4 Alfred Dann, letter to the Ministry of Labour, 30 October 1947, quoted in Colin Holmes, *John Bull's Island*, Macmillan, 1988, p.392.
5 Quoted in Colin Brook (ed.), *The Caribbean in Europe*, Frank Cass, 1986.
6 Interviewed in Daniel Lawrence, *Black Migrants, White Natives*, Cambridge, 1974, pp.39–40.
7 Quoted in Jonathon Green, *Them*, p.87.
8 Quoted in *ibid.*, p.91.
9 Quoted in *ibid.*, p.90.
10 Quoted in *ibid.*, p.239
11 Jawaharlal Nehru, quoted in Shompa Lahiri, *Indians in Britain*, p.184.
12 George Mikes, *How to Be a Brit*, Penguin, 1986, p.179.
13 Quoted in Zig Layton-Henry, *The Politics of Immigration*, Blackwell, 1992, p.94.
14 *The Times*, 16 September 1958, quoted by Edward Pilkington in Panikos Panayi (ed.), *Racial Violence in Britain*, p.183.
15 Quoted in Jonathon Green, *Them*, p.196.
16 Interviewed in Roxy Harris and Sarah White (eds), *Changing Britannia*, New Beacon, 1999, p.85.
17 'Commonwealth Migrants: Memorandum by the Secretary of State for the Home Department', 6 October 1961, quoted in Kathleen Paul, *Whitewashing Britain*, Cornell, 1997, p.166.

22 The Door Closes

1 Interviewed in Jonathon Green, *Them*, p.182
2 'Position of Asians in Kenya: Memorandum by Secretary of State for the Home Department', 30 October 1963, quoted in Kathleen Paul, *Whitewashing Britain*, p.180.
3 Quoted in Paul Foot, *The Rise of Enoch Powell*, 1969, p.119.
4 *Uganda Argus*, 19 August 1972, quoted in William Kuepper, G. Lynne Lackey and E. Nelson Swinnerton, *Ugandan Asians in Great Britain*, Croom Helm, 1975, p.55.
5 *The Economist*, 19 August 1972.

6 Interviewed in Jonathon Green, *Them*, p.202.
7 Keith Thompson, *Under Siege: Racism and Violence in Britain Today*, Penguin, 1988, p.xviii.
8 Timothy Mo, *Sour Sweet*, Abacus, 1983, p.1.

23 Little England

1 *World in Action*, Granada TV, 30 January 1978, quoted in Zig Layton-Henry, *The Politics of Immigration*, p.104.
2 Quoted by Nigel Harris, *The New Untouchables: Immigrants and the New World Order*, Penguin, 1995, p.125.
3 Interviewed in Jonathon Green, *Them*, p.239.
4 Interviewed in *ibid*, p.289.
5 Interview in Roxy Harris and Sarah White (eds), *Changing Britannia*, New Beacon, 1999, p.122.

24 Asylum Madness

1 *Observer*, 24 August 1997, quoted in Polly Pattullo, *Fire from the Mountain*, Constable, 2000, p.109.
2 Unless otherwise stated, the figures in this chapter are Home Office statistics. But they need to be treated with caution. All migration numbers are estimates or extrapolations. In Britain they are routinely based on passenger surveys, and on a very small sample. Some statisticians have suggested that they may include a variance of anything from 15 per cent to 40 per cent. They are useful for exposing trends – growths or declines. More often than not, they underestimate the true figure.

Conclusion: The Identity Parade

1 Samuel Butler, quoted in Christopher Hogwood, *Handel*, Thames & Hudson, 1984, p.266.
2 George Mikes, *How to Be a Brit*, p.260.
3 Quoted in Candida Lycett Green (ed.), John Betjeman, *Coming Home: An Anthology of Prose*, Methuen, 1997, p.141.
4 George Orwell, *England Your England*, Secker & Warburg, 1953, p.194.
5 Ferdinand Dennis, 'Journeys without maps', in Ferdinand Dennis and Naseem Khan (eds), *Voices of the Crossing*, Serpent's Tail, 2000, p.43.
6 Preface, *The Future of Multi-Ethnic Britain: The Parekh Report*, Profile, 2000, p.ix.

Select Bibliography

Adi, Hakim, *West Africans in Britain 1900–1960* (Lawrence & Wishart, 1988)

Agnihotri, Rama Kant, *Crisis of Identity: The Sikhs in England* (New Delhi, 1987)

Alderman, G., 'Anti-Jewish Riots in 1919', *S. Wales Welsh History Review*, No. 6, 1972

Allen Brown, R., *The Normans and the Norman Conquest* (Boydell, 1969)

Anderson, Gregory, *Victorian Clerks* (Manchester University Press, 1976)

Anwar, Muhammad, *The Myth of Return* (Heinemann, 1979)

Aris, Stephen, *Arnold Weinstock and the Making of GEC* (Aurum, 1998)

Ashton, Rosemary, *Little Germany: Exile and Asylum in Victorian England* (Oxford, 1986)

Aye Maung, N., 'Racially Motivated Crime', Home Office Research Paper No. 82

Banton, Michael, *The Coloured Quarter* (London, 1954)

Banton, Michael, *White and Coloured* (Oxford, 1959)

Barty-King, Hugh, *Eyes Right: The Story of Dollond and Aitchison* (Quiller, 1986)

Baucom, Ian, *Out of Place: Englishness, Empire and the Locations of Identity* (Princeton, 1999)

Bede, *A History of the English Church and People* (London, 1968)

Bentwich, Norman, *They Found Refuge* (Cresset, 1956)

Berghahn, M., *German-Jewish Refugees in England* (London, 1984)

Bermant, C., *Point of Arrival: A Study of London's East End* (Methuen, 1975)

Betjeman, John, *Coming Home: An Anthology of Prose*, Candida Lycett Green (ed.) (Methuen, 1999)

Bolt, C., *Victorian Ideas on Race* (London, 1971)

Booth, Charles, *Life and Labour of the People in London* (London, 1902)

Braidwood, Stephen, *Black Poor and White Philanthropists* (Liverpool University Press, 1994)

Braithwaite, E. R., *To Sir, With Love* (London, 1959)

Braithwaite, E. R., *Paid Servant* (New English Library, 1968)

Briggs, Asa, *Saxons, Normans and Victorians* (Bexhill, 1966)

Briggs, Asa, *A Social History of England* (Weidenfeld & Nicolson, 1983)

Briggs, N. C., and Gambier, R., *Huguenot Ancestry* (Phillimore, 1985)

Brook, Colin (ed.), *The Caribbean in Europe* (Frank Cass, 1986)

Burma, Ian, *Voltaire's Coconuts* (Weidenfeld & Nicolson, 1999)

Burton, Antoinette, *At the Heart of Empire* (University of California Press, 1998)

Carlyle, Thomas, 'Discourse on the Nigger Question', *Fraser's Magazine*, 1849

Carr, E. H., *The Romantic Exiles* (London, 1933)

Cesarani, David, *Jewish Chronicle and Anglo-Jewry* (Cambridge, 1994)

Chaudhuri, Nivad, *A Passage to England* (London, 1966)

Cheyette, Brian, *Constructions of Jewishness* (Cambridge, 1993)

Cheyette, Brian, *Neither Black nor White* (Thames & Hudson, 1995)

Chibnall, Marjorie, *Anglo-Norman England 1066–1166* (Oxford, 1986)

Chibnall, Marjorie (ed.), *The Ecclesiastical History of Orderic Vitalis* (Oxford, 1969)

Cohen, John M., *The Life of Ludwig Mond* (Methuen, 1956)

Coleman, D. A. (ed.), *Demography of Immigrant and Minority Groups in the United Kingdom* (Academic Press, 1982)

Coleman, Terry, *The Railway Navvies* (Penguin, 1968)

Colley, Linda, *Britons* (Pimlico, 1992)

Collins, W., *Jamaican Migrant* (London, 1965)

Colpi, Terri, *The Italian Factor* (Mainstream, 1991)

Colvin, I. D., *The Germans in England 1066–1598* (London, 1915)

Coogan, Tim, *Wherever Green is Worn: The Story of the Irish Diaspora* (Hutchinson, 2001)

Cooper, Edward, *Foreign Protestants in England 1618–1688* (London, 1862)

Cottret, Bernard, *Huguenots in England: Immigration and Settlement 1550–1700* (Cambridge, 1991)

Cuguano, O., *Thoughts and Sentiments on the Evil and Wicked Traffick of the Slavery and Commerce of the Human Species* (London, 1969 [1787])

Cundall, Frank, *Jamaica's Part in the Great War* (West Indies Committee, 1925)

Cunningham, William, *Alien Immigrants to England* (Frank Cass, 1969 [1887])

Curtis, L. P., *Anglo-Saxons and Celts* (London, 1968)

Curtis, L. P., *Apes and Angels: The Irish in Victorian Caricature* (Newton Abbott, 1971)

Dabydeen, David, *Hogarth's Blacks* (London, 1985)

Dabydeen, David, *A Harlot's Progress* (Cape, 1999)

Darby, H. C., *The Draining of the Fens* (Cambridge, 1956)

Davies, Norman, *The Isles* (Macmillan, 1999)

Davison, Robert, *Black British* (Oxford, 1966)

Dench, G., *Maltese in London* (Routledge, 1975)

Dennis, Ferdinand, *Behind the Frontlines* (Victor Gollancz, 1988)

Dennis, Ferdinand, and Khan, Naseem (eds), *Voices of the Crossing* (Serpent's Tail, 2000)

Denvir, J., *The Irish in Britain* (Kegan, Trench, Trubner, 1892)

Desai, Rashmi, *Indian Immigrants in Britain* (Oxford, 1963)

Dickinson, H. T., 'The Poor Palatines and the Parties', *English Historical Review*, 1967

Dictionary of Business Biography, Jeremy David (ed.) (Butterworth, 1981)

Dictionary of National Biography (Oxford, 1890)

Dobson, R. B., *Jews of Medieval York, 1190* (St Anthony's Press, 1974)

Doyle, Arthur Conan, *The Story of Mr George Edalji* (Egan, 1985)

Dresser, Madge, *Slavery Obscured* (Continuum, 2001)

Duffy, Maureen, *England: The Making of the Myth* (Fourth Estate, 2001)

Edwards, P., *Equiano's Travels* (London, 1967)

Ellingwood, D. C., and Pradhan, S. D., *India in World War I* (London, 1978)

Emecheta, Buchi, *Kehinde* (Heinemann, 1994)

Emecheta, Buchi, *Second Class Citizen* (Heinemann, 1994)

Endelman, T. M., *The Jews of Georgian England 1714–1830* (Philadelphia, 1979)

Endelman, T. M., *The Jews of Britain 1656–2000* (University of California Press, 2002)

Equiano, O., *The Interesting Narrative and Other Writings* (Penguin, 1995)

Feldman, David, *Englishmen and Jews (1840–1914)* (Yale, 1994)

Ferdinand, Dennis, *Behind the Frontlines* (Victor Gollancz, 1988)

Field, Frank (ed.), with Fleming, J. Arnold, *Flemish Influence in Britain* (Jackson, Wylie, 1930)

Fleming, J. Arnold, *Flemish Influence in Britain* (Jackson, Wylie, 1930)

Fishman, David, *East End Jewish Radicals* (Duckworth, 1975)

Foot, Paul, *Immigration and Race in British Politics* (Harmondsworth, 1965)

Foot, Paul, *The Rise of Enoch Powell* (Cornmarket, 1969)

Ford, Ford Madox, *The Spirit of People: An Analysis of the English Mind* (London, 1907)

Francis, Vivienne, *With Hope in their Eyes* (Nia, 1998)

Freeman, E. A., *The History of the Norman Conquest* (Oxford, 1877)

Fryer, Peter, *Staying Power* (Pluto, 1984)

Fryer, Peter, *Black People in the British Empire* (Pluto, 1989)

Fuller, Thomas, *The Church History of Britain (1655)*, J. S. Brewer (ed.) (Gregg, 1970)

Gainer, Bernard, *The Alien Invasion* (Heinemann, 1972)

Gardner, Juliet, *Over Here* (Collins & Brown, 1992)

Garetta, Vincent, 'Friends of Freedom', *Westminster History Review*, Vol. 3, 2000.

Garrard, J. A., *The English and Immigration* (London, 1971)

Garratt, Samuel, *Motives for Missions* (London, 1889)

Gartner, Lloyd P., *The Jewish Immigrant in England* (London, 1960)

Geddes, Andrew, *Immigration and European Integration: Towards Fortress Europe?* (Manchester University Press, 2000)

Gemery, Henry, and Hogendorn, Jan, *The Uncommon Market* (Academic, 1979)

George, Dorothy, *London Life in the Eighteenth Century* (Penguin, 1966)

Gershon, Karen, *We Came as Children* (Macmillan, 1989)

Gerzina, Gretchen, *Black England* (John Murray, 1995)

Gidoomal, Ram, Mahtani, Deepak, and Porter, David, *The British and How to Deal with Them* (Middlesex University Press, 2001)

Gilbert, John, *Famous Jewish Lives* (Odhams, 1970)

Gilbert, Martin, *The Boys: Triumph over Adversity* (Weidenfeld & Nicolson, 1996)

Gildas, *The Ruin of Britain and Other Works* (Phillimore, 1978)

Gilley, Sheridan, and Swift, Roger, *The Irish in the Victorian City* (Croom Helm, 1985)

Gilley, Sheridan, and Swift, Roger, *The Irish in Britain 1815–1939* (Pinter, 1989)

Gillman, Peter, and Gillman, Leni, *Collar the Lot* (Quartet, 1980)

Gilroy, Beryl, *Black Teacher* (Cassell, 1976)

Gilroy, Paul, *There Ain't no Black in the Union Jack* (Hutchinson, 1987)

Glass, R., *Newcomers: West Indians in London* (Allen & Unwin, 1963)

Gordon, W. Evans, *The Alien Immigrant* (Heinemann, 1903)

Grant, Bruce, *The Boat People* (Penguin, 1979)

Green, Jeffrey, *Black Edwardians: Black People in Britain 1901–14* (Frank Cass, 1998)

Green, Jonathon, *Them* (Secker & Warburg, 1990)

Guvert, Betty Kaplan, *Invisible Wings* (Greenwood Press, 1994)

Gwynn, Robin, *Huguenots of London* (Alpha, 1998)

Gwynn, Robin, *Huguenot Heritage: The History and Contribution of the Huguenots in Britain* (Sussex, 2001)

Haikin, Patricia, *Black Britons* (Oxford, 1971)

Hannaford, Ivan, *Race* (Johns Hopkins University Press, 1996)

Harding, Jeremy, *Refugees at the Rich Man's Gate* (Profile, 2000)

Hardyment, Christina, *Slice of Life* (BBC, 1995)

Harris, L. E., *Vermuyden and the Fens* (London, 1953)

Harris, Nigel, *The New Untouchables: Immigrants and the New World Order* (Penguin, 1995)

Harris, Roxy, and White, Sarah (eds), *Changing Britannia* (New Beacon, 1999)

Hashm, Farrukh, *The Pakistani Family in Britain* (CRC, 1969)

Helweg, A., *Sikhs in England* (Oxford, 1979)

Henriques, H. S. Q., *The Law of Aliens and Naturalisation (including text of Aliens Act 1905)* (Butterworth, 1906)

Herzen, My Life and Thoughts, J. D. Duff (tr.) (Oxford, 1980)

Hibbert, Christopher (ed.), *Queen Victoria in her Letters and Journals: A Selection* (John Murray, 1984)

Hibbert, Christopher (ed.), *George III: A Personal History* (Viking, 1998)

Hicks, Michael, *Who's Who in Late Medieval England* (Shepheard Walwyn, 1991)

Hill, C. P., *Who's Who in Stuart Britain* (Shepheard Walwyn, 1996)

Hiro, Dilip, *Black British, White British* (Grafton, 1991)

Hirschfeld, Gerhard, *Exile in Great Britain* (Berg, 1984)

Hobson, J. A., *Imperialism* (London, 1902)

Hogwood, Christopher, *Handel* (Thames & Hudson, 1984)

Hollifield, James, *Immigrants, Markets and States* (Harvard, 1992)

Holmes, Colin (ed.), *Immigrants and Minorities in British Society* (Allen & Unwin, 1978)

Holmes, Colin, *John Bull's Island: Immigration and British Society 1871–1971* (Macmillan, 1988)

Holmes, Colin, *A Tolerant Country?* (Faber & Faber, 1991)

Holmes, Martin, 'Evil May Day 1517', *History Today*, Vol. 15, No. 9, 1965

Hough, Richard, *Victoria and Albert* (Richard Cohen, 1996)

Howe, Glenford, *West Indians and World War I* (University of the West Indies, 1994)

Huxley, Thomas, *On Some Fixed Points in British Ethnology* (1871)

Hyamson, A. M., *The Sephardim of England* (Methuen, 1951)

Islam, Syed Manzurul, *The Mapmakers of Spitalfields* (Peepal Tree, 1997)

Jackson, John Arthur, *The Irish in Britain* (London, 1963)

James, Simon, *The Atlantic Celts: Ancient People or Modern Invention?* (British Museum, 1999)

Jeremy, David (ed.), *Dictionary of Business Biography* (Butterworth, 1981)

Johnson, Paul, *A History of the Jews* (Weidenfeld & Nicolson, 1987)

Jones, Ernest, *Sigmund Freud: Life and Work* (Penguin, 1964)

Katz, David, *Philosemitism and the Readmission of the Jews to England 1603–1655* (Clarendon, 1982)

Katz, David, *The Jews in the History of England* (Clarendon, 1997)

Kennedy, Carol, *ICI: The Company that Changed Our Lives* (Hutchinson, 1986)

Kerridge, Roy, *Real Wicked, Guy: A View of Black Britain* (Blackwell, 1983)

Kerridge, Roy, *The Storm Is Passing Over: A Look at Black Churches in Britain* (Thames & Hudson, 1995)

Killingray, David, *Africans in Britain* (Frank Cass, 1994)

Lafitte, François, *The Internment of Aliens* (Libris, 1988)

Lahiri, Shompa, *Indians in Britain* (Frank Cass, 2000)

Laing, Lloyd, and Laing, Jennifer, *Britain's European Heritage* (Alan Sutton, 1995)

Lamming, George, *The Emigrants* (Allison & Busby, 1980)

Lamming, George, *The Pleasures of Exile* (Allison & Busby, 1984)

Lang, David Marshall, *The Armenians: A People in Exile* (Allen & Unwin, 1981)

Lawrence, Daniel, *Black Migrants, White Natives* (Cambridge, 1974)

Layton-Henry, Zig, *The Politics of Immigration* (Blackwell, 1992)

Lees, Lynn Hollen, *Exiles of Erin* (Manchester University Press, 1979)

Le Quex, William, *Spies of the Kaiser* (London, 1909)

Leverton, Bertha (ed.), *I Came Alone* (The Book Guild, 1990)

Lewis, Philip, *Islamic Britain* (I. B. Tauris, 1994)

Little, Kenneth, *Negroes in Britain* (Kegan Paul, 1947)

Lipman, V. D., *Social History of Jews in England* (Watts, 1954)

Lipman, V. D. (ed.) *Three Centuries of Anglo-Jewish History* (London, 1961)

London, Jack, *The People of the Abyss* (Journeyman, 1977 [1903])

London, Louise, *Whitehall and the Jews* (Cambridge, 2000)

Lorimer, Douglas, *Colour, Class and the Victorians* (London, 1978)

Lynton, Mark, *Accidental Journey* (Overlook, 1995)

Mack Smith, Dennis, *Mazzini* (Yale, 1994)

Makiya, Kenan, *Cruelty and Silence* (Cape, 1993)

Mannsaker, Frances, 'East and West: Anglo-Indians', *Victorian Studies*, Vol. 24, No. 1, 1980

Marett, Valerie, *Immigrants Settling in the City* (Leicester University Press, 1989)

Martin, S. I., *Incomparable World* (Quartet, 1996)

Martin, S. I., *Britain's Slave Trade* (Channel 4 Books, 1999)

May, R., and Cohen, R., 'Liverpool Race Riots 1919', *Race and Class*, Vol. 16, 1974

Mayhew, Henry, *London and the London Poor: A Cyclopedia* (London, 1851)

McInnes, Colin, *City of Spades* (Penguin, 1964)

Melady, T. P., and Melady, M. B., *Uganda: The Asian Exiles* (Orbis, 1978)

Michelet, Jules, *Histoire de France*, G. H. Smith (tr.) (London, 1844)

Mikes, George, *How to Be a Brit* (Penguin, 1986)

Mo, Timothy, *Sour Sweet* (Abacus, 1983)

Modood, Tariq, and Berthoud, Richard, *Ethnic Minorities in Britain* (Policy Studies Unit, 1997)

Murdoch, Tessa, *The Quiet Conquest: The Huguenots* (Museum of London, 1985)

Murphy, Dervla, *Tales from Two Cities* (John Murray, 1987)

Myers, Norma, *Reconstructing the Black Past* (Frank Cass, 1966)

Nagar, Betty, *Jewish Pedlars and Hawkers* (Porphryogenitus, 1992)

Naipaul, V. S., *The Enigma of Arrival* (Viking, 1987)

Naipaul, V. S., *The Mimic Men* (Picador, 2002)

Ng, Kwee Choo, *The Chinese in London* (Oxford, 1968)

Okokon, Susan, *Black Londoners* (Sutton, 1998)

O'Neill, Gilda, *My East End* (Viking, 1999)

Orwell, George, *England Your England* (Secker & Warburg, 1953)

Palmer, Alan, *The East End* (John Murray, 1989)

Palmer, R. R., *The Year of the Terror* (Blackwell, 1917)

Panayi, Panikos, *The Enemy in Our Midst* (Oxford, 1991)

Panayi, Panikos (ed.), *Racial Violence in Britain in the Nineteenth Century* (Leicester University Press, 1996)

Parekh, Bhikhu (ed.), *The Future of Multi-Ethnic Britain* (Profile, 2000)

Parekh Report (Profile, 2002)

Patterson, Sheila, *Dark Strangers* (Tavistock, 1963)

Pattullo, Polly, *Fire From the Mountain* (Constable, 2000)

Paul, Kathleen, *Whitewashing Britain* (Cornell, 1997)

Peach, G. C. K., *West Indian Migration to Britain* (Oxford, 1968)

Pettegree, Andrew, *Foreign Protestant Communities in Sixteenth Century London* (Clarendon, 1986)

Pevsner, Nikolaus, *The Englishness of English Art* (London, 1956)

Phillips, Caryl, *The European Tribe* (Faber & Faber, 1987)

Phillips, Caryl, *Cambridge* (Faber & Faber, 1991)

Phillips, Caryl (ed.), *Extravagant Strangers* (Faber & Faber, 1997)

Phillips, Caryl, *A New World Order* (Secker & Warburg, 2001)

Phillips, Mike, *London Crossings* (Continuum, 2001)

Phillips, Mike, and Phillips, Trevor, *Windrush: The Irresistible Rise of Multi-Racial Britain* (HarperCollins, 1999)

Pilkington, Edward, *Beyond the Mother Country: West Indians and the Notting Hill White Riots* (I. B. Tauris, 1988)

Pine, L. G., *They Came with the Conqueror* (Evans, 1968)

Pollins, Harold, *Economic History of Jews in England* (Associated University Press, 1982)

Pollins, Harold, *Hopeful Travellers: Jewish Migrants and Settlers in Nineteenth Century Britain* (London Museum of Jewish Life, 1986)

Poole, A. L., *The Oxford History of England*, Vol. 3, *From Domesday Book to Magna Carta*, 1087–1216 (Oxford, 1951)

Porter, Bernard, *The Refugee Question in Mid-Victorian Politics* (Cambridge, 1979)

Powicke, Sir Maurice, *The Thirteenth Century* (Oxford, 1991)

Ramdin, Ron, *Reimaging Britain* (Pluto, 1999)

Ravenstein, E. G., *Census of the British Isles, 1871* (London, 1876)

Richardson, H. G., *The English Jewry under the Angevin Kings* (Methuen, 1960)

Richmond, A. H., *Colour Prejudice in Britain* (Routledge, 1954)

Rocker, Rudolf, *The London Years*, Joseph Leftwich (tr.) (London, 1956)

Rose, E. J. B., and Deakin, Nicholas, *Colour and Citizenship* (Oxford, 1969)

Roth, Cecil, *The Rise of Provincial Jewry* (London, 1950)

Roth, Cecil, *History of Jews in England* (Clarendon, 1978)

Routh, C. R. N., *Who's Who in Tudor England* (Shepheard Walwyn, 1990)

Russell, Bertrand, in 'Condition of India: Being the Report of the Delegation Sent to India by the India League in 1932' (London, 1934)

Sancho, I., *The Letters of the Late Ignatius Sancho* (London, 1968)

Scobie, E., *Black Britannia* (London, 1972)

Scouloudi, Irene (ed.), *Huguenots in Britain 1550–1800* (Macmillan, 1987)

Selvon, Samuel, *The Lonely Londoners* (Allan Wingate, 1956)

Sergeant, Harriet, *Welcome to the Asylum* (Centre for Policy Studies, 2001)

Seth, Andrew, and Randall, Geoffrey, *The Grocers* (Kogan Page, 1999)

Sewell, Tony, *Keep on Moving: The Windrush Legacy* (Voice Enterprises, 1998)

Shang, Anthony, *The Chinese in Britain* (London, 1984)

Shaw, Alison, *A Pakistani Community in Britain* (Blackwell, 1988)

Shaw, R. A., Gwynn, R. D., and Shaw, P. T., *Huguenots in Wandsworth* (Wandsworth Borough, 1985)

Sherman, A. J., *Island Refuge: Britain and Refugees from the Third Reich* (Frank Cass, 1994)

Shyllon, Folarin, *Black People in Britain 1555–1833* (Oxford, 1977)

Sigsworth, Eric, *Montague Burton: The Tailor of Taste* (Manchester, 1990)

Sivanandan, A., *Coloured Immigrants in Britain: A Select Bibliography* (IOR, 1967)

Smiles, Samuel, *Huguenots* (London, 1868)

Smith, Edward, *Foreign Visitors in England and What They Have Thought of Us* (London, 1889)

Smith, Graham, *When Jim Crow Met John Bull: Black American Troops in World War II in Britain* (London, 1987)

Smith, T. E., *Commonwealth Migration Flows and Figures* (Cambridge, 1981)

Smithies, B., and Fiddick, P., *Enoch Powell and Immigration* (Sphere, 1969)

Snowman, Daniel, *The Hitler Emigrés* (Chatto & Windus, 2001)

Spencer, R. G., *British Immigration Policy since 1939* (Routledge, 1997)

Spencer, Sarah, *Strangers and Citizens* (IPPR, 1994)

Sponza, Lucio, *The 1880s: A Turning Point* (Biddles, 1993)

Sponza, Lucio, *Italian Immigrants* (Leicester University Press, 1988))

Stalker, Peter, *The No-Nonsense Guide to International Migration* (Verso, 2001)

Statt, Daniel, *Foreigners and Englishmen: The Controversy over Immigration and Population 1660–1760* (University of Delaware Press, 1995)

Swinerton, E. N., *Ugandan Asians in Great Britain* (Croom Helm, 1975)

Sword, Keith, Ciechanowski, Jan, and Davies, Norman, *The Formation of the Polish Community in Great Britain* (London, 1958)

Talai, V. A., *Armenians in London* (1989)

Tannahill, J. A., *European Volunteer Workers in Britain* (Manchester, 1958)

Thompson, E. P., *The Making of the English Working Class* (Victor Gollancz, 1980)

Tidrick, Kathryn, *Empire and the English Character* (I. B. Tauris, 1992)

Tilbe, Douglas, *The Ugandan Asian Crisis* (London, 1972)

Tinker, H., *The Banyan Tree* (Oxford, 1977)

Thompson, Keith, *Under Siege: Racism and Violence in Britain Today* (Penguin, 1988)

Tovey, D'Blossiers, *Anglia Judaica, or the History and Antiquities of the Jew in England* (Weidenfeld & Nicolson, 1991 [1738])

Treasure, Geoffrey, *Who's Who in Late Hanoverian Britain* (Shepheard Walwyn, 1997)

Trevelyan, G. M., *History of England* (Longman's, 1926)

Tyerman, Christopher, *Who's Who in Early Medieval England* (Shepheard Walwyn, 1996)

Vadgama, Kusoom, *India in Britain* (Royce, 1984)

Visram, Rozina, *Ayahs, Lascars and Princes* (Pluto, 1986)

Visram, Rozina, *Asians in Britain* (Pluto, 2002)

Von Meysenbug, Malwida, *Rebel in a Crinoline*, Mildred Adams (ed.) (Allen & Unwin, 1937)

Wagner, Leopold, *Saunterings in London* (Allen & Unwin, 1928)

Walvin, James, *The Black Presence* (Orbach & Chambers, 1971)

Walvin, James, *Black Personalities in the Era of the Slave Trade* (Allen Lane, 1973)

Walvin, James, *Black Ivory* (HarperCollins, 1992)

Walvin, James, *Fruits of Empire* (Macmillan, 1997)

Walvin, James, *An African's Life: The Life and Times of Olaudah Equiano* (Cassell, 1998)

Wambu, Onyekachi (ed.), *Empire Windrush: Fifty Years of Writing About Black Britain* (Victor Gollancz, 1998)

Wasserstein, Bernard, *Britain and the Jews of Europe 1939–45* (Oxford, 1979)

Watson, James (ed.), *Between Two Cultures* (Blackwell, 1977)

Wiles, Alan (ed.) *Migration: An Economic and Social Analysis* (Cabinet Office, 2000)

Williams, Eric, *Capitalism and Slavery* (1944)

Wilson, David (ed.) *Life of Thomas Carlyle* (Kegan Paul, 1923–34)

Wilson, Francesca, *They Came as Strangers* (Hamish Hamilton, 1959)

Wistrich, Robert, *Anti-Semitism, the Longest Hatred* (London, 1991)

Wright, Peter, *The Coloured Worker in British Industry* (Oxford, 1968)

Yungblut, Laura Hunt, *Strangers Settled Here among Us* (Routledge, 1996)

Zangwill, Israel, *Children of the Ghetto* (Wayne State University Press, 1998)

Zubrzycki, Jerzy, *Soldiers and Peasants: The Sociology of Polish Migration* (SOES, 1988)

Index

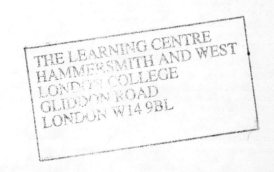